Strategic Perspectives in Destination Marketing

Mark Anthony Camilleri
University of Malta, Malta

A volume in the Advances in
Marketing, Customer Relationship
Management, and E-Services
(AMCRMES) Book Series

Published in the United States of America by
    IGI Global
    Business Science Reference (an imprint of IGI Global)
    701 E. Chocolate Avenue
    Hershey PA, USA 17033
    Tel: 717-533-8845
    Fax: 717-533-8661
    E-mail: cust@igi-global.com
    Web site: http://www.igi-global.com

Copyright © 2019 by IGI Global. All rights reserved. No part of this publication may be reproduced, stored or distributed in any form or by any means, electronic or mechanical, including photocopying, without written permission from the publisher.
Product or company names used in this set are for identification purposes only. Inclusion of the names of the products or companies does not indicate a claim of ownership by IGI Global of the trademark or registered trademark.

    Library of Congress Cataloging-in-Publication Data

Names: Camilleri, Mark Anthony, 1976- editor.
Title: Strategic perspectives in destination marketing / Mark Anthony
   Camilleri, editor.
Description: Hershey : Business Science Reference, [2018]
Identifiers: LCCN 2017058823| ISBN 9781522558354 (hardcover) | ISBN
   9781522558361 (ebook)
Subjects: LCSH: Place marketing. | Tourism--Marketing.
Classification: LCC G155.A1 S684 2018 | DDC 910.68/8--dc23 LC record available at https://lccn.loc.gov/2017058823

This book is published in the IGI Global book series Advances in Marketing, Customer Relationship Management, and E-Services (AMCRMES) (ISSN: 2327-5502; eISSN: 2327-5529)

British Cataloguing in Publication Data
A Cataloguing in Publication record for this book is available from the British Library.

All work contributed to this book is new, previously-unpublished material.
The views expressed in this book are those of the authors, but not necessarily of the publisher.

For electronic access to this publication, please contact: eresources@igi-global.com.

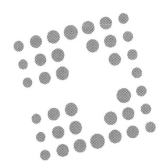

Advances in Marketing, Customer Relationship Management, and E-Services (AMCRMES) Book Series

ISSN:2327-5502
EISSN:2327-5529

Editor-in-Chief: Eldon Y. Li, National Chengchi University, Taiwan & California Polytechnic State University, USA

MISSION

Business processes, services, and communications are important factors in the management of good customer relationship, which is the foundation of any well organized business. Technology continues to play a vital role in the organization and automation of business processes for marketing, sales, and customer service. These features aid in the attraction of new clients and maintaining existing relationships.

The Advances in Marketing, Customer Relationship Management, and E-Services (AMCRMES) Book Series addresses success factors for customer relationship management, marketing, and electronic services and its performance outcomes. This collection of reference source covers aspects of consumer behavior and marketing business strategies aiming towards researchers, scholars, and practitioners in the fields of marketing management.

COVERAGE

- E-Service Innovation
- Social Networking and Marketing
- Mobile CRM
- Mobile services
- CRM strategies
- B2B marketing
- CRM in financial services
- Database marketing
- CRM and customer trust
- Customer Relationship Management

IGI Global is currently accepting manuscripts for publication within this series. To submit a proposal for a volume in this series, please contact our Acquisition Editors at Acquisitions@igi-global.com or visit: http://www.igi-global.com/publish/.

The Advances in Marketing, Customer Relationship Management, and E-Services (AMCRMES) Book Series (ISSN 2327-5502) is published by IGI Global, 701 E. Chocolate Avenue, Hershey, PA 17033-1240, USA, www.igi-global. com. This series is composed of titles available for purchase individually; each title is edited to be contextually exclusive from any other title within the series. For pricing and ordering information please visit http://www.igi-global.com/book-series/advances-marketing-customer-relationship-management/37150. Postmaster: Send all address changes to above address. ©© 2019 IGI Global. All rights, including translation in other languages reserved by the publisher. No part of this series may be reproduced or used in any form or by any means – graphics, electronic, or mechanical, including photocopying, recording, taping, or information and retrieval systems – without written permission from the publisher, except for non commercial, educational use, including classroom teaching purposes. The views expressed in this series are those of the authors, but not necessarily of IGI Global.

Titles in this Series

For a list of additional titles in this series, please visit:
https://www.igi-global.com/book-series/advances-marketing-customer-relationship-management/37150

Handbook of Research on Social Marketing and Its Influence on Animal Origin Food ...
Diana Bogueva (Curtin University, Australia) Dora Marinova (Curtin University, Australia) and Talia Raphaely (Curtin University, Australia)
Business Science Reference • ©2018 • 453pp • H/C (ISBN: 9781522547570) • US $325.00

Analyzing Attachment and Consumers' Emotions Emerging Research and Opportunities
Giuseppe Pedeliento (University of Bergamo, Italy)
Business Science Reference • ©2018 • 308pp • H/C (ISBN: 9781522549840) • US $185.00

Building Brand Identity in the Age of Social Media Emerging Research and Opportunities
Amir Ekhlassi (University of Tehran, Iran) Mahdi Niknejhad Moghadam (Sharif University of Technology, Iran) and Amir Mohammad Adibi (University of Tehran, Iran)
Business Science Reference • ©2018 • 189pp • H/C (ISBN: 9781522551430) • US $145.00

Neuromarketing and Big Data Analytics for Strategic Consumer Engagement Emerging ...
Joana Coutinho de Sousa (Unlimited-Hashtag, Portugal)
Business Science Reference • ©2018 • 200pp • H/C (ISBN: 9781522548348) • US $165.00

Holistic Approaches to Brand Culture and Communication Across Industries
Sabyasachi Dasgupta (O.P. Jindal Global University, India) Santosh Kumar Biswal (Symbiosis International University, India) and M. Anil Ramesh (Siva Sivani Institute of Management, India)
Business Science Reference • ©2018 • 281pp • H/C (ISBN: 9781522531500) • US $225.00

Multi-Platform Advertising Strategies in the Global Marketplace
Kenneth C. C. Yang (The University of Texas at El Paso, USA)
Business Science Reference • ©2018 • 377pp • H/C (ISBN: 9781522531142) • US $205.00

Digital Marketing Strategies for Fashion and Luxury Brands
Wilson Ozuem (University of Gloucestershire, UK) and Yllka Azemi (Indiana University Northwest, USA)
Business Science Reference • ©2018 • 460pp • H/C (ISBN: 9781522526971) • US $210.00

For an entire list of titles in this series, please visit:
https://www.igi-global.com/book-series/advances-marketing-customer-relationship-management/37150

701 East Chocolate Avenue, Hershey, PA 17033, USA
Tel: 717-533-8845 x100 • Fax: 717-533-8661
E-Mail: cust@igi-global.com • www.igi-global.com

Dedicated to my wife Adriana and to our special kids, Michela and Sam.

Table of Contents

Preface xv

Acknowledgment xviii

Chapter 1
The Business of Tourism: An Introduction 1
    Mark Anthony Camilleri, University of Malta, Malta

Chapter 2
How Foreign Tourist Intermediaries Perceive and Sell a Destination: The
Case of Portugal 28
    Ana Mano Gomes, Universidade de Aveiro, Portugal
    Rui Augusto da Costa, Universidade de Aveiro, Portugal
    António Carrizo Moreira, Universidade de Aveiro, Portugal

Chapter 3
Is the Tourism Destination a Core Attribute in the Choice of Cruise
Consumers? 58
    Donata Vianelli, University of Trieste, Italy
    Manuela Valta, University of Trieste, Italy

Chapter 4
Impacts of the Tourist Activity and Citizens' Evaluation About the Necessity
for Resting Periods 81
    Jose Maria Martin, Universidad Internacional de La Rioja, Spain

Chapter 5
The Use of Differential Pricing in Tourism and Hospitality 113
    Aurelio G. Mauri, Università di Lingue e Comunicazione, Italy
    Ruggero Sainaghi, Università di Lingue e Comunicazione, Italy
    Giampaolo Viglia, University of Portsmouth, UK

Chapter 6
eWOM: The Importance of Reviews and Ratings in Tourism Marketing 143
   Juan Pedro Mellinas, Universidad Internacional de La Rioja, Spain
   Sofía Reino, University of Hertfordshire, UK

Chapter 7
Communication Technologies in E-Tourism: A Review of Online Frameworks 174
   Maria Matiatou, Universidad de Alcalá, Spain

Chapter 8
Branding Porto: An Authentic-Based Approach to Place Identity Theory 198
   Clarinda Rodrigues, Linnaeus University, Sweden

Chapter 9
Buxton and the Peak District: Attracting Visitors to the Water Festival 220
   Jessica Maxfield, University of Derby, UK
   Peter Wiltshier, University of Derby, UK

Chapter 10
Perceived Destination Image: The Case of Gallipoli 240
   Neslihan Cavlak, Namık Kemal University, Turkey
   Ruziye Cop, Abant Izzet Baysal University, Turkey

Chapter 11
A Strategic Framework for Managing the Challenges of Developing Rural Tourism Destination Branding 268
   Samuel Adeyinka-Ojo, Curtin University, Malaysia

Chapter 12
The Role of Tour Operators in Destination Tourism Marketing in Malawi 295
   James Malitoni Chilembwe, Glasgow Caledonian University, UK & Mzuzu University, Malawi
   Victor Ronald Mweiwa, Malawi Institute of Tourism, Malawi
   Elson Mankhomwa, Malawi Institute of Tourism, Malawi

Chapter 13
Sustaining Tourism and Branding: The Core Responsibilities of Stakeholders in Destination Development 322
   Caner Çalişkan, Adiyaman University, Turkey
   Bekir Bora Dedeoglu, Nevsehir Haci Bektas Veli University, Turkey

Compilation of References 343

About the Contributors 403

Index 409

Detailed Table of Contents

Preface xv

Acknowledgment xviii

Chapter 1
The Business of Tourism: An Introduction 1
    Mark Anthony Camilleri, University of Malta, Malta

This chapter introduces its readers to the concept of tourism. It sheds light on the rationale for tourism, as it explains the tourists' inherent motivations to travel. It also describes different aspects that together make up the tourism industry. Tourists travel to destinations that are accessible to them. They require accommodation if they are visiting a place for more than 24 hours. Leisure and business travelers may also visit attractions and engage themselves in recreational activities. Hence, the tourist destinations should have the right amenities and facilities. In this light, this chapter clarifies how destinations may offer different products to satisfy a wide array of tourists. Tourism products can include urban (or city) tourism, seaside tourism, rural tourism, ecotourism, wine tourism, culinary tourism, health tourism, medical tourism, religious tourism, cultural (or heritage) tourism, sports tourism, educational tourism, business tourism (including meetings, incentives, conferences, and events), among others.

Chapter 2
How Foreign Tourist Intermediaries Perceive and Sell a Destination: The Case of Portugal 28
    Ana Mano Gomes, Universidade de Aveiro, Portugal
    Rui Augusto da Costa, Universidade de Aveiro, Portugal
    António Carrizo Moreira, Universidade de Aveiro, Portugal

Research on tourist destination images is vast and embraces many destinations, approaches, and methods. More attention has been given to the perspective of final customers, instead of the ones who sell the tourist products to them. This chapter aims to understand how foreign tourist intermediaries, from the top outbound countries, perceive and sell Portugal as a tourist destination. It aims also to analyze the travel motivations they expect Portugal can satisfy and the information sources used to collect information to create tourist products regarding this destination. Foreign tourist intermediaries have a very positive image of Portugal as a destination, associating it to a set of cognitive attributes and psychological motivations.

Chapter 3
Is the Tourism Destination a Core Attribute in the Choice of Cruise
Consumers?...58
    Donata Vianelli, University of Trieste, Italy
    Manuela Valta, University of Trieste, Italy

In the last 10 years, cruise tourism has been frequently analyzed in the academic literature on leisure tourism. However, analysis of consumer behavior and the consumer-buying process is still limited, especially if the European market is taken into consideration. To address this gap in the literature, the authors analyzed how different attributes are evaluated by consumers in their decision-making process. In particular, the authors identified the role of the tourism destination among the different attributes that influence cruisers' choices. Using primary survey data from a sample of 4,002 German, Spanish, Italian, and French consumers, the analysis identifies the existence of consumer segments that give different levels of importance to the numerous attributes, including the tourism destination.

Chapter 4
Impacts of the Tourist Activity and Citizens' Evaluation About the Necessity
for Resting Periods..81
    Jose Maria Martin, Universidad Internacional de La Rioja, Spain

Tourism's interactions with local communities and natural environments originate economic, social, and environmental impacts both positive and negative. The local community's assessment of these impacts is key to guarantee their support for tourism development since the planning process is subject to their opinion. Tourism seasonality can intensify these effects due to the influx of tourists during peak periods and generate periods of rest and recovery during the off-peak season. In this research, the locals' opinions on the need for a period of seasonal rest is studied, even if this period interrupts the economic activity linked to tourism. Using a group of Spanish touristic destinations shows that the residents in coastal destinations prefer the annual continuity of the activity and that they are much more critical of the environmental effects than social ones. On the contrary, the inhabitants of urban and rural destinations would rather enjoy resting periods.

Chapter 5
The Use of Differential Pricing in Tourism and Hospitality 113
> *Aurelio G. Mauri, Università di Lingue e Comunicazione, Italy*
> *Ruggero Sainaghi, Università di Lingue e Comunicazione, Italy*
> *Giampaolo Viglia, University of Portsmouth, UK*

Due to the widespread adoption of revenue management strategies within the hospitality business, pricing has become more and more a central topic both for academics and practitioners. In particular, pricing has evolved towards value-based approaches, dynamic and customized through the use of price differentiation. "Rate fences" are the criteria that hotels adopt to separate customer segments whose service values may differ. The purpose of this chapter is to analyze the academic literature as well as the business practices relating to this subject. The authors propose a logical link between rate fences and the hedonic pricing approach. Main topics are 1) rate fence classifications and 2) the effectiveness of rate fences and their impacts on perceptions of fairness. Overall, this contribution suggests that time-based rate fences are fundamental at the destination level, and they are strictly connected to seasonality. Destinations' policymakers and firms can consider strategies and tools for overcoming seasonality, including special events that may take place in a destination.

Chapter 6
eWOM: The Importance of Reviews and Ratings in Tourism Marketing 143
> *Juan Pedro Mellinas, Universidad Internacional de La Rioja, Spain*
> *Sofía Reino, University of Hertfordshire, UK*

It is difficult to find a traveler who has not written and/or read an online review at any stage of their travel. Most people will not book a hotel if this has no reviews and/or will not choose a destination before reading some opinions from other users. Tourism professionals can gain a comprehensive understanding of the dynamic relationships and key influential factors which are relevant to online reviews. A single business can have thousands of reviews. This creates a situation of information overload for hotel managers, who encounter themselves with increasingly larger numbers of information to analyze and act upon. The ability to effectively analyze data, using in occasions dedicated software becomes a crucial aspect of hotel management. The chapter ends with a reflection on how eWOM is leading to the generation of a new approach to business management.

Chapter 7
Communication Technologies in E-Tourism: A Review of Online
Frameworks..174
Maria Matiatou, Universidad de Alcalá, Spain

Information-intensive and technology-driven environments like e-tourism need to be constantly oriented towards improvement of their communication strategies and infrastructure considering their immediate impact on user experience and customer behavior. The full range of available technologies is rapidly stretching from sophisticated website features to personalized services based on recommender systems that associate user preference with destinations and hospitality services. Despite the development of these technologies, many challenges remain in designing, applying, and evaluating the web-based services in their critical role between visitor and destination experience. This chapter addresses the problem of how to support management decisions on information technology solutions that best promote destination brands, support visitors' decision-making process, and enhance user experience of a place, service, or destination.

Chapter 8
Branding Porto: An Authentic-Based Approach to Place Identity Theory........198
Clarinda Rodrigues, Linnaeus University, Sweden

Departing from the Porto brand case study, this chapter discusses the concept of destination brand identity from the supply-side perspective. Consequently, it proposes an authentic-based approach to place identity theory, in which destination authenticity is pointed out as a key driver to create a strong place brand identity. Moreover, it is suggested that destination managers should follow an eight-step approach to branding a destination. This dynamic view of place identity, which is supported by a continuous co-creation process involving local and external stakeholders, allows destination brand managers to mirror and reinforce the destination authenticity.

Chapter 9
Buxton and the Peak District: Attracting Visitors to the Water Festival 220
Jessica Maxfield, University of Derby, UK
Peter Wiltshier, University of Derby, UK

This chapter is designed to analyze and interpret the demand from a new and anticipated international visitor market to the small market and spa town of Buxton, Derbyshire. It offers an audience development plan for the newly renovated Crescent Hotel and Spa (CHS). The hotel is currently in the final stages of re-development following a major refurbishment to a culturally important, both environmentally and socially sensitive, icon in Buxton. Benefits to the town include heightened awareness of tourism's contribution, through income from staying visitors and a resultant boost to the incomes of a range of stakeholders in the supply chain. A secondary analysis of two case studies, best practices of Harrogate and Bath, has been considered as these are both similar spa towns. The chapter concludes with several recommendations for the CHS to encourage international tourists to visit and stay a while.

Chapter 10
Perceived Destination Image: The Case of Gallipoli 240
 Neslihan Cavlak, Namık Kemal University, Turkey
 Ruziye Cop, Abant Izzet Baysal University, Turkey

The perceived destination image is a strategic weapon that provides a competitive advantage for the tourism destinations. Perceptions are the elements that give meaning to destinations. In this respect, it is important for the destination marketers to know how tourists perceive the destination. It can be seen that tourists with different demographic and cultural backgrounds who visit the same destination can perceive its image differently. The tourism marketplace is highly competitive. Because of this, destination management organizations (DMOs) need to understand the actual and the desired perception of their destinations in order to take necessary measures. In this chapter, the concepts of destination and perceived destination image are emphasized. Secondly, the political environment, cultural attractiveness, social environment, and natural environment factors affecting the perceived destination image will be examined. Finally, the perceived destination images of domestic and foreign tourists visiting the Gallipoli in Turkey will be examined comparatively.

Chapter 11
A Strategic Framework for Managing the Challenges of Developing Rural
Tourism Destination Branding 268
 Samuel Adeyinka-Ojo, Curtin University, Malaysia

This chapter explores the importance and challenges of branding for rural tourism destination. In the wider context of destination branding construct, empirical studies on the strategies to manage the identifiable challenges have received fewer academic interests. In this chapter, triangulation of data sources was used in the collection of data that included in-depth interviews with 31 multiple stakeholders in Bario, Miri, and Kuching in Malaysia. Findings show destination branding is important and there are several factors inhibiting rural tourism destination brand development. In terms of contributions to the existing knowledge, this study has produced a strategic framework for managing the challenges of rural tourism destination branding. Implications for practice, host community, and directions for future studies are discussed.

Chapter 12
The Role of Tour Operators in Destination Tourism Marketing in Malawi 295
    James Malitoni Chilembwe, Glasgow Caledonian University, UK &
      Mzuzu University, Malawi
    Victor Ronald Mweiwa, Malawi Institute of Tourism, Malawi
    Elson Mankhomwa, Malawi Institute of Tourism, Malawi

Destination marketing is one of the tools used by tour operators to gain a tourism competitive advantage. Tourism is one of the biggest businesses in the global village. It is a business in a very competitive market environment that marketing tourism destinations cannot be done by destination management organizations (DMOs) alone but also intermediaries like tour operators. Marketing tourism destination nowadays is highly driven by technology which enhances tourists' destination knowledge prior to their visits. However, the downside of technology cannot be underestimated on the business environment. While there is a growing importance of technology usage which creates challenges for destination competitiveness, tour operators use their marketing strategies to help building positive destination images. These images are created to influence tourists' travel decision making and visits. This chapter, therefore, has examined the present tourism marketing strategies, activities, and approaches used by tour operators in creating positive images for tourism destination using 20 cases of Malawian tour operators.

Chapter 13
Sustaining Tourism and Branding: The Core Responsibilities of Stakeholders
in Destination Development..322
    Caner Çalişkan, Adıyaman University, Turkey
    Bekir Bora Dedeoglu, Nevsehir Haci Bektas Veli University, Turkey

Branding with local dynamics is crucial to sustain tourism for a destination's existence and future. In this case, many stakeholder groups are responsible for the participation, social cohesion, economy, and environment. Thus, the authors conducted face-to-face interviews with seven key persons related to regional tourism development in the research area, Adıyaman. Research results show that in Adıyaman, a strong partnership, cooperation, and cohesion for sustainable tourism and branding is needed. The use of local dynamics—such as values, natural resources, education, and manpower—is an important variable of sustainable tourism and branding process.

Compilation of References 343

About the Contributors 403

Index 409

Preface

The marketing of a destination relies on planning, organization and the successful execution of strategies and tactics. Therefore, this authoritative book provides students and practitioners with relevant knowledge of tourism planning and destination marketing. The readers are equipped with a strong pedagogical application of the socio-economic, environmental and technological impacts on the attractiveness of tourist destinations. At the same time, this publication presents contemporary conceptual discussions as well as empirical studies on different aspects of the travel and tourism industries.

The readers of this book will acquire a good understanding of the tourism marketing environment, destination marketing and branding, pricing of tourism products, tourism distribution channels, etourism, as well as on sustainable and responsible tourism practices, and among other topics. They will appreciate that the tourism marketers, including destination management organizations (DMOs) are increasingly using innovative tools, including; digital media and ubiquitous technologies to engage with prospective visitors. Hence, this book also sheds light on the latest industry developments in travel, tourism, hospitality and events.

Chapter 1 introduces the readers to the tourism concept as it describes the travel facilitators and motivators. Afterwards, it explains several aspects of the tourism product, including; the visitors' accessibility, accommodation, attractions, activities and amenities. It categorizes different travel markets; including; adventure tourism, business tourism (including meetings, incentives, conferences and events), culinary tourism, cultural (or heritage) tourism, eco-tourism (or sustainable tourism), educational tourism, health (or medical tourism), religious tourism, rural tourism, seaside tourism, sports tourism, urban (or city) tourism, wine tourism, among other niche areas.

Chapter 2 examines how foreign tourist intermediaries perceive Portugal as a tourist destination. It analyzes the promotional information that they use to attract visitors to this Southern European destination. This contribution recognizes that the tour operators have an important role in intermediating the relationship between the tourists and the tourism service providers. The authors suggest that tourism relies on the destination's image that is often being portrayed by the foreign tourism intermediaries.

Chapter 3 explores the cruising consumers' behaviors and their decision-making processes. The authors maintain that the destination, the social life on board as well as the cruise features are very important factors for consumer loyalty. In conclusion, they recommend that cruise lines should create synergies with local institutions in tourist destinations.

Chapter 4 investigates the Spanish inhabitants' opinions on the tourism industry's seasonality issues. The findings suggest that the local residents who live in the coastal destinations were in favor of having tourism activity throughout the year; as opposed to other host communities from urban and rural destinations (in Spain) who indicated that they would enjoy a break from tourist activity during the low / off peak seasons.

Chapter 5 provides a critical review about the pricing and revenue management strategies that are increasingly being adopted within the tourism and hospitality contexts. The authors introduce the readers to the concept of "rate fencing". This proposition suggests that businesses ought to differentiate among various customer segments, as they should attract and develop relationships with the most profitable ones.

Chapter 6 appraises the use of qualitative reviews and quantitative ratings in interactive media. The authors also engage in a discussion on the content analysis of the online users' generated content (UGC). They posit that it is in the interest of tourism and hospitality businesses to respond to positive and negative word of mouth publicity in reasonable time, as they may have to deal with fake and unverified reviews.

Chapter 7 clarifies how online travel businesses, including; *AirTickets, AirBnB and TripAdvisor* among others, are continuously investing in their communication technologies and infrastructures to improve their online users' experience. The author contends that innovative technologies, such as recommender systems and control frameworks are supporting the travel businesses' in their customer-centric approaches.

Chapter 8 discusses about the concept of the brand identity of destinations from the suppliers' perspective. The author puts forward a case study on the city of Porto, in Portugal. She explicates how this tourist destination has used an authenticity-based approach to leverage itself as a distinct brand identity among other destinations.

Chapter 9 proposes an ambitious plan to attract visitors to Buxton, Derbyshire. Firstly, the authors focus on the marketing endeavors of a local renovated hotel. Secondly, they provide relevant examples of how other wellness and spa towns in Britain, including; Bath and Harrogate are organizing events and festivals to attract international tourists throughout the year.

Preface

Chapter 10 explains how a perceived (positive) image can provide a sustainable competitive advantage to tourism destinations. The authors argue that the historical events as well as other socio-political factors can possibly affect the visitors' (pre-) conceptions of the Gallipoli peninsula in Turkey. However, they imply that the tourists' positive experiences could translate to positive publicity for this destination.

Chapter 11 elucidates the notion of destination branding in the rural context. The author maintains that there are both opportunities and challenges for tourism policy makers to preserve the traditional farms and rural dwellings, in order to safeguard their distinct identity. He posits that the rural environment can add value to the tourist destinations and their branding.

Chapter 12 posits that today's tour operators are highly driven by technology as prospective travelers are searching for online information about their destinations prior to their visits. The authors describe the digital marketing strategies and tactics that are used to promote Malawi, in Africa. They suggest that the inbound tour operators are increasingly using relevant content marketing through interactive technologies and social media to engage with prospective visitors.

Chapter 13 evaluates potential strategies that could be used to develop the tourism product in Adiyaman, Turkey. The authors identify the core responsibilities of the tourism stakeholders and put forward their key recommendations for the branding of this rural destination.

In sum, this authoritative publication is written in an engaging style that entices the curiosity of prospective readers. It explains all the theory in a simple and straightforward manner. This book reports on the global tourism marketing environments that comprise a wide array of economic, socio-cultural and environmental issues. It explains how technological advances have brought significant changes to the tourism industry and its marketing mix.

This book was written by academics for other scholars, researchers, advanced under-graduate and post-graduate students; as it provides a thorough literature review on different tourism topics, including; destination marketing and branding, sustainable and responsible tourism, tourism technologies, digital marketing, travel distribution and more. It is also relevant to the industry practitioners, including consultants, senior executives and managers who work for destination management organizations, tourism offices, hotels, inbound / outbound tour operators and travel agents, among others.

Acknowledgment

There are too many people to thank individually. I am very grateful to my family, particularly to my wife Adriana who has always encouraged me in my academic endeavors. Finally, I must thank IGI Global Publishers and their editorial team, including Marianne Caesar and Amanda Fanton, for their valuable support during this fruitful project.

Chapter 1
The Business of Tourism:
An Introduction

Mark Anthony Camilleri
University of Malta, Malta

ABSTRACT

This chapter introduces its readers to the concept of tourism. It sheds light on the rationale for tourism, as it explains the tourists' inherent motivations to travel. It also describes different aspects that together make up the tourism industry. Tourists travel to destinations that are accessible to them. They require accommodation if they are visiting a place for more than 24 hours. Leisure and business travelers may also visit attractions and engage themselves in recreational activities. Hence, the tourist destinations should have the right amenities and facilities. In this light, this chapter clarifies how destinations may offer different products to satisfy a wide array of tourists. Tourism products can include urban (or city) tourism, seaside tourism, rural tourism, ecotourism, wine tourism, culinary tourism, health tourism, medical tourism, religious tourism, cultural (or heritage) tourism, sports tourism, educational tourism, business tourism (including meetings, incentives, conferences, and events), among others.

INTRODUCTION

This chapter describes the main sectors within the travel, tourism and hospitality industries (Robinson, Fallon, Cameron & Crotts, 2016; Gee, Choy & Makens, 1984). It provides a good overview of the vertical and horizontal inter-relationships between different sectors (Camilleri, 2018a; Fick & Ritchie, 1991). Firstly, this chapter describes the nature of tourism and the individuals' inherent motivations

DOI: 10.4018/978-1-5225-5835-4.ch001

to travel. Secondly, it distinguishes the constituent parts that make up the tourism product, including; accessibility, accommodation, activities, attractions and amenities. Thirdly, it suggests that tourist destinations are increasingly attracting a wide array of travelers who may have different needs and wants.

DEFINING TOURISM

Individuals become tourists when they voluntarily leave their normal surroundings, where they reside, to visit another environment. These individuals will usually engage in different activities, regardless of how close or how far this environment (destination) is (Hall, 2008; Holloway & Taylor, 2006; Jafari, 2002). Therefore, tourists are visitors, and what they you do whilst visiting another place may be considered as tourism. Back in 1963, the United Nations Conference on International Travel and Tourism agreed to use the term 'visitors' (other than residents) to describe individuals visiting another country. This definition covered two classes of visitor: Tourists were classified as temporary visitors staying at least 24 hours in a destination. If they are travelling for recreation, health, sport, holiday, study or religious purposes, their visit could be categorized as leisure. Alternatively, excursionists, including cruise travelers may be considered as temporary visitors, if they stay in a destination for less than 24 hours. However, these definitions fail to take into account the domestic tourists. In 1976, the Institute of Tourism (which later became the Tourism Society) suggested that tourism is the temporary short-term movement of people to destinations outside the places where they normally live and work. Therefore, tourism includes the movement of people for all purposes, including day visits or excursions (Cooper, 2008; Holloway & Taylor, 2006).

This broader definition was slightly reformulated at the International Conference on Leisure Recreation Tourism that was organized by the Worldwide Network of Tourism Experts (AIEST) and the Tourism Society in Cardiff, in 1981: *Tourism may be defined in terms of particular activities, selected by choice, and undertaken outside the home environment. Tourism may or may not involve overnight stay away from home.* In 1991, the United Nations World Tourism Organization declared that *Tourism comprises the activities of persons travelling to and staying in places outside of their usual environment for not more than one consecutive year for leisure, business or other purposes.* At this stage, one could differentiate between domestic and international tourism (Yuksel, 2004). The former refers to travel that is exclusively undertaken within the national boundaries of the traveler's home country. The latter refers to travel within the borders of one's home country. Domestic travel will have an impact on the balance of payments and will reduce the outflow of money from the tourists' home country (Mathieson & Wall, 1982).

The Nature of Tourism

At this stage, it is important to realize that there are two types of travelers: There are those who travel for reasons of business. Others may travel for personal motives, including visits to friends and relatives (VFR travel); study; religious pilgrimages; sport; health, et cetera. For the first group, the decision to travel, and where to go, is largely beyond their control. The business travelers will have little discretion in the choice of their prospective destination, or on the timing of their trip. Generally, the purpose of their trip is not to enjoy the destinations' attractions and facilities. Business travel is usually arranged at short notice and for specific and brief periods of time; the duration of their itinerary may often be as short as a day (Swarbrooke & Horner, 2001). In this case, there could be a substantial journey time involved. For these reasons, business travelers need the convenience of frequent, regular transportation facilities, efficient, reliable services and good accommodation facilities (in terms of accommodation and catering) of a high standard, at their destination (Jafari, 2002). Very often, business travelers will be less concerned about the cost of travel, as their employer could be paying for their travel arrangements (Gustafson, 2012). Higher prices will not deter them from travelling, nor will lower prices encourage them to travel more often. Therefore, there seems to be inelastic demand for business travel (Gillen, Morrison & Stewart, 2003; Brons, Pels, Nijkamp & Rietveld, 2002; Arnott, De Palma & Lindsey, 1993). On the other hand, leisure travel is highly elastic for those travelers who are price-sensitive. The lower prices for holidays to particular destinations will usually lead to an increase in the aggregate numbers of travelers (Hall, 2008). Frugal tourists will usually shop around for affordable holidays (Xiang, 2013). Therefore, they may be prepared to delay their travel, or to book well in advance of their travel dates, if this would translate to a significant reduction in their travel costs (Russo, 2002).

The growing disposable income among many populations from developed and developing countries is having an effect of reducing price elasticity for many holiday makers, as upmarket winter sports holidays, cruises, special interest and long-haul travel continue to attract a greater proportion of travelers (UNWTO, 2017).

The Ability to Travel

Beyond price, there are other reasons why specific tourism products (for example airline service or certain types of holidays or resorts) are chosen, as opposed to others. The demand for tourism is dependent on whether the potential traveler has the ability to travel (i.e. travel facilitators) or the desire to travel (i.e. travel motivators). Leisure time and disposable income are two of the most important travel facilitators in tourism. They are called facilitators because they are factors that may actually facilitate or enable individuals to travel. There are other factors that may also affect the persons' ability to travel. Alternatively, these may limit the ability to travel. These factors include;

- **Age:** Can affect the ability to travel either through health restrictions, or through financial limitations;
- **Stage in the Family Life Cycle:** Travelers may have the money and the time at their disposal, but family commitment may preclude travelling;
- **Political Stability and Peace:** Although this issue may not prevent travelling; it may limit the tourists' choice of destinations. There may be restrictions that may be imposed on nationals of some countries for political reasons, including; conflicts, wars or acts of terrorism.

Different people will consider different qualities in destinations. For example, individuals may value sporting facilities, others may prefer social life and night clubbing. Travel for leisure and pleasure could involve a wide range of human emotions and drives that may be difficult to explain. However, the motivations to travel relate to the individuals' will to travel. The motivators are the factors which could explain why people do what they do, they also seem to justify the individuals' behavioral intention. They are intrinsic, and could relate to the human beings' inner feelings, emotions and beliefs, as they arise out of need and wants. Motivators may be conscious and subconscious and are often deeply embedded in one's psyche. Tourism planners, developers and promoters need to identify why people choose to travel, when some necessity compels them to do so. What motivates them to travel to a holiday destination? It is obvious that tourism satisfies some human needs. The question is, which ones? The travel motivators may be divided into four categories, as featured in Table 1.

Undoubtedly, a large number of people wish to travel. Therefore, the tourism industry has a vested interest in determining: What motivates individuals to travel? What motivates them to engage in specific tourism activities, and to choose one destination as opposed to another? The prime motivation to engage in pleasure travel is the desire to be elsewhere, even temporarily from the routine constraints and stresses of everyday life.

Sharpley (1994) contended that the motivation to travel may be attributed to extrinsic or intrinsic factors. Extrinsic tourist motivation is often influenced by a need to escape from the pressures and conditions of life in a tourist's home society. Therefore, the need for tourism could have been developed from the individuals' anti-thesis to work. Conversely, the individuals' intrinsic motivation to travel may arise from deep-rooted, psychological needs, such as self-esteem, or a need for companionship. Sharpley (1994) held that the tourists' motivation results from a

Table 1. Travel Motivators

Category	Motivations
Physical	Refreshment of body and mind for health purposes; participation in sports; pleasure (or fun); excitement; romance; shopping and entertainment; among others.
Cultural	Curiosity about foreign countries, people and places; interest in art, music, folklore and architecture; interest in historic places (remains, monuments and churches); experiencing specific events (for example Olympic Games, et cetera); among others.
Personal	Visiting friends and relatives; meeting new people and seeking friendships; seeking new and different experiences in different environments; escaping from one's own permanent social environment (desire for change); personal excitement of travelling; visiting places and people for spiritual reasons (including pilgrimages); among others.
Prestige and Status	Pursuit of hobbies; continuation of education and learning; seeking of business contacts and professional goals; conferences and meetings; ego enhancement and sensual indulgence; fashion, keeping up with others, et cetera.

(Source: Camilleri, 2018a)

variety of social, economic, demographic and psychological factors that are peculiar to each individual tourist. The author went on to suggest that these factors are not constant and may change through time.

THE TOURISM PRODUCT

The tourism industry's major function is to serve travelers. Its success depends on the positive inter-relationships of all sectors. It is hoped that this synergy among tourism service providers will translate to a positive experience to the individual tourist. Basically, tourism comprises four main sectors: (1) Transportation; (2) Accommodation; (3) Ancillary Services and; (4) Sales and Distribution.

Tourism would not exist to the extent that it does today if tourists are not able to travel from one destination to another, in a quick and efficient manner. Transportation is what makes this possible. The transportation available to the tourist can be divided into air, water and land. The tourists' need for transportation can be divided into three groups: transportation from the point of origin to the host country (destination) and return; transportation between host destinations, where tourists travel to more than one destination; and transportation within host destinations.

Generally, air travel will be used to reach distant destinations. For the shorter distances, tourists may travel by car, by train and sometimes by boat. Travel between host destinations could be undertaken by air, although this may well depend on how far they are from their country of residence. Different means of transportation are normally used within host destinations. Frequently, tourists would like to experience different forms of transportation, which often add color to their overall tourism experience. Many countries offer unusual forms of transportation including cable cars, funicular railways, monorail, punting, jet-boating and rafting, among other options. These alternative transport vehicles are an attraction within themselves. For instance, the Emirate of Dubai is currently evaluating the construction of a fast transport link through a hyperloop system that could potentially reduce travel times to tourists and residents alike. The hyperloop's vacuum-sealed pod transportation system is a futuristic passenger and freight transport system. Its promoters allege that this innovative technology could reach near-supersonic speeds.

TRANSPORTATION

Air Travel

Air transportation can be separated into national (or domestic) and international flights. Domestic flights depart from one point to another within the same country. International flights depart from a point in one country to a point within a different country. Travelers may travel through public or private companies. Airlines may offer scheduled, chartered, low-cost, commuter or regional services, operating to / from their country. Very often, they may also have smaller airlines which operate air taxi services, non-scheduled services and sight-seeing tours.

Scheduled and Chartered Services

The scheduled and chartered tour arrangements may have fixed itineraries as transportation service providers are expected to operate regardless of the numbers involved. Yet, in times of disruption or in any emergency, scheduled services usually accommodate distressed passengers, other than chartered services. The main difference between scheduled and chartered services is price. The majority of tourists who prefer to pre-organize long distance travel arrangements may usually opt for scheduled transportation, for this purpose. This is where the selected means of transportation operates according to a fixed timetable. Therefore, the scheduled flights will operate regardless of numbers.

The charter flights which encounter technical or other problems may not have the same ability to meet the needs and wants of their passengers. The chartered service is usually cheaper as the producer of the tour is able to negotiate better prices for the charter of a whole aircraft and/or for large block bookings at hotels.

Legacy Airlines

National airlines (also known as legacy carriers) carry the bulk of the world's scheduled air traffic under the flags of over one hundred nations. For example, American, Delta, United, Air Canada, Aero Mexico, British Airways, Lufthansa and Qantas would be considered legacy carriers. Many of these flag carriers have a long history, as they may have started their operations in the first half of the 20th century. They may also be considered as full-service carriers (particularly during long-haul journeys, where they provide in-flight service). They typically own a broad and varied fleet, with many different types of aircraft. Usually, these airlines may have an extensive route network, as they operate to domestic and international destinations. A trend among legacy carriers is to outsource short-haul and medium-haul flights to regional airlines.

Legacy airlines started differentiating their product as they created and innovated many of the comforts on board their aircraft, including; the inflight entertainment that passengers enjoy while travelling. Many legacy airlines offer a multitude of higher-end travel services and could even offer airport lounge facilities, among other services. They may offer these services as they collaborate with other airlines through partnerships and codeshare agreements, alliances and mergers.

Full-service, legacy carriers may be equated with 5-star hotels which offer complete luxury for their guests' sumptuous experiences (Camilleri, 2018b). The 5-star hotels offer many facilities, hire many employees and offer posh real estate as opposed to smaller hotels. Moreover, the smaller hotels may not be located in best location. They may have less employees, as most services are do-it-yourself. The low-cost hotels may offer only basic facilities to their guests.

Low-Cost Carriers

The concept of low-cost carriers (LCC) is based on the idea of delivering low fares to induce demand. Attaining low-cost requires high efficiency in every part of the business. Therefore, the key components of the LCC business model are the following; high aircraft utilization; no frills, including; no inflight entertainment, no business-class seating and the use of a single type of aircraft. The cabin interiors may be fitted with minimum comforts, no seat-back video screens, no reclining seats and blinds. These airlines may choose to carry advertising inside the cabin to increase revenue. Meals and beverages are usually paid for in full. Moreover, LCCs may typically cut overheads by flying to / from more remote airports (with lower access charges). Some airlines also extend the definition of "frills" to include standard services and conveniences; for example, a no-frills airline may charge passengers additional fees for check-in luggage, for using airport check-in desks, or for priority boarding, among other services. LCCs keep their costs down as they do not print their own tickets. Passengers are also encouraged to check-in online. Moreover, LCCs may be strict when it comes to no-show guests, as they do not allow cancellations. and may not offer refunds for missed flights.

LCCs' processes are kept as simple and straightforward as possible. They usually operate a single type of aircraft. This way, pilots, flight attendants, engineers, mechanics and operations personnel are specialized in a single type of aircraft. This means that there is no need for costly re-training of staff to operate different types of aircraft with their own specifications, and for maintaining an extensive inventory of spares.

Legacy vs. Low-Cost Carriers

For the time being, passengers could not combine their low-cost travel arrangements with other legacy airlines' reservations. LCCs operate a simple point-to-point network, unlike the legacy carriers who will usually provide onward connectivity options through other airlines (Camilleri, 2018c). If they have more than one travel itinerary that includes a low-cost carrier, they could not have their luggage labelled and passed from one flight to another (as it is the case for legacy airlines). Unlike the full-service carriers, LCCs do not use the same Global Distribution Systems (GDSs), which are very costly. LCCs have kept their distribution channels as simple as possible. They usually sell their tickets through the internet (Buhalis & Law, 2008), via their website or via price comparison sites, like Kayak, Google Flights and Momondo, among others. Their fares are usually paid by credit cards and debit cards. LCCs may not utilize many sales offices and they do not rely on the travel agents' services. This allows them to save costs, which are usually reflected in their prices. However, LCCs would usually contract specialized call centers for telephone sales and customer service issues.

Water-Borne Transportation

There are many forms of water-transportation, including ocean cruises, ferries and hovercrafts, passenger cargo ships, river cruises, house boats and yacht charters. Cruising in particular has staged a revival after many years of decline. Whereas cruises are designed for pleasure, ferries provide a necessary means of water transport for both passengers and cars, over short distances. Recently, short-sea (ferry) vessels have also achieved new levels of comfort and speed on many routes. Technological developments have helped to reduce high operating costs, while new forms of water transport have been developed, such as hovercrafts, jet foils and the twin hulled catamaran ferries.

The Ocean Liners

Line voyage services are those offering passenger transport on a port-to-port basis, rather than as part of a cruise. Ships supplying these routes are known as liners. Some former ocean liners operate as cruise ships, such as Marco Polo. However, their use is diminishing. The only dedicated transatlantic ocean liner in operation is Queen Mary 2 of the Cunard fleet. She also has the amenities of contemporary cruise ships and offers significant services like cruises.

Cruising

A cruise ship or cruise liner is a passenger ship that is used for pleasure voyages, where the voyage itself and the ship's amenities are a part of the experience, as well as the different destinations along the way, i.e., ports of call. Transportation is not the only purpose of cruising. In fact, many cruises return passengers to their originating port (this is known as a closed-loop cruise), with the ports of call that are usually in a specified region of a continent. The cruise ships are divided in the following categories:

- **Traditional Cruises:** Which provide a holiday at sea, sailing from and returning to the same port. This itinerary could last from 7 to 15 days with five or more ports of call.
- **Fly Cruises:** Involve the transportation of passengers by air from a home base to join a cruise ship at a certain port. Afterwards when the cruise trip is completed the passengers will return by air to their origin.
- **Cruise and Stay:** Is a combination of a fly-cruise and ground arrangement, where the passengers stay some time in one of the ports of call.
- **Mini-Cruises:** Are short cruises of 2-5 days duration and are often operated by car ferry operators during low season.
- **Educational Cruises:** Include special lessons on board and often relate to a special interest of the passengers.

Ferry Services and New Modes of Crossing Channels

The term ferry is one which embraces a variety of forms of short distance, water-borne transport. This includes urban transport, in cities, where outlying suburbs and surrounding towns are reached by water. Ferries of this type also attract tourists, either as a convenient form of local transportation or as an original way to view the city.

In spite of the introduction of new fast ferries, alternative and still faster forms of water transport are becoming popular on many short and medium range routes. With a certain degree of novelty, hovercrafts, hydrofoils and catamarans have improved water transportation services with benefits of speed and convenience. Hovercrafts rides on a cushion of air above the surface of the water. A hydrofoil is a lifting surface, or foil, that operates in water. They are similar in appearance and purpose to aero foils that are used by airplanes. A catamaran is a multi-hulled watercraft featuring two parallel hulls of equal size. Catamarans range in size from small (sailings or rowing vessels) to large (naval ships and car ferries). The structure connecting a catamaran's two hulls range from a simple frame strung with webbing to support the crew to a bridging superstructure incorporating extensive cabin and/or cargo space.

Other Water-Borne Transport

The attraction of water offers many other opportunities for tourist activity, both independently and in forms which have been commoditized and packaged for the tourist. Inland waterways, particularly; lakes, rivers and canals provide exceptional opportunities for recreation and tourism. Where there is a large river, there is normally some form of river cruising. Houseboats are usually found in canals or on rivers. These forms of accommodation offer flexibility for independent travelers who can navigate their own houseboat. They combine accommodation and travel on the waterways. Boat rentals and yacht charters are highly competitive businesses, particularly during the high season (i.e. in summer, as the weather permits).

Land Transportation

Travel on land gives a choice of travel by rail or road, with the latter offering travel by car, coach (or bus) and campervan.

Travel by rail is readily available in most parts of the world, and combined air-rail travel has become quite frequent. Generally speaking, trains offer two classes of service; first and second class. Long distance trains normally carry sleeping or couchette cars.

Cars are a popular means of transportation and these may be privately owned or rented. The increase in private car ownership has changed travel habits of tourists. For instance, the fly-drive packages have adapted to the needs of the motoring tourists. Very often, car rental companies collaborate with airlines as they offer services, such as: rental locations at most airports; rent-it here, leave-it-there systems (often referred to as one-way rentals); free world-wide reservation services with no cancellation fees; chauffeur driven services in many countries; and special "unlimited mileage" plans. In addition, taxi services are provided in all major cities in all continents.

The hotel and catering industry responded to these developments by building motels and hotels, roadside cafes and restaurants along transport routes as they benefited from accessibility.

ACCOMMODATION

The accommodation sector comprises different forms of hospitality facilities which can be conveniently categorized as service (where catering is included) or self-catering establishments. Service accommodation may consist of hotels, bed and breakfasts (B&B's), travel inns, and the like. Whereas self-catering accommodation may include; campsites, caravans and holiday rentals of villas, apartments and chalets, among others. Half-board accommodation will usually include breakfast and dinner, whilst the full-board service will involve the provision of lunch, as well. Hotels are the most significant and widely recognized service providers of overnight accommodation for tourists and business travelers. They may also form one of the key elements of package holidays.

Historically, accommodation was established along major transport routes, particularly where there are cross-roads. Subsequently, hotels were developed close to railways and airports. The accommodation which is situated close to major transport routes is designed to serve the transit market (i.e. people who are on their way to somewhere else). On the other hand, those tourists on vacation will generally want to stay as close as possible to the major centers of tourist activity (for example; near the seaside or in close proximity to the mountains, country towns, health spas or major cities). If the major attraction is the sea, tourists will want to stay as close to the sea as possible. For example, hotel guests may be willing to pay a premium price for a room that is located in the sea front. The business travelers may require accommodation which is close to their business activity. Whilst location is generally considered the most critical factor with regard to the profitability of an accommodation unit, other factors, such as price and facilities are also deemed important in the hospitality sector:

Price could be a limiting factor for many leisure travelers. At times, it may also place restrictions on the choice of accommodation. Many tourists travel on a budget. Therefore, they may only consider accommodation that is affordable to them (i.e. if it is within their price range). The size of the hotel establishment can also be considered as a crucial aspect of the hospitality product. Some individuals consider large hotels to be impersonal and "cold". Therefore, they may opt for smaller units. Others may perceive that the larger hotels are more likely to provide a guaranteed minimum level of service. The hotel amenities can also prove to be a very important criterion for tourists, particularly to the business travelers who may require certain specialized services.

Hotel Brands and the Corporate Chains

With the development of mass tourism, so have the large hotel chains and corporations within the accommodation sector. This expansion has also been aided by franchising, whereby hotels and motels are increasingly being operated by individual franchisees who are paying royalties to their parent companies, for the privilege of operating under their brand name. This form of expansion has been used with great success around the world as chains market their products more aggressively, advertise extensively and work closely with large tour operating organizations. In addition to their own websites, they provide an effective distribution network that is linked to global distribution systems, they tend to a have a higher presence in the industry than their market share would suggest.

Leading chains around the work have often diversified their brands by price and image to appeal to a wider variety of markets. International hotel chains retain a strong hold on the global accommodation market. Their policy is to create an international and uniform marketing image to distribute their product around the world.

A recent trend among hotel chains has been the development of budget-price properties. For example, in mainland Europe, Accor Hotels has exploited the deficiency in this sector by introducing the super budget chains, 'Formule 1' and 'Ibis Budget'. While others have popularized low budget brands such as bed and breakfast (B&B) hotels (for example, Britain's Premier Inn). These very low-priced hotels have managed to reduce costs by developing a unitary design as they automated many of their services. Super budget hotels, including Easyhotels offer very basic rooms, which may be quite small. The rooms may offer TVs (at a premium) and small showers and toilet cabinets. However, they may lack wardrobes or even bed side lights. They may not have communal areas or bars, and housekeeping services are usually charged. Sales are exclusively online and they may not advertise their properties. Moreover, no discounts are given to distributors, such as travel agents or tour operators.

Consortia

In an effort to counteract the distribution strengths of large chains, many independent hotels around the world have frequently banded together to form consortia. While this strategy may allow the group to benefit from economies of scale, such as mass purchasing, it reinforces their marketing strength. It enables them to improve their distribution through a united website. Therefore, consortia may benefit from websites of other leading suppliers, including travel search engines. While many of the larger consortia such as Best Western Hotels and Resorts and Inter-Continental Hotel Group operate on a global scale; others may operate on a national scale. Some privately-owned hotels have even united within a themed consortium, in order to market themselves more effectively at home and abroad. For instance, Choice Hotels International has established a strong national brand in overseas marketing. This is a highly appropriate strategy when developing a niche approach. For example, Small Luxury Hotels of the World focus on building an image of high standards, yet they strive to deliver a personal service. While Grand Heritage Hotels, an American owned consortium which is now drawing membership from high graded UK hotels emphasize luxury and status. Other specialist consortia operating in the UK include: Pride of Britain Hotels, Scotland's Personal Hotels and Great Inns of Britain, among others.

The Bed and Breakfast (B & Bs)

Tourists may want to meet and engage with the local people. They may enjoy an intimate relationship with the culture of the country they are visiting. For this reason, they may choose to seek accommodation in guesthouses or bed and breakfasts (B&Bs). These forms of accommodation establishments are generally family-run, and they may cater to leisure as well as business tourists. B&Bs in particular provide a very valuable service to the industry, in that they can offer the informality and friendliness that is sought by many tourists. Many of these small establishments (which may not have more than three bedrooms) would usually provide accommodation to holiday makers who are touring by car.

Farmhouse Accommodation and Agri-Tourism

Farmhouse holidays have also enjoyed considerable success in recent years. European countries with strong agricultural traditions have catered for tourists in farmhouse accommodation for many years. Farmers have often turned to tourism as a means of boosting revenue, particularly during the off-peak season. The simultaneous trend to healthier lifestyles and an increased appeal on natural foods and the outdoor life have also helped to make farm tourism popular among tourists. As a result, many tourist boards have provided assistance and training to those farmers who were interested in expanding their accommodation for tourism purposes. For example, both Ireland and Denmark have been packaging modestly priced farm holidays for the international market, in association with international tour operators and major ferry companies. In the case of Denmark, this has been a logical development to attract price sensitive tourists to what is generally perceived as an expensive destination.

Camping and Caravanning

Camping is one of the most popular outdoor recreational activities for many tourists. In 2015, the revenue from campgrounds and parks was estimated to reach around 5.8 billion U.S. dollars. Recreational vehicles including caravans are also a popular and convenient way of camping. These vehicles provide campers with home comforts such as kitchen facilities and living areas.

Second Homes and Time-Share Accommodation

Second homes may be used for seasonal, recreational, or occasional use. Alternatively, second homes may be described as properties that are owned or rented on a long lease. No doubt. the growth of second-home ownership has had an effect on the tourism industry.

Time-share is a specialized form of "vacation ownership" as it is associated with the ownership of a property. Multiple users will usually hold rights to use the property. Each sharer is allotted a specific period of time to use the property (typically, the duration of time-share accommodation is of one week, at the same time of every year). Therefore, the accommodation units may be partially owned on a lease, or may have a "right-to-use". The sharer holds no claim to ownership of the property. Timeshare offerings may be structured through deeded interests, right-to-use, club membership, share-based plans, et cetera.

Educational Accommodation

Educational accommodation, including; universities and other institutions of higher education may often rent their students' rooms during the summer months. The students' accommodation is usually situated near major tourist destinations, such as London, Cambridge, Oxford and Edinburgh, among other university cities. Several universities have experienced considerable success in this venture and have further expanded their involvement with the leisure market; by providing essential facilities that reflect the standards of budget holidaymakers.

The AirBnB Model of Shared Accommodation

The Sharing economy describes economic and social activities, involving; online transactions in an open-source community. It usually refers to peer-to-peer sharing via an online market place. The sharing economy may take a variety of forms, including using information technology to provide individuals with information, that enables them to optimize resources through an effective use of excess capacity. Airbnb is a good example of an online marketplace which enables individuals to lease or rent their accommodation. Airbnb allows online visitors to book accommodation for entire homes, private or shared rooms. Online users can filter their search results according to their affordable budgets. Moreover, Airbnb's user-friendly website allows its users to choose particular amenities, facilities and other options, which will suit their requirements. This form of "shared" accommodation is usually cheaper than hotels, particularly in urban areas. AirBnb does not own any accommodation; it is merely a broker and receives commissions from both guests and hosts, in conjunction with every booking.

ANCILLARY SERVICES

Most tourists on holiday will want to be amused, entertained and active during their visit. In this case, they will require information on their destination's ancillary services, including activities and attractions. Shopping, catering and WIFI facilities are also important aspects of the tourism product. The access to business centers, interpreters, financial services and communication facilities may also be necessary requirements in tourist destinations.

Tourist Publications and Online Content

Tourists will require information about their prospective destination both before they leave home and once they arrive. This information should give details on the local people and their way of life, language, currency, climate, amenities, transportation, accommodation and attractions. The tourists are unable to see, touch or feel the tourism product in advance. Hence, the supply of such material is critical to the success of any tourist destination. The content marketing of the destinations could be a deciding factor as to whether tourists will visit them or not. The provision of clear and informative material that is readily available online are considered as essential services to prospective visitors.

Today's travel marketers can increasingly impact their consumers through ubiquitous mobile devices, including smart phones and tablets. The usage of the mobiles has changed the consumers' attitudes, expectations, and even the way they buy hospitality products and travel related services. Local and "near me searches" have changed the travel path to purchase with in-destination or "in the moment" sales opportunities. Consumers expect the "mobile first" user experience with easy access to contact information, maps, directions and reviews. They expect accuracy in listing information, and immediate responses from brands.

Public Service and Amenities

A destination's infrastructure is not usually developed with the tourist in mind, but should include facilities and services that are required by tourists. Infrastructural elements include; roads, electricity and water supplies, communication facilities, sewage and waste disposal, policing and security, medical services and hygiene. In developed countries, these facilities are provided for residents. However, if a region has tourist potential, its infrastructure must take into account the likely needs for future expansion, due to a possible influx of tourists.

Financial Services

Tourists require access to financial services in order to fund their travel arrangements. Foreign exchange is probably the most important service required; tourists may also need insurance and credit facilities.

Insurance is an important service and could be an obligatory aspect of a tourist's travel arrangements. Travelers may need coverage for one or more of the following contingencies: medical care and hospitalization (and where necessary, repatriation); personal accident; cancellation or curtailment of holiday; delayed departure; baggage loss or delay; money loss and personal liability, among other products. Some policies may also include coverage for the collapse of the travel agent or tour operator (who sold the tourism products).

Travelers today have an ever-widening choice of how they could pay for travel services and goods while abroad. These include carrying foreign cash, in the form of banknotes (yet, this may lead to loss or theft); by using travel vouchers, credit cards or debit cards. Travelers' checks could be utilized in many parts of the world, as these products are sold by banks and commercial institutions. Travel vouchers may be used for the payment of travel services, including car hire and hotel accommodation.

Food and Beverage

For many travelers, the consumption of food and drink forms an important part of the travel experience. It is not unusual for the tourists' consumption patterns to change quite considerable whilst they are away from home. Many tourists gain great enjoyment from dining out, particularly, if they are not in the habit of doing this at home, whilst others may decide to consume convenience foods.

Entertainment

This category includes facilities such as cinema or movies, night clubs, theatres, plays and shows. As a general rule, they are often attended for the sole purpose of filling in the night time hours rather than being part of a planned itinerary.

Retail Facilities

Shopping can be seen as an attraction for some tourists, or it may be considered as a basic facility that tourists expect. The retail trade provides an important service to the tourist, in terms of supply. Tourists may need to purchase basic necessities such as toiletries, or may want to purchase souvenirs and gifts which reflect the destination they visited. Moreover, the purchase of duty-free goods at airports; or on on-board ships and aircraft; or at specially designated duty-free ports have been in demand by tourists, for a long time.

Education and Training

With the growing institutionalization of tourism industry sectors, there is a greater emphasis on professionalism. In many countries, many professional bodies have introduced their own programs of training and vocational education, which are often carried out through full time or part time courses at local colleges of further or higher education. Examples of these, include courses offered by the Institute of Hospitality, formerly known as the Hotel Catering International Management Association (HCIMA), the Chartered Institute of Transport (CIT) and the Institute of Travel and Tourism (ITT). In-service training for travel agents was first formalized with the introduction of the Certificate of Travel Agency Competence (COTAC), nationally validated by the City and Guilds of London Institute (CGLI) and supported by ABTA's National Training Board (now known as TTC training). Certificates in Travel (for travel agents) and Tour (for Tour Operators) replaced the former ABTA-approved ABTAC and ABTOC qualifications, but all too briefly (Holloway & Taylor, 2006).

Many universities in the world are increasingly introducing undergraduate degrees in travel and tourism. These higher education or vocational institutions are joining the already well established higher national diplomas, post graduate diplomas and master's degrees in the subjects of tourism and hospitality management. The popularity of degree level tourism programs has led to a huge expansion of courses on offer. Recent trends have led to the establishment of more specialized degrees, including masters' degrees. Leading universities in hospitality and tourism management, include: Hong Kong Polytechnic University, Griffith University, the University of Queensland, Pennsylvania State University Loughborough University, University of Surrey, Purdue University (West Lafayette), Virginia Polytechnic Institute and State University, Bournemouth University and the University of Birmingham, among others (ARWU, 2017).

Tourist Guides and Courier Services

There is no specific term which will conveniently identify those individuals whose function is to guide, inform and engage with groups of tourists. Whilst some tourist guides and couriers may be employed by carriers and tour operators, others may work independently or could provide freelance services to companies in the industry.

SALES AND DISTRIBUTION

In addition to the above mainstream sectors, there is a side of the tourism industry that is related to the provision of support services. In tourism, the consumer is nearly always moved to the product as opposed to a product being moved to the consumer (which is the case with most other services). The tourism product and the consumer are usually separated by geography, as they may be situated in the opposite sides of the world. The system by which a tourist product is sold to the tourist is known as the sales distribution system. In common with most other industries, the tourism sales distribution is carried out through service providers (including; airlines, hotels, transportation companies, etc.), wholesalers (tour operators) and retailers (or travel agents), both being known as intermediaries, or middlemen. In this day in age, consumers are increasingly purchasing tourism products through digital media (Camilleri, 2018d; Schegg & Stangl, 2017). Therefore, many service providers and tour operators are selling directly from their corporate web sites, or through travel search engines (where online visitors may compare prices).

In tourism, the producer (or manufacturer) equates with the supplier of service (i.e. the supplier of the transportation, accommodation or ancillary service). The wholesaler is known as the tour operator or tour wholesaler. The retailer is known as the travel agent. The suppliers are those organizations which provide the actual components of the tour (for example an airline will provide air transport; a hotel will provide accommodation and a motor coach company will provide surface transportation and some sightseeing arrangements). Other suppliers include organizations that offer activities (for example; trekking, jetboating, rafting and surfing, et cetera) and those that offer attractions such as theme parks, live-theatres, museums and the like.

The wholesalers are the tour operators who may also provide complete tours for sale, i.e. including transport, accommodation and land arrangements (these may be components of inclusive tours). Traditionally, tour operators have been classified as either inbound operators or outbound operators. Inbound operators arrange and package holidays for tourists entering the country in which the tour operator is based, whilst the outbound operators arrange and package tours outside of the country from where they are based (i.e. overseas). The retailer is the travel agent who sells the tours to the consumer.

Travel Agency Operations

Generally, the travel agents' job is to work out an itinerary that suit their customers' requirements in order to secure reservations from them. This can be achieved by either working through a tour operator or by approaching individual suppliers, directly. The travel agents are usually paid commission by the supplier/tour operator for sales made on their behalf. However, many airlines have either reduced their commissions (to travel agents) or eliminated them, completely.

The travel agents secure specific elements of the tourism product to meet their client needs. Therefore, the travel agents provide a location (either through brick and mortar premises, or online) where potential tourists can seek information on the tourism products;

- Travel advice on the various options available;
- A booking service to secure reservations, on the various aspects of the product, such as transport, accommodation, sight-seeing, etc.;
- Support in travel formalities. This may include the procurement of travel documents, including passports and visas;
- The issuance of tickets, vouchers and itineraries for all travel arrangements.

A passport (or identification document) is required to travel internationally, and in some cases a visa may also be needed. The inability to get these documents may hamper the individuals' ability to travel, at least internationally. Moreover, some destinations may have currencies that could not be exchanged in other countries. Alternatively, individuals may have certain restrictions on the transfer of their funds. These issues may restrict international travel, although they could boost domestic tourism.

Types of Tours

The tour is one of the most often used words in the travel industry. It is also one of the most confusing because of its different meanings. To one client it may mean an itinerary that is advertised in an attraction brochure. To another, 'tour' may simply mean visiting a city or a tourist attraction during a trip. In many cases, tours are put together by retail agents who will then obtain actual components of the tourism product; directly from suppliers or through local tour operators. These tours can be customized to suit the individual clients' requirements, or they may be prepared in advance and marketed by the retail agent. In these cases, the retail agents act as tour operators and can either sell tours through their agency, or sell them through other retail agents. Likewise, tour operators may sell directly to consumers as they may have their own front offices, or a user-friendly web site.

An itinerary may be independent or packaged. A package tour, for which the official term is 'inclusive tour' is an arrangement where transport and accommodation services are purchased by the tourist, at an all-inclusive price. The inclusive tours have the following characteristics: the travel arrangements are planned in advance; they may include transport, accommodation and surface arrangements; they are sold at an all-inclusive price, covering all features included in the tour; and must be paid in full prior to departure.

Inclusive tours can be divided into independent inclusive tours (IITs) or escorted inclusive tours (or group inclusive tours - GITs). The independent tours are designed for individual travel and can be completely or partially tailor-made, to suit the clients' needs. The itinerary may be flexible or may be fully planned in advance. The escorted tours have all the components of the independent, inclusive tour. However, they also offer the services of a qualified tour escort in addition to the normal arrangements. These tours are usually arranged for groups of people who will travel together throughout the tour.

Tours which only provide a combination of accommodation and other activities within the same city or area are known as package tours or packages. The actual arrangements are usually quite flexible and may provide several choices of hotels, restaurants and other activities. Inclusive tour charters (IT charters) are charter flights combined with land arrangements. This arrangement is usually made available to the consumer at fixed, all-inclusive prices, through retail agents. Cruises and rail tours can also be classified as tours because they provide the various components that are normally associated with tours, i.e. transportation, accommodation and some surface arrangements. All-inclusive tours can be formed by combining several packages and / or tours to form a complete itinerary. For example, tourists can fly to a destination and join a cruise. Afterwards, they may decide to purchase a tour to visit local attractions near the port, before returning to their cruise.

TOURISM ORGANISATIONS AND THEIR STAKEHOLDERS

Whilst the transportation, accommodation and the provision of ancillary services relate to supply of the tourism product; the sales sector is involved with demand. Therefore, retailers and tour operators have to deal with what their customers want. The first three sectors are concerned with supplying the traveler a specific service. These sectors may operate independently, or they may collaborate together. For example, a hotel will probably rely on guests arriving by some mode of transportation. Likewise, suppliers of activities and attractions may also require a transport operator to get visitors to their location. Hence, in many cases there is scope for the tourism businesses to forge a close relationship with other service providers.

Moreover, the tourism industry would not operate efficiently unless there is some form of regulation and structure (Camilleri, 2018e). The tourism industry participants may represent the government (for example national authorities, including tourist offices and agencies) or the private sector as they may be direct providers of tourist facilities or services, support organizations or development organizations. Their interests may be international, national, destinational or sectorial. At an international level, the geographical scope of an organization may be either worldwide (for example, the World Tourism Organization – UNWTO) or restricted to a specific region of the world (for example, the Association of European Airlines). Whilst at a national level, the organization's interest may be local or regional. Examples of these organizations may represent; surface transport sectors, hotels and other accommodation units, tour operators or wholesalers, travel agents, or training bodies).

National Tourism Offices

National governments usually establish tourist offices or tourism authorities to serve national goals in the realms of tourism planning and development. The tourism offices strengthen the public and private partnerships in international tourism marketing. Moreover, they may have an important regulatory role. Specifically, their responsibilities include;

- The promotion and advancement of the tourism destination.
- To advise government on tourism operations and to issue licenses.
- To contribute toward the improvement of the level of human resources in the tourism industry.
- To advise government on the planning and development of the tourism industry, as well as on the infrastructure supporting the industry.
- To assist and advise on any tourism-related issues and to undertake activities, events and projects to improve the tourism product. (MTTA, 1999)

TOURIST DESTINATIONS

We have already seen how the four sectors of the tourism industry work, and we also looked at the tourism product. We have identified how tourism sectors rely on each other to provide those ingredients the travelers are looking for.

Key Elements of Tourist Destinations

Regardless of how or why individuals travel, there are some fundamental requirements that travelers expect from destinations. Tourism researchers and developers say that there are several key elements that are essential to the success of a tourist destination. These are traditionally referred to as the 5A's - including; access, accommodation, attractions, activities and amenities.

- **Access:** For a destination to be viable to tourists, there must be some way to get to the country, the region, and the various attractions. This does not mean that there has to be first class or mass transportation available to everything, but it does mean that access must be made possible. Access relates to transport, but it can simply refer to a walking trail or a cycling track.
- **Accommodation:** If tourists are to be more than just one-day visitors, they must have somewhere to stay. It is important for tourist destinations to offer a wide array of accommodation facilities, in terms of different price ranges. Sometimes, the accommodation is virtually part of the attraction of the destination, especially if it overlooks a spectacular scenery or landmark.
- **Attractions:** Tourists rarely travel to a destination simply for the sake to stay in particular accommodation establishments. They usually travel to see what the destination has to offer them in terms of what they can see, do and experience. The features that attract a person to a particular destination are known as attractions. Attractions can be natural wonders, man-made attractions, special events, cultural or historic sites, arts and crafts, sport, music or dance, unusual or unique flora and fauna, night life (et cetera). Attractions are many and diverse. Therefore, the wider the variety of a destination's attractions would possibly appeal to a large number of tourists.
- **Activities:** Tourists may enjoy doing certain activities whilst at their destinations. These activities include; shopping, eating out, using sports facilities and engaging in outdoor recreational journeys (among other activities).
- **Amenities:** The destinations' amenities include the provision of electricity and water, sanitary facilities, safe drinking water, roads, police and emergency services, postal and communication facilities, media, et cetera. Crucially,

these structures ensure that the tourists stay safe and sound during their stay in a destination. Tourists need to have access to basic facilities to feel comfortable and secure.

Different Types of Destinations

Destinations possess tangible characteristics and consist of a number of physical attributes (Camilleri, 2018a), including; attractions, amenities, buildings, landscapes and so on. However, the tourists' perceptions are less tangible, such as; the hospitality of the locals (for example, Gemutlichkeit), the atmosphere generated by being in particular event, the sense of awe, alienation, or other emotions that could be generated by specific destinations (Murphy, Pritchard & Smith, 2000; Moutinho, 1987). Destinations have different appeals to different markets. Some individuals love crowds, others love isolation and find crowded places unbearable. The appeal of the destinations is varied as they offer immense opportunities for tourism to be developed in almost any country, and in any region; provided that they are targeted at the appropriate market (Hall, 2008).

Most of the destinations are managed to some extent, whether they are natural or constructed. The national parks are usually left in their natural state of beauty as far as possible. Nevertheless, they have to be managed through the provision of access, parking, facilities, accommodation (such as caravans and campsites), litter bins and so on. Broadly, we can categorize destinations by delineating them according to their offerings, as suggested in Table 2: Moreover, holiday destinations depend on their image and tourist perceptions (Beerli & Martin, 2004; Echtner & Ritchie, 1993). Very often, the destinations' image is often frozen in time and could no longer represent a true picture of the place. For as long as the tourists' perceptions remain positive, promotional bodies will seek to support these images in their advertising and promotion. Most well-known tourist destinations, like cities and beach resorts, may usually rely on the stereotypes which have been built over the years.

A Non-Exhaustive List of Tourism Destination Categories

- **Adventure Tourism:** May include active holidays, such as winter sports which are commonly associated with rural sites. Mountain resorts have often been developed to attract winter sports enthusiasts.
- **Culinary Tourism:** Or food tourism involves the exploration of food. This aspect of a destination may be considered as a vital component of the tourism experience. Very often, tourists will dine in local restaurants when they are on holiday. Various types of restaurant fall into several industry classifications based upon menu style, preparation methods and pricing. Additionally, how the food is served to the customer helps to determine this classification.

- **Cultural Tourism (or Culture Tourism):** Is concerned with the travelers' engagement with a country or region's culture. Tourists travel to learn about the lifestyle of other people. They may be interested in their history, art, architecture, religion(s), and other elements that helped them shape their way of life.
- **Ecotourism:** Is a form of tourism that is related to the responsible tourism to natural areas. Its focus is on the conservation of the environment, including flora and fauna. At the same time, it is intended to improve the well-being of the local people as it characterized by its low-impact, small-scale tourism (rather than mass tourism, which is more commercial).
- **Educational Tourism:** This may involve those tourists who travel to a destination for educational purposes. Very often, many students pursue specialized courses to learn foreign language(s) in tourist destinations.
- **Health Tourism:** May be offered by resorts and spas. They may be based in rural, seaside or urban areas.
- **Medical Tourism:** Involves those people who are travelling to obtain medical treatment in a different country. In the past, this term may have referred to those who travelled from less-developed countries to major medical centers that may be situated in highly developed countries (for treatments which may be unavailable in the tourists' home country).
- **MICE:** Meetings, incentives, conferences and exhibitions (or meetings, incentives, conferences, and Events) is a type of business tourism involving large groups of travelers who are brought together for a particular purpose. Their itineraries are usually planned well in advance.
- **Religious Tourism:** Is a type of tourism, where tourists may travel individually or in groups for pilgrimage, missionary, or leisure (fellowship) purposes.
- **Rural Tourism:** Includes lakes and mountain tourism, but may also comprise countryside touring, agri-tourism products, such as farm holidays, fruit picking, gardens, visits and stays in rural retreats, river and canal holidays, wild life parks and national parks, et cetera;
- **Seaside Tourism:** Includes seaside resorts, natural beaches, rental of boats and jet ski, fishing itineraries, coastal footpaths, scuba diving, et cetera;
- **Sports Tourism:** Refers to travel which involves either observing or participating in sporting events.
- **Urban Tourism:** Includes visits to cities, towns, capitals and the like.
- **Wine Tourism:** Refers to tourism that is related to wine tasting, consumption or purchase of wine. Wine tourism can consist of visits to wineries, vineyards and restaurants that are usually known for their unique vintages, as well as for their organized wine tours, wine festivals or other special events. (Source: Camilleri, 2017a)

CONCLUSION

The tourists travel to destinations that are accessible to them via land, sea or air. They require accommodation if they are visiting places for more than twenty-four hours. Leisure and business travelers may also visit attractions and engage themselves in recreational activities. Hence, the tourist destinations should have the right amenities and facilities to cater for the tourists. In this light, this chapter has clarified how destinations may offer different products that satisfy a wide variety of tourists.

This chapter has provided a good introduction to the business of tourism. It defined the notion of tourism and explained the tourists' inherent motivations to visit destinations. It also described different aspects of the tourism product. Tourism products can include; urban (or city) tourism, seaside tourism, rural tourism, ecotourism, wine tourism, culinary tourism, health tourism, medical tourism, religious tourism, cultural (or heritage) tourism, sports tourism, educational tourism, business tourism (including meetings, incentives, conferences and events), among others.

REFERENCES

Arnott, R., De Palma, A., & Lindsey, R. (1993). A structural model of peak-period congestion: A traffic bottleneck with elastic demand. *The American Economic Review*, 161–179.

Beerli, A., & Martín, J. D. (2004). Tourists' characteristics and the perceived image of tourist destinations: A quantitative analysis—a case study of Lanzarote, Spain. *Tourism Management*, 25(5), 623–636. doi:10.1016/j.tourman.2003.06.004

Brons, M., Pels, E., Nijkamp, P., & Rietveld, P. (2002). Price elasticities of demand for passenger air travel: A meta-analysis. *Journal of Air Transport Management*, 8(3), 165–175. doi:10.1016/S0969-6997(01)00050-3

Camilleri, M. A. (2018a). The Tourism Industry: An Overview. In *Travel Marketing, Tourism Economics and the Airline Product* (pp. 3–27). Cham, Switzerland: Springer. doi:10.1007/978-3-319-49849-2_1

Camilleri, M. A. (2018b). The Airline Product. In *Travel Marketing, Tourism Economics and the Airline Product* (pp. 3–27). Cham, Switzerland: Springer. doi:10.1007/978-3-319-49849-2_1

Camilleri, M. A. (2018c). Airline Schedules Planning and Route Development. In *Travel Marketing, Tourism Economics and the Airline Product* (pp. 3–27). Cham, Switzerland: Springer. doi:10.1007/978-3-319-49849-2_1

Camilleri, M. A. (2018d). Tourism Distribution Channels. In *Travel Marketing, Tourism Economics and the Airline Product* (pp. 3–27). Cham, Switzerland: Springer. doi:10.1007/978-3-319-49849-2_1

Camilleri, M. A. (2018e). The Marketing Environment. In *Travel Marketing, Tourism Economics and the Airline Product* (pp. 3–27). Cham, Switzerland: Springer. doi:10.1007/978-3-319-49849-2_1

Cooper, C. (2008). *Tourism: Principles and practice*. London, UK: Pearson Education.

Echtner, C. M., & Ritchie, J. B. (1993). The measurement of destination image: An empirical assessment. *Journal of Travel Research*, *31*(4), 3–13. doi:10.1177/004728759303100402

Fick, G. R., & Brent Ritchie, J. R. (1991). Measuring service quality in the travel and tourism industry. *Journal of Travel Research*, *30*(2), 2–9. doi:10.1177/004728759103000201

Gee, C. Y., Choy, D. J., & Makens, J. C. (1984). *The travel industry*. Westport, CT: AVI Publishing.

Gustafson, P. (2012). Managing business travel: Developments and dilemmas in corporate travel management. *Tourism Management*, *33*(2), 276–284. doi:10.1016/j.tourman.2011.03.006

Hall, C. M. (2008). *Tourism planning: policies, processes and relationships*. London, UK: Pearson Education.

Holloway, J. C., & Taylor, N. (2006). *The business of tourism*. London, UK: Pearson Education.

Jafari, J. (Ed.). (2002). *Encyclopedia of tourism*. Oxford, UK: Routledge.

Mathieson, A., & Wall, G. (1982). *Tourism, economic, physical and social impacts*. London, UK: Pearson Longman.

Moutinho, L. (1987). Consumer behaviour in tourism. *European Journal of Marketing*, *21*(10), 5–44. doi:10.1108/EUM0000000004718

Murphy, P., Pritchard, M. P., & Smith, B. (2000). The destination product and its impact on traveller perceptions. *Tourism Management*, *21*(1), 43–52. doi:10.1016/S0261-5177(99)00080-1

Robinson, P., Fallon, P., Cameron, H., & Crotts, J. C. (Eds.). (2016). *Operations management in the travel industry*. Oxford, UK: Cabi. doi:10.1079/9781780646107.0000

Russo, A. P. (2002). The "vicious circle" of tourism development in heritage cities. *Annals of Tourism Research, 29*(1), 165–182. doi:10.1016/S0160-7383(01)00029-9

Sharpley, R. (1994). *Tourism and tourist motivation*. Huntingdon, UK: Elm Publications.

Swarbrooke, J., & Horner, S. (2001). *Business travel and tourism*. Oxford, UK: Routledge.

UNWTO. (2016). *World Tourism Organization UNWTO: Tourism Highlights*. Retrieved from http://www.e-unwto.org/doi/pdf/10.18111/9789284418145

Xiang, Y. (2013). The characteristics of independent Chinese outbound tourists. *Tourism Planning & Development, 10*(2), 134–148. doi:10.1080/21568316.2013.783740

Yuksel, A. (2004). Shopping experience evaluation: A case of domestic and international visitors. *Tourism Management, 25*(6), 751–759. doi:10.1016/j.tourman.2003.09.012

Chapter 2

How Foreign Tourist Intermediaries Perceive and Sell a Destination:
The Case of Portugal

Ana Mano Gomes
Universidade de Aveiro, Portugal

Rui Augusto da Costa
Universidade de Aveiro, Portugal

António Carrizo Moreira
Universidade de Aveiro, Portugal

ABSTRACT

Research on tourist destination images is vast and embraces many destinations, approaches, and methods. More attention has been given to the perspective of final customers, instead of the ones who sell the tourist products to them. This chapter aims to understand how foreign tourist intermediaries, from the top outbound countries, perceive and sell Portugal as a tourist destination. It aims also to analyze the travel motivations they expect Portugal can satisfy and the information sources used to collect information to create tourist products regarding this destination. Foreign tourist intermediaries have a very positive image of Portugal as a destination, associating it to a set of cognitive attributes and psychological motivations.

DOI: 10.4018/978-1-5225-5835-4.ch002

INTRODUCTION

Over time, people tend to acquire images of locations or destinations through various communication inputs they receive (Gunn, 1988). Image is very important for tourism (Gallarza, Saura, & García, 2002; Gartner, 1994) as the projection of a proper image can be reflected in the tourists' perceived image (Gartner, 1994), which in turn influences the destinations' assessment and the behavior of potential visitors (Agapito, Valle, & Mendes, 2013; Baloglu, 1999; Bigné, Sánchez, & Sánchez, 2001). Moreover, the success or failure of tourism in many destinations strongly depends on the effective management of image, as well as on understanding of individuals' image of specific locations (Fakeye & Crompton, 1991; Elliot, Papadopoulos, & Kim, 2011). Stepchenkova and Mills (2010) defend that destination image research is one of the tourism scholarly areas with strong implications for destination management, marketing, and branding.

Many authors have conceptualized and defined tourist destination image. However, according to Jenkins (1999), the most complete definition is the one proposed by Lawson and Baud-Bovy (1977): *the expression of all objective knowledge, impressions, prejudice, imaginations, and emotional thoughts an individual or group might have of a particular place*. According to Gartner (1994), the perceived image of a destination consists of three components (Agapito, Valle, & Mendes, 2013; Baloglu & McCleary, 1999a; Beerli & Martín, 2004a; Stepchenkova & Mills, 2010; Tasci & Gartner, 2007): affective, cognitive and behavioral.

There has been plenty of research on the importance of destination image and how it influences tourists' behavior (e.g. Baloglu & McCleary, 1999a; Beerli & Martín, 2004a; Souiden, Ladhari, & Chiadmi, 2017). Selecting tourism intermediaries as the target population is a central contribution for research since tourism intermediaries are usually focused on promotional efforts, with functions such as developing and promoting destination tourism packages, besides informing potential visitors, these professionals are key influencers when it comes to the tourism sector. Furthermore, the majority of research regarding destination's image is focused on being understood through the perspective of the tourist, with limited literature focused on the perspective of these professionals.

In Portugal, studies on perceived image are not new. Some address Portugal as destination as a whole, while other studies examine only certain regions or cities. However, there is a lack of understanding how Portugal's perceived image is influenced by international tourist intermediaries (Mano, Costa, & Moutinho, 2014; Silva, Costa, & Moreira, 2018). As such, the main objective of this study is to investigate the importance of foreign tourist intermediaries in selling a destination (Camilleri, 2018a), considering the image they perceive and create. In order to accomplish this central objective, four specific goals were set to this research:

- **Goal 1:** To discuss the importance of the perceived image and its components for tourist destinations;
- **Goal 2:** To characterize the perceived image of Portugal as a tourist destination from the perspective of foreign tourist intermediaries;
- **Goal 3:** To identify the motivations of foreign tourist intermediaries to recommend Portugal to their customers;
- **Goal 4:** To identify the information sources used by foreign tourist intermediaries for the development and design of tourist products for Portugal.

Intermediaries can take several forms, among which we can distinguish for example, tour operators, travel agencies, search engines, research agencies (such as consultancy firms and universities), travel websites (such as TripAdvisor, Booking, Trivago, etc). They normally affect destination demand or influence the destination selection decisions of direct or indirect customers (Camilleri, 2018b, c; Line & Wang, 2017; Pearce, 2008). In this paper, we analyzed tour operators and travel agencies, which we call intermediaries for simplicity reasons.

PERCEIVED IMAGE OF TOURIST DESTINATIONS

Individuals tend to acquire images of locations or destinations via various information and communication channels (Echtner & Ritchie, 1991; Gartner, 1994; Govers, Go, & Kumar, 2007; Gunn, 1988; Pike, 2008; Tasci & Kozak, 2006) even in cases of no previous visit to the destinations. Positive or negative perceptions and values are assigned by the individual to these places, building images *well defined or [...] vague, more factual or fanciest, but in any case [...] indicative of preferences* (Gunn, 1988, p. 23). As such, as Silva et al. (2018) claim the tourism destination image is a mental representation of knowledge, beliefs, ideas, expectations, feelings and global impressions that individuals have regarding destinations. As such, one can claim that the subjective perspective tourists have regarding a location, influences their behavior (Alcañiz, García, & Blas, 2009; Bigné, Sánchez, & Sánchez, 2001; Rodríguez del Bosque & San Martín, 2008; Silva, Costa, & Moreira, 2018).

As the perceived image consists of a set of particular components that influence human aspects (cognition, emotion and behavior), it is essential to be informed about its components and attributes as it is influenced by the individual's own knowledge and beliefs, as well as by individual's feelings towards the object/destination under analysis.

Perceived Image Components

According to Gartner (1994), perceived image of a tourist destination consists of three components –cognitive, affective and behavioral – that were extensively analyzed over the past decades taking into account mainly the tourists' perspectives (Agapito, Valle, & Mendes, 2013; Baloglu & McCleary, 1999a; Beerli & Martín, 2004a; Stepchenkova & Mills, 2010; Tasci & Gartner, 2007).

The cognitive component involves a mental conception created by an individual regarding image attributes. It is a branch of the most intellectual and perceptual image related to the facts, beliefs and knowledge of an individual in relation to an object. In this process, the amount of received stimuli is fundamental to the creation of the corresponding cognitive image (Beerli & Martín, 2004a; Gartner, 1994; Stepchenkova & Mills, 2010).

The affective image represents what the individual feels about the object or location, which corresponds to a more emotional image. This component also reveals a more evaluative character (Agapito, Valle, & Mendes, 2013; Baloglu & McCleary, 1999a) related to the reasons that individuals have to select a destination, i.e., what individuals expect to achieve once in the destination. The third component relates to the behavioral image, which implies action in response to rational and emotional interpretations. In other words, this means how the individual processes the available information and acts regarding it (Gartner, 1994).

Although the concept of image embodies these components, the literature analyzed global image as a construct itself (Agapito, Valle, & Mendes, 2013; Alcañiz, García, & Blas, 2009; Baloglu & McCleary 1999a, 1999b; Custódio & Gouveia, 2007; Qu, Kim, & Im, 2011). This global image is the positive or negative evaluation of the place combining its three components (Beerli & Martín, 2004a).

Gartner (1994) suggests that destination image is formed hierarchically in such a way that cognitive components are formed first and, then, affective components. However, Qu, Kim, and Im (2011) defend that the cognitive and affective components of images can interact in unique ways when an overall image is built. In a different way, according to the model of the three-gaps of destination image formation (Govers, Go, & Kumar, 2007), cognitive, affective and behavioral image components are presented hierarchically at the same level considering their contribution to the perceived image. However, Li, Cai, Lehto, and Huang (2010) suggest a sequential relationship in which the cognitive component leads to affective evaluations and feelings, which finally leads to attitudes towards the destination (intentions, actions, behaviors) and to the overall image of the destination (Baloglu, 1999; Kim & Yoon, 2003; Qu, Kim, & Im, 2011; Stepchenkova & Mills, 2010).

In this respect, Baloglu and McCleary (1999b) analyzed the relationship among cognitive, affective and global image of a destination, confirming that the cognitive image has a positive influence on the overall destination image. This influence is even stronger when mediated by the affective dimension of the destination's image.

One of the typical characteristics involving studies on cognitive, affective and global image is that they normally analyze tourists' images on certain destinations. For example, based on responses from 1,530 potential tourists, Baloglu and McCleary (1999a) analyzed images from four different countries: Turkey, Greece, Italy, and Egypt, even before actual visitation. Beerli and Martín (2004a) analyzed 616 tourists to Lanzarote (Canary Islands), Spain. Alcañiz et al. (2009) analyzed 380 tourists in Peñíscola, Spain. Agapito et al. (2013) analyzed 379 tourists in Lagos, Portugal. In a different vein, Custódio and Gouveia (2007) conducted a survey of journalists covering the UEFA EURO 2004™ event based on 168 responses of 3500 questionnaires. However, the analysis of the perceived image by international tour operators and travel agencies to their outbound markets seems under-researched (Baloglu & Mangaloglu, 2001; Silva, Costa, & Moreira, 2018). For example, Alaeddinoglu and Can (2010) analyzes how UK-based travel intermediaries such as tour operators and travel agencies assess the destination image of Turkey based on a sample of 44 samples of 134 tour operators.

Perceived Image Analysis

The image of a tourist destination has an important role both in consumer behavior and in defining marketing strategies. Moreover, the use of convenient methodologies is critical for the measurement and evaluation of this concept when considering particular destinations. Echtner and Ritchie (1991) recognized this issue and its epistemological contribution ought to be highlighted.

Echtner and Ritchie's (1991) methodological inputs summarize the most commonly used methodologies and propose an approach that has been extensively adopted by many researchers (Alaeddinoglu & Can, 2010; Alcañiz, García, & Blas, 2009; Beerli & Martín, 2004a, 2004b; Carneiro, 2007; Chen & Hsu, 2000; Chen & Tsai, 2007; Gallarza, Saura, & García, 2002; García, Gómez, & Molina, 2012; Govers & Go, 2003; Grosspietsch, 2006; Jenkins, 1999; Konecnik & Gartner, 2007; McCartney, 2008; Qu, Kim, & Im, 2011; San Martín & del Bosque, 2008; Stepchenkova & Morrison, 2008).

Echtner and Ritchie (1991, p. 40) concluded that a product's image is perceived in terms of individual attributes – *perceptions of individual characteristics, dimensions and attributes of product image related to discursive forms of information processing* – and holistic impressions – *total impressions, auras and feelings incorporate the role of imagery, or holistic conceptualizations, in describing a product's image.*

Gallarza et al. (2002) reviewed the concept and measurement of destination image and based on the three dimensions of object, subject and attributes, they proposed a taxonomy of the methodological and statistical procedures for measuring the image of the destination image. Based on responses from 807 tourists visiting a holiday destination, San Martín and del Bosque (2008) found that destination image is a multidimensional concept formed by not only cognitive and affective evaluations of a place, but also the tourists' motivations and cultural values, as the shorter the cultural distance between destination and tourist, the more favorable the cognitive/affective image of the tourist destination is.

Based on the work of Echtner and Ritchie (1991), Qu et al. (2011) developed and tested a model of destination branding integrating the concepts of branding and destination image. They also suggest the incorporation of unique image as a new component of destination brand association. It is clear that the three dimensions of object, subject and attributes are still present.

According to Echtner and Ritchie (1991, p. 42), image can be described based on functional characteristics, namely those *directly observable or measurable*, and on psychological characteristics, which are *based on more abstract, intangible characteristics*. Both approaches can be applied to destinations, although a third analysis is suggested in this field: common versus unique characteristics. The first relates to *the impressions of a core group of traits on which all destinations are commonly rated and compared*, while the later relates to single events, features or auras (Echtner & Ritchie, 1991, p. 43). In this research, the authors attempted to achieve a full and complete measurement of the destination image capturing each of these three continuums and its six respective opposite poles. This led to a set of items to measure cognitive and affective image that were used in the data collection of this research and that are deeply explained in the methodology section. With this we can address goals 1 and 2, defined in the previous section.

There are many studies trying to capture the essence of destination image (Nghiêm-Phú, 2014), complementing previous studies (Echtner & Ritchie, 1991; Gallarza, Saura, & García, 2002; Pike, 2002; Stepchenkova & Mills, 2010). However, the analysis of destination image from the perspective of the intermediaries is still reduced (Alaeddinoglu & Can, 2010; Mariutti & Giraldi, 2014; Rezende-Parker, Morisson, & Ismail, 2003; Silva, Costa, & Moreira, 2018).

The main role of intermediaries as tour operators and travel agencies is to drive primary demand to the tourist destinations (Camilleri, 2018a; Kracht & Wang, 2010), connecting tourists with other industry stakeholders (Ford, Wang, & Vestal, 2012; Kracht & Wang, 2010), affecting destination choice (Alaeddinoglu & Can, 2010), and mediating the relationship between marketing communications strategy and global image (Silva, Costa, & Moreira, 2018), which is in line with the multi-stakeholder approach proposed by Line and Wang (2017).

This paper seeks to complement previous research on tourist intermediaries as Alaeddinoglu and Can (2010) compared UK-based mass and specialist travel intermediaries taking into account affective and cognitive images of Turkey, but did not analyze the motivations or information sources of those intermediaries. As such, in order to understand the main motivations of tourist intermediaries to recommend their destination choice (Portugal in this case) and the main information sources used by intermediaries when developing their products for Portugal as a destination choice. We address goals 3 and 4 put forward in the first section of this paper, regarding motivations and information sources used by foreign intermediaries.

METHODOLOGY

Data Collection and Sample

Most studies in social and behavioral sciences, and especially on tourist destination image, use quantitative methods (Gallarza, Saura, & García, 2002), based on primary data obtained through questionnaire surveys (Jones, 1996). As structured questionnaires facilitate the coding, processing of data and the analysis of the results, through closed answer questions, data collection was carried out through a structured questionnaire applied to tourism intermediaries based outside of Portugal. However, we used a semi-structured approach to capture the global image component through open answer questions (Echtner & Ritchie, 1991; Hsu, Wolfe, & Kang, 2004; Jenkins, 2003).

The target countries were selected taking into account the number of foreign visitors in Portugal, by country of residence. This is the most appropriate indicator since the aim was to select intermediaries from countries that send more visitors to Portugal. The top five countries according to this indicator in the recent years (2010-2013) are (Turismo de Portugal, 2013): The United Kingdom, Spain, Germany, France and Brazil.

This empirical study was based on a non-random convenience sample consisting of tour operators and travel agencies from those selected countries. This sampling technique was chosen for its ease of contact and speed and low cost of data collection as it was not possible to generate a random sample from all intermediaries across the world. However, in order to reach the largest possible number of tourist intermediaries, 282 questionnaires were sent via email to contacts achieved through an online comprehensive research and also through some tourism national organizations. As shown in Table 1, the response rate is 15.25%, with Spain and Brazil slightly underrepresented.

Table 1. Contacted Intermediaries and Obtained Responses

		UK	Spain	Germany	France	Brazil	Total
Contacted intermediaries by country	Un.	108	15	14	116	29	282
	%	38.30	5.32	4.96	41.13	10.28	100
Obtained responses (% relating to the number of contacted intermediaries in each country)	Un.	17	1	2	20	3	43
	%	15.74	6.67	14.29	17.24	10.34	15.25

Baloglu and Mangaloglu (2001) studied how tourist intermediaries based in the United States analyze the image of Mediterranean countries based on 46 responses, with a response rate of 14.9%. Although with higher response rates, Grosspietsch (2006) and Alaeddinoglu and Can (2010) obtained a similar number of responses (42 and 44, respectively) when analyzing the image of tourist destinations from international intermediaries. Based on these studies, one can argue that the rate and number of responses obtained in the present paper are within the parameters obtained in previous studies. Moreover, low response rates are common in organizational surveys, which usually range from 1 to 20 per cent (Baloglu & Mangaloglu, 2001; Paxson, 1995).

Measurement and Scales

The questionnaire was designed in two stages. Firstly, it was based on items and scales suggested on the literature – 41 papers and theses regarding tourist destination image were thoroughly analyzed in order to identify global, affective and cognitive images, as well as travel motivations and information sources. Secondly, it was subjected to a pre-test conducted on a convenience sample of seven Portuguese travel agencies, and subsequently improved.

The data were collected using a questionnaire consisting of previously validated scales adapted from previous research. With regard to the cognitive image, most of the authors base their measurements on Echtner and Ritchie (1991), with specific adaptations. As such, we used 33 of the attributes suggested by Echtner and Ritchie (1991), since all of these have already been widely tested. In addition, as some authors use other attributes we listed several complementary attributes for a thorough examination, bearing in mind the particular characteristics and the supply of the destination under study. This resulted in nine additional attributes for the analysis of cognitive image (Table 2).

A report on tourist satisfaction in Portugal (Intercampus, 2013) was also analyzed, in order to add attributes that are distinctive or particular of this destination (Jenkins,

2003; Li, Cai, Lehto, & Huang, 2010; MacKay & Fesenmaier, 1997; Qu, Kim, & Im, 2011). Three items were finally added to the analysis of cognitive image (Table 2).

All items of the cognitive image were randomly divided into four groups of 11-12 items each, which were interspersed among the remaining questions, in order to avoid response bias.

Most of the sources consulted regarding affective image are based on the work of a particular group of researchers (Russel, 1980; Russel & Pratt, 1980; Russel & Snodgrass, 1987; Russel, Ward & Pratt, 1981), who confirm that the affective image can be measured by the four bipolar scales used in this study: pleasant – unpleasant; exciting – boring; arousing – sleepy; relaxing – stressful. As such, destinations' affective image has been analyzed by a seven-point semantic differential scale (Table 2).

Regarding global image, as shown in Table 2, previous work on overall image of a destination (Alaeddinoglu & Can, 2010; Baloglu, 1999; Baloglu & McCleary, 1999b; Beerli & Martín, 2004a; Qu, Kim, & Im, 2011) was used to analyze Portugal's global image as tourist destination. Responses were given on a five-point Likert scale.

According to the literature, psychological motivations are related to: intellectual contexts; needs of escape and relaxation, belonging, excitement and adventure; social needs; and prestige. Beerli and Martín (2004a, 2004b) used thirteen items to investigate about intellectual, escape and relaxation, excitement and adventure, and prestige travel motivations. These thirteen items are complemented with other three: two related to belonging motivations; one related to social motivations, as shown in Table 2.

To reach the fourth specific goal of this paper, Gartner's (1994) list of information sources was included in the questionnaire, which was still adapted according to previous work (Baloglu, 1999; Baloglu & McCleary, 1999b; Carneiro, 2007; Govers, Go, & Kumar, 2007) and bearing in mind Portugal as the destination under study (Table 2). Both questions regarding motivations and information sources were measured through a five-point Likert-type scale.

Finally, the questionnaire was complemented with five socio-demographic questions about the respondents and their tourist intermediary institutions (Table 2). The questionnaire was administered (in Portuguese, English, French, German, and Spanish) through the online platform of the University of Aveiro, in July and August 2014.

We used descriptive statistics to display information on travel motivation and information sources, as well as to characterize the different attributes of cognitive and affective images. Descriptive statistics allow carrying further analysis in a later investigation phase. As a qualitative method to analyze the spontaneous associations to Portugal as part of the global image, a content analysis was performed, consisting essentially of the categorization of the mentioned words in classes, according to its

Table 2. Sources of the Questionnaire Items

Component	Attributes	Authors
Cognitive Image	List of 33 cognitive image attributes	(Echtner & Ritchie, 1991)
	Portugal is a country of slightly polluted environment.	(Alaeddinoglu & Can, 2010; Baloglu, 1999; Baloglu & Mangaloglu, 2001; Baloglu & McCleary, 1999b; Carneiro, 2007; Chen & Hsu, 2000; García, Gómez, & Molina, 2012; Kim & Richardson, 2003; O'Leary & Deegan, 2005)
	Portugal offers a wide range of theme parks.	(Jenkins, 1999; Qu, Kim, & Im, 2011)
	Portugal has opportunities and infrastructures for aquatic/nautical activities.	(Chi & Qu, 2008; Ibrahim & Gill, 2005; Jenkins, 1999; Lee & Lee, 2009; Mendes, Valle, & Guerreiro, 2011; Pike & Ryan, 2004; Qu, Kim, & Im, 2011)
	Portugal has many open spaces and opportunities for outdoor activities.	(Alcañiz, García, & Blas, 2009; Chi & Qu, 2008; Hsu, Wolfe, & Kang, 2004; Ibrahim & Gill, 2005; Jenkins, 1999; Qu, Kim, & Im, 2011)
	Portugal has interesting countryside and opportunities for rural tourism.	(Hsu, Wolfe, & Kang, 2004; Lee & Lee, 2009)
	Portugal has plenty of nature trails and opportunities for cycling, hiking and other mountain activities.	(Carneiro, 2007; Ibrahim & Gill, 2005)
	Portugal is suitable to practice golf.	(Chi & Qu, 2008; Lee & Lee, 2009; Mendes, Valle, & Guerreiro, 2011)
	Portugal offers gambling opportunities (casinos, bingos, among others).	(McCartney, 2008)
	Portugal is a pilgrimage place.	(McCartney, 2008)
	Portugal has good wines.	(Intercampus, 2013)
	Portugal is fluent in foreign languages.	
	Portugal is suitable to practice surf.	
Affective Image	List of 4 bipolar scales	(Agapito, Valle, & Mendes, 2013; Alaeddinoglu & Can, 2010; Baloglu, 1999; Baloglu & Mangaloglu, 2001; Baloglu & McCleary, 1999b; Beerli & Martín, 2004a, 2004b; Hosany, Ekinci, & Uysal, 2006; Kim & Richardson, 2003; Martínez & Alvarez, 2010; Pike & Ryan, 2004; Qu, Kim, & Im, 2011; San Martín & del Bosque, 2008)
Global Image	Closed question	(Alaeddinoglu & Can, 2010; Baloglu, 1999; Baloglu & McCleary, 1999b; Beerli & Martín, 2004a; Qu, Kim, & Im, 2011)
Psychological Travel Motivations	13 motivations related to the intellectual, escape and relaxation, excitement and adventure, and prestige	(Beerli & Martín, 2004a, 2004b)
	2 belonging motivations	(Carneiro, 2007; Li, Cai, Lehto, & Huang, 2010; Murphy, Benckendorff, & Moscardo, 2007)
	1 social motivation	(Baloglu, 1999; Baloglu & McCleary, 1999b; Carneiro, 2007; Murphy, Benckendorff, & Moscardo, 2007; San Martín & del Bosque, 2008)
Information Sources	List of 20 information sources	(Gartner, 1994; Baloglu, 1999; Baloglu & McCleary, 1999b; Carneiro, 2007; Govers, Go, & Kumar, 2007)
Socio-Demographic Questions		(García, Gómez, & Molina, 2012; Grosspietsch, 2006; Baloglu & Mangaloglu, 2001)

contents. Categories were defined *a posteriori*, without neglecting its five basic rules: mutual exclusion, homogeneity, relevance, objectivity and loyalty, and productivity (Jones, 1996).

The Research Sample

The demographic characteristics of the sample are shown in Table 3. The inquired intermediaries are mainly located in France and in the UK; only a small percentage are located in Brazil, Germany and Spain. According to their number of employees, almost all tourist intermediaries surveyed are micro, or small and medium-sized firms (95.35%) – 72.09% of them being micro and small firms. A significant part of these intermediaries has established business for more than 10 years. As such, one may argue that those intermediaries reveal some business stability and a thorough knowledge of the market. Most of the inquired intermediaries commercialize Portugal as a travel destination. Lastly, all respondents occupy management positions indicating a strong and reliable market knowledge.

In order to answer the four goals defined in the introduction we decided to use descriptive statistics to show how cognitive and affective images differ, as well as how travel motivations and information sources differ among tourist intermediaries. For that, we used SPSS Software Package Version 22.

To complement the descriptive statistics, we decided to create two groups based on global image, number of previous visits from tourist intermediaries and sales volume. The groups of previous visits are composed of $G_{pv}1$ – with 24 intermediaries that visited Portugal less than 10 times – and $G_{pv}2$ – with 16 intermediaries that previously visited Portugal 10 or more times. The two groups that composed the Sales Volume Group is composed by $G_{sv}1$ – with 22 intermediaries with a sales volume of €10 M or lower – and $G_{sv}2$ – with 18 intermediaries with a sales volume larger than 10 M€. The global image group was obtained using the anchor of seven-point liker scale and associating a negative global image to scores 1, 2 and 3, a neutral global image to score 4, and a positive global image to scores 5, 6 and 7. We created two groups: $G_{gi}1$ as neutral – with 13 intermediaries – and $G_{gi}2$ with positive global image – with 30 intermediaries.

After the selection of those groups we proceeded with the non-parametric Mann-Whitney U test, which is an alternative test to the independent sample T test. The Mann-Whitney U test does not make-assumptions related to the distribution of scores and does not require a normal distribution, and can be used with small samples (Moreira, Macedo, Lopes, & Moutinho, 2011).

Table 3. Demographic Characteristics of the Sample

Characteristics	Answers
Country of origin	France: 46.51% UK: 39.53% Brazil: 6.98% Germany: 4.65% Spain: 2.33%
Size (number of employees)	< 10: 30.23% 10-49: 41.86% 50-249: 23.26% > 250: 4.65%
Age	< 10: 4.76% 11-20: 28.57% 21-40: 54.76% > 40: 11.90%
Sales Volume	< €2 M: 17.5% €2000001-€5 M: 37.5% €5000001-€10 M: 25.0% > €10000001: 20.0%
Commercialization of tourist products to Portugal as a travel destination	Yes: 90.48% No: 9.52%
Respondents profile	Owner/President: 39.5% Product manager: 23.30% Marketing/Communications manager: 14% General manager: 11.6% Operations manager: 9.3% Sales manager: 2.3%

MAIN RESULTS: PORTUGAL VIEWED BY FOREIGN TOURIST INTERMEDIARIES

What Motivates Tourist Intermediaries to Recommend the Destination?

As foreign tourism intermediaries are the main object of this research, the main motivations behind intermediaries recommending their customers Portugal as a tourist destination are listed in Table 4. As one can see, all items range from 3.14 to 3.84, with a standard deviation lower than 1. Although the items show similar mean values among themselves, the motivations 'rest and relaxation', 'to escape daily routine', 'to see and do a variety of things with the whole family', 'to know different cultures and ways of life', 'to increase my knowledge of places, people and things', 'to alleviate stress and tension' and 'to spend quality time with family and friends away from home' have average values greater than 3.5, slightly standing out from the rest. In contrast, motivations concerning 'to go to fashionable places', 'to seek diversion and entertainment' and 'intellectual improvement' have average values below 3.2 points (Table 4).

Therefore, from the perspective of foreign tourist intermediaries, Portugal as a destination is likely to satisfy mainly belonging, escape and relaxation, motivations.

Which Information Sources Tourist Intermediaries Use to Create International Products/ Foreign Destinations?

Table 5 shows the information sources that are used by the travel intermediaries to promote their tourist destinations. We analyze the importance of the most and least used information sources by the surveyed tourist intermediaries in the design of international tourism products.

Table 4. Travel Motivations: descriptive statistics and Mann-Whitney U-tests

	Mean	SD	Previous Visits p-value*	Global Image p-value*	Sales Volume p-value*
Rest and relaxation	3.84	0.75	0.552	0.579	0.259
To escape daily routine	3.67	0.84	0.928	0.511	0.476
To see and do a variety of things with the whole family	3.67	0.85	0.972	0.834	0.123
To know different cultures and ways of life	3.63	0.93	0.809	0.102	0.937
To increase my knowledge of places, people and things	3.63	0.93	0.294	0.945	0.770
To alleviate stress and tension	3.60	0.88	0.552	0.730	0.259
To spend quality time with family and friends away from home	3.56	0.96	0.779	0.730	0.259
To go to places that friends have not visited	3.49	0.91	0.333	0.417	0.458
To tell friends about the experiences on vacation	3.42	0.82	0.948	0.763	0.060
To meet new people	3.40	0.88	**0.032**	0.133	0.371
To do exciting things	3.37	0.87	0.333	**0.011**	0.975
To attend cultural events	3.35	0.84	0.267	**0.048**	**0.032**
To seek adventure and pleasure	3.30	0.86	0.747	0.153	0.751
Intellectual improvement	3.19	0.88	0.946	0.850	0.143
To seek diversion and entertainment	3.16	0.97	0.469	0.817	**0.033**
To go to fashionable places	3.14	0.93	0.908	0.277	0.659

* Mann-Whitney U-test, Two-tailed p-value

Table 5. Information Sources: descriptive statistics and Mann-Whitney U-tests

	Mean	SD	Previous Visits p-value*	Global Image p-value*	Sales Volume p-value*
Your personal visit to Portugal or the personal visit of other representatives of your company	4.20	0.98		0.808	
Internet (in general)	3.90	1.11	0.855	0.938	0.065
International tourism fairs	3.60	1.43	0.855	0.136	0.979
Personal contact with employees of tour operators and travel agencies in the destination country via telephone, email or personal meetings	3.57	1.27	0.844	0.942	0.932
Internet: Official website of tourism in the destination country	3.57	1.15	0.638	0.984	0.822
Personal contact with employees of the public bodies in the destination country	3.57	1.15	0.794	0.751	0.878
Internet: Google search	3.48	1.19	0.794	1.000	0.863
Travel guides/tourist guidebooks	3.36	1.15	0.491	0.282	0.774
Internet: Websites of travel agencies and tour operators in the destination country	3.07	1.37	0.980	0.400	0.979
Recommendations of others who have visited the destination	3.07	1.22	0.780	0.196	0.823
Brochures, posters or reports of the public bodies in the destination country	3.05	1.15	0.444	0.426	0.487
Recommendations of family and friends	2.98	1.12	0.727	0.196	0.733
General newspapers and magazines	2.86	2.86	0.817	0.756	0.487
Newspapers and travel/tourism magazines	2.78	1.28	0.954	0.822	**0.010**
Brochures or posters of tour operators and travel agencies in the destination country	2.71	1.24	0.934	0.731	0.763
Advertising campaigns	2.71	1.15	0.954	0.608	0.193
Books, movies and documentaries	2.64	1.08	0.306	0.765	0.811
News and popular culture	2.48	1.07	0.730	0.984	0.288
Television and radio	2.40	1.19	0.869	1.000	0.079
Global Distribution Systems (GDS)	2.07	1.10	0.349	0.506	0.427

* Mann-Whitney U-test, Two-tailed p-value

Visits of the tourist intermediary's representatives to the destination country stand out positively from the 20 sources analyzed with a mean value of 4.20 and a standard deviation of 0.980, which shows the lowest variability among all the information sources. The importance of personal visits of tourism intermediaries as a major source of information in the creation of products regarding international destinations comes in line with the literature.

It is already known, that personal visits to destinations, as primary information source, result in more realistic, complex and different images from the ones formed through secondary sources of information, as a result of the personal experience and contact with the product (Gartner & Hunt, 1987; Moital, Costa, & Peres, 2005; Phelps, 1986; Tasci & Gartner, 2007). Table 5 suggests that five other sources of information stand out from the rest: 'Internet (in general)', 'international tourism fairs', 'Internet: official website of tourism in the destination country', 'personal contact with employees of tour operators and travel agencies in the destination country via telephone, email or personal meetings' and also 'personal contact with employees of the public bodies in the destination country'. This clearly indicates that the competitive intelligence that foreign tourist intermediaries use for the creation of their international products are based on the personal contact with organizations from the destination country, internet (including the official tourism website of the destination country) and international tourism fairs.

On the other hand, the sources of information used the least by tourist intermediaries are 'Global Distribution Systems (GDS)', 'television and radio', 'news and popular culture', 'books, movies and documentaries', 'advertising campaigns' and 'brochures or posters of tour operators and travel agencies in the destination country. As shown in Table 5, these correspond to the autonomous and the overt induced image formation agents (Gartner, 1994).

How is the Tourist Intermediaries Global, Affective and Cognitive Image Characterized?

Concerning the assisted global image, it is found that about 70% of the respondents consider that their image of Portugal as a tourist destination is very or strongly positive. Moreover, none of the respondents consider their image of Portugal as negative. The mean value of the global image is 5.91 (on a seven-point scale), meaning that, on average, tourist intermediaries have a very positive image of Portugal as a tourist destination. Moreover, its standard deviation is lower than 1, representing a narrow dispersion around the mean value.

To study the global image, a content analysis was also conducted to the three spontaneous associations to Portugal that respondents were asked to do. Thus, the 128 associations mentioned spontaneously were classified into 14 categories. Firstly, the full set of associations is analyzed, without regard to the order they were listed; secondly, those which stand out as first, second and third associations to Portugal as a tourist destination are taken into account; and lastly, the sites that constitute the category destinations are analyzed in depth.

It is noticeable that 'Sun, Sea and Sand' is the category that stands out the most, accounting for over 25% of the spontaneous associations. It is followed by references to historical and architectural heritage (11.72%), various destinations within the Portuguese territory (10.94%), friendliness and hospitality of the Portuguese people (7.81%), landscapes and natural attractions (7.03%) and also the gastronomy (7.03%). Although each of the remaining categories account for less than 7% of the mentioned spontaneous associations, it should be noted that references were also made to: culture, wine, golf, accessibility and location of Portugal, cities/villages or urban/rural, affordable prices, quality and pilgrimage. Although they have a low representation in the total of the spontaneous associations made, it is central that respondents associate Portugal to these elements, showing its importance in positioning Portugal as a tourist destination.

Regarding the second stage of analysis, the categories of 'Sun, Sea and Sand' and 'Historic and architectural heritage' are also the ones that stand out as first associations, which means that Portugal as a tourist destination has a strong position in these two areas. Apart from these, as first associations also arise 'Culture', specific destinations and 'Accessibility and location of Portugal'. As second associations, 'Sun, Sea and Sand' stands out again, which is followed this time by 'Scenery and natural attractions', 'Wine' and specific destinations. As for the third associations, 'Sun, Sea and Sand' continues to stand out in relation to the others, followed by the dichotomy 'Cities/villages', specific destinations and 'Gastronomy'.

Therefore, it appears that the category 'Sun, Sea and Sand' is the most transversal in the three levels of spontaneous association, as well as particular destinations. Although the 'Historical and architectural heritage' is highlighted as first associations, it decreases in the second and third groups. A similar situation occurs with references to culture. In contrast, 'Gastronomy', 'Cities/villages', 'Scenery and natural attractions', and also the 'Hospitality and friendliness' do not stand out as first associations, although they are proven to be important secondary and tertiary associations. Differently from the previous, the category 'Wine' stands out only on second associations, although it has been reported only once as a first and as a third association.

'Pilgrimage', 'Quality' and 'Affordable prices' are indeed the categories less mentioned. It should also be noted that golf, accessibility and location of Portugal, which although not often mentioned, appear in three levels of associations.

Finally, analyzing in detail the category related to particular destinations in Portugal, it appears that Porto is the most referred destination, followed by Lisbon, the Douro region, the Algarve region, and the Azores.

Regarding the affective image, one can conclude that foreign intermediaries consider Portugal a more pleasant than unpleasant destination, which is not only the most remarkable element of the affective image, but also the one with the lowest standard deviation. Respondents also see Portugal as a country more relaxing than stressful and more exciting than boring. The arousing-sleepy dimension stands close to an intermediate value between the two anchor extremes and also has the largest standard deviation of the four dimensions that compose affective image. This means that intermediaries did not find Portugal as an arousing destination (Table 6).

The scores of the 45 attributes of cognitive image clearly indicate how foreign intermediaries understand Portugal as a destination (Appendix). Attributes with larger scores (upper than or close to 4, on a scale of 1 to 5) are the ones related to cities' attractiveness and sightseeing, scenery and natural attractions, hospitality and friendliness of the Portuguese, accessibilities to the destination, interesting historical and cultural places to visit, good wines, weather and beaches, a high-quality tourist service, outdoor opportunities and facilities, political stability and, also, good quality accommodation.

On the other hand, attributes with lower mean values (less than 3) are the ones regarding the range of theme parks, exotic associations to Portugal, gambling opportunities at the destination, a crowdedness place and a pilgrimage destination (Appendix).

How Different Groups of Tourist Intermediaries Understand Affective and Cognitive Image, Travel Motivations and Information Sources

In order to complement the analysis of travel motivations, information sources, affective image, and cognitive image, we will take into account the Mann-Whitney U test, to compare how previous experience, global image and sales volumes of foreign travel intermediaries behave.

Table 6. Affective Image: Descriptive statistics and Mann-Whitney U-tests

	Mean	SD	Previous Visits	Global Image	Sales Volume
			p-value*	p-value*	p-value*
Arousing / Sleepy	3.23	1.38	0.202	0.166	0.846
Exciting / Boring	2.74	1.24	0.526	0.680	0.945
Relaxing / Stressful	2.35	1.13	0.071	0.501	0.360
Pleasant / Unpleasant	1.56	0.77	0.127	0.065	0.701

* Mann-Whitney U-test, Two-tailed p-value

In what concerns, what tourist intermediaries think and what the main travel motivations to visit Portugal are, one can conclude that 'to meet new people' is the only travel motivation with statistically significant differences (p value=0.032) between $G_{pv}1$ (intermediaries that visited Portugal less than 10 times) and $G_{pv}2$ (intermediaries that visited Portugal 10 times or more), as shown in Table 4. As the mean value of $G_{pv}2$ and $G_{pv}1$ are, 3.12 and 3.78, respectively, one can conclude that the more tourist intermediaries visit Portugal, the more they believe that the main tourists' travel motivation is 'to meet people'.

When considering $G_{gi}2$ (positive global image) and $G_{gi}1$ (neutral global image), one finds that 'to do exciting things' (p-value=0.011) – with mean values of 3.60 and 2.82 – and 'to attend to cultural events' (p-value=0.048) – with mean values of 3.57 and 2.87 – are the only two attributes that show significant statistical differences at a 5% level, as shown in Table 4. This means that one can claim that in general travel motivations are not influenced by the global image perceived by intermediaries, with the exception of the two items previously referred: 'to do exciting things' and 'to attend to cultural events'.

Finally, 'to attend to cultural events' (p-value=0.032) and 'to seek diversion and entertainment' (p-value=0.033) are the main motivations that differentiate the tourist intermediaries regarding the two groups on sales volume at a significance level of 5%, as shown in Table 4. The mean values of 'to seek diversion and entertainment' are 3.19 and 3.56, respectively for $G_{sv}1$ (sales volume of €10 M or lower) and $G_{sv}2$ (sales volume larger than €10 M). On the other hand, the mean values of 'to attend to cultural events' are 2.95 and 3.44, respectively for $G_{sv}1$ and $G_{sv}2$. This indicates that, in general, the size of tourist intermediaries does not differentiate Portugal in terms of travel motivations.

In what pertains to information sources, the groups analyzed using the Mann-Whitney tests are not very differentiating. As can be seen in Table 5, only 'newspapers and travel/tourism magazines' show statistically different results, for $G_{sv}1$ (sales volume of €10 M or lower) and $G_{sv}2$ (sales volume larger than €10 M), with an average mean of 2.67, 3.00, respectively. This means that information sources are generically used by tourist intermediaries, regardless their size, their global image or their previous number of visits to Portugal.

As shown in Table 6, there are no statistically significant differences among the four dimensions of affective image according to sales volumes groups, $G_{sv}1$ and $G_{sv}2$. When considering $G_{gi}2$ – positive global image – with a mean value of 1.34 and $G_{gi}1$ – neutral global image – with a mean value of 2.00, one can conclude that the pleasant/unpleasant dimension has statistically significant differences only at 10% level (p-value=0.65). Finally, with statistically significant differences at 10% level (p-value=0.071) one finds that the relaxing/stressful affective dimension differs between $G_{pv}1$ (mean value of 2.52) and $G_{pv}2$ (mean value 2.12). In general, one can claim that the analysis of the affective image shows relatively homogeneous results, when taking into account the Mann-Whitney U tests for the groups of number of previous visits, the global image or the size of the firm.

The appendix shows the results for the attributes of the cognitive image, taking into account the Mann-Whitney U tests for the differences of the sales volume groups ($G_{sv}1$ and $G_{sv}2$), global image groups ($G_{gi}1$ and $G_{gi}2$) and previous visits ($G_{pv}1$ and $G_{pv}2$). Clearly, only one attribute – is fluent in foreign languages – is statistically significantly different (p-value=0.016), at a 5% level, between $G_{pv}1$ and $G_{pv}2$, although there are two attributes that are statistically significant different at a 10% level ('offers low prices and a good value for money' and 'offers good shopping facilities'). When analyzing the differences between global image groups ($G_{gi}1$ and $G_{gi}2$) the conclusion is very similar as there are only three attributes ('is a destination with good fame and reputation', 'is fluent in foreign languages' and 'offers good shopping facilities') that show statistically significant differences at a 5% level.

Finally, taking into account the Mann-Whitney U tests for the differences of the sales volume groups ($G_{sv}1$ and $G_{sv}2$), one realizes that seven attributes – 'offers good opportunities for an adventure', with mean values of 2.82 and 3.33 for $G_{gi}1$ and $G_{gi}2$, respectively; 'offers access to parks and nature reserves', with mean values of 2.95 and 3.83 for $G_{gi}1$ and $G_{gi}2$, respectively; 'offers a good nightlife and entertainment', with mean values of 3.05 and 3.72 for $G_{gi}1$ and $G_{gi}2$, respectively; 'is a modern and urban country', with mean values of 3.18 and 3.72 for $G_{gi}1$ and $G_{gi}2$, respectively; 'has different customs, lifestyles, traditions and local crafts', with mean values of 3.50 and 4.06 for $G_{gi}1$ and $G_{gi}2$, respectively; 'is characterized by high quality tourist services (restaurants, accommodation, tourist offices, and other tourist services)', with mean values of 3.73 and 4.17 for $G_{gi}1$ and $G_{gi}2$, respectively; 'is a restful, relaxing and tranquil place', with mean values of 3.55 and 4.11 for $G_{gi}1$ and $G_{gi}2$, respectively; and 'offers a wide range of theme parks', with mean values of 1.95 and 3.67 for $G_{gi}1$ and $G_{gi}2$, respectively – show statistically significant differences at a 5% level.

The analysis of the different groups reveals that travel motivations and information sources are relatively similar among tourist intermediaries, which was expected given that they are a group of firms that seek market orientation based on the development of tourist products for their home market, taking into consideration what they interpret as most suitable for their business. One can claim that the differences found between groups, taking into account sales volume, are justified by the existence of some niches that are served differently by small and medium-sized firms.

CONCLUSION AND FUTURE RESEARCH

The foreign tourist intermediaries play an important role in transmitting their customers their perceived destination image. Moreover, this perceived image and its components play a central role in the creation and development of tourism products, as well as to the overall image of a tourism destination. It is also important to emphasize that tour operators have an important role in intermediating the relationship between tourists and business firms in the provision of services. Tour operators and travel agents act as information providers, linking supply and demand for destination's tourism products, having a great influence in the tourism distribution sector, and an important role in the tourist's decision-making processes.

Moreover, the success of tourism marketing policies depends on the effective management of destination's image, and how image is perceived by foreign tourism intermediaries. So, destination managers must develop a deep understanding of the characteristics, components and relationships of destination's image to develop appropriate decisions about development and management of tourism destinations and their image.

The conducted analysis confirmed that foreign tourist intermediaries consider Portugal as a tourist destination likely to satisfy belonging, escape and relaxation, and intellectual motivations. The main information sources used in designing international tourist products are the personal visits to the destination in order to enhance the importance of personal experience in the destination. In addition, the following information sources are also relevant: the Internet, the personal contact with employees of public bodies, destination country's travel agencies and tour operators, the official website to promote the destination and international industry fairs.

The foreign tourist intermediaries that sell their customers Portugal as a destination have, overall, a very positive image of Portugal, and associate it to a pleasant, relaxing and exciting, and at the same time arousing and sleepy destination. Foreign tourist intermediaries spontaneously associate Portugal to sun, sea and sand and to its historic and architectural heritage. In addition, the most mentioned destinations in such associations are Lisbon and Porto, the main cities of the country.

Another conclusion is that intermediaries also have a very positive cognitive image for certain attributes of Portugal as a destination such as the interesting and attractive cities to visit, beautiful scenery and natural attractions, hospitality and friendliness of the Portuguese, accessibility to the destination, diversity of sites and museums of historical and cultural interest, monuments and architectural heritage, good wines, pleasant weather and good beaches. In contrast, Portugal is not associated to a wide range of theme parks and to gambling opportunities. Also, the country it is not seen as an exotic destination, a crowded place, or a pilgrimage place.

Based on the global image, the number of previous visitors and the sales volume of travel agents and tour operators, it is possible to conclude that the groups of intermediaries are very homogeneous. For example, travel motivation and information sources tend to be similar, regardless of the number of previous visits to Portugal, the type of global image and the sales volume. This can be explained by the fact that these intermediaries are embedded, and strongly influenced by other business stakeholders and international competition, which leads them to relatively similar competitive strategies. It is possible to have a similar conclusion with regard to the affective image, which tends to be camouflaged by the business and / or market orientation, also influenced by business stakeholders.

It is important to note that the cognitive image has a similar behavior regarding: (a) the number of previous visits made by the intermediaries or; (b) the global image of the intermediaries. However, when analyzing the sales volume of intermediaries, there are eight attributes of the cognitive image that have different behaviors. Thus, it is important to refer that there may be differentiated options on the part of these intermediaries that will be worth analyzing more in depth in future studies.

FUTURE RESEARCH DIRECTIONS

Future research regarding this article's outputs needs to analyze not only what determines affective, cognitive and global image, in order to help marketing managers of Portugal as a tourist destination to improve their strategies, but also to address the consequents, in terms of loyalty and willingness to recommend the destination.

Of course, the image is something that is used by tourist intermediaries for business purposes. However, it would be interesting to analyze how image changes through time and in what way it would be possible to alter how foreign tourist intermediaries understand a tourist destination image.

From another point of view, it would be interesting in terms of managerial implications to Portugal as a destination to analyze which is the image projected by the Portuguese marketing campaigns and analyze to which extent they influence the perceived image of the intermediaries. It would also be interesting to compare intermediaries that generate a large percentage of their business having Portugal as a main destination with those intermediaries with a small presence in Portugal, in order to address if those differences are explained by the perceived image the intermediaries have about Portugal.

Finally, taking into account the business interest of the intermediaries it would be advisable to analyze how the perceived image of the destination is formed, how the number of visits to the tourist destination influences the perceived image, and whether the size of the intermediary is important in the generation of new tourist destinations packages. It would also be interesting to understand how perceived image changes influence new tourist destinations packages.

REFERENCES

Agapito, D., Valle, P. O., & Mendes, J. C. (2013). The cognitive-affective-conative model of destination image: A confirmatory analysis. *Journal of Travel & Tourism Marketing, 30*(5), 471–481. doi:10.1080/10548408.2013.803393

Alaeddinoglu, F., & Can, A. S. (2010). Destination image from the perspective of travel intermediaries. *Anatolia: An International Journal of Tourism and Hospitality Research, 21*(2), 339–350. doi:10.1080/13032917.2010.9687107

Alcañiz, E. B., García, I. S., & Blas, S. S. (2009). The functional-psychological continuum in the cognitive image of a destination: A confirmatory analysis. *Tourism Management, 30*(5), 715–723. doi:10.1016/j.tourman.2008.10.020

Baloglu, S. (1999). A path analytic model of visitation intention involving information sources, socio-psychological motivations, and destination image. *Journal of Travel & Tourism Marketing, 8*(3), 81–90. doi:10.1300/J073v08n03_05

Baloglu, S., & Mangaloglu, M. (2001). Tourism destination images of Turkey, Egypt, Greece, and Italy as perceived by US-based tour operators and travel agents. *Tourism Management, 22*(1), 1–9. doi:10.1016/S0261-5177(00)00030-3

Baloglu, S., & McCleary, K. W. (1999a). A model of destination image formation. *Annals of Tourism Research, 26*(4), 868–897. doi:10.1016/S0160-7383(99)00030-4

Baloglu, S., & McCleary, K. W. (1999b). U.S. international pleasure travelers' images of four Mediterranean destinations: A comparison of visitors and non-visitors. *Journal of Travel Research, 38*(2), 144–152. doi:10.1177/004728759903800207

Beerli, A., & Martín, J. D. (2004a). Factors influencing destination image. *Annals of Tourism Research, 31*(3), 657–681. doi:10.1016/j.annals.2004.01.010

Beerli, A., & Martín, J. D. (2004b). Tourists' characteristics and the perceived image of tourist destinations: A quantitative analysis - a case study of Lanzarote, Spain. *Tourism Management, 25*(5), 623–636. doi:10.1016/j.tourman.2003.06.004

Bigné, J. E., Sánchez, M. I., & Sánchez, J. (2001). Tourism image, evaluation variables and after purchase behaviour: Inter-relationship. *Tourism Management*, 22(6), 607–616. doi:10.1016/S0261-5177(01)00035-8

Camilleri, M. A. (2018a). The Tourism Industry: An Overview. In Travel Marketing, Tourism Economics and the Airline Product (pp. 3-27). Cham: Springer.

Camilleri, M. A. (2018b). Tourism Distribution Channels. In Travel Marketing, Tourism Economics and the Airline Product (pp. 105-115). Cham: Springer. doi:10.1007/978-3-319-49849-2_6

Camilleri, M. A. (2018c). Tourism Supply and Demand. In Travel Marketing, Tourism Economics and the Airline Product (pp. 139-154). Cham: Springer. doi:10.1007/978-3-319-49849-2_8

Carneiro, M. J. (2007). *Modelação da escolha de destinos turísticos: Uma análise de posicionamento* (PhD thesis). University of Aveiro, Aveiro, Portugal.

Chen, C.-F., & Tsai, D. (2007). How destination image and evaluative factors affect behavioral intentions? *Tourism Management*, 28(4), 1115–1122. doi:10.1016/j.tourman.2006.07.007

Chen, J. S., & Hsu, C. (2000). Measurement of Korean tourists' perceived images of overseas destinations. *Journal of Travel Research*, 38(4), 411–416. doi:10.1177/004728750003800410

Chi, C. G., & Qu, H. (2008). Examining the structural relationships of destination image, tourist satisfaction and destination loyalty: An integrated approach. *Tourism Management*, 29(4), 624–636. doi:10.1016/j.tourman.2007.06.007

Custódio, M. J., & Gouveia, P. M. (2007). Evaluation of the cognitive image of a country/destination by the media during the coverage of mega-events: The case of UEFA EURO 2004 in Portugal. *International Journal of Tourism Research*, 9(4), 285–296. doi:10.1002/jtr.615

Echtner, C. M., & Ritchie, J. R. (1991). The meaning and measurement of destination image. *Journal of Tourism Studies*, 2(2), 2–12.

Elliot, S., Papadopoulos, N., & Kim, S. (2011). An integrative model of place image: Exploring relationships between destination, product, and country images. *Journal of Travel Research*, 50(5), 520–534. doi:10.1177/0047287510379161

Fakeye, P., & Crompton, J. (1991). Image differences between prospective, first-time, and repeat visitors to the lower Rio Grande valley. *Journal of Travel Research*, 30(2), 10–16. doi:10.1177/004728759103000202

Ford, R. C., Wang, Y., & Vestal, A. (2012). Power asymmetries in tourism distribution networks. *Annals of Tourism Research, 39*(2), 755–779. doi:10.1016/j.annals.2011.10.001

Gallarza, M. G., Saura, I. G., & García, H. C. (2002). Destination image: Towards a conceptual framework. *Annals of Tourism Research, 29*(1), 56–78. doi:10.1016/S0160-7383(01)00031-7

García, J. A., Gómez, M., & Molina, A. (2012). A destination-branding model: An empirical analysis based on stakeholders. *Tourism Management, 33*(3), 646–661. doi:10.1016/j.tourman.2011.07.006

Gartner, & Hunt, J. D. (1987). An analysis of state image change over a twelve-year period (1971-1983). *Journal of Travel Research, 26*(2), 15–19.

Gartner. (1994). Image formation process. *Journal of Travel & Tourism Marketing, 2*(2-3), 191–216.

Govers, R., & Go, F. M. (2003). Deconstructing destination image in the information age. *Information Technology & Tourism, 6*(1), 13–29. doi:10.3727/109830503108751199

Govers, R., Go, M., & Kumar, K. (2007). Promoting tourism destination image. *Journal of Travel Research, 46*(1), 15–23. doi:10.1177/0047287507302374

Grosspietsch, M. (2006). Perceived and projected images of Rwanda: Visitor and international tour operator perspectives. *Tourism Management, 27*(2), 225–234. doi:10.1016/j.tourman.2004.08.005

Gunn, C. A. (1988). *Vacationscape: Designing tourist regions*. University of Minnesota: Van Nostrand Reinhold.

Hosany, S., Ekinci, Y., & Uysal, M. (2006). Destination image and destination personality: An application of branding theories to tourism places. *Journal of Business Research, 59*(5), 638–642. doi:10.1016/j.jbusres.2006.01.001

Hsu, C. H. C., Wolfe, K., & Kang, S. K. (2004). Image assessment for a destination with limited comparative advantages. *Tourism Management, 25*(1), 121–126. doi:10.1016/S0261-5177(03)00062-1

Ibrahim, E. E., & Gill, J. (2005). A positioning strategy for a tourist destination, based on analysis of customers' perceptions and satisfactions. *Marketing Intelligence & Planning, 23*(2), 172–188. doi:10.1108/02634500510589921

Intercampus. (2013). *Estudo satisfação de turistas – Análise de resultados*. Lisbon: Turismo de Portugal, IP.

Jenkins, O. (1999). Understanding and measuring tourist destination. *International Journal of Tourism Research*, *1*(1), 1–15. doi:10.1002/(SICI)1522-1970(199901/02)1:1<1::AID-JTR143>3.0.CO;2-L

Jenkins, O. (2003). Photography and travel brochures: The circle of representation. *Tourism Geographies*, *5*(3), 305–328. doi:10.1080/14616680309715

Jones, R. A. (1996). *Research methods in the social and behavioral sciences.* New York: Sinauer Associates.

Kim, H., & Richardson, S. L. (2003). Motion picture impacts on destination images. *Annals of Tourism Research*, *30*(1), 216–237. doi:10.1016/S0160-7383(02)00062-2

Kim, S., & Yoon, Y. (2003). The hierarchical effects of affective and cognitive components on tourism destination image. *Journal of Travel & Tourism Marketing*, *14*(2), 1–22. doi:10.1300/J073v14n02_01

Konecnik, M., & Gartner, W. C. (2007). Customer-based brand equity for a destination. *Annals of Tourism Research*, *34*(2), 400–421. doi:10.1016/j.annals.2006.10.005

Kracht, J., & Wang, Y. C. (2010). Examining the tourism distribution channels: Evolution and transformation. *International Journal of Contemporary Hospitality Management*, *22*(5), 736–757. doi:10.1108/09596111011053837

Lawson, F., & Baud-Bovy, M. (1977). *Tourism and recreational development.* London: Architectural Pres.

Lee, G., & Lee, C.-K. (2009). Cross-cultural comparison of the image of Guam perceived by Korean and Japanese leisure travelers: Importance–performance analysis. *Tourism Management*, *30*(6), 922–931. doi:10.1016/j.tourman.2008.11.013

Li, M., Cai, L. A., Lehto, X. Y., & Huang, Z. J. (2010). A missing link in understanding revisit intention - The role of motivation and image. *Journal of Travel & Tourism Marketing*, *27*(4), 335–348. doi:10.1080/10548408.2010.481559

Line, N. D., & Wang, Y. (2017). A multi-stakeholder market oriented approach to destination marketing. *Journal of Destination Marketing & Management*, *6*(1), 84–93. doi:10.1016/j.jdmm.2016.03.003

MacKay, K. J., & Fesenmaier, D. R. (1997). Pictorial element of destination in image formation. *Annals of Tourism Research*, *24*(3), 537–565. doi:10.1016/S0160-7383(97)00011-X

Mano, A., Costa, R., & Moutinho, V. (2014). O estado atual e perspetivas futuras de investigação da imagem de destino turísticos: O caso de Portugal. *Revista Turismo & Desenvolvimento*, *2*(21/22), 391–402.

Mariutti, F., & Giraldi, J. (2014). Country brand identity: An exploratory study about the Brazil brand with American travel agencies. *Tourism Planning & Development*, *11*(1), 13–26. doi:10.1080/21568316.2013.839469

McCartney, G. (2008). Does one culture all think the same? An investigation of destination image perceptions from several origins. *Tourism Review*, *63*(4), 13–26. doi:10.1108/16605370810912182

Mendes, J. C., Valle, P. O., & Guerreiro, M. (2011). Destination image and events - A structural model for the Algarve case. *Journal of Hospitality Marketing & Management*, *20*(3-4), 366–384. doi:10.1080/19368623.2011.562424

Moital, M., Costa, C., & Peres, R. (2005). Lisbon as a city break destination: Competitive analysis as perceived by London travel agents. *Journal of Tourism and Development*, *2*(1), 67–80.

Moreira, A. C., Macedo, P., Lopes, M., & Moutinho, V. (2011). *Exercícios de estatística com recurso ao SPSS*. Lisbon: Sílabo.

Murphy, L., Benckendorff, P., & Moscardo, G. (2007). linking travel motivation, tourist self-image and destination brand personality. *Journal of Travel & Tourism Marketing*, *22*(2), 45–59. doi:10.1300/J073v22n02_04

Nghiêm-Phú, B. (2014). A review of destination image studies from 2008 to 2012. *European Journal of Tourism Research*, *8*, 35–65.

O'Leary, S., & Deegan, J. (2005). Ireland's Image as a tourism destination in France: Attribute, importance and performance. *Journal of Travel Research*, *43*(3), 247–256. doi:10.1177/0047287504272025

Paxson, M. C. (1995). Increasing survey response rates: Practical instructions from the total design method. *The Cornell Hotel and Restaurant Administration Quarterly*, *36*(4), 66–73.

Pearce, D. G. (2008). A needs-function model of tourism distribution. *Annals of Tourism Research*, *35*(1), 148–168. doi:10.1016/j.annals.2007.06.011

Phelps, A. (1986). Holiday destination image — the problem of assessment: An example developed in Menorca. *Tourism Management*, *7*(3), 168–180. doi:10.1016/0261-5177(86)90003-8

Pike, S. (2002). Destination image analysis: A review of 142 papers from 1973-2000. *Tourism Management, 23*(5), 541–549. doi:10.1016/S0261-5177(02)00005-5

Pike, S. (2008). *Destination marketing: An integrated marketing communication approach.* Oxford, UK: Butterworth-Heinemann, Elsevier.

Pike, S., & Ryan, C. (2004). Destination positioning analysis through a comparison of cognitive, affective, and conative perceptions. *Journal of Travel Research, 42*(4), 333–342. doi:10.1177/0047287504263029

Qu, H., Kim, L. H., & Im, H. H. (2011). A model of destination branding: Integrating the concepts of the branding and destination image. *Tourism Management, 32*(3), 465–476. doi:10.1016/j.tourman.2010.03.014

Rezende-Parker, A. M., Morisson, A. M., & Ismail, J. A. (2003). Dazed and confused? An exploratory study of the image of Brazil as a travel destination. *Journal of Vacation Marketing, 9*(3), 243–259. doi:10.1177/135676670300900304

Rodríguez del Bosque, I., & San Martín, H. (2008). Tourist satisfaction a cognitive-affective model. *Annals of Tourism Research, 35*(2), 551–573. doi:10.1016/j.annals.2008.02.006

Russel, J., Ward, L., & Pratt, G. (1981). Affective quality attributed to environments: A factor analytic study. *Environment and Behavior, 13*(3), 259–288. doi:10.1177/0013916581133001

Russell, J. (1980). A circumplex model of affect. *Journal of Personality and Social Psychology, 39*(6), 1161–1178. doi:10.1037/h0077714

Russell, J., & Pratt, G. (1980). A description of the affective quality attributed to environments. *Journal of Personality and Social Psychology, 38*(2), 311–322. doi:10.1037/0022-3514.38.2.311

Russell, J., & Snodgrass, J. (1987). Emotion and the environment. In D. Stokols & I. Altman (Eds.), *Handbook of Environmental Psychology* (Vol. 1, pp. 245–281). New York: John Wiley & Sons.

San Martín, H., & del Bosque, I. R. (2008). Exploring the cognitive–affective nature of destination image and the role of psychological factors in its formation. *Tourism Management, 29*(2), 263–277. doi:10.1016/j.tourman.2007.03.012

Silva, M., Costa, R., & Moreira, A. (2018). The influence of travel agents and tour operators' perspectives on a tourism destination. The case of Portuguese intermediaries on Brazil's image. *Journal of Hospitality and Tourism Management, 34*, 93–104. doi:10.1016/j.jhtm.2018.01.002

Souiden, N., Ladhari, R., & Chiadmi, N. (2017). Destination personality and destination image. *Journal of Hospitality and Tourism Management, 32*, 54–70. doi:10.1016/j.jhtm.2017.04.003

Stepchenkova, S., & Mills, J. E. (2010). Destination image: A meta-analysis of 2000 - 2007 Research. *Journal of Hospitality Marketing & Management, 19*(6), 575–609. doi:10.1080/19368623.2010.493071

Stepchenkova, S., & Morrison, A. M. (2008). Russia's destination image among American pleasure travelers: Revisiting Echtner and Ritchie. *Tourism Management, 29*(3), 548–560. doi:10.1016/j.tourman.2007.06.003

Tasci, A. D. A., & Gartner, W. C. (2007). Destination image and its functional relationships. *Journal of Travel & Tourism Marketing, 45*(4), 413–425.

Tasci, A. D. A., & Kozak, M. (2006). Destination brands vs destination images: Do we know what we mean? *Journal of Vacation Marketing, 12*(4), 299–317. doi:10.1177/1356766706067603

Turismo de Portugal (2013). *Anuário das estatísticas do turismo 2012*. Lisbon: Turismo de Portugal, IP.

APPENDIX

Table 7. Cognitive Image: Descriptive Statistics and Mann-Whitney U-tests

	Mean	SD	Previous visits p-value*	Global image p-value*	Sales volume p-value*
... has interesting and attractive cities/sightseeing	4.35	0.81	+	+	+
... has beautiful scenery and natural attractions	4.28	0.80	0.561	0.303	0.545
... is characterized by the hospitality and friendliness of the local population	4.23	0.72	0.469	0.108	0.399
... is an easily accessible destination	4.21	0.97	+	+	+
... has sites and museums of historical and cultural interest	4.14	0.86	0.553	0.073	0.399
... has interesting monuments and architectural heritage	4.12	1.01	0.270	0.133	0.585
... has good wines	4.07	0.81	0.869	0.070	0.263
... has great beaches	3.95	0.90	0.833	0.256	0.446
... has very good weather/climate	3.95	0.75	0.395	0.681	0.732
... has political stability	3.93	0.99	0.947	0.817	0.846
... offers a wide range and high-quality accommodation	3.93	0.94	0.946	0.220	0.263
... has many open spaces and opportunities for outdoor activities	3.93	0.83	0.938	0.681	0.142
... is characterized by high-quality tourist services (restaurants, accommodation, tourist offices, and other tourist services)	3.93	0.59	0.626	0.295	**0.031**
... offers low prices and a good value for money	3.88	0.85	0.062	0.231	0.270
... is a destination with good fame and reputation	3.84	0.87	0.264	**0.032**	0.463
... has a delicious and quality local cuisine	3.81	1.03	0.709	0.165	0.270
... has interesting countryside and opportunities for rural tourism	3.79	1.06	0.709	0.530	0.270
... is a suitable place for children and families	3.77	0.95	0.809	0.857	0.732
... is a restful, relaxing and tranquil place	3.77	0.68	0.320	0.764	**0.013**
... has many places of interest to visit and a wide range of recreational activities	3.74	0.88	0.809	0.102	0.131
... has different customs, lifestyles, traditions and local crafts	3.72	0.83	0.149	0.579	**0.049**
... has opportunities and infrastructures for aquatic/nautical activities	3.60	0.93	0.799	0.730	0.770
... has opportunities and facilities for sport activities	3.60	0.90	0.626	0.859	0.859
... is suitable to practice golf	3.58	1.16	0.709	0.894	0.695
... provides a high level of personal safety	3.56	0.80	0.391	0.596	0.382
... presents a high level of hygiene and cleanliness	3.53	0.70	0.391	0.596	0.545
... has good transportation and local infrastructures	3.44	0.80	0.561	0.133	0.125
... is a modern and urban country	3.42	0.76	0.845	0.073	**0.005**
... is fluent in foreign languages	3.40	0.96	**0.016**	**0.030**	0.798
... offers a good nightlife and entertainment	3.35	0.97	0.747	0.596	**0.004**
... is an economically developed country	3.35	0.72	0.846	0.133	0.545
... offers access to parks and nature reserves	3.33	1.09	0.396	0.969	**0.013**

continued on following page

Table 7. Continued

	Mean	SD	Previous visits p-value*	Global image p-value*	Sales volume p-value*
... has plenty of nature trails and opportunities for cycling, hiking and other mountain activities	3.33	0.84	0.947	0.649	0.136
... offers good shopping facilities	3.28	0.96	0.096	**0.003**	0.399
... has availability of quality tourist information and facilities for providing help and information	3.19	0.82	0.630	0.604	0.659
... has a wide range of cultural events such as fairs, exhibitions and festivals	3.16	0.92	0.739	0.471	0.424
... is suitable to practice surf	3.05	1.31	0.947	0.801	0.136
... offers good opportunities for an adventure	3.05	1.02	0.739	0.981	**0.033**
... is a country of slightly polluted environment	3.05	0.95	0.946	0.981	0.622
... offers good opportunities to learn and increase knowledge	3.00	1.06	0.135	0.271	0.263
... is a pilgrimage place	2.86	1.15	0.836	0.604	0.659
... is a crowded destination	2.42	1.03	0.561	0.716	0.798
... offers gambling opportunities (casinos, bingos, among others)	2.42	0.98	0.747	0.716	0.371
... is an exotic destination	2.37	1.05	0.561	0.090	0.307
... offers a wide range of theme parks	2.30	1.08	0.747	0.763	**0.030**

* Mann-Whitney U-test, Two-tailed p-value
+ Unable to compute

Chapter 3
Is the Tourism Destination a Core Attribute in the Choice of Cruise Consumers?

Donata Vianelli
University of Trieste, Italy

Manuela Valta
University of Trieste, Italy

ABSTRACT

In the last 10 years, cruise tourism has been frequently analyzed in the academic literature on leisure tourism. However, analysis of consumer behavior and the consumer-buying process is still limited, especially if the European market is taken into consideration. To address this gap in the literature, the authors analyzed how different attributes are evaluated by consumers in their decision-making process. In particular, the authors identified the role of the tourism destination among the different attributes that influence cruisers' choices. Using primary survey data from a sample of 4,002 German, Spanish, Italian, and French consumers, the analysis identifies the existence of consumer segments that give different levels of importance to the numerous attributes, including the tourism destination.

DOI: 10.4018/978-1-5225-5835-4.ch003

Is the Tourism Destination a Core Attribute in the Choice of Cruise Consumers?

INTRODUCTION

In recent years, an increasing number of studies on the topic of cruise tourism have been conducted both in mature and emerging markets (Kester, 2003; Forgas-Coll, Palau-Saumell, Sánchez-García, & Maria Caplliure-Giner, 2014; Fan, Qiu, Hsu, & Liu, 2015). Many reasons justify this increasing attention in the literature (Vianelli, 2011), the first of which is that the industry is still growing. In the last 20 years, the number of passengers has been steadily increasing from nearly four million at the end of the 1980s to approximately 24.7 million in 2016 (Clia, 2017). Another aspect that makes analysis of the cruise market interesting is the growing diversification of the supply and demand, which must meet the consumers' needs from both the functional and emotional perspectives (Camilleri, 2018a, b). Furthermore, in contrast to other tourism products, cruise evaluation is based on a complex bundle of different characteristics, where the destination is fundamental to clients' choices, but it is only one attribute of the product. Finally, the cruise business has a significant impact on port economy through embarkation and disembarkation (Braun, Xander, & White, 2002; Chase, 2002; Douglas & Douglas, 2004). In fact, cruise passengers might return to a port of disembarkation for a more in-depth exploration of a tourist destination that they briefly saw during their cruise (Gabe, Lynch, & McConnon Jr, 2006).

Despite the growing attention on cruise tourism in the academic literature, consumer research mainly examines purchase and post-purchase evaluations, whilst studies on consumer decision-making and on cruise destination remain very limited. The aim of this research is to analyze consumer behavior of European consumers of four different nationalities in the decision-making stage of a cruise product. The authors will capture consumers' choices in terms of attributes of the cruise service. More specifically, the role of the tourism destination in influencing consumers' decisions will be analyzed in comparison with other attributes of the cruise product. Moreover, numerous studies on cross-national differences in consumer behavior in different consumption sectors have underlined that cultural differences can have a strong influence on consumer behavior (Alon, Jaffe, Prange, & Vianelli, 2016). In our research context, we want to analyze if the tourism destination plays the same role in the choice of consumers of different nationalities, underlining the existence of a European consumer, of if some differences can be identified.

This chapter follows a twofold structure. It first reviews cruise tourism literature and relates it to past research to explain the European context of cruise demand. In developing the literature review, relevant insights into international research are provided, by reporting the most important attributes of a cruise product that have been investigated as well as those needing further analysis. Then, the study presents the empirical findings of 4,002 European consumers from Germany, Spain, Italy, and France, surveyed in five ports of cruise embarkation. The results have relevant managerial implications by providing companies with information from real customers. Attributes that cruise companies can focus on are identified, in order to develop efficient communication strategies towards final customers and travel agencies in different European countries. Furthermore, the role the tourism destination plays in the consumer's choice of the cruise product is highlighted, in order to reveal opportunities for collaboration between the cruise companies and the local institutions promoting the destination, with the common goal of enhancing brand value both for the cruise company and the tourism destination.

THE EVOLUTION OF CRUISE TOURISM IN EUROPE

Cruise tourism was born in the 1970s in the Caribbean area and the main target was upper-class clients in the United States (US). Only in the 1990s did cruise tourism begin to develop in the European market, first in the United Kingdom (UK) and then followed by other countries. In recent years, the Asiatic regions also saw developments in this type of tourism, which is estimated to have generated capacity growth of 302% from 2008 to 2013 (Fan, Qiu, Hsu, & Liu, 2015). The US still represents more than half of the total demand; nevertheless, the highest demand growth is in the European market, which points to plenty of opportunities for the future (Table 1). In fact, despite the recession having a negative impact on the number of cruisers in some countries, such as Italy and Spain, the European market is growing. The five main countries are currently Germany (with a market share of 30%), the UK (28%), Italy (11%), France (9%), and Spain (7%). Especially in countries such as Germany where the growth rate is high (11.3% in 2016), most of the cruisers are *first timers,* who show a clear preference for short cruises no longer than a week. The average age is high, approximately 50 years old, especially compared to the US market, even if the number of young families choosing a cruise for their vacation is increasing.

The growth in demand that we have witnessed in recent years has been strongly stimulated by the marketing strategies of cruise companies. Price reductions have made it possible to transform the cruise product from an elite product predominantly reserved for the niche segment of the older and wealthier, to a mass product also geared towards younger clientele. The duration of the cruise has been shortened, making it more accessible to passengers who are looking for a short break, but which will allow them to visit a large number of destinations. Furthermore, investments in online and offline communications have increased significantly, both for the end consumer and the travel agencies.

Table 1. The development of the cruise market worldwide (millions of passengers)

Country	2012	2013	2014	2015	2016	2015–2016
US	10.67	10.71	11.33	11.28	11.52	2.1%
Europe	6.13	6.36	6.39	6.46	6.67	3.2%
• Germany	1.54	1.68	1.77	1.81	2.02	11.6%
• UK and Ireland	1.70	1.72	1.64	1.78	1.88	5.6%
• Italy	0.83	0.86	0.84	0.80	0.75	-6.2%
• France	0.48	0.52	0.59	0.61	0.57	-6.6%
• Spain	0.57	0.47	0.45	0.47	0.49	4.2%
Other European countries	1.01	1.11	1.10	0.99	0.96	-3.1%
Rest of the world	4.50	5.27	5.47	6.75	7.61	11.3%
Total world	21.3	22.34	23.19	24.70	25.80	4.5%

Source: Data Adaptation European Cruise Council (2010); Statista (2017)

ATTRIBUTES OF THE CRUISING PRODUCT EVALUATION: A LITERATURE REVIEW

Cruising demand is made up of a heterogeneous set of individuals who are characterized by a differentiated socio-demographic profile. Individuals choose a cruise vacation based upon their preferences, attitudes, and motivations, which differ greatly in choice behavior and complexity compared to other types of tourist products. In fact, a whole series of variables characterizing the cruise and affecting the purchase stand alongside the evaluation of the tourism destination. Cruise companies must take into account consumers' characteristics to define a product offer appropriate for the needs of target customers. Cruise companies also need to understand the importance of the itinerary with respect to other attributes, while developing effective marketing and communication strategies, and maximizing satisfaction during the cruise. In summary, the academic literature examines variables that relate to the perception of the cruise product with its multiple characteristics, the experience (*first timers* versus *cruise repeaters*), brand loyalty, and familiarity (*brand* and *non-brand repeaters*).

Regarding the characteristics of the cruise, among the most important attributes are the destination and the excursions (Crompton, 1992; Crompton & Ankomah, 1993; Decrop, 1999). These characteristics are easily comprehensible since the cruise itself is a tourism product. Nevertheless, De la Vina and Ford (2001) noticed that the choice of a new destination does not have the same importance for all passengers. The authors found that the choice of a new destination is more critical for *cruise repeaters*, thus becoming a very important element for the company's management approach. Closely related to the destination choice, Teye and Leclerc

(1998) highlighted how a port's location and embarkation characteristics as well as the quality of the excursions influence the consumers' cruise choices.

Compared to other tourism products, numerous physical and emotional characteristics are taken into consideration by consumers (Mancini, 2000; Duman, 2002; Krieger, Moskowitz, & Rabino, 2005). Especially when comparing the destinations of similar cruises, a first element that is taken into account for the cruise choice is the price (Kalyanaram & Winer, 1995; Duman, 2002). Fan et al. (2015) report that cruising is perceived as more expensive than land-based trips but with a high value for money. In the case of the cruise product, consumers' price evaluations are rather complex because they may reflect thoughts on promotions, other expenses made during the vacation, the cost of an alternative cruise, or indeed, the cost of another type of vacation. Thus, the price can be significantly affected by many aspects during the buying decision. Moreover, pricing policies have allowed cruise companies to attract younger segments of the population, thereby shifting the cruise products from luxury goods to mass products (Cartwright & Baird, 1999). Although many studies have analyzed the influence of the price variable with reference to the cruise industry, their results are often discordant. For example, Petrick (2005) identified consumer segments with varying degrees of sensitivity. After purchasing the cruise, the most sensitive passengers were those who were loyal to the brand and judged the price to be fair. However, differences in pricing were not significant when comparing *cruise repeaters* and *first timers*. Duman and Mattila (2003) had very interesting results. In a study sample of 392 cruisers, they found that the most price-sensitive segments were younger consumers, and the *cruise repeaters*, who enjoyed cruise trips more often, made more experienced evaluations.

Other variables influencing cruise choice are the opportunity to enjoy a great meal and experiencing a vacation in a dreamy atmosphere (Qu & Ping, 1999). Consumers also enjoyed guided activities on the ship and being free of any thoughts about organizing their own activities. Emotions and desires for socialization, in particular, are very significant elements of value creation for the cruiser (Duman & Mattila, 2005). Nevertheless, consumers need to carry out their activities with absolute freedom (Yarnal & Kerstetter, 2005; Forgas-Coll, Palau-Saumell, Sánchez-García, & Maria Caplliure-Giner, 2014). The criticality of such aspects may, however, vary with regard to the degree of involvement, lifestyle, and socio-demographic characteristics of the customer (Nichols & Snepenger, 1988; Pizam & Mansfeld, 1999).

Several other factors influence consumers' cruise choices. Communication activities developed directly by the cruise companies both with the end-users and through travel agencies act as influencers. Since the tourist service is characterized by a lack of standardization and difficulties controlling a priori quality, financial and emotional risks associated with the cruise decision increase. When evaluating a purchase, word-of-mouth or personal information sources are much more important than impersonal ones coming from the media (Murray, 1991; Sirakaya & Woodside, 2005).

Recent research (Vianelli, 2011) has found that information is often replaced and/or filtered by the evaluation of a company's image, both in terms of brand and perceptions of fit between the cruise product and one's own cruise idea. The brand plays an important role among the variables that can reduce uncertainty about choosing a company (Petrick, Li, & Park, 2007). However, research has shown that the brand is not as strong compared to other attributes. The brand does not compensate, for example, a negative allegation made about a cruise company (Ahmed, Johnson, Ling, Fang, & Hui, 2002). It rather reveals a very low awareness of the cruise company (Marti, 2005).

Loyalty is also an element that needs careful consideration. A loyal customer can develop a different purchase process compared to other customers. Loyal customers focus their evaluation choice on the novelties introduced by the company, new routes, etc., while others are less attached to features previously experienced with the company. Besides representing a reliable basis for a company's turnover (Berger, Weinberg, & Hanna, 2003), careful evaluation of the *brand repeater* is crucial. The literature has shown that *brand repeaters* play an essential role in terms of word of mouth (Reid & Reid, 1993; Petrick, 2004c). However, research has also stressed that loyal consumers, both the *cruise repeaters* and the *brand repeaters*, are the most sensitive to price as well the most attentive to the privileges derived from joining loyalty programs (Vianelli, 2011). Other research has shown that loyal customers are the most attracted to promotions; consequently, companies should develop appropriate yield management policies (Petrick, 2004a).

Finally, several studies have discussed the importance of prior experience with service evaluations. The academic literature emphasizes that those who already know a particular service and its characteristics have higher expectations (Nerhagen, 2003). In cruise ship management, Petrick (2004b) highlighted that the perception of quality is strongly influenced by the company's image, emotional dimension, and price for both *first timers* and *brand repeaters*. However, while *first timers*' purchases are more determined by price, *cruise repeaters* display a lot of the emotional dimension. In particular, as the tourist destination is a critical feature of repurchasing, research has found that the destination of the cruise is particularly important for *cruise repeaters*, who are also *brand repeaters* (Vianelli, 2011). Therefore, the quality of the destination and the variety of excursions are particularly influential elements of a suitable cruise product that meets consumers' needs.

THE ROLE OF THE TOURISM DESTINATION IN INFLUENCING THE EVALUATION OF A CRUISE

Research Methodology

The object of this research concerns an analysis of consumer behavior in the decision-making process. We examine the attributes that mainly influence consumers' choices in the cruise industry, while also focusing on the role of the tourism destination at the port of landing. To do so, we differentiate customers into the following categories: *first timers* and *cruise repeaters*, *brand* and *non-brand repeaters*, and *nationality*.

We surveyed customers in five European ports of cruise embarkation, focusing on German, French, Spanish and Italian consumers. These nationalities have been selected because they are among the ones that exhibit the highest market share per passenger in Europe. Customers were interviewed before embarking. The face-to-face interviews followed a three-part structured survey, translated in four different languages. The first part of the survey aimed to identify the customer profile (*cruise* versus *non-cruise repeater* and *brand* versus *non-brand repeater*). In the second part, we identified the discriminant cruise elements of the customer's choice. As a discriminant element, we included the tourism destination of the cruise. We measured our variables on a seven-point Likert scale, ranging from 1 (not important at all) to 7 (extremely important). The third part of the survey asked for psychographic and socio-demographic information. The final sample consisted of 4,002 customers. *First timers* accounted for 51.1%, against 49.1% for *cruise repeaters*. Of the latter, 67.9% were *brand repeaters*. A breakdown of the socio-demographic characteristics of the sample is described in Table 2.

The empirical analysis followed a two-phase procedure. First, we conducted a factorial analysis on the variables influencing consumers' cruise choices. The Bartlett's test was significant (.000, <. 05), showing an acceptable amount of variable correlations and allowing us to proceed with the factorial analysis. The sample size analysis (Kaiser-Meyer-Olkin measure of sampling adequacy [MSA]) was higher than 0.50 (0.920), confirming the appropriate use of the factorial analysis. Running SPSS 22 to perform the factorial analysis (Table 3), we identified the main factorial dimensions and assigned both factorial and single variable importance. The variables showed communalities, i.e. the extent to which an item correlates with all other items, higher than 0.50. We interpreted this result as good significance of the factorial analysis performed, The Cronbach's alpha for single factors, measuring scale reliability, exceeded the acceptance level of 0.70 (with a range between 0.697 and 0.853), showing that the internal consistency of the scale is acceptable. The factorial analysis allowed us to identify the most important variables that differentiate consumers' choice of cruise company.

Table 2. Socio-demographic characteristics of cruise consumers in the research sample

Countries	N°	%
Italy	1,372	34.3
Germany	963	24.1
Spain	809	20.2
France	858	21.4
Gender		
Male	1,965	49.1
Female	2,037	50.9
Age	N°	%
18–24	268	6.7
25–34	782	19.5
35–44	644	16.1
45–54	811	20.3
55–64	811	20.3
More than 64	686	17.1
Education	N°	%
Primary school	247	6.2
Secondary school	1,155	28.9
High school	1,338	33.4
University	1,077	26.9
n.a.	185	4.6

A cluster analysis was also performed. We first segmented the population and then analyzed the relationship between the clusters and the psychographic and socio-demographic variables, including the country of origin. For each cluster, the role the tourism destination played in the cruise choice was analyzed.

FINDINGS

For companies and institutions involved in the cruise business, including local municipalities that could see the cruise business as an opportunity to improve awareness of the tourism destination, it is very important to understand the variables that influence the cruise-buying process. The factor analysis carried out on the attributes that can have an impact on the choices of potential cruisers clearly identified six fundamental dimensions influencing the consumer-buying process (Table 3).

- **Communication:** The cruise-buying process strongly relies on information that comes from multiple sources of communication. Information can be disseminated through advertising of the cruise company outside and inside the agency, advertising media, and internet sites. Also travel agents are an important source of communication. They act as influencers by offering their personal advice. Furthermore the availability of the cruising brand in a high number of travel agencies makes the clients more confident in buying one cruise brand over another one, or opting for a cruise instead of another type of organized vacation, such as a vacation village or bus tour.
- **Social Life on Board:** This factor includes all the variables related to socialization, entertainment, experiential activities during the cruise and brand awareness. More specifically, this dimension captures the image of the vacation, which is not only the products and services, but also the way of life, with the freedom to decide whether to share the cruise experience with other passengers or to stay on one's own.
- **Cruise Features:** In the consumer-buying process, cruise features are taken into consideration. The cruise product is quite complex, and the consumer must evaluate numerous characteristics. These include perceptions of the quality of the food provided by the cruise company, the ship's cabins, the amenities inside the ship, etc. The price is also considered in this dimension, reflecting the quality perception and, consequently, the value of the products and services that cruisers are willing to buy. Loyalty programs are strongly connected with price perception. Finally, the evaluation of cruise features includes the consumer's perception of how the cruise fits with his/her expectations.
- **Tourism Destination:** The attractiveness of the destination and the excursions, together with the number of opportunities to visit different places, and the perception of the atmosphere perceived by the cruisers, is a factor that clearly describes the tourism destination as one of the attributes taken into consideration by cruisers in their buying process.

As pointed out in Table 3 the average importance of the four factors differ. When clients evaluate the different characteristics of a cruise, the *Tourism destination* factor is, together with *Cruise features*, one of the most important dimensions considered in their choice. In fact, *Cruise features* and *Tourism destination* are the factors with the highest average values (5.20 and 5.06, respectively), followed by the evaluation of the *Social life on board. Communication* seems to be the least important in influencing the buying process. Nevertheless, these results have to be further analyzed, considering the different types of clients. In fact. there are some variables that show significant differences (ANOVA test < 0.005) when comparing

Is the Tourism Destination a Core Attribute in the Choice of Cruise Consumers?

Table 3. Variables that influence the cruise-buying process: results of the factorial analysis – rotated component matrix

	Factor 1 Communication	Factor 2 Social life on board	Factor 3 Cruise features	Factor 4 Tourism destination	α	Factor Ave	Item Ave	DS
In-store advertising (posters, catalogues, etc. inside the travel agency)	0.786				0.853	4.39	4.53	1.82
Advertising the cruise company in the travel agency windows (outside)	0.761						4.22	1.81
TV advertising, radio, journals, social networks	0.703						3.89	1.84
Travel agent's advice	0.677						4.78	1.87
The possibility to buy the cruise in a high number of travel agencies	0.631						4.62	1.87
Number of communication channels used by the company (TV, radio, newspapers, internet, …)	0.608						4.24	1.82
A nice internet site, easy to use, with exhaustive information	0.413						4.47	1.89
Entertainment on the ship (music, casino, etc.)		0.667			0.706	4.92	5.02	1.65
Opportunities to socialize and make friends		0.666					4.09	1.83
Freedom to do what I want and when		0.640					5.29	1.48
Brand awareness		0.432					5.29	1.63
Best price			0.736		0.697	5.20	5.12	1.62
Food quality			0.713				5.65	1.45
Characteristics of the ship (ship's cabins, etc.)			0.632				5.48	1.45
Existence and benefits of the loyalty program			0.445				4.21	1.89
The cruise corresponds to my product expectations			0.419				5.58	1.40
A high number of itineraries or destinations				0.819	0.711	5.06	5.32	1.52
High-quality tourism destinations/excursions				0.681			5.23	1.56
Informal atmosphere				0.474			4.64	1.64
% of variance	33.9%	8.5%	6.0%	5.7%				
Eigenvalues	6.450	1.623	1.157	1.090				

Extraction method: Principal component analysis; Rotation method: Varimax with Kaiser Normalization. Rotation converged in 7 iterations. Variance explained at 54.3%.

first timers versus *cruise repeaters, brand repeaters* versus *non-brand repeaters* (Table 4), and different nationalities (Table 5).

In particular, as pointed out in Table 4, the destination becomes the most important variable when we compare *cruise repeaters* to *first timers*.

In fact, considering the number of itineraries and destinations, this choice variable is higher for *cruise repeaters* (Ave = 5.48) against *first timers* (Ave = 5.21), with 55.2% of *cruise repeaters* saying that this characteristic is important or very important, against 47% of *first timers*. The same difference can be pointed out for the high quality of tourism destinations and excursions with Ave = 5.27 for *cruise repeaters* and 53% of them considering this variable highly important, against Ave = 5.12 for *first timers* and 45.6% of them considering the quality of the destination and the excursions of high importance.

Cruise repeaters can be *brand repeaters* or *non-brand repeaters*. In this case as well, the evaluation of the destination as a key attribute differs. On average, *brand repeaters*, both in terms of the number and the quality of tourism destinations and excursions, consider these attributes more important (Ave = 5.53 against Ave = 5.27 for the number, and Ave = 5.41 against Ave = 5.20 for the quality). Similarly, for the number of itineraries, 58.3% of *brand repeaters* consider this highly important against 48.6% of *non-brand repeaters*. Regarding quality, it is considered of high importance in the choice of a cruise by 55.2% of *brand repeaters*, against 48.2% of *non-brand repeaters*.

Surprisingly, the differences among cruisers from different countries are not significant when they evaluate the tourism destination of the cruise. This indicates that when evaluating the destination as a key attribute of the cruise choice, cruisers behave as European consumers and cruise companies can communicate these attributes with a standardized global approach.

Considering the destination as one of the key attributes of cruisers' choices and drawing a comparison with other key attributes, some interesting results emerge.

As already pointed out, *cruise repeaters*, especially when they are *brand repeaters*, consider the destination a distinctive attribute of the cruise product. They are expert cruisers, and thus, they buy the cruise again only if they can enjoy new and interesting destinations. For *first timers*, everything is new; therefore, they take into consideration all the attributes without having a specific preference. The destination is important, but its role in influencing the *first timer*'s choice is not very different from other cruise attributes. *Cruise* and *brand repeaters* are more polarized in their evaluations; for example, for 71.0% of *cruise repeaters* and 75.1% of *brand repeaters*, food quality is important or extremely important, against 55.0% and 62.0% of *first timers* and *non-brand repeaters*, respectively.

Table 4. A comparison between the averages and the highest degree of importance: first timers vs. cruise repeaters and brand vs. non-brand repeaters

Factors	First timers Ave	Cruise repeaters Ave	Anova	First timers %	Cruise repeaters %	Brand repeaters Ave	Non-brand repeaters Ave	Anova	Brand repeaters %	Non-brand repeaters %
In-store advertising (posters, catalogues, etc. inside the travel agency)	4.57	4.50	.254	34.3	34.9	4.54	4.37	.063	37.2	30.0
Advertising the cruise company in the travel agency windows (outside)	4.21	4.23	.196	26.7	28.9	4.29	4.14	.108	30.6	25.1
TV advertising, radio, journals, social network	3.90	3.87	.678	21.7	22.5	3.94	3.78	.094	24.6	18.2
Travel agent's advice	4.87	4.67	.045	44.6	41.9	4.78	4.72	.678	41.5	42.5
The possibility to buy the cruise in a high number of travel agencies	4.54	4.68	.083	36.5	41.1	4.71	4.68	.680	42.2	38.4
Number of communication channels used by the company (TV, radio, newspapers, internet, …)	4.22	4.25	.233	26.9	29%	4.37	4.03	.000	31.8	23.2
A nice internet site, easy to use, with exhaustive information	4.43	4.51	.747	34.9	35.9	4.49	4.56	.508	36.4	34.9
Entertainment on the ship (music, casino,….)	4.86	5.24	.000	39.9	49.2	5.32	4.87	.000	53.5	40.4
Opportunities to socialize and make friends	4.07	4.15	.336	24.9	25.5	4.19	3.94	.004	27.0	22.6

continued on following page

Table 4. Continued

Factors	First timers Ave	Cruise repeaters Ave	Anova	First timers %	Cruise repeaters %	Brand repeaters Ave	Non-brand repeaters Ave	Anova	Brand repeaters %	Non-brand repeaters %
Freedom to do what I want and when	5.23	5.40	.005	49.2	52.0	5.45	5.13	.000	55.5	44.6
Brand awareness	5.30	5.25	.108	53.6	53.5	5.96	4.92	.000	58.8	42.4
Best price	4.93	5.39	.000	41.1	52.6	5.34	5.30	.661	53.6	50.5
Food quality	5.38	5.93	.000	55.0	71.0	6.05	5.63	.000	75.1	62.0
Characteristics of the ship (cabins, etc.)	5.39	5.55	.001	54.5	73.4	5.62	5.46	.019	62.0	57.0
Existence and benefits of the loyalty program	3.92	4.75	.000	19.6	38.5	4.88	4.07	.000	45.2	24.5
The cruise corresponds to my product expectations	5.48	5.71	.000	56.7	64.6	5.79	5.44	.000	67.8	57.9
A high number of itineraries or destinations	5.21	5.48	.000	47.0	55.2	5.53	5.27	.000	58.3	48.6
High-quality tourism destinations/excursions	5.12	5.27	.000	45.6	53.0	5.41	5.20	.000	55.2	48.2
Informal atmosphere	4.55	4.67	.000	30.5	36.1	4.82	4.56	.002	37.8	32.5

* The highest degree of importance is the sum of the % answers equal to "6 = important" and "7 = extremely important" in a Likert scale of 1 to 7

Is the Tourism Destination a Core Attribute in the Choice of Cruise Consumers?

Table 5. *A comparison between the averages and the highest degree of importance for different nationalities*

Factors:	Italy Ave	Germany Ave	Spain Ave	France Ave	ANOVA	Italy %	Germany %	Spain %	France %
In-store advertising (posters, catalogues, etc. inside the travel agency)	4.78	4.24	4.48	4.48	.000	41.7	27.9	31.7	33.6
Advertising the cruise company in the travel agency windows (outside)	4.42	4.16	4.25	3.94	.000	33.9	26.3	25.2	21.8
TV advertising, radio, journals, social networks	4.32	3.57	3.78	3.68	.000	31.3	15.6	18.0	18.4
Travel agent's advice	4.86	4.47	4.94	4.87	.000	45.7	38.3	43.9	44.0
The possibility to buy the cruise in a high number of travel agencies	4.73	4.39	4.66	4.66	.000	41.8	35.2	36.4	39.9
Number of communication channels used by the company (TV, radio, newspapers, internet, ….)	4.54	3.91	4.15	4.22	.000	35.7	20.8	25.3	26.1
A nice internet site, easy to use, with exhaustive information	4.47	4.45	4.46	4.51	.933	38.5	31.9	34.1	35.7
Opportunities to socialize and make friends	4.59	3.84	4.16	3.48	.000	37.4	16.1	26.6	15.0
Entertainment on the ship (music, casino, etc.)	5.36	4.82	5.01	4.69	.000	55.1	37.1	43.6	36.3
Freedom to do what I want and when	5.50	5.42	5.11	4.97	.000	57.8	54.3	42.7	42.4
Brand awareness	5.88	4.61	5.10	5.29	.000	70.5	35.1	47.0	52.9
Best price	4.92	5.54	4.92	5.17	.000	42.1	59.9	36.7	48.6
Food quality	5.66	5.98	5.39	5.49	.000	62.9	73.2	54.1	59.6
Characteristics of the ship (ship's cabins, etc.)	5.51	5.61	5.31	5.44	.000	59.0	62.1	51.0	55.5
Existence and benefits of the loyalty program	4.29	4.45	4.11	3.89	.000	30.8	30.6	27.2	25.0
The cruise corresponds to my product expectations	5.71	5.62	5.48	5.41	.000	65.1	62.6	56.9	54.6
An high number of itineraries or destinations	5.36	5.40	5.28	5.22	.045	52.7	55.8	48.0	45.9
High-quality tourism destinations/excursions	5.26	5.28	5.13	5.21	.187	49.8	53.8	43.8	48.3
Informal atmosphere	4.64	4.92	4.56	4.39	.000	33.9	41.3	30.7	25.5

* The highest degree of importance is the sum of the % answers equal to "6 = important" and "7=extremely important" in the Likert scale 1 to 7

Considering nationality, it was found that the destination is equally highly relevant for consumers from all the four countries. However, we cannot reach the same conclusions for the other attributes. In particular, Italian cruisers give the highest importance to advertising and brand image. Furthermore, along with Spanish consumers, the social life they can experience on a cruise is very relevant to their choice. In contrast, French consumers are the segment that, in general, is less interested in socialization. Finally, German consumers are the least influenced by advertising and brand image, while they consider cruise features extremely important in their choice, especially food quality and price. These differences can be explained consistently using Hofstede's dimensions (Hofstede, 2010).

Italy is a "me" centered country where individualism plays an important role. This means that Italians have a greater attitude towards brand, and, as consequence, brand image becomes more critical in consumer's choice of the cruise. Within the European countries, Spaniards, together with Portuguese, score the lowest in individualism. This underscores Spaniards' attitude toward social life and experiences. Scoring high both in individualism and power distance, French are independent mindset and emotionally independent with regard to groups in which they belong. This explains French's disinterest in socialization. Among the examined countries, Germany is scoring the lowest in power distance. This means that Germans are more prone towards equality and sharing common lifestyle principles. Such inclination well explains Germans' interest in price and cruise quality.

Tourism Destination and Consumer Segments

As pointed out in the descriptive analysis of European cruisers, the most important factors that influence consumers' choices are tourism destination, cruise features, and the social life on the cruise. This last factor is on average the least important, but its importance varies depending on the type of consumer; for example, it is more relevant for Italian and Spanish consumers.

In order to capture the complexity of cruiser's buying behavior, a cluster analysis was carried out, with the aim of taking into consideration all the tendencies of these factors for different types of consumers when they evaluate buying a cruise vacation. Three out of four factors were considered as macro-variables for the application of the cluster analysis (Euclidean distance – K-means clustering). In this way, it was possible to identify groups of subjects that present similar behaviors in relation to the four factors considered in the analysis. It was found that, considering the objective of this research, four segments were able to give us a good interpretation of the phenomena (Table 6). Furthermore, in the table of variance analysis (ANOVA), which evaluates the statistical quality of the clustering process, the F test showed

Table 6. Cluster analysis based on cruisers' decision-making process

Factors	Segments						ANOVA	
	The social life lovers (n=618)	The tourism destination lovers (n=567)	The rational cruisers (n=1143)	The cruise experience lovers (n=624)	The ship lovers (n=578)	The passive cruisers (n=472)	F	Sig.
Social Life on Board	,73523	-1,19686	,55261	,64853	-,81408	-,72360	1184,617	,000
Cruise Features	-1,09940	-,13184	,54580	,26926	,91170	-1,19628	1080,210	,000
Tourism Destination	,37300	,92113	,59919	-1,15819	-,53349	-,86145	1114,860	,000

significant values (Sig. < 0.05) for all the variables, thereby presenting average values significantly different in each segment.

The final segments, described below, show some limited differences in the socio-demographic variables and in the type of consumers (*first timers* vs. *cruise repeaters* and *brand* vs. *non-brand repeaters*). Nevertheless, it is possible to say that some nationalities are more represented in some of the segments.

- **The Social Life Lovers:** This segment includes cruisers who buy the cruise, taking into consideration especially the perception of the social life they can experience on the ship, where it is possible to socialize and make friends, thanks to the numerous entertainment opportunities offered during the cruise. When considering the nationalities in this segment, we find most of the Italian and Spanish consumers; in fact, 22.5% and 16.9% of Italian and Spanish cruisers are included in this group, against only 7.3% and 11.9% of German and French consumers, respectively. Furthermore, in this segment, we find a high percentage of *first timers*, who are probably attracted by the emotional dimensions of the cruise experience, which they perceive to be more attractive compared to other types of vacations. In terms of socio-demographic characteristics, most of the senior consumers are found in this segment (i.e., older than 55 years old), and most of the cruisers with a primary school degree are concentrated in this segment (32%).
- **The Tourism Destination Lovers:** These cruisers are the ones who give more importance to the number and quality of tourism destinations and excursions offered by the cruise, and to the atmosphere they can experience visiting a destination. Different from the other segments, the on-board activities are not considered in their choice, and their attention is mainly focused on on-shore activities. In other words, it is possible to say that they are the opposite of the *Ship lovers* and the *Cruise experience lovers*, who totally focus on on-

board activities and do not take into consideration the destinations and the excursions offered by the cruise. Most of the French consumers are included in this segment (19.8%) as well as a high percentage of German consumers (15.0%).

- **The Rational Cruisers:** This segment includes cruisers who, in their buying process, pay attention to all the attributes that characterize a cruise vacation. Before making a decision, they attentively evaluate the cruise features, the number and quality of tourism destinations and excursions, and the information about the social life on board with all the entertainment activities. However, these consumers are labelled the Rational cruisers because they prefer to focus on objective characteristics that have to be attentively evaluated before making a decision. Considering the type of consumers, all of the nationalities are represented, but most of the German consumers (33.5%) and Italian consumers (32.2%) are included in this segment. Furthermore, considering the socio-demographic characteristics, it is relevant to point out that most of the cruisers in this segment are young.
- **The Cruise Experience Lovers:** This segment is characterized by cruisers who, in their buying process, take into account all on-board characteristics, such as food quality, ship amenities, price, social life, etc. However, the real distinction from the other segments is that they are not interested at all in the tourism destinations and the excursions offered during the vacation. For these cruisers, the ship is the real destination; thus, only what they find on board the ship influences their buying process. In this segment, all nationalities with different socio-demographic characteristics and different behaviors (*first timers* and *cruise repeaters, brand* and *non-brand repeaters*) are represented.
- **The Ship Lovers:** Differently from the previous segment, these consumer not only consider the tourism destination not important in their choice, but also they avoid to take into consideration any form of social activity. Only cruise features such as food quality, ship amenities, price, etc. are important in their choice. Also for *Ship lovers*, the ship is the real destination; thus, only the evaluation of the characteristics of the ship can influence their buying process. A high percentage of French (20.4%) and German (20.6%) consumers are included in this segment.
- **The Passive Cruisers:** The buying process of this segment is not characterized by an attentive evaluation of the characteristics of the cruise product. Neither the cruise features nor the social life with all the entertainment activities on the ship or the tourism destination with all the different places that can be visited during the cruise have a real impact on their choice behavior. It is not the case that there is a high percentage of *first timers* in this segment, but it is not so different from segments that are more rational and active in

their evaluations. Since they are passive, this segment is influenced more by advertising and the travel agent's advice.

In conclusion, considering the analysis of all the segments, it appears that the tourism destination is not always important in cruisers' choices. In some cases, they are more focused on the ship as a vacation destination itself; in other cases, some consumers are not active in the buying process in general; thus, the tourism destination is not involved in their decision. However, the destinations and the local excursions, even if they may not be central to the buying process, are generally important dimensions of cruisers' choices.

CONCLUSION AND MANAGERIAL IMPLICATIONS

This research has contributed to enriching the analysis of the role of the destination in the context of cruise tourism. The issue is relevant because most of the tourism business is associated with a destination that clients decide to visit. However, in the case of cruises, where 3,000 or even 5,000 cruisers decide to spend a week or more on board a ship that is like a small village, what they like to do when the ship reaches a port can be very different. During the interviews carried out in this research, it was possible to identify opposing consumers' sentiments that clearly reflect the quantitative results of this research and could predict the statistical results. On one hand, some consumers said things like, *I hate when we reach a destination because in the port of disembarkation, it is not possible to play at the casino, and we are expected to leave the ship*. On the other hand, other cruisers, especially *first timers*, said,

I am excited about visiting so many places, with excursions in a number of different destinations in a very comfortable way, sleeping every night in the same room, but I am worried that there are so many people on this ship and the impossibility of leaving the ship when I want.

Despite these opposing consumer attitudes, the focus on the tourism destination is clearly central in most of the consumers' choices and has to be taken into consideration by cruise companies.

First, the research has pointed out that the destination is very important, especially for *cruise repeaters*. Among them, *brand repeaters* give the highest importance to the tourism destination. For these reasons, from a managerial point of view, loyalty programs should not only be developed with a price perspective, but they should also be used to promote a specific tourism destination. In connection with this, more than what has been done in the past, local tourism bureaus should highlight that a specific tourism destination can also be visited by joining the cruise of a partner cruise company. This approach could be a way to create synergies with local institutions, which would be advantageous for both the cruise companies and the local touristic destinations.

Second, in promoting a tourism destination by the cruise companies, it was interesting to find that for the specific choice factor of tourism destination, it was possible to identify a homogeneous European consumer, thus allowing for a standardized communication strategy. Nevertheless, it is important for cruise companies to be aware of the existence of different segments with different attitudes that are not dependent on nationality. For some consumers, the destination is the most important cruise factor to be taken into consideration, while for others, it is important but other elements come first (e.g., food quality, cruise features, etc.).

Finally, the destination is only one dimension that has an impact on cruise choice. If, as the results of this study show, it is true that consumers of different nationalities are very similar in their evaluations of the role of the destination on their final choice, on the other side, it was also possible to identify different segments for the other dimensions (e.g., social life and cruise features), reflecting different preferences also according to nationality. For example, like Italian and Spanish consumers, German consumers take into consideration the destination, but to target them it is also important to associate the destination with all the characteristics of the cruise features, while for Italian and Spanish consumers, it is important to underline the tourism destination but to also increase communications about the social life on board.

REFERENCES

Ahmed, Z. U., Johnson, J. P., Ling, C. P., & Fang, T. W. A. K. (2002). Country-of-Origin and Brand Effects on Consumers' Evaluations of Cruise Lines. *International Marketing Review*, *19*(2/3), 279–323. doi:10.1108/02651330210430703

Alon, I., Jaffe, E., Prange, C., & Vianelli, D. (2016). *Global Marketing: Contemporary theory, practice and cases*. New York: Routledge-Taylor & Francis.

Berger, P. D., Weinberg, B., & Hanna, R. C. (2003). Customer lifetime value determination and strategic implications for a cruise-ship company. *Journal of Database Marketing & Customer Strategy Management*, *11*(1), 40–52. doi:10.1057/palgrave.dbm.3240204

Braun, B. M., Xander, J. A., & White, K. R. (2002). The impact of the cruise industry on a region's economy: A case study of Port Canaveral, Florida. *Tourism Economics*, *8*(3), 281–288. doi:10.5367/000000002101298124

Camilleri, M. A. (2018a). The Tourism Industry: An Overview. In *Travel Marketing, Tourism Economics and the Airline Product* (pp. 3–27). Cham, Switzerland: Springer. doi:10.1007/978-3-319-49849-2_1

Camilleri, M. A. (2018b). Tourism Supply and Demand. In *Travel Marketing, Tourism Economics and the Airline Product* (pp. 3–27). Cham, Switzerland: Springer. doi:10.1007/978-3-319-49849-2_1

Cartwright, R., & Baird, C. (1999). *The development and growth of the cruise industry*. Oxford, UK: Butterworth-Heinemann.

Chase, G. L. (2002). *The economic impact of cruise ships in the 1990s: Some evidence from the Caribbeans.* Published Doctoral Thesis, UMI 3041166.

Clia. (2017). *2016 Annual Report, Statistics and Markets*. Retrieved from http://www.cruising.org/about-the-industry/research/2016-annual-report

Crompton, J. L. (1992). Structure of vacation destination choice sets. *Annals of Tourism Research*, *19*(3), 420–434. doi:10.1016/0160-7383(92)90128-C

Crompton, J. L., & Ankomah, P. K. (1993). Choice set propositions in destination decisions. *Annals of Tourism Research*, *20*(3), 461–476. doi:10.1016/0160-7383(93)90003-L

De la Vina, L., & Ford, J. (2001). Logistic regression analysis of cruise vacation market potential: Demographic and trip attribute perception factors. *Journal of Travel Research*, *39*(4), 406–410. doi:10.1177/004728750103900407

Decrop, A. (1999). Triangulation in qualitative tourism research. *Tourism Management*, *20*(1), 157–161. doi:10.1016/S0261-5177(98)00102-2

Douglas, N., & Douglas, N. (2004). Cruise ship passenger spending patterns in Pacific Island ports. *International Journal of Tourism Research*, *6*(4), 251–261. doi:10.1002/jtr.486

Duman, T. (2002). *A model of perceived value for leisure travel products*. Published Doctoral Thesis in Leisure Studies, UMI 3065879.

Duman, T., & Mattila, A. S. (2003). A logistic regression analysis of discount receiving behavior in the cruise industry: Implications for cruise marketers. *International Journal of Hospitality & Tourism Administration, 4*(4), 45–57. doi:10.1300/J149v04n04_03

Duman, T., & Mattila, A. S. (2005). The role of affective factors on perceived cruise vacation value. *Tourism Management, 26*(3), 311–323. doi:10.1016/j.tourman.2003.11.014

Fan, D. X., Qiu, H., Hsu, C. H., & Liu, Z. G. (2015). Comparing Motivations and Intentions of Potential Cruise Passengers from Different Demographic Groups: The Case of China. *Journal of China Tourism Research, 11*(4), 461–480. doi:10.1080/19388160.2015.1108888

Forgas-Coll, S., Palau-Saumell, R., Sánchez-García, J., & Maria Caplliure-Giner, E. (2014). The role of trust in cruise passenger behavioral intentions: The moderating effects of the cruise line brand. *Management Decision, 52*(8), 1346–1367. doi:10.1108/MD-09-2012-0674

Gabe, T. M., Lynch, C. P., & McConnon, J. C. Jr. (2006). Likelihood of cruise ship passenger return to a visited port: The case of Bar Harbor, Maine. *Journal of Travel Research, 44*(3), 281–287. doi:10.1177/0047287505279107

Hofstede, G., Hofstede, G. J., & Minkov, M. (2010). *Cultures and organizations: software of the mind*. McGraw-Hill Professional.

Kalyanaram, G., & Winer, R. S. (1995). Empirical generalizations from reference price research. *Marketing Science, 14*(3), G161–G169. doi:10.1287/mksc.14.3.G161

Kester, J. (2003). Cruise Tourism. *Tourism Economics, 9*(3), 337–350. doi:10.1177/135481660300900307

Krieger, B., Moskowitz, H., & Rabino, S. (2005). What customers want from a cruise vacation: Using internet-enabled conjoint analysis to understand the customer's mind. *Journal of Hospitality & Leisure Marketing, 13*(1), 83–111. doi:10.1300/J150v13n01_06

Mancini, M. (2000). *Cruising: A guide to the cruise line industry*. New York: Delmar Publishing.

Marti, B. E. (2005). Cruise line logo recognition. *Journal of Travel & Tourism Marketing, 18*(1), 25–31. doi:10.1300/J073v18n01_03

Murray, K. B. (1991). A test of services marketing theory: Consumer information acquisition activities. *Journal of Marketing*, 55(1), 10–25. doi:10.2307/1252200

Nerhagen, L. (2003). Travel mode choice: Effect of previous experience on choice behavior and valuation. *Tourism Economics*, 9(1), 5–30. doi:10.5367/000000003101298240

Nichols, C. M., & Snepenger, D. J. (1988). Family decision-making and tourism behavior and attitudes. *Journal of Travel Research*, 26(4), 2–6. doi:10.1177/004728758802600401

Petrick, J. F. (2004a). Are Loyal visitors desired visitors? *Tourism Management*, 25(4), 463–470. doi:10.1016/S0261-5177(03)00116-X

Petrick, J. F. (2004b). First timers' and repeaters' perceived value. *Journal of Travel Research*, 43(1), 29–38. doi:10.1177/0047287504265509

Petrick, J. F. (2004c). The roles of quality, value and satisfaction in predicting cruise passengers' behavioral intentions. *Journal of Travel Research*, 42(4), 397–407. doi:10.1177/0047287504263037

Petrick, J. F. (2005). Segmenting cruise passengers with price sensitivity. *Tourism Management*, 26(5), 753–762. doi:10.1016/j.tourman.2004.03.015

Petrick, J. F., Li, K., & Park, S. (2007). Cruise Passengers' Decision-Making Processes. *Journal of Travel & Tourism Marketing*, 23(1), 1–15. doi:10.1300/J073v23n01_01

Pizam, A., & Mansfeld, Y. (Eds.). (1999). *Consumer behavior in travel and tourism. Binghamtom*. Haworth Press.

Qu, H., & Ping, W. Y. E. (1999). A service performance model of Hong Kong Cruise travelers' motivation factors and satisfaction. *Tourism Management*, 20(2), 237–244. doi:10.1016/S0261-5177(98)00073-9

Reid, L. J., & Reid, S. D. (1993). Communicating tourism suppliers: Services building repeat visitor relationships. *Journal of Travel & Tourism Marketing*, 2(2/3), 3–20.

Sirakaya, E., & Woodside, A. G. (2005). Building and testing theories of decision making by travelers. *Tourism Management*, 26(6), 815–832. doi:10.1016/j.tourman.2004.05.004

Teye, V. B., & Leclerc, D. (1998). Product and service delivery satisfaction among north American cruise passengers. *Tourism Management*, 19(2), 153–160. doi:10.1016/S0261-5177(97)00107-6

Vianelli, D. (2011). Il comportamento di scelta del prodotto crocieristico nel mercato italiano. *Micro & Macro Marketing*, 20(1), 19–38.

Yarnal, C. M., & Kerstetter, D. (2005). Casting off: An exploration of cruise ship space, group tour behavior, and social interaction. *Journal of Travel Research, 43*(4), 368–379. doi:10.1177/0047287505274650

Chapter 4
Impacts of the Tourist Activity and Citizens' Evaluation About the Necessity for Resting Periods

Jose Maria Martin
Universidad Internacional de La Rioja, Spain

ABSTRACT

Tourism's interactions with local communities and natural environments originate economic, social, and environmental impacts both positive and negative. The local community's assessment of these impacts is key to guarantee their support for tourism development since the planning process is subject to their opinion. Tourism seasonality can intensify these effects due to the influx of tourists during peak periods and generate periods of rest and recovery during the off-peak season. In this research, the locals' opinions on the need for a period of seasonal rest is studied, even if this period interrupts the economic activity linked to tourism. Using a group of Spanish touristic destinations shows that the residents in coastal destinations prefer the annual continuity of the activity and that they are much more critical of the environmental effects than social ones. On the contrary, the inhabitants of urban and rural destinations would rather enjoy resting periods.

DOI: 10.4018/978-1-5225-5835-4.ch004

INTRODUCTION

As any other economic activity, tourism interacts with the environment in which it is developed. The manifestation of these interactions takes place in the so-called tourism impacts (Mathieson & Wall, 1982). The first studies on tourism impacts were focused on the analysis of the positive economic effects, while the negative effects of this activity, both environmental and sociocultural, were only studied later (Keogh, 1989). Several studies have identified the environmental effects that tourism has. Negative impacts linked to an increase of the environmental pressure on the one hand; and positive ones derived from a more conservationist approach on the other (Puczkó & Ratz, 2000). The negative effects on the environment and the life of the local communities are intensified in destinations with a high concentration of visitors at certain times of the year since this generates periods of high pressure on the natural resources (Martin, Jimenez, & Molina, 2014). This phenomenon, known as tourism seasonality has therefore, the capability to aggravate the negative effects of tourism (Camilleri, 2018a). Besides the interferences with the environment caused by a period of peak activity, tourism seasonality implies an accompanying effect, the existence of off-peak seasons in terms of tourist arrivals. When evaluating these ''off-peak seasons'', there are very different and controversial opinions, because as explained further on, many authors point out the damages derived from a period of less activity whereas others present the possible beneficial effects (Lusseau & Higham, 2004).

This study proposes an analysis that starts off with the citizen assessment in order to weight the advantages of a period of less activity or no activity at all. This evaluation considers the benefits for the environment and the community that a resting period implies but it also weights the potential harms an off-peak season causes on the regional economy. To evaluate this process of exchange we use the theoretical framework proposed by the Social Exchange Theory (SET) as a reference, according to which, locals shape their attitude towards tourism comparing the potential benefits with the costs associated of the activity itself (Ap, 1992). To evaluate the seasonal resting period is somewhat complex, while for some citizens it might be beneficial, for others it can generate heavy losses. With the ultimate aim of overcoming this problem, a non-forced oriented fieldwork has been formulated. In this fieldwork based on neutral questions, the citizen is offered the possibility to rank every impact on a positive-negative scale.

This analysis is of great importance during the development of tourist destinations planning processes and when defining growth strategies for said processes; given that to guarantee the success of a certain destination the support and commitment of the local community are required (Gursoy, Chi, & Dyer, 2010). In this sense, understanding the attitudes of the citizens towards the need for a seasonal resting period is essential. This study tries to reflect on this matter, on the environmental and social impacts of the tourist activity, on the need for a period of seasonal rest; and on the citizen attitude towards this possibility.

In summary, the contribution of this research is based on determining if the citizen perception of tourism impacts changes accordingly to the degree of seasonality of the destination while discriminating environmental, social and economic impacts. By doing so, we intend to shed some light on whether the population of destinations that enjoy periods of rest has a different point of view from those residing in locations with a homogeneous number of arrivals throughout the year. Equally, we try to answer if the inhabitants of these regions prefer a more seasonal destination, which would also imply periods of rest where the economic and work activities become discontinuous. This analysis is proposed according to the type of destination so that the assessment is associated with the real degree of seasonality.

To illustrate these ideas and increase the empiric evidence regarding them, a case study is applied to a particular reality. The analysis of the locals' perception is proposed in relation to the environmental, social and economic impacts originated by tourism; as well as the assessment of the necessity to have a seasonal resting period. This application takes place in three different types of touristic destinations in Spain: three urban destinations, three coastal destinations, and three rural destinations. Choosing this area of study is widely justified because of the diversity of the touristic product in Spain and the important role that tourism plays in the economy of the country, as shown later. The proposed analysis departs from the contextualization of the importance of the citizen support to guarantee the success of the destination; and the description of the types of impact that might condition their attitudes. The chapter goes on with the exposition of the causes and effects of tourism seasonality, including arguments in favor of a seasonal resting period. Then, it continues with the methodological development that leads to the case study and the consequent exposition of the results. The study then continues to discuss the results obtained and their consequences on formulating public policies. Lastly, the conclusions and the limitations of the research are presented, as well as proposing future possible lines of research related to this study.

THE IMPORTANCE OF THE PUBLIC SUPPORT FOR THE SUCCESS OF THE DESTINATION

Tourist development implies several economic, sociocultural and environmental changes in the lives of the residents, some of which are more beneficial than others (Camilleri, 2018b; Lee, 2013). The nature of these changes, the perspective of their evolution and the way in which they are perceived by the residents are crucial to gain the support of the host community. The participation and support of local residents are imperative for the sustainability of the tourism industry in any destination (Gursoy, Chi, & Dyer, 2010). Therefore, it is indispensable to understand the residents' point of view in relation to the potential negative impacts and to maximize the benefits perceived so that a higher level of support from the community is gained (Prayag, Hosany, Nunkoo, & Alders, 2013).

Shaping the attitudes of the citizens towards tourism is conditioned by a set of factors well identified in the tourism literature. The definition of this attitude is influenced by the nature and intensity of the impacts; as well as the level of development of the tourist destination. Doxey (1975) suggested an index of the residents' irritation (Irridex), which progresses according to the consolidation of the destination in a continuum over time and is divided into the next phases: euphoria, to apathy, to annoyance, to antagonism as certain saturation points are reached. Ap and Crompton (1993), identified the residents' reaction to tourism with four stances: embracement, tolerance, adjustment, and withdrawal. The level of citizen support seems to be related to the stage of development of the tourist destination. Upchurch and Teivane (2000), connected the citizens' support with the tourist area life cycle theory, proposed by Butler (1980). It shows that the more consolidated the tourist development is in an area, the more evident and intense are its effects. According to this explanation, the relationship tourism-society goes through phases of exploration, involvement, development, consolidation, stagnation and then decline or renewal (Gjerald, 2005).

Residents' attitudes have been the subject of many studies, with a particular focus on identifying the factors that influence or determine them (Bujosa & Rossello, 2007). The factors considered to have an influence on the shaping of the locals' support are quite varied. Butler (1974), suggested the importance of the number of arrivals in the destination, the length of the stay, the ethnic and economic characteristics of the visitors and the activities in which they engage. The characteristics of the destination influence too, the perception of the impacts. Hence, aspects such as the economic state of the area, the degree of local involvement in tourism, the spatial characteristics of tourism development, the viability of the host culture and other characteristics are very influential (e.g. political attitudes and religious backgrounds of the host population) (Gjerald, 2005). Other aspects which shape the perception of the residents are the community attachment, the length of residence in an area, the economic dependency on tourism, age and language, the nature and duration of the contact with tourists and the area of residence (Huei-Wen & Huei-Fu, 2016).

Given that the community itself is one of the key role players in the tourism sphere, it is of great importance the way in which these impacts are perceived by the residents since the support for tourist activity derives from it (Deery, Jago & Fedline, 2012). The inhabitants' negative attitudes towards tourism may be a challenge to the development and sustainability of tourist destinations (Diedrich & García, 2009) because the success of the industry depends on local attractions and the hospitality of the host community (Gursoy, Jurowski, & Uysal, 2002). Thus, hostile behaviors against tourists become a limiting factor as opposed to a friendly attitude that would support the development of the destination. Tourists tend to avoid spots where they do not feel welcome (Yoon, Gursoy, & Chen, 1999). It is of extreme relevance for the travelers how the locals treat them; otherwise, they will search for a new place to visit (Diedrich & García, 2009).

Tourism is not developed in an isolated way but instead, within social and environmental contexts with particular characteristics and differentiated needs (Camilleri, 2018b). For instance, the residents are aware that the environment in which it is developed needs time to recover or even the community itself might need a resting period after which, they can return to their daily routine once the peak season has passed. By contrast, some of them might consider more important the economic gain of an activity that occurs throughout the year, putting aside the aforementioned needs. Either way, this assessment will condition the social preferences and must be taken into consideration or the local support, which is a key factor for tourist development, might be jeopardized (Dyer, Gursoy, Sharma, & Carter, 2007).

Researchers have recognized the necessity of including local communities in the early planning stages of a destination (Liu, Sheldon, & Var, 1987). Monitoring the opinions and attitudes of the residents is as necessary as incorporating them into the development of tourism projects, which will help planners to control the negative factors perceived by the residents and boost the important ones (Dyer, Gursoy, Sharma, & Carter, 2007). Moreover, during the tourism-planning and decision-making processes, it is also important to count with the cooperation of the residents since this will help develop more positive attitudes towards tourism (Vargas, Oom, Da Costa, & Albino, 2015). Currently, this issue is not addressed properly despite its significance. Local and national governments are not developing effective mechanisms that favor the local population's participation in the decision-making process. The sustainable development initiatives are more successful if the residents are encouraged to express their wishes, goals, and needs when making decisions, so that they are offered the possibility to generate opportunities that favor them socially and economically (Marien & Pizan, 2005). In this context, the study points out the need to count with the citizen opinion on whether to have a seasonal resting period or not.

TYPES OF TOURISM IMPACTS AND THEIR RELATIONSHIP WITH CITIZEN SUPPORT

Tourism impacts are sorted into three groups: social, environmental and economic (Fennell, 2007). Understanding the nature of these impacts is indispensable and how they are perceived by the citizens is crucial. A lack of support from the community would most likely lead to the demise of the tourism industry in a specific area (Slabbert & Saayman, 2011). Several studies have analyzed the relationship between the impacts perceived by the residents and their support for tourism development (Nunkoo & Ramkissoon, 2012). In this sense, some studies point out that the residents often tend to have a positive attitude towards tourism if it is seen as a tool for development, especially in developed countries (Gursoy, Chi, & Dyer, 2010). Tourism can result in better levels of sustainability, but its success depends heavily upon the goodwill of the residents (Park, Lee, Choi, & Yoon, 2012). The manner in which residents perceive tourism impacts is crucial to predict their support and participation in promoting sustainable tourism development (Gursoy, Jurowski, & Uysal, 2002). In short, the host communities' support for tourism depends on the perception of the positive and negative impacts (Telfer & Sharpley, 2008). Whereas the perception of the positive effects helps gather support for tourist activity, the negative ones might cause the withdrawal of said support (Sharpley, 2014). This perception might be conditioned by demographic factors (Sinclair-Maragh, 2017). Evidence has been found on the different support for tourism shown in rural and urban areas (Rasoolimanesh, Ringle, Jaafar, & Ramayah, 2017). Also the influence of community residents' perceptions of tourism impacts and their life satisfaction is dependent on whether the residents are affiliated or not affiliated with the tourism sector (Woo, Uysal, & Sirgy, 2018).

The first studies on tourism impacts were focused on the assessment of the positive economic effects of this activity. These studies were developed by public planners, as well as academics and private investors who needed to justify new tourism development processes. Complementary studies were developed focused on the negative aspects of this activity as an evolution and to evaluate the ecologic and sociocultural impacts (Keogh, 1989). Tourism impacts comprehend positive effects, such as generating new employment opportunities for the residents (Andereck & Nyaupane, 2011), the improvement of the citizens' quality of life, the strengthening of the business network, the preservation of the tangible heritage, the consolidation of the local identity and the restoration of the local pride (Andereck, Valentine, Knopf, & Vogt, 2005), the improvement of the destination's public image, an increase of leisure opportunities, the intercultural interaction, the environmental valuation and the enhancement of public transportation and facilities among others (Almeida, Peláez, Balbuena, & Cortés, 2016). Tourism generates negative impacts in the three aforementioned categories: 1.) ecologic; 2.) sociocultural, and; 3.) economic. These impacts are quite varied, and their intensity and manifestation depend heavily upon the type of destination, its context and type of visitors. The effects that stand out the most are the crowding of infrastructures and public spaces, the alteration of the local lifestyle, more expensive local stores and properties, alcohol, drugs and security problems, environmental damages, increased waste production, loss of cultural identity, interferences with the fauna and flora, noise generation, intensive use of the natural resources among many others (Almeida, Peláez, Balbuena, & Cortés, 2016).

As Cohen (1984) argues, sociocultural impacts are one of the most important issues in tourism research because they have a direct influence on the locals' lives. Destination planners and managers should focus more on generating and promoting non-economic benefits such as social and cultural ones, because they are more important than economic benefits in influencing residents' life satisfaction (Lin, Chen, & Filieri, 2017). The environmental impacts should be considered equally important since many tourist destinations base their attractive on the natural environment around them and its deterioration would lead to the future unsustainability of tourism. In this analysis, the citizen evaluations of the sociocultural, economic and environmental impacts are compared with one another. This is done in order to show the different perceptions in each type of destination but also, to find out how important they are for the residents and determining the need for a seasonal resting period according to each group of impacts.

Sharpley (1994), justified the importance of social impacts for the regular citizen, arguing that they have an immediate and noticeable effect on host communities in tourist destinations. These impacts can be classified into two different groups; socioeconomic and sociocultural. Socioeconomic impacts comprehend the individual's economic independence, labor force displacement, changes in form of employment, changes in land values and ownership, improved standard of living; and changes in the political and economic systems. While the sociocultural impacts are related to the growth of undesirable activities, social dualism, demonstration effect, culture as a commercial commodity and growth of hostility to tourists. The analysis of social impacts is more complex compared to the analysis of the economic impacts due to the fact that the quantification of benefits and costs is more subjective (Gjerald, 2005). Thus, this assessment is conditioned upon the own attitude of the residents towards tourism, which results from the evaluation of the individual costs and benefits generated by the tourist activity.

The local's support for tourism is conditioned upon the changes generated in their residential settings, some more beneficial than others (Lee, 2013). Therefore, it is indispensable to follow the evolution of these changes and the interactions generated in the planning process of the destination in order to guarantee and preserve a long-term citizen support. This knowledge contributes too, to design of policies that help reduce the negative impacts perceived by the residents; and to define possible actions that increase the benefits of the tourism in order to secure the citizen support (Prayag, Hosany, Nunkoo, & Alders, 2013). Sharpley (2014), claims that perceiving positive impacts encourages the community to support tourism development and participate in it. On the contrary, perceiving negative effects will have the opposite effect, a lack of support for the development of this activity. Several studies have analyzed the relationships between the perceptions of the residents, the support for tourism development and community participation in the context of the stakeholder theory (Nicholas, Thapa, & Ko, 2009).

Literature on tourism has established a few theories to explain how the residents shape their perception of tourism. The first studies that defined the citizen attitude and the assessment of the impacts were criticized for being too descriptive and the scarcity of reasons given to explain why the residents reacted to tourism in the way they did (Gursoy & Rutherford, 2004). The evolution of analysis techniques has made possible to generate new theories that explain how the citizen perceptions and attitudes towards tourism are shaped. Theories such as Fishbein and Ajzen's (1975), the Theory of Reasoned Action (e.g., Dyer, Gursoy, Sharma, & Carter, 2007), the Social Representation Theory (e.g. Andriotis & Vaughan, 2003), the Doxey's Irridex (Holden, 2006), Butler's model of Intercultural Perception (Colantonio & Porter, 2006) or the Social Carrying Capacity Theory (Savarides, 2000). Without disregarding the contributions made by each one of these theories, none of them capture the communities' feelings and reactions as precisely as the Social Exchange Theory by George Homans (1958) does.

The Social Exchange Theory (SET) is the most accepted framework to explain the reactions of the residents to the development of tourist destinations since it allows for the capturing of differing views based on experiential and psychological outcomes (Prayag, Hosany, Nunkoo, & Alders, 2013). According to this theory, the attitude of the residents is shaped based on an evaluation "of the expected benefits or costs obtained in return for the services they supply" (Ap, 1992). Thus, in case that the residents perceive more positive impacts than negative (cost/benefit), the expected outcome is that they will support tourism development (Lee, 2013).

The reasoning on which this theoretical framework has been built is that local communities tolerate the tourist activity in their environment in exchange for some kind of compensation in the face of the evident negative impacts that will take place, perceived as costs. These "rewards" can take different forms, such as employment creation, revenue increase or the improvement of the standard of life. According to the residents' expectations, if a non-adequate compensation is not perpetuated, the support for tourism will result damaged and hostile reactions against this activity will then take place (Ward & Berno, 2011). Given that the residents' reaction towards tourism development is a heterogeneous variable, past studies have widened the framework of the SET to include determinants that influence the residents' support, for example, the state of the local economy, residents' economic gain, ecocentric and environmental attitudes and the use of tourism resources (Gursoy, Chi, & Dyer, 2010).

Considering this, we can define three elements within the tourism development exchange process: economic, sociocultural and environmental elements (Nunkoo & Ramkissoon, 2012). In each of these axes, tourism has proved to have the potential to generate both positive and negative impacts in local communities (Prayag, Hosany, Nunkoo, & Alders, 2013). Therefore, from an environmental point of view, tourism can be responsible for the rise in the levels of contamination or the acoustic pollution and crowding (Nunkoo & Ramkissoon, 2010). On the other hand, positive effects such as the improvement of the area's appearance and the enhancement of natural and cultural protection should not be overlooked (Vargas, Plaza, & Porras, 2009). In the economic sphere, tourism can help increase the job opportunities and improve the standards of life, but it can also increase the cost of living in the area where it has been developed (Nunkoo & Ramkissoon, 2012). Finally, from a sociocultural point of view, tourism development can increase the residents' quality of life, help preserve the monuments and the archeological sites, it will even help to protect the cultural identity of the area and gain pride. In the same line, it encourages the cultural exchange between residents and tourists as well as providing more leisure opportunities. However, tourism can also cause a rise in criminality, alcohol consumption and even prostitution (Dyer, Gursoy, Sharma, & Carter, 2007).

Tourism's negative effects may be amplified by a larger number of visitors at certain times of the year since the pressure on resources and the interferences with the local community are more severe. This phenomenon is related to tourism seasonality. Besides the effects derived from peak seasons, tourism seasonality implies valley seasons as well, in which the activity is reduced. This has effects on the employment and the commercial activity. In the next section of the chapter, we will reflect on the phenomenon of seasonality and the points against and in favor of having a period of rest that helps the environment and the host community to recover.

TOURISM SEASONALITY AND ITS EFFECTS

In a broad sense, seasonality is a phenomenon that affects several economic sectors being tourism most likely conditioned because of it (Cisneros & Fernandez, 2015). Taking the general definition proposed by Hylleberg (1992) into account, seasonality is defined as, *the systematic, although not necessarily regular, intra-year movement caused by changes in the weather, the calendar and timing of decisions, directly or indirectly through the production and consumption decisions made by the agents of the economy.*

Narrowing down that definition to the sphere of tourism, several definitions have been proposed but none of them are accepted widely (Koenig-Lewis & Bischoff, 2005). Because of its extended use and acceptation, Butler's definition (1994) can also be taken into account *a temporal imbalance in the phenomenon of tourism, which maybe be expressed in terms of dimensions of such elements as number of visitors, expenditure of visitors, traffic on highways and other forms of transportation, employment and admissions to attractions.*

To understand this phenomenon correctly it is imperative to know its causes. One of the classifications proposed, differences between three groups of factors as the cause of seasonal trends. These groups are: weather (temperature, sunshine hours), calendar effects (religious festivities, festivals) and timing (school holidays, business holidays, fiscal years, accounting periods, dates of paid of the dividends and bonuses, etc.) (Hylleberg, 1992); these factors can also be grouped either in natural or institutional. Many alternative ways have been proposed to classify the factors that condition tourism seasonality, as the one defined by Lundtorp et al. (1999). This classification differentiates between push-factors, such as the climate, the sportive season, events, etc.; and pull-factors, such as the institutional factors, calendar, trends, etc. The orientation of the destination is also a key element when determining the seasonal tendencies. Destinations which are less climate-dependent and able to offer a steady or diversified product throughout the year will also enjoy lower seasonal trends (Martin, Jimenez, & Molina, 2014). Seasonal tourism impacts cover different dimensions and have become more intense because of mass tourism (Wall & Yan, 2003).

As presented earlier, the negative consequences of tourism seasonality take place during both peak and low seasons. In the first case, they imply levels of over-saturation, which affect mainly the environment and the local communities, while on the second case; a lower tourist activity does not take full advantage of the potential of the area for tourism and results in economic losses. Both of these imbalances constitute the problems caused by the tourism's seasonal variations, which modify the tourism development scheme that many regions rely on. The effects of tourism seasonality are generally classified into three different categories: effects on the labor market, environmental, economic and social effects (Hinch & Jackson, 2000).

Within the economic effects are included the inefficient use of facilities, resources, and infrastructures due to the alternation of saturated and underutilization periods (Rosselló, Riera, & Sausó, 2004). In this category are also included the drops in economic benefits caused by underexploited periods (Cuccia & Rizzo, 2011). Moreover, the viability of the destination can be jeopardized since the quality of the service offered to the customers is greatly reduced during peak periods (Capo, Riera, & Rosselló, 2007). On the contrary, during valley seasons the destination might seem dull to the visitor and impact negatively on their perception because many businesses may be closed. During peak periods, the maintenance of the facilities is also affected (Koc & Altinay, 2007). Economic effects are equally important for the host community since residents linked to tourism must ensure enough savings for the rest of the year (Murphy, 1985). As a consequence of the pressure that tourism has during certain periods, it can also increase the standard of living.

Environmental and ecologic effects are mainly generated in periods with a higher concentration of visitors. They include traffic congestion in rural roads, interferences with the animal and vegetal life, physical erosion, overexploitation of aquifers, enlarged waste production, etc. (Andereck, Valentine, Knopf, & Vogt, 2005). Sociocultural effects include the prejudices, both against the local community because of interferences during the peak periods and against the visitors themselves due to traffic congestion and high traffic volume, lack of parking spots, long queues in establishments, increase in the price of services, etc. (Kuvan & Akan, 2005). During the high tourism season, public and leisure infrastructures become saturated and traffic congestion and parking problems occur (Sheldon & Abenoja, 2001), which often cause inconvenience to local residents (Liu & Var, 1986). Generally, when the tourist pressure is higher, extra staff must be hired in order to provide certain public services. This results in the increase of local taxes because the government considers the stable population as a criterion for resources allocation (Murphy, 1985). During the peak season, the tourist will not be able to enjoy adequate services whereas in the low season many local businesses might be closed (Butler, 1994). This affects the reputation and the image of the destination (Flognfeldt, 2001). Likewise, during peak periods, certain negative impacts of the tourist activity related to certain kinds of tourism are intensified, such as the alcohol and drug consumption (Diedrich & Garcia, 2009). Lastly, the effects on employment are related to the manner in which seasonality affects the local community and employers. This is one of the most studied issues implied by tourism seasonality (Flognfeldt, 2001). Tourism seasonality is problematic when trying to hire adequate staff (Murphy, 1985), and mostly when trying to maintain an adequate quality standard (Baum, 1999), since short-term employees do not receive proper staff training, among other aspects. In addition to this, these kinds of job usually attract low-qualified people (Mill & Morrison, 1998). Tourism-dependent regions that suffer from tourism seasonality build low-quality job markets, characterized by discontinuous job positions with low chances of promotion and labor conditions with room for improvement.

BENEFITS OF A SEASONAL RESTING PERIOD

Despite the evident negative effects of tourism seasonality, several studies suggest the benefits that a seasonal resting period has, especially in regard to environmental and sociocultural contexts. This period also involves a chance of recovery for local ecosystems, as well as a return to normality for the communities living in the tourist area (Higham & Hinch, 2002). Hartmann (1986) noted that it is erroneous to assess seasonality solely from an economic point of view and to isolate tourist services from their social and environmental contexts. This author also points that the lengthy 'dead' season is the only chance for the ecological and social environments to recover fully. Grant et al. (1997) argue that positive economic impacts can also be found as a result of tourism seasonality. For instance, during low seasons maintenance works can be performed on buildings and attractions. During the periods with a heavy flow of visitors, tourism resources can suffer because of this pressure, whether they are natural or historic. This is why some authors agree on the necessity of counting with resting periods in areas with a high tourism pressure (Ioannides & Petersen, 2003). Regarding the job market, there are also attitudes in favor of seasonality that note the positive aspects. Some jobs with a high level of seasonality are extremely beneficial for collectives with irregular work needs, such as students and those who need to compliment other seasonal jobs, like agricultural job positions (Flognfeldt, 2001). Mourdoukoutas (1988) noted that many people choose seasonal jobs that fit in with their non-market activities during the off-peak periods, e.g. students, artists or house-wives. Collectives, such as farmers think that becoming involved in seasonal tourist activities like providing accommodations, might increase their income as well as their social status (Mill & Morrison, 1998). As exposed before, it is possible to establish a long-term symbiotic relationship between tourism and other economic sectors (Ball, 1989). In this line, Flognfeldt (2001), points out that a seasonal job can complement traditional employment and unemployment patterns. This author studied several business strategies in the rural environment in Norway, including mixed employment (e.g. tourism and teaching), use of student and migrant workers, and moving away to work or study in the off-peak periods.

The rest of local communities is one of the most positive elements when a drop in the number of arrivals occurs, particularly in highly-trafficked destinations at certain times of the year. Murphy (1985) shows that for some communities *the lull before and after the storm helps to make the season more bearable and the industry tolerable*. Some residents take advantage of off-peak periods to use local amenities and facilities (Murphy, 1985). These periods also permit the rest and stress reduction of local communities and helps them preserve their identity, local customs, traditions, and lifestyle since all of these factors are affected during peak periods with a higher concentration of visitors (Hartmann, 1986). Butler (1994) stresses that the strategies to lengthen the main season or to attract more visitors outside the season need the full support of host communities if they are to be successful in all aspects. As already mentioned, *seasonality is not necessarily bad for everyone* (Murphy, 1985). Some authors have proposed creating a second peak season as an alternative to just one period of high concentration or to a stable level of activity throughout the year. The second peak season could allow stakeholders to smooth over some negative effects of single-peak seasonality such as, for example, the efficient use of available facilities (Vergori, 2017).

Some hotels have developed successful strategies to face off-peak periods (Murphy, 1985). For example, they offer reduced prices to attract demand during periods with a low flow of visitors, special weekend offers, continuity in main attractions and special packages for a certain segment of the population, such as the elderly or company tourism, etc. These strategies make possible for businesses like these to stay open during the whole year and maintain high-qualified staff hired. However, it appears that this option is not well received in small guesthouses and family-owned B&Bs, in which the same motivation to generate activity during off-peak periods does not exist (Murphy, 1985).

METHODOLOGY

This study reflects on tourism impacts, how important it is the citizen perception of said impacts and the necessity of either counting with a seasonal resting period or not. The methodological approach is essential to evaluate this perception. The first studies focused on the assessment of the citizen's perception of the tourism impacts or their attitude towards this activity categorized the impacts as positive or negative; economic, sociocultural and environmental impacts or simply costs and benefits. Despite this, little attention has been paid to the own evaluation of the citizens of which of these impacts they consider to be positive or negative (Andereck, Valentine, Knopf, & Vogt, 2005).

Even though several studies performed on the citizen attitude towards tourism have been carried out, a generally accepted classification of the perception of the residents about the impacts of tourism has not been proposed yet (Stylidis, Biran, Sit, & Szivas, 2014). One of the methodologies of analysis is the costs-benefits approach (Lee, 2013). The studies that follow this methodology separate the potential impacts in costs or benefits (positive or negative), usually indicating negative relationships between perceived costs and support for tourism development and a direct positive relationship between perceived benefits and support (Lee, 2013). The problem of this system is that it only offers a partial vision of how the residents perceive the impacts since they have already been arranged in costs or benefits (Gursoy & Rutherford, 2010).

An alternative approach is the domain related costs-benefits approach. This methodology tries to enhance the understanding of the relationship impacts perceived-residents' support, considering both the nature (positive/negative or costs/benefits) and domain (economic, sociocultural, environmental) of the impacts. Here, studies have delineated impacts into several areas (domains) of perceived positive and negative environmental, sociocultural and economic impacts. Similar to the costs-benefits approach, the domain related costs-benefits approach hypothesizes direct positive relationships between the economic, sociocultural and environmental benefits and support, and direct negative relationships between the economic, sociocultural and environmental costs and residents' support (Dyer, Gursoy, Sharma, & Carter, 2007). This approach reflects the compromise between the diverse domains of positive and negative impacts of tourism development that residents of a particular destination are willing to make (Dyer, Gursoy, Sharma, & Carter, 2007) and explains a great portion of the variance of residents' support (Gursoy & Rutherford, 2004). Both methodologies are based on a previous categorization of potential impacts (into positive or negative economic, sociocultural or environmental impacts, or simply costs and benefits). Therefore, in none of these approaches the citizen is given freedom to show if they perceive a certain impact as positive or negative, they are just able to agree or disagree with a pre-coded scale of positive or negative statements (Andereck, Valentine, Knopf, & Vogt, 2005).

In order to overcome the limitations of these methodologies, other studies propose a non-forced approach to measure impacts. This approach provides the residents with a series of neutrally phrased statements, asking for their own perceptions of directionality, namely the extent to which they consider tourism to have a positive or negative effect on the various domains of community life (Andereck, Valentine, Knopf, & Vogt, 2005). Jurowski et al., (1997) classified impacts into perceived economic, social and environmental. They suggest direct positive relationships between all three types of impacts and the residents' support for nature-based tourism development. This methodology of analysis adjusts perfectly to the aim of this study since the individual assessments of the tourism impacts are explored. Previous studies based on a non-forced approach noted that the more positive the residents' perception of the tourism impacts is; the more likely is the support for tourism to thrive. According to this approach, the nature of the perceived impacts (positive/negative perception) is reflected in the overall score of each impact (mean scores higher/lower than the midpoint of the scale indicate more positive/negative perception) (Deccio & Baloglu, 2002).

The aim of this case study is focused on the analysis of the locals' assessment of tourism impacts, and on the necessity to count with a seasonal resting period. In other words, whether the residents would rather have a period with lower tourist pressure to be able to counteract the negative impacts or on the contrary, they would prefer to reject this time of tranquility to maintain a constant and stable economic activity throughout the year. The consolidation of this applied analysis is focused on three groups of Spanish tourist destinations (Table 1): the three most important

Table 1. Tourist destinations under analysis. Number of visitors staying in tourist accommodations in 2016

Urban Destinations	Travelers
City of Madrid	9,068,040
City of Barcelona	7,484,276
City of Granada	1,837,517
Coastal Destinations	**Travelers**
Balearic Islands: Mallorca	7,345,866
Andalusia: Costa del Sol	4,716,864
Valencia: Costa Blanca	3,839,623
Rural Destinations	**Travelers**
Pirineo Navarro	125,759
North side of Extremadura	107,043
National Park: Picos de Europa	57,668

(Source: Spanish National Institute of Statistics)

urban destinations in Spain in terms of number of tourists accommodated in hotels: Madrid, Barcelona and Granada; the three most popular coastal areas: Balearic Islands, Costa del Sol in Andalusia and Costa Blanca in Valencia; and lastly, the three rural areas with the largest number of arrivals in Spain: Pirineo Navarro, the north area of Extremadura and National Park Picos de Europa.

Although there is a vast bibliography on the analysis of tourism impacts, as Gjerald (2005) argues, the fact that local communities and their residents are different all over the world leaves space for comparison and stating new discoveries in this field. As Merriam (1988) noted and is widely accepted by many other researchers, the case study is a methodology that fits in situations where it is not possible to differentiate the variables that define the phenomenon itself. This methodology is individualistic (it focuses on a particular situation), descriptive (it provides an extensive description), heuristic (offers insight) and inductive (goes from general data to the concept) (Gjerald, 2005). This work process allows for the discovery of new theoretic knowledge on tourism impacts perceived by the residents in their environment. According to Mehmetoglu (2004), the study case permits to combine the "thick description" of the context, which comes from ethnography, with an analytical approach based on theory.

A quantitative survey was carried out via telephone during June 2017 in the selected destinations, which are representative of the three main types of tourism in Spain. The survey was not limited to just tourist areas but as a requisite, the residents must have been living in the city for over five years and be over 25 years old. 600 residents were surveyed in each destination. This process is based on a methodological framework consisting of a non-forced approach. According to Fennell (2007), tourism impacts are measured from social, ecologic and economic points of view. The questionnaire was designed using items proposed in the bibliography on the aspects subject to assess in the analysis of socioeconomic impacts (Dyer, Gursoy, Sharma, & Carter, 2007). Following a non-forced approach in an initial selection, the measurement items of the perceived impacts were phrased in a neutral position (with a bipolar scale ranging from 1 = strong negative to 5 = strong positive, with 3 indicating no change) so that respondents had the freedom to indicate the extent to which they perceived those impacts as positive or negative (Andereck, Valentine, Knopf, & Vogt, 2005). The application of Cronbach's α and Factor Analysis have ensured the reliability and validity of the items that make up the questionnaire by examining the relationship between these items and their constructs. Equally, other descriptive analyses have been developed in order to ascertain the strength or the quality of respondents' positive and negative perceptions, as well as their support for a resting period. Moreover, t-test and analysis of variance (ANOVA) have been used to determine heterogeneity among respondents.

RESULTS

Tourism is considered as one of the strategic sectors of the Spanish economy. Worldwide, Spain ranked third in terms of international tourism receipts, generating USE 57 billion; a figure that is lower than the United States (USD 204.5 billion) and China (USE 114 billion) (Hosteltur, 2016). In 2015, this activity accounted for an 11.7% of the national GDP and generated directly 1.4 million jobs (Exceltur, 2016). This contribution is far from any other economic sector of the country. The increase in the number of arrivals has been a determining factor for the recovery of the Spanish economy after the 2007 crisis. In 2009, Spain welcomed 52.2 million tourists, a figure that rose to 75.3 million in 2016. This growth meant a strong impulse in the Spanish economic activity. Only in 2015, tourism accounted for a growth of 0.5 points of the GDP within a total variation of 2.5%. Moreover, tourism was also responsible for one out of every seven job positions created that year. However, a rise in the number of arrivals also means a big challenge, since some tourist destinations receive more and more visitors each year and this implies too an increase of the potential negative effects of this activity and more interferences with the lives of local communities. Severe traffic congestion, the increase in the prices of the rents in tourist neighborhoods, acoustic pollution, etc., have resulted in attitudes of rejection towards tourism in the last few years in certain Spanish tourist spots. This sentiment has taken form in the assault of restaurants, stores and yachts, attacks on tourist buses, damages to bicycles in tourist locations and other vandalism acts, mostly in Barcelona and its surroundings but also in the Balearic Islands and to a minor extent in other areas of the country. The Tourism Activity Report of Barcelona (2015) shows the number of residents who consider tourism to have reached its limit in this city went from a 25% in 2012 to a 43.1% in 2015. This shows that a dormant social conflict has settled in a city with a largely tourism-dependent economy.

Using Spain as the case study proves an advantage because of its heterogeneous tourist product and the importance that tourism has in its economy. The Spanish national tourist product is organized in three categories: coastal, urban and rural. Each one of these destinations manifests their own particular characteristics in terms of influx of tourists and seasonality, as well as very different impacts as a result of these figures. According to Martin et al. (2014), the coastal destinations are the ones that suffer from a more intense seasonality and also have a bigger flow of visitors. This situation might get worse, for instance, as some studies have pointed out, peer-to-peer online rental platforms may increase the concentration of tourists (Martin et al., 2018). Urban destinations are on the other side of the spectrum since the arrivals are more stable throughout the year. In this type of destinations, the volume of visitors is overall more reduced; however, certain tourist spots have seen the number or arrivals greatly increased. This has aggravated the pressure that the local residents suffer in urban centers. The seasonality level in rural destinations is at an average level. Moreover, the lower number of tourist arrivals reduces this problem during peak season (Martin, Salinas, Rodríguez, & Jiménez, 2017).

The results of Factor Analysis and reliability testing to evaluate the dimensionality of the adapted items in the questionnaire are shown in Table 2. A value of 0.819 for the Kaiser-Meyes measure of sampling adequacy proves that these data are adequate for the analysis according to the principal component method (Kaiser, 1974). The results of the promax rotation analysis show that the items that make up the questionnaire (adapted from previous studies) need to be divided across four variables (social impacts, economics impacts, environmental impacts and attitude towards seasonality) in order to make the results compatible with those previous studies. Factor 1 (social impacts) includes 11 items. Factor 2 (economic impacts) includes 9 items. Both, Factor 3 (environmental impacts) and Factor 4 (attitude towards seasonality) include 3 items. Cronbach's α for factor 1 was 0.801, with a loading range of 0.614–0.812. For Factor 2, Cronbach's α was 0.714, with a loading range of 0.611–0.861. For Factor 3, Cronbach's α was 0.811, with a loading range of 0.612–0.801. For Factor 4, Cronbach's α was 0.781, with a loading range of 0.747–0.802. These results indicate an acceptable degree of reliability and validity for the items used to measure local residents' perceptions towards tourism development, their support for tourism development and community participation.

Table 2. The results of factor analysis and reliability testing for the adapted items

Adapted Items	Loading	Cronbach's α
Average Social Impacts		**0.801**
The preservation of cultural/historical sites	0.698	
Peace and quite	0.614	
Litter	0.812	
Traffic	0.801	
Crowding and congestion	0.751	
Drug and alcohol abuse	0.755	
Urban sprawl and population growth	0.645	
Conflicts over zoning/land use	0.807	
The preservation of my way of life	0.792	
The availability of retail shops	0.688	
Prestige and image of the city	0.678	
Average Economic Impacts		**0.714**
Tax revenue		
The value of my house and/or land	0.611	
Enough good jobs for residents	0.861	
The strength and diversity of the local economy	0.699	
Increase of residents' income	0.651	
The price of real estate is rising	0.845	
The job options for young people	0.655	
Fair prices for goods and services	0.855	
Fair price for apartments rentals	0.716	
Average Environmental Impacts		**0.811**
Environmental protection	0.612	
Protection of the natural resources	0.692	
Environmental preservation	0.801	
Attitude Towards Seasonality		**0.781**
Interest of having a resting period from an economic point of view.	0.802	
Interest of having a resting period from a social point of view.	0.771	
Interest of having a resting period from an environmental point of view.	0.747	

Extraction Method: Principal Component Analysis; Rotation Method: Promax with Kaiser Normalization.

The summated scaling method (Hair, Tatham, Anderson, & Black, 2010) was used to calculate the values for social impacts, economic impacts, environmental impacts and attitude towards seasonality. The analysis of the results of the surveys carried out (Table 3) shows that the assessment of the social impacts in urban destinations (2,4) is considered to be more negative than in rural and coastal destinations (2, 8 and 3, 5). In touristic cities, the higher concentration of visitors in specifically delimited areas can have a heavier impact on the local communities as manifested in the answers. In particular, the problems perceived to a greater extent in urban destinations are related to traffic congestion, crowding, peace and tranquility, alcohol and drug abuse and population increase. This last fact might be associated with the increase in the prices of rentals in touristic areas as a consequence of their transformation in touristic apartments. In coastal destinations, the most noted effects are related to crowding, alcohol and drug abuse and cases of public peace disturbance. In rural destinations, the assessment of the social impacts is much more positive except the negative evaluation of the traffic.

The altogether assessment of the economic effects derived from tourism is more positive than the evaluation of the social impacts. This perception reaches a maximum of 3.8 in coastal destinations, followed closely by a 3.7 in rural destinations and 3.2 in urban destinations. The negative impacts perceived in this case are mostly focused on the increase in prices of goods, rents and properties. It is worth mentioning that the increase in the prices of rentals in urban destinations is perceived as a negative element, whereas in coastal and rural destinations it is perceived as something positive. This might be due to the chance of obtaining profits from a second residence, which is something more common in coastal areas than in urban ones. As far as ecologic impacts are concerned, the most pessimist assessment belongs to coastal destinations (2.5 against 3.1 and 4.2 in urban and rural destinations respectively). The perception of the environmental damages in cities appears to be more limited, matching with a lower environmental impact. In coastal destinations, the unbearable pressure caused by a large number of visitors increases the negative evaluation. Although the tourism developed in rural destinations is entirely linked to the environment, the lower number of tourists shuns the idea of negative perception. Moreover, the role of tourism in environmental preservation is in high esteem in rural destinations.

The last aspect under examination is referred to the citizen assessment of the necessity for a seasonal resting period with no tourist activity at all. The overall assessment of the necessity of having a seasonal resting period shows that in urban destinations there is a bigger necessity for a resting period, a need that is not that needed in coastal destination. Taking the social impacts into consideration, the different evaluation of the communities on whether to have a resting period are evident. With a score of 3.8, urban destinations consider this break more necessary. On the other hand, coastal destinations are less prone to this; with 2.4 points; and, rural destinations stand halfway those two scores. If we keep in mind the environmental reasons, the residents in coastal destinations value the need of having a resting period with 3.9 points, showing their will to count with a resting period. On the other side of the spectrum are the residents of urban destinations with a value of 1.9 points. Rural destinations reach a score of 2.1, closer to coastal areas. When it comes down to the economy, the local community agrees on the idea that a seasonal resting period could be detrimental, being especially notorious in coastal destinations.

Heterogeneity was assessed using an independent-sample t-test and one-way ANOVA across level of seasonality. To obtain these results, each citizen was assigned to one of the next groups (high seasonality or low seasonality). The criterion used to draw the line between high and low seasonality is the Gini Index, the most stable among seasonality measurement systems (Lundtorp, 2001), which allows for the measurement of the concentration of tourist arrivals. Taking the average GI value of the Spanish tourism sector as a reference (Martin, Jimenez, & Molina, 2014), those destinations with a higher GI value are considered to be "high seasonality" destinations and those with a lower GI value are considered to be "low seasonality" destinations. Therefore, in order to assess these groups, we have taken into consideration the GI associated with the place of residence of each respondent.

Before analyzing heterogeneity, the normality of the distribution of the variables (social impacts, economic impacts, environmental impacts and attitude towards seasonality) should be assessed. We employed the skewness and kurtosis thresholds to assess normality. The rule-of-thumb threshold used to accept normality and to perform independent-sample t-test and one-way ANOVA is the value between -2 and 2 (George & Mallery, 2003). Some studies have suggested a cut-off value of 2 for skewness and 7 for kurtosis (Hair, Tatham, Anderson, & Black, 2010). Table 4 shows that the skewness and kurtosis values were between -1 and 1 for each of the variables. Therefore, the variables met the criterion for assumed normality, permitting analysis by way of independent-sample t-testing and one-way ANOVA.

The results of independent-sample t-testing across level of seasonality are shown in Table 5. The tests that were performed showed a significant difference between results according to the level of seasonality. The inhabitants of destinations suffering from a higher level of seasonality show less awareness of tourism's negative impacts. Therefore, it is proven that a seasonal resting period reduces this perception. However, as discussed previously, these are the inhabitants that demand more stability throughout the year. The results of the ANOVA test across seasonality level (Table 6) show significant differences in the four items analyzed. This means that the perception of tourism impacts is different in environments with different levels of seasonality.

Table 3. Tourism impacts' assessment and necessity for a seasonal resting period in each type of destination

	Urban Destinations	SD	Coastal Destinations	SD	Rural Destinations	SD
Average Social Impacts	2.4		2.8		3.5	
The preservation of cultural/historical sites	3.8	0.79	2.1	0.25	4.1	0.22
Peace and quite	1.7	0.58	1.9	0.26	2.7	0.65
Litter	1.9	0.91	2.9	0.41	2.6	0.21
Traffic	3.2	0.57	2.1	0.69	1.4	0.19
Crowding and congestion	1.5	0.59	1.6	0.24	3.7	0.55
Drug and alcohol abuse	1.8	0.84	1.6	0.98	4.2	0.36
Urban sprawl and population growth	1.9	0.47	4.1	0.57	4.2	0.99
Conflicts over zoning/land use	2.1	0.77	3.7	0.69	3.9	1.21
The preservation of my way of life	2.4	0.91	3.6	0.25	4.2	0.22
The availability of retail shops 0.76	2.1	0.74	3.6	0.47	3.9	0.69
Prestige and image of the city	4.4	0.43	3.9	0.33	4.1	0.33
Average economic impacts	3.2		3.8		3.7	
Tax revenue	4.4	0.48	4.7	0.12	3.5	0.66
The value of my house and/or land	2.3	0.67	4.6	0.09	4.1	0.14
Enough good jobs for residents	4.2	0.97	4.5	0.58	3.7	0.92
The strength and diversity of the local economy	3.1	1.12	2.9	0.43	3.9	0.66
Increase of residents' income	3.7	0.94	4.2	0.44	3.8	0.17
The price of real estate is rising	2.3	0.68	4.4	0.69	3.9	0.79
The job options for young people	3.9	0.44	4.1	0.57	3.2	0.61
Fair prices for goods and services	2.8	0.12	2.7	0.98	4.1	0.39
Fair price for apartments rentals	1.7	0.94	2.4	0.68	3.2	0.49
Average environmental impacts	3.1		2.5		4.2	
Environmental protection	3.1	0.33	2.5	1.02	4.1	0.65
Protection of the natural resources	3.1	0.45	2.4	0.59	4.2	0.45
Environmental preservation	3.2	0.96	2.7	1.11	4.2	0.38
Attitude towards seasonality (interest of having a resting period)	3.1		2.4		2.8	
Interest of having a resting period from an economic point of view.	1.7	0.64	1.2	0.66	1.5	0.62
Interest of having a resting period from a social point of view.	3.8	0.32	2.4	0.57	2.8	0.97
Interest of having a resting period from an environmental point of view.	1.9	0.12	3.9	0.86	2.1	0.28

Source: Own Elaboration. 1=very negative, 5=very positive. When assessing seasonality 1 (a resting period is not necessary), 5 (a resting period is very much needed).

Table 4. Results of normality test

Variables	Skewness	Kurtosis
Social impacts	-0.311	-0.0135
Economic impacts	0.211	-0.271
Environmental impacts	-0.743	0.941
Attitude towards seasonality	-0.181	0.110

Table 5. Results of t-test across seasonality level.

| | Mean | | |
	Hight Seasonality	Low Seasonality	t-value
Social impacts	2.11	3.12	2.91**
Economic impacts	3.03	3.91	3.15**
Environmental impacts	2.61	4.11	3.17**
Attitude towards seasonality	4.12	2.01	3.21**

**p < .01.

Table 6. Results of one-way ANOVA across seasonality level

| | Mean | | | |
	Hight Seasonality	Low Seasonality	F	p-value
Social impacts	2.11	3.12	4.28	< 0,05
Economic impacts	3.03	3.91	6.11	<0.05
Environmental impacts	2.61	4.11	8.92	<0.01
Attitude towards seasonality	4.12	2.01	4.87	<0.05

CONCLUSION

In tourism planning processes, whether they involve new destinations or already consolidated areas, the opinion of the citizens is more relevant than generally thought. Considering the citizen opinion and keeping in mind the perception of negative and positive impacts derived from the tourism will help plan tourist destinations from an economic and social point of view. The viability of a destination can be jeopardized without citizen support.

Tourism generates a series of impacts, both positive and negative in the environments where it is developed. These impacts can be grouped in three different categories: economic, social and environmental. Based on a daily interaction, the citizens will evaluate how tourism impacts on their lives. This assessment is understood as a process of exchange where positive benefits are generated for the community, as well as costs derived from the negative impacts. Locals will value the outcome of this process and shape their opinion and support for the tourist activity.

A great deal of negative impacts is more intense in destinations with higher levels of seasonality. Seasonality, understood as the irregular influx of tourists throughout the year, generates inefficiency in the three aforementioned contexts. However, the literature on tourism has also highlighted the benefits that a seasonal resting period has. These periods of recovery interfere with the economic and job activities developed in the destinations. They also help the environment recover and allow creating periods of rest for local communities, who will then be able to go back to their routines.

The assessment on the need of having a seasonal resting period has been developed through a fieldwork consisting of surveys in three different types of Spanish destinations (urban, coastal and rural destinations). This process has also shown that the citizens of coastal destinations, which suffer from higher levels of seasonality, are less prone to a seasonal resting period. On the contrary, the residents of urban destinations (the less seasonal destinations), hold in high esteem to count with period of rest regarding the social impacts. Thus, the host communities would rather enjoy the opposite level of seasonality shown by their environment.

Aside from the above, this study shows that the inhabitants of coastal destinations are more concerned about environmental impacts than the inhabitants of other destinations. This is the most extended reason for justifying a seasonal resting period. This is not equally considered in urban destinations, where a seasonal resting period is justified to a greater extent. In these destinations, the reason to demand a seasonal resting period is the pressure put on local communities. In rural destinations there is not such a strong need for a seasonal resting period, although the most widespread reason would be social impacts. The results are coherent with the assessment of the impacts derived from tourism. The social impacts have a bigger weight in urban destinations, and the ecological impacts are more important in coastal destinations, where the economic benefits of tourism are more prominent. Moreover, this study shows significant differences in the assessment of the impacts derived from tourism. The citizens of destinations with continuous activity throughout the year perceive negative impacts to a larger extent whereas those that enjoy a seasonal resting period show less awareness.

The theoretical implications of these results justify the need to consider the citizen assessment towards seasonality and tourism impacts as a heterogeneous factor that varies according to the nature of the destination. The data presented complete the bibliography on tourism seasonality, where seasonal periods of rest are a controversial issue. This study shows that this assessment is not unique, but different in each destination.

From a practical point of view, these findings should be considered when planning touristic destinations. As noted in the bibliography, the perception and attitude of the citizens is key to guarantee success of the destination. For coastal destinations we must assume the will of the citizens to have longer peak seasons, provided that the planning is environmentally sustainable. Meanwhile, in urban destinations, public policies able to minimize social impacts and guarantee a place for calmness are required. Therefore, it is not advisable to analyze seasonality as a general concept, but instead it must be contextualized based on the characteristics of each tourist segment, the interactions with the social and ecologic environment and the characteristics of each destination. It is key to design policies able to push non-economic benefits since the citizen commitment to tourism development depends on them. This assert, encapsulated in the bibliography on tourism must be even more present in urban destinations given the results obtained.

This study initiates a line of research not explored yet: the relationship between perceiving tourism impacts and the level of seasonality. The implications are not less since a deeper understanding of the citizen attitudes is needed in order to plan destinations socially sustainable. The further development of this line of research should particularly analyze different types of tourism in distinct socioeconomic environments so that it is possible to know under which circumstances the citizens demand seasonal periods of rest even when they must assume economic losses. Equally, these studies will help understand under which circumstances tourism activity can be developed continuously without aggravating the negative impacts perceived by the citizens and in which cases the seasonal concentration of activity is the root of the issue. Developing this line of research should also involve the analysis of strategies able to diminish these impacts by means of public policies that guarantee that local communities are not harmed. In this sense, the limitations of this study are evident, since it offers a first analysis that should be enhanced with additional research in order to reinforce the conclusions with information coming from different scopes. There is a second limitation originated from the need to be able to perform temporal analyses since the economic cycle might condition the citizen response. Due to space limitation and focus, this study has not performed a comparative analysis using variables such as the place of residence of the citizen, the locals´ relationship with tourism and other sociodemographic aspects.

REFERENCES

Almeida, F., Peláez, M. A., Balbuena, A., & Cortés, R. (2016). Residents' perceptions of tourism development in Benalmadena (Spain). *Tourism Management*, *54*, 259–274. doi:10.1016/j.tourman.2015.11.007

Andereck, K. L., & Nyaupane, G. P. (2011). Exploring the nature of tourism and quality of life perceptions among residents. *Journal of Travel Research*, *50*(3), 248–260. doi:10.1177/0047287510362918

Andereck, K. L., Valentine, K. M., Knopf, R. C., & Vogt, C. A. (2005). Residents' perceptions of community tourism impacts. *Annals of Tourism Research*, *32*(4), 1056–1076. doi:10.1016/j.annals.2005.03.001

Andriotis, K., & Vaughan, R. D. (2003). Urban residents' attitudes toward tourism development: The case of Crete. *Journal of Travel Research*, *42*(2), 172–185. doi:10.1177/0047287503257488

Ap, J. (1992). Residents' perceptions on tourism impacts. *Annals of Tourism Research*, *19*(4), 665–690. doi:10.1016/0160-7383(92)90060-3

Ap, J., & Crompton, J. L. (1993). Residents' strategies for responding to tourism impacts. *Journal of Travel Research*, *32*(1), 47–50. doi:10.1177/004728759303200108

Ayuntamiento de Barcelona. (2015). *Tourism Activity Report of Barcelona*. Barcelona, Spain: Ayuntamiento de Barcelona.

Ball, R. M. (1989). Some aspects of tourism, seasonality and local labour markets. *Area*, *21*(1), 35–45.

Baum, T. (1999). Seasonality in tourism: Understanding the challenges. *Tourism Economics*, *5*(1), 5–8. doi:10.1177/135481669900500101

Bujosa, A., & Rossello, J. (2007). Modelling environmental attitudes toward tourism. *Tourism Management*, *28*(3), 688–695. doi:10.1016/j.tourman.2006.04.004

Butler, R. W. (1974). Social implications of tourism development. *Annals of Tourism Research*, *2*(2), 100–111. doi:10.1016/0160-7383(74)90025-5

Butler, R. W. (1980). The concept of a tourist area cycle of evolution: Implications for management and resources. *Canadian Geographer*, *25*(1), 5–12. doi:10.1111/j.1541-0064.1980.tb00970.x

Butler, R. W. (1994). Seasonality in tourism: issues and problems. In A.V., Seaton (Eds.), Tourism: the State of the Art. Chichester, UK: Wiley.

Camilleri, M. A. (2018a). Tourism Supply and Demand. In *Travel Marketing, Tourism Economics and the Airline Product* (pp. 3–27). Cham, Switzerland: Springer. doi:10.1007/978-3-319-49849-2_1

Camilleri, M. A. (2018b). The Marketing Environment. In *Travel Marketing, Tourism Economics and the Airline Product* (pp. 3–27). Cham, Switzerland: Springer. doi:10.1007/978-3-319-49849-2_1

Capó, J., Riera, A., & Rosselló, J. (2007). Accommodation determinants of seasonal patterns. *Annals of Tourism Research*, *34*(2), 422–436. doi:10.1016/j.annals.2006.10.002

Cisneros, J. D., & Fernandez, A. (2015). Cultural tourism as tourist segment for reducing seasonality in a coastal area: The case study of Andalusia. *Current Issues in Tourism*, *18*(8), 765–784. doi:10.1080/13683500.2013.861810

Cohen, E. (1984). The sociology of tourism: Approaches, issues, and findings. *Annual Review of Sociology*, *10*(1), 373–392. doi:10.1146/annurev.so.10.080184.002105

Colantonio, A., & Potter, R. B. (2006). *Urban tourism and development in the socialist state: Havana during the 'special period*. La Habana, Cuba: Ashgate Publishing.

Cooper, D. R., & Schindler, P. S. (2003). *Business research methods*. New York: McGraw Hill.

Cuccia, T., & Rizzo, I. (2011). Tourism seasonality in cultural destinations: Empirical evidence from Sicily. *Tourism Management*, *32*(3), 589–595. doi:10.1016/j.tourman.2010.05.008

Deccio, C., & Baloglu, S. (2002). Non-host community resident reactions to the 2001 Winter Olympics: The spillover impacts. *Journal of Travel Research*, *41*(1), 46–56. doi:10.1177/0047287502041001006

Diedrich, A., & García, E. (2009). Local perceptions of tourism as indicators of destination decline. *Tourism Management*, *30*(4), 512–521. doi:10.1016/j.tourman.2008.10.009

Doxey, G. V. (1975). Leisure, tourism and Canada's aging population tourism in Canada: Selected issues and options. *Western Geographical Series*, *21*, 57–72.

Dyer, P., Gursoy, D., Sharma, B., & Carter, J. (2007). Structural modeling of resident perceptions of tourism and associated development on the Sunshine Coast, Australia. *Tourism Management*, *28*(2), 409–422. doi:10.1016/j.tourman.2006.04.002

Exceltur. (2016). *Valoración turística empresarial de 2015*. Madrid, Spain: Exceltur.

Fennell, D. A. (2007). *Ecotourism*. New York: Routledge.

Fishbein, M., & Ajzen, I. (1975). *Belief, attitude, intention, and behavior*. Reading, MA: Addison-Wesley.

Flognfeldt, T. (2001). Long-term positive adjustments to seasonality: consequences of summer tourism in the Jotunheimen Area, Norway. In T. Baum & S. Lundtorp (Eds.), *Seasonality in Tourism* (pp. 109–117). Oxford, UK: Pergamon. doi:10.1016/B978-0-08-043674-6.50010-6

George, D., & Mallery, P. (2003). *SPSS for Windows step by step: A simple guide and reference. 11.0 update* (4th ed.). Boston: Allyn & Bacon.

Gjerald, O. (2005). Sociocultural Impacts of Tourism: A Case Study from Norway. *Journal of Tourism and Cultural Change*, *3*(1), 36–58. doi:10.1080/14766820508669095

Grant, M., Human, B., & Le Pelley, B. (1997). Seasonality. In *Insights. Tourism Intelligence Papers*. London, UK: British Tourist Authority.

Gursoy, D., Chi, C. G., & Dyer, P. (2010). Locals' attitudes toward mass and alternative tourism: The case of Sunshine Coast, Australia. *Journal of Travel Research*, *49*(3), 381–394. doi:10.1177/0047287509346853

Gursoy, D., Jurowski, C., & Uysal, M. (2002). Resident attitudes. A structural modeling approach. *Annals of Tourism Research*, *29*(1), 79–105. doi:10.1016/S0160-7383(01)00028-7

Gursoy, D., & Rutherford, D. G. (2004). Host attitudes toward tourism: An improved structural model. *Annals of Tourism Research*, *31*(3), 495–516. doi:10.1016/j.annals.2003.08.008

Hair, J. F., Tatham, R. L., Anderson, R. E., & Black, W. (2010). *Multivariate data analysis* (7th ed.). Englewood Cliffs, NJ: Prentice Hall.

Hartmann, R. (1986). Tourism, seasonality and social change. *Leisure Studies*, *5*(1), 25–33. doi:10.1080/02614368600390021

Higham, J., & Hinch, T. D. (2002). Tourism, sport and seasons: The challenges and potential of overcoming seasonality in the sport and tourism sectors. *Tourism Management*, *23*(2), 175–185. doi:10.1016/S0261-5177(01)00046-2

Hinch, T. D., & Jackson, E. L. (2000). Leisure Constraints Research: Its Value as a Framework for Understanding Tourism Seasonability. *Current Issues in Tourism*, *3*(2), 87–106. doi:10.1080/13683500008667868

Holden, A. (2006). *Tourism studies and the social sciences*. New York: Routledge.

Hosteltur. (2016). *Informe de Coyuntura Turística 2015*. Madrid, Spain: Hosteltur.

Huei-Wen, L., & Huei-Fu, L. (2016). Valuing Residents' Perceptions of Sport Tourism Development in Taiwan's North Coast and Guanyinshan National Scenic Area. *Asia Pacific Journal of Tourism Research, 21*(4), 398–424. doi:10.1080/10941665.2015.1050424

Hylleberg, S. (1992). General introduction. In S. Hylleberg (Ed.), *Modelling Seasonality* (pp. 3–14). Oxford, UK: Oxford University Press.

Ioannides, D., & Petersen, T. (2003). Tourism 'non-entrepreneurship' in peripheral destinations: A case study of small and medium tourism enterprises on Bornholm, Denmark. *Tourism Geographies, 5*(4), 408–435. doi:10.1080/1461668032000129146

Ivanov, S., & Ivanova, M. (2011, September). *Triple bottom line analysis of potential sport tourism impacts on local communities – a review*. Paper presented at the Black Sea Tourism Forum. Sport tourism – Possibilities to extend the tourist season, Varna, Bulgaria.

Jurowski, C., Uysal, M., & Williams, D. R. (1997). A theoretical analysis of host community resident reactions to tourism. *Journal of Travel Research, 36*(2), 3–11. doi:10.1177/004728759703600202

Kaiser, H. F. (1974). An index of factorial simplicity. *Psychometrika, 39*(1), 31–36. doi:10.1007/BF02291575

Keogh, B. (1989). Social Impact. In G. Wall (Ed.), *Outdoor recreation in Canada* (pp. 233–275). Toronto, Canada: Wiley.

Koc, E., & Altinay, G. (2007). An analysis of seasonality in monthly per person tourist spending in Turkish inbound tourism from a market segmentation perspective. *Tourism Management, 28*(1), 227–237. doi:10.1016/j.tourman.2006.01.003

Koenig-Lewis, N., & Bischoff, E. E. (2005). Seasonality Research: The State of the Art. *International Journal of Tourism Research, 7*(4-5), 201–219. doi:10.1002/jtr.531

Kuvan, Y., & Akan, P. (2005). Resident's attitudes toward general and forest-related impacts of tourism: The case of Belek, Antalya. *Tourism Management, 26*(5), 691–706. doi:10.1016/j.tourman.2004.02.019

Lee, T. H. (2013). Influence analysis of community resident support for sustainable tourism development. *Tourism Management, 34*, 37–46. doi:10.1016/j.tourman.2012.03.007

Lin, Z., Chen, Y., & Filieri, R. (2017). Resident-tourist value co-creation: The role of residents' perceived tourism impacts and life satisfaction. *Tourism Management*, *61*, 436–442. doi:10.1016/j.tourman.2017.02.013

Liu, J., Sheldon, P. J., & Var, T. (1987). Resident perception of the environmental impacts of tourism. *Annals of Tourism Research*, *14*(1), 17–37. doi:10.1016/0160-7383(87)90045-4

Liu, J., & Var, T. (1986). Resident attitudes toward tourism impacts in Hawaii. *Annals of Tourism Research*, *13*(2), 193–214. doi:10.1016/0160-7383(86)90037-X

Lundtorp, S. (2001). Measuring tourism seasonality. In T. Baum & S. Lundtorp (Eds.), *Seasonality in Tourism* (pp. 23–50). Oxford, UK: Pergamon. doi:10.1016/B978-0-08-043674-6.50006-4

Lundtorp, S., Rassing, C. R., & Wanhill, S. (1999). The off-season is 'no season': The case of the Danish island of Bornholm. *Tourism Economics*, *5*(1), 49–68. doi:10.1177/135481669900500104

Lusseau, D., & Higham, J. E. S. (2004). Managing the impacts of dolphin-based tourism through the definition of critical habitats: The case of bottlenose dolphins (Tursiops spp.) in doubtful sound, New Zeeland. *Tourism Management*, *25*(6), 657–667. doi:10.1016/j.tourman.2003.08.012

Marien, C., & Pizan, A. (2005). Implementing sustainable tourism development through citizen participation in the planning process. In S. Wahab & J. J. Pigram (Eds.), *Tourism, development and growth: The challenge of sustainability*. London, UK: Routledge.

Martin, J. M., Jimenez, J. D., & Molina, V. (2014). Impacts of seasonality on environmental sustainability in the tourism sector based on destination type: An application to Spain's Andalusia region. *Tourism Economics*, *20*(1), 123–142. doi:10.5367/te.2013.0256

Martin, J. M., Rodríguez, J. A., Zermeño, K. A., & Salinas, J. A. (2018). Effects of Vacation Rental Websites on the Concentration of Tourists—Potential Environmental Impacts. An Application to the Balearic Islands in Spain. *International Journal of Environmental Research and Public Health*, *15*(2), 347–333. doi:10.3390/ijerph15020347 PMID:29462863

Martin, J. M., Salinas, J. A., Rodríguez, J. A., & Jiménez, J. D. (2017). Assessment of the Tourism's Potential as a Sustainable Development Instrument in Terms of Annual Stability: Application to Spanish Rural Destinations in Process of Consolidation. *Sustainability*, *9*(10), 1692–1712. doi:10.3390u9101692

Mathieson, A., & Wall, G. (1982). *Tourism: Economic, physical and social impacts.* Harlow, UK: Addison Wesley Longman.

Mehmetoglu, M. (2004). *Kvalitativ Metode for Merkantile Fag [Qualitative Methods for Business Studies].* Bergen, Norway: Fagbokforlaget.

Merriam, S. (1988). *Case Study Research in Education. A Qualitative Approach.* San Francisco, CA: Jossey-Bass Publishers.

Mill, R. C., & Morrison, A. M. (1998). *The Tourism System, an Introductory Text.* Dubuque, IA: Kendall/Hunt.

Mourdoukoutas, P. (1988). Seasonal employment and unemployment compensation: The case of the tourist industry of the Greek island. *American Journal of Economics and Sociology, 47*(3), 315–329. doi:10.1111/j.1536-7150.1988.tb02044.x

Murphy, P. E. (1985). *Tourism: A community approach.* London, UK: Methuen.

Nicholas, L. N., Thapa, B., & Ko, Y. J. (2009). Residents' perspectives of a World Heritage Site: The Pitons Management Area, St. Lucia. *Annals of Tourism Research, 36*(3), 390–412. doi:10.1016/j.annals.2009.03.005

Nunkoo, R., & Gursoy, D. (2012). Residents' support for tourism: An identity perspective. *Annals of Tourism Research, 39*(1), 243–268. doi:10.1016/j.annals.2011.05.006

Nunkoo, R., & Ramkissoon, H. (2010). Modeling community support for a proposed integrated resort project. *Journal of Sustainable Tourism, 18*(2), 257–277. doi:10.1080/09669580903290991

Nunkoo, R., & Ramkissoon, H. (2012). Power, trust, social exchange and community support. *Annals of Tourism Research, 39*(2), 997–1023. doi:10.1016/j.annals.2011.11.017

Park, D. B., Lee, K. W., Choi, H. S., & Yoon, Y. (2012). Factors influencing social capital in rural tourism communities in South Korea. *Tourism Management, 33*(6), 1511–1520. doi:10.1016/j.tourman.2012.02.005

Prayag, G., Hosany, S., Nunkoo, R., & Alders, T. (2013). London residents' support for the 2012 Olympic Games: The mediating effect of overall attitude. *Tourism Management, 36,* 629–640. doi:10.1016/j.tourman.2012.08.003

Puczkó, L., & Rátz, T. (2000). Tourist and resident perceptions of the physical impacts of tourism at Lake Balaton, Hungary: Issues for sustainable tourism management. *Journal of Sustainable Tourism, 8*(6), 458–478. doi:10.1080/09669580008667380

Rasoolimanesh, S. M., Ringle, C. M., Jaafar, M., & Ramayah, T. (2017). Urban vs. rural destinations: Residents' perceptions, community participation and support for tourism development. *Tourism Management*, *60*, 147–158. doi:10.1016/j.tourman.2016.11.019

Roselló, J. A., Riera, A., & Sausó, A. (2004). The economic determinants of seasonal patterns. *Annals of Tourism Research*, *31*(3), 697–711. doi:10.1016/j.annals.2004.02.001

Saveriades, S. (2000). Establishing the social tourism carrying capacity for the tourist resorts of the east coast of the Republic of Cyprus. *Tourism Management*, *21*(2), 147–156. doi:10.1016/S0261-5177(99)00044-8

Sharpley, R. (1994). *Tourism, Tourists and Society*. Huntingdon, UK: ELM Publishers.

Sharpley, R. (2014). Host perceptions of tourism: A review of the research. *Tourism Management*, *42*, 37–49. doi:10.1016/j.tourman.2013.10.007

Sheldon, P. J., & Abenoja, T. (2001). Resident attitudes in a mature destination: The case of Waikiki. *Tourism Management*, *22*(5), 435–443. doi:10.1016/S0261-5177(01)00009-7

Sinclair-Maragh, G. (2017). Demographic analysis of residents' support for tourism development in Jamaica. *Journal of Destination Marketing & Management*, *6*(1), 5–12. doi:10.1016/j.jdmm.2016.03.005

Slabbert, E., & Saayman, M. (2011). The influence of culture on community perceptions: The case of two South African arts festivals. *Event Management*, *15*(2), 197–211. doi:10.3727/152599511X13082349958352

Stylidis, D., Biran, A., Sit, J., & Szivas, E. (2014). Residents' support for tourism development: The role of residents' place image and perceived tourism impacts. *Tourism Management*, *45*, 260–274. doi:10.1016/j.tourman.2014.05.006

Telfer, D. J., & Sharpley, R. (2008). *Tourism and development in the developing world*. Abingdon, UK: Routledge.

Upchurch, R. S., & Teivane, U. (2000). Resident perceptions of tourism development in Riga, Latvia. *Tourism Management*, *21*(5), 499–507. doi:10.1016/S0261-5177(99)00104-1

Vargas, A., Oom, P., Da Costa, J., & Albino, S. (2015). Residents' attitude and level of destination development: An international comparison. *Tourism Management*, *48*(3), 199–210. doi:10.1016/j.tourman.2014.11.005

Vargas, A., Plaza, M. A., & Porras, N. (2009). Understanding residents' attitudes toward the development of industrial tourism in a former mining community. *Journal of Travel Research, 47*(3), 373–387. doi:10.1177/0047287508322783

Vergori, A. S. (2017). Patterns of seasonality and tourism demand forecasting. *Tourism Economics, 23*(5), 1011–1027. doi:10.1177/1354816616656418

Wall, G., & Yan, M. (2003). Disaggregating visitor flows — the example of China. *Tourism Analysis, 7*(3/4), 191–205.

Ward, C., & Berno, T. (2011). Beyond social exchange theory: Attitudes toward tourists. *Annals of Tourism Research, 38*(4), 1556–1569. doi:10.1016/j.annals.2011.02.005

Woo, E., Uysal, M., & Sirgy, M. J. (2018). Tourism Impact and Stakeholders' Quality of Life. *Journal of Hospitality & Tourism Research (Washington, D.C.), 42*(2), 260–286. doi:10.1177/1096348016654971

Yoon, Y., Gursoy, D., & Chen, J. S. (1999). An investigation of the relationship between tourism impacts and host communities' characteristics. Anatolia: An International. *Journal of Tourism and Hospitality Research, 10*(1), 29–44.

Chapter 5
The Use of Differential Pricing in Tourism and Hospitality

Aurelio G. Mauri
Università di Lingue e Comunicazione, Italy

Ruggero Sainaghi
Università di Lingue e Comunicazione, Italy

Giampaolo Viglia
University of Portsmouth, UK

ABSTRACT

Due to the widespread adoption of revenue management strategies within the hospitality business, pricing has become more and more a central topic both for academics and practitioners. In particular, pricing has evolved towards value-based approaches, dynamic and customized through the use of price differentiation. "Rate fences" are the criteria that hotels adopt to separate customer segments whose service values may differ. The purpose of this chapter is to analyze the academic literature as well as the business practices relating to this subject. The authors propose a logical link between rate fences and the hedonic pricing approach. Main topics are 1) rate fence classifications and 2) the effectiveness of rate fences and their impacts on perceptions of fairness. Overall, this contribution suggests that time-based rate fences are fundamental at the destination level, and they are strictly connected to seasonality. Destinations' policymakers and firms can consider strategies and tools for overcoming seasonality, including special events that may take place in a destination.

DOI: 10.4018/978-1-5225-5835-4.ch005

INTRODUCTION

Pricing research has primarily developed in microeconomics and marketing, although with different approaches. Whereas pricing studies in microeconomics are largely theoretical, research in marketing is principally oriented toward managerial decisions (Rao, 2009). In this regard, Nagle (1984) observed that economic models are abstractions and are not intended to describe realistically the methods firms use in making their pricing decisions and the manner in which consumers respond to those decisions.

Despite the centrality of pricing for firms' performance, until a couple of decades ago, research on pricing was relatively limited: *price is so important to the firm's success, one wonders why pricing has not received more attention* (LaPlaca, 1997, p. 192). However, in more recent years, the subject has received increasing attention, in part due to studies related to yield and revenue management. Within this context, price differentiation plays a central role, and the means (price fences) used to make different customer segments pay a different price are a key point. In practice, fences are able to augment or reduce the features and value of products, thus facilitating price differentiation. This brings the hedonic pricing approach to mind, even if the link between rate fences and hedonic price it is still in its infancy. Consequently, the authors propose to expand this connection.

Finally, the topic is approached with regard to considering elements and fences that are more destination dependent. Time-based rate fences are fundamental at the destination level, and they are connected to seasonality. Destinations' policy makers and firms can therefore consider strategies and tools for overcoming seasonality, including special events that may take place in a destination.

This chapter offers three main contributions. First, it reconciles the price discrimination conceptualizations used in marketing and economics. Second, it presents the interplay between rate fences and hedonic pricing, offering managers clear guidance on how to approach these managerial levers. Third, it applies these tools to hospitality and tourism, showing the peculiarities and possible synergies between hotels and destination for revenue maximization.

PRICE DISCRIMINATION AND PRICE DIFFERENTIATION

In recent years, pricing has received increased attention from academics and operators, a change which can be related both to technological progress and to an evolution in the approaches firms commonly employ to choose their prices.

First, in the current digital environment, price has acquired a special and more central role. In fact, new technologies offer innovative and effective managerial instruments for pricing policies, but they also make pricing more difficult and complex to manage (Mauri, 2014). Second, academics have emphasized the importance of customer value in applying profitable pricing policies. Customer value has been defined by Zeithaml (1988, p. 14) as a *consumer's overall assessment of the utility of a product based on perceptions of what is received and what is given*. In fact, value-based pricing has become a key conception in firms' strategies and tactics. Therefore, the notion of reservation price is brought to mind (Kalish & Nelson, 1991):

A consumer's reservation price for a specific product is simply the price at which the consumer is indifferent between buying and not buying the product, given the consumption alternatives available to the consumer (Jedidi & Zhang, 2002, p. 1352). The reservation price captures a consumer's valuation of a product's attributes, assuming consumption opportunities elsewhere and the budget constraints she faces. Following the same line of reasoning, the concept of "customised pricing" has been developed and employed, which refers to situations where sellers have the option to set different prices for different clients based on both the customer and the product being purchased (Phillips, 2005). Nowadays, new technologies have significantly developed the technical capabilities of firms to apply customised pricing.

Firms often segment customers according to their price sensitivity and charge them differently, which has been labelled price discrimination or price differentiation (or else differential pricing, Varian, 1996). In this regard, authors have provided different definitions and have employed the terminology in various ways. As Varian (1989) observed, *price discrimination is one of the most prevalent forms of marketing practices* (p. 598). The conventional (and stricter) definition is that price discrimination is present when the same commodity is sold at different prices to different consumers. However, most economists agree that price discrimination also exists when similar, but not identical, products are sold at prices that do not reflect differences in costs (Clerides, 2004). According to Stigler's (1987) widely-accepted definition, price discrimination is present when two or more similar goods are sold at prices that are in different ratios to marginal costs.

Cassady Jr. (1946a), in an article published in the Journal of Marketing, stated that price discrimination may encompass various situations: (1) variations in the prices set for homogeneous products (including services furnished); (2) identical prices in connection with the exchange of non-homogeneous product-services; or (3) differences in both prices and product-services, with price differences varying disproportionately to differences in the product-services exchanged. Technically, then, price discrimination may be defined as the unequal treatment of those with whom a buyer or seller has dealings (Cassady Jr., 1946a).

To practice price discrimination successfully, firms need detailed knowledge of the distribution of consumers' willingness to pay (Besanko, Dubé, & Gupta, 2003). Technological progress has offered firms new tools to better implement price differentiation. In fact, the availability of new information technologies and advanced database analytics, as well as the widespread use of Internet transactions, permit firms to collect and process detailed customer information on a large scale and in a timely and cost-effective manner (Zhang, 2009).

A firm's ability to apply differential pricing mainly depends upon two essential factors: its ability to identity groups of customers with different levels of willingness to pay and its ability to price them independently (Raza, 2015). Differential pricing refers to segmentation of the market and differences in pricing grounded on these segments' price elasticity of demand (Mauri, 2012a), which measures the consequence of price changes on the quantity demanded.

PRICE DIFFERENTIATION IN THE HOTEL BUSINESS

Hotel firms are paying more and more attention to pricing as a consequence of widespread revenue management. In fact, pricing is the central lever of revenue management (Kimes & Chase, 1998; Ivanov, 2014), and differential pricing is widely applied within tourism industries. Consequently, price discrimination methods have become standard operating procedures for many hospitality firms (Raab, Mayer, Kim, & Shoemaker, 2009). Hotels are able to take advantage of differential pricing for various segments because the market for hotels can be divided into narrow customer segments (Yelkur & Nêveda DaCosta, 2001).

Price discrimination can help firms to increase revenue in two ways. First, by charging higher (premium) prices to less price-sensitive market segments, firms can augment their revenues. Second, at the same time, by charging lower prices to price-sensitive market segments in order to raise the sales volume of the service, firms can thus offset price reductions. For example, within the hotel industry, it is possible to distinguish between business travelers, who are commonly price-insensitive, and leisure travelers, who are usually price-sensitive (Heo & Lee, 2009). Price differentiation can also be applied to ancillary hotel services, such as spas. For instance, a study based on clients' preferences for spa rates and restrictions identified four market segments (Guo, Guillet, Kucukusta, & Law, 2016).

Proper market segmentation and price discrimination are crucial for effective pricing and revenue management implementation. After a market segmentation structure has been defined, firms use several conditions and restrictions to separate price categories, which are means, such as less information, purchase processes, time, and refund penalties, to "fence" customers into different market segments and make it difficult or time consuming for them to move from one market segment to another. A 'fence' is a device that is designed to preserve market segmentation and limit spillover between segments (Zhang, 2011).

Fences for Differentiating Prices

Rate fences are the rules and the criteria that hotels, or other service firms, can use to separate customer segments whose service values may differ. In fact, in order to make different customers actually pay different prices, hotels must introduce barriers that result in clients purchasing services by following diverse patterns. According to Hanks et al. (1992, p. 21), rate fences are *logical, rational rules or restrictions that are designed to allow customers to segment themselves into appropriate rate categories based on their needs, behaviour, or willingness to pay*. To minimize "buy-downs", e.g. customers who actually pay a lower rate when they would have been willing to pay a higher price, it is essential to adopt proper rate fencing (Vinod, 2004). Sanders (2011) formulates the following example of how a firm, varying the product, may apply price discrimination:

- Adding and subtracting product features;
- Adding and subtracting convenience;
- Adding and subtracting durability;
- Adding and subtracting design appeal;
- Adding and subtracting speed of delivery and processing;
- Changing the level of customer service;
- Advertising, branding, and perhaps generating a cool factor and snob appeal.

The subtraction of a feature is linked to the notion of restrictions. Restrictions are defined as sets of requirements that are used to discount prices, differentiate products, and discourage diversion. Within airlines, examples are fourteen-day advance booking requirements, cancellation penalties, Saturday-night stayovers, and midweek departure requirements (McGill & Van Ryzin, 1999).

The air transportation sector has developed a significant tradition of price discrimination and price fences, the most common of which are advance purchase, round trips, and Saturday-night stay restrictions. While the advance-purchase and round-trip requirements can also have cost-saving aspects, their main function is to create "fences" to exclude business travelers, whose demand often occurs on short notice. The Saturday-night stay restriction has no cost-saving justification, but represents an effective way to block business travelers who are supposedly willing to spend weekends with their families or in other leisure activities not at their business destinations. Another price-discriminating method is to limit the notice of availability of last-minute low fares to certain distribution channels (Levine, 2002).

It is important to underline that correctly designed rate fences allow hotel guests to self-segment on the basis of their willingness to pay (Kimes & Wirtz, 2003). Furthermore, rate fences permit and justify a pricing structure based on multiple prices (Kimes & Chase, 1998). Price discrimination is considered fairer if based on the mutual perception of fairness as well as on the adoption of clear and logical fences. Fences make services less homogeneous and, thus, less comparable. On the other hand, unjust and/or incomprehensible fencing may create perceived unfairness, resulting in negative consequences.

A policy of price differentiation, through the use of rate fences, also makes it possible to sell services to customers who can only afford to pay lower rates. These clients, in fact, are usually inclined to accept certain restrictions on their purchase and consumption experiences in order to obtain cheaper prices.

Rate Fence Classification

There are several means of classifying fences (Lovelock & Wirtz, 2004; Mauri, 2012b; Mauri & Soone, 2009; Wirtz & Kimes, 2007; Zhang, 2011; Zhang & Bell, 2012). Below, we offer a comprehensive examination of the subject by referring to both academic contributions and hotels' actual practices. To do so, the authors reviewed publications containing the wording "rate fences". A basic approach distinguishes between two groups of rate fences that hotels can employ to customize their rates: physical fences and non-physical fences (Hanks, Noland & Cross, 1992). Table 1 presents a classification of rate fences, in addition to also providing some examples. We distinguish among three types of non-physical fences:

- Fences based on transaction characteristics;
- Fences based on consumption characteristics;
- Fences based on buyer characteristics.

Physical fences regard tangible aspects of the firm's offer. Within hotels, physical rate fences include the physical location and view of the rooms, size and furnishings, presence of amenities, and extra-services.

On the other hand, non-physical rate fences comprise consumption characteristics (e.g. time or duration of use and frequency or volume of consumption), transaction characteristics (e.g. booking time), and buyer features. Furthermore, it is also important to observe that different rate fence types may be combined among themselves. This taxonomy is also adopted by Lovelock and Wirtz (2004).

Table 1. A classification of rate fences in the hotel industry

Physical Fences (Product-Related)	Basic Product (type, size, furnishing, view, and location of the room)
	Amenities (Wi-Fi, free breakfast, airport transfer)
	Service Level (dedicated call centers/staff members, priority waiting list)
	Bundling (of products, amenities, and/or services)
Non-Physical Fences: Transaction Characteristics	Time of booking (advance purchase, last minute)
	Method of Payment (cash/credit card, pre-paid)
	Location of reservation
	Flexibility of usage (fees/penalties for cancelation and reservations changes)
	Information offered (opaque pricing)
Non-Physical Fences: Consumption Characteristics	Channel of booking (direct/indirect, traditional/OTAs/social media)
	Time (high/low season, weekday/weekend) and duration of use (minimum stay, stay over on the weekend)
Non-Physical Fences: Buyer Characteristics	Location of consumption (Prices vary by location (between cities, city center versus edges of city)
	Frequency or volume of consumption (frequent guests' programs, volume agreed rates)
	Association membership (Alumni, AAA)
	Individual/groups (size and type of group)
	Customer age (child, senior)
	Reason for stay (leisure, business)

(Sources: Adapted from Lovelock & Wirtz, 2004; Mauri, 2012b; Mauri & Soone, 2009; Wirtz & Kimes, 2007; Zhang, 2011).

Supplementary to the previous taxonomy, we can introduce a second classification focused on the key element of time, distinguishing between time-based and non-time-based fences. The role of time has already been observed by Cassady Jr., who defined the phenomenon as *two identical items sold at different prices at different times (temporal discrimination)* (1946a, p. 11), stating that *this use of temporal price discrimination has many applications in service industries and market distribution* (1946b, p. 149). Time-based fences may relate to both transaction characteristics (e.g. time of booking) and/or temporal consumption characteristics (e.g. time and duration of use).

These aspects are crucial to profitable price settings, firstly because prices can be linked dynamically to market demand and to available inventory, and secondly because purchasing behaviors, analyzed from the point of view of time, permit useful customer segmentation, an example being the diverse timing of leisure and

Table 2. A further classification of hotel rate fences types

Type of Fences			Fences
Physical Fences	Product-Related	Non-Time-Based	Room features, amenities, services
Non-Physical Fences	Transaction characteristics		Rate rules, purchase channel
		Time-Based	Time of booking (time before the date of stay)
	Consumption characteristics		Time and duration of use
		Non-Time-Based	Location of use
	Customer characteristics		Customer features, frequency of use

(Source: Mauri, 2012b; Mauri & Soone, 2009).

business bookings. Empirical evidence has shown that time-based fences are the most accepted fence category by hotel guests (Mauri & Soone, 2009). Thus, we can combine the first and second fence classifications to obtain the scheme in Table 2

Rate Fences, Price Differentiation, and Self-Selection

It has been observed that rate fences let hotel guests self-segment on the basis of their willingness to pay (Kimes & Wirtz, 2003). In fact, in some cases, customers can play a role in rate fixing. In this regard, Chi-Cheng et al. (2012) distinguish between "posted price discrimination" (i.e. firms set prices and afterwards consumers have to "take-it-or-leave-it") and "participative price discrimination" (such as auctions and pay what-you-want, in which buyers determine the prices). In other words, in some cases, customers do not have any choice except to accept the specific rate the company has addressed to them. In some other cases, customers may have a certain discretionary power, for instance, in changing the booking channel (if a parity rate is not applied) or changing the period of stay.

Sometimes, when the seller cannot identify the customer type, he can design product features, restrictions, and rate fences in such a way that the customer voluntarily chooses the product-price combination meant for him (Moorthy, 1984). For example, booking time is frequently related to travel purpose (i.e. leisure or business). Ng (2006) underlines that firms could employ segmentation based on self-selection.

According to this line of argument, a further classification of rate fences can be operationalized. In fact, a classification can be made distinguishing between fences that establish insuperable hurdles (fences to which the guest must be subject) and fences that are based on self-selection by customers (Mauri, 2012b).

In the first type of fences, we can include, for instance, age and other customer features. In this case, customers have to submit themselves to the firms' choices. Conversely, the second situation can comprise behavioral fences linked to customers' choices, such as in-advance purchases, Saturday-night stayovers, and surcharges for one-way tickets.

In reality, the degree of self-selection can be described as a continuous variable (rather than a discrete one), as it can take on different values over a minimum/maximum continuum. For instance, there may be an apparent liberty of choice, but the actual situation will drive guests to operate in a specific way.

The fact that fences are "suffered" or can be "chosen" by customers may have consequences for the level of perception of fairness. In fact, Dickson and Kalapurakal (1994) argue that price discrimination is usually considered fairer as long as all customers have the possibility of achieving all price levels.

Rate Fences: Effectiveness and Fairness

Over the past decades, revenue management has been increasingly used in the hospitality sector. However, up until recent times, scant research had investigated the effects of these practices on the relationships between hotels and their customers (Mauri, 2007; Wirtz, Kimes, Theng, & Patterson, 2003). In recent years, however, we have observed that an interesting stream of studies has arisen in this domain. A complete summary of the research on perceptions of fairness of revenue management in the hospitality industry is presented by Heo and Lee (2011).

A successful implementation of revenue management must avoid the risk of perceptions of unfairness by hotel guests. Otherwise, the achieved gains of revenue management could be counterbalanced, or even overcome, by losses due to brand loyalty detriment.

The theme of perceptions of fairness has mainly been studied with regard to pricing policies. However, perceived unfairness may also depend on decisions that affect the nature of the service itself and/or reduce the service quality. Moreover, some techniques for inventory control, such as capacity restrictions and overbooking, may also contribute to perceived unfairness.

In the following discussion, we will synthesize some of the concepts and branches of research. The topics of justice, equity, and fairness have received special attention by social science researchers (e.g. equity and justice theories). The subject has also been studied by services marketing researchers. In fact, customers' levels of satisfaction and their future loyalty to a brand depend upon whether the customers believe that they have been treated fairly by the firm, i.e. whether justice has been done.

However, the rich stream of contributions is characterized by the use of different terminologies, in that the terms justice, equity, and fairness are all employed. Oliver (2009) stated that *in elementary terms, equity is a fairness, rightness, or deservingness comparison to other entities, whether real or imaginary, individual or collective, person or nonperson*. Greenberg (1987) discussed the concept of organizational justice, connecting it to Equity Theory (Adams, 1963). In particular, three forms of justice are generally considered (Greenberg, 1990):

- **Distributive Justice:** As the fairness associated with the outcomes of decisions and the distribution of resources;
- **Procedural Justice:** As the fairness of the processes that lead to outcomes;
- **Interactional Justice:** As the degree to which the people affected by a decision are treated with dignity and respect.

Customers can judge their market encounter according to these three aspects of justice. For instance, Smith et al. (2015) investigate how hotel cancelation policies affect distributive and procedural fairness.

Morrisson and Huppertz (2010) observe that an equity judgment requires an interaction between three actors: the client, a referent person (i.e. another client), and the service provider (the firm). In this process, the referent standard is external (the customer observing what the other participants receive) and posterior (the customer establishes this norm only after having perceived what the other clients obtained).

If, on the one hand, equity exists, then, on the other hand, inequity may take place. In fact, equity occurs on a continuum constrained by negative inequity, where outcomes are less than deserved, and positive inequity, where outcomes are superior to what was deserved (Oliver, 2009; Weiss, Suckow & Cropanzano, 1999). However, do people pursue ideal equity or do they chase their own advantage? According to Messick and Sentis (1979), it is possible to distinguish between two attitudes:

- **Proportional Fairness (Equity):** Equal treatment for all the parties involved;
- **Preference:** Maximization of one's own outcome relative to those of other parties.

In particular, the preference viewpoint states that a party in a transaction will feel more fairness when inequity is in his/her favor (Oliver, 2009). This case can be called advantageous or favorable inequity, with regard to which Skitka (2009) affirmed that outcome fairness and outcome favorability are distinctly different constructs.

Customers may perceive revenue management as an opportunistic behaviour of the firm and then judge these practices as unfair. As a result, customers' trust and loyalty towards the hotel brand may deteriorate significantly. Fairness perceptions have been discovered to be related to company profitability (Kahneman, Knetsch & Thaler, 1986). In addition, if customers consider a firm's practices to be unfair, negative consumer responses are expected.

According to the established literature, fairness has been defined as a judgment of whether an outcome and/or the process to reach an outcome are reasonable, acceptable, and just (Bolton, Warlop & Alba, 2003; Campbell, 1999; Monroe & Xia, 2005). It is important, in this respect, to underline that fairness evaluations are inevitably comparative (Xia, Monroe & Cox, 2004). Furthermore, equity theory (Adams, 1963) suggests that an individual can make two different types of equity judgments: internal and external. External equity judgments occur when the consumer compares his/her ratio of outcomes to inputs in an exchange with the ratio of a reference person (Morrisson & Huppertz, 2010). When consumers are vulnerable or disadvantaged, a violation of justice principles can trigger perceptions of unfairness. The following factors can influence the perceptions on fair pricing (Xia, Monroe & Cox, 2004).

- Transaction similarity and choice of comparative other parties;
- Cost–profit distribution and attributes of inequality;
- Buyer–seller relationship and trust;
- Social norms and meta-knowledge of the marketplace.

Starting with the first factor, transaction similarity, transactions may differ for multiple reasons: the service characteristics, the quantity, the purchase method, the timing, etc. However, the features of the parties involved are also important (Major & Testa, 1989; Martins & Monroe, 1994). For example, most clients do not perceive it as unjust to charge a couple and a little child a lower rate than three adults for the same hotel room, since the subjects concerned are different. In this sense, if customers notice rate differences, perceptions of unfairness are greater if they consider the transactions similar.

Second, a perception that a price is unfair results not only from a perceived higher price but also from consumers' understandings of the reason why the higher price was set. The seller's cost plays an important role in buyers' assessments of whether a price is acceptable and fair (Bolton, Warlop & Alba, 2003). Customers typically perceive a given price increase as fair if it is a consequence of an increase in the seller's costs. On the contrary, they perceive it as unfair if it is linked to increased consumer demand. However, because of information asymmetry in transactions, consumers rarely have a clear picture of the producer's real cost structure.

Third, a transaction has to be considered in the broader context of buyer–seller relationships that are mainly based on repeated transactions (McMahon-Beattie, 2006). Trust is a major concept in buyer–seller relationships (Gambetta, 1988). In particular, in the marketing literature, trust has emerged as a key factor in the establishment and maintenance of the long-term relationships crucial to a firm's success (Dwyer, Schurr & Oh, 1987; Garbarino & Johnson, 1998).

Finally, social norms and meta-knowledge of the marketplace represent shared rules of behaviour in economic exchanges. However, culture, beliefs, knowledge, and norms may evolve over time. In fact, some studies have discovered that revenue management has recently become more acceptable to customers in the hotel sector (Camilleri, 2018a; Kimes & Wirtz, 2003). It is also noteworthy that social norms and the degree of familiarity with these techniques may vary among different market segments (based on geography, nationality, social class, age, etc.). A study by Wirtz and Kimes (2007) has illustrated the moderating role of customer familiarity with revenue management pricing, framing of prices, and fencing conditions on perceptions of fairness; social nature has also been identified as a key factor for reference prices (Viglia, Mauri, & Carricano, 2016).

Furthermore, research reveals that more frequent users of hotels, younger hotel guests, and more educated people are likely to perceive hotels' revenue management practices to be fair, compared to other subjects (Heo & Lee, 2011). According to Heo and Lee (2010), greater familiarity does not appear to guarantee better perceptions of fairness by customers, although providing information on hotels' pricing policies can enhance customers' perceptions of procedural fairness (Choi & Mattila, 2004). Cultural issues matter because customer preferences may vary according to culturally diverse consumers, and this information can enable the design of hotel pricing policies (Liu, Guillet, Xiao, & Law, 2014; Song, Noone, & Mattila, 2017).

Hedonic Pricing

The 'hedonic pricing' model considers goods and services as collections of attributes or characteristics, and the set of attributes can include both quantitative and qualitative elements. This approach can be applied to any market for a differentiated product (Monty & Skidmore, 2003). The core of the hedonic pricing approach is the idea that the price of any product is the sum of the unobserved prices of the bundle of attributes associated with it. Consequently, the objective is to understand the implicit prices for these individual attributes (Chen & Rothschild, 2010).

The authors believe that a logical connection between rate fences and the hedonic pricing approach can be established, even if we did not find such a connection in previous studies. The extent to which rate fences are successful with customers depends on the specific characteristics of the hotel, the booking process, and the stay, and these characteristics can be individually evaluated through a hedonic pricing approach.

Hedonic price theory stems from the idea of approaching goods and services as a bundle of objective attributes (Rosen, 1974). In the hospitality industry, one can consider the whole hotel experience as a homogeneous product or unpack it into several components, such as the value of a good Wi-Fi connection, a convenient location, the quality of breakfast, etc. In other words, the hedonic pricing model assumes that the price of a composite product, like a hotel stay, is the sum of the implicit values of each attribute that composes the product (Andersson, 2010). In this sense, hospitality and tourism markets are very suitable for hedonic research (Papatheodorou, Lei, & Apostolakis, 2012).

However, the choice of hotel attributes is relevant, and the evidence of their impact on rates differs from study to study according to the particular nature of the case under analysis. For this reason, there is no shared basis for approaching this issue (Chen & Rothschild, 2010), and hotel room pricing can be studied from both demand-side and supply-side perspectives (Camilleri, 2018b; Chen & Rothschild, 2010).

Traditional models tend to break down each hotel observation (e.g. Thrane, 2005). In this sense, consumer valuations of hotels depend on several specific hotel attributes, including star ratings, tangible elements of the room, hotel location, and amenities (Abrate, Fraquelli, & Viglia, 2012; Heo & Hyun, 2015; Hung, Shang & Wang, 2010; Juaneda, Raya, & Sastre, 2011; Schamel, 2012; Zhang, Ye & Law, 2011).

When assessing the role of different attributes, location stands out in its importance (Lee & Jang, 2011; Zhang, Ye, & Law, 2011). In particular, Lee and Jang (2011) found that airport hotels can obtain a price premium, which increases depending on the convenience of reaching the city center. Further, because of the role of new consumer trends, environmentally friendly attributes can increase consumers' willingness to pay.

In addition to these hotel-specific attributes, a few studies have identified the effect of transactional attributes on hotel room rates, including types of distribution channels, cancellation polices, and hotel ratings (Chen, Schwartz & Vargas, 2011; Noone & Mattila, 2009; Öğüt & Taş, 2012; Schamel, 2012; Tso & Law, 2005). Within transactional attributes, lead times play a central role (Chen & Schwartz, 2008b; Schamel, 2012; Schwartz, 2000; 2008). While traditionally this point is connected with the difference between business and leisure travelers, research (Schwartz, 2000) has also found that clients' willingness to pay increases as booking time approaches the date of stay, unrelated to the market segments (Camilleri, 2018c).

According to Schwartz (2000), the change of willingness to pay depends on consumers' information search costs. In the Internet-based marketplace, consumers can easily observe the change in room rates, and this has been found to affect their propensity to book a hotel (Chen & Schwartz, 2008a). As Chen and Schwartz (2008a) argue, the changing patterns of such internal reference prices in hotels can affect consumers' room rate expectations and their subsequent booking behaviour.

Research by Zhang and Law (2011) found that, in terms of explaining variance in room prices, the attributes are different amongst economic, mid-scale, and luxury hotels. In this sense, an ascending order of accommodation needs is observed when we move from economy to luxury hotels.

More recent literature has gone further, encompassing tactical determinants of price level in the hedonic formulation (Abrate & Viglia, 2016; Alegre & Sard, 2015). Interestingly, this approach also works well with rural accommodations, such as agritourism establishments (Viglia & Abrate, 2017).

Authors have identified several attributes that could affect pricing and tested models that included some of them. Table 3 presents some of these articles and the attributes cited within. These features embrace many aspects, both qualitative and quantitative, regarding the room, the hotel facilities and characteristics, the location, and, finally, the destination in general. Even some quality signals, like ratings and reviews, can drive price changes. The authors of these articles provide the order of the features. The presented features are the most common. Little attempt at a classification has been made by previous research.

The Seasonality of Destinations

Destinations may be connected to hotel rate fences at three levels:

1. Features of the destination that influence hedonic price and rate fences;
2. Destination management organizations (DMOs) policies addressed to improve the attractiveness of the area;
3. Cooperation among different actors (firms) within a destination.

Hedonic price and rate fences are affected by the features of a destination, among which seasonality plays a major role, discriminating between high and low seasonality (White & Mulligan, 2002). Economic and managerial studies have analyzed the demand fluctuations, over time, for various types of services. The tourism and hospitality industries are particularly affected by this phenomenon, usually defined as "seasonality" (Chung, 2009). Tourism seasonality is an extensive, multifaceted theme area, which has received significant attention, especially in recent years (Koenig-Lewis & Bischof, 2005). Among the first studies of tourism to do so, BarOn

Table 3. List of attributes affecting hedonic pricing in hotels

Coenders, Espinet & Saez (2003) Size (number of rooms), Category (number of stars), Beach (hotels located right in front of the sea), Room (hotels whose rooms are equipped with at least one of the following without price surcharge: television, air conditioning, or mini-bar), Parking (hotels with a parking place), Sport (hotels offering at least one of the following sport facilities: tennis, squash, golf, or mini-golf, with or without extra payment), Town.	Chen & Rothschild (2010). Hotel is associated with a chain, Hotel room size (m2), Hotel located in city center, Bathroom with both bath and shower present in the hotel room, Buffet-type breakfast, LED TV present in the hotel room, Business center present in the hotel, Bar/café present in the hotel, Internet access is available in the hotel room, Shuttle bus is available in the hotel, Conference facilities are present in the hotel, Swimming pool is present in the hotel, Fitness center is present in the hotel.
Masiero, Heo & Pan (2015). View (City, Harbor), Floor, Access to hotel club, Free mini bar, Guest smartphone, Cancelation policy.	Espinet et al. (2003) Town in which hotel is located, Star category, Number of rooms, Accepts credit cards, Special access for disabled, Admits pets, Air-conditioning, Satellite TV, Lift, Cafeteria, Shops, Safe, Heating, Money change, Close to town center, Discotheque, Located in a historical building, Located in a picturesque building, Car repair, Gymnasium, Golf, Kindergarten, Suites with a living room, Garden or terrace, Bicycle rental, Mini-golf, Mini-bar in the room, Park for children, Parking place, Hairdresser, Outdoor swimming pool, Indoor swimming pool, Music or radio in the room, Conference halls, Sauna, Hairdryer in the room, 24-hour service, Medical care, Squash, Telephone in the room, TV in the room, Tennis court, Simultaneous translation, Video in the room, Games and recreational activities, Casino, Recently renovated, Water and wine included in full board price, Number of operators who include it in their catalogues, Children's swimming pool, Restaurant, Close to the beach, Balcony in the room, View of the sea, Year of first opening.
Zhang, Ye & Law (2011). Official hotel class, Average of travelers' five-point room ratings, Location, Cleanliness, and Service.	
Viglia & Abrate (2017). Restaurant, Pool, Meeting room, Services for disabled people, Pets allowed, Game area for kids, Bike rental, TV, Wi-fi service, Air conditioning, Parking, Menu with typical own products, Direct selling of own products, Tasting experiences/food wine events, Value of reviews	Abrate & Viglia (2016) Squared meters room, Balcony, Congress center, Number of rooms, Free Internet, Star ratings, Number of competitors with available room.

(1975) and Butler (1994) highlighted the link between seasonality and/or demand patterns and destinations features.

The term seasonality comes from the word season and therefore refers to demand fluctuations according to the four quarters into which the year is normally divided. Indeed, it is important to observe that demand variations can occur and may be observed in different timespans (Lundtorp, 2001; Mauri, 2012a): a pluriannual period (demand oscillations during phases of economic cycles, so-called long-run waves); a year (demand fluctuations in diverse seasons and months); a week (demand variations between weekdays and weekends); and a day (demand variations hour by hour). Each of these fluctuations can be important for travel and hospitality industries. Furthermore, they can overlap. For example, in many destinations, there are summer and weekend peak days that coincide (Rosselló & Sansó, 2017), in addition to there also being a possible overlap on special dates (e.g. public holidays and events days). Kuznets (1933) observes that the annual recurrence and the limited duration of oscillations distinguish seasonal variations from other movements, such as trends and cyclical and random modifications.

Concerning seasonality, academic contributions have principally regarded three aspects: causes, effects, and remedies. In the tourism context, demand variability is usually described as originating from two types of factors: natural and institutional (Allcock, 1989). Natural seasonality is due to temporal changes in natural phenomena at the destination level, which are usually associated with climate, season of the year, etc. (Butler & Mao, 1997). On the other hand, institutional seasonality rests on religious, cultural, ethnic, and social factors, such as business holidays (Baum & Hagen, 1999). The most important form of institutional seasonality is represented by school vacations during the summer (Baron, 1999). Butler (1994) observed that there are three additional reasons for seasonality, which are social pressure or fashion, sports seasons, and even inertia.

Demand variability can be considered as a whole and/or can be analyzed by dividing it into single market segments. Some studies agree that different segments have dissimilar seasonality patterns (e.g. Baggio & Sainaghi, 2016; Fernández-Morales & Mayorga-Toledano, 2008; Sainaghi & Baggio, 2017). Visitors' profiles imply different travel behaviour patterns, which can be variously affected by demand variability causes (Mauri, 2012a). Koc and Altinay (2007) found that the seasonal pattern in per person tourist spending is considerably different from the seasonal pattern in tourist arrivals.

Rate Fences, Hedonic Pricing, and Destinations

The authors have illustrated several types of rate fences and established a logical link with hedonic pricing. In this section, we aim to highlight which features and price components are more destination sensitive. Price elements are dependent on market segments' needs and preferences, hotel characteristics, and destination features. Coenders et al. (2003) found that hotel attributes are not the sole determinants of price and that tourists do not only pay for a hotel room but also for its environment. Hamilton (2007) observed that the type of coastal landscape influences the price of accommodation. First time visitors can be more price sensitive when compared to repeat visitors, and they associate a larger weight to desirable attributes such as view; in this sense, hotel guests are willing to pay more for a room with a harbor view when compared to one with a city view (Masiero, Heo & Pan, 2015).

The types of travelers involved in a destination also play a key role, at both a horizontal level (i.e. leisure vs business) and for vertical segments (i.e. leisure luxury vs leisure economy). Market segmentation can be defined vertically when the segments are ordered along the increasing or decreasing magnitude of a particular segmentation measure. On the other hand, horizontal segmentation identifies market segments as a result of differentiating consumers by the diversity of a criterion (Oh & Jeong, 2010). For example, a city may attract three types of travelers: business, exhibition (trade-fair), and leisure (Sainaghi & Canali, 2011). Research has found different customer preferences for hotel rate restrictions based on their socio-demographic characteristics and travel behaviour (Denizci Guillet, Liu & Law, 2014; Denizci Guillet, Law & Xiao 2014).

At the destination level, destination management organizations (DMOs) or other forms of governance (d'Angella, De Carlo & Sainaghi, 2010) can influence the attractiveness of the area and, therefore, the rate fences. In focusing on destination processes, the examples below illustrate the ability: 1) to influence seasonality; 2) to create a new product; 3) to plan events, or; 4) to generate new attractions (Sainaghi, 2006).

Concerning seasonality, the city of Milan organizes important trade-fair events (Sainaghi & Canali, 2011), the most attractive of which is the "Salone del mobile", a trade-fair dedicated to furnishings. Attendants should reserve their accommodation in advance, as there is a high risk of sell out. This example illustrates that the destination can influence clients in anticipating their reservation time. More generally, the same effect is generated by many other events. For example, a recent study (Sainaghi & Mauri, 2018) reveals that during trade fair events the average daily rate (ADR) increases by 67€ (from 124€ to 57€) during weekend days and 22€ (from 151 to 173) during midweek days. These wide gaps suggest the ability of these events to influence potential clients.

The DMOs can change the local seasonality with regard to developing new products. The city of Livigno, an Italian alpine destination, has created the Ski pass free, a special offer dedicated to winter trails. As described by Sainaghi and De Carlo (2016), this initiative was able to more than double overnight bookings for hotels and the number of skiers for ski companies. Since the existence of this promotion, lodging firms have increased their rates. This example is particular close to rate fences, in fact the basic idea of Ski pass free is to include the ski pass free of charge to all the clients that promote an hotel or an apartment in Livigno during the seasonal tails. The cost of the free of charge ski pas is divided by lodging firms (50%) and ski businesses (50%).

During 2015, the city of Milan hosted a special event: The World Expo, which attracted more than 20 million visitors (Guizzardi, Mariani & Prayag, 2017). In a recent study, Sainaghi and Mauri (2018) measured the profound impact of the Expo on both hotels' seasonality and operating performance. In particular, based on a sample composed by 30 thousand hotel rooms (representative of 80% of Milan), the authors have analyzed the ability of this event to reconfigure the seasonal patterns of the City. The results are impressive and show an average increase of RevPAR equal to 59%. Furthermore, during the weakest period (weekend and non-working days) the occupancy is rise by 50%, the average daily room (ADR) by 41%, triggering a RevPAR augment by 112%.

In Milan, the creation of a new trade-fair attraction (one of the biggest in Europe) has developed a new location advantage for hotels. Revenue managers can, therefore, divide customers according to their preferences to remain close to the trade-fair area, thus creating a rate fence (Sainaghi & Canali, 2009a; 2009b). Other examples include the construction of an "artificial" attraction to change the location advantage to inside a destination, and, in an alpine region, the creation of new cable equipment to link an isolated location with an existing ski area so as to completely change the hotel's attractiveness (Sainaghi, 2017).

CONCLUSION

Hotel rate fences have been traditionally studied at firm level, as techniques to increase hotel performance. However, in the case of a network product or a territorial destination product, the attention should be given to the total tourist expenditures. Tourist expenditures is a key metric for destinations and their analysis helps in assessing and improving the impact of tourism on a regional economy (Nicolau & Masiero, 2013). From a temporal point of view, travel and on-site expenditures can be considered separately. The first expenditures (i.e. airline ticket and hotel cost) determine the choice of the destination. While the other purchases commonly follow, during the stay. In other words, accommodation assumes not only the role of a central service, but it is the means that permits customers to be in the destination and to purchase other services and goods in the area. By that logic, a cooperative approach followed by all the different firms and businesses operating within a destination (i.e. hotels, restaurants, entertainment, sports, etc.) could be oriented to add a new element to define hotel rate fences. A criterion able to identify tourist profiles expected to buy a variety of products in the destination. This criterion should be combined with profit sharing mechanisms able to motivate cooperation among hotels and other firms applying a framework of destination-centric revenue management (DCRM) (Kuokkanen, 2016): the effort of independent business owners in a tourism destination to combine their activities in attracting customers, jointly creating more demand and profits.

Firms have constantly to evaluate the benefits and possibilities between a cooperative and competitive approach (Kylanen & Mariani, 2012). Although many tourism businesses within a destination recognize their interdependence and the need to align their activities by establishing relationships, the choice of coordinating, and delivering collaborative marketing activities is not an easy one (Wang & Krakover, 2008). Collaboration can take place both under and outside of the governance of a DMO. However, the presence of a DMO is increasingly considered as an effective means of achieving collaboration among the various components of the destination (Fyall, Garrod, & Wang, 2012).

The connections between hotel rate fences and destination appears to be multifaceted. Synergy between destinations' governance and hotel revenue management policies may improve operating and financial performance of all the actors of a destination.

REFERENCES

Abrate, G., Fraquelli, G., & Viglia, G. (2012). Dynamic pricing strategies: Evidence from European hotels. *International Journal of Hospitality Management*, *31*(1), 160–168. doi:10.1016/j.ijhm.2011.06.003

Abrate, G., & Viglia, G. (2016). Strategic and tactical price decisions in hotel revenue management. *Tourism Management*, *55*, 123–132. doi:10.1016/j.tourman.2016.02.006

Adams, J. S. (1963). Towards an understanding of inequity. *Journal of Abnormal and Social Psychology*, *67*(5), 422–436. doi:10.1037/h0040968 PMID:14081885

Alegre, J., & Sard, M. (2015). When demand drops and prices rise. Tourist packages in the Balearic Islands during the economic crisis. *Tourism Management*, *46*, 375–385. doi:10.1016/j.tourman.2014.07.016

Allcock, J. B. (1989). Seasonality. In S. F. Witt & L. Moutinho (Eds.), *Tourism marketing and management handbook* (pp. 387–392). Englewood Cliffs, NJ: Prentice-Hall.

Andersson, D. E. (2010). Hotel attributes and hedonic prices: An analysis of internet-based transactions in Singapore's market for hotel rooms. *The Annals of Regional Science*, *44*(2), 229–240. doi:10.100700168-008-0265-4

Baggio, R., & Sainaghi, R. (2016). Mapping time series into networks as a tool to assess the complex dynamics of tourism systems. *Tourism Management*, *54*, 23–33. doi:10.1016/j.tourman.2015.10.008

Bar-On, R. R. (1999). The measurement of seasonality and its economic impacts. *Tourism Economics*, *5*(4), 437–458. doi:10.1177/135481669900500409

BarOn. R. V. (1975). Seasonality in tourism. London: The Economic Intelligence Unit.

Baum, T., & Hagen, L. (1999). Responses to seasonality: The experiences of peripheral destinations. *International Journal of Tourism Research*, *1*(5), 232–299. doi:10.1002/(SICI)1522-1970(199909/10)1:5<299::AID-JTR198>3.0.CO;2-L

Besanko, D., Dubé, J.-P., & Gupta, S. (2003). Competitive price discrimination strategies in a vertical channel using aggregate retail data. *Management Science*, *49*(9), 1121–1138. doi:10.1287/mnsc.49.9.1121.16565

Bolton, L. E., Warlop, L., & Alba, J. W. (2003). Consumer Perceptions of Price (Un) Fairness. *The Journal of Consumer Research*, *29*(4), 474–491. doi:10.1086/346244

Butler, R., & Mao, B. (1997). Seasonality in Tourism: Problems and Measurement. In P. Murphy (Ed.), *Quality Management in Urban Tourism* (pp. 9–23). Chichester, UK: Wiley.

Butler, R. W. (1994). Seasonality in tourism: Issues and problems. In A. V. Seaton (Ed.), *Tourism. The state of the art* (pp. 332–340). Chichester, UK: Wiley.

Camilleri, M. A. (2018a). Tourism Supply and Demand. In *Travel Marketing, Tourism Economics and the Airline Product* (pp. 139–154). Cham: Springer. doi:10.1007/978-3-319-49849-2_8

Camilleri, M. A. (2018b). Pricing and Revenue Management. In *Travel Marketing, Tourism Economics and the Airline Product* (pp. 155–163). Cham: Springer. doi:10.1007/978-3-319-49849-2_9

Camilleri, M. A. (2018c). Market Segmentation, Targeting and Positioning. In *Travel Marketing, Tourism Economics and the Airline Product* (pp. 155–163). Cham: Springer. doi:10.1007/978-3-319-49849-2_9

Campbell, M. C. (1999). Perceptions of Price Unfairness: Antecedents and Consequences. *JMR, Journal of Marketing Research*, *36*(2), 187–199. doi:10.2307/3152092

Cassady, R. Jr. (1946a). Some Economic Aspects of Price Discrimination under non-perfect market conditions. *Journal of Marketing*, *11*(1), 7–20. doi:10.2307/1246801

Cassady, R. Jr. (1946b). Techniques and purposes of price discrimination. *Journal of Marketing*, *11*(2), 135–150. doi:10.2307/1246769

Chen, C. C., & Schwartz, Z. (2008a). Room rate patterns and customers' propensity to book a hotel room. *Journal of Hospitality & Tourism Research (Washington, D.C.), 32*(3), 287–306. doi:10.1177/1096348008317389

Chen, C. C., & Schwartz, Z. (2008b). Timing matters: Travelers' advanced-booking expectations and decisions. *Journal of Travel Research, 47*(1), 35–42. doi:10.1177/0047287507312413

Chen, C. C., Schwartz, Z., & Vargas, P. (2011). The search for the best deal: How hotel cancellation policies affect the search and booking decisions of deal-seeking customers. *International Journal of Hospitality Management, 30*(1), 129–135. doi:10.1016/j.ijhm.2010.03.010

Chen, C. F., & Rothschild, R. (2010). An application of hedonic pricing analysis to the case of hotel rooms in Taipei. *Tourism Economics, 16*(3), 685–694. doi:10.5367/000000010792278310

Chi-Cheng, W., Yi-Fen, L., Ying-Ju, C., & Chih-Jen, W. (2012). Consumer responses to price discrimination: Discriminating bases, inequality status, and information disclosure timing influences. *Journal of Business Research, 65*(1), 106–116. doi:10.1016/j.jbusres.2011.02.005

Choi, S., & Mattila, A. S. (2004). Hotel revenue management and its impact on customers' perceptions of fairness. *Journal of Revenue and Pricing Management, 2*(4), 303–314. doi:10.1057/palgrave.rpm.5170079

Chung, J. Y. (2009). Seasonality in tourism: A review. *Ereview of Tourism Research, 7*(5), 82–96.

Clerides, S. K. (2004). Price discrimination with differentiated products: Definition and identification. *Economic Inquiry, 42*(3), 402–412. doi:10.1093/ei/cbh069

Coenders, G., Espinet, J., & Saez, M. (2003). Predicting random level and seasonality of hotel prices: A latent growth curve approach. *Tourism Analysis, 8*(1), 15–31. doi:10.3727/108354203108750148

D'Angella, F., De Carlo, M., & Sainaghi, R. (2010). Archetypes of destination governance: A comparison of international destinations. *Tourism Review, 65*(4), 61–73. doi:10.1108/16605371011093872

Denizci Guillet, B., Law, R., & Xiao, Q. (2014). Rate fences in hotel revenue management and their applications to Chinese leisure travelers: A fractional factorial design approach. *Cornell Hospitality Quarterly, 55*(2), 186–196. doi:10.1177/1938965513507497

Denizci Guillet, B., Liu, W., & Law, R. (2014). Can setting hotel rate restrictions help balance the interest of hotels and customers? *International Journal of Contemporary Hospitality Management*, *26*(6), 948–973. doi:10.1108/IJCHM-01-2013-0020

Dickson, P., & Kalapurakal, R. (1994). The Use and Perceived Fairness of Price-Setting Rules in the Bulk Electricity Market. *Journal of Economic Psychology*, *15*(3), 427–448. doi:10.1016/0167-4870(94)90023-X

Dwyer, F. R., Schurr, P. H., & Oh, S. (1987). Developing buyer-seller relationship. *Journal of Marketing*, *51*(2), 11–27. doi:10.2307/1251126

Espinet, J. M., Saez, M., Coenders, G., & Fluvià, M. (2003). Effect on prices of the attributes of holiday hotels: A hedonic prices approach. *Tourism Economics*, *9*(2), 165–177. doi:10.5367/000000003101298330

Fernández-Morales, A., & Mayorga-Toledano, M. C. (2008). Seasonal concentration of the hotel demand in Costa del Sol: A decomposition by nationalities. *Tourism Management*, *29*(5), 940–949. doi:10.1016/j.tourman.2007.11.003

Fyall, A., Garrod, B., & Wang, Y. (2012). Destination collaboration: A critical review of theoretical approaches to a multi-dimensional phenomenon. *Journal of Destination Marketing & Management*, *1*(1), 10–26. doi:10.1016/j.jdmm.2012.10.002

Gambetta, D. (1988). Can we trust? In D. Gambetta (Ed.), *Trust: Making and Breaking Cooperative Relations*. Oxford, UK: Basil Blackwell.

Garbarino, E., & Johnson, M. S. (1999). The different roles of satisfaction, trust, and commitment in customer relationships. *Journal of Marketing*, *63*(2), 70–87. doi:10.2307/1251946

Greenberg, J. (1987). A taxonomy of organizational justice theories. *Academy of Management Review*, *12*(1), 9–22.

Greenberg, J. (1990). Organizational justice: Yesterday, today, and tomorrow. *Journal of Management*, *16*(2), 399–432. doi:10.1177/014920639001600208

Guizzardi, A. Mariani, & Prayag, G. (2017). Environmental impacts and certification: evidence from the Milan World Expo 2015. *International Journal of Contemporary Hospitality Management*, *29*(3), 1052-1071.

Guo, Y., Denizci Guillet, B., Kucukusta, D., & Law, R. (2016). Segmenting spa customers based on rate fences using conjoint and cluster analyses. *Asia Pacific Journal of Tourism Research*, *21*(2), 118–136. doi:10.1080/10941665.2015.1025085

Hamilton, J. M. (2007). Coastal landscape and the hedonic price of accommodation. *Ecological Economics*, *62*(3), 594–602. doi:10.1016/j.ecolecon.2006.08.001

Hanks, R. D., Cross, R. G., & Noland, R. P. (1992). Discounting in the hotel industry: A new approach. *The Cornell Hotel and Restaurant Administration Quarterly*, *33*(1), 15–23.

Heo, C. Y., & Hyun, S. S. (2015). Do luxury room amenities affect guests' willingness to pay? *International Journal of Hospitality Management*, *46*, 161–168. doi:10.1016/j.ijhm.2014.10.002

Heo, C. Y., & Lee, S. (2009). Application of revenue management practices to the theme park industry. *International Journal of Hospitality Management*, *28*(3), 446–453. doi:10.1016/j.ijhm.2009.02.001

Heo, C. Y., & Lee, S. (2010). Customers' Perceptions of Demand-driven Pricing in Revenue Management Context: Comparisons of Six Tourism and Hospitality Industries. *International Journal of Revenue Management*, *4*(3/4), 382–402. doi:10.1504/IJRM.2010.036030

Heo, C. Y., & Lee, S. (2011). Influences of consumer characteristics on fairness perceptions of revenue management pricing in the hotel industry. *International Journal of Hospitality Management*, *30*(2), 243–251. doi:10.1016/j.ijhm.2010.07.002

Hung, W. T., Shang, J. K., & Wang, F. C. (2010). Pricing determinants in the hotel industry: Quantile regression analysis. *International Journal of Hospitality Management*, *29*(3), 378–384. doi:10.1016/j.ijhm.2009.09.001

Ivanov, S. (2014). *Hotel Revenue Management: From Theory to Practice*. Varna: Zangador.

Jedidi, K., & Zhang, Z. J. (2002). Augmenting conjoint analysis to estimate consumer reservation price. *Management Science*, *48*(10), 1350–1368. doi:10.1287/mnsc.48.10.1350.272

Juaneda, C., Raya, J. M., & Sastre, F. (2011). Pricing the time and location of a stay at a hotel or apartment. *Tourism Economics*, *17*(2), 321–338. doi:10.5367/te.2011.0044

Kahneman, D., Knetsch, J. L., & Thaler, R. (1986). Fairness and the Assumptions of Economics. *The Journal of Business*, *4*(59), 285–300. doi:10.1086/296367

Kalish, S., & Nelson, P. (1991). A comparison of ranking, rating and reservation price measurement in conjoint analysis. *Marketing Letters*, *2*(4), 327–335. doi:10.1007/BF00664219

Kim, J., Natter, M., & Spann, M. (2009). Pay What You Want: A New Participative Pricing Mechanism. *Journal of Marketing, 73*(1), 44–58. doi:10.1509/jmkg.73.1.44

Kimes, S. E., & Chase, R. B. (1998). The Strategic Levers of Yield Management. *Journal of Service Research, 1*(2), 156–166. doi:10.1177/109467059800100205

Kimes, S. E., & Wirtz, J. (2003). Has Revenue Management Become Acceptable? *Journal of Service Research, 6*(2), 125–135. doi:10.1177/1094670503257038

Koc, E., & Altinay, G. (2007). An analysis of seasonality in monthly per person tourist spending in Turkish inbound tourism from a market segmentation perspective. *Tourism Management, 28*(1), 227–237. doi:10.1016/j.tourman.2006.01.003

Koenig-Lewis, N., & Bischoff, E. E. (2005). Seasonality research: The state of the art. European Business Management School. *International Journal of Tourism Research, 7*(4-5), 201–219. doi:10.1002/jtr.531

Kuokkanen, H. (2016). Behavioural pricing opportunities in tourism destinations: A collaborative approach. *International Journal of Revenue Management, 9*(2-3), 186–200. doi:10.1504/IJRM.2016.077020

Kuznets, S. S. (1933). *Seasonal variations in industry and trade (No. 22)*. New York: National Bureau of Economic Research.

Kylanen, M., & Mariani, M. M. (2012). Unpacking the temporal dimension of coopetition in tourism destinations: Evidence from Finnish and Italian theme parks. *Anatolia, 23*(1), 61–74. doi:10.1080/13032917.2011.653632

LaPlaca, P. J. (1997). Contributions to marketing theory and practice from industrial marketing management. *Journal of Business Research, 38*(3), 179–198. doi:10.1016/S0148-2963(96)00128-2

Lee, S. K., & Jang, S. (2011). Room rates of US airport hotels: Examining the dual effects of proximities. *Journal of Travel Research, 50*(2), 186–197. doi:10.1177/0047287510362778

Levine, M. E. (2002). Price discrimination without market power. *Yale Journal on Regulation, 19*, 1.

Liu, W., Guillet, B. D., Xiao, Q., & Law, R. (2014). Globalization or localization of consumer preferences: The case of hotel room booking. *Tourism Management, 41*, 148–157. doi:10.1016/j.tourman.2013.09.004

Lovelock, C. H., & Wirtz, J. (2004). *Services Marketing*. Englewood Cliffs, NJ: Prentice Hall.

Lundtorp, S. (2001). Measuring tourism seasonality. In T. Baum & S. Lundtorp (Eds.), *Seasonality in tourism* (pp. 23–48). Amsterdam: Pergamon. doi:10.1016/B978-0-08-043674-6.50006-4

Major, B., & Testa, M. (1989). Social Comparison Processes and Judgments of Entitlement and Satisfaction. *Journal of Experimental Social Psychology*, *25*(2), 101–120. doi:10.1016/0022-1031(89)90007-3

Martins, M., & Monroe, K. B. (1994). Perceived Price Fairness: A new Look at an Old Construct. *Advances in Consumer Research. Association for Consumer Research (U. S.)*, *21*(1), 75–78.

Masiero, L., Heo, C. Y., & Pan, B. (2015). Determining guests' willingness to pay for hotel room attributes with a discrete choice model. *International Journal of Hospitality Management*, *49*, 117–124. doi:10.1016/j.ijhm.2015.06.001

Masiero, L., Nicolau, J. L., & Law, R. (2015). A demand-driven analysis of tourist accommodation price: A quantile regression of room bookings. *International Journal of Hospitality Management*, *50*, 1–8. doi:10.1016/j.ijhm.2015.06.009

Mauri, A. G. (2007). Yield management and perceptions of fairness in the hotel business. *International Review of Economics*, *54*(2), 284–293. doi:10.100712232-007-0015-4

Mauri, A. G. (2012a). *Hotel revenue management: Principles and practices*. Pearson.

Mauri, A. G. (2012b). *Hotel Revenue Management and Guests' Perceived Fairness. Theoretical Issues and Empirical Findings from a Multiple-Year Survey*. Smashwords.

Mauri, A. G. (2014). Foreword: marketing and pricing in the digital environment. In G. Viglia (Ed.), *Behavioral Pricing, Online marketing behavior, and analytics*. New York: Palgrave Macmillan.

Mauri, A. G., & Soone, I. (2009). Yield/Revenue Management and Perceptions of Fairness in Hotel Business: Empirical Evidences. *Proceedings 12th International QMOD and Toulon-Verona Conference on Quality and Service Sciences (ICQSS)*.

McGill, J. I., & Van Ryzin, G. J. (1999). Revenue management: Research overview and prospects. *Transportation Science*, *33*(2), 233–256. doi:10.1287/trsc.33.2.233

McMahon-Beattie, U. (2006). Trust and revenue management. *Journal of Revenue and Pricing Management*, *4*(4), 406–407. doi:10.1057/palgrave.rpm.5170162

Messick, D. M., & Sentis, K. P. (1979). Fairness and preference. *Journal of Experimental Social Psychology, 15*(4), 418–434. doi:10.1016/0022-1031(79)90047-7

Monroe, K. B., & Xia, L. (2005). The Many Routes to Price Unfairness Perceptions. *Advances in Consumer Research. Association for Consumer Research (U. S.), 32*(1), 387–391.

Monty, B., & Skidmore, M. (2003). Hedonic pricing and willingness to pay for bed and breakfast amenities in Southeast Wisconsin. *Journal of Travel Research, 42*(2), 195–199. doi:10.1177/0047287503257500

Moorthy, K. S. (1984). Market segmentation, self-selection, and product line design. *Marketing Science, 2*(4), 288–307. doi:10.1287/mksc.3.4.288

Morrisson, O., & Huppertz, J. W. (2010). External equity, loyalty program membership, and service recovery. *Journal of Services Marketing, 24*(3), 244–254. doi:10.1108/08876041011040640

Nagle, T. (1984). Economic Foundations for Pricing. *The Journal of Business, 57*(1), 3–26. doi:10.1086/296232

Ng, I. C. L. (2006). Differentiation, self-selection and revenue management. *Journal of Revenue and Pricing Management, 5*(1), 2–9. doi:10.1057/palgrave.rpm.5160019

Nicolau, J. L., & Masiero, L. (2013). Relationship between price sensitivity and expenditures in the choice of tourism activities at the destination. *Tourism Economics, 19*(1), 101–114. doi:10.5367/te.2013.0192

Noone, B. M., & Mattila, A. S. (2009). Hotel revenue management and the Internet: The effect of price presentation strategies on customers' willingness to book. *International Journal of Hospitality Management, 28*(2), 272–279. doi:10.1016/j.ijhm.2008.09.004

Öğüt, H., & Onur Taş, B. K. (2012). The influence of internet customer reviews on the online sales and prices in hotel industry. *Service Industries Journal, 32*(2), 197–214. doi:10.1080/02642069.2010.529436

Oh, H., & Jeong, M. (2010). Evaluating stability of the performance-satisfaction relationship across selected lodging market segments. *International Journal of Contemporary Hospitality Management, 22*(7), 953–974. doi:10.1108/09596111011066626

Oliver, R. L. (2009). *Satisfaction: A Behavioral Perspective on the Consumer* (2nd ed.). Armonk: M.E. Sharpe.

Papatheodorou, A., Lei, Z., & Apostolakis, A. (2012). Hedonic price analysis. Handbook of research methods in tourism: Quantitative and qualitative approaches, 170-182. doi:10.4337/9781781001295.00015

Phillips, R. (2005). *Pricing and Revenue Optimization*. Palo Alto, CA: Stanford University Press.

Raab, C., Mayer, K., Kim, Y. S., & Shoemaker, S. (2009). Price-sensitivity measurement: A tool for restaurant menu pricing. *Journal of Hospitality & Tourism Research (Washington, D.C.)*, *33*(1), 93–105. doi:10.1177/1096348008329659

Rao, V. R. (2009). *Handbook of pricing research in marketing*. Edward Elgar Publishing. doi:10.4337/9781848447448

Raza, S. A. (2015). An integrated approach to price differentiation and inventory decisions with demand leakage. *International Journal of Production Economics*, *164*, 105–117. doi:10.1016/j.ijpe.2014.12.020

Rosen, S. (1974). Hedonic prices and implicit markets: Product differentiation in pure competition. *Journal of Political Economy*, *82*(1), 34–55. doi:10.1086/260169

Rosselló, J., & Sansó, A. (2017). Yearly, monthly and weekly seasonality of tourism demand: A decomposition analysis. *Tourism Management*, *60*, 379–389. doi:10.1016/j.tourman.2016.12.019

Sainaghi, R. (2006). From Contents to Processes: Versus a Dynamic Destination Management Model (DDMM). *Tourism Management*, *27*(5), 1053–1063. doi:10.1016/j.tourman.2005.09.010

Sainaghi, R. (2017). *Destination management e strategie competitive nel settore funiviario: il caso SIT (Alta Valcamonica)*. Milano: Edizioni LUMI.

Sainaghi, R., & Baggio, R. (2017). Complexity traits and dynamics of tourism destinations. *Tourism Management*, *63*, 368–382. doi:10.1016/j.tourman.2017.07.004

Sainaghi, R., & Canali, S. (2009a). Posizionamento competitivo delle urban destination e performance delle imprese alberghiere: Il caso Milano. *Economia & Management*, *9*(3), 83–100.

Sainaghi, R., & Canali, S. (2009b). *Commercial mix, seasonality and daily hotel performance: the case of Milan. Strategic management engineering: Enterprise, environment and crisis*. Chengdu, Sichuan, China: Sichuan University Press.

Sainaghi, R., & Canali, S. (2011). Exploring the effects of destination's positioning on hotels' performance: The Milan case. *Tourismos: An International Multidisciplinary Journal of Tourism*, 6(2), 121–138.

Sainaghi, R., & De Carlo, M. (2016). How to Create Destination Capabilities in the Field of New Product Development. In H. Pechlaner & E. Innerhofer (Eds.), Competence-Based Innovation in Hospitality and Tourism (pp. 185-196). Routledge.

Sainaghi, R., & Mauri, A. (2018). The Milan World Expo 2015: Hospitality operating performance and seasonality effects. *International Journal of Hospitality Management*, 72, 32–46. doi:10.1016/j.ijhm.2017.12.009

Sanders, L. (2011). *Developing New Products and Services: Learning, Differentiation, and Innovation*. Business Expert Press. doi:10.4128/9781606492420

Schamel, G. (2012). Weekend vs. midweek stays: Modelling hotel room rates in a small market. *International Journal of Hospitality Management*, 31(4), 1113–1118. doi:10.1016/j.ijhm.2012.01.008

Schwartz, Z. (2000). Changes in hotel guests' willingness to pay as the date of stay draws closer. *Journal of Hospitality & Tourism Research (Washington, D.C.)*, 24(2), 180–198. doi:10.1177/109634800002400204

Schwartz, Z. (2008). Time, price, and advanced booking of hotel rooms. *International Journal of Hospitality & Tourism Administration*, 9(2), 128–146. doi:10.1080/15256480801907885

Skitka, L. J. (2009). Exploring the "lost and found" of justice theory and research. *Social Justice Research*, 22(1), 98–116. doi:10.100711211-009-0089-0

Smith, S. J., Parsa, H. G., Bujisic, M., & van der Rest, J. P. (2015). Hotel cancelation policies, distributive and procedural fairness, and consumer patronage: A study of the lodging industry. *Journal of Travel & Tourism Marketing*, 32(7), 886–906. doi:10.1080/10548408.2015.1063864

Song, M., Noone, B. M., & Mattila, A. S. (2017). A Tale of Two Cultures: Consumer Reactance and Willingness to Book Fenced Rates. *Journal of Travel Research*.

Stigler, G. (1987). *A Theory of Price*. New York: Macmillan.

Thrane, C. (2005). Hedonic price models and sun-and-beach package tours: The Norwegian case. *Journal of Travel Research*, 43(3), 302–308. doi:10.1177/0047287504272034

Tso, A., & Law, R. (2005). Analysing the online pricing practices of hotels in Hong Kong. *International Journal of Hospitality Management, 24*(2), 301–307. doi:10.1016/j.ijhm.2004.09.002

Varian, H. R. (1989). Price discrimination. Handbook of industrial organization, 1, 597–654.

Varian, H. R. (1996). Differential pricing and efficiency. *First Monday, 1*(2). doi:10.5210/fm.v1i2.473

Viglia, G., & Abrate, G. (2017). When distinction does not pay off-Investigating the determinants of European agritourism prices. *Journal of Business Research, 80*, 45–52. doi:10.1016/j.jbusres.2017.07.004

Viglia, G., Mauri, A., & Carricano, M. (2016). The exploration of hotel reference prices under dynamic pricing scenarios and different forms of competition. *International Journal of Hospitality Management, 52*, 46–55. doi:10.1016/j.ijhm.2015.09.010

Vinod, B. (2004). Unlocking the value of revenue management in the hotel industry. *Journal of Revenue and Pricing Management, 3*(2), 178–190. doi:10.1057/palgrave.rpm.5170105

Wang, Y., & Krakover, S. (2008). Destination marketing: Competition, cooperation or coopetition? *International Journal of Contemporary Hospitality Management, 20*(2), 126–141. doi:10.1108/09596110810852122

Weiss, H. M., Suckow, K., & Cropanzano, R. (1999). Effects of justice conditions on discrete emotions. *The Journal of Applied Psychology, 84*(5), 786–794. doi:10.1037/0021-9010.84.5.786

White, P. J., & Mulligan, G. F. (2002). Hedonic estimates of lodging rates in the four corners region. *The Professional Geographer, 54*(4), 533–543. doi:10.1111/0033-0124.00348

Wirtz, J., & Kimes, S. E. (2007). The Moderating Role of Familiarity in Fairness Perceptions of Revenue Management Pricing. *Journal of Service Research, 9*(3), 229–240. doi:10.1177/1094670506295848

Wirtz, J., Kimes, S. E., Ho Pheng Theng, J., & Patterson, P. (2003). Revenue management: Resolving potential customer conflicts. *Journal of Revenue and Pricing Management, 2*(3), 216–228. doi:10.1057/palgrave.rpm.5170068

Xia, L., Monroe, K. B., & Cox, J. L. (2004). The Price Is Unfair! A Conceptual Framework of Price Fairness Perceptions. *Journal of Marketing, 68*(4), 1–15. doi:10.1509/jmkg.68.4.1.42733

Yelkur, R., & Nêveda DaCosta, M. M. (2001). Differential pricing and segmentation on the Internet: The case of hotels. *Management Decision*, *39*(4), 252–262. doi:10.1108/00251740110391411

Zeithaml, V. A. (1988). Consumer perceptions of price, quality and value: A means-end model and synthesis of evidence. *Journal of Marketing*, *5*(3), 2–22. doi:10.2307/1251446

Zhang, M. (2011). Fencing in the practice of revenue management. In I. Yeoman & U. McMahon-Beattie (Eds.), *Revenue management. A practical pricing perspective*. Basingstoke, UK: Palgrave Macmillan. doi:10.1057/9780230294776_11

Zhang, M., & Bell, P. (2012). Price fencing in the practice of revenue management: An overview and taxonomy. *Journal of Revenue and Pricing Management*, *11*(2), 146–159. doi:10.1057/rpm.2009.25

Zhang, Z., Ye, Q., & Law, R. (2011). Determinants of hotel room price: An exploration of travelers' hierarchy of accommodation needs. *International Journal of Contemporary Hospitality Management*, *23*(7), 972–981. doi:10.1108/09596111111167551

Zhang, Z. J. (2009). Competitive targeted pricing: perspectives from theoretical research. Handbook of Pricing Research in Marketing, 302. doi:10.4337/9781848447448.00023

Chapter 6
eWOM:
The Importance of Reviews and Ratings in Tourism Marketing

Juan Pedro Mellinas
Universidad Internacional de La Rioja, Spain

Sofía Reino
University of Hertfordshire, UK

ABSTRACT

It is difficult to find a traveler who has not written and/or read an online review at any stage of their travel. Most people will not book a hotel if this has no reviews and/or will not choose a destination before reading some opinions from other users. Tourism professionals can gain a comprehensive understanding of the dynamic relationships and key influential factors which are relevant to online reviews. A single business can have thousands of reviews. This creates a situation of information overload for hotel managers, who encounter themselves with increasingly larger numbers of information to analyze and act upon. The ability to effectively analyze data, using in occasions dedicated software becomes a crucial aspect of hotel management. The chapter ends with a reflection on how eWOM is leading to the generation of a new approach to business management.

DOI: 10.4018/978-1-5225-5835-4.ch006

INTRODUCTION

The Internet and social media have given place to what is commonly known as the *democratization of content* and this phenomenon is changing the way that consumers and companies interact. Business strategies are shifting from influencing consumers directly and induce sales to mediating the influence that Internet users have on each other. A consumer review is *a mixture of fact and opinion, impression and sentiment, found and unfound tidbits, experiences, and even rumor* (Blackshaw & Nazarro, 2006). Consumers' comments are seen as honest and transparent, but it is their subjective perception what shapes the behavior of other potential consumers.

With the emergence of the Internet, tourists search for information and reviews of destinations, hotels or services. Several studies have highlighted the great influence of online reputation through reviews and ratings and how it affects purchasing decisions by others (Schuckert, Liu, & Law, 2015). These reviews are seen as unbiased and trustworthy, and considered to reduce uncertainty and perceived risks (Gretzel & Yoo, 2008; Park & Nicolau, 2015). Before choosing a destination, tourists are likely to spend a significant amount of time searching for information including reviews of other tourists posted on the Internet. The average traveler browses 38 websites prior to purchasing vacation packages (Schaal, 2013), which may include tourism forums, online reviews in booking sites and other generic social media websites such as Facebook and Twitter.

Nowadays, it is difficult to find a traveler that has not used Internet in any stage of their travel (Camilleri, 2018a, b). A few years ago, in 2013, Google produced a study that laid out the five major stages of travel: dreaming, planning, booking, experiencing and sharing (Figure 1). These five stages of travel define the consumer's behavior before, during, and after their trip. Internet influences travelers at each of these stages through other travelers' opinions, mainly in the form of Social Media and Online Reviews.

- **Dreaming:** Travelers are less likely to respond to advertising than to content that entertains, informs, and surprises them. People find travel inspiration on social media, so businesses can reach the dreamer by encouraging their followers to share their travel stories and interact with their online community.
- **Planning:** The decision is taken, and travelers focus on the logistics: when to travel, how long to spend, how to get there, accommodation, activities, etc... The customer is now in the planning stage where, they'll be visiting around 20-40 different websites and will search for online reviews about almost everything.
- **Booking:** Guests are ready to make their purchase decisions and have reached the right-hand side stages of the diagram in Figure 1. At this point the key

Figure 1. The five stages of travel by Google
(Source: Robertson, 2015).

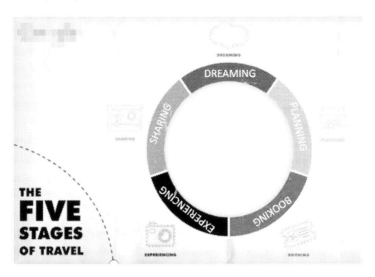

aspect that businesses need to look out for is to make the transaction as smooth and seamless as possible. Some people will not make a reservation if they do not read reviews about the service before. Most Online Travel Agencies (OTAs) nowadays include reviews in their hotel profile and the same applied to many other tourism businesses.

- **Experiencing:** Some travelers plan everything previously, but some of them leave minor decisions to the moment when they are already traveling. Examples of this relate to restaurant bookings and/or tickets for visitor attractions, which can be done on the go using a Smartphone or on site, directly. This may allow for certain flexibility, such as when visitors plan for an outdoor activity and the weather is not good. A great customer experience has always been important in tourism to increase loyalty and positive word-of-mouth. However, this is even more relevant nowadays, because customers' opinions will have a wider audience when shared online.
- **Sharing:** Many people may wait until they return home from their holidays before sharing photos and comments in Social Media. However, some travelers may not even wait and will start sharing information about tourism products and services while travelling, perhaps may even do it while they are still consuming them. Regardless of when this happens, this is the stage at which travelers produce the information that will influence others and be used by those individuals going through their dreaming, planning and booking stages.

Although opinions about tourism services and destinations can be shared in social media like Facebook, Twitter or Instagram, the focus of the remainder of this chapter will be on tourism-specific review websites; with particular focus on those providing hotel reviews, such as TripAdvisor, HolidayCheck, Booking.com, Expedia and Travelocity. This chapter is divided in several sections that analyze the main points to understand online reviews in tourism marketing:

- Key Terminology related to online reviews, ratings and social media.
- Motivations to write and read reviews on Internet.
- Rating systems features and information management.
- Information reliability and fake reviews.
- Reviews importance.

The final section of this chapter (conclusion) analyzes the implications of eWOM for business management in the tourism industry. Furthermore, it includes a series of practical recommendations to the management of online reviews and reputation.

KEY TERMINOLOGY

Social media has been defined as a group of Internet-based applications that build on the ideological and technological foundations of Web 2.0, and that allow the creation and exchange of user-generated content (Kaplan & Haenlein, 2010). Therefore, Web 2.0, which is a related term, refers to the ideological and technological foundations that allow the creation and exchange of User Generated Content (UGC), which may take the form of text, photos and/or videos. .. Thus, contrary to the traditional web, also known as Web 1.0, where users were passive viewers of content, Web 2.0 allows users to interact and to collaborate with each other, giving place to virtual communities.

The Web 2.0 ethos focuses on the user, by providing easy-to-use websites (even by non-experts), and facilitating editing, publication and information exchange. Smartphones connected to Internet and applications (Apps) adapted to this devices have increased the number of users and content shared in this way. Social media, forums and reviews websites are the best examples of this concept, that was firstly defined in 2005 (O'Reilly, 2005).

New concepts, like "Tourism 2.0" and "Travel 2.0" have been introduced to describe how the Web 2.0 have influenced the way we travel (Camilleri, 2018a; Christou, Sigala, & Gretzel, 2012). These terms refer to the business revolution that has taken place in the tourism and leisure industries facilitated by the new generation of technologies, which have changed the way travelers search, evaluate, purchase and consume touristic services.

Following the reference made to UGC in the above-mentioned definition of social media by Kaplan and Haenlein (2010), UGC can be defined as any type of content that has been created and shared by unpaid contributors. It may take the form of pictures, videos, testimonials, ratings, tweets, reviews, etc.

A fundamental principle of consumer behavior refers to the fact that users have the ability to significantly influence on each other, something traditionally called as "word of mouth" (WOM). When these opinions are shared through the Internet this is called "electronic word of mouth" (eWOM) (Dellarocas, 2003; Goldsmith & Horowitz, 2006). The big difference between WOM and eWOM is that in eWOM, recommendations are typically from unknown individuals. Therefore, personal ties are lacking in eWOM, which may reduce the level of perceived credibility of the sources.

eWOM is formally defined as *all informal communications directed at consumers through Internet-based technology related to the usage or characteristics of particular goods or services, or their sellers* (Litvin, Goldsmith, & Pan, 2008). The characteristics of eWOM tend to be described as:

- **High Diffusion Capacity:** The user can access opinions of unknown people around the world.
- **Massive Use by Users of Different Ages and Collectives:** Sharing between all the different points of view.
- **The Message Can Be Propagated Quickly in Several Ways:** Blogs, web pages, social networks, etc.
- **Multidirectional Discussion:** Among users who actively participate with their responses to the information presented.
- **Durability Over Time:** As discussions are uploaded to the network for current and future reference.
- **Credibility:** For being information offered by users spontaneously and without commercial pretensions.
- **It is Free:** Users do not get any economic reward for writing content and do not have to pay for read other's reviews.

The phenomenon of eWOM has been extensively researched, including studies focusing on reasons to use eWOM (both in terms of writing reviews and reading); research looking into its influence on consumer choice; and projects supporting the development of methodologies to synthesize the vast levels of information created through eWOM (Litvin, Goldsmith, & Pan, 2017). Reflecting on the power of eWOM, James Surowiecki proposed the concept of "Wisdom of Crowds" in his book of 2004

The wisdom of crowds: Why the many are smarter than the few and how collective wisdom shapes business, economies, societies and nations (Surowiecki, 2004). The author argues that diverse collection of independently deciding individuals is likely to make certain types of decisions and predictions better than individuals or even experts. Related to this term is that one of "Collective Intelligence" suggested by Toby Segaran in his book of 2007 *Programming Collective Intelligence: Building Smart Web 2.0 Applications* (Segaran, 2007). Through this book, this author shows how to mine the enormous amount of data created by people on the Internet, accessing interesting datasets from websites and collecting data from users, which can be very valuable to support managerial decision-making.

Ethnography researchers have also paid attention to opinions about different issues shared by Internet users. Their focus is on data collection and analysis of content in social media and websites that allow consumers participation. To name these new techniques, experts have used different terms, like "Virtual Ethnography" (Hine, 2000), "Netnography" (Kozinets, 2002), "Webnography" (Puri, 2007) or "Ciber-ethnography" (Keeley-Browne, 2011).

MOTIVATIONS TO WRITE AND READ REVIEWS

People spend a lot of time sharing content in social media or writing reviews in different webs or Apps. Incentive hierarchies have been created by a number of websites in an attempt to motivate users to contribute. This is the case of TripAdvisor, for example. They incentivize users by awarding them increasingly higher status on the platform after fulfilling a certain threshold, e.g. if they generate certain number of reviews (Liu, Schuckert, & Law, 2016). Likes on the content shared through Facebook or retweets on Twitter can also be a motivation for people who share their travel experiences. However, overall, sharing content online is ultimately an altruistic behaviour, and entails no economic compensation. This phenomenon can be considered equivalent to that one that takes place offline or in "real life", where consumers also share information about products and services with others with the only desire to help them making informed decisions (Camilleri, 2018b; Resnick & Zeckhauser, 2002)..

Motivations behind writing and sharing online reviews have been discussed in the academic literature (Hennig-Thurau, Gwinner, Walsh, & Gremler, 2004; Schuckert, Liu, & Law, 2015). The motivation for posting negative reviews ranges from taking revenge to warning others (Wetzer, Zeelenberg, & Pieters, 2007). However, some authors argue that contributors are mostly driven by intrinsic and positive motives such as enjoyment, concerns for other consumers or wanting to help rather than vengeance (Yoo & Gretzel, 2008).

The Internet facilitates users voicing their complaints. Zaugg (2006) suggests that this is because the psychological costs of sharing negative feedback are lower online than face-to-face or through telephone interaction. The reason is because immediate distressing reactions can be avoided, thus lowering the threshold to complain. Furthermore, complaining online to the company may reduce both economic and psychological complaint cost for customers (Hong & Lee, 2008). Product and service reviews on the Internet show the best and the worst of people (Whitty & Joinson, 2008). On the one hand, anonymity favors users to give more honest opinions; on the other, that anonymity, encourages some users to lie more than they would in real life and it is a way to show complaints after an unsatisfactory hotel experience (Chiappa & Dall'Aglio, 2012).

Consumers seek the opinions of others online for a variety of reasons. This ranges from basic utilitarian motives such as to get information, to more hedonic motives. Furthermore, it is evident that some of the factors seem more deliberate and planned, while other motivations are more spontaneous in nature. Previous research identified 8 main factors that motivate consumers for seeking opinions online (Goldsmith & Horowitz, 2006):

Factor 1: Perceived risk: ... *so the chances of me making a bad decision are reduced.*
Factor 2: Influence of others: ...*because I have seen others successfully seek out information electronically.*
Factor 3: Price consciousness: ...*because it helps me find products that are priced the lowest.*
Factor 4: Ease to use: ... *because the amount of effort I have to make to find information is small.*
Factor 5: Accidentally: ...*because I just come across it when surfing the Net.*
Factor 6: It's cool: ... *in order to be more popular among my friends.*
Factor 7: Saw on TV: ...*when I see a TV ad that makes me want to go online and learn more.*
Factor 8: To get information: ...*because I can get a variety of information from people who have positive and negative opinions.*

Consumers can be motivated by one or more of these factors, and they may also be influenced even by others additional factors not registered in this list. Nonetheless, the main point is that they seek for opinions, they trust them, at least to some extent, and their behavior is influenced by the content.

RATING SYSTEMS FEATURES AND INFORMATION MANAGEMENT

Online consumer reviews contain comments and ratings (some also contain photos and videos). Comments display reviewers' assessments of the positive and/or negative experiences as voiced in the textual content of reviews (qualitative information). Ratings are numeric summary statistics (quantitative information), prominently shown in the form of five or ten point star recommendations at the surface level of the review. Recent research shows that high priority is given to rating symbols rather than textual material (Aicher, Asiimwe, Batchuluun, Hauschild, Zöhrer, & Egger, 2016).

In the case of hotels, when a list of hotels is displayed, this includes quantitative information about hotel ratings and the number of reviews (Figure 2). If the consumer goes to the hotel profile, additional ratings can also be found for single items (e.g. service, location, cleanliness, etc....). Single reviews with individual ratings and text are also provided and can be organized following different criteria (Figure 3).

The display of just a global rating or 4-8 categories (e.g. "Room cleanliness", "Service & staff", etc. in Figure 3) trivializes a very complex issue. As suggested

Figure 2. Hotel information in Expedia hotel list
(Source: Expedia.com)

Figure 3. Reviews information in a single hotel profile (Expedia)
(Source: Expedia.com)

by Zhou, Ye, Pearce, and Wu (2014), many hotel attributes can influence travelers satisfaction, as shown by their research using reviews from Agoda.com in China. The authors identified 6 broad categories and 23 different attributes that influence customer satisfaction (Table 1).

The percentage of consumers consulting online review sites prior to their travels is increasing and because of that, there is an emerging research stream examining the effects of online reviews on tourism destinations, businesses and attractions. The existence of hundreds, thousands and even millions of online reviews on certain matters, provides researchers valuable information to learn about individuals. During the last few years, hotel reviews databases have gained great importance, generating a large number of publications on this topic, as a valuable source of information for academic researchers and hoteliers (Cantallops & Salvi, 2014; Kwok, Xie, & Richards, 2017). Whenever applicable, researchers are replacing the data sets collected through questionnaires and interviews by those collected from online services, with Booking and TripAdvisor being the most prominent sources (Stanisic, 2016).

This could hardly be achieved with traditional methodologies, without an extremely important economic cost. Even with a high economic investment, it would be impossible to cover large databases like TripAdvisor (500 million reviews about tourism businesses and places) or Booking.com (130 million reviews about hotels). It allows researchers to extract information manually about hundreds of hotels which include thousands of reviews. By using web data extraction software the process can be automated, allowing researchers getting information about thousands of hotels with millions of reviews, in a fast way.

Table 1. Twenty-three hotel attributes that influence customer satisfaction

Attribute Category	Attribute Category
Physical setting (Room)	Room/bathroom amenities, room size and layout, room cleanliness, additional welcome facilities
Physical setting (Hotel)	Availability of Wi-Fi, public facilities (lounge, lobby, pool, and fitting center), dated level (old/new), noise level, entertainment facilities
Physical setting (Food)	Food variety (including Western food), food quality, dining environment, availability of special food services (room service; vegetarian and gluten free options)
Value	Room, food and beverage, and other prices
Location	Nearness to attractions, city center, airport/railway stations; accessibility
Staff	Friendliness of staff members, language skills of staff members, efficiency of staff members in solving problems

(Source: Zhou, Ye, Pearce, & Wu, 2014)

UGC is easy to access, as it is freely available on the web. However, the large levels of content which is available makes managing it a very complex task. As an example, medium size hotels can easily have more than 1.000 reviews and dozens of new reviews from dozens of websites uploaded every month. This is the case of The Venetian Hotel in Las Vegas which in 2017 had 24,000 reviews in Expedia, 25,600 in TripAdvisor and 13,500 in Google. Major attractions like Sagrada Familia (Barcelona), Eifel Tower (Paris) or Colosseum (Rome) exceed 100.000 reviews in TripAdvisor, while museums like The Metropolitan Museum of Art (New York), The British Museum (London) or Musee du Louvre (Paris) range from 45,000 to 80,000 reviews. Restaurants, Natural parks, Amusement parks, Beaches, Outdoor activities or Concerts are also evaluated in these websites.

Online reviews can be examined from different dimensions, such as emotional expressions, helpfulness, framing, reviewers' gender, reviewer' geographical origin, credibility, trust, review valence, review length, review complexity, volume, etc… With such high levels of information researchers need to make use of Big Data solutions to help with the analysis. And this is even the case when analyzing quantitative data like date, valence, reviewer profile, used device, etc... However, content can also be analyzed with a qualitative methodology, focusing on sentiment analysis, natural language processing and machine learning capabilities.

The increased use of Big Data collected from online review websites for research purposes is supported by automatically controlled systems, which acquire information about millions of reviews from thousands of hotels (Radojevic, Stanisic, & Stanic, 2015) quickly, cheaply and conveniently. Once this large databases are obtained, researchers attempt to analyze and understand online traveler reviews through the use of sophisticated technologies (Govers & Go, 2004; Ye, Law, & Gu, 2009; Ye, Zhang, & Law, 2009). The difficulty to manage such extremely high levels of information is not only of concern to academic researchers, but also relevant to hotel, restaurants, attractions and destinations who need this information to make management decisions. Furthermore, reviews about their establishments are found across dozens of websites, each of them with different scoring systems. Since looking through every single webpage is often unfeasible, a number of systems have been produced to summarize and digest this information. These systems are called "hotel reputation management" software (Reviewpro, Revinate, Olery, etc…) and they help capturing, measuring, and optimizing the guest experience, based on reviews and social media content (Figure 4). According to Hensens (2015), services offered by these companies generally include:

- The pulling together of reviews and ratings in one dashboard from different review platforms.

Figure 4. Hotel reputation management brands
(Source: Compiled by the authors)

- The integration and weighting of scores through an algorithm providing a holistic score, typically on a scale from 1-100.
- The comparison of hotel performance within a group, or a competitive set.
- **Sentiment Analysis:** Identify positive and negative mentions related to guests' experiences in several categories.

Although these software solutions were initially developed for hotels, some are also capable of capturing and grouping enough information to be used by tourism destinations under their product "Destination Analytics" (ReviewPro, 2017).

Differences Between Online Reviews Databases

There are dozens of webpages that collect comments and ratings on hotels and other tourist services. Although the type of information collected is similar, there are certain differences that must be taken into account when using these databases:

1. **Number of Reviews:** Booking and TripAdvisor host the largest number of hotel reviews worldwide, but other websites are also very popular. There are some websites that have limited geographic coverage, such as HRS in the German-speaking market, CTRIP in China or Priceline in North America, but they host a number of reviews similar to Booking or TripAdvisor in their areas.
2. **Delete Reviews:** There are also differences depending on the criterion of expiration and deletion of reviews. While there are websites that do not eliminate reviews, even if they are more than ten years old (TripAdvisor), others such as Booking or Priceline proceed to erase reviews after a certain period of time (usually 24 months).

3. **Scales:** Scoring systems used by different websites are not identical. Although systems with a 1-5 or 1-10 scale predominate, there are systems such as HolydayCheck using a scale of 1-6, TravelRepublic (0-10), Agoda (2-10) or Booking (2,5-10).
4. **Collecting Reviews:** Some webs only allow travelers who stayed in a property to write a review. They send an email to its clients once they checked-out inviting them to provide their feedback (Figure 5) whereas other websites allow anyone with an account to post a review on whatever hotels. However, this facilitates fake reviews to be posted.

Types of Websites Where Online Reviews Can Be Found

Taking into account their differences, websites collecting hotel online reviews can be grouped as follows:

1. **Online Travel Agencies (OTA):** This companies are emailing its clients once they checked-out with a link inviting them to review and provide their feedback about their stay. We include in this group websites like Booking, TravelRepublic, Priceline, HRS or Expedia.
2. **Online Travel Agencies Using External Data:** Some OTAs collect reviews and also include the information provided by TripAdvisor, like Hotels.com. Other OTAs do not collect reviews and show information about reviews and

Figure 5. E-mail sent by Booking.com
(Source: Campaignmonitor.com)

scores from TripAdvisor (B the travel brand, Halcon Viajes) or from TrustYou (Lastminute.com, Rumbo.es).

3. **Online Travel Portals:** These are websites where anyone can register and give their opinion on different aspects of their trip, including their experience in hotels. Best examples are TripAdvisor, HolidayCheck or Zoover. These websites are not travel agencies themselves, but they provide the possibility to search hotels and link with online travel agencies, even in recent years have incorporated the possibility of making reservations directly on the platform. Although these websites claim to implement control mechanisms to prevent fraud, it is possible to introduce fake reviews.

4. **Metasearch Websites (Trivago, Kayak, Skyscanner, HotelsCombined, etc…):** These websites offer a price comparison service, identifying the lowest possible prices for hotels throughout the different booking platforms. Along with price information, metasearch websites show a valuation of the property based on the reviews of guests. This information is extracted by an aggregation of information from the different booking platforms.

INFORMATION RELIABILITY AND FAKE REVIEWS

Online reviews are just subjective opinions wrote by users (as opposed to those written by professionals) based on their very unique experience and perception. Users may not necessarily collect accurate information, and their reviews can often be full of emotions (Clark, 2013) and biased. However, they are perceived as reducing uncertainty when evaluating alternatives and making a decision to buy (Gretzel & Yoo, 2006). Somehow, users believe that commercial information is not completely honest while online reviews are more neutral and objective (Bray, Schetzina, & Steinbrick, 2006; Fernback & Thompson, 2014; Wang, Yu, Fesenmaier, Yoo, Lee, Gretzel, & Fesenmaier, 2009).

Although influenced or stimulated by traditional marketers and marketing activities, eWOM is nonetheless owned and controlled by consumers, and it often carries far higher credibility and trust than traditional media, as explained above these lines. Nowadays eWOM platforms grow and traditional tools lose impact. Around the world, trust levels for each type of advertising format vary (Nielsen, 2015). *Recommendations from people I know* is always the first option but second position is *branded websites* or *consumer opinions posted online*, depending on the geographical area. European and North Americans respondents are most skeptical about advertising formats, showing lower percentages in almost all cases, but still trust in "consumer opinions posted online" with a second position in both cases.

TripBarometer is based on the results of a month-long survey conducted on behalf of TripAdvisor by research firm StrategyOne (Tripbarometer, 2013). It takes into account the responses of 35,042 people, from 26 countries spanning 7 regions. Results show that 69% of travelers rely on travel review websites when they make their travel plans (Figure 6), while 93% say that their booking decisions are influenced by online reviews. Not only are people reading about others' travel experiences, they're also sharing their own (51% say that they have written an online review). Hotel managers know how important these reviews are and 81% are now inviting guests to submit reviews. Furthermore, 65% write management responses to negative hotel reviews, while a lower percentage (50%) respond to the positive reviews.

In late 2013, on behalf of TripAdvisor, PhoCusWright commissioned an independent study among 12,000 travelers across the globe (TripAdvisor, 2014b). Results showed that more than 80% read at least 6-12 reviews before making their accommodation decisions, and they also think the site makes them feel confident in their travel decisions.

Fake Reviews

UGC may be considered as spontaneous and passionate feedback provided by real consumers, as previously explained. However, this is not always the case. Fake reviews are an important phenomenon which heavily impacts on the fate of tourism

Figure 6. Travel planning is dominated by online resources (Source: Tripbarometer, 2013).

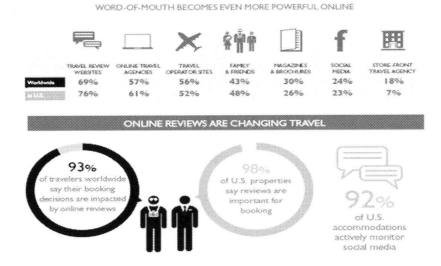

businesses (Yoo & Gretzel, 2009). There is growing evidence to suggest the existence of fake reviews, a practice that undermines the credibility of the process (Mayzlin, Dover, & Chevalier, 2014; Simonson, 2016). This phenomenon is observed in the restaurant context using Yelp.com (Luca & Zervas, 2016). A considerable amount of research has focused on the identification of fake reviews (Hu, Bose, Koh, & Liu, 2012; Lappas, 2012; S. Xie, Wang, Lin, & Yu, 2012), but none of the proposed methods is 100% reliable. While OTAs only allow to write reviews to customers who have stayed in that particular hotel, anyone can write a review in websites like TripAdvisor, Yelp or HolidayCheck. This is a controversial issue that doesn't stop users from reading and trusting reviews, despite of where it comes from.

Generic social media websites, such as Facebook, Twitter or Instagram, also has plenty of fake content, usually described as Astroturfing (Lee, Tamilarasan, & Caverlee, 2013). It is used by organizations to give the illusion of genuine public support to their brands. It is easy to buy "packs" of thousands of fake followers, likes or retweets for a reduced price. It is also possible to use that fake profiles with "Bots" (Ferrara, Varol, Davis, Menczer, & Flammini, 2016), which is a software that automatically controls hundreds or thousands of social media accounts. It can autonomously perform actions such as tweeting, retweeting, liking, following or unfollowing.

TripAdvisor is the world's largest travel site: more than 535 million reviews, available in 49 markets and 415 million average unique monthly visitors. The authenticity of TripAdvisor' reviews has often been questioned (Ayeh, Au, & Law, 2013; Filieri, Alguezaui, & McLeay, 2015). This is because any internet user can register on this website (with a real or fake identity) and provide information about hotels where they have been hosted or where they may have never been. Due to these allegations, TripAdvisor has developed a list of guidelines of what would be considered as fraudulent reviews (TripAdvisor, 2014c):

- Writing a review for his/her own property.
- Asking friends or relatives to write positive reviews.
- Submitting a review on behalf of a guest.
- Copying comment cards and submitting them as reviews.
- Pressuring a TripAdvisor member to remove a negative review.
- Offering incentives such as discounts, upgrades, or any special treatment in exchange for reviews.
- Hiring an optimization company, third party marketing organization, or anyone to submit false reviews.
- Impersonating a competitor or a guest in any way.

There are cases of hotels that include positive reviews of their establishment, as well as cases of hotels that generate negative reviews about competitors (Dohse, 2013). In addition there have also been cases of guest threatening to write a negative review unless a refund, upgrade, or other type of request was met by the establishment, which is something recognized by TripAdvisor as fraudulent use of the review website.

TripAdvisor claims to use sophisticated methods of controlling fraudulent content. However, such measures simply hinder and limit the inclusion of fake reviews and do not completely avoid the problem. Some pranksters have conducted experiments, proving that it is possible to include fake reviews on TripAdvisor and even creating businesses that do not really exist. Some of these actions have been successful passed control systems and appeared in mass media:

Pranksters 'trick TripAdvisor' into naming made-up eatery as an Italian town's top-ranking restaurant (Mirror).

Five-star fake! TripAdvisor prankster fools the foodies: Disgruntled user posts spoof reviews in anger at site not being policed properly (Daily Mail).

Hostel for the homeless soars to top 100 of TripAdvisor's best places to stay after jokers give it a five-star rating (Daily Mail).

Mary Johnston Is Ready For Reviews: Woman Listed As Tourist Attraction On Tripadvisor (Huffington Post)

It is very easy to create an email account in a free service like Hotmail or Gmail, using a fake name and register in TripAdvisor to write anonymous reviews. It is almost impossible to be detected as a fake reviewer. However, there are certain behaviors which TripAdvisor considers suspicious and may trigger an account to be blocked or examined. For example, when someone tries to repeat this process several times in just one day or a week, TripAdvisor may suspect of such amount of reviews from the same location, using the same web browser and all of them very positive or negative.

For establishments with a low number of reviews, it may be possible to substantially vary their score with a few fraudulent reviews, but it is much more complicated for medium and large establishments. These businesses receive hundreds of reviews from real customers and would have to generate a lot of fake reviews to produce significant variations in overall scores. Such a big amount of reviews could activate TripAdvisor detection systems.

eWOM

Although it is clear that fake reviews on TripAdvisor exist, the percentage that they represent (of the total 500 million registered reviews in the website) is unknown. TripAdvisor control systems are likely to make it difficult for fake reviews to be included, so their percentage is likely to be minimal. Even if there are one million fake reviews, it would only mean a 0.2% of total number of reviews, and therefore, the remainder 99.8% of the reviews would be real.

When TripAdvisor detects that a hotel may be receiving fake positive reviews, it acts in various ways, as indicated on its own website. The first is, *A property may drop by several pages in the TripAdvisor popularity index*, the second is, *The property will no longer be eligible for inclusion in TripAdvisor's Travelers Choice awards, Top 10 lists, press releases, etc.* and finally, *A large red penalty notice, explaining that the property's reviews are suspicious may appear on the listing page*. (Figure 7).

It is very important to note that there is no possibility for the hotel to be removed from the website, even if it is proven that this has breached TripAdvisor's regulations, which is exactly what some properties would prefer. The hotel profile will always remain on the website and users will always be able to provide reviews and photographs, even without the business owner agreement.

The focus of the above analysis has been placed on TripAdvisor to illustrates the issue of fake reviews in the tourism industry. However, it is worth note that this issue applies to other similar websites, as previously mentioned.

THE REVIEWS' IMPORTANCE

In the hotel sector, it has been demonstrated that online reviews and ratings have a significant impact on potential consumers and their purchase decisions. Research has demonstrated that the impact of reviews can be noticed on both the number of bookings and possibility of price increment:

Figure 7. Red badge on hotel profile
(Source: Tripadvisor.com)

- A 10% increase in traveler review ratings boosting online bookings by more than 5% (Ye, Law, & Gu, 2009).
- Higher customer rating significantly increases the online sales of hotels and that a 1% increase in online customer ratings increases sales per room by up to about 2.6% depending on the destination. It also increase prices by 1% in cities like Paris and London (Öğüt & Onur Taş, 2012).
- A 1-point increase in a hotel's 100-point ReviewPro Global Review Index™ (GRI) leads up to a 0.89% increase in price (ADR), a 0.54% increase in occupancy, and a 1.42% increase in Revenue per Available Room (RevPAR) (Anderson, 2012).
- A 1-point increase in a 1-10 scale is associated to an increase in the occupancy rate of 7.5% (Viglia, Minazzi, & Buhalis, 2016).

Such is the importance of online reviews that the United Nations World Tourism Organization has suggested the need to integrate them into conventional hotel classification (UNWTO, 2014). Otherwise, there have been suggestions that conventional start classifications as they currently stand may disappear (Hensens, 2015).

Star classification systems provide accurate and objective information of accommodation establishments. However, they have drawn critics as the criteria required for each star level varies across countries (Hensens, 2015). Major complaints are that they are widely misunderstood by the public, overly complex, and overemphasize physical amenities over quality service (Schrader, 2013).

Classification systems assess the availability of certain facilities and amenities whereas online guest reviews measure whether establishments meet customers' expectations. Thus guest reviews provide a quality check upon facilities and amenities. Hotel online reviews offer an independent reference on the standard and quality of hotel services. However, the criteria is subjective. Some experts argue that guest reviews and scores are better at providing a benchmark on the quality and range of services than that of star classification systems (Henses, 2015). According to this author, start rating systems as they exist are likely to disappear. And it is true that many travelers, especially of the youngest generations, may even feel that official stars are just a secondary element and pay considerably more attention to guest reviews, location, WIFI quality, etc… when making their decisions to book.

The suggestion by United Nations World Tourism Organization to integrate online review ratings into hotel classification (UNWTO, 2014) would serve complementary purposes. This would be done in an attempt to complement the usual objective quantitative measures offered by hotel stars systems with the subjective qualitative information provided by hotel online reviews. Several countries are moving towards integrated models (Australia, Switzerland, Abu Dhabi, and Norway) taking a variety of approaches. The main aspect of these models relates to the way the information from the two sources of information is presented. Full integration models imply that the hotel can move up or down a star level depending on its perceived quality, as measured by online guest reviews. However, comparative performance models display online ratings and hotel classification details separately, rather than integrated.

CONCLUSION

After analyzing how rating systems work and their importance for the tourism industry, this final section considers the practical recommendations needed to manage them. As a conclusion of the previous sections, it could be argued that management actions should help to improve customers' satisfaction. This would lead establishments to increase their ratings and as a consequence, to increase sales, occupancy, their Average Daily Rate (ADR), etc… However, managing online reputation is not as simple. It requires taking into account multiple factors and implementing changes at the managerial level. Actions can be divided in two main groups:

1. Increase ratings in order to get more sales.
2. Analyze information in order to improve services and customers satisfaction.

The first group can be addressed through two main strategies, commonly recommended by experts: to obtain more reviews and to respond reviews. The second group includes more complex processes that will allow managers to extract learning out of online reviews and gain value to improve their services.

Encourage Customers to Write Reviews

TripAdvisor popularity Index algorithm is based on three key ingredients: the quality (average score), quantity (number of reviews) and how recent reviews are. It is not easy to increase ratings. However increasing the number of reviews and obtaining recent comments, is relatively easier to achieve, given that it does not require economic investments or significant changes in service protocols.

TripAdvisor recommends hotels to encourage their guests to submit user reviews upon their return home and this recommendation is made with substantial emphasis. There is also a blog entry in TripAdvisor webpage called "More reviews, higher ranking" (Camilleri, 2018b; TripAdvisor, 2014a) referring to an academic paper with the title *Online Customer Reviews of Hotels: As Participation Increases, Better Evaluation Is Obtained* (Melián-González, Bulchand-Gidumal, & González López-Valcárcel, 2013).

Despite an initial period of tension and lawsuits filed by hotels against websites like TripAdvisor (between 2010 and 2012) regarding the publication of fake reviews, the relationship between these parties has improved (McEvilly, 2015). Three of the largest hotel groups in the world, Four Seasons, Wyndham and Accor, even encourage guests to write reviews on TripAdvisor after their stay.

It is also very interesting for businesses to have a database as large as possible for statistical reasons. The greater the number of registered reviews, the more reliable the information used for the analysis will be. It can also be a way to protect against possible attacks of fake negative reviews, since its relative weight will be lower if the establishment has more registered reviews.

However, hoteliers should avoid selectively encouraging only the guests they believe will write positive reviews and in some countries, such as the UK, this may even be considered unlawful (CMA, 2016). A common practice of this would be that case in which staff ask guests how they enjoyed their stay as they are checking out, and only if the person had a good experience, they would then be asked to write a review in TripAdvisor. Otherwise, if their experience was negative they would not be asked to post a review. This is fraudulent behavior, which if untracked, may help hotels effective improving their ratings. However, it is very difficult for TripAdvisor to detect.

Respond Reviews

While, this is not always the case, many websites that collect reviews offer hotel owners the ability to respond to any comment that users post about their establishments. When this is the case, it is sufficient for the owner to be correctly registered in the corresponding website and it does not imply any additional payment. Responding to review may help hotels improving their image. According to a TripAdvisor study, 62% of travelers say that responses to reviews posted by the hotel management make them more likely to book a stay at a hotel (TripAdvisor, 2014b). This shows a substantial level of empathy with managers who reply to reviews, and the likelihood to help minimizing the impact of negative reviews. Several studies have shown that responding to customer reviews improves hotel scores and sales, so it has become an almost imperative issue in online reputation management. The work by Xie, Zhang, Zhang, Singh, and Lee (2016) showed that managerial response leads to an average increase of 0.235 stars in the TripAdvisor ratings and a 17.3% increase in the volume of subsequent consumer.

Responding to all reviews may sometimes not be possible, as it would require a substantial amount of time for those establishments receiving a high volume of reviews. Furthermore, many of the required answers are likely to be highly repetitive. This is particularly the case of the responses to positive comments.

There are plenty of guides and advice to proceed in writing the answers, although it is not possible to determine exactly how to act in each individual situation. There will be exceptional cases in which experience, sensitivity and common sense will have to be used. Most expert recommendations have a number of common points or general parameters to follow (Brinzan, 2016):

1. **Guests Should Be Thanked and Greeted by Their Name:** Even if the review is negative, you should thank them for the time and interest taken. It should not be forgotten that no traveler has an obligation to write reviews.
2. **The Name and Position of the Person Replying Should Identified:** This task entails great level of responsibility, so it will have to be performed by a duly trained person with a high degree of independence.
3. **Responses Should Be Posted Quickly (and always within 2-3 days):** Sometimes it is necessary to carry out a small investigation to identify the client and/or the problem raised.
4. **When the Review is Negative, the Response Should Include the Word "Sorry", Even if the Problem is not the Responsibility of the Establishment:** This practice would help showing empathy and concern.
5. **The Response Should Include an Explanation of the Measures to be Taken:** It is very positive to state that the problem has been detected and that it will be tried to solve. The more details can be given about this, the more satisfied the user will feel and more confidence will generate in those who later read it.
6. **The Answer Should Never Include an Offer for Compensation:** Offering a discount or free service publicly can encourage others to include negative reviews in an attempt to also obtain compensation.
7. **Responses Should be Customized:** Using standardized responses should be avoided, as it may give the impression that incidents are not actually read or investigated.
8. **Direct Confrontations with Customers Should be Avoided:** It does not matter whether we know that *"the customer is not right"*. The answers should always be polite and friendly, even if their aim is to make the client understand that their complaints are ungrounded.

The New Business Management Approach

Businesses, organizations in general and tourism destinations should consider UGC in their marketing plans and communication mix. While managers do not have control over the comments placed online by users, they are able to decide how to act upon these. Business managers and owners may not necessarily agree with the content of the comments placed online, and may even question the knowledge and level of experience of the users posting them. As discussed in a previous section of this chapter, the existence of fake reviews may add further frustration to the already burdensome task of reading, investigating and acting upon the content of reviews by managers. However, ignoring posts is the least effective approach, based on the impact that both reviews and management responses have on bookings, as discussed through a previous section of this chapter.

The importance of responding to reviews for reputation management has already been discussed in a previous section of this chapter. However, there is one more way in which managers may act upon this data. The information that travelers provide through UGC can be, within limits, compared to that one given by traditional service auditors. Furthermore, this information is also comparable to that one that used to be collected through surveys. However, there are some differences that can make the data obtained through UGC even more attractive for businesses than that one given by service auditors and/or customer surveys. First of all, this information is provided for free. Contrary to service auditors and/or surveys, which cost money to run, this information is freely available online. Secondly, it is coming from actual customers, and the customers of establishment. Thus, they provide a detailed insight into the preferences of the type of customer who is likely to stay in that type of hotel are. And thirdly, customers comment on issues that matter to them, rather than on those categories pre-coded by hotel managers when designing their surveys. By collecting and analyzing reviews proactively, businesses can identify and address operational and service-related issues in order to increase satisfaction. This information can help managers making decisions about the "product" they sell and whether this fits the requirements of the market. And based on that, this data may form a very fundamental aspect of the internal audit incorporated in any marketing plan. And while the focus of this analysis has been predominantly placed on the hotel sector, the same applies to destinations, transport, visitor attractions and other tourism organizations.

As explained in previous sections there are companies providing specialized software that captures and measures reviews and social media content. However, little research has been done to investigate the processes by which this information can be turned into knowledge and then integrated effectively throughout the company. And it is herewith argued that this research is duly needed.

Improving customers' satisfaction is indeed a matter that involves all staff. Thus, it is not enough that information is effectively analyzed by managers, but also that efficient processes to share this knowledge with staff need to be developed. From a quantitative point of view, it is possible to keep track of variations in scores over time, and even to associate a part of the employees salary to scores, as NH and Melia are doing (Delgado, 2014).

In addition, detailed studies can be carried out on the effectiveness of the changes that are introduced. For example, if complaints about coffee or breakfast croissants have been detected and the hotel have changed the suppliers of these products, it is possible to check whether those changes have had a real effect. It is as easy as comparing the percentage of reviews complaining about these aspects before and after making the changes. If we talk about a tourist attraction and the complaints refer to the pre-reservation system, online reviews can also be used to check if the changes made are effective.

This new approach to business management, requires managers to put to a side any preconceptions about what adequate service is, which may be based on their education and/or business experience. The ability to analyze data, its adequate interpretation and the implementation of appropriate actions based on this information, becomes instead a leading role. To take on this new approach it is necessary to be aware of the nature and importance of eWOM, as we have discussed in this chapter.

Finally, consumers' satisfaction is commonly defined as the difference between expectations and performance (Parasuraman, Zeithaml, & Berry, 1988). If marketing communication delivers on the promises (i.e. expectations are met) then consumers will be satisfied but if the company fails to deliver what they promised, consumers will be dissatisfied and write complains, often online. Therefore, this online feedback may also be used to reflect upon the reliability of the promotional material about the establishment.

REFERENCES

Aicher, J., Asiimwe, F., Batchuluun, B., Hauschild, M., Zöhrer, M., & Egger, R. (2016). Online Hotel Reviews: Rating Symbols or Text… Text or Rating Symbols? That Is the Question! In Information and Communication Technologies in Tourism 2016 (pp. 369–382). Springer.

Anderson, C. (2012). The Impact of Social Media on Lodging Performance. *Cornell Hospitality Report*, *12*(15), 6–11.

Ayeh, J. K., Au, N., & Law, R. (2013). "Do We Believe in TripAdvisor?" Examining Credibility Perceptions and Online Travelers' Attitude toward Using User-Generated Content. *Journal of Travel Research*, *52*(4), 437–452. doi:10.1177/0047287512475217

Blackshaw, P., & Nazarro, M. (2006). *Consumer-generated media (CGM) 101: Word-of-mouth in the age of the web-fortified consumer*. New York: Nielsen.

Bray, J., Schetzina, C., & Steinbrick, S. (2006). *Six travel trends for 2006*. PhoCusWright.

Brinzan, D. (2016). *How to Respond Properly to Online Hotel Reviews*. Retrieved 24 November 2017, from https://www.hermesthemes.com/respond-properly-online-hotel-reviews/

Camilleri, M. A. (2018a). Tourism Distribution Channels. In *Travel Marketing, Tourism Economics and the Airline Product*. Cham: Springer. doi:10.1007/978-3-319-49849-2_6

Camilleri, M. A. (2018b). Integrated Marketing Communications. In *Travel Marketing, Tourism Economics and the Airline Product*. Cham: Springer. doi:10.1007/978-3-319-49849-2_5

Cantallops, A. S., & Salvi, F. (2014). New consumer behavior: A review of research on eWOM and hotels. *International Journal of Hospitality Management, 36*, 41–51. doi:10.1016/j.ijhm.2013.08.007

Chiappa, G. D., & Dall'Aglio, S. (2012). Factors influencing Travellers' e-Ratings and e-Complaints about Hotel Services: Insights from an Italian Tourism Destination. In *Information and Communication Technologies in Tourism 2012* (pp. 448–459). Vienna: Springer; doi:10.1007/978-3-7091-1142-0_39

Christou, E., Sigala, M., & Gretzel, U. (2012). *Social Media in Travel, Tourism and Hospitality: Theory, Practice and Cases*. Farnham, UT: Routledge.

CMA. (2016). *Online reviews: letting your customers see the true picture - GOV.UK*. Retrieved 24 November 2017, from https://www.gov.uk/government/publications/online-reviews-and-endorsements-advice-for-businesses/online-reviews-giving-consumers-the-full-picture

Delgado, C. (2014). El huésped 2.0 siempre tiene la razón. *El País*. Retrieved from https://elpais.com/economia/2014/08/09/actualidad/1407601275_385548.html

Dellarocas, C. (2003). The digitization of word of mouth: Promise and challenges of online feedback mechanisms. *Management Science, 49*(10), 1407–1424. doi:10.1287/mnsc.49.10.1407.17308

Dohse, K. (2013). *Fabricating Feedback: Blurring the Line Between Brand Management and Bogus Reviews (SSRN Scholarly Paper No. ID 2333170)*. Rochester, NY: Social Science Research Network. Retrieved from https://papers.ssrn.com/abstract=2333170

Fernback, J., & Thompson, B. (2014). *Virtual communities: abort, retry, failure?* Retrieved from http://www.well.com/user/hlr/texts/vccivil.html

Ferrara, E., Varol, O., Davis, C., Menczer, F., & Flammini, A. (2016). The Rise of Social Bots. *Communications of the ACM*, *59*(7), 96–104. doi:10.1145/2818717

Filieri, R., Alguezaui, S., & McLeay, F. (2015). Why do travelers trust TripAdvisor? Antecedents of trust towards consumer-generated media and its influence on recommendation adoption and word of mouth. *Tourism Management*, *51*, 174–185. doi:10.1016/j.tourman.2015.05.007

Goldsmith, R. E., & Horowitz, D. (2006). Measuring Motivations for Online Opinion Seeking. *Journal of Interactive Advertising*, *6*(2), 2–14. doi:10.1080/15252019.2006.10722114

Govers, R., & Go, F. M. (2004). Projected destination image online: Website content analysis of pictures and text. *Information Technology & Tourism*, *7*(2), 73–89. doi:10.3727/1098305054517327

Gretzel, U., & Yoo, K. H. (2008). Use and impact of online travel reviews. *Information and Communication Technologies in Tourism*, *2008*, 35–46.

Hennig-Thurau, T., Gwinner, K. P., Walsh, G., & Gremler, D. D. (2004). Electronic word-of-mouth via consumer-opinion platforms: What motivates consumers to articulate themselves on the internet? *Journal of Interactive Marketing*, *18*(1), 38–52. doi:10.1002/dir.10073

Hensens, W. (2015). The future of hotel rating. *Journal of Tourism Futures*, *1*(1), 69–73. doi:10.1108/JTF-12-2014-0023

Hine, C. (2000). *Virtual ethnography*. Sage. doi:10.4135/9780857020277

Hong, J.-Y., & Lee, W.-N. (2008). Consumer Complaint Behavior in the Online Environment. In *Web Systems Design and Online Consumer Behaviour*. Idea Group Inc (IGI). Retrieved from https://www.igi-global.com/chapter/consumer-complaint-behavior-online-environment/18274

Hu, N., Bose, I., Koh, N. S., & Liu, L. (2012). Manipulation of online reviews: An analysis of ratings, readability, and sentiments. *Decision Support Systems*, *52*(3), 674–684. doi:10.1016/j.dss.2011.11.002

Kaplan, A. M., & Haenlein, M. (2010). Users of the world, unite! The challenges and opportunities of Social Media. *Business Horizons*, *53*(1), 59–68. doi:10.1016/j.bushor.2009.09.003

Keeley-Browne, E. (2011). Cyber-Ethnography: The Emerging Research Approach for. In Handbook of Research on Transformative Online Education and Liberation: Models for Social Equality. Hershey, PA: Information Science Reference.

Kozinets, R. V. (2002). The field behind the screen: Using netnography for marketing research in online communities. *JMR, Journal of Marketing Research, 39*(1), 61–72. doi:10.1509/jmkr.39.1.61.18935

Kwok, L., Xie, K. L., & Richards, T. (2017). Thematic framework of online review research: A systematic analysis of contemporary literature on seven major hospitality and tourism journals. *International Journal of Contemporary Hospitality Management, 29*(1), 307–354. doi:10.1108/IJCHM-11-2015-0664

Lappas, T. (2012). Fake Reviews: The Malicious Perspective. In *Natural Language Processing and Information Systems* (pp. 23–34). Berlin: Springer. doi:10.1007/978-3-642-31178-9_3

Lee, K., Tamilarasan, P., & Caverlee, J. (2013). Crowdturfers, Campaigns, and Social Media: Tracking and Revealing Crowdsourced Manipulation of Social Media. *Seventh International AAAI Conference on Weblogs and Social Media.*

Litvin, S. W., Goldsmith, R. E., & Pan, B. (2008). Electronic word-of-mouth in hospitality and tourism management. *Tourism Management, 29*(3), 458–468. doi:10.1016/j.tourman.2007.05.011

Litvin, S. W., Goldsmith, R. E., & Pan, B. (2017). A retrospective view of electronic word of mouth in hospitality and tourism management. *International Journal of Contemporary Hospitality Management.* doi:10.1108/IJCHM-08-2016-0461

Liu, X., Schuckert, M., & Law, R. (2016). Online incentive hierarchies, review extremity, and review quality: Empirical evidence from the hotel sector. *Journal of Travel & Tourism Marketing, 33*(3), 279–292. doi:10.1080/10548408.2015.1008669

Luca, M., & Zervas, G. (2016). Fake It Till You Make It: Reputation, Competition, and Yelp Review Fraud. *Management Science, 62*(12), 3412–3427. doi:10.1287/mnsc.2015.2304

Mayzlin, D., Dover, Y., & Chevalier, J. (2014). Promotional reviews: An empirical investigation of online review manipulation. *The American Economic Review, 104*(8), 2421–2455. doi:10.1257/aer.104.8.2421

McEvilly, B. (2015). *How Online Review Sites Are Affecting Your Hotel.* Retrieved from https://www.hospitalitynet.org/opinion/4070901.html

Melián-González, S., Bulchand-Gidumal, J., & González López-Valcárcel, B. (2013). Online customer reviews of hotels: As participation increases, better evaluation is obtained. *Cornell Hospitality Quarterly, 54*(3), 274–283. doi:10.1177/1938965513481498

Nielsen. (2015). *The Nielsen Global Trust in Advertising Survey*. Retrieved from https://www.nielsen.com/content/dam/nielsenglobal/apac/docs/reports/2015/nielsen-global-trust-in-advertising-report-september-2015.pdf

O'reilly, T. (2005). *What is Web 2.0: Design patterns and business models for the next generation of software*. Sebastopol, CA: O'Reilly Media.

Öğüt, H., & Onur Taş, B. K. (2012). The influence of internet customer reviews on the online sales and prices in hotel industry. *Service Industries Journal, 32*(2), 197–214. doi:10.1080/02642069.2010.529436

Parasuraman, A., Zeithaml, V. A., & Berry, L. (1988). SERVQUAL: A multiple-item scale for measuring consumer perceptions of service quality. *Journal of Retailing, 64*(1), 12–40.

Park, S., & Nicolau, J. L. (2015). Asymmetric effects of online consumer reviews. *Annals of Tourism Research, 50*(Supplement C), 67–83. doi:10.1016/j.annals.2014.10.007

Puri, A. (2007). The web of insights-The art and practice of webnography. *International Journal of Market Research, 49*(3), 387–408. doi:10.1177/147078530704900308

Radojevic, T., Stanisic, N., & Stanic, N. (2015). Solo travellers assign higher ratings than families: Examining customer satisfaction by demographic group. *Tourism Management Perspectives, 16*, 247–258. doi:10.1016/j.tmp.2015.08.004

Resnick, P., & Zeckhauser, R. (2002). Trust among strangers in Internet transactions: Empirical analysis of eBay's reputation system. In *The Economics of the Internet and E-commerce* (pp. 127–157). Emerald Group Publishing Limited. doi:10.1016/S0278-0984(02)11030-3

ReviewPro. (2017). *Destination Analytics*. Retrieved 30 October 2017, from https://www.reviewpro.com/products/destination-analytics/

Robertson, D. M. H. (2015). Heritage interpretation, place branding and experiential marketing in the destination management of geotourism sites. *Translation Spaces, 4*(2), 289–309. doi:10.1075/ts.4.2.06rob

Schaal, D. (2013). *Travelers Visit 38 Sites Before Booking a Vacation, Study Says*. Retrieved 30 October 2017, from https://skift.com/2013/08/26/travelers-visit-38-sites-before-booking-a-vacation-study-says/

Schrader, K. (2013). *Types of Hotel Ratings Other Than the Star Rating*. Retrieved 24 November 2017, from http://traveltips.usatoday.com/types-hotel-ratings-other-star-rating-108407.html

Schuckert, M., Liu, X., & Law, R. (2015). Hospitality and tourism online reviews: Recent trends and future directions. *Journal of Travel & Tourism Marketing, 32*(5), 608–621. doi:10.1080/10548408.2014.933154

Segaran, T. (2007). *Programming Collective Intelligence: Building Smart Web 2.0 Applications*. O'Reilly Media, Inc.

Simonson, I. (2016). Imperfect Progress: An Objective Quality Assessment of the Role of User Reviews in Consumer Decision Making, A Commentary on de Langhe, Fernbach, and Lichtenstein. *The Journal of Consumer Research, 42*(6), 840–845. doi:10.1093/jcr/ucv091

Stanisic, N. (2016). *Recent Trends in Quantitative Research in the Field of Tourism and Hospitality (SSRN Scholarly Paper No. ID 2875849)*. Rochester, NY: Social Science Research Network.

Surowiecki, J. (2004). *The Wisdom of Crowds: Why the Many are Smarter Than the Few and how Collective Wisdom Shapes Business, Economies, Societies, and Nations*. Doubleday.

TripAdvisor. (2014a). *More reviews, higher rating*. Retrieved from https://www.tripadvisor.com/TripAdvisorInsights/n2086/more-reviews-higher-rating

TripAdvisor. (2014b). *PhoCusWright insights plus TripAdvisor tips, Part 1*. Retrieved 29 October 2017, from https://www.tripadvisor.com/TripAdvisorInsights/n2121/phocuswright-insights-plus-tripadvisor-tips-part-1

TripAdvisor. (2014c). *What is considered fraud?* Retrieved from http://www.tripadvisorsupport.com/hc/en-us/articles/200615037-What-is-considered-fraud-

Tripbarometer. (2013). *TripBarometer Reveals Travel, Green and Mobile Trends*. Retrieved 29 October 2017, from https://www.tripadvisor.com/TripAdvisorInsights/n627/tripbarometer-reveals-travel-green-and-mobile-trends-infographic

UNWTO. (2014). *Online Guest Reviews and Hotel Classification Systems: An Integrated Approach*. Madrid: UNWTO.

Viglia, G., Minazzi, R., & Buhalis, D. (2016). The influence of e-word-of-mouth on hotel occupancy rate. *International Journal of Contemporary Hospitality Management, 28*(9), 2035–2051. doi:10.1108/IJCHM-05-2015-0238

Wang, Y., Yu, Q., & Fesenmaier, D. R. (2002). Defining the virtual tourist community: Implications for tourism marketing. *Tourism Management*, *23*(4), 407–417. doi:10.1016/S0261-5177(01)00093-0

Wetzer, I. M., Zeelenberg, M., & Pieters, R. (2007). "Never eat in that restaurant, I did!": Exploring why people engage in negative word-of-mouth communication. *Psychology and Marketing*, *24*(8), 661–680. doi:10.1002/mar.20178

Whitty, M. T., & Joinson, A. (2008). *Truth, Lies and Trust on the Internet* (1st ed.). London: Routledge.

Xie, K. L., Zhang, Z., Zhang, Z., Singh, A., & Lee, S. K. (2016). Effects of managerial response on consumer eWOM and hotel performance: Evidence from TripAdvisor. *International Journal of Contemporary Hospitality Management*, *28*(9), 2013–2034. doi:10.1108/IJCHM-06-2015-0290

Xie, S., Wang, G., Lin, S., & Yu, P. S. (2012). Review Spam Detection via Temporal Pattern Discovery. In *Proceedings of the 18th ACM SIGKDD International Conference on Knowledge Discovery and Data Mining* (pp. 823–831). New York, NY: ACM. 10.1145/2339530.2339662

Ye, Q., Law, R., & Gu, B. (2009). The impact of online user reviews on hotel room sales. *International Journal of Hospitality Management*, *28*(1), 180–182. doi:10.1016/j.ijhm.2008.06.011

Ye, Q., Zhang, Z., & Law, R. (2009). Sentiment classification of online reviews to travel destinations by supervised machine learning approaches. *Expert Systems with Applications*, *36*(3), 6527–6535. doi:10.1016/j.eswa.2008.07.035

Yoo, K. H., & Gretzel, U. (2008). The influence of involvement on use and impact of online travel reviews. In Hospitality Information Technology Association (HITA) conference (pp. 15–16). Academic Press.

Yoo, K.-H., Lee, Y., Gretzel, U., & Fesenmaier, D. R. (2009). Trust in travel-related consumer generated media. *Information and Communication Technologies in Tourism*, *2009*, 49–59.

Zhou, L., Ye, S., Pearce, P. L., & Wu, M.-Y. (2014). Refreshing hotel satisfaction studies by reconfiguring customer review data. *International Journal of Hospitality Management*, *38*(Supplement C), 1–10. doi:10.1016/j.ijhm.2013.12.004

ADDITIONAL READING

Anderson, C. K., & Han, S. (2016). Hotel Performance Impact of Socially Engaging with Consumers. *Cornell Hospitality Report, 16*(10), 3–9.

European Union (2014). *Study on Online Consumer Reviews in the Hotel Sector*. Retrieved from: https://publications.europa.eu/en/publication-detail/-/publication/7d0b5993-7a88-43ef-bfb5-7997101db6d5

Future Foundation. (2014). *Big Data, the impact on travel and tourism*. Retrieved from: https://www.wttc.org/research/other-research/big-data-the-impact-on-travel-tourism/#undefined

HOTREC. (2011). *"Hotel review" sites add value to the hospitality industry*. HOTREC position paper. Retrieved from: http://www.hotrec.eu/Documents/Document/20110908181823-D-0907-241a-MS_-_HOTREC_position_paper_on_hotel_review_sites.pdf

Lynn, M., & Riaz, U. (2015). *Thumbs Down... to Thumbs Up, Burnish hospitality brands by responding to social media*. Accenture. Retrieved from: https://www.accenture.com/t20150714T141615__w__/us-en/_acnmedia/Accenture/Conversion-Assets/DotCom/Documents/Global/PDF/Dualpub_15/Accenture-Social-Media-and-Hospitality.pdf

Minazzi, R. (2015). *Social media marketing in tourism and hospitality*. Heidelberg: Springer. doi:10.1007/978-3-319-05182-6

ReviewPro. (2013). *New ReviewPro guide for hoteliers: How to respond to reviews*. Retrieved from: https://www.reviewpro.com/blog/new-reviewpro-guide-for-hoteliers-how-to-respond-to-reviews/

Tripadvisor (2015). *Key Insights from "Using Guest Reviews to Pave the Path to Greater Engagement"*. Retrieved from: https://www.tripadvisor.com/TripAdvisorInsights/n2656/research-key-insights-using-guest-reviews-pave-path-greater-engagement

Tripadvisor (2016). *Our guidelines for traveller reviews*. Retrieved from: https://www.tripadvisorsupport.com/hc/en-gb/articles/200614797

KEY TERMS AND DEFINITIONS

Big Data: Extreme volume of data coming from a variety of sources that has the potential to be mined and used for business decisions.

EWOM: Electronic word of mouth. Any statement made by real customers about a product or service available in the Internet.

Fake Reviews: The practice of falsely representing oneself as a real consumer when writing reviews.

OTAs: Online travel agencies (OTAs) are online companies which sell travel related services via the Internet.

Tourism 2.0: Travel sites that use Web 2.0.

UGC: User generated content (UGC) is content (text, scores, photos, videos, etc.) that has been created and shared in the internet by unpaid contributors.

Web 2.0: It refers to the technology currently present in many websites that allows users to create and exchange content in an easy and quick way.

Chapter 7
Communication Technologies in E-Tourism:
A Review of Online Frameworks

Maria Matiatou
Universidad de Alcalá, Spain

ABSTRACT

Information-intensive and technology-driven environments like e-tourism need to be constantly oriented towards improvement of their communication strategies and infrastructure considering their immediate impact on user experience and customer behavior. The full range of available technologies is rapidly stretching from sophisticated website features to personalized services based on recommender systems that associate user preference with destinations and hospitality services. Despite the development of these technologies, many challenges remain in designing, applying, and evaluating the web-based services in their critical role between visitor and destination experience. This chapter addresses the problem of how to support management decisions on information technology solutions that best promote destination brands, support visitors' decision-making process, and enhance user experience of a place, service, or destination.

INTRODUCTION

Effective use of communication technologies has always been integral to the successful implementation of marketing strategies. Internet and Web technology holds an important role in destination marketing because of the information-intensive nature of the tourism industry. Travelers depend on device mediated content to make a decision;

DOI: 10.4018/978-1-5225-5835-4.ch007

they cannot directly experience the destination from a distance as production and consumption of the tourism product happen at the same time. The convergence of information technology with the tourism experience leads to a paradigm shift from tourism to smart tourism where new problems, new experiences and new ways of handling destination image emerge (Hunter, Chung, Gretzel, & Koo, 2015). This convergence along with the rapid evolution of the Internet is an influential factor that shapes travelers' behavior (Kenteris, Gavalas, & Economou, 2009).

In this increasingly autonomous ecosystem of decision-making, knowledge management technologies provide software solutions to allow collaboration and sharing of organizational information. Driven by economic, social and technological change, this domain has grown rapidly since the 90s. Tourism and destination marketing can use knowledge systems and data driven information solutions that facilitate information flow, thus improve customer experience and gear value co-creation. Kim et al. (2009) identify user resistance to implementation of information systems due to the 'status quo bias 'and the switching costs that affect perceived value. This resistance may feed an unfriendly knowledge adoption environment sustained by weak links between research and the tourism industry. The chapter's objective is to fill in this gap with insights that promote understanding and propose user-friendly, technology-based solutions.

Websites are the "hubs" where product, service and company information is shared with the public. It is therefore imperative that their effectiveness in transmitting messages and delivering information is measured and evaluated. A great marketing strategy may never reach its full potential without appropriate performance evaluation to demonstrate the strengths and weaknesses of the company's website. The chapter addresses this equally critical space with a discussion on established models of website evaluation. The purpose is to enlighten stakeholders on the role and progress of these emerging technologies in the e-tourism environment, and establish a reliable frame of reference for industry specialists.

Only creative and innovative companies will survive the competition by embracing a continuous business process of re-engineering (Buhalis, 1998). This process will ensure that vision, rational organization, commitment and training are aligned to empower destination organizations to capitalize on the unprecedented opportunities emerging through ITs.

TECHNOLOGIES IN E-TOURISM

Knowledge Management Technologies in e-Tourism

How a tourism organization manages and communicates its knowledge is a strategic priority. Codifying knowledge ensures deposit for efficient transfer so that appropriate audiences receive information on time.

Semantic web solutions enter the equation because of their relevance to information technologies that enable knowledge transfer through automation and interoperability of applications. Because appropriate interfaces with people in web environments require capturing and codifying explicit knowledge into processable and interdependent chunks of information, the semantic web and its building blocks are put into action. As Livi (2008) suggests, information communication technologies in tourism emerge as information brokers and e-intermediaries, enabling browser functions—navigation and information retrieval—, user discussions, customer-to-company interaction and online purchase actions (Camilleri, 2018a).

Big data, collaboration and consumer web technologies such as portals, discussion boards, blogs and expert systems already impact the tourism industry along the following lines:

- Can deliver more relevant and richer business insights.
- Will contribute to innovation for the industry with new products and services.
- Will improve learning of customer preferences and therefore customer relationships.
- The use of information will help build connections with travelers, anticipating their needs and offering them expected services at the right time.
- Will facilitate immediate reaction.
- Can continuously improve customer experience and decision support.
- Easier and cheaper to process than small data after getting familiar with the appropriate techniques.

Web content in dedicated hotel websites (Hepp, Siorpaes, & Bachlechner, 2006) often does not contain sufficient information that allows potential guests to make a reservation decision without additional communication in different mediums (e-mail or phone call). For semantic web technology to facilitate explicit (automation in information extraction and processing) and implicit information, data must be augmented and re-structured from haystack piles to ontological annotations.

Recommender systems are filter systems that facilitate choices and organize existing information into meaningful predictors of user preferences. RS can carry out a number of functions and have considerable implications in the ways tourism websites operate.

Recommendation engines (systems) can rely on:

1. The properties of the items that a user likes and how they impact other preferences, or
2. The likes and dislikes of other users, which the recommender system applies to compute a similarity index between users and come up with appropriate suggestions.

A combination of both methods leads to a much more robust recommendation engine.

Existing recommender systems in e-Tourism do not only align information with online bookings. To provide added value for both sides of the service continuum, they have to aggregate input from web users and direct it to the appropriate recipients, integrating their cultural features and preferences. Recommender systems applied to websites of DMOs shorten research time and increase time spent on evaluation and planning. They allow organizations to improve their online presence and sales at lower costs compared to private systems that do not take into account all destination parameters or match products/services to specific needs (Rabanser, & Ricci, 2005). RS make use of different business models used in e-tourism: Brokerage, Advertising, Infomediary, Manufacturer, Community or Subscription are matched to suitable recommender systems with personalized interface and content such as TripAdvisor or Booking.Com.

A recommender system can obtain the cognitive state of the user/customer and carry out suggestions to change it, thus increasing the level of customization in the long run. There are five types of recommender systems: 1) content-based; 2) collaborative filtering; 3) demographic; 4) knowledge-based, and; 5) hybrid. Identifiers of elements that the system needs vary according to the type and number of information sources. If we are to identify an existing system or develop a new system in tourism websites, two things must be considered:

1. The layers and functions of architectural design.
   a. **Presentation:** The section that presents information and allows users to interact with the system.
   b. **Services:** Brings together APIs for data mining algorithms, case-reasoning systems, and libraries for environments for scalable performant applications that allow generation of recommendations.

c. **Data Access:** Data extractor and task manager for insert, delete, update and query operations.
d. **Data:** Information that encapsulates metadata provided by the RS such as videos, images, Social Networks, learning object repositories for tourism.
2. The functions of each component.
   a. **Graphical User Interface:** Handles interaction between user/ RS, manages events, validates user input data and handles user requests on HTTP-based protocol.
   b. **Recommendation Algorithms:** Configures implemented algorithm and handles correlation and similarity metrics.
   c. **Data Extractor:** Retrieves information for RS databases using SQL and NonSQL queries.
   d. **Data Provider:** Provides the persistence mechanism information required by the data extractor (Learning Object Repository, Social Networks, Web, Linked data).

Personalized content depends greatly on knowledge acquisition techniques of recommender systems as the basis of the user's profile. Performance of RS is also enhanced by clearly defined shared information and formulation of individual recommendations. Domain knowledge supported by common sets of heuristics can be useful in recommending sources of information (databases, web sources—links, pages crawled—, external events. Recommendation techniques can be very culturally specific: rule filters rank items by order of potential interest; machine-learning employs similarity matching to rank interest; and collaborative filtering groups users with similar preferences in items.

Information contained in web sources that rely solely on human user is a serious shortcoming of existing technologies. Next generation tourism information systems contain semantic web technologies that bring together information repositories to facilitate research, extraction, interpretation and decision making.

Siricharoen (2008) spoke of four prototypical scenarios:

1. **First Scenario:** SEMANTIC SEARCH ENGINE FOR TOURISM
   Current possibilities do not allow for combined data from different tourism areas (e.g. attending a festival plus lodging information. Querying distributed data is allowed by Semantic Search that considers multiple concepts simultaneously (name of festival, nearby places/activities, travel, lodging).
2. **Second Scenario:** BROWSING TOPIC PORTALS
   An intermediate web space with topic/local information is needed to integrate abundant information and exploring possibilities for a particular area. This helps

the user/visitor avoid web pages with overlapping content. Similar websites from authorized sources are included in the census of the present study.

3. **Third Scenario:** SEMANTICS-BASED ELECTRONIC MARKETS
   Match between providers/requesters of tourism services needs a fast pace, adjusted to last minute availabilities, such as late vacancies and last minute offers. The complex character of the touristic product (location, time, quality of hospitality, region, prices) dictates the need for a rich conceptual model to allow the tourism domain benefit of electronic markets.

4. **Fourth Scenario:** WEB SERVICES FOR TOURISTS
   Cross-checking of different databases (date of an event/visit versus time available from personal calendar) to come up with a unique proposal that does not require linear, time consuming search.

Semantic Web technologies provide the perfect toolbox for the area of e-tourism. SW is evolving to a global database with distribution features that require accessibility, trust and credibility. Ontologies are key building blocks of the SW as formal specifications of a shared conceptualization.

To the extent that an ontology structure holds definitions of concepts, binary relationships between concepts and attributes, it draws automatically from human perception of these concepts and their culturally specific interpretation. Semantic annotations are all about deeper and richer associations of meanings, and as such they make machine-readable information more intelligent. Such associations between different categories of tourism related information must take into account places, seasons, activities, transportation, attractions, and other knowledge pieces of varying granularity in order to effectively support navigation, browsing, parametric search, user expectations and ultimately user experience. The merged ontology language DAML+OIL formally represents a domain and the logic behind this representation, which creates the space for considerations related to cultural identity. Because decisions are based on one's own self-conception and positioning into a group, assumptions, process and interpretation of content become culturally specific. Jakkilinki (2005) in his study *Ontology-Based Intelligent Tourism Information Systems: An overview of Development Methodology and Applications* speaks of intelligent plug-ins that allow multiple users to share the ontology as an applet on the web. Ontologies promise a shared and common understanding of tourism concepts that stretches across people and application systems, thus operates at a supra-cultural space of mutual acceptance. Collaborative systems can be conceptualized and operationalized within converging frameworks and value systems.

A space worth examining for the relevance to this study is the *Geospatio-Temporal Semantic Web*, a cluster of geospatial and spatio-temporal ontologies to provide mappings between places of historical and cultural interest (Lytras 2011). Semantic

Web Applications and technologies offer a variety of tools (semantic wikis, web browsers, Content Management Systems) to be picked up and offer, among other, new possibilities for intelligent websites/portals with improved local search, knowledge representation and decision support. Connecting to GTSW extension of the WWW through appropriate technical standards (RDFs, SPARQL, OWLs), interfaces via hyperlinks, hashtags and ontologies, is literally putting the digital landscape of the industry onto a gigantic, open-access map. Providing models and methods to deal with such places of historic/cultural interest will contribute to substantial benefit when searching content using maps in semantic cultural heritage portals. Such portals can be successfully embedded as gateways/external links within National Tourism Websites, Destination Marketing portals and websites of Professional Associations in Hospitality industry. Due to the high volume of online transactions and the diversified market and information sources, the tourism industry can benefit tremendously/substantially from sophisticated E-Commerce and Semantic Web technology.

Tourism Information Systems (TIS) are a new type of business systems that serve and support e-tourism and e-travel organizations, such as airlines, hoteliers, car rental companies, leisure suppliers, and travel agencies. One class of these systems relies on travel related information sources, such as Web sites, to create tourism products and services. The information extracted from these sources can serve as the springboard for a variety of tasks, including dynamic packaging, travel planning, and price comparison.

The development of dynamic packaging applications is particularly interesting. Dynamic packaging can be defined as the combining of different travel components, bundled and priced in real time, in response to the request of the consumer or booking agent.

An effective approach to the development of a dynamic packaging platform encompasses the use of the latest information technologies such as semantic web, web services, and web processes. E-tourism is a perfect application area for semantic web technologies, since information dissemination and exchange are the key backbones of the travel industry.

"How-to" knowledge is less effectively captured and codified by retention techniques than "what-is" and "who knows". Yet it is more actionable and critical to strategic analysis and decision making. Building efficient and sensitive communication tools belongs to the realms of this tacit knowledge that is linked to strategic performance, stems from an elevated awareness of the organizational values/mission, and is based on decision support frameworks that enable articulation and transfer of this knowledge. Decisions on the distinct features of corporate websites result from deploying such virtual decision environments (VDEs) to their full potential to benefit from tools of interactive modelling, "what if" simulation analysis of complex situations. This also is a direct reflection of the organizational identity.

Development of mobile applications is another distinct service that needs to be strategically tackled. Technology is more than ever portable and has homogenizing effects in consumer behavior. It addresses high individualistic needs for flexible and personalized information management, with tourism being an ideal application field. Mobile internet is fast transcending from the top of Maslow's hierarchy (1987) to the middle layers, satisfying essential everyday needs for safety and information. The internet is a sensitive medium recently adopting higher context features and technically capable of providing possibilities for transaction through a website. But to make this transaction happen, it has to take into account several factors besides language and products: navigation modes, tone, pictures, color and text associations. These considerations apply equally to the more traditional desktop or laptop user culture and the tablet/mobile audience of younger age, more information and technology oriented. The emerging mobile recommender systems (Gavalas, Konstantopoulos, Mastakas, & Pantziou, 2014) bring to mobile device users rich tourist experiences, context-aware services and multimedia content tailored to their preferences.

Website Assessment for Operationality, Usability and Competence

Websites are increasingly used as the principal source of organizational information (Camilleri, 2018b). As a consequence they need to be consistently monitored round the clock and evaluated for their quality and performance. Lines of evaluation vary from mechanistic checklist of content authority, accuracy, objectivity, currency, coverage, to the more contextual, quality-oriented approach based on promoting peer- and editorially-reviewed resources, comparison, and corroboration.

In their seminal meta-analysis *Progress in Tourism Management: A Review of Website Evaluation*, professors Law, Qi and Buhalis (2010) refer to the following sets of tools:

1. Faba-Perez, Guerrero-Bote, Moya-Anegon (2005): A technique that compares web page measures (text elements, link formatting, Web Impact Factor).
2. Suh, Lim, Hwang, Kim (2004): Automated tools to analyze numerically measurable data (traffic and time-based data).
3. Cox and Dale (2002): Scoring system with binary classifications for websites.
4. Hardwick and MacKenzie (2003): 3 scoring systems for evaluation of miscarriage websites.
5. Yeung (2004): Longitudinal study of the functional characteristics of commercial websites in Hong Kong.

6. Heldal, Sjovold, Heldal (2004): Combination of branding, human-computer interaction and usability could enhance website evaluation.
7. Liang and Lai (2002): Consumer based approach to derive functional requirements for e-store design, empirical findings. Quality of design has a direct effect on purchasing decision.
8. Kim and Stoel (2004): WebQual scale to examine the dimensional hierarchy of apparel websites, quality of websites selling apparel products could be conceptualized as a 12-dimension construct.
9. Jang (2004): Online information search will become a major trend among travelers.
10. Law and Hsu (2006) online reservations for travel products and services become an important application.
11. Corigliano and Baggio (2006): Quality and performance of commercial websites needs to be monitored.
12. Leung and Law (2006): Longitudinal study, networking was the most popular research area with the highest growth rate. Travel website-related studies have become important to industrial practitioners and academic researchers.
13. Morrison, Taylor and Douglas (2004): Review of application of the Balanced Scorecard method in tourism website evaluation studies, proposed a modified BSC method for future tourism and hospitality website evaluation. Also benchmarking approach combines user perceptions with website performance to help owners identify strengths/weaknesses of their websites and those of their competitors, plus best practices in the industry.
14. Hashim, Murphy and Law (2007): Website design frameworks, five dimensions of website quality based on the most researched online features of tourism and hospitality websites: 1) information and process 2) value added 3) relationships 4) trust 5) design and usability. Most popular attributes of hotel websites: reservations, contact info, promotions, products/services.
15. Law and Bai (2006) review of published articles in respected Journals and conferences (JofInfTech&Tourism, IFITT Intnl Federation for Info Tech and Travel & Tourism), largest publication channels on technology applications in travel and tourism.
16. Buhalis and Law (2008) e-tourism related studies in the past 20 years, predicted the future of e-tourism for the next 10 years.

We are highlighting the Faba-Pérez et al. (2005) model as it carries direct application value. The Web Impact Factor it proposes is a relative indicator, most studied in bibliometric analyses, and is expressed by the fraction

$$WIF = \frac{Number\ of\ the\ web\ space's\ inlinks}{Number\ of\ the\ web\ space's\ pages}$$

where Web Space is defined as pages + sites and sets of pages on other servers
Key points:

1. Informetric Indicators study: a) electronic information available on the Internet and; b) the search and retrieval of info through hypertext links
2. **Citation**→ outlinks and inlinks of web spaces analogous to references and citations of traditional scientific publications

Indicators proposed:
Indicators Based on Formal Characteristics:

1. Number of pages
2. Weight of web spaces according to the weighted sum of their formal characteristics
3. Weight and logarithm of the number of pages

Webometric Measures Based on a Web Space's Links (WI Factor):

1. Inlinks received by web spaces
2. Betweenness, measure of centrality used in Noc Net Analysis that determines to what degree a node acts as intermediary between other nodes by location between them
3. Google page rank (algorithm) for popularity displayed in Google's toolbar for each of the web spaces

- **Pages and Log (Pages):** Number of internal pages associated with each of the Web spaces
- **Weight:** Measure of formal characteristics of web spaces that are determined automatically for each page. Each characteristic is assigned a weight according to their relevance for retrieval of any requested information. Range of weights assigned from -0.5 to 0.3 (desirable and non-desirable characteristics) for the following:

1. **New Pages:** Changed in the last month
2. **External Links:** Are outlinks from the origin Web space to another, greater or lesser number determines "**brightness**" of the originating web space

3. **Metadata:** Presence of different types of META tags. Dublin Core Metadata Element Set DCMES subset consists of 15 elements relating to:
   a. **Content**
      i. Coverage
      ii. Description
      iii. Type
      iv. Relation
      v. Source
      vi. Subject
      vii. Title
   b. **Intellectual Property**
      i. Contributor
      ii. Creator
      iii. Publisher
      iv. Rights
   c. **Aspects of Document Configuration**
      i. Date
      ii. Format
      iii. Identifier
      iv. Language
4. **Main Metadata:** Metadata considered of special relevance for access to the information (Author, Creator, Keywords, Subject, Description, Title, Date)
5. **Hypertextual Density**: Number of HTML links per page of the Web space
6. **Multimedia Density**: Number of multimedia objects per page of the Web space
7. **Small Pages:** Smaller than 3 KB (use Website Page Site Checker)
8. **Broken Links (External and Internal):** Broken outlinks in a web space, possible causes File Not Found, Cannot Connect, Host Not Found, Time Out
9. **Pages with No Title:** Blank, null or white space in the Title HTML tag
10. **Slow Pages:** Larger than 50 KB that take more than 20 or 30 seconds to load
11. **Broken Anchors**: Problems with hypertext linking to places within a document
12. **Links with Non-Critical Problems:** Outlinks in Web spaces that do not function correctly because of minor problems (i.e. temporary or permanent redirect)
13. **Pages with No Image Attributes** (no height, width or Alt attribute assignments)
14. **Old Pages:** Not changed for the last 6 months
15. **Deep Pages:** That require more than four clicks to get to from front page.

Weight formula:

$$Ws = \sum_{i=1}^{n} wixi$$

where *wi* is the weight assigned to the i-th characteristic, n is the number of characteristics of each Web space, *xi* is the number of occurrences of the i-th characteristic.

On the side of qualitative metric systems, we can make the following remarks:

Introducing innovation diffusion theory (IDT) originally proposed by Rogers (1995), and comparing it with the technology acceptance model (TAM), Park and Gretzel (2006), (Information and Communication Technologies in Tourism, 2008) established a model that comprises five measurements: relative advantage, compatibility, complexity, trust, and subjective norm. An additional metric worth considering is the new Fulfillment Related Factor, which refers to the delivery of products and services within a service level promise (Wolfinbarger & Gilly 2003; Field, Heim & Sinha, 2004)

Tourism Website Assessment Tools and the Modified Balanced Scorecard Approach

With the growth of internet marketing it is imperative that performance of organizational websites is measured and benchmarked against competition and industry standards.

Below follows a comprehensive summary of existing literature, a warehouse of tools and models built along different dimensions, performance criteria and evaluators.

Approaches for evaluating tourism and hospitality websites include the modified BSC approach, from its beginning in 1999 to present, as well as other website evaluation approaches. The study classifies them into four groups according to the reason, time, efficiency and effectiveness of the evaluation. It concludes with a call to action for industry leaders, academics and consultants to develop a unified procedure for website evaluation in tourism and hospitality.

Tierney (2000) suggests that maintenance and setup costs, facilitation of improvements, judgement of site performance and comparison to best practices dictate the need for evaluation. Online sales are a good indicator of effective tourism sites; however many destination marketing organizations do not have this feature.

Murphy, Forrest, Wotring and Brymer (1996a) analyzed the websites of 36 hotels and grouped features in functional dyadic categories (promotion/marketing, service/information, interactivity/technology, management, developing a classification system for categories of content.

In another study, Murphy, Forrest and Wotring (1996b) analyzed restaurant websites for specific features such as e-mail, online sales promotion, reservations, frequent specials, coupons, directions, contests), concluding that Web is not sufficiently used to address diverse audiences.

Kasavana et al. (1997) did not evaluate specific sites but rather developed marketing benchmarks for hospitality Websites (audience measurement, audience recall, bandwidth, user friendliness, use of e-commerce, use of new technologies to advance online marketing) without assessing specific sites. Ho (1997) outlined four types of value creation in Websites: timeliness, customization, built-in propositions, and excitement by graphics, in his examination of 1,000 N. American sites from different industries.

Cano and Prentice (1998) traced tourism promotion websites in Scotland and concluded they were underperforming as destination hotspots/marketing tools. Connolly, Olsen and Moore (1998) examine the use of Internet by hotels as a distribution channel and question the return on investment on the significant costs of website development. Kasanava (2002) identifies difficulties in devising specific metrics to measure the effectiveness of a website.

The present chapter traces the timeline of the valuable management approach called modified Balanced Scorecard in the evaluation of tourism and hospitality websites, from its birth in 1999 to present time, starting from the history of its influential predecessor, the original BSC model.

Developed in 1992 by Robert Kaplan and David Norton, the original BSC is an exceptional assessment tool for organizational performance, one that breaks away from the backward looking financial measures and steps into the broader field of measures tied to the organization's vision and strategy. Performance is measured from four perspectives: customer, financial, internal business, and innovation, a holistic view that examines business results as outcomes of cause-effect relationships and captures financial as well as non-financial elements of corporate strategy. Niven (2002) stresses the importance of BSC as a tool that communicates to stakeholders in concrete performance measures how the organization is mobilizing its values to achieve its vision and objectives. The core philosophy of BSC is that *measurement gets things done*. The model embraces an amalgam of lead and lag indicators defined by Niven (2002) as future versus historical performance drivers, integrating the "New Economy" forward thinking with the continuity of tradition and best practices from the past. Balance is achieved by decomposing organizational vision into strategy and then into operations, the receiving end of individual contribution from each member of the organization (Camilleri, 2018c; Rohm, 2002). Evaluation of the model dictates that it is too inward looking, out of step with forward thinking and technology related skills that both require integration of environmental factors and future indicators. In tourism and hospitality, BSC was successfully adopted by hotel chains and lodging services in the United States (1998-1999), raising customer satisfaction and retention.

The need for more systematic website performance measurement was brought up by Morrison, Taylor, Morrison and Morrison (1999), with Taylor suggesting a modified approach of the BSC model for website evaluation across different industries. The revised approach identifies four perspectives for hotel website evaluation: customer, technical, marketing, and internal. Each of these perspectives is operationalized with a set of critical success factors (CSFs), Daniel (1961), Rockart (1979). Hotel websites effectiveness is evaluated on the bases of 25 CSFs according to Morrison et al. (1999; 2004).

Ismail's contribution should be carefully noted for taking the Morrison model at the next level and helping overcome its main limitations. Ismail, Labropoulos, Mills and Morrison (2002). Likert scales encourage subjectivity into responses. Financial aspects such as website ROI are not sufficiently scrutinized, plus the internal perspective was not sufficiently represented, failing to produce a significant number of CSFs related to and controlled by internal audiences/stakeholders.

Blum and Fallon (2002) contend that website evaluation can run along a business axis, a customer axis, and a business/customer combined axis. The business perspective views website as a transformation/transaction tool, the customer perspective focuses on design issues and consumer behavior theory; the combined perspective is the ground where the modified BSC is established. Limitations of the original model include the un-balanced scores for the four dimensions and the one-point-in-time or static analysis which cannot capture the changing dynamics of websites within a time frame.

Ismail et al. (2002) applied the modified BSC model to evaluate the marketing of culture on websites of European national tourism organizations (NTOs). This approach is invaluable as existing literature and forerunner of the present study, because it evaluates the corresponding official tourism portals and websites in Greece, analyzing their cultural information contents and weighing the degree of cultural competence (embedded awareness and sensitivity). Customers become site visitors and evaluation criteria are reorganized into: a) navigation quality; b) ease of contact; c) site attractiveness, and; d) integration of travel and tourism links.

Likert scales were substituted with dichotomous scales to capture presence or absence of site features and remove subjectivity noted in the original study. Kendall's Coefficient of Concordance non-parametric technique was used in this sophisticated approach to recognize type of data, and revealed that countries with rich cultural heritage such as Greece and Portugal did not use Web resources effectively. It is interesting to observe the two countries' Mediterranean subculture and how their common high context, non-linear indicators influence their ability to leverage technology in a detached, rational fashion.

Feng, Morrison and Ismail (2003) used the modified BSC to evaluate content of Destination Marketing Organization websites –and their local tiers--in China and the U.S., measuring Web page design, marketing strategies, marketing information (replaced cultural aspects in the initial model) and technical quality. The results indicated superiority of US DMO websites, particularly in regard to the marketing strategies and information. The modified BSC was also applied by So and Morrison (2002) to evaluate National Tourism Organization websites in East and South Asia. The four perspectives were similar to the Feng et al. (2003) study, weighting the four perspectives for equal contribution to the total score of each NTO website. Countries making the most effective use of their Websites were Singapore, Hong Kong, and South Korea.

The modified BSC has been successfully applied since 1999 to Convention and Visitor Bureau websites under the Certified Destination Management Executive program. Although it was found to be a valid a practical tool, the standard version was further modified and transformed into an improved, more flexible tool to address more users: customers, expert groups, and different industry sectors. New perspectives were added to capture authority, fine quality and responsiveness elements, such as legal compliance, trip planner assistance and link popularity. Other website evaluation models include Content Analysis, employed by the following scholars:

Benchendorff and Black (2000), who evaluate 16 Regional Tourism Authorities in Australia and suggest the Internet Marketing Star concept. The tool evaluates site planning, design, content, and management features.

Blum and Fallon (2002) analyzed 53 websites of Welsh visitor attractions of seven distinct categories according to product, price, promotion, place, customer relations and technical characteristics. They found that some features were not adequately used, such as place for online transactions, promotion and customer relations. Perdue (2001) evaluated ski resorts in North America along four features; quality and speed of site accessibility, ease of navigation, visual attractiveness, and quality of information content. The regression analysis helped test a conceptual model which showed that navigation, visual attractiveness and information content were integral in the perception of a resort through its website.

In the business-to-business context, Evans et al., (1999) introduce a website assessment tool that focuses on five categories: home page, overall design and performance, text content, audio-visual elements, interaction and involvement. In their case study they demonstrate that different audiences weight website elements differently according to their needs and preferences.

It is important that we build a framework that connects all of the above studies along the following functions:

1. Common characteristics between the studies

2. Distinct technical and marketing features
3. Presence or absence of acceptability factors
4. Emphasis on informative content and not the mode of delivery

Other studies evaluated unique characteristics of sites, such as online flight reservation services, namely flight schedules, availability, airfares, online ordering information, by Law and Leung (2002). Jeong and Lambert (2001) used the experimental design model to test eight hypothetical hotel websites for usage rates of relationship marketing functions such as feedback, loyalty programs or value-added services and customized research. Countryman (1999) interestingly applied his study on marketing concepts of state tourism websites in the U.S. for presence of marketing concepts in their design and creation. Evaluation criteria included accessibility, segmentation, positioning, consumer research, content, design and hyperlinks, to conclude that the particular websites do not exhaust the possibilities of the Internet and its interactive nature. The study has shown that market segmentation is not sufficiently integrated to provide specialized information to particular audiences such as travel agents and event planners.

Similarly, Wan, Su and Shih (2000) analyzed the content of hotels and wholesalers' websites in Taiwan, to measure friendliness, variety of information, community and online reservation systems. The study revealed that despite the good user interface, variety of information was rated low; few websites included a virtual community; and finally hotels made use of online reservations much more consistently than tour operators.

Chung and Law (2003) measured performance of Hong Kong hotels according to information provided along five website dimensions: facilities, customer contact, reservations, surrounding area and websites management. Choi (2003) discovered that restaurant Web marketing is at a very premature stage to integrate the e-commerce potential.

Nielsen and Tahir (2002) used a qualitative usability text to measure through a discussion method, different website features and come up with a final screen output.

As per Sterne (2002) and Net Genesis/SPSS Inc. (2003b), success of websites can be measured with nontraditional tools, the e-metrics. These web metrics refer to B2C and B2B sites, measuring respectively units like net dollar/visitor, click stream, customer drop-off rates, customer satisfaction, loyalty index; B2B sites are measured for performance, user efficiency, and average time spent on the website. E-metrics is the extended range of important yardsticks, including customer behavior indices such as stickiness, slipperiness, focus and velocity, costs related to promotional investment in websites, and best customers as determined by recency, frequency and monetary value. There is, however, a diagnosed need for standardized measurement criteria to evaluate tourism and hospitality websites to ensure objectivity and reliability.

Websites are significant investments for companies and transaction platforms with customers through their embedded e-commerce functions; performance and ROI data are paramount as indicators of website ability as a medium.

Although the mBSC model has the potential to provide this standardized approach in the evaluation of tourism and hospitality websites, it also has limitations and can be applied more effectively across different industry sectors and by various groups of evaluators, including but not limited to experts, customers and managerial staff. The enhanced outcome will be a synthesis of multiple perspectives which will help overcome mBSC's limitations, improve inter-rater reliability and validate the internal as well as the external perspective on the functionality of corporate websites. Effectiveness is built on understandability and acceptability, the hidden regulators that are audience-unique, culture specific determinants of successful communication. Timeframes are also important in validating the results of the mBSC approach; instead of capturing one snapshot in time, added value is gained from repeated evaluations and comparison of scores between different points in time (Kim, Morrison, & Mills, 2003; So & Morrison, 2003). Changes in websites can be tracked and progression can be traced with studies involving the time factor. Website-traffic analysis is another useful tool provided by log file analyzer programs (Inan, 2002). The conversion rate, another useful measure used by several DMOs, indicates proportions of website visitors who actually visit the destination. These are valuable tools that are tied to organizational objectives and resources in order to measure accurately the website's capabilities (Kaplan & Norton, Harvard Business Review, 1992).

The above literature discussion assumes indirectly that traffic is a measure of website design and content acceptability. The present paper challenges—or at least questions—this position. Traffic is not necessarily translated to interest, residence, navigation or favorable decisions that result in transactions; it may simply record random web browsing with no further implications. To this point, integration of *cultural sensors* and *hidden regulators* in website design and content, and the ways it can affect *purposeful traffic* and online interactivity has not been systematically addressed.

Overall, there are several evaluation approaches for tourism and hospitality websites:

- Business, Customer, and Combined Business and Customer (Blum & Fallon, 2002)
- Formative (during the time of activity implementation to ensure regularity and appropriate assessment of strengths/weaknesses) or Summative (after activity implementation has been completed and results are documented)

- Efficiency (measured levels of customer activity in response to specific actions—inquiries, coupons, Web page visits) versus Effectiveness (ability to meet and measure pre-defined objectives).

The modified BSC is prominently used in the summative measurement of effectiveness, marketing perspective, customer service and website design as reasons for conducting website evaluation.

CONCLUSION

The author has examined two fundamental information technologies that shape and support digital marketing in the area of tourism: Firstly, the recommender system is a data-driven IT solution that is intended to offer suggestions to customers, users or visitors. Secondly, the control framework traces and quantifies navigation and usability parameters within a website.

Companies such as AirTickets, AirBnB and TripAdvisor adapt their business models on technologies of information filtering systems and business intelligence that transforms raw data to organizational knowledge, and data on user preferences into concrete proposals. Simplicity is key: The user is attracted by the ease of choice, as offers, suggestions and reviews are on immediate view, and purchasing decisions only a few clicks away.

Because of their increased communication role, organizational websites are powerful marketing vehicles: as such, they need to be monitored, updated and evaluated on a regular basis in order to yield data on browsing habits, purchase behaviors and user preferences.

It is important that implications emerging from enabler technologies are recognized and highlighted. Adoption of edge technologies is diffused over longer periods of time as compared to short-lived flashy trends but deliver stable, long-term benefits related to customer satisfaction and effective destination promotion. The key role of research is to facilitate these adoption patterns (Cooper, 2006) and help overcome gaps rooted in the digital divide and the reserved attitude towards knowledge intensive environments.

REFERENCES

Benckendorff, P. J., & Black, N. L. (2000). Destination marketing on the Internet: A case study of Australian Regional Tourism Authorities. *Journal of Tourism Studies*, *11*(1), 11–21.

Blum, V., & Fallon, J. (2001). Welsh visitor attraction web sites: Multipurpose tools or technological tokenism? *Information Technology & Tourism, 4*(3-1), 191-201.

Buhalis, D. (1998). Strategic use of information technologies in the tourism industry. *Tourism Management, 19*(5), 409–421. doi:10.1016/S0261-5177(98)00038-7

Buhalis, D., & Law, R. (2008). Progress in information technology and tourism management: 20 years on and 10 years after the Internet—The state of eTourism research. *Tourism Management, 29*(4), 609–623. doi:10.1016/j.tourman.2008.01.005

Camilleri, M. A. (2018a). Tourism Distribution Channels. In *Travel Marketing, Tourism Economics and the Airline Product* (pp. 3–27). Cham, Switzerland: Springer. doi:10.1007/978-3-319-49849-2_1

Camilleri, M. A. (2018b). Integrated Marketing Communications. In *Travel Marketing, Tourism Economics and the Airline Product* (pp. 3–27). Cham, Switzerland: Springer. doi:10.1007/978-3-319-49849-2_1

Camilleri, M. A. (2018c). Strategic Planning and the Marketing Effectiveness Audit. In *Travel Marketing, Tourism Economics and the Airline Product* (pp. 3–27). Cham, Switzerland: Springer. doi:10.1007/978-3-319-49849-2_1

Cano, V., & Prentice, R. (1998). Opportunities for endearment to place through electronic 'visiting': WWW homepages and the tourism promotion of Scotland. *Tourism Management, 19*(1), 67–73. doi:10.1016/S0261-5177(97)00092-7

Choi, Y. S. (2003). The Web marketing strategy for fine dining restaurants. *Advances in Hospitality and Tourism Research,* Volume 8*: Proceedings of the Annual Graduate Education and Graduate Student Research Conference in Hospitality and Tourism*, 98-99.

Chung, T., & Law, R. (2003). Developing a performance indicator for hotel Websites. *International Journal of Hospitality Management, 22*(1), 119–125. doi:10.1016/S0278-4319(02)00076-2

Corigliano, M. A., & Baggio, R. (2006). On the significance of tourism website evaluations. *Information and Communication Technologies in Tourism, 2006*, 320–331.

Countryman, C. C. (1999). Content analysis of state tourism Websites and the application of marketing concepts. *Advances in Hospitality and Tourism Research,* Volume 4*: Proceedings of the Annual Graduate Conference in Hospitality and Tourism*, 210-218.

Cox, J., & Dale, B. G. (2002). Key quality factors in Web site design and use: An examination. *International Journal of Quality & Reliability Management, 19*(7), 862–888. doi:10.1108/02656710210434784

Daniel, R. H. (1961, September). Management data crisis. *Harvard Business Review*, 111–112.

Evans, J. R., & King, V. E. (1999). Business-to-business marketing and the world wide web: Planning, managing, and assessing web sites. *Industrial Marketing Management, 28*(4), 343–358. doi:10.1016/S0019-8501(98)00013-3

Faba-Pérez, C., Zapico-Alonso, F., Guerrero-Bote, V. P., & Moya-Anegón, F. D. (2005). Comparative analysis of webometric measurements in thematic environments. *Journal of the American Society for Information Science and Technology, 56*(8), 779–785. doi:10.1002/asi.20161

Field, J. M., Heim, G. R., & Sinha, K. K. (2004). Managing Quality in the E-service System: Development and Application of a Process Model. *Production and Operations Management, 13*(4), 291–306. doi:10.1111/j.1937-5956.2004.tb00219.x

Feng, R., Morrison, A. M., & Ismail, J. A. (2003). East versus west: A comparison of online destination marketing in China and the U.S. *Journal of Vacation Marketing, 10*(1), 43–56. doi:10.1177/135676670301000105

Gavalas, D., Konstantopoulos, C., Mastakas, K., & Pantziou, G. (2014). Mobile recommender systems in tourism. *Journal of Network and Computer Applications, 39*, 319–333. doi:10.1016/j.jnca.2013.04.006

Hardwick, J. C. R., & MacKenzie, F. M. (2003). Information contained in miscarriage-related websites and the predictive value of website scoring systems. *European Journal of Obstetrics, Gynecology, and Reproductive Biology, 106*(1), 60–63. doi:10.1016/S0301-2115(02)00357-3 PMID:12475583

Hashim, N. H., Murphy, J., & Law, R. (2007). A review of hospitality website design frameworks. *Information and communication technologies in tourism 2007*, 219-230.

Heldal, F., Sjøvold, E., & Heldal, A. F. (2004). Success on the Internet—optimizing relationships through the corporate site. *International Journal of Information Management, 24*(2), 115–129. doi:10.1016/j.ijinfomgt.2003.12.010

Hepp, M., Siorpaes, K., & Bachlechner, D. (2006). Towards the semantic web in e-tourism: can annotation do the trick? *14th European Conference on Information System (ECIS 2006)*.

Hunter, W. C., Chung, N., Gretzel, U., & Koo, C. (2015). Constructivist research in smart tourism. *Asia Pacific Journal of Information Systems*, *25*(1), 105–120. doi:10.14329/apjis.2015.25.1.105

Inan, H. (2002). *Measuring the success of your Website*. Frenchs Forest, NSW: Pearson Education Australia.

Ismail, J. A., Labropoulos, T., Mills, J. E., & Morrison, A. M. (2002). A snapshot in time: The marketing of culture in European Union NTO Websites. *Tourism, Culture & Communication*, *3*(3), 165–179. doi:10.3727/109830401108750760

Jakkilinki, R., Sharda, N., & Ahmad, I. (2005). *Ontology-based Intelligent Tourism Information Systems: An overview of development methodology and applications*. Paper presented at the International Conference TES2005 (Tourism Enterprise Strategies: Thriving – and Surviving – in an Online Era), Victoria University, Melbourne, Australia.

Jang, S. (2005). The past, present, and future research of online information search. *Journal of Travel & Tourism Marketing*, *17*(2-3), 41–47. doi:10.1300/J073v17n02_04

Jeong, M., & Lambert, C. (2001). Adaptation of an information quality framework to measure customers' behavioral intentions to use lodging Web sites. *International Journal of Hospitality Management*, *20*(2), 129–146. doi:10.1016/S0278-4319(00)00041-4

Kaplan, R. S., & Norton, D. P. (1996). *Using the balanced scorecard as a strategic management system*. Academic Press.

Kaplan, R. S., & Norton, D. P. (1992, January). The balanced scorecard–measures that drive performance. *Harvard Business Review*, 71–79. PMID:10119714

Kasavana, M. L., & Cahill, J. J. (1997). *Managing computers in the hospitality industry*. Educational Inst of the Amer Hotel.

Kasavana, M. L. (2002). eMarketing: Restaurant websites that click. *Journal of Hospitality & Leisure Marketing*, *9*(3/4), 161–178.

Kenteris, M., Gavalas, D., & Economou, D. (2009). An innovative mobile electronic tourist guide application. *Personal and Ubiquitous Computing*, *13*(2), 103–118. doi:10.100700779-007-0191-y

Kim, D. Y., Morrison, A. M., & Mills, J. E. (2003). (in press). Tiers or tears? An evaluation of the Web-based marketing efforts of major city convention centers in the U.S. *Journal of Convention & Exhibition Management*.

Kim, H. W., & Kankanhalli, A. (2009). Investigating user resistance to information systems implementation: A status quo bias perspective. *Management Information Systems Quarterly, 33*(3), 567–582. doi:10.2307/20650309

Kim, S., & Stoel, L. (2004). Apparel retailers: Website quality dimensions and satisfaction. *Journal of Retailing and Consumer Services, 11*(2), 109–117. doi:10.1016/S0969-6989(03)00010-9

Law, R., & Bai, B. (2006). Website development and evaluations in tourism: a retrospective analysis. *Information and communication technologies in tourism 2006*, 1-12.

Law, R., & Hsu, C. H. (2006). Importance of hotel website dimensions and attributes: Perceptions of online browsers and online purchasers. *Journal of Hospitality & Tourism Research (Washington, D.C.), 30*(3), 295–312. doi:10.1177/1096348006287161

Law, R., & Leung, R. (2000). A study of airlines' online reservation services on the Internet. *Journal of Travel Research, 39*(2), 202–211. doi:10.1177/004728750003900210

Law, R., Qi, S., & Buhalis, D. (2010). Progress in tourism management: A review of website evaluation in tourism research. *Tourism Management, 31*(3), 297–313. doi:10.1016/j.tourman.2009.11.007

Liang, T. P., & Lai, H. J. (2002). Effect of store design on consumer purchases: An empirical study of on-line bookstores. *Information & Management, 39*(6), 431–444. doi:10.1016/S0378-7206(01)00129-X

Livi, E. (2009). Information technology and new business models in the tourism industry. In *Emerging Issues and Challenges in Business & Economics: Selected Contributions from the 8th Global Conference* (Vol. 24, p. 315). Firenze University Press.

Lytras, M. D., & Global, I. G. I. (2011). Geospatio-temporal semantic web for cultural heritage. In *Digital culture and e-tourism: Technologies, applications and management approaches* (pp. 12–14). Hershey, PA: IGI Global.

Maslow, A., & Lewis, K. J. (1987). *Maslow's hierarchy of needs*. Salenger Incorporated.

Morrison, A. M., Taylor, J. S., & Douglas, A. (2004). *Website evaluation in tourism and hospitality*. Academic Press.

Morrison, A. M., Taylor, J. S., Morrison, A. J., & Morrison, A. D. (1999). Marketing small hotels on the World Wide Web. *Information Technology & Tourism*, 2(2), 97–113.

Murphy, J., Forrest, E. J., Wotring, C. E., & Brymer, R. A. (1996). Hotel management and marketing on the Internet: An analysis of sites and features. *The Cornell Hotel and Restaurant Administration Quarterly*, 37(3), 770–782.

Murphy, J., Forrest, E., & Wotring, C. E. (1996). Restaurant marketing on the worldwide web. *The Cornell Hotel and Restaurant Administration Quarterly*, 37(1), 61–71. doi:10.1177/001088049603700117

NetGenesis/SPSS Inc. (2003a). *E-metrics. Business metrics for the new economy.* Retrieved June 28, 2003, from http://www.spss.com/netgenesis

Nielsen, J., & Tahir, M. (2002). *Homepage usability: 50 Websites deconstructed.* Indianapolis, IN: New Riders Publishing.

Niven, P. R. (2002). *Balanced scorecard step-by-step: Maximizing performance and maintaining results.* John Wiley & Sons.

Page Size Checker | online Tool to check web page size. (n.d.). Retrieved from https://smallseotools.com/website-page-size-checker/

Park, Y. A., & Gretzel, U. (2007). Success factors for destination marketing web sites: A qualitative meta-analysis. *Journal of Travel Research*, 46(1), 46–63. doi:10.1177/0047287507302381

Rabanser, U., & Ricci, F. (2005). Recommender systems: Do they have a viable business model in e-tourism? *Information and Communication Technologies in Tourism*, 2005, 160–171.

Rogers Everett, M. (1995). Diffusion of innovations. New York: Academic Press.

Rockart, J. F. (1979). Chief executives define their own data needs. *Harvard Business Review*, 57(2), 238–241. PMID:10297607

Rohm, H. (2002). Performance measurement in action. *Perform*, 2(2), 2–5.

Siricharoen, W. V. (2008). Learning Semantic Web from E-Tourism. *Agent and Multi-Agent Systems: Technologies and Applications*, 516-525. doi:10.1007/978-3-540-78582-8_52

So, S.-I., & Morrison, A. M. (2003). Internet marketing in tourism in Asia: An evaluation of the performance of East Asian National Tourism Organization Websites. *Journal of Hospitality & Leisure Marketing*.

Sterne, E. (2002). *Web metrics. Proven methods for measuring Web site success.* New York: Wiley Publishing, Inc.

Suh, E., Lim, S., Hwang, H., & Kim, S. (2004). A prediction model for the purchase probability of anonymous customers to support real time web marketing: A case study. *Expert Systems with Applications, 27*(2), 245–255. doi:10.1016/j.eswa.2004.01.008

Tierney, P. (2000). Internet-based evaluation of tourism web site effectiveness: Methodological issues and survey results. *Journal of Travel Research, 39*(2), 212–219. doi:10.1177/004728750003900211

Wan, C. S., Su, A. Y., & Shih, C. C. (2000). A study of Website content analysis of international tourist hotels and tour wholesalers in Taiwan. *Advances in Hospitality and Tourism Research,* Volume 5*: Proceedings of the Annual Graduate Conference in Hospitality and Tourism Research*, 132-137.

Wolfinbarger, M., & Gilly, M. C. (2003). ETailQ: Dimensionalizing, Measuring and Predicting eTail Quality. *Journal of Retailing, 79*(3), 183–198. doi:10.1016/S0022-4359(03)00034-4

Yeung, W. L., & Lu, M. (2004). Functional characteristics of commercial web sites: A longitudinal study in Hong Kong. *Information & Management, 41*(4), 483–495. doi:10.1016/S0378-7206(03)00086-7

Zeithaml, V. A., Parasuraman, A., & Malhotra, A. (2000). *A Conceptual Framework for Understanding E-service Quality: Implications for Future Research and Managerial Practice.* Marketing Science Institute Working Paper Series, Report NO. 00-115.

Chapter 8
Branding Porto:
An Authentic-Based Approach to Place Identity Theory

Clarinda Rodrigues
Linnaeus University, Sweden

ABSTRACT

Departing from the Porto brand case study, this chapter discusses the concept of destination brand identity from the supply-side perspective. Consequently, it proposes an authentic-based approach to place identity theory, in which destination authenticity is pointed out as a key driver to create a strong place brand identity. Moreover, it is suggested that destination managers should follow an eight-step approach to branding a destination. This dynamic view of place identity, which is supported by a continuous co-creation process involving local and external stakeholders, allows destination brand managers to mirror and reinforce the destination authenticity.

INTRODUCTION

Porto is pointed out as a unique and exceptional city in many ways. Known as the "Cidade Invicta" (unvanquished city), Porto easily seduces its visitors through its history, architecture, culture, gastronomy, trade, encounters and discoveries. Furthermore, Porto has all the charm of towns that happily cohabit with the river, allowing tourists to stroll along river Douro (river of gold), to cruise on the majestic river or to visit the Porto wine caves. Moreover, Porto is also a sea city where you can bath in the Atlantic Ocean and enjoy a fresh drink and tasty food in a cozy esplanade.

DOI: 10.4018/978-1-5225-5835-4.ch008

Nevertheless, to attract tourists to an almost unknown destination in Europe, Porto Municipality had to make efforts in branding the city to the world. One of main steps was taken in 2014 when the municipality created a new visual identity representing Porto as a global city, the city for everyone. This new visual identity, which was awarded in the European Design Awards 2015, reflects creatively the passionate feelings of the city: ancient, very noble, and always local, where you can feel cozy and at home. Moreover, Porto has interestingly been referred in the media as a mysterious holiday destination (The Guardian, 2017), a city full of surprises (The Guardian, 2009), a food and design hub (New York Times, 2016) and a charming destination (Le Figaro, 2014). This is undoubtedly the result of an intense campaign of public relations initiated in 2014 by Porto City Hall, combined with nation branding digital campaigns targeting international tourists always eager for exciting and affordable experiences. Adding to that, well-known events such as Red Bull Race have been used to promote the city as a hub of fun and amusement.

Thus, this chapter´s aim is twofold: firstly, it intends to review the main theories on place branding, with a focus on destination image, destination authenticity and place brand identity. Secondly, it discusses the process of branding authentic destinations through the illustration of the Porto case study. To conclude, this chapter offers novelty by discussing theoretically and empirically how strong place brand identities can be created and how destination authenticity contributes to mirror the destination core values.

PLACE BRANDING

Place branding research has gained much attention among academics and practitioners in the last decades. The rising interest in the field of destinations, nations and cities is deeply anchored on the need to design effective place branding strategies to attract foreign investment, talented or skilled manpower and visitors. Indeed, a destination brand is increasingly considered a valuable asset for urban development and a relevant tool for cities to distinguish themselves and improve their positioning (Camilleri, 2018a; Ashworth & Kavaratzis, 2009). Moreover, extant research shows that tourists usually visit destinations which falls in their destination awareness set (Yousaf, Amin, & Gupta, 2017) and fulfill their hedonic and sensory needs (Agapito, do Valle, & Mendes, 2014).

Nevertheless, it is commonly accepted that destination brands are complex assets and that place brand managers have very little control on the process of branding a city (Yousaf, Amin, & Gupta, 2017). Indeed, destination brands as a product are the result of a continuous and interactive process between government, international funding bodies, private stakeholders and residents (Ashworth & Kavaratzis, 2009).

At different levels, all of these actors contribute to the creation of unique and distinct place brand associations, linked to the economic, social, political, cultural and technological aspects of a place (Camilleri, 2018b). Hence, destination branding is considered a challenging task for place brand managers in developing a sustainable and long-term brand strategy able to protect both the interests of private stakeholders, residents and tourists (Yousaf, Amin, & Gupta, 2017).

DESTINATION IMAGE

Destination image is usually conceptualized as the sum of beliefs, ideas, and impressions that a person has of a destination (Crompton, 1979). Being mental representations of destinations (Baloglu & McCleary, 1999), the perceptions of destinations attributes (Echtner & Ritchie, 2003) are individual and cultural-based (Son & Pearce, 2005).

As a multi-dimensional construct, destination image has been mainly evaluated from different perspectives, including both cognitive, functional and affective aspects (e.g. Agapito, do Valle, & Mendes, 2013). Cognitive destination image is defined as the beliefs and knowledge that tourists have in regard to the destination tangible attributes (Pike & Ryan, 2004; do Valle, Mendes, & Guerreiro, 2012), such as natural and cultural environment and all the unique experiences associated to a particular destination (Wang & Hsu, 2010; Lu, Chi, & Liu, 2015). Moreover, Bonn et al. (2005) postulate that cognitive destination image includes environmental, service and perception of safety dimensions. On the other hand, affective destination is represented by feelings that tourists hold about a destination (Lin, Morais, Kerstetter, & Hou, 2007; Agapito, do Valle, & Mendes, 2013).

In another empirical study conducted by Alcañiz et al. (2009) a functional-psychological continuum was proposed to measure destination image, including natural attractions, local transportations, shopping facilities, accommodation availability and climate as functional destination components; and hospitality/friendliness, service and restaurant quality, and value for money as psychological destination components. In the same vein, Wang and Hsu (2010) examined a Chinese tourism destination and identified five components, namely tourism service quality, amenities, tourism resources, travel environment and supporting factors.

Although most of the research conducted in the last four decades views destination image as a tri-dimensional concept, a multisensory approach is gaining importance amongst tourism scholars. Son and Pearce (2005) and Huang and Gross (2010) conducted qualitative studies on how Australia´s multisensory images are storage and interpreted by tourists. Both studies concluded that Australia´s most memorable visual images are the Kangaroos, the Opera House and Koalas, whereas the most memorable tactile images relate to touching native Australian animals, sand and trees. Interestingly, a recent qualitative study conducted by Xiong et al. (2015) on Phoenix, Hunan Province, China, demonstrated that the destination image was influenced by all the five senses, although visual image received the most attention and tactile image the least attention.

It is commonly accepted that destination image influences tourists' decision-making process, destination price and post-trip evaluations (Zhang, Fu, Cai, & Lu, 2014). Moreover, extant studies in the field of tourism indicate that a positive image impacts on tourists' satisfaction with destinations (Gursoy, Chen, & Chi, 2014; Ryan & Gu, 2007; Sun, Chi, & Xu, 2013; Tasci & Gartner, 2007). Additionally, research shows that tourists' revisit intentions and willingness to spread positive word-of-mouth about a particular destination are directly influenced by destination image or indirectly influenced by destination image through tourists' satisfaction (Castro, Armario, & Ruiz, 2007; Chi & Qu, 2008). A recent meta-analysis of Zhang et al. (2014) shed light on the significance of the impact of destination image on tourism loyalty with varying degrees. More specifically, the authors stressed that the overall image has the greatest impact on tourists' loyalty, followed by affective and conative image. Furthermore, destination image has the greatest impact on composite loyalty, followed by attitudinal and behavioral loyalty.

In sum, destinations are perceived by tourists as a complex amalgam of destination experiential and functional attributes. The perceived destination images are the result of indirect experiences with a destination (e.g. branding campaigns to promote a destination, international press, word-of-mouth, among many others) and direct experiences (e.g. personal experiences in the destination as a result of a trip or a long stay). In this context, it is crucial that the perceptions that tourists hold of a destination as a result of their indirect experiences do not conflict with the perceptions arising from their direct experiences. Otherwise, the process of destination image formation will be seriously harmed by the gap between the place brand identity and the destination image.

DESTINATION AUTHENTICITY

Destination authenticity has been acknowledged as an essential concept in tourism in the last decade (Knudsen, Rickly, & Vidon, 2016; Kolar & Zabkar, 2010). Moreover, the relationships between authenticity and experiences have been widely discussed by tourism scholars (e.g. MacCannel, 1973; Rickly Boyd, 2012; Wang, 1999) and practitioners.

As Zhu (2012) notes there is a call for authenticity in tourism activities, which is a movement that reflects the desires of tourists for genuine and credible representations of culture and heritage. In this regard, three major approaches of authenticity have been proposed in the tourism literature: initially the objective authenticity and constructive authenticity grounded on an object-centered approach and more recently the existential authenticity grounded on a self-searching approach.

It is worth noting that Wang's (1999) approach on existential authenticity suggests a strong sense of the authentic self as a real feeling when engaging in non-ordinary tourism activities, which are free from the societal constraints of daily life and that lead to feelings of self-making, pleasure and relaxation. The author argues that existential authenticity can be divided into two different dimensions: intra-personal authenticity and inter-personal authenticity. The intra-personal dimension of existential authenticity includes the bodily feelings (sensual pleasures, feelings or other bodily impulses), and self-making and self-identity (routinization breaks and adventure feelings). On the other hand, the inter-personal dimension of existential authenticity is mainly related to the sense of authentic togetherness in family ties and touristic Communitas.

Nevertheless, Brown (2013) claims that tourism works as catalyst for existential authenticity. This perspective conceptually shifts focus from the limited timeframe of tourism experiences suggested by Wang (1999) and Steiner and Reisinger (2006). Thus, instead of tourists be plunged back again to inauthenticity at the end of the trip after a temporary release from the inauthenticity of everyday life, Brown (2013) argues that tourism has a more valuable role as a catalyst for authentic living. Indeed, the author explains that tourism offers an opportunity for both pleasure and self-exploration and might work as a therapeutic pause in life.

In the context of cultural heritage tourism, authenticity is pointed out as a critical component of meaningful experiences (Kolar & Zabkar, 2010) that connects tourists to destination attractions. Nevertheless, few empirical studies have explored visitors´ perceptions of authenticity. One notable exception is a study by Lu et al. (2015), whom investigated the influence of perceived authenticity, tourists´ involvement, and destination image on tourists´ experience. Their findings indicated that perceived authenticity and tourists´ involvement in local activities contributed directly to the formation of destination image. Moreover, it was demonstrated that destination image fully mediates the relationship between perceived authenticity and tourists´ satisfaction, whereas it partially mediates the link between tourists´ involvement and satisfaction.

Another recent study by Ram et al. (2016) explored how tourists perceived authenticity in terms of its genuineness when visiting major attractions and demonstrated that places infused with heritage experience value are perceived as more authentic. Similar findings were reported by Budruk (2008) in a study about the Canyon de Chelly National Monument, in Arizona. Indeed, it was demonstrated that the visitors were motivated by the desire to enjoy nature, to experience and learn about Navajo culture, and to socialize with the family. Moreover, visitors perceived Canyon de Chelly as an authentic experience, which was uplifted by the preservation of archaeological resources as well as learning about customs and values of local people, and meeting with locals. Interestingly, the higher the visitors level of place identity and the greater their age, the higher their perceptions of those cultural heritage tourists.

This is consistent with the idea that some people need to look into the past to identify and understand themselves (Steiner & Reisinger, 2006). Using the lens of Lacanian psychoanalysis, Knudsen et al. (2016) argue that authenticity is a fantasy and that it plays a relevant role in tourism. Although life is characterized by fundamental alienation, the authors argue that there are certain places where alienation is absent. Hence, tourists can visit, learn, emulate or even re-create themselves. Moreover, authenticity as a fantasy goes beyond the motivation for experience, it is deeply anchored on a psychological demand of alienation of everyday life.

Moreover, extant research show that perceived authenticity contributes to the formation of a positive destination image (Sönmez & Sirakava, 2002; Naoi, 2004; Frost, 2006). Specifically, a favorable image of a tourism destination triggers positive predisposition to experience authenticity (Jiang, Ramkissoon, Mavondo, & Feng, 2017).

Identity and Authenticity in Destination Image Construction

Mass tourism has been heavily criticized by scholars for generating pseudo-events and commodifying cultures (Steiner & Reisinger, 2006), a process that tends to standardize tourism experiences and prevents tourists from living authentic experiences when in contact with foreign cultures (Marine-Roig, 2015).

It is worth noting that destination image is socially constructed and is the sum of images emerging from several tourist sources (brochures, guidebooks, specialized magazines), from non-touristic images (films, books and documentaries) and from tourists themselves (Camilleri, 2018a; Marine-Roig, 2015). As mentioned earlier, tourists perceive destinations differently and the overall image that they hold about a destination is grounded on a combination of cognitive, affective, conative and sensory dimensions.

As noted by Marine-Roig (2015), a plethora of agents – local agents, independent media, intermediaries, friends and relatives – project the destination image. Consequently, the destination image can be considered a constructive circle in constant spin between the destination (object) and the tourist (subject). Interestingly, Marine-Roig (2015) advocates that identity can be seen as more related to the tourist object (i.e. the destination, the attraction, a particular experience). On the other hand, authenticity is considered as something eminently related to the tourist subject and consequently to the perceived image.

Place brand identity is a significant construct of place branding and has been scarcely examined in the context of tourism. As Ruzzier and de Chernatony (2013) highlighted it is crucial to clearly and consistently communicate with multiple target audiences so that places can distinguish themselves from one another. In that regard, it is interesting to stress that all destination brand touch points are significant in delivering a coherent message to tourists. This assumption reflects the shift from a focus only on how the place brand is currently perceived (brand image) to how a brand wants to be perceived in its encounters (brand identity).

Scholars and practitioners recognize the role of brand identity as a relevant tool to effectively differentiate and manage brands in highly competitive markets (Aaker, 2002; Kapferer, 2012). In that regard, traditionally brand identity is postulated as an inside-out and top-down managerial process, in which brand managers act as communicative cores to convey the brand identity to external and internal stakeholders (Komun, Gyrd-Jones, Al Zagir, & Brandis, 2017). In other words, brand managers task is to clearly specify the brand´s meaning (sender´s side) and to ensure that consumers internalize brand information (receiver´s side) (Kapferer, 2012).

In the last decades, several brand identity frameworks have been developed (Aaker, 2012; de Chernatony, 1999; Kapferer, 2012; Upshaw, 1995) and widely used by scholars and practitioners. One of the most well-known frameworks is the brand identity prism proposed by Kapferer (1986) which simultaneously incorporates the company´s (physical, relationship, personality, culture, and consumer reflection) and the consumers´ inputs (self-image). It is worth noting however that the notions of brand identity, brand positioning and brand image frequently overlap both in practice and in the literature (da Silveira, Lages, & Simões, 2013).

Tourism literature also suggests that place branding strategies usually apply a top-down approach (e.g. Kotler & Gertner, 2002). In other words, the process of building and communicating a brand is leaded by economic or tourism agencies with little involvement of residents and other local stakeholders in the branding process. Consequently, the sense of place is left aside when branding a destination which can threaten the long-term sustainability of a destination brand. Another stream of research suggests a bottom-up approach to place branding, as an effective means to achieve authenticity, brand sustainability and commitment of several local stakeholders (e.g. Aitken & Campelo, 2011). This view is supported by Silveira et al. (2013), who claimed that the increasingly dynamic environment and the rising role of stakeholders as brand co-creators call for the reconceptualization of brand identity. Hence, the authors propose an innovative managerial brand identity framework grounded on the idea that brand identity is dynamic and constructed over time by brand managers and other stakeholders.

In the field of tourism, an identity-based approach to place branding theory have been developed in the last two decades. Nevertheless, most of the models are very limited in their approach to building and developing a destination identity. One notable exception is however the place brand identity model proposed by Ruzzier and de Chernatony (2013).

Illustrated through the case study of Old West Country – a marketing consortium consisting of several rural counties in the state of New Mexico in USA, Cai (2002) proposed a conceptual model that is centered on building destination identity through spreading activation. Their findings suggested dynamic linkages among the 3As (brand elements mix, image building, brand associations) and the 3Ms (marketing activities). Moreover, the model also suggested that spreading activation takes place under the four conditions (4Cs) of existing organic image, destination size and composition, existing induced image and positioning and target markets. Cai (2009) has enhanced his model by stressing the importance of different stakeholders, their long-term relationships and interdependences along all the stages of brand identity development.

In contrast to previous studies focused on the demand-driven, tourists´ perceived destination image, Konecnik and Go (2008) explored the concept of place brand identity from the supply-side perspective. Hence, drawing on Aaker and Joachimsthaler's (2000) brand leadership model, the authors introduced a theoretical framework for developing place identity by investigating the tourism destination brand Slovenia. The proposed framework recognizes the significant importance of input of local Slovenian residents as effective means to support Slovenia´s tourism marketing campaigns.

Balakrishnan (2009) suggested that the destination brand process revolves around five key destination brand components, namely vision and stakeholders' management, target customers and product portfolio matching, positioning and differentiation strategies using brand components, communication strategies and finally feedback and response management strategies. As highlighted by Balakrishnan (2009), destination branding is a long-term process which requires focus and commitment in terms of time, people and resources. Moreover, it may imply changes in policies, culture and mindset. Hence, the proposed framework moves away from conventional visual brand elements and integrates branding at a strategic level.

More recently, Ruzzier and de Chernatony (2013) developed a new place brand identity model, which has its roots in marketing, tourism and sociological theory. The conceptual model focus on the country brand of Slovenia and proposes a coordinated and holistic approach involving key influencers and enactment stakeholders. It incorporates general brand identity elements from de Chernatony's brand identity model, such as vision, values, personality and distinguishing preferences as a key aspect of positioning. Moreover, it includes two additional elements: mission to guide countries´ future directions and benefits that enable countries to attract stakeholders and differentiate one country from other countries.

According to Ruzzier and de Chernatony (2013), brand identity elements (mission, vision, values, personality, distinguishing preferences and benefits) constantly interact in order to fulfill the brand promise. This is achieved through the place brand´s functional and emotional values to create the desired experiential promise. Furthermore, the place brand identity model is grounded on the community-based branding framework (Cai, 2009) and suggests the involvement of all stakeholders to encourage a long-term relationship and interdependence between influential stakeholders and key enactors as they deliver the country´s brand promise.

This dynamic identity-based approach to place branding theory is supported by Kavaratzis and Hatch (2013), who drawn upon the organizational identity model proposed by Hatch and Schultz (2002). Indeed, those scholars argue that the true nature of place branding is anchored on the interaction and dialogue between all the stakeholders. Inevitably, this dynamic view of place identity does not limit the nature of branding to the creation of new logos and the development of catchy slogans. Instead, marketing communication tools are suggested as means to mirror and reinforce the destination values and mission. Moreover, Kavaratzis and Hatch (2013) highlight that the involvement of local communities in place branding is the most authentic basis to express the real soul of a destination. Hence, the co-creation of a destination brand is acknowledged as significant in expressing place identity effectively.

Indeed, destination brands go much beyond an appealing visual identity (Ashworth & Kavaratzis, 2009) and marketing communication efforts. Destination brands are blends of heritage, ambiances and collective experiences that drive emotional resonance in multiple encounters. Hence, the more a destination brand resonates with its stakeholders (locals, tourism agents, organizations and governmental agencies) and reflects the destination values, the more authentic it will be perceived by tourists. Consequently, it is important to align all tangible and intangible brand identity elements in a coherent and appealing manner, so as to convey the authenticity of a destination through effective communication marketing strategies. Against this background, an authentic destination brand is a strong identifier that might impact: (a) on tourists´ decision-making process when choosing a holiday destination; (b) on investors when screening for a place to start their business or install their headquarters or; (c) on foreigners when looking for a new place to live.

Branding a Destination Through Authenticity

Assuming that tourists, investors and residents might be attracted to places that fulfil their hedonic and authenticity needs, the question is raised of how destination

Branding Porto

brand managers should build a strong place brand identity? In other words, how can place brand identity be strategically created and managed in order to engage tourists emotionally?

The brand "Porto." is one striking example of how place brand identity was successfully created by engaging multiple stakeholders. As shown in the case box, Porto Municipality applied a bottom-up approach to place branding facilitating the process of co-creation of its new visual identity.

Although leading the process of building and communicating the Porto brand, the Municipality relied on the commitment of local stakeholders in the branding process. However, this authentic sense of place expressed by local stakeholders was complemented with overall perceptions that external stakeholders hold about the city. By involving internal and external stakeholders in the process of creating its visual identity, the Porto brand was able to express itself through the voices and feelings of those who have experienced the city in many ways. Inevitably, the city as a destination kept faithful to its core values – a cosmopolitan, cozy and friendly city open to the world.

It should be stressed that all the Porto brand identity elements – its mission, its values, its personality – all interacted constantly to deliver the destination experiential brand promise. Porto was never intended to be a destination product, targeting tourists worldwide through massification of its offering. The city kept its authenticity along the centuries and gained awareness through positive word-of-mouth as the result of direct tourism experiences and media. The visual identity, as one component of the overall place brand identity, expressed the soul of the city through a logo and other icons. Moreover, communication tools such as public relations and social media contributed to generate higher levels of destination awareness. In other words, it raised attention to the experiential aspects of Porto as a destination or a place to live – its heritage, its culture, its gastronomy, its natural beauty, among many other aspects.

It is worth noting that local and external stakeholders immediately resonated with the new Porto visual brand identity. Indeed, the visual identity worked as an "umbrella" to express their sense of place. A sense of place that residents express with proud when referring to their city. A sense of place that tourists carry in their hearts after visiting the city and share with others in social media. A sense of place that governmental agencies and private organizations convey in their daily activities. Indeed, this sense of place has been visually translated in the Porto´s new visual identity. Porto´s interactive grid incorporates several icons connected to architecture (Clérigos Tower, Town Hall, House of Music, Ribeira), culture (Serralves, Soares dos Reis Museum, Porto Wine Museum), encounters (Cristal Palace Gardens), landscapes (Douro river and beaches), gastronomy (Porto wine caves, local restaurants and esplanades), festivities (St John festivities, open air concerts), among many others.

In sum, Porto as a destination brand was always faithful to its core values, its mission and its personality. When facing the need to express its visual brand identity, Porto Municipality adopted a bottom-up approach to place branding involving both local and external stakeholders. This dynamic view of place identity did not limit the nature of branding to the creation of a new city logo and the development of a catchy slogan. Instead, the new logo and the overall marketing communication tools were used to mirror and reinforce the destination authenticity. Interestingly, after 2014 Porto´s communication strategy relies mainly on the positive word-of-mouth in the international press and social media. Journalists and tourists, from different nationalities, have shared their experiences of sensing Porto as an authentic destination through its heritage, gastronomy, festivities and events such as the Red Bull Race. Moreover, photographers and writers have acted as brand ambassadors in social media by sharing thrilling stories of how they have *fallen in love* with Porto. Additionally, more and more flight companies operating in Porto describe the city as a charming, romantic and unique destination. Moreover, European Best Destinations awards in 2012, 2014 and 2017 contributed to spread positive word-of-mouth internationally. In conclusion, Porto has relied mainly on different stakeholders to co-create its brand by sharing their feelings and experiences. Allowing the city to be promoted through the eyes of different stakeholders, Porto positioned itself as an authentic and unique destination.

Grounded on the Porto brand case study, the author claims that destination authenticity has a significant role in the place brand identity creation. From a strategic point of view, it is suggested that place brand managers should follow an eight-stepwise approach to market a destination infused with authentic experiential value:

Step 1: Brainstorm with local stakeholders (residents, organizations, companies, municipality, among many others) in order to identify the destination core values and its offering in terms of experiential and utilitarian benefits. The co-creation of a destination brand should be initiated by place brand managers at an early stage to guarantee that all the stakeholders are deeply involved in developing the destination brand as a valuable asset. Moreover, local stakeholders can easily share their sense of place, which will allow place brand managers to define in an authentic manner the destination cores values and how the destination offering could be developed to attract tourists.

Step 2: Collect data from external stakeholders and analyze the perceived destination image. It is commonly accepted that local and external stakeholders perceive and feel destinations differently. Hence, it is crucial to collect all the available data that allows a place brand manager to see the destination through the eyes of external stakeholders (e.g. tourists, journalists, writers, photographers, etc).

That data is available in different formats such as pictures, films, articles, blogs, social media, among many others.

Step 3: Discuss if and how the intended brand identity matches with the perceived destination image. After collecting all the available data from external stakeholders, place brand managers should analyze the beliefs, ideas, and impressions that external stakeholders have of a destination. After clearly identified the destination image, place brand managers can cross it with the intended place brand identity discussed previously with local stakeholders. If a match between the intended place brand identity and the destination image is identified, it means that authenticity is a common denominator. The unmatched items should be thoroughly analyzed, as well the (dis)advantages of incorporating them or not in the intended place brand identity.

Step 4: Elaborate a briefing to support the process of visual identity creation. After the place brand identity is clearly defined, place brand managers are advised to write a briefing to advertising agencies or graphic designers. The briefing should contain detailed information about: (a) the place brand identity; (b) the research conducted to create the place brand identity and; (c) how visual identity should reflect the place brand identity.

Step 5: Involve local stakeholders in the process of choosing the new visual identity. Since the new visual identity should reflect the place brand identity discussed with local stakeholders in Step 1, it is crucial to involve them in the final decision-making process. Achieving a consensus in this step will also guarantee that local stakeholders act as destination ambassadors throughout all the process.

Step 6: Communicate the new visual identity of the destination by involving several local and external stakeholders. The communication of the new visual identity is a very important step and should be carefully organized to meet its objectives. Engaging local and external stakeholders in catchy and unique public events may generate positive word-of-mouth and elicit strong emotional feelings towards the destination brand.

Step 7: Define the communication strategy anchored on an authentic destination offering. In order to guarantee that the destination brand is perceived as authentic, place brand managers should guarantee that there is a good match between the tourism offerings and the communication strategy. Moreover, allowing local and external stakeholders to promote the destination, will contribute to create place brand awareness and a strong and authentic destination image.

Step 8: Assess continuously the place brand identity and the destination image to guarantee authenticity when delivering the brand promise. Being the destination brand part of a dynamic and competitive environment, it is crucial to assess both place brand identity and destination image at least every two years. Furthermore, having a visual identity that is flexible allows to continuously discover, experience and promote the destination in completely different ways without losing its authenticity.

In this context, it is crucial that the perceptions that tourists hold of a destination as a result of their indirect experiences do not conflict with the perceptions arising from their direct experiences. Otherwise, the process of destination image formation will be seriously harmed by the gap between the place brand identity and the destination image.

CONCLUSION

Attracting tourists to an almost unknown destination entails great challenges to place brand managers. How can a destination brand stand out in the crowd and make itself attractive to tourists, investors or people looking for a new place to live or settle a business? One way is to market the destination as unique and authentic.

Indeed, the rising interest on place branding is linked to the need to design more effective place branding strategies. Multiple reasons justify this political need: attract foreign investment, talented or skilled manpower and visitors. Consequently, a destination brand is considered a valuable asset for urban development and significant investments have been made worldwide to promote several places.

Nevertheless, destination brands as a product are the result of a continuous and interactive process between governmental agencies and a plethora of stakeholders. At different levels, the stakeholders contribute to the creation of unique and distinct place brand associations, which are linked to the economic, social, cultural, political and technological aspects of the place. In order to develop a sustainable and long-term place brand strategy, it is crucial however to reflect an authentic sense of place into a strong and coherent place brand identity.

Authentic destinations rely on its core values, mission and personality to convey its place brand identity. From a strategic point of view, authentic destinations express its brand promise consistently in all brand touching points. The destination brand does not rely on the massification of tourism as a product. Instead, it grows in a sustainable manner relying on the multiple and daily actions of its internal and external stakeholders.

Departing from the Porto brand case study, this chapter discussed the concept of place brand identity from the supply-side perspective. Consequently, it is proposed an authentic-based approach to place identity theory, in which destination authenticity is pointed out as a key driver to create a strong place brand identity. Moreover, it is suggested that place brand managers should follow an eight-stepwise approach to branding a destination. This dynamic view of place identity, which is supported by a continuous co-creation process involving local and external stakeholders, allows place brand managers to mirror and reinforce the destination authenticity.

Case Study Porto: A City Opened to the World

Porto means harbor. A harbor that is open to the world, to new cultures and to new ideas. In 2012, during the mandate of the Mayor Rui Rio, Porto was elected the Best European Destination. It was the first international recognition of a city that combines history, modern and ancient architecture, gastronomy and wines, and authenticity in welcoming tourists. All of these ingredients, together with low cost flights offerings and a new airport, attracted a bunch of tourists to visit a peripheral and unknown European city. Indeed, Porto has benefited from being a safe place in terms of terrorism and natural catastrophes, at the same time it offers a low-cost living style.

As a cosmopolitan city, Porto is considered nowadays an attractive place to visit, live, study and work. Recent market research studies show that there is an increase in the total number of stays, price paid by each stay and expenditures. Spanish, followed by French and Brazilian, are among the majority of tourists that visit Porto. It should be stressed that Porto benefited strongly of having diversified its flight connections in the last years though regular companies such as Lufthansa, Turkish Airlines, United Airlines, Canada Airlines, Iberia, British Airlines, KLM and Air France, among many others.

Another relevant tourism segment concerns young and well qualified tourists, who looks to Porto as a weekend destination and wants mainly to enjoy its bars, pubs and discos. But Porto has more to offer to young people, especially the ones working and living in the city. With a thrilling atmosphere, the city is both a hub for start-ups investment and a place to enjoy life at its fullest. Indeed, many young tech entrepreneurs are buying old buildings in the city center and reconverting them into their offices.

Interestingly, the city welcomes around 3500 Erasmus students yearly. Most of these students are said to have fallen in love by the city and are good ambassadors, promoting the city worldwide when they return to their home country. Indeed, Porto University is considered by the City Hall a relevant partner in promoting the city as a tourist destination and a place to live.

Porto City Hall: A New Political Paradigm

In 2014, Rui Moreira was elected Mayor of Porto City Hall. Being an independent, with an entrepreneurial background, he easily attracted international media attention.

Soon after his election, his photo was published in the cover page of New York Times. Many other interviews followed in Liberation, Le Monde, El Pais, among many other international media. Being very charismatic, fluent in several languages and an independent politician, Rui Moreira started to be invited as a speaker to attend several international conferences. This economic diplomacy, combined with marketing campaigns in traditional and digital media, facilitated the brand awareness towards Porto as a destination.

In the same year, Porto was awarded the Best European Destination for the second time. In parallel, à shift in the political paradigm took place calling for the creation of a strong place brand with a unique visual brand identity. A brand that goes beyond the political interests of the municipality. A brand that will have the shortest statement in the world – Porto. It stands by itself!

Porto

The creation of the visual identity of Porto began many months before its presentation. The process started with the claim that Porto City Hall needed a new logo, which could easily satisfy the ambition to have a stronger corporate visual identity. Nevertheless, the Mayor of the Porto City Hall and some members of his team, understood the need as a more challenging task. Would it be possible to graphically sum up Porto? Would it be possible to create a visual identity that mirrors Porto´s soul? Indeed, Porto had never relied on a strong visual identity to brand itself as a unique destination as other cities such Amsterdam and New York. Although, Porto as a destination benefited already from some brand awareness, obtained mainly from its election in 2012 as the Best European Destination, more efforts were needed to promote the city effectively worldwide.

The point of departure started with a discussion of what Porto was as a destination brand. This reflection took several months and involved several members of the Porto City Hall, including its Mayor Rui Moreira. Porto was scanned through the eyes of the City Hall members and through the eyes of outsiders, such as films, videos and photographs available online. A plethora of perspectives on Porto, allowed the City Hall team to realize that the City Hall was part of the Porto brand. It lived side by side with a vibrant city where tourists arrived in low-cost flights and sailed in high-cost cruises, strolled around the city to enjoy its architecture, visited the Porto wine caves, enjoyed both traditional and international food, lost themselves at Saint John festivities, relaxed on the armchairs of the House of Music, Tivoli and Coliseum, immersed themselves in museums and cultural foundations such as Serralves, went to the local market Bolhão, or/and ended up in each other´s arms in the romantic gardens of the Cristal Palace.

Branding Porto

As the result of the brainstorming process, it was believed that Porto was very concrete and immaterial at the same time. Porto was linked to its heritage, to its people, to the cosmopolitan modernity of its school of architecture, but it was much more than that. Only a strong visual brand identity could reflect its real core brand values. Consequently, a briefing was produced by the Communication Adviser to the Mayor, Nuno Nogueira Santos, and sent to ... designers.

The briefing stated that the Porto brand should be simple and express Porto as a destination, but not through a single figurative iconographic element such as Clérigos Tower or Luis I Bridge. Additionally, the new visual identity should also incorporate corporate elements as the City Hall, its services and its municipal companies. Moreover, it should be contemporary, flexible, international, reflect Porto´s cultural and heritage value and ... most of all convey emotions and love for the city. This view on Porto as a brand reflected the Porto City Hall´s ambition to move beyond the corporate image to a broader concept of a destination brand. On the other hand, it was a provocative claim and it required the acceptance of different stakeholders, from the City Hall to other municipal companies, from its residents to private investors, from tourism agencies to the tourists themselves.

The designer Eduardo Aires was given the task of interpreting the Porto brand and to create a new visual identity. The visual identity program aimed at defining and identifying Porto – its nature and its soul. Having lived in Porto for over 35 years, Eduardo Aires had a relationship of proximity with the city, a sense of belonging that was crucial to understand the branding challenge. One of the first tasks was to understand how other city stakeholders perceived the city and what was more salient in their perception. Interestingly, a collective consensus became clear to the designer: there was a shared feeling around several iconic urban elements such as the bridges, Clérigos Tower, House of Music, Pavilhão Rosa Mota, Ribeira´s picturesque houses, Douro river, Port wine or the St John´s festivities in summer time. This iconic web reflected all the essence of the city.

Hence, the designer decided to express the ancient city in only one word – "Porto." In this regard, the word and image have juxtaposed and become one single entity giving shape to a simplistic but strong statement. The typographically image is a block in which the five characters – Porto – are very close together in a very sensual manner. Indeed, there is no kind of disruptive design discourse in the word Porto, since all the letters intertwine together in a harmonious manner. The lettering represents the city in a neutral way, which allows the logo to be timeless. This is crucial to offer the brand Porto to live beyond the scope of a specific municipal government – "the city before the City Hall". Furthermore, the word Porto was easy to spell and to memorize in several international markets, which stressed its elasticity. Finally, the designer proposed to add a dot to the word Porto. The city of Porto is no longer abstract, is unique and different – it is Porto. Period. It is worth noting that the dot is the only universal character that is represented graphically in the same way in all the languages. Thus, "Porto." was easily understood and appreciated in many international markets where the brand was promoted as an European destination.

Having "Porto." as a departure point, the designer decided to use the word as a magnet that attracts everything around the city. Consequently, several pictograms were created representing a plethora of iconic monuments, places, experiences and activities that brings life to the city. Additionally, the pulse of Porto was represented by a grid that intertwines all of its elements into a city route.

The above-mentioned proposal won the City Hall contest to create a new visual brand identity. The visual brand identity is anchored on a visual element, which is typographically clean, legible and without connotations besides the word itself. Porto. Period is the pure expression of the city authenticity and uniqueness. Moreover, the pictograms reflect the city experiences and interests and add dynamism to the visual brand identity. In conclusion, it was not the City Hall that got a new logo but Porto that had its brand as a destination. Most interestingly, this new visual brand identity was well accepted by politics, private stakeholders, tourism operators, tourists and residents, among many others. It is evident that Porto brand was able to reflect the core values of the city and engage emotionally its stakeholders. Being so authentic made it possible to be accepted nationally and internationally.

Today, Porto brand is a vehicle of promotion by itself due to its several design awards. It called the international attention in so many ways in the international press and it has been copied as well. Nevertheless, it is a reason of proud to Porto citizens, municipality employees and many immigrants around the world. Some even asked to keep it close to their heart and asked for a T-Shirt! It seems that most of them have identified themselves with the simplicity and authenticity of the city. Porto as a destination brand stands as an example of an open system where anyone can co-create by adding new elements. A dynamic system that allows to continuously discover the city and experience it in completely different ways!

REFERENCES

Aaker, D. A. (2002). *Building strong brands*. New York, NY: Free Press.

Aaker, D. A., & Joachimsthaler, E. (2000). *Brand leadership*. New York: The Free Press.

Agapito, D., do Vale, P., & Mendes, J. (2014). The sensory dimension of tourist experiences: Capturing meaningful sensory-informed themes in Southwest Portugal. *Tourism Management, 42*, 224–237. doi:10.1016/j.tourman.2013.11.011

Agapito, D., do Valle, P., & Mendes, J. (2013). The cognitive-affective-conative model of destination image: A confirmatory analysis. *Journal of Travel & Tourism Marketing*, *30*(5), 471–481. doi:10.1080/10548408.2013.803393

Aitken, R., & Campelo, A. (2011). The fours Rs of place branding. *Journal of Marketing Management*, *27*(9), 913–933. doi:10.1080/0267257X.2011.560718

Alcañiz, E. B., García, I. S., & Blas, S. (2009). The functional psychological continuum in the cognitive image of a destination: A confirmatory analysis. *Tourism Management*, *30*(5), 715–723. doi:10.1016/j.tourman.2008.10.020

Ashworth, G., & Kavaratzis, M. (2009). Beyond the logo: Brand management for cities. *Journal of Brand Management*, *16*(8), 520–531. doi:10.1057/palgrave.bm.2550133

Balakrishnan, M. S. (2009). Strategic branding of destinations: A framework. *European Journal of Marketing*, *43*(5/6), 611–629. doi:10.1108/03090560910946954

Balakrishnan, M. S. (2009). Strategic branding of destinations: A framework. *European Journal of Marketing*, *43*(5/6), 611–629. doi:10.1108/03090560910946954

Baloglu, S., & McCleary, K. W. (1999). A model of destination image formation. *Annals of Tourism Research*, *26*(4), 868–897. doi:10.1016/S0160-7383(99)00030-4

Bonn, M. A., Joseph, S. M., & Dai, M. (2005). International versus domestic visitors: An examination of destination image perceptions. *Journal of Travel Research*, *43*(3), 294–301. doi:10.1177/0047287504272033

Brown, L. (2013). Tourism: A catalyst for existential authenticity. *Annals of Tourism Research*, *40*, 176–190. doi:10.1016/j.annals.2012.08.004

Budruk, M., White, D. D., Wodrich, J. A., & Van Riper, C. (2008). Connecting Visitors to People and Place: Visitors' Perceptions of Authenticity at Canyon de Chelly National Monument, Arizona. *Journal of Heritage Tourism*, *3*(3), 185–202. doi:10.1080/17438730802139004

Cai, L. A. (2002). Cooperative branding for rural destinations. *Annals of Tourism Research*, *29*(3), 720–742. doi:10.1016/S0160-7383(01)00080-9

Cai, L. A. (2009). Tourism branding in a social exchange system. In L. A. Cai, W. C. Gartner, & A. M. Munar (Eds.), *Tourism branding: Communities in action* (pp. 89–104). Emerald Group Publishing Limited. doi:10.1108/S2042-1443(2009)0000001009

Camilleri, M. A. (2018a). The Tourism Industry: An Overview. In *Travel Marketing, Tourism Economics and the Airline Product* (pp. 3–27). Cham, Switzerland: Springer. doi:10.1007/978-3-319-49849-2_1

Camilleri, M. A. (2018b). The Marketing Environment. In *Travel Marketing, Tourism Economics and the Airline Product* (pp. 3–27). Cham, Switzerland: Springer. doi:10.1007/978-3-319-49849-2_1

Castro, C. B., Armario, E. M., & Ruiz, D. M. (2007). The influence of market heterogeneity on the relationship between a destination's image and tourists' future behavior. *Tourism Management*, *28*(1), 175–187. doi:10.1016/j.tourman.2005.11.013

Chi, C. G.-Q., & Qu, H. (2008). Examining the structural relationships of destination image, tourist satisfaction and destination loyalty: An integrated approach. *Tourism Management*, *29*(4), 624–636. doi:10.1016/j.tourman.2007.06.007

Crompton, J. L. (1979). An Assessment of the Image of Mexico as a Vacation Destination and the Influence of Geographical Location upon that Image. *Journal of Travel Research*, *17*(4), 18–24. doi:10.1177/004728757901700404

Da Silveira, C., Lages, C., & Simões, C. (2013). Reconceptualizing brand identity in a dynamic environment. *Journal of Business Research*, *66*(1), 28–36. doi:10.1016/j.jbusres.2011.07.020

De Chernatony, L. (1999). Brand management through narrowing the gap between brand identity and brand reputation. *Journal of Marketing Management*, *15*(1–3), 157–179. doi:10.1362/026725799784870432

Do Valle, P. O., Mendes, J., & Guerreiro, M. (2012). Residents' participation in events, events image, and destination image: A correspondence analysis. *Journal of Travel & Tourism Marketing*, *29*(7), 647–664. doi:10.1080/10548408.2012.720151

Echtner, C. M., & Ritchie, J. R. B. (2003). The meaning and measurement of destination image. *Journal of Tourism Studies*, *14*(1), 37–48.

European Best Destinations. (2017). Retrieved October 1, 2017, from https://www.europeanbestdestinations.com/best-of-europe/european-best-destinations-2017/

Frost, W. (2006). Brave hearted Ned Kelly: Historic films, heritage tourism and destination image. *Tourism Management*, *27*(2), 247–254. doi:10.1016/j.tourman.2004.09.006

Gursoy, D., Chen, J., & Chi, C. G.-Q. (2014). Theoretical examination of destination loyalty formation. *International Journal of Contemporary Hospitality Management*, *26*(5), 809–827. doi:10.1108/IJCHM-12-2013-0539

Hatch, M. J., & Schultz, M. (2002). The Dynamics of Organisational Identity'. *Human Relations*, *55*(8), 989–1018. doi:10.1177/0018726702055008181

Huang, S. S., & Gross, M. J. (2010). Australia's destination image among mainland Chinese travelers: An exploratory study. *Journal of Travel & Tourism Marketing*, *27*(1), 63–81. doi:10.1080/10548400903534923

Jiang, Y., Ramkissoon, H., Mavondo, F. T., & Feng, S. (2017). Authenticity: The Link Between Destination Image and Place Attachment. *Journal of Hospitality Marketing & Management*, *26*(2), 105–124. doi:10.1080/19368623.2016.1185988

Kapferer, J.-N. (2012). *The new strategic brand management. Advanced insights and strategic thinking*. London: Kogan Page.

Kavaratzis, M., & Hatch, M. J. (2013). The dynamics of place brands: An identity-based approach to place branding theory. *Marketing Theory*, *13*(1), 69–86. doi:10.1177/1470593112467268

Knudsen, D. C., Rickly, J. M., & Vidon, E. S. (2016). The fantasy of authenticity: Touring with Lacan. *Annals of Tourism Research*, *58*, 33–45. doi:10.1016/j.annals.2016.02.003

Kolar, T. & Zabkar, V. (2010). A consumer-based model of authenticity: An oxymoron or the foundation of cultural heritage marketing? *Tourism Management*, *31*(5), 652–664. doi:. tourman.2009.07.01010.1016/j

Konecnik, M., & Go, F. (2008). Tourism destination brand identity: The case of Slovenia. *Journal of Brand Management*, *15*(3), 177–189. doi:10.1057/palgrave.bm.2550114

Kornum, N., Gyrd-Jones, R., Al Zagir, N., & Brandis, K. A. (2017). Interplay between intended brand identity and identities in a Nike related brand community: Co-existing synergies and tensions in a nested system. *Journal of Business Research*, *70*(January), 432–440. doi:10.1016/j.jbusres.2016.06.019

Kotler, P., & Gertner, D. (2002). Country as brand, product and beyond: A place marketing and brand management perspective. *Journal of Brand Management*, *9*(4/5), 249–261. doi:10.1057/palgrave.bm.2540076

Le Figaro. (2014). Retrieved October 1, 2017, from http://madame.lefigaro.fr/art-de-vivre/porto-insolite-charmante-240414-851138

Lin, C. H., Morais, B., Kerstetter, D. L., & Hou, J. S. (2007). Examining the Role of Cognitive and Affective Image in Predicting Choice across Natural, Developed, and Theme-Park Destinations. *Journal of Travel Research, 46*(2), 183–194. doi:10.1177/0047287507304049

Lu, L., Chi, C. G., & Liu, Y. (2015). Authenticity, involvement, and image: Evaluating tourist experiences at historic districts. *Tourism Management, 50*, 85–96. doi:10.1016/j.tourman.2015.01.026

MacCannell, D. (1973). Staged authenticity: Arrangements of social space in tourist settings. *American Journal of Sociology, 79*(3), 589–603. doi:10.1086/225585

Marine-Roig, E. (2015). Identity and authenticity in destination image construction. *Anatolia, 26*(4), 574–587. doi:10.1080/13032917.2015.1040814

Moreira, R., Santos, N. N., & Aires, E. (2014). *Porto*. Porto: Câmara Municipal do Porto.

Naoi, T. (2004). Visitors' evaluation of a historic district: The roles of authentic city and manipulation. *Tourism and Hospitality Research, 5*(1), 45–63. doi:10.1057/palgrave.thr.6040004

New York Times. (2016). Retrieved October 1, 2017, from https://www.nytimes.com/2016/02/10/t-magazine/travel/porto-portugal-hotels-galleries-restaurants.html

Pike, S., & Ryan, C. (2004). Destination positioning analysis through a comparison of cognitive, affective, and conative perceptions. *Journal of Travel Research, 42*(4), 333–342. doi:10.1177/0047287504263029

Ram, Y., Björk, P., & Weidenfeld, A. (2016). Authenticity and place attachment of major visitor attractions. *Tourism Management, 52*, 110–122. doi:10.1016/j.tourman.2015.06.010

Rickly Boyd, J. (2012). Authenticity & Aura: A Benjaminian approach to tourism. *Annals of Tourism Research, 30*(1), 269–289. doi:10.1016/j.annals.2011.05.003

Ruzzier, K., & de Chernatony, L. (2013). Developing and applying a place brand identity model: The case of Slovenia. *Journal of Business Research, 66*(1), 45–52. doi:10.1016/j.jbusres.2012.05.023

Ryan, C., & Gu, H. (2007). Destination branding and marketing: the role of marketing organisations. In H. Oh (Ed.), *The handbook of destination marketing*. Oxford, UK: Elsevier.

Son, A., & Pearce, P. (2005). Multi-faceted image assessment. *Journal of Travel & Tourism Marketing*, *18*(4), 21–35. doi:10.1300/J073v18n04_02

Sönmez, S., & Sirakaya, E. (2002). A distorted destination image? The case of Turkey. *Journal of Travel Research*, *41*(2), 185–196. doi:10.1177/004728702237418

Steiner, C. J., & Reisinger, Y. (2006). Understanding Existential Authenticity. *Annals of Tourism Research*, *33*(2), 299–318. doi:10.1016/j.annals.2005.08.002

Sun, A., Chi, C. G.-Q., & Xu, H. (2013). Developing destination loyalty: The case of Hainan Island, China. *Annals of Tourism Research*, *43*, 547–577.

Tasci, A. D. A., & Gartner, W. C. (2007). Destination image and its functional relationships. *Journal of Travel Research*, *45*(4), 413–425. doi:10.1177/0047287507299569

The Guardian. (2017). Retrieved October 1, 2017, from https://www.theguardian.com/travel/2017/jul/31/destination-unknown-the-new-way-to-book-a-mystery-holiday-srprs-me

Upshaw, L. (1995). *Building brand identity*. New York: John Wiley.

Wang, C., & Hsu, M. K. (2010). The relationships of destination image, satisfaction, and behavioral intentions: An integrated model. *Journal of Travel & Tourism Marketing*, *27*(8), 829–843. doi:10.1080/10548408.2010.527249

Wang, N. (1999). Rethinking authenticity in tourism experience. *Annals of Tourism Research*, *26*(2), 349–370. doi:10.1016/S0160-7383(98)00103-0

Xiong, J., Hashim, N. H., & Murphy, J. (2015). Multisensory image as a component of destination image. *Tourism Management Perspectives*, *14*, 34–41. doi:10.1016/j.tmp.2015.03.001

Yousaf, A., Amin, I., & Gupta, A. (2017). Conceptualising Tourist Based Brand-Equity Pyramid: An Application of Keller Brand Pyramid Model to Destinations. *Tourism and Hospitality Management*, *23*(1), 119–137. doi:10.20867/thm.23.1.1

Zhang, H., Fu, X., Cai, L. A., & Lu, L. (2014). Destination image and tourist loyalty: A meta-analysis. *Tourism Management*, *40*, 213–223. doi:10.1016/j.tourman.2013.06.006

Zhu, Y. (2012). Performing heritage: Rethinking authenticity in tourism. *Annals of Tourism Research*, *39*(3), 1495–1513. doi:10.1016/j.annals.2012.04.003

Chapter 9
Buxton and the Peak District:
Attracting Visitors to the Water Festival

Jessica Maxfield
University of Derby, UK

Peter Wiltshier
University of Derby, UK

ABSTRACT

This chapter is designed to analyze and interpret the demand from a new and anticipated international visitor market to the small market and spa town of Buxton, Derbyshire. It offers an audience development plan for the newly renovated Crescent Hotel and Spa (CHS). The hotel is currently in the final stages of re-development following a major refurbishment to a culturally important, both environmentally and socially sensitive, icon in Buxton. Benefits to the town include heightened awareness of tourism's contribution, through income from staying visitors and a resultant boost to the incomes of a range of stakeholders in the supply chain. A secondary analysis of two case studies, best practices of Harrogate and Bath, has been considered as these are both similar spa towns. The chapter concludes with several recommendations for the CHS to encourage international tourists to visit and stay a while.

INTRODUCTION

This chapter is designed to analyse and interpret the demand from a new and anticipated international visitor market to the small market and spa town of Buxton, Derbyshire through the offer of a water festival. The Crescent Hotel and Spa (CHS) is currently in the final stages of re-development following a major refurbishment to a culturally

DOI: 10.4018/978-1-5225-5835-4.ch009

Copyright © 2019, IGI Global. Copying or distributing in print or electronic forms without written permission of IGI Global is prohibited.

important, both environmentally and socially sensitive, icon in Buxton. An audience development model (ADM) will be developed to identify ways to attract a new type of tourist to Buxton. The purpose of this study is to: (a) adopt the concept of a water festival through an ADM; (b) to compare Buxton to similar spa towns in the UK and; (c) to analyse key international markets (Camilleri, 2018a,b). This analysis and adoption of the festival are important to determine the success rate diversification in Buxton. Several UK destinations have successful festival/ event tourism and as Buxton is developing a new concept for this market it is important to determine what key competitors have done in the past to develop a strong diversification strategy for tourism success. Therefore, this chapter examines the impact of a new water festival, as this activity could attract new tourists to Buxton and the Peak District.

BACKGROUND

Buxton is located in the heart of the Peak District National Park and is the oldest and most visited National Park in the UK. Buxton currently caters for; outdoor/ walking tourists, cyclists; as there are many trails within and around the area; day trippers and lastly; wellness tourists as this is a developing tourism segment (Visit Buxton, 2016). Buxton offers a range of activities and has a wide number of accommodation types to meet the demand of many tourism segments (Visit Buxton, 2016; Bill, 2010), however, the CHS will be the first five-star hotel and resort in the area, therefore implying a change to the demand for the town. Buxton has a population of 24,000 people and has a reputation as 'The Bath of the North', this is due to Buxton being situated on thermal springs. Each year the town receives 1.3 million visitors, which generates £74 million to the local economy; mostly from food and beverage retailers (High Peak Borough Council, 2012).

Water Festival

The CHS is a grade 1 listed heritage building and renovation work started in April 2016, the work is expected to last for 20 months to restore the whole building. Six months after the start date the pump room was finished and is currently used as a venue for meetings at which the community is updated on the progress of the renovation of the building. Once the renovations are completed this will become the reception area for the visitor centre. The finish date is anticipated to be 2019. The funding for the project has come from various private and public section organisations, including the Heritage Lottery Fund and Derbyshire County Council. The hotel itself is built adjacent to thermal springs and will have 80 bedrooms, café, restaurant, shops, visitor centre, tour guides and a spa complex.

The CHS is expected to increase visitor numbers by 7% per annum, create a new upscale market to the town and the creation of a unique selling point for tourism (Buxton and Thermal Spa, 2016). It has created 350 construction jobs plus in-excess of 140 permanent jobs within the hotel. Buxton will become the cornerstone of local growth, a £4.5 million boost to the economy. The adjacent four-star Old Hall Hotel is also being refurbished as part of the project (Buxton and Thermal Spa, 2016).

It has been established that the target market for the CHS is international, this is because this links with the tourism development plans for the area. It has been established that the spa market attracts Japanese (Kamata & Misui, 2015), Chinese and European markets and expected to grow to an estimated worth of £7.57 billion (Mintel, 2011).

The proposed water festival is an annual event will be held during low seasons in the CHS, to highlight the importance of water, the heritage of Buxton and to attract international tourists to the spa (Mackenzie, 2017). The water festival will be designed to highlight to tourists the range of water treatments available and how these have developed over the years. This will be a unique experience and highlight different treatments that would not normally be on offer (Mackenzie, 2017).

LITERATURE REVIEW

Basic Terminology

Thermal water comes from the ground surface exceeding 30 degrees, spas are located close to the thermal water and use the thermal water to provide medical products (Besse, 2015). Within this research the terms spa, wellness and health tourism will be used interchangeably, to provide an understanding of how the creation of a spa water festival in Buxton could impact the town through the development of a ADM. Spa tourism is a tool used to market destinations (Vallbona & Dimitrovski, 2016). The creation of a spa hotel to a town provides a new approach to highlight the history of the town (Walton, 2014).

Audience Development Model

An ADM is used as a tool to plan and develop a new product into a new/ existing market. An ADM will be used for the CHS creation of a water festival. ADMs have been used since 1987 to understand tourist motivations (Keller, 1987). In 2004 Wiggins (2004) redesigned the traditional ADM to improve the understanding of certain target markets. This development helped to get more in-depth knowledge. The purpose of an ADM is a tool used to make informed decisions to increase the chances of success within new businesses and innovation (Trimi & Berbegal-Mirabent, 2012). Strategic planning and destination marketing is important for destination management organisation (DMOs) to differentiate themselves to the target market (Pike, 2015). It is important for the CHS to meet the needs of international markets by creating a unique product specially designed for their needs. It has been identified that indispensable stages in creating ADMs are: market research, understand the target market, create objectives, action plan, monitor and evaluate (Davidson & Rogers, 2012, p. 39). Figure 1 shows the various steps of developing a new product. These steps are used as a guideline for an ADM.

An ADM, has been used as the basis of the research to understand the stages involved in creating a water festival through the CHS to attract a new international market, which is different to the current demand.

New Tourism Market

Halkier, Kozak and Svensson (2014) observed that it is difficult to develop tourism solely by marketing to new customers, thus highlighting the importance of retaining existing consumer relationships. The CHS need to build on the tourism which already exists within Buxton, by using the thermal water which is available in the area to develop and increase wellness tourism. Song, Cao and Zheng (2016), identified that the development of international markets means that companies need to innovate with new products. As the tourism strategy in Buxton is to attract an international market the development of a CHS water festival would be used as a new product for this specific market. Table 1 shows the 6 main aims for tourism in the Peak District and Derbyshire and how the CHS will meet these aims.

Figure 1. Audience Development Model
(Source: Adapted from Booz, 1981; 2013 cited in Hassanien, Dale & Clarke, 2010)

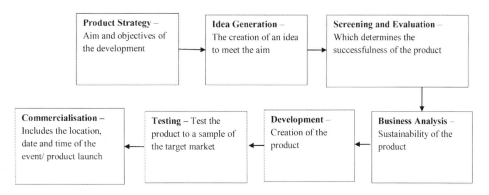

Table 1. *The Tourism Strategies of Buxton, the Peak District and Derbyshire*

Visit Peak District and Derbyshire Tourism Aims	Buxton – CHS
Maximise the impact of the visitor economy in key destinations and hubs	The CHS will develop a hotel and spa resort and create a water festival to increase the tourism product offering in Buxton.
Capital Investment to improve the visitor offer	The CHS have funding from many public and private organisations to develop the Crescent and the Old Hall Hotel.
Create a leading cultural, festivals and events destination	The CHS will develop a water festival which highlights the heritage and culture of the destination.
Maximise the potential for growth through tactical marketing campaigns	This will be done through the Visit Peak District and Derbyshire DMO rather than the CHS.
Develop a successful thriving tourism industry	The CHS will be a part of the tourism products which are offered.
Develop a consistent brand for the Peak District	The CHS will be a part of the wellness brand which is created for Buxton and the Peak District.

(Source: Dilley, 2015, p5)

To attract new, whilst retaining existing customers, businesses need to have the right product; the product which has the 'highest customer perceived value' (Kotler, Armstrong, Harris, & Piercy, 2013, p13). This is hard for a company to identify as each consumer group may express different needs and expectations. The perceived value of the product is not just necessarily based on the price of the product, but more how the customer feels the innovation of the product will enhance their life further (Kotler, Armstrong, Harris, & Piercy, 2013).

Spa Tourism

One of the oldest forms of tourism is spa tourism which has developed through new emergent forms such as health and wellness tourism throughout the years, and these changes have been driven by leisure and international tourists (Erdeli, Dinca, Gheorghilas, & Surugiu, 2011, p16). The development of spas started in Roman times and throughout the last 200 years have fluctuated in popularity (Gordon, 2012). Wellness tourism is the creation of holidays and physical revitalisation (Stathi & Avgerinos, 2001). Spa tourism represents a healthy alternative to traditional sun, sand and sea mass tourism holidays (Doughty & Zwirner, 1994).

Traditionally wellness was linked with feeling good and being fit. The five elements which are linked with modern day wellness are; physical activity, spiritual activity, health and natural nutrition, relaxation and face and body care (Banja, 2016). The reason for this change is due to the lifestyle changes of tourists as life is more stressful, tourists are more tense, exhausted and require tranquillity (Banja, 2016). Spacilova (2014) argues that the sense of wellness is not only linked with the physical, mental and social aspects of a person's life but also with the sexual, emotional, spiritual, educational, occupational, financial, environmental, ethical and existential aspects of a person's life. Wellness tourism attracts tourists to improve themselves both mentally and physically (Marak, Oparka & Wyrzykowski, 2014). Therefore, spas are used to educate people on diet, nutrition and exercise through forms of detoxification (Spacilova, 2014). Another example of a wellness product from Greece is a hydrotherapy package which is used to encourage international markets (Stathi & Avgerinos, 2001). The health and leisure tourism market is a global industry which western countries currently dominate (Walton, 2012). However, the British spa tourism development is behind in comparison to other European countries (Doughty & Zwiner, 2003). This highlights the need for development of the CHS and the creation of a water festival in the town to provide a competitive advantage against other European countries.

The three main features of a heritage tourism destination are the people, the buildings and the events (Ashworth, 2002). Event tourism is used as marketing tool to promote destinations (Getz & Page, 2015). This is important for Buxton as the CHS and the water festival can be used as marketing tools to encourage tourists to learn about the history of the town and the thermal water.

Wellness tourism is one of the fastest growing segments in the tourism industry (Kim, Chiang & Tang, 2016). Health and wellness has become a globalised industry, this new growth in the industry has become standardised, therefore creating the need for a unique selling point (Smith & Puczko, 2014). Further research conducted by Hopkinson, (2014) has identified that market towns rely on having a unique selling point to attract tourists. Tabacchi, (2010) stated that a spa that does not have a competitive edge or differentiated product will struggle to survive. Spas are an important revenue stream for hotels (Kucukusta & Denizci Gulliet, 2014), this highlights the importance of the water festival as this will act a differentiated product and provide a new experience for tourists.

The development of health tourism is a growing segment across European countries that are located on thermal springs. This is due to the increase of healthy living concepts and the use of natural products (Puczkó & Rátz, 2006). Health tourism destinations are becoming increasingly popular with international tourists and are a way to reduce seasonality in destinations due to consistent demands throughout the year (Jónás-Berki, Csapó, Pálfi, & Aubert, 2015). Events are also used to reduce seasonality in market towns, it is also essential to have a mixture of tourists and residents in the area to maintain the demand for local services (Hopkinson, 2014). This suggests that holding a water festival which attracts international tourists in the low season for Buxton will minimise seasonality and help to support local businesses. This also links with the aims and objectives of the Visit Peak District and Derbyshire tourism strategy for the area.

Festival Tourism

Within this research festival tourism is related to the Buxton water festival to act as a catalysis for increased tourism and to support the local heritage of the destination. Festivals are defined as people travelling to a destination for short periods of time to participate in specific themed events (Bruwer, 2015). Festivals act as tourism attraction in the destination (Quinn, 2006) and they have proven to be a way to share a destination's culture, the man-made and natural environment at the location and showcase local businesses. Festivals in towns and cities attract a wide range of visitors and stakeholders including resort guests, casual visitors to the spa and wellness centre, the owner-operators, suppliers, residents of Buxton, and financiers (Sachs & Ruhli, 2011). To attract and retain customers the town needs to have the right event/festival on offer to meet their needs and expectations (Kotler, Armstrong, Harris, & Piercy, 2013).

Seventy percent of tourism destinations open all year round with reduced opening hours to attract tourists during low demand periods, of which, 39% host special events as a way to encourage more tourists (Connell, Page & Meyer, 2015). A water festival could be a way to increase tourism numbers in Buxton, increasing demand during low periods. Lee, Lee and Wicks (2004) postulated that there are four cluster types of event tourists; culture and family, multipurpose, escape and event of which there are six motivational characteristics; cultural exploration, family togetherness, novelty, escape, event attractions and socialisation. Classifying event tourists supports the development of a specific tourism product (Lee, Lee & Wicks, 2004).

Target Market Needs

It has already been established that one objective of this development is to attract international tourists (Bradley, 2016; Mackenzie, 2016). Song, Cao and Zheng (2016), suggested that the development of global markets means that companies need to develop new products. The CHS water festival is designed to attract new customers with an innovative new product. Wellness tourists have similar needs to sport and eco tourists, therefore creating a way to cross market products (Rawlinson & Wiltshier, 2016). When a town has international significances, the tourism in that area can be boosted (Molnár, 2014). Spa tourism destinations have attracted international markets since the nineteenth century as these destinations were branded as sophisticated (Frost & Laing, 2016). Joukes (2016) has identified that to attract international tourists you need to guarantee that the spa is high quality through international accreditations. Table 2 identifies the needs of the various international markets and how the water festival can meet them.

Table 2 highlights that the water festival and the CHS meets the needs of the tourists from Japan, US, Europe and China. Linking the information presented in table two with the ADM presented in Figure 1, understanding the needs of international tourists can be linked with screening and evaluation and business analysis.

Table 2. Buxton's Potential Markets

International Markets	Consumer Needs	Water Festival
China	• Chinese tourists find it cheaper to travel aboard and go shopping in designer outlets (Mintel Group Ltd, 2016). • In a recent study by Mintel almost all of respondents from China wanted to visit the UK, with a large number interested in Historical attractions and shopping. Almost half of the respondents wanted to visit film locations and 63% of people that have already visited would recommend the UK to others (Mintel Group Ltd, 2014).	• The water festival can fulfil this need by using high end products, also The CHS will have designer outlets around the building • As the CHS is linked with Chatsworth house, many tourists can stay at The CHS and have day trips to Chatsworth. This will bring in more guests especially for this market as Pride and Prejudice, The Duchess and The Wolfman were all filmed there (Partners of Chatsworth, 2016).
Japan	• Medical Tourism within the country is becoming a developing niche tourism market. • Shopping tourism is also an increasing niche tourism market (Mintel Group Ltd, 2016).	• The water festival which The CHS hotel and spa is creating will be educating tourists on the benefits of water and tourists will experience water treatments.
Europe	• In 2014 a study was conducted by Mintel of which 37% of Germans wanted a UK wide package and a third of the respondents were interested in visiting the seaside and country locations (Mintel Group Ltd, 2014).	• This is interesting as this shows the development of tourists and the experience which they are seeking. This is a positive thing for The CHS as tourists are seeking something other than large cities.
US	• The research also found that the US are good brand ambassadors for the UK. • 36% of US respondents also want a UK wide package and are known as London plus tourists as they want to visit other destinations not just the capital. (Mintel Group Ltd, 2014).	• Similarly, with the European market the US are looking for different packages away from the capital city.

(Source: Compiled by the Authors, 2016)

Dryglas (2016) has identified that spa tourists can be classified into two main types commercial and non-commercial. Commercial tourists tend to visit a spa for medical purposes whereas a non-commercial tourist visits mainly for therapeutic purposes. Non-commercial tourists tend to be younger, healthier than commercial tourists and travel to relax. Spas attracts both wellness and medical tourists. Motivations of these types of tourists are: rejuvenation, socialisation, hedonism, obsession with health and beauty, relaxation and escapism (Dimitrivski & Todorovic, 2015). Yoo, Lee and Lee (2015) have identified that the 6 motivational factors that tourists visiting a wellness festival are; social interaction, novelty, nature, family togetherness, cultural exploration and relaxation (p165). Fundamental to these motivational factors is an active interest in health (Yoo, Lee & Lee, 2015). Table 3 highlights the three main types of spa and wellness tourists, the typical characteristics of these tourist types and the link with The CHS Water Festival.

Table 3. The Characteristics of Spa Consumers

	Characteristics	Water Festival
Entry Level - 25% of the market	• Price and Convenience are important factors • They mainly exercise to lose weight • They want to be involved within wellness, but they are not committed	A wide range of water treatments will be offered at various prices. The tour which is available will also be useful to educate this segment. The CHS development is aiming to make the hotel and spa accessible to all tourism segments (Mackenzie, 2016).
Mid-Level - 62% of the market	• Knowledgeable about wellness • Involved in wellness activities • They exercise for the health benefits rather than to simply lose weight • Follow new wellness trends • Eat healthily and use whole foods	This segment is one of the largest and therefore should be targeted as a key audience for the water festival. The mid-level category will be interested in the health benefits of the water itself and the water treatments available.
Core - 13% of the market	• This segment are the trend setters within wellness • Feel they have responsibilities towards the environment and society • They source food locally and use eco-friendly products • Follow a wellness lifestyle	The water festival will demonstrate the traditional practices with water and identify the benefits of water treatments for the mind and body.

(Mintel Group Ltd, 2016)

Impacts

Tourism is a competitive industry, which links the tourism policy in the destination to maximise the socio-cultural, environmental and economic benefits whilst minimising the negative tourism impacts (Pike, 2016). Spas in a destination improves the populations health, increases tourism, boosts the economy and increases international credibility (Opolskiej, Migala & Szczyrba, 2006). The creation of an event/ festival in a tourism destination improves the destinations public image, stimulates jobs, increases income, promotes the local products and develops tourism in the destination (Stankova & Vassenska, 2015). Tourism in a destination creates economic diversity (Molnár, 2014) and having both mineral water and a spa in a destination creates branding and publicity (Walton, 2014). The negative environmental impacts of tourism include pollution, litter and damage to the land, paths and roads (Mason, 2016). Other negative impacts can include the increased land values due to the increase of second homes and increased food costs due to an increased demand during high tourism seasons (Mason, 2016). Local people can also feel resentment towards tourists, there can be overcrowding in destinations at population attractions and farmers are encouraged to sell their land for development and end in low paid jobs (Archer, Cooper & Ruhanen, 2005). To minimise the negative impacts of a new tourism product and hotel development within the town the best practices of Harrogate and Bath have been analysed in the next section. This is also to understand the competition against Buxton and to identify areas of success which The CHS could adopt to attract further custom.

THE FINDINGS

This section will look at the best practices of Bath and Harrogate to identify development objectives for the CHS. Currently the CHS is working with key organisations such as Chatsworth House and similar destinations such as Harrogate in the development process to gain valuable information to create the right spa hotel (Mackenzie, 2016).

Case Study: Harrogate

Harrogate spa is a private day spa which offers tours which provide an insight into the history and facilities of the baths to spa visitors and paying members of the public (Harrogate Turkish Baths and Spa, 2016). Harrogate Baths, offer guided tours around the building every Wednesday 9:00-10:00 which costs £3.75 per person (Harrogate Turkish Baths and Spa, 2016). Similarly, to Harrogate, The CHS will offer spa tours, however as The CHS is also a hotel. A suggestion for The CHS would be to have set days and times for these tours to limit the disturbance to hotel guests whilst still giving consumers in Buxton a chance to experience the spa. Through the Harrogate tourism information website, a brochure of activities, attractions and accommodation within the town can be ordered and delivered to any country in the world (Visit Harrogate, 2016). As the CHS and the surrounding areas are looking to attract international tourists, it is a suggestion that information is available in other languages, this will act as additional marketing and promotion of the destination especially in overseas destinations. A way in which Harrogate shares insider tips is though tourism organisations such as local tour operators (Yorkshire Tour Company, 2017). This is a positive marketing method to encourage both international and domestic tourists to visit other parts of Harrogate as well as the thermal springs. The Harrogate tourism strategy 2017-2021 aim is to continue the planned work on developing the royal pump room museum and increase leisure tourism within museums (Harrogate Borough Council Department of Economy and Culture, 2017). This is a positive concept for the CHS as this reaffirms Buxton's tourism strategy and highlights the success of The Crescent.

Case Study: Bath

Bath is a traditional day spa; the building includes The Pump Room which has been converted into a restaurant for afternoon tea and has a learning centre. Bath spa is a world heritage centre (Bath and North-East Somerset Council, 2016). The main differences between Bath and the CHS is that Bath is an open attraction and not a hotel, which allows visitors into the Baths between 9:30-17:00, 363 days a year. Tourists can wander freely through the site, being the Temple of Sulis Minerua and offers free audio tours and a public guided tour every hour (Bath and North-East Somerset Council, 2016). The pricing structure in Bath is dependent on the season and whether tourists want to visit the Roman Baths separately compared to other attractions in the area. When visiting all three attractions a discounted rate is offered:

The use of a group discount from this example in Bath (Bath and North-East Somerset Council, 2016) helps to encourage tourists to visit more than one attraction at once. This can be highlighted as an example for the CHS and Visit Peak District to help meet the tourism objectives of the area to increase the visitor experience. Residents of Bath also get free entry to these attractions, when using a Discovery card, which is also free to apply for (Bath and North-East Somerset Council, 2016). This encourages the local community to understand the heritage of the town and enables more word of mouth recommendations about the destination. Through the Roman Bath visitor page, information sheets are provided in several languages including English, Chinese, Dutch, French, German, Italian, Japanese and Spanish

Table 4. The Pricing Structure for Bath

Person Type	Price
Roman Baths	
Adult	£15.50
Child	£9.80
Senior/ Student	£13.75
Roman Baths, Victoria Art Museum and Fashion Museum Group Ticket	
Adult	£21.50
Child	£11.75
Senior/ Student	£18.50

(Source: Bath and North-East Somerset Council, 2016)

(Bath and North-East Somerset Council, 2016). Bath attracts a wide range of tourists not just domestic and therefore has a need to translate tourist literature into several languages. This is a consideration for CHS as during the water festival there will be a lot of information which may need to be translated. An additional way that Bath advertises is through several newspapers (Mawer, 2017) and magazine articles (Conde Nest Publication Ltd, 2017) which have published insider tips on the destination. The 2017-2020 tourism strategy which Bath has created has identified that, there aim is to create a distinctive world class heritage spa destination (p2), to become a 'must see and explore' international spa destination (p3) and to spread visitors throughout the year (p3) (Visit Bath, 2017). The Bath tourism strategy also states that they are increasing national and international investment in creative industries (p4), completing research on case study destinations to find information on health and wellbeing impacts (p6) and producing national and international marketing (p8) (Reeve, 2015). Along with Harrogate, Baths' tourism plan is linked with Buxton and the CHS tourism policy and highlights the potential of tourism in this area.

This section has created some clear recommendations for Buxton in the terms of how to manage tours and the creation of a spa tourism product. This type of tourism in Buxton compared to Bath and Harrogate can be replicated if the best practices of those destinations are followed.

CONCLUSION

The objectives of this study were to: (a) adopt the concept of a water festival through an ADM; (b) to compare Buxton to similar spa towns in the UK and; (c) to analyse key international markets. This chapter has provided new insights to the ADM in an

Buxton and the Peak District

emerging resort. An ADM is used to improve the understanding of a target market (Keller, 1987) and to make informed decisions for development (Trimi & Berbegal-Mirabent, 2012). The CHS are designing a water festival to attract spa, wellness and health tourists. On opening the CHS expect to increase tourism by 7% (Buxton and Thermal Spa, 2016), the water festival will be an annually event to boost tourism during low seasons, by providing a unique experience. Spa tourism has been identified as a healthier alternative to the sun, sea and sand mass tourism holidays (Doughty & Zwirner, 1994). This is due to a change is lifestyle as tourists have increased stress levels and are exhausted (Banja, 2016). Spas attracts both wellness and medical tourists, motivations of these types of tourists are: rejuvenation, socialisation, hedonism, obsession with health and beauty, relaxation and escape (Dimitrivski & Todorovic, 2015). Currently the CHS project is working through idea generation stage two of the ADM to meet the project aim of attracting an international market. Local businesses may need to adapt and diversify their tourism offering to meet the international target market needs (Camilleri, 2018c), including tourists from Japan, China and the USA. These markets have been highlighted as opportunities within the Peak District region (Bradley, 2016; Mackenzie, 2016). The positive impacts of the water festival are the boost to the local economy and the increase international credibility (Opolskiej, Migala & Szczyrba, 2006). The highlighted negative impacts are increased pollution and litter in the destination (Mason, 2016). Two case studies, those being Bath and Harrogate, have established best practices for Buxton to emulate. These benchmarked destinations have highlighted the importance of integrating a range of tours around the spa area, establishing the balance between day visitors and overnight visitors and the importance of linking an event tourism strategy, specifically the water festival with attractions and businesses in the local area.

In conclusion, Figure 2 shows how, the ADM can be used to develop the water festival in Buxton. The bold boxes identify the next stages which need to be undertaken.

Figure 2. Adapted Audience Development Model
(Source: Compiled by the Authors, 2017)

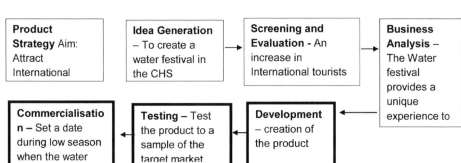

The limitations of this study were time and cost, as it is suggested that the CHS will run a trail of the water festival in order to get primary research from the tourists. Future research could be conducted to understand the specific needs of tourists visiting Buxton for wellness and spa purposes.

RECOMMENDATIONS

The key recommendations which the CHS could adapt to meet initial target market demands and minimise any negative impacts have been highlighted below.

The introduction of a group attraction ticket where tourists can visit several attractions through one ticket, similar to the scheme used in Bath (Bath and North-East Somerset Council, 2016). This will encourage more tourists to visit smaller attractions in the area and generate more local income. Bradley (2016) The Secretary of State for culture, media and sport has identified that a plan for a discount scheme, where tourists buy one ticket at a discounted rate for multiple attractions, is being developed. The CHS should build key relationships with local tourism boards and organisations, develop a tourism action plan and trial the water festival on local people. Before advertising the water festival, the CHS should build a joint advertisement campaign. This should be targeted to the international market with Marketing Peak District and Derbyshire, highlighting the number of reasons why they should visit this region. In conjunction with key stakeholders the CHS should develop a tourism action plan to attract the international markets to The CHS and to the water festival (Hassanien, Dale & Clarke, 2010) and Booz (1981; 2013) (cited in Hassanien, Dale & Clarke, 2010). A trail water festival could be completed on exiting visitors before the official opening in 2019 to ensure the success of the festival. The CHS should include multilingual brochures and guides, discount scheme and tours around the spa area for hotel guests and day visitors. The CHS will provide tours around the spa for hotel guests throughout the day to educate tourists on the history and the development of the building. This links with the aim of The CHS and the ADM which has been shown above (Buxton CHS and Thermal Spa, 2016).

REFERENCES

Archer, B., Cooper, C., & Ruhanen, L. (2005). *The Positive and Negative Impacts of Tourism*. Oxford, UK: Elsevier. doi:10.1016/B978-0-7506-7789-9.50011-X

Ashworth, G. (2002). The Image of Georgian Bath 1700–2000: Towns, Heritage and History. *Journal of Historical Geography*, *28*(2), 303–304. doi:10.1006/jhge.2002.0433

Banja, V. (2016). Tourism in Function of Development of the Republic of Serbia: Spa Tourism in Serbia and Experiences of other countries. *1st International Scientific Conferences.*

Bath and North-East Somerset Council. (2016). *The Roman Baths Bath.* Available at: http://www.romanbaths.co.uk/visit

Besse, B. A. (2015). *The situation of the Hagymatikum of Makó on the Hungarian spa market, possible ways of attracting more visitors there* (Doctoral dissertation, bgf).

Bill, J. (2010). Perceptions of Tourism Products. *Tourism Management*, *31*(5), 607–610. doi:10.1016/j.tourman.2009.06.011

Bradley, K. (2016). *2016 Annual Tourism Conference and Exhibition.* Derbyshire, UK: Marketing Peak District and Derbyshire.

Bruwer, J. (2015). Service performance and satisfaction in a South African festival scape. *Anatolia – An International Journal of Tourism and Hospitality Research*, *26*(3), 434-446.

Buxton CHS and Thermal Spa. (2016). *Buxton CHS and Thermal Spa.* Available at: http://buxtonCHS.com/

Camilleri, M. A. (2018a). The Marketing Environment. In *Travel Marketing, Tourism Economics and the Airline Product* (pp. 3–27). Cham, Switzerland: Springer. doi:10.1007/978-3-319-49849-2_1

Camilleri, M. A. (2018b). Strategic Planning and the Marketing Effectiveness Audit. In *Travel Marketing, Tourism Economics and the Airline Product* (pp. 3–27). Cham, Switzerland: Springer. doi:10.1007/978-3-319-49849-2_1

Camilleri, M. A. (2018c). Understanding Customer Needs and Wants. In *Travel Marketing, Tourism Economics and the Airline Product* (pp. 3–27). Cham, Switzerland: Springer. doi:10.1007/978-3-319-49849-2_1

Conde Nest Publication Ltd. (2017). *Best of Bath.* Available at: http://www.cntraveller.com/recommended/uk/best-of-bath-somerset-uk

Connell, J., Page, S. J., & Meyer, D. (2015). Visitor attractions and events: Responding to seasonality. *Tourism Management*, *46*, 283–298. doi:10.1016/j.tourman.2014.06.013

Davidson, R., & Rogers, T. (2012). *Marketing Destinations and Venues for Conferences and Conventions* (2nd ed.). Routledge.

Dilley, J. (2015). *The Peak District and Derbyshire Growth Strategy for the Visitor Economy 2015-2020.* Available at: http://mediafiles.thedms.co.uk/Publication/DS/cms/pdf/Growth%20Plan%20draft%20v1.pdf

Dimitriviski, P., & Todorovic, A. (2015). Clustering Wellness Tourists in spa Environment. *Tourism Management Perspectives*, *16*, 259–265. doi:10.1016/j.tmp.2015.09.004

Doughty, D., & Zwimer, W. (2003). Urban Setting. The Urban Experience: A People-Environment Perspective, 135.

Doughty, D., & Zwirner, W. (1994). *A spa culture for the nineties and thereafter: Health and relaxation in an urban setting.* Academic Press.

Dryglas, D. (2016). Profile of tourists visiting European spa resorts a case study of Poland. *Journal of Policy Research in Tourism, Leisure and Events, 9*(3), 298-317.

Erdeli, G., Dinca, A. I., Gheorghilas, A., & Surugiu, C. (2011). Romanian spa tourism: A communist paradigm in a post communist era. *Human Geographies*, *5*(2), 41–56. doi:10.5719/hgeo.2011.52.41

Frost, W., & Laing, J. (2016). *History of spa tourism.* The Routledge Handbook of Health Tourism.

Getz, D., & Page, S. (2015). Progress and Prospects for Event Tourism Research. *Tourism Management*, *52*, 593–631. doi:10.1016/j.tourman.2015.03.007

Gordon, B. M. (2012). Reinventions of a spa town: The unique case of Vichy. *Journal of Tourism History*, *4*(1), 35–55. doi:10.1080/1755182X.2012.671377

Halkier, H., Kozak, M., & Svensson, B. (2014). Innovation and Tourism Destination Development. *European Planning Studies*, *22*(8), 1547–1550. doi:10.1080/09654313.2013.784571

Harrogate Borough Council Department of Economy and Culture. (2017). *Culture Five Year Forward Plan 2017-2021.* Available at: https://localdemocracy.harrogate.gov.uk/ViewSelectedDocument.asp?DocumentID=38883

Harroate Borough Council Department of Economy and Culture. (2017). *Culture Five Year Forward Plan 2017-2021.* Available at: https://localdemocracy.harrogate.gov.uk/ViewSelectedDocument.asp?DocumentID=38883

Harrogate Turkish Baths and Spa. (2016). *Turkish Baths and Health Spa.* Available at: http://www.turkishbathsharrogate.co.uk/

Hassanien, A., Dale, C., & Clarke, A. (2010). *Hospitality Business Development.* Oxford, UK: Butterworth Heinemann.

High Peak Borough Council. (2012). *Buxton.* Available at: http://www.highpeak.gov.uk/hp/council-services/profile-of-the-main-areas/buxton

Hopkinson, M. (2014). *Yorkshire Market Towns: not just for shopping: A research survey by PLACE.* Academic Press.

Jónás-Berki, M., Csapó, J., Pálfi, A., & Aubert, A. (2015). A Market and Spatial Perspective of Health Tourism Destinations: The Hungarian Experience. *International Journal of Tourism Research, 17*(6), 602–612. doi:10.1002/jtr.2027

Joukes, V. (2016). Efficient Networking Makes Mineral Spa Towns More Attractive: A Handful of Examples. Cultural Management and Tourism in European Cultural Routes: from theory to practice, 136.

Kamata, H., & Misui, Y. (2015). Why do they choose a spa destination? The case of Japanese Tourists. *Tourism Economics, 21*(2), 283–305. doi:10.5367/te.2014.0450

Keller, J. (1987). Development and Use of the ARCS Model of Instruction Design. *Journal of Instructional Development, 10*(3), 2–10. doi:10.1007/BF02905780

Kim, E., Chaing, L., & Tang, L. (2016). Investigating Wellness Tourists: Motivation, Engagement and Loyalty: In search of the Missing Link. *Journal of Travel and Tourism Marketing, 34*(7), 867-879.

Kotler, P., Armstrong, G., Harris, L., & Piercy, N. (2013). *Principles of Marketing* (6th ed.). Essex, UK: Pearson Education Limited.

Kucukusta, D., & Denizci Gulliet, B. (2014). Measuring Spa-goers Preferences: A Conjoint Analysis Approach. *International Journal of Hospitality Management, 41,* 115–124. doi:10.1016/j.ijhm.2014.05.008

Lee, C. K., Lee, Y. K., & Wicks, B. E. (2004). Segmentation of festival motivation by nationality and satisfaction. *Tourism Management, 25*(1), 61–70. doi:10.1016/S0261-5177(03)00060-8

Mackenzie, L. (2016). *2016 Annual Tourism Conference and Exhibition.* Derbyshire: Marketing Peak District and Derbyshire.

Marak, J., Oparka, S., & Wyrzykowski, J. (2014). *Factors conditioning the creation of the combined product "Health Resort, Spa and Wellness Tourism" in a region.* Tourism Role in the Regional Economy.

Mason, P. (2016). *Tourism Impacts Planning and Management* (3rd ed.). Oxon, UK: Routledge.

Mawer, F. (2017). 36 Hours in…Bath. *Telegraph.* Available at: http://www.telegraph.co.uk/travel/destinations/europe/united-kingdom/england/somerset/bath/articles/36-hours-in-bath/

Mintel Group Ltd. (2011). *Spa Tourism – International – October - 2011.* Available at: http://academic.mintel.com.ezproxy.derby.ac.uk/display/545413/

Mintel Group Ltd. (2014a). *Inbound Tourism – UK – November 2016.* Available at: http://academic.mintel.com.ezproxy.derby.ac.uk/display/723354/

Mintel Group Ltd. (2014b). *Legacy of mega events in tourism – International – November 2010.* Available at: http://academic.mintel.com.ezproxy.derby.ac.uk/display/482892/

Mintel Group Ltd. (2016a). *Leisure Review – UK – December 2016.* Available at: http://academic.mintel.com.ezproxy.derby.ac.uk/display/809667/

Mintel Group Ltd. (2016b). *The Evolution of Wellness Tourism –August 2016.* Available at: http://academic.mintel.com.ezproxy.derby.ac.uk/display/786404/

Mintel Group Ltd. (2016c). *Travel and Tourism – China – February 2016.* Available at: http://academic.mintel.com.ezproxy.derby.ac.uk/display/764551/

Mintel Group Ltd. (2016d). *Travel and Tourism – Japan – February 2016.* Available at: http://academic.mintel.com.ezproxy.derby.ac.uk/display/764590/

Mintel Group Ltd. (2017). *Spa, Salon and In-store Treatments – UK – September 2017.* Available at: http://academic.mintel.com.ezproxy.derby.ac.uk/display/793777/

Molnár, J. K. E. (2014). Potential for Tourism Development in Industrial Towns Based on Cultural Heritage, The Cases of Svit and Martfu. Enhancing Competitiveness of V4 Historic Cities to Develop Tourism, 178.

Opolskiej, Z. N. P., Migala, M., & Szczyrba, Z. (2006). Article. *Spas and Spa Tourism in the Czech Republic, 1*(312), 147–162.

Partners of Chatsworth. (2016). *Chatsworth on Film.* Available at: http://www.chatsworth.org/press-and-filming/filming

Pike, S. (2015). *Destination Marketing Essentials* (2nd ed.). London: Taylor and Francis.

Pike, S. (2016). *Destination Marketing Essentials* (2nd ed.). London: Routledge.

Puczkó, L., & Rátz, T. (2006). 10 Product Development and Diversification in Hungary. Tourism in the new Europe: The challenges and opportunities of EU enlargement, 116.

Quinn, B. (2006). Problematising 'festival tourism' arts festivals and sustainable development in Ireland. *Journal of Sustainable Tourism*, *14*(3), 288–306. doi:10.1080/09669580608669060

Rawlinson, S., & Wiltshier, P. (2016). *Developing a wellness destination*. The Routledge Handbook of Health Tourism.

Reeve, K. (2015). *Cultural and Creative Strategy Review: Bath and North-East Somerset 2015-2020*. Academic Press.

Sachs, S., & Ruhli, E. (2011). *Stakeholders Matter*. Cambridge, UK: Cambridge University Press. doi:10.1017/CBO9781139026963

Smith, M., & Puczko, L. (2014). *Routledge Advances in Tourism*. London: Routledge.

Song, W., Cao, J., & Zheng, M. (2016). Towards an integrative framework of innovation network for new product development project. *Production Planning and Control*, *27*(12), 967–978. doi:10.1080/09537287.2016.1167980

Spacilova, K. (2014). *Destination Spa Darkov: A study reviewing options for a full spa experience* (Maters Dissertation Thesis).

Stankova, M., & Vassenska, I. (2015). Raising cultural awareness of local traditions through festival tourism. *Tourism & Management Studies*, *11*(1).

Stathi, A., & Avgerinos, A. (2001). Bathing in the healing waters. A case-study of the development of thermal spas in Greece. *World Leisure Journal*, *43*(1), 41–51. doi:10.1080/04419057.2001.9674218

Tabacchi, M. (2010). Current Research and Events in the Spa industry. *Cornell University*, *51*(1), 102–117.

Trimi, S., & Berbegal-Mirabent, J. (2012). Business Model Innovation in Entrepreneurship. *International Entrepreneurship and Management Journal*, *8*(4), 449-465.

Vallbona, M. C., & Dimitrovski, D. (2016). Well-being as driving force for economic recuperation of traditional spas, Lleida, Spain. *Tourism in Function of Development of The Republic of Serbia, 1st International Scientific Conferences,* 173.

Visit Bath. (2017a). *Executive Summary: Destination Marketing Strategy 2017-2020.* Available at: https://visitbath.co.uk/dbimgs/Summary%20of%20Bath%20Destination%20Marketing%20Strategy%20October%202017.pdf

Visit Bath. (2017b). *Executive Summary: Destination Marketing Strategy 2017-2020.* Available at: https://visitbath.co.uk/dbimgs/Summary%20of%20Bath%20Destination%20Marketing%20Strategy%20October%202017.pdf

Visit Buxton. (2016). *Visit Buxton Leading Spa Town.* Available at: http://www.visitbuxton.co.uk/

Visit Harrogate. (2016). *Visit Harrogate.* Available at: http://www.visitharrogate.co.uk/

Walton, J. K. (2012). Health, sociability, politics and culture. Spas in history, spas and history: An overview. *Journal of Tourism History, 4*(1), 1–14. doi:10.1080/1755182X.2012.671372

Walton, J. K. (2014). Family firm, health resort and industrial colony: The grand hotel and mineral springs at Mondariz Balneario, Spain, 1873–1932. *Business History, 56*(7), 1037–1056. doi:10.1080/00076791.2013.839661

Wiggins, J. (2004). Motivation, ability and opportunity to participate a reconceptualization of the RAND model of audience development. *Marketing Management, 7*(1), 22-33.

Yoo, I. Y., Lee, T. J., & Lee, C. K. (2015). Effect of health and wellness values on festival visit motivation. *Asia Pacific Journal of Tourism Research, 20*(2), 152–170. doi:10.1080/10941665.2013.866970

Yorkshire Tour Company. (2017). *Insider Tips Seven amazing experiences in Harrogate to make a great day out.* Available at: http://www.theyorkshiretourcompany.com/single-post/2017/03/13/Insider-tips---Seven-amazing-experiences-in-Harrogate-to-make-a-great-day-out

Chapter 10
Perceived Destination Image:
The Case of Gallipoli

Neslihan Cavlak
Namık Kemal University, Turkey

Ruziye Cop
Abant Izzet Baysal University, Turkey

ABSTRACT

The perceived destination image is a strategic weapon that provides a competitive advantage for the tourism destinations. Perceptions are the elements that give meaning to destinations. In this respect, it is important for the destination marketers to know how tourists perceive the destination. It can be seen that tourists with different demographic and cultural backgrounds who visit the same destination can perceive its image differently. The tourism marketplace is highly competitive. Because of this, destination management organizations (DMOs) need to understand the actual and the desired perception of their destinations in order to take necessary measures. In this chapter, the concepts of destination and perceived destination image are emphasized. Secondly, the political environment, cultural attractiveness, social environment, and natural environment factors affecting the perceived destination image will be examined. Finally, the perceived destination images of domestic and foreign tourists visiting the Gallipoli in Turkey will be examined comparatively.

DOI: 10.4018/978-1-5225-5835-4.ch010

INTRODUCTION

This chapter aims to present and discuss the concept of perceived destination image as shown in the literature. The process of perceived destination image formation is dynamic. The factors which influence the destination image are severally important and they complete each other. The perceived destination image plays a very essential role in the destination marketing process, because it provides crucial information about how the place is perceived by tourists. Different groups of people may see the features of a same destination from different perspectives. This chapter proposed that; tourists which have different demographic characters and travel behaviors might have different perceptions of the same destination. At the end of the chapter there is a case study about Gallipoli to support this proposal. This study also highlights the presence of image heterogeneity that different tourists may gain different benefits from a destination.

Destination image is a strategic weapon that provides a competitive advantage for the tourism industry. It plays a critical role in the description, promotion and organization of destinations. Because of this holistic nature, the image emerges as a very important concept in terms of the success of destinations. In this sense, destinations with a positive image are more often considered and preferred by customers (Echtner & Ritchie, 1991: p. 2)

There are many factors that affect the decision-making process of a tourist destination. Accommodation, cultural attractions, weather, landscapes, political factors, exchange rates are some of the factors that influence perceptions about a destination of tourists. For this reason, destination marketers are looking for the most important factors that influence the image of the destination. In addition, destination image influences the customers' future destination selection, recommendation behaviour and repeat visits (Fayeke & Crompton, 1991: p. 15; Stepchenkova & Mills, 2010: p. 585).

The studies show that destination image affects tourists' destination selection process (Camilleri, 2018a,b; Baloglu & McCleary, 1999; Chon, 1992; Chon, 1990; Chi & Qu, 2008). Destination image means all of the beliefs, thoughts and expressions that a tourist has about a destination or place (Crompton, 1979: p. 18). For this reason, the tourists mostly prefer the destinations which have positive image.

The objectives of the chapter are; to define the concepts of destination and perceived destination image, to examine the political environment, cultural attractiveness, social environment and natural environment that are the factors affecting the perceived destination image and to reveal the perceived destination images of domestic and foreign tourists visiting the Gallipoli Peninsula Historical National Park in Turkey comparatively.

BACKGROUND

Tourism is an industry that contributes positively to the social, economic, cultural and environmental development of regions. Especially for the developing countries, the contribution of the national income, the foreign exchange income, the balance of payments and the new employment fields created by the developed business lines of tourism industry are very important. The tourism industry is one of the leading industries to provide employment opportunities in the world today. International tourism has become the most important service sector for developed and developing countries with its contribution to the welfare of countries and the increasing influence of countries' foreign exchange reserves. The tourism industry offers its customers the opportunity to visit different destinations with opportunities such as sightseeing, entertainment and learning.

In recent years, perceived destination image had drawn much attention in tourism industry because it is mainly related with the sales of tourist goods and services. It affects the whole consumption experience of the tourists. Perceived destination image literature has been studied by many researchers. Major studies have been undertaken by numerous researchers (Echtner & Ritchie, 1991; 1993; Fayeke & Crompton, 1991; Gallarza, Saura, & Calderón, 2002; Pike, 2002; Baloglu & Mangaloglu, 2001; Bigne, Sanchez, & Sanchez, 2001; Beerli & Martin, 2004; Hallab & Kim, 2006; Taşçı, Gartner & Cavuşgil, 2007; Li & Stepchenkova, 2012; Jenkins, 1999; Gravili & Rosato, 2017).

Perceived destination image measurement becomes very popular both in academic and applied tourism researches recently. Mainly, the quantitative approach has been using by the majority of the perceived destination image studies. It is seen that, 75 percent of the 86 articles researchers used quantitative approach (Dolnicar & Grün, 2012: p. 1). Most of the researchers are using questionnaires in order to understand the responders' image about the destination. Destinations' images are measured with the destination attributes rating scales.

DESTINATION AND DESTINATION IMAGE CONCEPTS

Destinations are places where the supply side of tourism activities offers various attractions, transportation, accommodation, food and beverage services, sales and support services. In the tourism market where competition is very intense, destinations offer different kinds of goods and services. This makes it difficult for the tourists to choose between the destinations.

Studies about perceived destination image began in the early 1970s when Hunt (1975) suggested that image is an important factor in the development of tourism. After his study, the destination image has begun to take a critical place in the field of tourism researches (Hosany, Ekinci & Uysal, 2006: p. 638).

There is no only one definition of destination image because it was conceptualized by many researchers from different fields. The image of a destination is intangible and subjective so it may change from one to another. It is also an interdisciplinary subject. This have made the theoretical analysis of destination image more complex and frustrated the adoption of a clear definition (Gravili & Rosato, 2017: p. 28). Some of the main definitions of "destination image" from the literature is shown in the Table 1.

Image is one of the critical components that ensures tourism destinations to differ from each other and that effects the decision-making process of tourists (Baloglu & Brinberg, 1997: p. 11). Therefore, we must know the images of destinations and the way they are perceived by tourists. However, researches made on the images of touristic destinations reveal that several challenges are faced due to the characteristic features of tourism product. First of all, tourism product has a complicated and multi-dimensional characteristic. Secondly, in tourism marketing, clients must be available physically in the area where the scenario shall be played. On the other hand, tourism service includes several subjectivities. The image of an area is comprised of the joint component of local community, other tourists, stores and employees. One of the other challenges of the tourism industry is that its products have an abstract nature. Therefore, destination image is much more critical than concrete sources in tourism researches. That is because perception may become much more powerful than facts in terms of motivating clients for taking action or not (Gallarza, Saura & Calderón García, 2002: p. 57).

THE IMPORTANCE OF PERCEIVED DESTINATION IMAGE FOR THE TOURISM INDUSTRY

It is very critical to find out how and why tourists select the destinations they have chosen since it is more important than selling a destination to find out how that client gave that decision to purchase relative destination. Since touristic product has an abstract characteristic and since it is consumed in the area where it originates, it is very critical for the image of a destination to reflect the facts. Therefore, following issues effect the creation process of the image of a destination; information provided by travel agencies, TV, radio and internet news, stories told by those, who visited the relative destination, and experiences of those, who actually visited the destination.

Table 1. Destination Image Definitions

(Hunt, 1975: p. 1)	"Impressions that a person or persons hold about a state in which they do not reside"
Lawson and Baud Bovy (1977) (In Jenkins, 1999: p. 2).	"The expression of all objective knowledge, impressions, prejudice, imaginations, and emotional thoughts an individual or group might have of a particular place"
(Crompton, 1979: p. 18)	"Sum of beliefs, ideas, and impressions that a person has of a destination"
Richardson and Crompton (1988) (In Echtner & Ritchie, 2003: p. 41)	"Perceptions of vacation attributes"
(Gartner, 1989: p. 16)	"A complex combination of various products and associated attribute"
(Echtner & Ritchie, 1991: p. 8)	"The perceptions of individual destination attributes and the holistic impression made by the destination"
(Fayeke & Crompton, 1991: p. 15).	"The mental construct developed by a potential tourist on the basis of a few selected impressions among the flood of total impressions"
Kotler et al., (1994) (In Gallarza, Saura & Calderón García, 2002: p. 60)	"The image of a place is the sum of beliefs, ideas, and impressions that a person holds of it"
Santos Arrebola (1994) (In Gallarza, Saura & Calderón García, 2002: p. 60)	"Image is a mental representation of attributes and benefits sought of a product"
(Milman & Pizam, 1995: p. 21)	"A sum total of the images of the individual elements or attributes that make up the tourism experience"
Parenteau (1995) (In Gallarza, Saura & Calderón García, 2002: p. 60)	"Is a favorable or unfavorable prejudice that the audience and distributors have of the product or destination"
(Ahmed, Sohail, Myers, & San, 2006: p. 59)	"What tourists think or perceive about a state as a destination, its tourism resources, its tourist services, the hospitality of its host, its social and cultural norms, and its rules and regulations which influence their consumer behaviour"
Chen & Tsai, 2007: p. 1116)	"The visitor's subjective perception of the destination"
(Alcaniz, Gracia & Blas, 2009: p. 716)	"As the overall perception of the of a destination and a representation of the destination in the tourist's mind

Gunn (1988), conceptualized the effects that various sources make on creation of a destination image and role they play on the establishment of destination image, and established a travel experience model that is comprised of seven phases (as cited in Echtner & Ritchie, 1991: p. 3). Gunn names the first phase of its model as "organic image". In this phase, destination image is comprised of non-touristic and non-commercial information, such as information obtained from general media (news, magazines, books and films), information obtained from school or family and friends. Second phase of the model uses more of commercially provided information that is obtained from travel magazines, brochures, travel agencies and travel guides. Organic image may change as a result of any information obtained in this way. This image available in the second phase is referred to as "induced image". Sources of the information obtained in relation with the goods and services are usually commercial sources. In other words, mass media makes a limited effect on creation of a product image. Destination image is obtained more from commercial sources in general because there are certain differences between the touristic image and national image of a country. This means that non-commercial sources include historical, political, economic and social factors. Therefore, differences may be observed between organic image and induced image from time to time (Echtner & Ritchie, 1991: 3). In the third phase, travel decision is given according to the image perceived in consideration of time, money and other limitation. In the fourth phase, effects that various components, such as views, guidebooks and road signs etc., which are observed while travelling in the destination, make on destination image are assessed. In the fifth phase, accommodation and activities, personal experiencing and modification of image and creation of changed/induced image take place in the destination. Sixth phase is comprised of inward journey and assessment and discussion of experience with fellow travelers, and seventh phase, which is the last phase, is comprised of assessments made after travel and new backlogs (Jenkins, 1999: p. 3).

First of all, benefit that is obtained from consumption of touristic products is experimental. Actions that the tourists shall perform are shaped in the destination. Before actual consumption, which is based on perception completely, tourists must conceive accurately the positive feelings that they shall experience. Tourists obtain information on the destinations from various sources in time. Such information is organized in their minds. Tourist behaviors are generally a result of perceptions (Leisen, 2001: p. 49). Destination selection of those, who travel, is mostly based on the image that such destination created on them (Baloglu & McCleary, 1999: p. 868; Hunt, 1975: p. 1; Chon, 1991: p. 68). On the other hand, destination image makes tourists to make a selection out of these destinations where time and money are limited, but where variety and competition are plenty. Therefore, tourists select the destination, from which they perceive the most positive image (Gartner, 1989: p. 16).

Tourism industry is an image industry. Destinations that have the image of a positive destination are preferred more, visited repeatedly and information related with the destination spread from mouth to mouth by marketing (Qu, Kim & Im, 2011: p. 468). On the other hand, it causes loss of money and time to transform any negative image, which is formed in relation with any destination, to positive. For example, India gave start to a campaign with the slogan of "Incredible India" in 2002 in order to tarnish its image as the world's dirtiest country and to increase the number of coming tourists. Dramatic investments and advertisements expenses were made for the campaign. Image campaign had become successful, and while the number of tourists coming to India was 2.65 million in 2000, it increased to 5.38 in 2008 (Kerrigan, Shivanandan & Hede, 2012: p. 320).

In the tourism industry, image plays a very critical role in the holiday resort selections of consumers. For example, Bodrum is one of the first resorts that come to mind when one says entertainment tourism in the summer. Antalya is one of the cities that have the image of sea-sand-sun. In the USA, Las Vegas has the image of gambling tourism, and Istanbul and Roman are among the cities that have the image of cultural tourism. It was asked to tourists to tell the first thing that comes to their minds about Belgium, Denmark, Germany, Spain and France (Öztürk, Yeşiltaş, Kozak, Özel, & Aksöz, 2013: p. 120). First concepts that came to the minds of tourists may be seen in Table 2.

Consequently, image is one of the critical components that affect the ratio of success or failure achieved by destinations. If destinations wish to compete successfully in the tourism markets where competition is intense, they must make an effort to improve their images. Because image affects the post-purchase behaviour, mouth-to-mouth communication and any future purchase intention of tourists (Bigne, Sanchez & Sanchez, 2001: p. 616).

FACTORS FORMING THE PERCEIVED DESTINATION IMAGE

Perceived destination image is assessment of a destination together with its cognitive and emotional components in its integrity. It is accepted that perceived destination image affects the behaviour variables of consumers in several ways (Baloglu & McCleary, 1999: p. 868; Echter & Ritchie, 1993: p. 12; Chen & Hsu, 2000: p. 415; Fayeke & Crompton, 1991: p. 10; Gartner, 1994: p. 209). Researchers endeavor to determine the components that define, change and strengthen destination image due to its potential effect of tourist behaviors (Tascı, 2007: p. 23).

Table 2. The Image of Five Countries

Country Name	First Five Image About The Countries				
Belgium	Brussel	Chocolate	Tintin	Beer	Capital of European Union
Denmark	Vikings	Hans Cristian A.	Copenhagen	Lego	Football
Germany	Beer	Berlin	High way	Goethe	Seriousness
Spain	Barcelona	Bull Fighting	Paella	Art	Juan Carlos
France	Paris	Wine	Gerard Depardieu	Food	Fashion

Source: (Öztürk, Yeşiltaş, Kozak, Özel, & Aksöz, in Destinasyon Yönetimi, 2013: p. 120)

Political environment related with the destination, cultural attractions, natural environment and social environment components are the components that create destination image. Tourism industry is built on an intact and clean environment, attractive natural areas, authentic history and cultural traditions and hospitable local community. Therefore, it is very critical for the visitors to perceive the characteristics specific to relative destination positively during their actual visits.

Political Environment

Political environment is one of the most important supply resources that affect the image of a destination. Today's tourism world, which always communicates, gets affected quite a lot from the events and incidents that take place out of its control. Even small-scaled crises may make significant effects on destinations (Alvarez & Campo, 2014: p. 70). Political instability is defined as any country that is taken under control by overthrowing a government or by a coup made by a group or a situation where public order may not be maintained anymore. Tourism industry is very fragile against political events, such as riots, rebellions, terrorism, wars and regional tensions (Sonmez, 1998: p. 420). It is observed that such negative events that take place due to political reasons make negative effects directly on the tourism activities that are related with any region or country. Tourism demand may sometimes overcome such damaging effects in a very short period. However, crisis environment may become more permanent when certain tourism destinations are subjected to political events and confusions continuously (Alvarez & Campo, 2014: p. 70).

Various components, such as peace, safety and security etc. are at the top of the prerequisites for development of regions or countries in touristic terms, and they are listed among the most basic indicators of touristic development. If a destination does not have certain components, such as peace, safety and security etc., then such destination may not gain a good competitive power in national and international markets, even though it has many other natural, cultural, economic and social attractions in comparison to other destinations. It makes a positive contribution to the destination as long as the tourism industry feeds on peace (Cavlek, 2002: p. 478).

As in the case of their daily lives, people may come across to a range of safety risks in touristic destinations as well. Today, it has become difficult, almost impossible to avoid such situations (Pizam, 1999: p. 5). People may live in areas, which they refer to as insecure, but no one may make people to have a holiday in a place, which they perceive as insecure. Today, basic demand of consumers is provision of a high-quality supply, i.e. service, and presentation of such quality in a suitable environment. Any act of violence that is exhibited towards tourists does not only cause activities to halt in relative destination, but also causes activities to decrease, even stop completely in the regions and countries that are neighbors to that destination in general. Consequently, tourism industry makes a great contribution to national economies. Therefore, host country must take all types of measures beforehand in order to keep itself away from any political crises at all times (Cavlek, 2002: p. 479).

One of the most critical aspects of political instability is terrorism. Terrorism is defined as usage of any method, which includes pressure, intimidation and any type of violence, against civilians, official, local and general governments in order to achieve certain political, religious and/or economic objectives. It is inevitable for such political environment components that threaten daily life to not to make any negative effect on the tourism industry. Terrorist attacks damage the collaboration established between tourism and tourism related entities. Such attacks cause certain destinations, in which tourists define with the concepts of safe, attractive and relaxed, to be perceived negatively. Also, such attacks affect the revenues of tourism entities and other entities negatively by decreasing tourist arrivals and touristic expenses (Sönmez, Apostolopoulos & Tarlow, 1999: p. 13).

Political instability makes a quite destructive effect on tourism industry. This sensitivity of tourism industry towards negative power of political instability is important. Scope and size of political instability is one of the most critical components, which determine the image of destinations, in terms of potential holiday-makers from the countries that send tourists. This is because destination image indicates the perceived stability and security of a destination in a certain way in the eyes of potential tourists (Seddighi, Nuttall & Theocharous, 2001: p. 182).

Due to intangible nature of travel experience, it is very important to have a political positive image for touristic destinations (Sönmez, Apostolopoulos & Tarlow, 1999: p. 15). Security and safety perceptions are the most critical determinants of the decision to travel. Tourists may easily cancel their plans to travel to a certain destination, which they deem as risky (Rittichainuwat & Chakraborty, 2009: p. 413).

Tourists generally wish to visit the destinations, which they perceive as developed economically (Shahzad, Shahbaz, Ferrer, & Kumar, 2017: p. 224). In this respect, economic development levels of regions make a positive effect on perceived destination image (Li & Stepchenkova, 2012: p. 250; Martinez & Alvarez, 2010: p. 760; Kim, Hallab & Kim, 2012: p. 464). Economically developed countries also develop and invigorate the tourism industry in their countries. Country specific tourism resources are determined, infrastructure of the same is prepared and tourism activities may be increased with the positive effect of economic development level. Thus, it is ensured that international tourists show interest in the region in particular (Chen & Chiou-Wei, 2009: p. 818).

Cultural Environment

World tourism market is being revolutionized every day in order to present varieties to their potential visitors. Destinations race with each other in order to present various other holiday alternatives in addition to traditional alternatives, such as sea, sand and sun etc. (Boyd, 2002: p. 211).

In the tourism market where competition is very intense, it is becoming inevitable for destinations to look several ways in order to make differences in their goods and services. One of the most critical ways of creating such diversity is the requirement from the destinations to create a unique brand identity and image. The reason why destinations wish to become diverse is that they aim to arouse interest for their different and mysterious atmosphere to be visited by clients.

Protection and enrichment of the historical areas and cultural events available in the destinations are very critical for promotion and marketing of tourism industry (Long & Perdue, 1990: p. 10; Taylor, Fletcher & Clabaugh, 1993: p. 30). Tourists are interested dramatically in antique ruins, castles, ancient houses, fortresses, war fields and other structures that carry the traces of the past. Major historical sites and ruins, which are left from ancient civilizations and which are available within the borders of developing countries, are very important for the tourists. Pyramids and sculptures that are available in Egypt, Kremlin Palace that is available in Moscow, Buckingham Palace that is available in London, and White House and High Court Building that are available in Washington etc. are being visited by many tourists (İçöz, 2005: p. 46). Many tourists wish to re-explore history by visiting these places.

Destinations that have a cultural appearance different than the one available in the area where people always live always seem attractive to tourists. It mystifies the tourists to present various cultural components that belong to a destination in a unique way, such as any believes, architectural works, museums, art galleries, exhibitions, expos and hand works etc., and they show many alternatives that may be explored by tourists (Alhemoud & Armstrong, 1996: p. 77).

The attractiveness of the local foods of a destination is also one of the most important components that the tourists wish to explore. One of the most entertaining events, which tourists enjoy the most during their travels (Quan & Wang, 2004: p. 302) and which adds value to the image of a destination, is to eat food (Boyne, Hall & Williams, 2003: p. 132; Du Rand, Heath & Alberts, 2003: p. 98). Foods are listed in the first or second place in the list of travel motivations of tourists, and foods add an additional value to destination image as well. The number of tourists, who travel to eat food, is increasing day by day in recent years, and it is becoming one of the events, which tourists enjoy the most during their travels and in which they do not refrain from spending any amount of money. Local cuisines are one of the most important indicators of the abstract heritage of destinations, and tourists go through an actual cultural experience as they consume those foods that come from relative region (Okumus, Okumus & McKercher, 2007: p. 253). Different food culture related with a region is one of the most critical destination marketing components, which draw tourists to any region. On the other hand, foods play a critical role in differentiation of destinations from each other significantly. Cuisines are categorized into brands by nations, such as Chinese, French, Italian, Turkish and Mexican etc. This situation gives the opportunity to establish a positive collaboration between food styles and destination (Okumus, Okumus & McKercher, 2007: p. 253).

Tourists consider it as very important for the destinations to have different attractiveness levels. Attraction centers related with any destination may establish a bond between tourists and destinations. Attractive aspects of any destination may direct people to travel in order to do something and to see certain areas, and they also provide a uniform satisfaction to visitors. Destinations mostly become attractive as a result of the natural resources they contain. Regions that have various resources, such as sea, river and creeks etc., may provide a variety of entertainment and recreation facilities. Various activities, such as trekking, skiing, scenery viewing, camping, hunting and wild life photography etc., may also provide a different taste to tourists, and make the relative region attractive. Cultural resources, such as archaeological excavations, historical sites and local manners and customs etc., are also listed among activities that attract tourists in recent years. Large entertainment centers, such as theme parks and gaming areas that are available in other countries, particularly in the USA, may be listed among places that are preferred by tourists (Gunn, 1989: p. 5).

War is one of the biggest disasters that human beings ever experienced. However, historical and environmental outputs of war are seen as a motivational source from the perspective of tourism for visiting the areas that are damaged due to the war (Bigley, Lee, Chon, & Yoon, 2010: p. 372). For example, war ruins, such as war fields, cemeteries, monuments, museums and evidences of living history, undertake the role of historical resources for development of "war tourism" activities and relative infrastructure (Smith, 1998: p. 204).

Visitation of areas related with death and cruelty is referred to as thana tourism (Seaton, 1996) or dark tourism (Foley & Lennon, 1996), and demand for this type of tourism is increasing in recent years. Seaton (1996: p. 240) defines thana tourism or dark tourism as the location, to where one travels completely or partially with the motivation to face death actually or symbolically.

Social Environment

One of the critical components that effect destination image is the developed social environment experience that the destination shall make the tourists experience. Destinations, which create various nightlife activities, which provide a quality shopping experience, which provide suitable mass transportation facilities and which have restaurants of top quality, are preferred more by tourists (Kim, Hallab & Kim, 2012: p. 502). Tourism destinations are locations that produce wide range of goods and services under the same trademark. These goods and services provide a uniform experience to tourists. The experience that tourists go through by these goods and services make certain positive or negative effects on customer satisfaction and destination image (Buhalis, 2000: p. 98).

Holidays are times when people get away from the routines, which they go through every day, and when they look for an opportunity to have some fun, try something different and to have some rest on their own, with their families or friends. Therefore, tourists have many expectations from a destination. Casinos, popular bars, discos, restaurants, cafes, cinemas, theatres and concerts are among the reasons that trigger many tourists to travel. In the direction of the surveys made by various research companies in recent years, various cities, such as London, Amsterdam, Cuba, Ibiza, Barcelona, Berlin and Prague etc., are listed among the top entertaining cities of the world.

Another issue that makes an effect on destination image is the shopping facilities that are available in the destination. As a tourist activity, shopping is considered as one of the most important events presented by a tourism destination. While shopping is an event, to which tourists participate continuously, it is also one of the most critical reasons that make tourists travel. It is emphasized that travelers tend to spend a significant part of their travel budgets on souvenirs. Several researches reveal that tourists spend any of surplus funds they have on souvenirs, and then on accommodation, food and entertainment respectively (Letho, Jang, Achana, & O'Leary, 2004: p. 320; Turner & Reisinger, 2001: p. 16).

Shopping activities are considered as a part of destination planning or marketing karma by many destinations. Shopping, which also plays a critical role in terms of destination image, causes certain destinations to focus on this theme. A customer who is satisfied with an operation or from a product tends to be a loyal customer of that business or/and product (Kalyoncuoğlu & Faiz, 2017: p. 131). Various cities, such as Paris, Hong Kong and Thailand etc., refer to themselves as the capital of shopping (Letho, Jang, Achana, & O'Leary, 2004: p. 321).

Existence of a range of quality food-beverage entities on the travelled destination causes such destinations to be preferred. It is a very critical component for the food and beverage standards that are provided by service personnel to be at an acceptable level. Tourists consume foods and beverages in restaurants, bars, pubs and cafes in the destinations they travel all day long. High quality and reliable service makes a positive effect on destination image.

On the other hand, a mass transportation facility, which has a high service quality, which is sustainable and reliable, makes a positive contribution to the destination image. Transportation is among the secondary characteristics that make contribution to the attractiveness of destinations. Also, it is one of the critical components of a destination, which is a uniform product (Thompson & Schofield, 2007: p. 136). Tourists use mass transportation means during their travels in the destination. Most significant reasons of this behavior is that mass transportation means are cheaper, easier, reliable and comfortable.

Various mass transportation means, such as trains, metros, trams, buses and ferries etc., are used by the tourists to explore the destination they went. Tourists use metro the most in several European countries in particular, such as Munich, Paris and London etc. Ferry service is critical for several river and island settlements, and they operate in connection with bus transportation. Ferry transportation has become so important that various destinations, such as Sydney and Hong Kong etc., use it in their logos (Le-Klaahn & Hall, 2015: p. 788).

Natural Environment

Tourism destination supply is a multi-dimension concept that covers not only tourism economic goods, such as entertainment, accommodation, transportation, foods and beverages etc., but also components of natural environment. These attraction centers, which are dependent on the natural resources of destinations, constitute the basis of the demand made for any potential destination (Mihalic, 2013: p. 615).

Natural environment, which is one of the environmental components that constitute a destination, has a great effect on destination image. Most significant reason of this situation is that destinations generally exist with the natural resources they have. Destinations generally obtain competitive advantage and attract tourists to themselves thanks to those unique environmental components (Hassan, 2000: p. 239). Characteristics of natural environment are comprised of an intact and clean natural environment, impressive natural scenery, peaceful areas available in the destination and magnificent beaches (Kim, Hallab & Kim, 2012).

The importance of natural environmental components has increased even more for destinations in recent years. Poon (1989) defines "new tourist" as a person, who is environment friendly, who demands more the experiences that are based on natural environment and who are sensitive against environmental pollution in destinations (Mihalic, 2013: p. 614). Today, tourism demand is getting away from crowded, polluted and intense city environments, and shifts towards the natural environment that is authentic, intact, clean and that has the breeze of the past. People are more interested in open-air events, natural sceneries and peaceful environments, which shall ensure that they are integrated to the environment (Kastenholz & Lima, 2011: p. 62).

This intense interest in experiencing nature increases even more with the presentation of natural environment to touristic consumption. This situation causes rural areas to be used in particular as a touristic platform for various activities, such as recreation and entertainment etc. Natural environment has become accessible by too many people with the increase in spare time and human mobility. Events that are held in natural environment may vary according to the characteristics of relative region. This situation causes each destination to submit various entertainment and recreation facilities and different experiences. This situation ensures that natural environment provides a frame to people to create their own experiences (Breejen, 2007: p. 1418).

One of the reasons why people travel is to get away from the environment that they always live and to go to peaceful areas, which may help them to relax. Therefore, environmental quality is a critical component that affects the destination selection processes of potential tourists. Destinations must increase their environmental qualities in order to attract potential tourists and thus, to gain competitive advantage.

For example, large tourism destinations, such as Egypt, China and India etc. are experiencing pollution and deterioration in terms of environmental components (air, water and garbage heaps etc.) in the process that began with urbanization and industrialization and that still continues. The number of foggy days has increased and air pollution has reached to a critical level in recent years (Zhang, Zhong, Xu, Wang, & Dang, 2015: p. 2398). According to the report published by China Tourism Academy Journal, the number of overseas tourists decreased in the ratio of 0.45% in 2014 in comparison to 2013, and tourist satisfaction has decreased in the ratio of 1.49%. International media and English press in particular notified that the air pollution in China may cause bronchitis, asthma and sinusitis, and that children and elderly may be affected dramatically from this situation in particular [http://www.cctv-america.com/2015/11/18/chinas-air-pollution-affects-tourism-in-2014, (2016, October 18)]. This situation may have affected the destination image of China negatively.

People visit destinations for entertainment, recreation and spending their spare times neatly. People are getting relaxed, taking joy and becoming peaceful by being in a peaceful natural environment that is not polluted and deteriorated. Hull and Harvey (1989) made a study to research the effect of whether the intensity and size of trees available in parks, plant cover and paths make any impact on emotions. In the study, it is revealed that as the intensity of trees in the park increases, as their sizes get bigger and as the number of paths increases, people are becoming more relaxed and peaceful (Prem, Arrowsmith & Jackson, 2004: p. 33). On the other hand, Ulrich et al., (1991) reveals that an impressive natural scenery decreases stress and that it makes an effect to repair human health.

Destinations by the seaside are the locations that provide service to tourists throughout the summer. Tourists living in the northern section tend to spend a part of their holidays in southern coasts where they may enjoy sun and water sports.

European tourists prefer Mediterranean beaches in the summer, and Northern Americans prefer southern coasts, such as Florida, California and Caribbean etc. New exotic destinations that are located at a far distance are also attractive to tourists, who are looking for something different. Distances are becoming less and less thanks to globalization, and people wish to experience different experiences. Goa, Bali and Thailand are among the locations that attract tourists in recent years (Buhalis, 2000: p. 102).

Natural environment is the most critical determinant in the destination selection and destination visit process of tourists. However, natural environmental components may exist by various tourism creative sources, such as accommodation, food-beverage, transportation and entertainment etc. Destinations that are rich in natural environmental sources may not become more than a potential tourism destination as long as there is no tourism creative sources. Tourism sources must be created in order to become an actual tourism destination (Mihalic, 2013: p. 619).

METHODOLOGY

The aim of this study is to reveal the Turkish and Anzac tourists' perceived image of Gallipoli in Turkey. There are some studies in the literature on the perceived destination image. Some of these studies are briefly summarized in the following table. In Table 3 shows some studies about destination image.

Setting and Sample

Target population of the research is comprised of local and foreign tourists, who visited 2016 – Gelibolu Peninsula Historical National Park and who accommodated minimum one night therein. The objective of the research is to obtain information on the demographics, destinations and visit cultures of Turkish and Anzac tourists, who visited Gelibolu Peninsula Historical National Park, which has certain historical and cultural values, which managed to draw attention both in the national and international arena and which has a great importance for Turkish tourism, and to learn the image they have in relation with the destination.

Gallipoli Peninsula Historical National Park

It has become one of the fastest growing tourism activities to visit war fields with the opening of war fields to tourism in recent years. Gelibolu Peninsula Historical National Park is a site where Çanakkale land and sea wars have taken place, and which has a rich plant cover thanks to its historical and cultural values. National Park

Perceived Destination Image

Table 3. Selected Studies About Perceive Destination Image

Author	Region	Sample size	Dimensions	Findings
(Hunt, 1975)	Utah, Montana, Colorado and Wyoming	1000 tourists who don't visit the destination	Territory type, climate, population features and entertainment character	The destination perceptions of tourists who do not visit the region suggests that, most of the entertainment venues and activities of tourists are impressive in all the provinces, but that there are significant differences in the characteristics of territory type, climate and residential population.
(Fayeke & Crompton, 1991)	Rio Grande, Texas	568 prospective, first-time, and repeat long-stay winter visitors to the destination	Social activities, natural and cultural attractions, accommodation and transport, entertainment and leisure activities	There are differences in all dimensions between destination visitors and first-time visitors
(Yılmaz, Icigen, Ekin, & Utku, 2009)	Antalya	1,237 tourists	Environmental conditions, destination advantages, activities, attractiveness, facilities and climate	This study want to reveal the perceived destination image differences between the tourists who just arrived (arriving tourists) and the tourists who are about the leave the destination (departing tourists). It is found that there are significant differences in terms of Environmental Conditions, Attractiveness, and Climate factors between two groups, indicating that the destination possesses a more positive image for departing tourists.
(Wang & Davidson, 2010)	Australia	380 Chinese tourist	Natural attraction and general environment, quality and variety of goods/services, cultural and well-known attractions and accessibility	While tourists are satisfied with the natural surroundings and landscapes, they are not satisfied with accessibility, shopping, museums and entertainment. In the study, which measures the destination image in two stages, pre and post, the post-visit evaluations are found to be slightly more positive
(Tang, 2014)	Wenchuan, China (after the great Wenchuan earthquake of 2008)	346 tourists	travel motivation, destination image and overall satisfaction	A statistically significant relationship between travel motivation and overall visitor satisfaction, as well as relationships between travel motivation and types of destination image
(Lee, Lee & Lee, 2014)	Seoul, South Korea	520 tourists	Affection, amenity and hygiene, diverse attractions, easy accessibility	There is a statistically significant change between the perceived destination image of the tourists' previsit and postvist. The customer's perceived destination image evaluations seem to be more positive after the visit.
(Onder & Marchiori, 2017)	San Francisco, Detroit, Kansas City, Las Vegas, New Orleans, Orlando, Phoenix, and Seattle	2658 (505 tourists visited and 2153 tourists have never been visited the destinations)	Cognitive, affective and conative components	Two studies are conducted to reach this aim. Firstly, an online survey was done to the tourists in order to understand the image of the destination of the selected US cities. Then the videos of the destinations of the same cities are displayed by participating in the analysis of the web sites of the cities. Although the results show a general agreement between the two studies, the uniqueness of the weather conditions, the natural environment and the shopping areas are revealed.
(Atadil, Sarıkaya & Altıntas, 2017)	Dubai and Shanghai	426 (prospective Chinese and Arab tourists)	Accessibility to information and resources, overall destination image, credibility and quality, competitiveness	While the perceptions of Chinese and Arab tourists are similar in terms of competitiveness but they do not differ in other dimensions

holds the center stage both in national and international arena due to aforementioned characteristics.

Gelibolu Peninsula Historical National Park is a very important and meaningful war field for Turks, New Zealanders and Australians. There is an issue that makes Çanakkale War very important and more interesting than all of the other wars. Turkish and Anzac soldiers established warm relations after a very short time from the break out of war, and they managed to remain friends with each other after the war. The word "Anzac" is comprised of the capital letters of the following words; "Australian and New Zealander Army Corps". This concept is greeted with sympathy by all of the three countries. It represents a degree that is mentioned with honor by Australians and New Zealanders. Thousands of Australians and New Zealanders attend to the ceremonies organized in Anzac Bay in April 25 every year. Anzacs, who come from a distance of 22.000 kilometers, are a proof of the friendship inherited to them by their grandfathers (Mütelcimler, 2005: p. 17).

Tourism activities have a great importance in a dynamic country like Turkey, which has quite a young population, and a unique history, and cultural and natural beauties. Although Turkey has improved itself in the field of tourism by years, it lags way behind when compared to other countries. In our country where the numbers of coming tourists increase every day, expenses made by tourists do not represent the same ratio of increase. Turkey may not escape from its image of "cheap country". In brief, it may be observed clearly that the quality of coming tourists is much more important than the number of coming tourists. Most of the foreign tourists, who visit Gelibolu Peninsula Historical National Park, are comprised of Australians and New Zealanders. According to the demographics of tourists, it's see that their levels of education and income are very high. The fact that the tourists visiting a certain destination have a high level of income and education is very important both for the region and country. Another aspect of tourism is that it provides assistance to development of rural regions. It causes new activities and business fields to be opened by giving prominence to the attraction centers in the region and thus, increasing the demand for tourism. Thus, new accommodation entities, restaurants, bars, travel agencies and transportation entities are required in the region. Occurrence of new business opportunities causes employment opportunities to emerge in the region. The population of Gelibolu Peninsula Historical National Park is less than 10.000, and it is a rather small destination. Therefore, field work was performed in Çanakkale - Gelibolu Peninsula Historical National Park since it is important in both regional and national terms to learn how tourists visiting the National Park perceive the destination.

Measurement

The data was collected from the Turkish and Anzac tourists who have visited Gallipoli by using the face-to-face questionnaire. The questionnaire consists of statements of the tourists' perceived destination image about Gallipoli. The questionnaire was both English and Turkish. The perceived destination image scale which was developed by Kim, Hallab, and Kim, (2012), were used to collect the data. The questionnaire items were scored on a five-point Likert scale, ranging from 1= strongly disagree to 5= strongly agree. The questions in the scale consist of four parts; political environment, cultural attractiveness, social environment and natural resources. This scale, which is prepared in the form of 5 Likert type, consists of 22 questions in total. Frequency analysis, factor analysis, t test and correlation were performed in the analysis of the research data.

It was aimed to obtain data that may allow generalization of the findings related with the sample used in the research in consideration of the variables available in conceptual model. Thus, it's detected that 493 surveys are usable, i.e. 250 surveys by Turkish tourists and 243 surveys by Anzac tourists, and therefore, research sample was determined as 493.

FINDINGS

Among the Anzac foreign tourists participating in the survey 50.6% are male, 45.6% are aged between 21-30, while 58.4% of Anzac foreign respondents are single and around 48.6% hold a graduate degree. The 49.1% of foreign respondents earn $8001 and over for a month. The Turkish tourists participating in the survey 52% are male, 28% are aged between 21-30, while 51.2% of the Turkish respondents are married and around 36.4% hold a under graduate degree. The 29.9% of Turkish respondents earn less than $500 for a month. According to the demographic factors, the education and income level of Anzac tourists are quite high. High level of education and income level of the foreign tourists may affect both the destination and country positively.

The travel behaviour of the Anzac and Turkish participants about Gallipoli is also different from each other. Among % 31.4 of Anzac tourists participating in the survey have information about the destination from the internet while the % 24.8 of Turkish participants receive the information about the destination mostly from the travel agency. % 72.4 of foreign participants and % 81.6 of Turkish participants come to Gallipoli for holiday. % 61.7 of the foreign tourist stay in the destination for less than five days and % 49.8 of them have never visited the destination before. The % 92.4 of Turkish participants stay in the destination for less than five days and % 36.8 of them have never visited the destination before. % 46.9 of the foreign participants appear to prefer to travel with organized tour while % 45.6 of Turkish participants prefer to travel with their friends. In addition, while the vast majority of foreign participants (% 35.8) planned their trips in 3-6 months, the % 80.4 of Turkish participants' pre-planning time took less than 3 months. It's revealed that, the Anzac tourists come quite a distance to Turkey, stayed there less than 5 days. It appears that although coming from a very far distance, majority of Australian and New Zealander tourists spend less than five days at the destination. Besides, its historical and cultural attractions, Gallipoli have also a colorful social environment and natural beauties. However, it is demonstrated that, although presenting such attractions, both local and foreign tourists spend very limited time in Gallipoli.

Regarding the scale used in the research, independent samples t-test was used to compare Turkish and Anzac visitors in every aspect. In the difference tests based on the total (493 participants) of Turkish (250 participants) and Anzac (243 participants) groups, we examined whether there is any statistical difference between these two groups.

As a result of the comparative analysis, it's revealed that there are differences between the destination image perceived by Turkish and Anzac tourists visiting Gelibolu Peninsula Historical National Park. Accordingly, it is understood that the Turkish tourists visiting Gelibolu Peninsula Historical National Park perceived the destination with an image that is more positive compared to the image perceived by Anzac tourists in general. In the main dimension of the perceived destination image, the foreign tourists' average (3.77) is lower than the average of the Turkish tourists (4.03).

In the research, it is revealed that there are differences between destination image sub-dimensions of cultural attractiveness of destination and perception of natural environment and political environment images out of the destination image sub-dimensions that are perceived by the Turkish and Anzac tourists visiting Gelibolu Peninsula Historical National Park ($p<0,05$). Turkish participants perceived cultural environment (4.42) more positively than Anzac participants (4.18). Turkish participants perceived political environment (4.15) more positively than Anzac participants (3,63). Turkish participants perceived political environment (4.03) more positively than Anzac participants (3,74). It is understood that Turkish tourists perceive the destination more positively than foreign tourists in cultural, natural and political terms.

On the other hand, it's revealed that Turkish and Anzac tourists perceive social environment components ($p>0,05$), which are among the sub-dimensions of perceived destination image, in the same way. Turkish participants perceived social environment (4.15) more positively than Anzac participants (3,47) but it's not statistically significant ($p>0,05$). Turkish and Anzac tourists perceive the social environment of the destination positive in the same way.

CONCLUSION

This chapter is focused on the subject of perceived destination image, which is of great importance for tourism destinations. Different tourist groups may perceive the characteristics that the destinations have in a different way. It is very important for heterogeneous destinations to know how they are perceived by the visitors. For this purpose, perceived destination image is told in the first place, and then, components that affect perceived destination image are revealed and finally, a quantitative research is made to demonstrate that perceived destination image varies from person to person. Research was made on two tourist groups that visited the same location in the same period of time, that had different demographics and that has different travel cultures. As a result of the t-test that was made on the scale averages of these two groups, it's revealed that the tourist groups, who visit the same destination in the same period of time, go through different experiences than each other in the relative destination, and thus, that the destinations they visit are different from each other. In the political environment sub-dimension, which is one of the destination image sub-dimensions perceived in the study, it was revealed that the average of foreign visitors was lower than the average of local visitors. Accordingly, in comparison to foreign visitors, local visitors perceived that Gelibolu Peninsula Historical National Park has a destination image of a more stable and safe environment and that it is internationally accessible, clean and hygienic, developed economically, and that it is a destination with cheap accommodation facilities, and that it is a destination where it is easier to obtain information on the region. Also, in the cultural attractiveness sub-dimension, which is one of the sub-dimensions of perceived destination image, it is observed that the average of foreign visitors was lower than the average of local visitors. Accordingly, it is understood that the local visitors had the image that Gelibolu Peninsula Historical National Park is a destination that has historical and cultural attraction centers and that has impressive foods and atmosphere. In the natural environment sub-dimension, which is one of the sub-dimensions of perceived destination image, it is observed that the average of foreign visitors was lower than the average of local visitors. Accordingly, in comparison to foreign visitors, local visitors perceive Gelibolu Peninsula Historical National Park as a less polluted and deteriorated, more peaceful natural environment and a destination with more magnificent beaches. On the other hand, in the social environment sub-dimension of perceived destination image, we did not detect any significant difference between the opinions of local and foreign visitors. Accordingly, we revealed that they perceived below issues similarly in terms of destination image; quality of shopping facilities, impressive nightlife, comfort provided by mass transportation facilities, and availability of high quality restaurants, which are considered among the social environment components of Gelibolu Peninsula Historical National Park.

This study is about Turkish and Anzac tourists, who visited the destination, and who experienced the destination. There are also other variables that affect perceived destination image. Therefore, other affecting components are not included to the study.

In today's tourism markets, in which competition increases day by day, it is critical to create a positive destination image in order to achieve a sustainable destination management and marketing process. The fact that the destinations have various levels of attractions and images may establish a bond between tourists and destinations. It's important to know that what kind of images that destinations have and how they are perceived by tourists in order to find out how and why tourists select certain destinations to travel. Because even more important than selling a destination is to determine how a client gives the decision to buy that destination. If tourists have a positive experience in any destination, such situation would ensure that such destination has a positive image. Thus, tourists would prefer such destination, which has a positive image, even more, and they would make positive recommendations.

REFERENCES

Ahmed, Z. U., Sohail, M. S., Myers, C., & Chan Pui, S. (2006). Marketing of Australia to Malaysian Consumers. *Services Marketing Quarterly*, *28*(2), 57–78. doi:10.1300/J396v28n02_04

Alcañiz, E. B., García, I. S., & Blas, S. S. (2009). The Functional-psychological Continuum in the, Cognitive Image of a Destination: A Confirmatory Analysis. *Tourism Management*, *30*(5), 715–723. doi:10.1016/j.tourman.2008.10.020

Alhemoud, A. M., & Armstrong, E. G. (1996). Image of Tourism Attractions in Kuwait. *Journal of Travel Research*, *34*(4), 76–80. doi:10.1177/004728759603400413

Alvarez, M. D., & Campo, S. (2014). The Influence of Political Conflicts on Country Image and Intention to Visit: A Study of Israel's Image. *Tourism Management*, *40*, 70–78. doi:10.1016/j.tourman.2013.05.009

Atadil, H. A., Sarıkaya, E., & Altıntaş, V. (2017). An Analysis of Destination Image for Emerging Markets of Turkey. *Journal of Vacation Marketing*, *23*(1), 37–54. doi:10.1177/1356766715616858

Baloglu, S., & Brinberg, D. (1997). Affective Images of Tourism Destinations. *Journal Of Tourism Research*, *35*(4), 11–15.

Baloglu, S., & Mangaloglu, M. (2001). Tourism Destination Images of Turkey, Egypt, Greece, and Italy as Perceived by US-based Tour Operators and Travel Agents. *Tourism Management*, *22*(1), 1–9. doi:10.1016/S0261-5177(00)00030-3

Baloglu, S., & McCleary, K. W. (1999). A Model Of Destination Image Formation. *Annals of Tourism Research, 26*(4), 868–897. doi:10.1016/S0160-7383(99)00030-4

Beerli, A., & Martin, J. D. (2004). Factors Influencing Destination Image. *Annals of Tourism Research, 31*(3), 657–681. doi:10.1016/j.annals.2004.01.010

Bigley, J. D., Lee, C. K., Chon, J., & Yoon, Y. (2010). Motivations for War-related Tourism: A Case of DMZ Visitors in Korea. *Tourism Geographies, 12*(3), 371–394. doi:10.1080/14616688.2010.494687

Bigne, J. E., Sanchez, M. I., & Sanchez, J. (2001). Tourism Image, Evaluation Variables and After Purchase Behaviour: Inter-relationship. *Tourism Management, 22*(6), 607–616. doi:10.1016/S0261-5177(01)00035-8

Boyd, S. (2002). Cultural and heritage tourism in Canada: Opportunities, principles and challenges. *Tourism and Hospitality Research, 3*(3), 211–233. doi:10.1177/146735840200300303

Boyne, S., Hall, D., & Williams, F. (2003). Policy, Support and Promotion for Food-Related Tourism Initiatives. *Journal of Travel & Tourism Marketing, 14*(3-4), 131–154. doi:10.1300/J073v14n03_08

Breejen, L. (2007). The experiences of long distance walking: A case study of the West Highland Way in Scotland. *Tourism Management, 28*(6), 1417–1427. doi:10.1016/j.tourman.2006.12.004

Buhalis, D. (2000). Marketing the competitive destination of the future. *Tourism Management, 21*(1), 97–116. doi:10.1016/S0261-5177(99)00095-3

Camilleri. (2018a). The Tourism Industry: An Overview. In *Travel Marketing, Tourism Economics and the Airline Product* (pp. 3-27). Cham, Switzerland: Springer.

Camilleri. (2018b). Integrated Marketing Communications. In *Travel Marketing, Tourism Economics and the Airline Product* (pp. 3-27). Cham, Switzerland: Springer.

Cavlek, N. (2002). Tour operators and destination safety. *Annals of Tourism Research, 29*(2), 478–496. doi:10.1016/S0160-7383(01)00067-6

Chen, C., & Chiou-Wei, S. Z. (2009). Tourism expansion, tourism uncertainty and economic growth: New evidence from Taiwan and Korea. *Tourism Management, 30*(6), 812–818. doi:10.1016/j.tourman.2008.12.013

Chen, J. S., & Hsu, C. H. C. (2000). Measurement of Korean Tourists' Perceived Images of Overseas Destinations. *Journal of Travel Research, 38*(4), 411–416. doi:10.1177/004728750003800410

Chen, J. S., & Tsai, D. C. (2007). How destination image and evaluative factors affects behavioral intentions? *Tourism Management*, *29*(4), 1115–1122. doi:10.1016/j.tourman.2006.07.007

Chi, C. G., & Qu, H. (2008). Examining the structural relationships of destination image, tourist satisfaction and destination loyalty: An integrated approach. *Tourism Management*, *29*(4), 624–636. doi:10.1016/j.tourman.2007.06.007

Chon, K. (1990). The role of destination image in tourism: A review and discussion. *Tourism Review*, *45*(2), 2–9.

Chon, K. (1991). Tourism destination image modification process: Marketing implications. *Tourism Management*, *12*(1), 68–72. doi:10.1016/0261-5177(91)90030-W

Chon, K. (1992). The role of destination image in tourism: An extension. *Tourism Review*, *47*(1), 2–8.

Crompton, J. L. (1979). An Assessment of the Image of Mexico as a Vacation Destination and the Influence of Geographical Location Upon That Image. *Journal of Travel Research*, *17*(4), 18–23. doi:10.1177/004728757901700404

Dolnicar, S., & Grün, B. (2013). Validly Measuring Destination Image in Survey Studies. *Journal of Travel Research*, *52*(1), 3–14. doi:10.1177/0047287512457267

Du, R., Gerrie, H. E., & Alberts, N. (2003). The Role of Local and Regional Food in Destination Marketing. *Journal of Travel & Tourism Marketing*, *14*(3-4), 97–112.

Echter, C. M., & Ritchie, J. R. B. (1993). The Measurement Of Destination Image: The Empirical assessment. *Journal of Travel Research*, *31*(4), 3–13. doi:10.1177/004728759303100402

Echtner, C. M., & Ritchie, J. R. B. (1991). The Meaning and Measurement of Destination Image. *Journal of Tourism Studies*, *2*(2), 37–48.

Fayeke, P. C., & Crompton, J. L. (1991). Image Differences between Prospective, First-Time, and Repeat Visitors to the Lower Rio Grande Valley. *Journal of Travel Research*, *30*(2), 10–16. doi:10.1177/004728759103000202

Foley, M., & Lennon, J. J. (1996). JFK and dark tourism: A fascination with assassination. *International Journal of Heritage Studies*, *2*(4), 198–211. doi:10.1080/13527259608722175

Gallarza, G. M., Saura, I. G., & Calderón, H. (2002). Destination image: Towards a Conceptual Framework. *Annals of Tourism Research*, *29*(1), 56–78. doi:10.1016/S0160-7383(01)00031-7

Gartner, C. W. (1989). Tourism Image: Attribute Measurement of State Tourism Products Using Multidimensional Scaling Techniques. *Journal of Travel Research*, *28*(2), 16–20. doi:10.1177/004728758902800205

Gravili, S., & Rosato, P. (2017). Italy's Image as a Tourism Destination in the Chinese Leisure Traveler Market. *International Journal of Marketing Studies*, *9*(5), 28–55. doi:10.5539/ijms.v9n5p28

Gunn, A. C. (1989). *Tourism Planning*. New York: Taylor and Francis.

Hallab, Z., & Kim, K. (2006). US travelers' perceptions of Mississippi as a tourist destination. *Tourism Analysis*, *10*(4), 393–403. doi:10.3727/108354206776162822

Hassan, S. S. (2000). Determinants of Market Competitiveness in an Environmentally Sustainable Tourism Industry. *Journal of Travel Research*, *38*(3), 239–245. doi:10.1177/004728750003800305

Hosany, S., Ekinci, Y., & Uysal, M. (2006). Destination image and destination personality: An application of branding theories to tourism places. *Journal of Business Research*, *59*(5), 638–642. doi:10.1016/j.jbusres.2006.01.001

Hunt, D. J. (1975). Image as a Factor In Tourism Development. *Journal of Tourism Research*, *13*(3), 1–7.

İçöz, O. (2005). *Turizm Ekonomisi*. Ankara: Turhan Kitabevi.

Jenkins, H. O. (1999). Understanding and Measuring Tourist. *International Journal of Tourism Research*, *1*(1), 1–15. doi:10.1002/(SICI)1522-1970(199901/02)1:1<1::AID-JTR143>3.0.CO;2-L

Kalyoncuoğlu, S. & Faiz, E. (2017). Akıllı Telefon Pazarı İçin Müşteri Sadakatinin Oluşturulmasında Memnuniyetin, Algılanan Değerin ve Değiştirme Maliyetinin Etkisi. *Üçüncü Sektör Sosyal Ekonomi, 52*(1), 128-149.

Kastenholz, E., & Lima, J. (2011). The Integral Rural Tourism Experience From the Tourist's Point of View– A Qualitative Analysis of Its Nature and Meaning. *Tourism & Management Studies*, *7*(8), 62–74.

Kerrigan, F., Shivanandan, J., & Hede, A. (2012). Nation Branding: A Critical Appraisal of Incredible India. *Journal of Macromarketing*, *32*(3), 319–327. doi:10.1177/0276146712445788

Kim, K., Hallab, Z., & Kim, J. N. (2012). The moderating effect of travel experience in a destination on the relationship between the destination image and the intention to revisit. *Journal of Hospitality Marketing & Management*, *21*(5), 486–505. doi:10.1080/19368623.2012.626745

Kozak, N. (2006). *Turizm Pazarlaması*. Ankara: Detay Yayıncılık.

Lee, B., Lee, C., & Lee, J. L. (2014). Dynamic Nature of Destination Image and Influence of Tourist Overall Satisfaction on Image Modification. *Journal of Travel Research*, *53*(2), 239–251. doi:10.1177/0047287513496466

Letho, Y. X., Jang, S., Achana, F. T., & O'Leary, J. T. (2004). Tourist shopping preferences and expenditure behaviours: The case of the Taiwanese outbound market. *Journal of Vacation Marketing*, *10*(4), 320–332. doi:10.1177/135676670401000404

Li, X., & Stepchenkova, S. (2012). Chinese Outbound Tourists' Destination Image of America: Part I. *Journal of Travel Research*, *51*(3), 250–266. doi:10.1177/0047287511410349

Long, T. P., & Perdue, R. R. (1990). The Economic Impact of Rural Festivals And Special Events: Assessing The Spatial Distribution of Expenditures. *Journal of Travel Research*, *28*(4), 10–14. doi:10.1177/004728759002800403

Martinez, S. C., & Alvarez, D. M. (2010). Country Versus Destination Image in a Developing Country. *Journal of Travel & Tourism Marketing*, *27*(7), 748–764. doi:10.1080/10548408.2010.519680

Mihalic, T. (2013). Performance of Environmental Resources of a Tourist Destination: Concept and Application. *Journal of Travel Research*, *52*(5), 614–630. doi:10.1177/0047287513478505

Milman, A., & Pizam, A. (1995). The Role of Awareness and Familiarity with a Destination: The Central Florida Case. *Journal of Travel Research*, *33*(3), 21–27. doi:10.1177/004728759503300304

Mütelcimler, E. (2005). *Korkak Abdul'den Coni Türk'e Gelibolu*. İstanbul: Alfa Basım Yayım Dağıtım.

Okumuş, B., Okumuş, F., & McKercher, B. (2007). Incorporating local and international cuisines in the marketing of tourism destinations: The cases of Hong Kong and Turkey. *Tourism Management*, *28*(1), 253–261. doi:10.1016/j.tourman.2005.12.020

Onder, I., & Marchiori, E. (2017). A Comparison of Pre-visit Beliefs and Projected Visual Images of Destinations. *Tourism Management Perspectives*, *21*, 42–53. doi:10.1016/j.tmp.2016.11.003

Öztürk, Y., Yeşiltaş, M., Kozak, M., Özel, Ç. H., & Aksöz, O. (2013). *Destinasyon Yönetimi*. Eskişehir: Anadolu Üniversitesi Yayınları.

Pike, S. (2002). Destination Image Analysis – a Review of 142 Papers from 1973 to 2000. *Tourism Management*, *23*(5), 541–549. doi:10.1016/S0261-5177(02)00005-5

Pizam, A. (1999). A Comprehensive Approach to Classifying Acts of Crime and Violence at Tourism Destinations. *Journal of Travel Research*, *38*(1), 5–12. doi:10.1177/004728759903800103

Prem, C., Arrowsmith, C., & Jackson, M. (2004). Determining Hiking Experiences in Nature-based Tourist Destinations. *Tourism Management*, *25*(1), 31–43. doi:10.1016/S0261-5177(03)00057-8

Qu, H., Kim, L. H., & Im, H. H. (2011). A Model of Destination Branding: Integrating the Concepts of the Branding and Destination Image. *Tourism Management*, *32*(3), 465–476. doi:10.1016/j.tourman.2010.03.014

Quan, S., & Wang, N. (2004). Towards a Structural Model of the Tourist Experience: An Illustration. *Tourism Management*, *25*(3), 297–305. doi:10.1016/S0261-5177(03)00130-4

Rittichainuwat, B. N., & Chakraborty, G. (2009). Perceived Travel Risks Regarding Terrorism and Disease: The case of Thailand. *Tourism Management*, *30*(3), 410–418. doi:10.1016/j.tourman.2008.08.001

Seaton, A. V. (1996). Guided by the Dark: From Thanatopsis to Thanatourism. *International Journal of Heritage Studies*, *2*(4), 234–244. doi:10.1080/13527259608722178

Seddighi, H., Nuttall, M., & Theocharous, A. (2001). Does cultural background of tourists influence the destination choice? an empirical study with special reference to political instability. *Tourism Management*, *22*(2), 181–191. doi:10.1016/S0261-5177(00)00046-7

Shahzad, S. J. H., Shahbaz, M., Ferrer, R., & Kumar, R. R. (2017). Tourism-led growth hypothesis in the top ten tourist destinations: New evidence using the quantile-on-quantile approach. *Tourism Management*, *60*, 223–232. doi:10.1016/j.tourman.2016.12.006

Smith, V. L. (1998). War and Tourism: An American Ethnography. *Annals of Tourism Research*, *25*(1), 202–227. doi:10.1016/S0160-7383(97)00086-8

Sonmez, S., Apostolopoulos, Y., & Tarlow, P. (1999). Tourism in Crisis: Managing the Effects of Terrorism. *Journal of Travel Research*, *38*(1), 13–18. doi:10.1177/004728759903800104

Sonmez, S. F. (1998). Tourism, Terrorism and Political Instability. *Annals of Tourism Research*, *25*(2), 416–456. doi:10.1016/S0160-7383(97)00093-5

Stepchenkova, S., & Mills, J. E. (2010). Destination Image: A Meta-Analysis of 2000–2007. *Journal of Hospitality Marketing & Management*, *19*(6), 575–609. doi:10.1080/19368623.2010.493071

Tang, Y. (2014). Travel Motivation, Destination Image and Visitor Satisfaction of International Tourists After the 2008 Wenchuan Earthquake: A Structural Modelling Approach. *Asia Pacific Journal of Tourism Research*, *19*(11), 1260–1277. doi:10.1080/10941665.2013.844181

Tascı, A. D. A. (2007). Assessment of factors influencing destination image using a multiple regression model. *Tourism Review*, *62*(2), 23–30. doi:10.1108/16605370780000311

Taşçı, A. D. A., Gartner, W. C., & Cavusgil, S. T. (2007). Conceptualization And Operationalization of Destination Image. *Journal of Hospitality & Tourism Research (Washington, D.C.)*, *31*(2), 194–223. doi:10.1177/1096348006297290

Taylor, D. T. F., Robert, R., & Clabaugh, T. (1993). A Comparison of Characteristics, Regional Expenditures, and Economic Impact of Visitors to Historical Sites with Other Recreational Visitors. *Journal of Travel Research*, *32*(1), 30–35. doi:10.1177/004728759303200105

Thompson, K., & Schofield, P. (2007). An investigation of the relationship between public transport performance and destination satisfaction. *Journal of Transport Geography*, *15*(2), 136–144. doi:10.1016/j.jtrangeo.2006.11.004

Turner, L., & Reisinger, Y. (2001). Shopping satisfaction for domestic tourists. *Journal of Retailing and Consumer Services*, *8*(1), 15–27. doi:10.1016/S0969-6989(00)00005-9

Ulrich, R. S., Simons, R. F., Losito B. D. & Fiorito, E. (1991). Stress recovery during exposure to natural and urban environments. *Journal of Environmental Psychology, 11*, 201-230.

Wang, Y., & Davidson, M. C. G. (2010). Pre- and post-trip perceptions: An insight into Chinese package holiday market to Australia. *Journal of Vacation Marketing, 16*(2), 111–123. doi:10.1177/1356766709357488

Yılmaz, Y., Yılmaz, Y., Icigen, E. T., Ekin, Y., & Utku, D. B. (2009). Destination Image: A Comparative Study on Pre and Post Trip Image Variations. *Journal of Hospitality Marketing & Management, 18*(5), 461–479. doi:10.1080/19368620902950022

Zhang, A., Zhong, L. Y., Xu, Y., Wang, H., & Dang, L. (2015). Tourists' Perception of Haze Pollution and the Potential Impacts on Travel: Reshaping the Features of Tourism Seasonality in Beijing, China. *Sustainability, 7*(3), 2397–2414. doi:10.3390u7032397

KEY TERMS AND DEFINITIONS

Cultural Environment: An environment with unique characteristics created by each community.

Destination: Places offering goods and services to tourists during their holidays.

Image: People's perception of something.

Natural Environment: It is an environment living and non-living beings interact in harmony, which gives people peace and happiness.

Perceived Destination Image: The feelings and thoughts that tourists have of a place.

Political Environment: The environment in which a country, central and local governments, and their affiliates provide and exercise political authority.

Social Environment: It is an environment that allows the individual to have a good time.

Chapter 11
A Strategic Framework for Managing the Challenges of Developing Rural Tourism Destination Branding

Samuel Adeyinka-Ojo
Curtin University, Malaysia

ABSTRACT

This chapter explores the importance and challenges of branding for rural tourism destination. In the wider context of destination branding construct, empirical studies on the strategies to manage the identifiable challenges have received fewer academic interests. In this chapter, triangulation of data sources was used in the collection of data that included in-depth interviews with 31 multiple stakeholders in Bario, Miri, and Kuching in Malaysia. Findings show destination branding is important and there are several factors inhibiting rural tourism destination brand development. In terms of contributions to the existing knowledge, this study has produced a strategic framework for managing the challenges of rural tourism destination branding. Implications for practice, host community, and directions for future studies are discussed.

DOI: 10.4018/978-1-5225-5835-4.ch011

INTRODUCTION

The goal of every destination is to position itself in such a way that the visitors' experiences of that place will bring about repeat visits and create unsolicited ambassadors for the destination (Morgan, Pritchard & Pride, 2010). This phenomenon has led many rural destinations to look into the potentials and strategies involved in developing their destination brand. Extant studies on place and destination branding, tourism destination marketing, and phases involved in building a tourism destination branding indicate there are challenges of destination brand development (Baker & Cameron, 2008; Morrison, 2013), particularly in a rural place. Notably, in the wider context of destination branding construct, strategies to manage the identifiable challenges have received fewer academic interests.

Furthermore, the capability in terms of location advantage may not be readily available for a rural destination. According to Cai (2002), destination branding involves selecting a consistent mix of brand elements to identify and distinguish a destination through positive image building. Morrison and Anderson (2002) describe destination branding as a way of disseminating the uniqueness of a destination identity through differentiable features from other competing locations. The purpose of rural tourism destination brand building is to create a unique identity for rural place that differentiates it from competing rural destinations. There are similarities in the way rural tourism destinations are promoted and marketed. This view is consistent with Greaves and Skinner's (2010) study that rural destination in the United Kingdom promote themselves on their superb scenery, offer for relaxation, outdoor leisure activities, quality accommodation, locally-sourced food, a range of attractions and a full calendar year of rural events and festivals.

The current study was conducted in Bario a rural destination and predominantly a rice farming community without amenities such as good roads, water, electricity, hotels and modern houses. This rural community is located in the heart of Kelabits highlands in Sarawak, East Malaysia. Bario is situated 3, 200 feet above sea level or at an altitude of about 1,100m (Jiwan, Paul, Teo & Jiwan, 2006). This rural place has a population of about 1,200 people (Malaysian Government, 2011). Accessibility to this village is via an 18 - seater Otter aircraft twice a day depending on the weather conditions. Bario lacks a network of good roads as a result it takes about 14 hours in a four-wheel drive on a logging road from Miri the gate way city to the village.

It should be noted that less than 10 per cent of total tourist arrivals in Malaysia visit rural tourism destinations due to poor planning resulting in tourist discomfort, low patronage and a negatively impacting overall satisfaction (Government of Malaysia, 2010). Likewise, some of the few rural destinations in Malaysia that have attracted tourists in the past are no longer attractive to tourists to visit due to the greed of the tourism economy, a lack of planning and an overuse of these rural destinations (Mohamed & Muhibudin, 2012). Currently, there is a lack of brand positioning in rural tourism destinations in Malaysia and this is detrimental to the growth and development of rural tourism.

Therefore, in order to reposition the battered image of rural tourism in Malaysia, the Malaysian government has recognized that there is a need to develop a destination brand for rural tourism (Government of Malaysia Tenth Malaysia Plan, 2010, p. 327). More importantly, the aims of this study are from two perspectives. First, it is to identify the challenges of developing a brand for rural tourism destination; and second, is to outline the strategies that could be adopted to manage these challenges of developing a brand from the context of rural tourism destination. In order to have a good knowledge of the existing gaps, the next section is focused on the relevant literature work on issues affecting rural tourism space, branding and destination branding concepts, importance of destination branding, challenges of destination branding, and managing identified factors affecting branding process especially in rural destinations.

LITERATURE REVIEW

Sundries Issues in Rural Tourism Destination

The first issue this section addresses is to provide answers to the following pertinent question: Is a rural place developed as a tourism destination still rural? A rural place can be developed as tourism space and still maintain its status as a rural destination. For example, Leineperi is a village of 300 inhabitants and rural tourism destination in Finland; it is known as an important heritage site and one of the country's best-preserved old industrial villages (Mittila & Lepisto, 2013). Despite the modern development in the village it retains its status as a rural place. Leineperi has a museum, and the village brand is basically based on iron, its cultural history, seasonal markets, and themed events that focus on mental art, craftsmanship, organic and local food (Mittila & Lepisto, 2013).

On the other hand, a rural place can be developed as tourism destination, but the quantum and quality of infrastructures provided in such a destination should be the criteria that should be considered if such a rural place is categorized as urbanized. This should also be pointed out in the event that the infrastructures development alters the authentic experience and "ruralness" of such a place. For example, Langkawi in Malaysia used to be *a rural fishing village, Langkawi today has transformed into a developed rural tourism destination* (Nair 2015, p. 154). The level of sophisticated infrastructures developed in Langkawi, which include an international airport, and five and six stars hotels by both government and private investors may have altered the status. However, based on the Langkawi Tourism Blueprint (2011-2015), the goal is to transform Langkawi into one of the leading islands in the world (LADA, 2011). The burning issue is whether we can say that Langkawi though a developed rural destination is still rural or urban destination. In this context, it will depend on the Malaysia government's criteria that states if the population of a place is less than 10,000 (Malaysian Government, 2011), such place can be regarded as a rural destination.

The second issue this section set out to explore is when does a rural place become urban? The criteria used vary from one country to the other (Obonyo & Fwaya, 2012). Based on the arguments in the preceding section, most countries have used population to determine if a place is rural or urban irrespective of the level of both infrastructures and private amenities. In Malaysia for example, population is mainly used. The next issue is to look into what are the consequences of such changes in terms of the development on rural places? According to Mostowfi (2000), only those rural regions with specific cultural, authentic, natural or social charm would attract tourists. Similarly, rural tourism comes into existence when the rural culture is the key component of the tourism product offering (OECD, 1994). The consequences of such changes may alter the visitors' perception that the rural identity has changed. This may lead to loss of rural tourists in the short term but in the long run, the destination may be able to attract different groups of tourists depending on the new tourism products on offer.

Moreover, the characteristics of a rural destination, specifically from the tourism perspective are also taken into consideration. This is because the characteristics of a rural place are the identity that distinguishes a rural space from other tourism destinations. Basically, there are certain features of a rural space which include remoteness or countryside (Petric, 2003); non-urban settings (Pakurar & Olah, 2008); natural environment (Aref & Gill, 2009); rural leisure activities and scenery (Lo, Songan & Mohamad, 2011); authentic experience (Kim & Jamal, 2007); lack of amenities and infrastructures (Cai, 2002; Haven-Tang & Sedgley, 2014); difficult accessibility (Bala, 2002); traditional and lifestyle (Petric, 2003); without mass tourism (Lebe & Milelner, 2006); low population (Ghaderi & Henderson, 2012); and farming occupation and rural people (Pourova, 2002).

To sum up, the issue of whether branding effectively changes the nature of a place and the likely impacts on its social fabric; especially in relation to the rural space will depend on the ability of destination multiple stakeholders to manage the success or failure of a rural tourism place. Based on the extant literature, branding of a rural place would change the nature of the place and it would have both social and economic impacts on the rural tourism destination. Notably, the first impact of branding on a destination is to create favorable destination image, awareness in the minds of the visitors, tourist loyalty, repeat visit, increase in quality of tourism service and standard of living (Tasci, 2011). On top of that, branding of a destination is a catalyst for economic development and tourism growth (Turtureanu, 2005; Schubert, Brida, & Risso, 2011). Other impacts include infrastructures development (Camilleri, 2018a; Tasci, 2011; Lo, Songan, & Mohamad, 2011, p.104). In addition, there is potential of becoming a high yielding tourism destination (Dwyer, Forsyth, Fredline, Jago, Deery, & Lundie, 2006; Northcote & Macbeth, 2006). However, despite the positive impacts of branding on tourism destination, it could affect the social fabrics negatively. For example, due to an increased number of tourist arrivals, it could lead to increase in crime, drug use, prostitution, language and cultural effects, negative changes in values and custom, increase in price levels (Camilleri, 2018b; Kayat, 2011; Kayat, 2008), and carrying capacity may be affected. In view of these challenges, it is expedient that the importance of destination branding and likely negative effects should be communicated to the multiple stakeholders. This is lacking in the literature and hence, there is a lack of support from the host community and multiple stakeholders.

Branding and Destination Branding Concepts

Keller (2003) describes branding as a strategic business choice grounded in ancient times, which involves marking livestock, crafts and guilds, and the purpose is to develop signs of ownership for protection against stealing and counterfeiting the original, in terms of identification and differentiation with the promise of certain qualities. This definition attempts to address some fundamental concepts such as strategy, ownership, protection, differentiation and qualities which are important components of branding concepts. Esu and Arrey (2009) referred to branding as all the processes and marketing activities involved in creating a brand.

Destination branding is a term commonly used by scholars in tourism literature to explain how to develop a unique identity for a tourism destination that helps the actual and potential tourists to differentiate a given tourism location from another destination (Greaves & Skinner, 2010). This view is consistent with Morgan, Pritchard, and Piggot's (2002) study where they argue that it is imperative for tourism destinations to develop a unique identity – to create a niche and clearly distinguish a destination from other competing destinations. Destination branding is used to promote specific (or named) tourism destination or location. This tourism destination could be a city, town, village or iconic centers. From the context of a rural place, the aim of tourism destination branding is to create a unique identity for a rural destination that differentiates it from similar rural tourism places.

The Importance of Destination Branding

The importance of destination branding on tourists and tourists' reaction when making decisions on where to spend their holidays is a phenomenon that destination marketing and branding managers should have a good understanding in terms of planning and implementation. Haven-Tang and Sedgley (2014) argue that the common features of rural destinations and lack of distinct differentiation make it a difficult effort to attract visitors, and to create a sense of destination awareness and identity. For example, there are several rural destinations in Malaysia that offer similar rural tourism products. These tourism products include jungle trekking or hiking, beautiful beaches, homestays, water rafting, water sports, farming tourism, adventure tourism and cultural tourism, which can be found in rural destinations across the country. However, the question is how we separate the 'wheat from the shaft' or better put, how would a tourist differentiate a preferred rural tourism destination among other competing destinations that offer similar products which could lead to a repeat experience. The answer is to adopt the concept of destination brand into rural tourism. This view is consistent with Greaves and Skinner (2010)'s study where destination brand is used to explain the unique identity of a tourism destination that helps the actual and potential tourists to differentiate a given tourism location from another destination.

Challenges of Destination Branding

Extant literature review indicates that there are challenges which could inhibit destination brand building. For example, Baker and Cameron (2008) observe that despite the benefits of destination branding, there are different challenges faced by destination marketers in developing a destination brand. These issues are classified into three namely: financial, political and environmental challenges (Morgan & Pritchard, 2010). In most cases, destination management and marketing organizations (DMMOs) have very limited financial resources coupled with political strive or instability in some destinations, economic downsizing, terrorism, wars, outbreak of diseases, negative media coverage and other environmental disasters which affect destination image and brand building efforts (Morgan & Pritchard, 2010).

In addition, another constraint to tourism destination branding is the lack of sole control over product and marketing programs, unlike normal products and services where a single organization can handle or provide direction for its marketing activities (Morgan & Pritchard, 2010). Furthermore, destination politics is also identified as one of the challenges of destination brand building. According to Baker and Cameron (2008), destination politics is concerned with the complexity of the tourism offerings as well as the issue of multiple stakeholders and the complex relationship among the stakeholders which poses an obstacle for an effective tourism destination branding process. Other obstacles include difficulty of communicating brand benefits and brand promise (Baker & Cameron, 2008).

Moreover, Anholt (2010) summarizes eight key challenges in developing a destination brand. These challenges are: (1) understanding visitors and non-visitors; (2) achieving stakeholder buy-in of the destination brand; (3) destination brand architecture (relationship between national and regions brands); (4) stretching the brand through partnership (seeking for suitable brand partners for example airlines, NGOs, government ministries, development agencies); (5) user-generated content and social networking (considering the threat and opportunity); (6) brand coherence: image and cliché (distinguishing between stereotypes and icons); (7) branding on a budget (no budget is too small for a destination brand), and; (8) brand lifespan and re-branding (otherwise known as destination brand fashion curve to illustrate destination brand life cycle which consists of *fashionable, famous, familiar, fatigued and refreshment*, unlike the phases of product life cycle such as *introduction, growth, maturity, saturation and decline*).

With regards to Anholt's suggestion on brand life cycle, it is consistent with Weinreich (1999) that instead of considering brand life cycle, destination brand managers should look into destination brand S-curve, that is, *fashionable, famous, familiar, fatigued and refreshment* which shows a brand's life and development. Braun, Kavaratis and Zenker (2010) also mention that in developing a destination brand, one of the constraints include the local residents' characteristics and reputation. This claim is consistent with Foley and Fahy (2004) that one of the major challenges of destination branding is that the large society or the general public of the tourism destination do not yet view or consider destination as a brand like products and services.

Besides that, Tapachai and Waryszak's (2000) study views the challenges of developing destination branding from destination image related problems from the tourist's opinion based on five values. For example epistemic values deals with the experience of a new culture; emotional values deal with the atmosphere of a resort; functional values include the number of shops available at the destination for shopping purposes; conditional values is the availability of cheap travel; and social values include the suitability for all ages (tourists). Supphellen and Helgeson (2004) observe that destination marketers need to take into consideration heterogeneity of tourists motives of different target visitors to visit a destination and this has been identified as a challenge for destination branding integrated marketing communication. Besides this, the UNWTO (2007, p.5) mention that in developing a destination brand, tourism destinations are faced with different challenges which include 'budget limitations, political interference, an often volatile external environment, delivery challenges, corruption and differentiation issues'.

Moreover, Morrison (2013) mentions several challenges of destination branding. These include:

1. Destination mix products and services;
2. Lack of DMMOs total control over destination branding mix;
3. Involvement of multiple players;
4. Lack of long-term commitment by destination players;
5. Tourism destination as an experience product;
6. Lack of sufficient funding;
7. Political issue and influence, and;
8. Public criticism on destination brands advertising.

In addition, Moilanen and Rainisto's (2009) contribution that states that developing a destination brand is different significantly from the branding of physical consumer goods. They suggest the following as challenges of building a destination and place brand, namely:

1. New concepts, new range of usage;
2. Difficulties in controlling;
3. Collective character of place marketing;
4. The customer builds the product, and limited possibilities to opt out - 'forced network';
5. Defining a brand's objective in a network and closeness to politics;
6. Product factor's inequality;
7. Product's development;
8. Tourism product's experience centricity;
9. Changing seasons and a brand; and
10. Limited financial resources.

It should be noted that there exists commonalities in the challenges of destination branding identified by previous studies. Hence, these factors affecting destination brand building can be summed up in seven major categories. These include lack of adequate financial resources, political and environment issues, multiple stakeholders, complexity of tourism products, host community and destination politics, user-generated content (UGC) and social networking, and destination image-related issues from the tourist's standpoint.

Managing the Challenges of Destination Branding

It should be noted that there are limited or no studies that have developed the strategies for managing the challenges of destination brand building. However, based on the literature that has focused on the challenges of destination brand development, it is possible to point out the potential strategies of managing these challenges (Camilleri, 2018c). For example, these potential strategies include stakeholders' involvement, developing unique and distinguishable destination, destination brand benefits communication, adequate funding/budget, identifying and managing distinctive tourism attractions, and develop unique and distinguishable destinations (Foley & Fahy, 2004; Baker & Cameron, 2008; Morgan & Pritchard, 2010). Therefore, the empirical inquiry conducted in this study focuses on the challenges and strategies of managing the challenges of destination brand building from the rural tourism context.

METHODOLOGY

This study was designed to further understand rural tourism from the perspective of destination brand building. This study adopted the qualitative research methodology (Cresswell, 2014; Guba & Lincoln, 1994) because it is the most appropriate in answering the research questions, while the purposive sampling technique was employed in recruiting the participants. Bario, the study context is chosen and categorized as a rural destination based on the Malaysian government criteria of having a population of less than 10,000. Bario local inhabitants are estimated at 1,200 based on the 2010 population figure (Malaysian Government, 2011).

Triangulation of data sources were used in the collection of data that included in-depth interviews which can provide rich information into people's experiences, opinions, values, attitudes and feelings (May, 2001); participant observation (Tilstone, 1998; Jorgensen, 1989) and documentary evidence (Kalkstein-Silkes, 2007). The most important benefit of triangulation in this study is that findings are more convincing and accurate if it is based on multiple sources of evidence or information (Yin, 2009, p.116). The data were collected from multiple stakeholders. More specifically, this study is structured to answer the following research questions: (a) What are the importance of destination branding in the context of rural tourism?; (b) What are the challenges of developing a destination brand for rural tourism?, and; (c) What are the strategies of managing the challenges of rural tourism destination brand development?

To achieve the aims of this study, the researcher conducted in-depth interviews with 31 participants in Bario's rural community, Miri and Kuching which are gateway cities to Bario in Sarawak between May and July 2014 until the point of data saturation was achieved (Jennings, 2010; Strauss & Corbin, 2008). The selection criteria are that the participants should be stakeholders in rural tourism destination and tourists should have visited Bario in the past or first timers should have spent at least five nights. This is important in order for the tourists to share their lived experiences and why they decided to revisit Bario. The selection of participants followed studies on stakeholders in rural tourism destination (Quinlan, 2008; Nair, Munikrishnan, Rajaratnam & King, 2015, p. 333).

The in-depth interviews adopted a semi-structured format in order to elicit detailed data (Lofland & Lofland, 1995). The in-depth interviews were recorded by using a digital tape recorder with an average of 45 minutes per interview (Rasmussen, Ostergaard, & Beckmann, 2006) and transcribed after the interviews were concluded (Gubrium & Holstein, 2001). This study adopted the six stages of thematic analysis to analyze the in-depth interviews (Braun & Clarke, 2006). Thematic analysis was deemed fit because it is a qualitative analytic method that involves identifying themes by systematically reading the data very carefully and then re-reading the data several times (Fereday & Muir-Cochrane, 2006).

In addition, a total of 10 days of participant observation was conducted in Bario which generated 12 pages of field notes. These field notes from the participant observation were used as supplementary data and the content was analyzed for the themes developed from the in-depth interviews. Cresswell (2007, pp.134-135) identifies seven steps that are necessary in participant observation which were adopted in this study. In addition, the recommendations of Tilstone (1998) were followed, where the participant observation should address the context (date, time of the day, length of observation, and events) and content of the phenomenon being studied (stakeholders' participation and involvement in activities that suggest challenges in rural destination brand building and strategies to reduce the bottlenecks).

Moreover, documentary evidence was used to supplement the data obtained from both in-depth interviews and participant observation. The criteria used for the selection of the documentary evidence are to assess the sources of the printed materials if they are reliable. In this study, the following criteria were adopted in the selection of the documentary evidence namely authenticity, credibility, representativeness and meaning (Scott, 1990, pp.7-35). This is important to guide against threats to validity and reliability (Scott, 1990). The selection of documentary evidence is in harmony with the previous study where brochures (or documentary evidence or printed materials) were used in three rural destinations of Indiana in the United States of America (Kalkstein-Silkes, 2007).

RESULTS AND DISCUSSION

In this study, 31 participants were contacted and interviewed in May and July 2014 in Bario, and the cities of Miri and Kuching. These include participants from the Ministry of Tourism (MoT); the Sarawak Tourism Board (STB) which is the local DMMOs saddled with the responsibilities of marketing and promoting tourism in Bario; the sole airline company operating flight services in and out of Bario; the Miri Tourism Task Force (MTTF); and State Department of Immigration headquarters in Kuching. These participants were regarded as stakeholders in tourism development and destination branding of Bario. Notably amongst them are ten international tourists, a researcher from the University of London who was interviewed in Bario, two local tourists, seven local residents and tourism entrepreneurs, an airline pilot at Miri airport, and three key informants from MoT and STB. Likewise, there are three participants from non-government organizations and tourism volunteers, two destination branding experts, one participant from MTTF, and finally one participant was also interviewed from the Department of Immigration (DOI). The inclusion of the interview from DOI was due to the unique position of Sarawak as a state in the eastern part of the country which has different immigration laws and autonomy compared with other states in west Malaysia. In order to protect the anonymity of the interviewees, a participant code (PC) number was used to represent each of the participants.

Destination Branding

The participants' opinions on what they think should be the importance of destination branding from a rural destination standpoint is presented in the following statements. A tourist from New Zealand said:

Basically... destination branding should set a standard... it would also lead to tourist loyalty if the experience meets their expectation. They will always see Bario as their choice destination and become brand ambassador to Bario by word of mouth and provide unsolicited publicity. (PC3)

Likewise, when asked about the importance of a destination brand in a rural destination, a local resident, homestay operator and community leader commented:

Bario will be placed on the world map, well known, and Bario will be developed in terms of social amenities like road, electricity and many more. Repeat visit and development of the local economy. (PC30)

On top of that, a director with the Sarawak Tourism Board (DMMO for Bario) affirmed the importance of a of destination branding:

Destination branding brings tourist loyalty, increase tourist arrivals, government providing infrastructures, attracts more tourism investment, favorable destination image and identity. (PC1)

Findings from the analyses of participants' views on the importance of destination branding show that destination branding leads to tourist loyalty and an increase in tourist arrivals because tourists would become destination ambassadors through the word of mouth by sharing their positive experiences, which comes as a result of quality service and satisfaction. These findings are consistent with previous studies that claim tourist satisfaction is a determinant of destination loyalty (Aaker, 1991; Moore, Rodger & Taplin, 2013). Destination branding could lead to high yield tourist destination which has a link with the tourist's willingness to pay (WTP) more due to increase in tourist spending (Northcote & Macbeth, 2006), and Bario has potential to transform itself from a low to high yield rural tourism destination (Adeyinka-Ojo & Khoo-Lattimore, 2013). Summary of these findings on the importance of destination branding is presented in Table 1.

Table 1. Importance of Destination Branding

Importance of destination branding in rural tourism destination uncovered in this study	Favorable destination image and awareness
	Tourist loyalty and repeat visit
	Increase in quality service and standard of living
	Tourism revenue and sales taxes
	Modern homestay and maintenance of culture
	Catalyst for economic development and tourism growth
	Infrastructures development
	High yield tourism destination
	Promoting sustainable tourism
	Preservation of traditional farming occupation
	Human capacity development
	Agriculture and non- tourism investment

(Source: Compiled by the Author)

Challenges of Developing a Destination Brand

The purpose of this section is to present the findings and highlights the opinions of participants in the in-depth interview sessions as it affects the challenges of building a destination brand from the context of rural tourism. Comments from these participants are presented in the following statements.

The key informant from the Ministry of Tourism in Sarawak points out:

...One of the challenges would be a lack of good leadership at the lower lever. If there is no leadership who has the interest of the community, things will not work and it may be difficult to liaise with other stakeholders. Another issue here is the lack of funds to carry out branding development and how it can be launched at the destination. The challenge of fulfilling what the destination has promised the tourists - because if you promise and you cannot fulfil it could backfire resulting in tourists not trusting the destination. The geographic location l think is another challenge especially when the destination is not easily accessible. There is a lot of politics which l would not mention... The issue of security and safety is another challenge due to terrorism or kidnapping as a result, especially for foreign tourists, immigration may tighten control on the number of visitors coming especially if there are concerns for citizens from certain countries. (PC23)

Findings from the statements of this key informant from the Ministry of Tourism (MOT) highlights most of the challenges in developing a destination brand specifically in rural tourism. These findings are consistent with literature sources on the challenges of building a destination brand. For example, the issues of funding, politics and the environment have been reported in previous studies (Baker & Cameron, 2008; Morgan & Pritchard, 2010). Furthermore, comments from a local resident and teacher in one of the community schools in Bario reveal additional challenges of developing a destination brand stating:

...One of the challenges is how to get the participation of the host community; the second is the quality and availability of branding experts. The issue of finance is also very crucial, the willingness of other stakeholders to show commitment to the branding project. Another issue is the political environment of the destination whether it has a negative image or positive image including the local politics in terms of government commitment to tourism. (PC14)

One of the major challenges in the tourism industry is the lack of skilled manpower. In destination brand development, there are very few destination brand experts in the industry and this has been a challenge to most tourism destinations. The tourism industry is growing globally but there is a lack of skilled manpower to manage this industry. Findings from this section is consistent with what is obtained in practice. However, a lack of destination branding experts is less reported in the existing literature as a challenge of developing a destination brand. This finding is viewed as a contribution to this study. When asked about the challenges of destination brand building, a tourist from Germany stated:

Accessibility and transportation could be one of the challenges of destination brand. Another challenge is that ... the destination is not well known, where the image is known to very few people. For example, many people may not know about Bario until they get to Malaysia. Branding is a big project as it requires good funding and political will, I mean, government support - basically these are the main challenges. (PC9)

One of the homestay operators, who is also a local resident and tour guide states that:

Destination awareness could be a challenge including the image of the place in the tourism market. Also, the geographical location whether it is a city, town or a remote destination because it will affect the accessibility by the tourist. Funding is also a major challenge in tourism destination branding; the presence of multiple stakeholders with different economic and political interests is a major issue. This is followed by local politics, safety and security concern;[and] host community attitudes in terms of whether they are on the same page with other stakeholders is very important. (PC17)

The issue of accessibility is one of the main challenges in tourism destination. There are several studies on destination accessibility (Ritchie & Crouch, 2003; UNWTO, 2007; Cooper, 2012). These studies have not mentioned accessibility as one of the challenges of developing a destination brand. This is a new insight that needs to be considered in the destination brand building process. For example, a director from one of the NGOs and volunteers in Bario echoes:

Hmm.. I think one of the challenges is the geographical location of the tourism destination. If a place is located where the accessibility is very difficult, it may be difficult to brand. The second is more or less a political problem, where the perception about the country is not favorable - this would affect branding and tourists would avoid the place... because of safety and security concerns. We also have the problem of finding people who know much on how a rural tourism destination can be branded and developed... most of the people are not well trained because what l can see there is advertisement and promotion just to create awareness, but l don't think it has much impact on the people. The last one which l think is very important is the issue of a lack of adequate funding. (PC31)

This section was concluded with comments from a marketing and branding expert:

OK, the major challenge would be a lack of financial resources because even bigger destinations suffer the same fate. Political and environmental challenges such as political interference, conflicts, natural disasters, apathy and opposition from the local community cannot be overemphasized. The issue of a lack of human resources and infrastructures to handle the brand can lead to an inability to deliver the brand promise to the tourist. (PC26)

These findings revealed that there are different challenges in destination brand building as pointed out by the participants. There are commonalities in the findings, these challenges are consistent with the existing literature (Tapachai & Waryszak, 2000; UNWTO, 2007; Baker & Cameron, 2008; Morgan & Pritchard, 2010; Braun, Kavaratis, & Zenker, 2010). However, findings indicate that there are contributions generated from this section to the existing knowledge.

These new findings include the following: (a). lack of destination branding experts and manpower; (b). lack of local leadership to drive the brand vision; (c) safety and security concern and; (d) geographic location and accessibility. These new findings have not been reported in the extant literature sources on the challenges of destination brand building. Based on these discoveries they would be taken into cognizance as components of strategic framework in managing challenges of destination brand building in rural tourism place. Findings also show that funding or lack of adequate financial resource is one the main challenges in developing a destination brand either at the rural or national levels. This is because according to the participants, the branding of a tourism destination is like commercial activities of buying and selling that needs adequate funding or budget allocation from the government to ensure its success.

In addition, due to the issue of multiple stakeholders with different economic interests and lack of central ownership of the destination, this may constitute a lack of commitment on the parts of these stakeholders in terms of funding. These views are consistent with Morgan and Pritchard (2004; 2010, p.62) that *managers in destination organisations face peculiar branding challenge in particular they have small budgets*. Likewise, other studies have also pointed out that the first challenge, confronting destination branding managers and marketers is their limited budgets (Baker & Cameron, 2007), and limited financial resources (Moilanen & Rainisto, 2009).

Moreover, Baker and Cameron (2007) opined that due to the presence of multiple stakeholders and the complexity of the relationships which exists among them, this poses a challenge in the process of destination branding. Other challenges enumerated by the participants agree with existing literature sources on environmental issues, lack of sole control, politics, host community characteristics behaviour and reputation or internal stakeholder groups, and destination image related problems (Morgan & Pritchard, 2010; Braun, Kavaratzis,& Zenker, 2010; Baker & Cameron, 2007; Waryszak, 2000). Based on the analyses of the views expressed by the respondents interviewed, findings on the challenges of developing a destination brand are presented in Table 2.

In addition, one of the challenges in the existing literature on destination brand building as a result of technological development is the issue of user-generated content (UGC) and social networking which can impact on the destination brand development (Anholt, 2010). This is not featured in the study's findings but UGC and social networking could either be a threat or opportunity because DMMOs have little control over the content. Nevertheless, having highlighted these challenges, one may ask if there are strategies to manage them. Therefore, findings from the notion of managing the challenges of the tourism destination branding process will be discussed in the following section.

Table 2. Challenges of Developing a Destination Brand

Challenges of destination brand building uncovered in this study	Multiple stakeholders and lack of commitment
	Funding or lack of financial resource
	Political and environmental issues
	Host community behaviours
	Difficulty of communicating brand benefits, failure to fulfil brand promise
	Destination image and awareness
	Identifying unique tourism offerings
	Lack of local leadership to drive the brand vision
	Geographic location and accessibility
	Lack of destination branding experts and manpower
	Safety and security concern

(Source: Compiled by the Author)

Managing the Challenges of Destination Brand Building

This section suggests strategies that could be adopted to manage the challenges of developing a brand from the context of rural tourism destinations. There are limited or no specific studies from the existing literature as a platform or foundation to build upon in terms of panacea from the academic or practitioner standpoint of addressing destination brand building challenges. However, most of the findings are generated from the different views expressed by the participants. The following are the extracts from the participants' comments. A local resident, farmer and tour guide points out:

Well, I think the external stakeholders should be involved because… if the stakeholders can agree to work together, the challenge would not be too much to manage. Again, the local community involvement is very important here to guarantee sustainable safety and security. Also needed are effective communication and less of political interference and provision of grants or funds from the tourism ministry. (PC20)

Comments include that of a local resident in Bario:

Host community and other stakeholders' commitment; government making provision for reasonable budget allocation; and identifying and managing the distinctive tourism assets and appeal compared to other tourism places. Engagement of marketing and destination branding experts to work within the available amount of funds. (PC17)

Stakeholders and the local community's involvement have been widely studied in the literature on community-based tourism (Jamal & Getz, 1995; Jones, 2005; Lepp, 2007; Kayat, 2008; Ezeuduji & Rid, 2011; Lee, 2012). Findings from these previous studies did not mention specifically the inclusion of the host community in managing the challenges of developing a destination brand. The study context is a rural community and the main stakeholders are the local residents which makes the involvement of members of the local residents indispensable as a key factor in the management of challenges of building a destination brand. Besides that, when asked how the challenges of developing a destination brand can be managed, a volunteer from the United Kingdom states:

First is the stakeholders' involvement, and also to communicate the brand benefits to them. There should be enough funding for … brand planning and development. The engagement of tourism branding and marketing experts who can nurture the destination brand using the tourism assets found in that destination. Regular and effective promotional strategies are also important. The destination should make it clear whether it is a mass tourism or premium destination. (PC29)

This is followed by comments from a tourist from New Zealand:

A strong local leadership who can build a strong relationship with other stakeholders... because to build a destination brand there should be adequate funding or budget from the government. (PC3)

In his own contribution on managing the challenges of destination brand building, a key informant from the Department of Immigration commented:

I think the challenges of [the] destination branding process can be addressed through effective community leadership, collaboration by stakeholders and government support through tourism ministry. There must also be provision of enough funds to plan, develop and launch the brand. (PC28)

Findings reveal that the status of the destination should be well-defined, either as a mass or premium destination with few but quality number of tourists who are willing to spend more days or extend their length of stays (LoS) and are willing to pay (WTP) more. More importantly, from the rural destination standpoint, the presence of a strong local leadership to drive the brand vision is essential. This is necessary in order to establish relationship with stakeholders and non-stakeholders for the successful development of the local destination brand. This view is consistent with Ezeuduji and Rid (2011) that motivation to participate in tourism or other factors that allow active involvement of the local community could become critical to successful rural tourism. Summary of these findings from views from the participants are presented in Table 3.

In order to complement the findings from the in-depth interviews section which is the main data collection adopted in this study, a summary of findings from the triangulation of data sources are presented in Table 4.

IMPLICATIONS AND CONCLUSION

The key findings cut across the importance and challenges of destination branding in the context of a rural place, and suggested strategies from the participants' views, participant observation and documentary evidences. Literature sources have reported less on how these challenges can be managed. For example, findings outlined in this section could be regarded as contributions to existing literature sources. This study highlighted 12 importance of destination branding notably is the preservation of traditional farming occupation which is important to the rural dwellers in terms of their occupation identity. Findings produce 11 factors affecting the destination

Table 3. Managing the Challenges of Destination Brand Building

Strategies for managing the challenges of destination brand building uncovered in this study	Effective communication of destination brand benefits strategy
	Host community and multiple stakeholders involvement
	Adequate funding/budget
	Less political interference
	Premium destination development strategy
	Identifying and managing distinctive tourism attractions
	Strong leadership and relationship building with stakeholders and non-stakeholders
	Partnering with destination branding and marketing experts
	Food and cultural festival, and Local MICE
	Sustainable safety and security

(Source: Compiled by the Author)

Table 4. Findings from Triangulation of Data Sources

In-Depth Interviews	Participant Observation	Documentary Evidence
Challenges of developing a destination brand for rural tourism		
(a) Lack of brand Communication benefits (b) Inability to outline brand promise	(a) Lack of brand communication benefits to the stakeholders (b) Bario is not yet a destination brand hence there is no brand promise in place	(a) Low level of education, although most of the local people in Bario can communicate in English (b) Lack of awareness of potential brand benefits and promise if any
Strategies of managing the challenges of rural tourism destination brand development		
(a) Food and cultural festival (b) Local meetings, incentives, conferences and exhibitions (L-MICE)	(a) Food and cultural festival (b) Local MICE – WWF/ Kalimantan Indonesia and Kelabit highlands Malaysia Meetings	(a). Promote local food, culture and tourism through Bario food and cultural festival (b). Local MICE events or developmental conferencing

(Source: Compiled by the Author)

brand development in rural tourism which include lack of destination branding experts and manpower.

Interestingly, three of the strategies for managing the challenges of developing a destination brand unearthed in this study would be considered as contributions. These are: (a) a strong local leadership and relationship building to liaise with other stakeholders especially the government for financial assistance and support from stakeholders and non-stakeholders; (b) sustainable safety and security, and; (c) partnering with destination branding and marketing experts. Likewise, there are another eight strategies for managing destination brand challenges uncovered in this study, namely:

1. Effective communication of brand benefits;
2. Host community and multiple stakeholders' involvement;
3. Adequate funding/budget;
4. Less political interference;
5. Premium destination development strategy;
6. Identifying and managing distinctive tourism attractions;
7. Food, cultural festival and local MICE, and;
8. User-generated content (UGC) is also important despite a lack of control by the destination management and marketing organisations (DMMOs).

Where positive experiences are shared UGC and social networking could enhance the image of the destination (Anholt, 2010) and by extension, destination brand development. These eight strategies have been applied to other aspects of the destination brand building process. Unfortunately, their application to the rural space is very limited.

For example effective consultation and communication of the brand benefits to the stakeholders, especially the host community, identify distinctive tourism attractions that offer right tourism products to the right visitors, have been applied in other segments of destination branding. Hence these strategies are not new even though they suggest new insights to the management of destination brand building challenges. In a nutshell, these findings are the key strategies required to manage effectively the challenges of building destination brand. This study has uncovered different challenges of destination brand building from the literature and from the analyses of in-depths interviews, participant observation and documentary evidence. These findings are crafted and conceptualized into 11 components of strategic framework for managing the challenges of the destination branding (SFMCDB) process in rural tourism space presented in Figure 1.

Figure 1. Strategic Framework for Managing the Challenges of Developing Rural Tourism Destination Branding
(Source: Compiled by the Author)

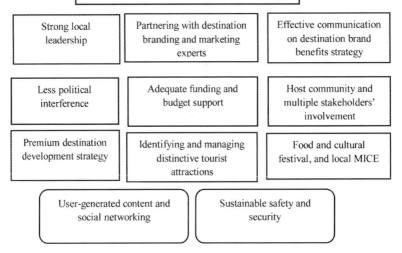

Essentially, this study has implications to theory, practice and the host community. For example, findings outline the theoretical contributions to the existing knowledge as lack of destination branding experts and manpower, lack of local leadership to drive the brand vision, lack of awareness of potential brand benefits, and geographic location and accessibility to the rural destination. From the practical implication point of view, findings highlight that the tourism destination marketers and branding practitioners should develop strong leadership and relationship building with the stakeholders and non-stakeholders. Likewise, local food and cultural festival should be used as strategies in rural destination brand development. On top of that, there is a need to evolve partnering strategy with marketing and destination branding experts. Destination marketers should also monitor UGC and social networking related activities that affect the rural tourism destination. The implications to the host community is that they should be involved in the destination brand building process and support initiatives from interested stakeholders to boost safety and security of the tourism attractions and of course the rural tourism community. In conclusion, it is suggested that future studies should be focused on multiple rural tourism destinations possibly to extend the components of strategic framework for managing challenges of destination branding and to adopt mixed research methodology to validate the findings from this study.

ACKNOWLEDGMENT

The funding for this project is made possible through the research grant obtained from the Malaysian Ministry of Education Long Term Research Grant Scheme (LRGS) Programme [Reference No.: JPT.S (BPKI)2000/09/01/015Jld.4(67)].

REFERENCES

Aaker, D. A. (1991). *Managing brand equity*. New York: Free Press.

Adeyinka-Ojo, S. F., & Khoo-Lattimore, C. (2013). Slow food events as a high yield strategy for rural tourism destinations: The case of Bario, Sarawak. *Worldwide Hospitality and Tourism Themes*, 5(4), 353–364. doi:10.1108/WHATT-03-2013-0012

Anholt, S. (2010). *Handbook on tourism destination branding*. Madrid: ETC/UNWTO.

Aref, F., & Gill, S. (2009). Rural tourism development through rural cooperatives. *Nature and Science*, 7(1), 670–673.

Baker, M. J., & Cameron, E. (2008). Critical success factors in destination marketing. *Tourism and Hospitality Research*, 8(2), 79–97. doi:10.1057/thr.2008.9

Bala, P. (2002). *Changing borders and identities in the Kelabit highlands: anthropological reflections on growing up in a Kelabit village near the international border*. Kuching, Malaysia: Unit Penerbitan Universiti Malaysia, Sarawak.

Braun, E., Kavaratzis, M., & Zenker, S. (2010). My city – my brand: the role of residents in place branding. *50th European Regional Science Association Congress*.

Braun, V., & Clarke, V. (2006). Using thematic analysis in psychology. *Qualitative Research in Psychology*, 3(2), 77–101. doi:10.1191/1478088706qp063oa

Cai, L. A. (2002). Cooperative branding for rural destination. *Annals of Tourism Research*, 29(3), 720–742. doi:10.1016/S0160-7383(01)00080-9

Camilleri, M. A. (2018a). The Tourism Industry: An Overview. In *Travel Marketing, Tourism Economics and the Airline Product* (pp. 3–27). Cham, Switzerland: Springer. doi:10.1007/978-3-319-49849-2_1

Camilleri, M. A. (2018b). Tourism Supply and Demand. In Travel Marketing, Tourism Economics and the Airline Product (pp. 139-154). Cham: Springer. doi:10.1007/978-3-319-49849-2_8

Camilleri, M. A. (2018c). Strategic Planning and the Marketing Effectiveness Audit. In *Travel Marketing, Tourism Economics and the Airline Product* (pp. 3–27). Cham, Switzerland: Springer. doi:10.1007/978-3-319-49849-2_1

Cooper, C. (2012). *Essentials of Tourism*. Pearson Education Limited.

Cresswell, J. W. (2007). *Qualitative inquiry and research design: Choosing among five approaches* (2nd ed.). Thousand Oaks, CA: Sage.

Cresswell, J. W. (2014). *Research Design: Qualitative, quantitative, and mixed methods approaches* (4th ed.). Thousand Oaks, CA: Sage Publications Inc.

Dwyer, L., Forsyth, P., Fredline, L., Jago, L., Deery, M., & Lundie, S. (2006). *Concepts of Tourism yield and their measurement – technical reports*. Cooperative Research Centre for Sustainable Tourism.

Esu, B. B., & Arrey, V. M. E. (2009). Branding cultural festival as a destination attraction: A case study of Calabar carnival festival. *International Business Research*, 2(3), 182–192. doi:10.5539/ibr.v2n3p182

Ezeuduji, I. O., & Rid, W. (2011). Rural tourism offer and local community participation in The Gambia. *Tourismos: An International Multidisciplinary Journal of Tourism*, 6(2), 187–211.

Fereday, J., & Muir-Cochrane, E. (2006). Demonstrating rigor using thematic analysis: A hybrid approach of inductive and deductive coding and theme development. *International Journal of Qualitative Methods*, 5(1), 1–11. doi:10.1177/160940690600500107

Ghaderi, Z., & Henderson, J. C. (2012). Sustainable rural tourism in Iran: A perspective from Hawraman Village'. *Tourism Management Perspectives*, 2-3, 47–54. doi:10.1016/j.tmp.2012.03.001

Government of Malaysia. (2010). *Tenth Malaysia Plan. The Economic Planning Unit*. Putrajaya, Malaysia: Prime Minister's Department.

Greaves, N., & Skinner, H. (2010). The importance of destination image analysis to UK rural tourism. *Marketing Intelligence & Planning*, 28(4), 486–507. doi:10.1108/02634501011053586

Guba, E. G., & Lincoln, Y. S. (1994). Competing paradigms in qualitative research. In N. K. Denzin & Y. S. Lincoln (Eds.), *Handbook of Qualitative Research*. Thousand Oaks, CA: Sage Publications Inc.

Gubrium, J. A., & Holsten, J. A. (2001). *Handbook of interview research: Context and method*. Thousand Oaks, CA: Sage. doi:10.4135/9781412973588

Haven-Tang, C., & Sedgley, D. (2014). Partnership working in enhancing the destination brand of rural areas: A case study of made in Monmouthshire, Wales, UK. *Journal of Destination Marketing & Management, 3*(1), 59–67. doi:10.1016/j.jdmm.2013.12.001

Jamal, T., & Getz, D. (1995). Collaboration theory and community tourism planning. *Annals of Tourism Research, 22*(1), 186–204. doi:10.1016/0160-7383(94)00067-3

Jennings, G. (2010). Tourism research (2nd ed.). Milton, Australia: Wiley & Sons Australia Limited.

Jones, S. (2005). Community-based ecotourism: The significance of social capital. *Annals of Tourism Research, 32*(2), 303–324. doi:10.1016/j.annals.2004.06.007

Jorgensen, D. L. (1989). *Participant observation: A methodology for human studies*. Newbury Park, CA: Sage Publications. doi:10.4135/9781412985376

Kalkstein-Silkes, C. A. (2007). *Food and food related festivals in rural destination branding* (Doctoral Thesis). Purdue University.

Kayat, K. (2008). Stakeholders' perspectives toward a community-based rural tourism development. *European Journal of Tourism Research, 1*(2), 94–111.

Kayat, K. (2011). *Homestay Programme as a Malaysian Tourism Product*. Sintok, Kedah: UUM Press.

Keller, K. L. (2003). *Strategic brand management: Building, measuring and managing brand equity*. Upper Saddle River, NJ: Prentice Hall International.

Kim, H., & Jamal, T. (2007). Touristic quest for existential authenticity. *Annals of Tourism Research, 34*(1), 181–201. doi:10.1016/j.annals.2006.07.009

Langkawi Development Agency (LADA). (2011). *The Langkawi tourism blueprint (2011-2015)*. Langkawi, Kedah, Malaysia: LADA Publications.

Lebe, S. S., & Milfelner, B. (2006). Innovative organization approach to sustainable tourism development in rural areas. *Kybernetes, 35*(7-8), 1136–1146. doi:10.1108/03684920610675139

Lee, T. H. (2012). Influence analysis of community resident support for sustainable tourism development. *Tourism Management, 30*, 1–10. doi:10.1016/j.tourman.2012.03.007

Lo, M.-C., Songan, P., & Mohamad, A. Z. (2011). Rural destinations and tourists' satisfaction. *Journal of Services Research*, *11*(2), 59–74.

Lofland, J., & Lofland, L. H. (1995). Analysing social settings: A guide to qualitative observation and analysis (3rd ed.). Belmont, CA: Wadsworth.

Malaysian Government. (2011). *Population and housing census of Malaysia: preliminary count Report 2010*. Retrieved from: https://www.statistics.gov.my

May, C. (2001). *From direct response to image with qualitative and quantitative research*. Presentation at the 32nd Annual Conference of the Travel and Tourism Research Association, Fort Myers, FL.

Mittila, T., & Lepsisto, T. (2013). The role of artists in place branding: A case study. *Place Branding and Public Diplomacy*, *9*(3), 143–153. doi:10.1057/pb.2013.15

Mohammed, B. (2002). Strategic positioning of Malaysia as a tourism destinations: A review. In *Sustainable Tourism Research Cluster*. Universiti Sains Malaysia.

Mohammed, B., & Muhibudin, M. (2012). From idyllic fishing village to beach resorts: the case of Pangkor Island. *Proceedings of the Regional Symposium on Rural Tourism: Scaling up Community-Based Ecotourism*.

Moilanen, T., & Rainisto, S. (2009). *How to Brand Nations, cities and Destinations – a planning book for place branding*. Palgrave Macmillan. doi:10.1057/9780230584594

Moore, S. A., Rodger, K., & Taplin, R. H. (2013). Moving beyond visitor satisfaction to loyalty in nature-based tourism: A review and research agenda. *Current Issues in Tourism*, 1–17. doi:10.1080/13683500.2013.790346

Morgan, N., Pritchard, A., & Pride, R. (Eds.). (2010). Destination Branding: Creating the unique destination proposition (2nd ed.). Oxford, UK: Elsevier Butterworth-Heinemann.

Morgan, N., & Pritchard, A. (2010). Meeting the destination branding challenge. In N. Morgan, A. Pritchard, & R. Pride (Eds.), Destination Branding: Creating the unique destination proposition (2nd ed.). Oxford, UK: Elsevier Butterworth-Heinemann.

Morgan, N., Pritchard, A., & Piggott, R. (2002). New Zealand, 100% pure.the creation of a powerful niche destination brand. *Journal of Brand Management*, *9*(4-5), 335–354. doi:10.1057/palgrave.bm.2540082

Morrison, A., & Anderson, D. (2002). *Destination branding*. Retrieved from: http://www.macvb.org/intranet/presentation/DestinationBranding

Morrison, A. M. (2013). *Marketing and managing tourism destinations*. London: Routledge. PP.

Mostowfi, B. (2000). *Agro-tourism and sustainable development, case study: Landscape design for Karyak village* (Master's thesis). University of Tehran, Tehran, Iran.

Nair, V. (2015). Langkawi's tourism blueprint (2011-2015): Transformation from rural tourism to developed rural tourism destination. *Proceeds of 21st Asia Pacific Tourism Association Conference*, 154-156.

Nair, V., Uma Thevi, M., Sushila Devi, R., & King, N. (2012). Redefining rural tourism in Malaysia: A conceptual perspective. *Asia Pacific Journal of Tourism Research*, *20*(3), 314–337. doi:10.1080/10941665.2014.889026

Northcote, J., & Macbeth, J. (2006). Conceptualising yield: Sustainable tourism management. *Annals of Tourism Research*, *33*(1), 199–220. doi:10.1016/j.annals.2005.10.012

Obonyo, G. O., & Fwaya, E. V. O. (2012). Integrating tourism with rural development strategies in Western Kenya. *American Journal of Tourism Research*, *1*(1), 1–8.

Organisation for Economic Co-operation and Development (OECD). (1994). *Tourism strategies and rural development*. OECD.

Pakurar, M., & Olah, J. (2008). Definition of rural tourism and its characteristics in the northern great plain region. *System*, *7*, 777–782.

Petric, L. (2003). Constraints and possibilities of the rural development with special stress on the case of Croatia. European Regional Science Association, 1-28.

Pourová, M. (2002). *Agroturistika [Agrotourism]*. Praha: CREDIT.

Quinlan, T. (2008). *A stakeholder approach to the branding of urban tourism destinations* (Master Thesis). Waterford Institute of Technology, Ireland.

Rasmussen, S. E., Ostergaard, P., & Beckmann, C. S. (2006). *Essentials of social Science Research Methodology*. Southern Denmark University Press.

Ritchie, J. R. B., & Crouch, G. I. (2003). *The Competitive Destination: A Sustainable Tourism Perspective*. Wallingford, UK: CABI Publishing. doi:10.1079/9780851996646.0000

Schubert, S. F., Brida, J. G., & Risso, W. A. (2011). The impacts of international tourism demand on economic growth of small economics dependent on tourism. *Tourism Management*, *32*(2), 377–385. doi:10.1016/j.tourman.2010.03.007

Scott, J. (1990). *A matter of record: Documentary sources in social research.* Cambridge, UK: Polity Press.

Strauss, A. L., & Corbin, J. M. (2008). *Basics of qualitative research: Techniques and procedures for developing grounded theory.* London: Sage publications Limited.

Supphellen, M., & Helgeson, J. G. (2004). A conceptual and measurement comparison of self-congruity and brand personality. *International Journal of Market Research, 46*(2), 205–233. doi:10.1177/147078530404600201

Tapachai, N., & Waryszak, R. (2000). An examination of the role of beneficial image in tourist destination selection. *Journal of Travel Research, 39*(1), 37–44. doi:10.1177/004728750003900105

Tasci, A. D. A. (2011). Destination branding and positioning. In Y. Wang & A. Pizam (Eds.), *Destination marketing and management theories and applications.* Oxfordshire, UK: CABI. doi:10.1079/9781845937621.0113

Tilstone, C. (Ed.). (1998). *The technique of observation. In Observing teaching and learning: principle and practice* (pp. 32–53). London: David Fulton Publishers.

Turtureanu, I. A. (2005). *Economic impact of tourism, Acta Universitatis Danubius.* Romania: University of Galati.

United Nations World Tourism Organisation. (2007). *A practical guide to tourism destination Management UNWTO.* Madrid: Author.

Weinreich, N. (1999). *Hands-On Social Marketing: A Step-by-Step Guide.* Thousand Oaks, CA: SAGE Publications.

Yin, R. K. (2009). Case study research: Design and methods (4th ed.). Thousand Oaks, CA: Sage Publications, Inc.

Chapter 12
The Role of Tour Operators in Destination Tourism Marketing in Malawi

James Malitoni Chilembwe
Glasgow Caledonian University, UK & Mzuzu University, Malawi

Victor Ronald Mweiwa
Malawi Institute of Tourism, Malawi

Elson Mankhomwa
Malawi Institute of Tourism, Malawi

ABSTRACT

Destination marketing is one of the tools used by tour operators to gain a tourism competitive advantage. Tourism is one of the biggest businesses in the global village. It is a business in a very competitive market environment that marketing tourism destinations cannot be done by destination management organizations (DMOs) alone but also intermediaries like tour operators. Marketing tourism destination nowadays is highly driven by technology which enhances tourists' destination knowledge prior to their visits. However, the downside of technology cannot be underestimated on the business environment. While there is a growing importance of technology usage which creates challenges for destination competitiveness, tour operators use their marketing strategies to help building positive destination images. These images are created to influence tourists' travel decision making and visits. This chapter, therefore, has examined the present tourism marketing strategies, activities, and approaches used by tour operators in creating positive images for tourism destination using 20 cases of Malawian tour operators.

DOI: 10.4018/978-1-5225-5835-4.ch012

INTRODUCTION

Destination marketing plays a major role in influencing tourism development in a community (Wang & Pizam, 2011). Sustainable tourism defines destination marketing as a process of communicating with potential visitors to influence tourists' destination preference, tourists' intention to travel, and ultimately, tourists' final decisions and product choices (Pike, 2015). Moreover, in many developing countries, ministries or departments of tourism are responsible for destination marketing; and in most cases, they work jointly with tour operators. Tourists, too, play a role through their behavior—which is frequently monitored by authorities to determine tourism impacts (Camilleri, 2018; Murray, Lynch & Foley, 2016) as well as to determine the ramifications of destination marketing and image creation beyond the realms of marketing effectiveness (Orel & Kara, 2014). It is therefore important to determine not only the numbers of tourists, but also the type and quality (including behavior) of tourists, that a destination receives—which, in turn, influences the impact of tourism in a destination community. In order to achieve the activity, it also requires that the services of Destination Management Organizations (DMOs) – or tourism ministries and departments – be supported by tour operators. As Van Rensburg (2014) notes, one of the reasons why a tour operator needs to work closely with departments of tourism is due to its closeness and interaction with tourists even before decisions are made by tourists to visit destinations. Tour operators, according to Djurica (2010), are always in the forefront of discussing destinations with potential tourists, responding to potential tourists' questions, and convincing tourists to consume tourism products; additionally, they are also involved in clarifying destination products and creating the destination image. In tourism and destination image creation, tour operators consider a number of marketing strategies—the most important one being marketing communication through their tourist brochures, advertisements, and destination websites.

On the other hand, a destination image is the perception in which tourists and non-tourists view a destination—that is often ascribed to its image (Kokkranikal, Cronje & Butler, 2011). A destination image is highly and most frequently researched in relation to how tourists perceive the destination and how the image influences the decision-making process (Qu & Qui, 2015). According to Pike (2015), that image has the power to undeniably influence behavior on tourist behavior, too. Many developed countries use DMOs to portray a destination image and vision; and yet, in many developing countries, opportunities are lost by side-lining DMOs. While little is being done, tour operators in developing countries like Malawi take an active role by designing their own brochures and destination websites to appeal to tourists' desire to get them visit destinations. Unlike DMOs which market destinations by putting emphasis on appealing to what they believe tourists want, tour operators are always in consistent contact with tourists and know exactly what tourists want. In this case, there is a need to incorporate tour operators in destination marketing rather than side-lining them.

Tour operators use their promotional materials to create a destination tourism image (Djurica, 2010). They also function as intermediaries in tourism distribution systems linking producers and consumers. Tour operators have expertise in packaging tourism products and allow for more offerings to a wider range of tourism and interested party consumers. It is important to focus on induced images when applying a destination image as a vital element of marketing strategy (Kokkranikal, Cronje, & Butler, 2011). It is further noted that the inclusion of tour operators can be a deliberate attempt by travel traders and DMOs to develop a destination image that matches their tourism development (Pike, 2015).

Understanding Tour Operators (Tour Wholesalers)

Tour operators are the ones who assemble the component parts of a holiday or who actually package holidays (Chilembwe & Mweiwa, 2014). For example, the provision of travel means the provision of accommodation, facilities, transfers, excursions, and other services. Tour operators, in other words, function like wholesalers because they are involved in the buying of large content (in bulk) from providers of travel services such as hotels, car rentals, and airlines. Tour operators break products into smaller-sized, manageable packages ('particles') and sell these packages as finished products in the form of inclusive tours—selling either directly to consumers or through travel agencies.

Chilembwe and Mweiwa (2014) observe that there are also 'principles' (organizations) which provide a service and product—which make up the packaged holiday. According to Cloquet (2013), the above may be divided into specialist tour operators (for example, safari tours), which are less well-known; or mass tour operators, which are more famous (because they deal with many consumers and control their own airlines, accommodation and resorts). In order to market tourism products, there is a need to apply different marketing strategies for specialized and mass tour operators because the two are different (Mariani, 2016; Wall-Reinius, Loannides & Zampoukos, 2017). The target group is different, too; just as is their purpose for taking part in the tour. Tour Operators are involved in several activities including the promotion and marketing of tourism destinations and associated products and services on offer (See Table 1 below).

Table 1. *Different types of tour operators and some of their activities*

Inbound Tour Operators	Outbound Tour Operators
• Deal with and handle incoming foreign tourists • Provide tourists with arrival and departure categories' services (transfers, accommodation, transportation, sightseeing, entertainment, currency, and insurance services) • Contribute to the health, growth, and promotion of tourism and destinations	• Are specialized in designing and promoting multinational tours (in foreign countries) • Sell tours to individuals or groups of people from local or foreign countries for a prescribed period of time • Arrange travel documents for tourists – along with transportation (beginning from where the tour starts), accommodation, and sightseeing.
Domestic Tour Operators	**Ground Tour Operators**
• Promote and market products within their locality (country, region, or area) • Promote tour packages on their own or through outlets and other retail travel agents • Contribute to the cause of national integration • Sometimes coordinate with other domestic operators in different countries (if tourists are touring multiple countries)	• Are also known as reception operators, destination management companies, or handling agencies • Provide land arrangements at a destination • Provide ground services for large tour operators where there are no local branches/ offices • Secure, coordinate, supervise, and handle accounts or payments of all services related to the tour in the region or area

(Source: Compiled by the Researchers, 2017)

Tour Operators' Marketing Initiatives

Tour operators should establish an overall marketing strategy which may differ according the types and size of the business. Lubbe (2000), citing Kotler and Armstrong (2012), provides three main strategies that tour operators (wholesalers) can apply:

1. Going for the lowest prices, building on the economics of scale that their size brings them, and negotiating capabilities;
2. Concentrating on specific products and on building up a reputation for quality, to justify higher prices; and
3. Targeting specific sectors of the market, and specializing in certain categories of tours.

However, the suggested marketing strategies can only benefit tour operators themselves rather than the tourism destination. The marketing strategies for the tourism destination should aim at reaching or covering beyond a single country and continent within a short period of time. In addition, they should also consider targeting different categories of people in terms of their culture, language, social and economic status (Kotler & Armstrong, 2012).

Tour operators also use brochures to present their product offerings to tourism consumers (Chilembwe & Mweiwa, 2014). A brochure communicates a holiday product to the customer. According to Wall-Reinius et al. (2017), tour operators – regardless of size – use brochures to sell a wide range of products and services. Some tour operators produce separate brochures to target a specific period of the year (for example, summer, winter, long-haul travel, or short breaks (Boniface & Cooper, 2005).

Role of the Tour Operator in Destination Marketing

Marketing tourism destination requires a shared vision and a knowledge exchange between actors in a network comprised, in part, by tour operators (Murray, Lynch & Foley, 2016). In addition, it requires creating shared values to strengthen the competitive positioning of the tourism destination (Camilleri, 2014; 2016). It also requires an integrated destination communique to multiple actors to communicate consistent messages to tourists across the globe (Murray, Lynch, & Foley, 2014). In this case; tourism ministries and destination managers play a number of roles with the help of several other interest actors in destination marketing ranging from tracking marketing trends to using marketing information in the development of marketing campaigns. Therefore, there is a need to include tour operators in the network of firms to assist in creating marketing campaigns and building destination trust among visitors (Murray, Lynch, & Foley, 2016). Tour operators not only market destinations through their activities but also have a role in selling tour packages and airline products as well as hotel accommodations (Van Rensburg, 2014). The power of tour operators' rests on their creating impressions on tourists so that those tourists engage in repeat visits—hence, operators are indirectly marketing the tourist destination. Orel and Kara (2014) contend that destination marketing leads to tourists' satisfaction.

Destination Positioning and Image

Destination positioning is the process of establishing and maintaining a distinctive place for a destination in the minds of travelers in the targeted markets (Kotler & Armstrong, 1994; cited in Qu & Qui, 2015). Undeniably, destination image has the power to influence on tourist behavior, too (Pike, 2015). Unlike in developed countries which use DMOs to portray a destination image and vision, many developing countries use tour operators alongside tourism ministries to create a destination image (Ministry of Tourism, 2009). The tourism industry is one of those industries which is using destination image and positioning to market destination products. The ever-increasingly-competitive nature of the tourism market – which functions this way in order for actors to differentiate tourism destinations from their competitors – is a well-known concept (Pike, 2009; Pike 2015). Therefore, tour operators have a role in ensuring that their actions in selling tourism products and services create self-congruity and destination branding. According to Qui and Qui (2015), a construct of self-congruity and destination brand personality is a multi-dimensional aspect including actual self-concept, ideal self-concept, social self-concept, and ideal social concept. It has a positive bearing effect not only on key destination decision-making preferences but also on destination belief, intention to return, and destination recommendation by tourists (Li, 2009; Yuksel & Bili, 2009; Usakli & Baloglu, 2011). Moreover, using destination personality helps to identify an authentic brand identity—one that has strong symbolic meanings with regards to uniqueness of the tourism destination (Daye, 2010).

Tour Operators, Information Technology, and Marketing

Nowadays, tour operators have turned to social media marketing technologies in tourism (Rahman, 2017). Several products are being developed by tour operators including the creation of full-color video clips and related social activities to attract tourists (Hamari, Koivisto, & Sarsa, 2014; Amuquandoh, 2010; Leung, Law, Hoof, & Buhalis, 2013). Meanwhile, Morrison (2013) observes that information technology is playing a big role in marketing tourism products and services to online destination markets. Online destination image and online word-of-mouth promotion play a role in destination marketing (Kotoua & Ilkan, 2017a). Tour operators too have not lagged behind in marketing their tourism destination products using the internet. As more tourists' surf through the internet using their electronic gadgets (devices such as laptops, tablets, and smartphones), tour operators have also increased online marketing channels to different tourism destinations to promote their products and services (Shankar, Venkatesh, Hofacker, & Naik, 2010; Rogers & Davidson, 2015). Travelers visit several websites, review products, and check graphical images before deciding whether to purchase tourism products (Li & Yeh, 2010). A recent study by Kotoua and Ilkan (2017b) reveals that simple websites are no longer making an impact on destination marketing due to technological advances. They further suggest that websites should provide different tools and marketing channels to facilitate the surfing and informational needs of travelers. In this case, tour operators have a role in creating websites that have an impact on customers' retention, marketing, and experience. Websites created should not only be of high quality in appearance but should also be easy to navigate and should be approved through customers feedback as being user friendly (Chung, 2015; Wells, Valacich, & Hess, 2011).

In addition, tour operators need to take opportunities for social media marketing techniques, for example, online word-of-mouth promotion. This has a personal influence that affects tourists' selection of destinations (Kotoua & Ilkan, 2017b). Others call online word-of-mouth promotion as e-word-of-mouth promotion, and it is considered to be a legitimate medium of communication which has gained recognized acceptability as such in the tourism industry (Barreto, 2014; Yang, 2013). It is also more effective and can reach millions of potential tourists as compared to traditional word-of-mouth promotion (Bilgihan, Barreda, Okumus, & Nusair, 2016; Kozinets, De Valck, Wajnicki, & Wilner, 2010; Frias, Rodriguez, Castaneda, Sabiote, & Buhalis, 2012). Tour operators have a role in providing up-to-date website information about their products and services including related information regarding destinations. Kotoua and Ilkan, (2017a) confirm that online websites should provide valuable destination marketing information to tourists through social media and online word-of-mouth promotion.

Apart from tour operators' websites, travelers also interact with destination organization websites (Xu, He, & Hua, 2014) and make informed decisions based on social media websites (Sun, Fong, Law, & Luk, 2016). Tourists make destination choices for their holidays after searching information online, while others get information from fellow tourists to make sure that they are choosing the right destination (Flanagin, Metzger, Pure, Markov, & Hartsell, 2014). Similarly, the Woodside, Mir, and Duque (2011) study found a significant relationship between tourism destination dominance and marketing website usefulness.

It is, therefore, not about how much information (content) that is put on websites but rather how much the content of the website is useful in attracting potential visitors (Woodside, Mir, & Duque, 2011). Additionally, Orel and Kara (2014) assert that tour operators' role in this regard is to make a contribution to tourism destination dominance and to produce useful websites that appeal to visitors. Tour operators can, again, use information technology to reduce costs; enhance operational efficiency; and improve customer experience and service quality through marketing tourism products at various destinations.

Moreover, tour operators focus on market segments because they have information obtained through market search (Buhalis & Michopoulou, 2011). One of the most important segments requiring tour operators' consideration is the 'accessibility market' to make tourism products accessible to all people (physically challenged as well as the aging population). Tour operators are there to support tourism firms by selecting places of tourists' interest that have facilities with accessibility to the destination, to make trips enjoyable for everyone. Puhretmair (2004), cited in Buhalis and Michopoulou (2011), said:

Global competition, legislation [,] and [an] increasingly ageing population demonstrate that competitive tourism destinations and organizations should undertake steps to improve their accessibility and provide appropriate information (p. 146).

This means that a number of tourism players (Destination Management Organizations, tourism ministries, tourism planners, and tour operators as well as travel agents) should work together on addressing issues of market accessibility for consumers.

Destination Promotion Through Supporting the Local Economy

On the other hand, tour operators have a responsibility to support the growth of the local economy through their activities. Local tourism economy includes tourist attractions (Mokkonen, 2016). According to Kotoua and Ilkan (2017b), touristic attractions can be divided into two main components: cultural and natural attractions. Through vigorous marketing campaigns and the proper provision of an educational environmental, tour operators have a role in protecting and preserving cultural attractions. They are there to select the attractions that appeal to tourists at the right time and the right place. They also have a role to play in collaborating with tourism planners and suggesting ways to (and how to) improve those tourism destinations. They should contribute to joint marketing programs that should bring in more revenue to the local economy; improve tourism infrastructure; and concentrate on innovative tourism destination marketing as well as on tourism sustainability. Furthermore, they are bound to participate freely (voluntarily) in corporate social responsibility initiatives through provision of awareness of destination environment to their tourists. The awareness of destination features (brand labels) may help visitors to become responsible travelers to their selected destination.

CASE STUDIES OF TOUR OPERATORS IN MALAWI

This is a case study approach in which twenty tour operators were selected (see the appended Table 1) and identified cases worthy of analysis based on their websites. These tour operators' local and foreign owned firms are actively operating in Malawi. The researchers wanted to understand the common ground between both local and foreign tour operators engaged in marketing Malawi as a tourist destination. This was done by checking the content that tour operators include in their websites for marketing Malawi tourism products. This includes the functionality and quality of contents – for example, videos, Skype, and pictures – and their visual appeal to website researchers. Also checked was the frequency with which the websites were updated and the frequency with which technological marketing communications were used to convey messages about new or promotional products. The researchers also analyzed whether tour operators have a membership for a national or regional tour-operating association or whether they are operating independently. Are they in a specific or particular kind of partnership – or do they just engage in general networking with other local or foreign tour operators? Do they have internal marketing personnel responsible for the firm's marketing or not? Are the tour operators' websites really portraying a good image of Malawi? And of the comments received from consumers of the tourism products by the tour operators, are the comments positive or negative?

Data Collection

This study only targeted those tour operators which had been in business for a minimum of three years, had a minimum of five employees, and had an operational website. The research also considered the social media marketing technologies: Twitter, Facebook, Instagram, Brochures, Pinterest, Blogs, Online videos, online reviews, and tour operators' networking/collaborations or partnerships. These are tour operators which carry out most of their day-to-day operations with the help of information technology.

This study collected and employed both secondary and primary data. Saunders et al. (2012: p. 304) describes secondary data as being *information that has been collected, processed, or analyzed by other researchers and stored for further [reference] or [for another] purpose*. In the case of this study, it was sourced from the internet—particularly, from tour operators' websites. The researchers have also used reputable and highly-ranked peer-reviewed journals, books, and industry reports in their analysis. The study needed secondary data for understanding the concepts and also to critically analyze the situation at hand regarding the role of tour operators in destination marketing (more specifically, in the Malawian context).

The study also considered the use of primary data to verify some information available from tour operators' websites. Primary data according to Saunders et al (2012: p. 307) is *raw data that was not in existence before and it is collected afresh and for the first time*. In this study, primary data was collected from five tour operators in Malawi. One representative (a marketing manager) from each of five tour operators was interviewed through social media (Skype) after they consented to participate in the study.

Study Area

The study is conducted in Malawi—mainly in the cities of Blantyre and Lilongwe. These two cities are chosen because they are the country's biggest cities; therefore, there is a greater availability of tour operators as compared to other cities within the national borders. Most of the larger tour operators have also established their head offices or local branches for international entities in either one of the two selected cities (hence the choice). Researchers are convinced that data from these two cities would give a true representation of the rest of the cities in Malawi. Blantyre is located in the Southern Region of the country, and it is Malawi's commercial capital – whereas Lilongwe, the capital city, is located in the Central Region (see Figure 1 below).

Sampling Technique

Babbie (2010) defines sampling as the process of selecting a sample (or samples) of the population to represent the entire population. In the case of this study, researchers used purposive sampling. The twenty tour operators selected (see Table 1) were

Figure 1. Map of Malawi showing the cities of Blantyre and Lilongwe
(Source: World Atlas, 2017)

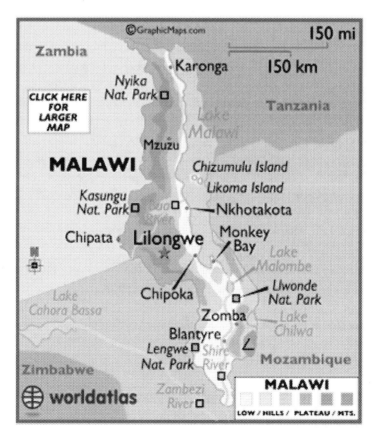

intentionally chosen as case studies based on the availability of websites to supply the required information (see Table 2). The five marketing managers interviewed by Skype were also purposively selected just to confirm the information supplied by their websites. Saunders, Lewis, and Thornhill (2012) suggest that the selection of respondents should be based on those that can provide meaningful responses in order to address the problem. Therefore, the selection of five managers was considered on the basis that they are the people responsible for carrying out tour-operation-related marketing activities using websites and other existing technologies.

Ethical Consideration

Permission was first sought from tour operators, especially those marketing managers who supplied supplementary and verifiable information regarding tour marketing activities. This was done before in-depth interviews, just to verify what they put on their websites for marketing purposes.

Data Analysis

The bulk of the data has been collected through websites; therefore, researchers have used website contents and analyzed data statistically despite that a sample size was very small. Data from interviews was analyzed thematically. The common issues were identified and picked, and the contents were recorded in a handbook. These findings were then related to secondary data; from these, the conclusions were derived. The choice of data analysis technique was based on nature of the study which is both qualitative and quantitative.

Limitations of the Study

The researchers have wanted to place a clear demarcation between locally-owned and foreign-owned tour operators. However, it has been difficult to separate the two decisively, because 50% of the tour operators selected 'wear' two operational 'masks.' They are both local and foreign. Therefore, it became difficult to make a judgment with regards to quality, content, visibility, rankings, and online reviews as distinguished based on whether tour operators were locally owned or foreign owned. Thus, in this case, the results, analysis, and judgment of information has been generalized as referring genetically to Malawian tour operators. Again, the results of this study cannot be generalized to developed economies of the world. However, there is still the possibility that the findings of this study can be generalized in some developing countries which are involved in the business of tour operations.

RESULTS AND DISCUSSION

The study targeted twenty tour operators (see Table 2) and identified cases of analysis based on their websites. The tour operators were locally-owned and foreign-owned but operating in Malawi. The researchers checked contents that tour operators had included in their websites (for their having done so for the purpose of marketing Malawi tourism products). Assessments included the functionality and quality of contents (for example, videos; Skype; pictures) and how appealing are they to website researchers. In addition, the study targeted those tour operators who had been in business for a minimum of three years, had a minimum of five employees, and had an operational website. The research also considered the social media marketing technologies such as: Twitter, Facebook, Instagram, online brochures, Pinterest, blogs, TripAdvisor reviews, online videos, and tour operators' networking/ collaborations or partnerships. It should be noted that tour operators have been operating for several decades. In case of Malawi, it is traced back to 1980's when first tour operators (15%) entered the market (see Figure 2). Since then, the market of tour operating has had been growing and, from 1990 to 2009 many operators (30% and 25%) respectively joined the sector. However, between the years 2010 to 2015, the sector started experiencing decline due to advancement of marketing technologies and required more resources to venture into business market as Figure 2 shows the summary of historical development.

Despite that there is 20% of tour operating firms which have been indicated that period of opening firm is not known, such firms have been included in this study because researchers have seen these firms operating for years.

Figure 2. Percentages of tour operating firms ventured into business from 1980–2015
Source: Researchers' data, 2017

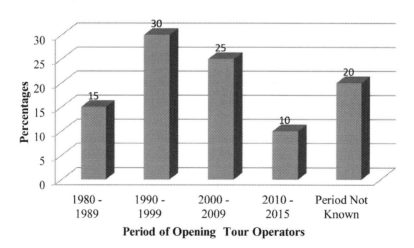

Marketing of Destination Adventure Tourism Products

Marketing is the process by which companies' valuing of the customer is expressed by their building a strong customer relationship with them in order to capture value from the customers in return (Kotler & Armstrong, 2012). Furthermore, marketing tourism products requires representing and describing products and creating an experience that exceeds expectations (Masosn, 2008). It is important and necessary to consider what tourists experience when they come into contact with the products, and to consider their expectations regarding a destination—and using those expectations as an opportunity for marketing both the destination and its associated products (Khadka, 2012). Understanding the nature of the tourism product offerings helps marketers to develop marketing strategies which promote destination products without undue assumptions about tourist destination (Font & Carey, 2005). An increased growth in the adventure tourism market over the years has been facilitated by the growing demand of adventure tourism (Khadka, 2012; ACS Distance Education, n.d.)—which is, in part, a creation of tour operators; as adventure activities have increasingly become part of tourists' holidays during visits. Destinations are often marketed by regional or local tourism promotional agencies or associations of public provenance (Lake, 2015), but they depend on private commercial operators to provide the retail products at the destination and (generally) also to run the adventure activities (Font & Carey, 2005; Buckley, 2010; Kotler & Armstrong, 2012; Briggs & Turay, 2016). Tour operators should incorporate destination positioning when designing and planning activities for the marketing of adventure tourism products. They should also consider the satisfaction of the customers' needs and wants—and those of the future customer, who needs need to be identified and anticipated (Khadka, 2012; Giddy & Webb, 2016). According to Carter, (2006) and Kotler and Armstrong (2012), the concept of integrated marketing communication tools can be used in the development of strategies to ensure the yielding successful results. Integrated marketing communication is a management concept designed to integrate the five components of the promotional mix – advertising, sales promotion, online marketing, public relations and direct marketing – which can effectively work together in a unified force to promote adventure tourism products Buckley (2010) states that although the literature shows that there is a conception of tourism marketing, not much has been investigated with regards to tour operators' marketing styles in relation to adventure tourism—particularly in developing countries.

Tour operators' marketed adventure tourism products basically form the body of general tourism destination marketing but with a focus on adventure products, the quality of the products, and the quality of marketing tools (Carter, 2006; Page, 2007; Bauer, 2010; Buckley, 2010). Now more than ever, tourism is being recognized as being a major economic contributor in many destinations worldwide (UNWTO,

2017). Therefore, this entails that there is a need to do more research on adventure tourism marketing in order to better position and brand tourism destinations. Tour operators have a duty to promote and encourage responsible travel and adventure tourism which adds value for foreign exchange and supports export industries along with environmental, social, cultural, historic resources and their protection. Boniface and Cooper (2005) observe that tourism, as a worldwide phenomenon, affects a vast number of people and places and has the potential to touch or influence many more. Adventure activities have a lot of benefits with regards to the personal health of the individual doing the activities. Hence, tour operators should take the opportunity to market such products and to position some of the places of tourists' interest as adventure tourism destinations. It is interesting to note that there are 10 benefits that one can get from adventure sports (Andrews, 2015). Benefits include burning calories, keeping the blood flowing, and stretching the body little by little—thus helping individuals become stronger. Other benefits include adventure sports being a great way of having fun while providing visitors with new experiences and opportunities to live life to the fullest as they escape from the daily routine. There is thrill of life when tourists watch destination online videos and visit the places give them new experiences resulting in great memories one can always cherish. Therefore, tour operators may innovate by developing marketing strategies to attract tourists according to client preference and business trends in order to maximize the promotion and marketing of the destination.

Information Technology (Social Media Marketing)

In the study, twenty companies were used to understand the trends in the usage of technology as a modern marketing tool. The study has shown that all (100%) the twenty tour operators selected had developed websites; they have Twitter, Facebook and also used e-brochure. In addition, 95% used guides and 95% networking, 85% used Instagram, 75% used blogs, 70% used Pinterest, 60% you tube/ video and only 25% used skype (see Figure 3) for more details.

This suggests that although website is used by all tour operating firms, other technological means are also important to supplement their websites as evident in Figure 3. The social marketing media technologies that were found to be widely and mostly used among tour operating firms are: Twitter, Facebook, Instagram, online brochures, guides, Pinterest, blogs, videos, and networking (see Table 2). It was observed from the online comments (reviews) from different websites' users that such visitors were indeed interested in visiting and using the websites. It is therefore, proper to say, it is not only about how much information (contents) you put on websites but how much usefulness of the content in the websites to attract potential visitors. In addition, besides tour operators' websites, travelers also interact with destination

Figure 3. Technological marketing strategies of resident tour operators based in Malawi
Source: Researchers' data, 2017

organization websites – as noted by Xu, He, and Hua (2014) – and make informed decisions based on social media websites (Sun, Fong, Law, & Luk, 2016). Tourists make destination choices for their holiday after searching information online; while others get information from fellow tourists to make sure that they are choosing the right tourism destination (Flanagin, Metzger, Pure, Markov, & Hartsell, 2014).

An interesting website is always shared with others (Xu, He, & Hua, 2014). Tourists apply marketing online word-of-mouth promotion to their colleagues about tourism destinations. According to Kotoua and IIkan (2017b), online word-of-mouth marketing has a personal influence that affects tourists' selection of destinations. E-word of mouth promotion is one of the modern communication media accepted in methods of marketing in the tourism industry (Barreto, 2014). It is also more effective and can reach millions of potential tourists as compared to traditional word-of-mouth marketing (Bilgihan, Barreda, Okumus, & Nusair, 2016; Kozinets, De Valck, Wajnicki, & Wilner, 2010; Frias, Rodriguez, Castaneda, Sabiote, & Buhalis, 2012). Similarly, Kotoua and IIkan, (2017a) confirm that online websites should provide valuable destination marketing information to tourists through social media and online word-of-mouth promotions.

Tour operators strive to provide up-to-date website information about their products and services—including destinations. During interviews, when questioned how often they update their websites, one marketing manager had this to say:

Updating websites to portray current activities during the season is part of a tour operators' role; and we try to position the destination image. Although- sometimes, we face financial hiccups because we need to change or redesign the whole website altogether if our focus has changed (Regina – Interview on 12 August, 2017)

Tour operators find the use of brochures to be effective when it comes to the presenting their product offerings. A brochure communicates the holiday product to the customers. According to Mokkonen, (2016) through tour brochures, tour operators – as a matter of principle – include tourist attractions that can be divided into cultural and natural attractions. Indeed, tour operators are actively involved in the marketing of destinations.

Most of the tour operators (see Appendix 2, Table 2) function based on networking. They work hand in hand with local or foreign individual operators and agencies, in executing their marketing campaigns. Some operators are in partnership with organizations overseas, making it easy for them to market tourism destinations through their product offerings.

In doing so, they promote and market a destination through media coverage. Meanwhile, other tour operators have branded their websites by depicting Malawi as being a cultural destination; while other destinations are depicted as being natural attractions with friendly people to whom one would naturally be attracted.

FUTURE RESEARCH DIRECTIONS

The study indicates that all 20 tour operators use websites, Facebook, Twitter and e-brochure in marketing destination products; however; other technological systems are also used to supplement their marketing campaigns. It is also noted that tour operators spend a lot of money for website designers to come up with an attractive website. Website pages should occasionally be updated in addition to promoting the website for it to appear most frequently on the front page of results returned when using search engines. However, it is not clear as to how much money, on average, tour operators spend on marketing budgets and campaigns—or the proportional profitability of their doing so. Having investigative-level insight with regards to expenditures on e-marketing strategies, as could be revealed through, would give a more detailed picture of the field to young entrepreneurs and graduates who are interested in venturing into the tour operation business.

CONCLUSION

The marketing of tourism destinations requires a shared vision and a knowledge exchange between network actors in which tour operators are part of the network. It also requires an integrated destination communique to multiple actors to communicate consistent messages to tourists across the global spectrum, as is also noted by Murray et al. (2014). While destination managers play a number of crucial roles in marketing tourism destinations, there is a need to include tour operators in the network of firms to assist in creating marketing campaigns and building destination imagery for, and trust with, visitors. Tour operators market destinations through activities such as selling tour packages, airline products, and hotel accommodations (Van Rensburg, 2014). Therefore, they have the prerequisite skills, power, and ability to impress the tourists and create a positive tourism destination image (Qu & Qui, 2015). Modern tour operators use social media in marketing technologies which reach millions of potential consumers in tourism (Rahman, 2017). Creating a tourism destination image and online word-of-mouth promotions has a positive impact on the local economy. Tour operators apply effective online word-of-mouth marketing which has a personal influence on tourists and one that affects their selection of destinations (Kotoua & IIkan, 2017b). While most tourists surf through the internet using their electronic gadgets (such as laptops, tablets, and smartphones), tour operators have also increased their online marketing techniques and channels to include different tourism destinations to promote their products and services (Shankar, Venkatesh, Hofacker, & Naik, 2010; Rogers & Davidson, 2015). Tour operators have created useful sites on the worldwide web. This study, therefore, concludes that tour operators mostly use websites, Twitter, Facebook and e-brochure, all (100%) when marketing tourism destination products. In addition, their tourism marketing campaigns are supplemented by other technological systems such guides and networking (95%), Instagram (85%), blogs (75%), 70% used Pinterest (70%), you tube or video (60%) and only 25% go for skype. The results also suggest that websites should not only be of high quality with regards to their appearance but should also be easy to navigate and user-friendly as well (Chung, 2015; Wells, Valacich, & Hess, 2011). Tour operators, more often than not, update their website information about their products, services including destination trends; using technology effectively as a model and a standard marketing tool for many businesses. Therefore, technological social media marketing methods such as renowned websites, Twitter, Facebook, online brochure, networking and guides are expected to continue dominating in marketing tourism destinations in Malawi as a formal media, and social media and beyond borders—among businesses operating tours. However, the future of Malawi tour operating firms has a great potential to embrace other emerging tourism products marketing technologies such as Instagram, Pinterest, blogs, and videos.

ACKNOWLEDGMENT

This research received no specific grant from any funding agency in the public, commercial, or not-for-profit sectors.

REFERENCES

ACS Distance Education (ACSEDU). (n.d.). *Marketing adventure tourism: Ecotourism and adventure tourism.* Retrieved August 19, 2017, from http://www.acsedu.com/courses/ecotourism-and-adventure-activities-courses.aspx

Amuquandoh, F. E. (2010). Residents' perceptions of the environmental impacts of tourism in the Lake Bosomtwe Basin, Ghana. *Journal of Sustainable Tourism, 18*(2), 223–238. doi:10.1080/09669580903298531

Andrews, C. G. (2015). Ten reasons why adventure travel is good for you. *Good Nature Travel—The Official Travel Blog of Natural Habitat Adventures & WWF.* Retrieved July 4, 2017, from http://goodnature.nathab.com/ten-reasons-why-adventure-travel-is-good-for-you

Antigua and Barbuda Tourism Development. (2003). *Tourism's economic impacts increasing the contribution to prosperity. Antigua LP.* Antigua and Barbuda: KPMG Consulting.

Babbie, E. R. (2010). *The practice of social research* (12th ed.). Belmont, CA: Wadsworth Cengage.

Barreto, A. M. (2014). The word of mouth phenomenon in the social media era. *International Journal of Market Research, 56*(5), 631–654. doi:10.2501/IJMR-2014-043

Bauer, A. (2010). *Marketing adventure tourism: What works and what doesn't.* Munich, Germany: Munich University of Applied Sciences. Accessible from the Shannon College of Hotel Management. Retrieved from http://www.shannoncollege.com/wp-content/uploads/2009/12/A.-Bauer-THRIC-2010-Full-Paper.pdf

Bilgihan, A., Barreda, A., Okumus, F., & Nusair, K. (2016). Consumer perception of knowledge-sharing in travel-related online social networks. *Tourism Management, 52*, 287–296. doi:10.1016/j.tourman.2015.07.002

Boniface, B. G., & Cooper, C. (2005). *Worldwide destinations: The geography of travel and tourism.* Oxford, UK: Butterworth-Heinemann.

Briggs, P. B., & Turay, S. (2016). *Malawi: The Bradt travel guide* (7th ed.). Guilford, CT: Globe Pequot Press.

Buckley, R. C. (2010). *Adventure tourism management*. Oxford, UK: Butterworth-Heinemann.

Buhalis, D., & Michopoulou, E. (2011). Information-enabled tourism destination marketing: Addressing the accessibility market. *Current Issues in Tourism, 14*(2), 145–168. doi:10.1080/13683501003653361

Camilleri, M. A. (2014). Advancing the sustainable tourism agenda through strategic CSR perspectives. *Tourism Planning & Development, 11*(1), 42–56. doi:10.1080/21568316.2013.839470

Camilleri, M. A. (2016). Responsible tourism that creates shared value among stakeholders. *Tourism Planning & Development, 13*(2), 219–235. doi:10.1080/21568316.2015.1074100

Camilleri, M. A. (2018). The Marketing Environment. In *Travel Marketing, Tourism Economics and the Airline Product* (pp. 3–27). Cham, Switzerland: Springer. doi:10.1007/978-3-319-49849-2_1

Carter, C. (2006). World adventure capital. In R. Buckley (Ed.), Adventure Tourism (pp. 429-442). Wallington, Australia: The Centre for Agriculture and Bioscience International (CABI) Publishing.

Chilembwe, J. M., & Mweiwa, V. (2014, September 14). Tour guides: Are they tourism promoters and developers? Case study of Malawi. *International Journal of Research in Business Management, 2*(9), 29–45.

Chilembwe, J. M., & Sepula, M. B. (2017). Corporate social responsibility practices in the tourism and hospitality industry in Malawi. In C. Koutra (Ed.), *Social Responsibility: Application of Good Practices and Malpractices in Tourism and Hospitality Industry in the Developing World*. New York, NY: Nova Science Publishers.

Chung, N. K., & Koo, C. (2015). The use of social media in travel information search. *Telematics and Informatics, 32*(2), 215–229. doi:10.1016/j.tele.2014.08.005

Cloquet, I. (2013). Looking into the overlooked: Incoming tour operators and early tourism Development in Gabon. *Current Issues in Tourism, 16*(7-8), 647–663. doi:10.1080/13683500.2013.785480

Daye, M. (2010). Challenges and prospects of differentiating destination brands: The case of the Dutch Caribbean islands. *Journal of Travel and Marketing, 27*(1), 1–13. doi:10.1080/10548400903534725

Djurica, M. 2010). Tourism destination marketing management. *Proceedings of the Tourism and Hospitality Management 2010 Conference*, 890-901.

Flanagin, A. J., Metzger, M. J., Pure, R., Markov, V., & Hartsell, E. (2014, March). Mitigating risk in eCommerce transactions: Perception of information credibility and the role of user-generated ratings in product quality and purchase intention. *Electronic Commerce Research, 14*(1), 1–13. doi:10.100710660-014-9139-2

Font, X., & Carey, B. (2005). *Marketing sustainable tourism products.* Leeds, UK: Leeds Metropolitan University.

Frias, D. M., Rodriguez, M. A., Castaneda, J. A., Sabiote, C. M., & Buhalis, D. (2012). The formation of tourist destination's image via information sources; The moderating effect of culture. *International Journal of Tourism Research, 14*(5), 437–450. doi:10.1002/jtr.870

Hamari, J., Koivisto, J., & Sarsa, H. (2014). Does gamification work? A literature review of empirical studies on gamification. In *Proceedings of the 47th Hawaii International Conference on System Sciences*, 3025-3034. Institute of Electrical and Electronics Engineers (IEEE). Retrieved from http://doi.ieeecomputersociety.org/10.1109/HICSS.2014.377

Khadka, S. (2012). *Marketing of adventure and nature tourism—A case study of Shambala Trekking Agency in Nepal* (Thesis). Central Ostrobothnia University of Applied Sciences, Ostrobothnia, Finland. Retrieved from https://www.theseus.fi/bitstream/handle/10024/41135/Khadka%20Sujata.pdf

King, R. A., Racherla, P., & Bush, V. D. (2014). What we know and don't know about online word-of-mouth: A review and synthesis of the literature. *Journal of Interactive Marketing, 28*(3), 167–183. doi:10.1016/j.intmar.2014.02.001

Kokkranikal, J., Cronje, P., & Butler, R. (2011). Tourism policy and destination marketing in developing countries: The chain of influence. *Tourism Planning & Development, 8*(4), 359–380. Retrieved from https://www.tandfonline.com/doi/figure/10.1080/21568316.2011.603885

Kotler, P., & Armstrong, G. (2012). *Principles of marketing* (14th ed.). Upper Saddle River, NJ: Prentice Hall.

Kotoua, S., & Ilkan, M. (2017a). Online tourism destination marketing in Kumasi Ghana. *Asia Pacific Journal of Tourism Research*, *22*(6), 666–680. doi:10.1080/10941665.2017.1308394

Kotoua, S., & Ilkan, M. (2017b). Tourism destination marketing and information technology in Ghana. *Journal of Destination Marketing & Management*, *6*(2), 127–135. doi:10.1016/j.jdmm.2017.04.007

Kozinets, R. V., De Valck, K., Wajnicki, A. C., & Wilner, S. J. (2010). Networked narratives: Understanding word-of-mouth marketing in online communities. *Journal of Marketing*, *74*(2), 71–89. doi:10.1509/jmkg.74.2.71

Lake, L. (2015). *Marketing 101: What is branding?* Retrieved June 13, 2017, from http://www.marketing.abou.com/cs/brandmktg/a/whatisbranding.htm

Leung, D., Law, R., Hoof, H. V., & Buhalis, D. (2013). Social media in tourism and hospitality: A literature review. *Journal of Travel & Tourism Marketing*, *30*(1), 3–22. doi:10.1080/10548408.2013.750919

Li, X. P. (2009). An examination of [the] effects of self-concepts, destination personality and SC-DP congruence on tourist behavior. Blacksburg, VA: Virginia Polytechnic Institute and State University.

Li, Y. M., & Yeh, Y. S. (2010). Increasing trust in mobile commerce through design aesthetics. *Journal of Computers in Human Behavior*, *26*(4), 673–684. doi:10.1016/j.chb.2010.01.004

Makkonen, T. (2016). Cross-border shopping and tourism destination marketing: The case of Southern Jutland, Denmark. *Scandinavian Journal of Hospitality and Tourism, 16*(Sup1), 36-50. 10.1080/15022250.2016.1244506

Mariani, M. M. (2016). Coordination in inter-network co-operation: Evidence from the tourism sector. *Industrial Marketing Management*, *53*, 103–123. doi:10.1016/j.indmarman.2015.11.015

Mason, P. (2008). *Tourism impacts, planning and management*. Oxford, UK: Butterworth-Heinemann.

Ministry of Tourism. (2009). *National tourism policy for Malawi*. Lilongwe, Malawi: Malawi Government. Retrieved from http://www.e-travelworld.cn/malawi/Publications/documents/NATIONAL%20TOURISM%20POLICY.pdf

Morrison, A. (2013). Destination management and estimation marketing: The platform for excellence in tourism destinations. *Luyou Xuekan*, *28*(1), 6–9. Retrieved from http://www.lyxk.com.cn/EN/Y2013/V28/I1/6

Murray, N., Lynch, P., & Foley, A. (2014). Destination visioneering: A case study of best Practice. *Proceedings of the Irish Academy of Management Conference*. Limerick, Ireland: University of Limerick.

Murray, N., Lynch, P., & Foley, A. (2016). Unlocking the magic in successful tourism destination marketing: The role of sensing capability. *Journal of Marketing Management, 32*(9), 877–899. doi:10.1080/0267257X.2016.1192557

Orel, F. D., & Kara, A. (2014). Supermarket self-checkout service quality, customer satisfaction, and loyalty: Empirical evidence from an emerging market. *Journal of Retailing and Consumer Services, 21*(2), 118–129. doi:10.1016/j.jretconser.2013.07.002

Page, S. L. (2007). *Tourism management: Managing for change*. Oxford, UK: Elsevier.

Pike, S. (2009). Destination brand positions of a competitive set of near-home destinations. *Tourism Management, 30*(6), 857–866. doi:10.1016/j.tourman.2008.12.007

Pike, S. (2015, December 17). *Destination marketing: Essentials* (2nd ed.). New York, NY: Routledge.

Qui, Y., & Qui, H. (2015). Nonutilitarian tourism destination positioning: A case study in China. *International Journal of Tourism Research, 17*(4), 388–398. doi:10.1002/jtr.2005

Rahman, S. (2017). Tourism destination marketing using Facebook as a promotional tool. *IOSR Journal of Humanities and Social Science, 22*(2), 87–90. doi:10.9790/0837-2202018790

Rogers, T., & Davidson, R. (2015). *Marketing destinations and venues for conferences, conventions and business events: A convention and event perspective (Events management)*. New York, NY: Routledge.

Saunders, M., Lewis, P., & Thornhill, A. (2012). *Research methods for business students* (6th ed.). Harlow, UK: Pearson Education.

Shankar, V., Venkatesh, A., Hofacker, C., & Naik, P. (2010). Mobile marketing in the retailing environment: Current insights and future research avenues. *Journal of Interactive Marketing, 24*(2), 1–12. doi:10.1016/j.intmar.2010.02.006

Sun, S., Fong, L. H. N., Law, R., & Luk, C. (2016). An investigation of Gen-Y's online hotel information search: The case of Hong Kong. *Asia Pacific Journal of Tourism Research, 21*(4), 443–456. doi:10.1080/10941665.2015.1062405

United Nations World Tourism Organization. (2017). *Tourism for sustainable development in least developed countries: Leveraging resources for sustainable tourism with the enhanced integrated framework*. Geneva, Switzerland: United Nations Conference on Trade and Development. Retrieved from https://www.e-unwto.org/doi/pdf/10.18111/9789284418848

Usakli, A., & Baloglu, S. (2011). Brand personality of tourist destinations: An application of self-congruity theory. *Tourism Management*, *32*(1), 114–127. doi:10.1016/j.tourman.2010.06.006

Van Rensburg, M. J. (2014). Relevance of travel agents in the digital age. *African Journal of Hospitality, Tourism and Leisure*, *3*(2), 1–9. Retrieved from https://core.ac.uk/download/pdf/43178196.pdf

Wall-Reinius, A., Loannides, D., & Zampoukos, K. (2017). Does geography matter in all-inclusive resort tourism? An investigation of the marketing approach of major Scandinavian tourist operators. *Tourism Geographies: An International Journal of Tourism Space, Place and Environment*, 1-19. 10.1080/14616688.2017.1375975

Wang, Y. C., & Pizam, A. (2011). Destination marketing and management: Theories and application. Oxford, UK: The Centre for Agriculture and Bioscience International (CABI) Publishing. doi:10.1079/9781845937621.0000

Wells, J. D., Valacich, J. S., & Hess, T. J. (2011). What signal are you sending? What website quality influences perceptions of product quality and purchase intentions. *Management Information Systems Quarterly*, *35*(2), 373–396. doi:10.2307/23044048

Woodside, A., Mir, V. R., & Duque, M. (2011). Tourism's destination dominance and marketing website usefulness. *International Journal of Contemporary Hospitality Management*, *23*(4), 552–564. doi:10.1108/09596111111130038

World Atlas. (2017). *Map of Malawi*. Retrieved September 18, 2017 from http://www.worldatlas.com/webimage/countrys/africa/mw.htm

Xu, L., He, P., & Hua, Z. (2014). A new form of hotel to collaborate with a third-party website: Setting online-exclusive rooms. *Asia Pacific Journal of Tourism Research*, *20*(6), 635–655. doi:10.1080/10941665.2014.924975

Yang, H. (2013). Market mavens in social media: Examining young Chinese consumers' viral marketing attitude, eWOW motive, and behaviour. *Journal of Asia-Pacific Business*, *14*(2), 154–178. doi:10.1080/10599231.2013.756337

Yuksel, Y., & Bilim, Y. (2009). Interactions between visual appeals, holiday motivations, destination personality and self-image: The implication for destination advertising. *Journal of Travel and Tourism Research*, *9*, 75–104.

ADDITIONAL READING

Buckley, R., Shakeela, A. S., & Guitart, D. (2014). Adventure tourism and local livelihoods. *Annals of Tourism Research*, *48*, 266–291. doi:10.1016/j.annals.2014.06.006

Chan, N. L., & Guillet, B. D. (2011). Investigation of social media marketing: How does the hotel industry in Hong Kong perform in marketing on social media websites? *Journal of Travel & Tourism Marketing*, *28*(4), 345–368. doi:10.1080/10548408.2011.571571

Hay, S., Page, S. J., & Buhalis, D. (2013). Social media as a destination marketing tool: [Its use] by national tourism organisations. *Current Issues in Tourism*, *16*(3), 211–239. doi:10.1080/13683500.2012.662215

Herrero, A., San Martin, H., & Hernandez, J. M. (2015). How online search behavior is influenced by user-generated content on review websites and hotel interactive websites. *International Journal of Contemporary Hospitality Management*, *27*(7), 1573–1597. doi:10.1108/IJCHM-05-2014-0255

Kang, M., & Schuett, M. A. (2013). Determinants of sharing travel experiences in social media. *Journal of Travel & Tourism Marketing*, *30*(1-2), 390–391. doi:10.1080/10548408.2013.751237

Kay, J. A., & Lee, S.-H. (2014). Beyond adoption of travel technology: Its application to unplanned travel behaviour. *Journal of Travel & Tourism Marketing*, *31*(5-6), 667–680. doi:10.1080/10548408.2014.888968

Kayar, C. H., & Kozak, N. (2010). Measuring destination competitiveness: An application of the Travel and Tourism Competitiveness Index (2007). *Journal of Hospitality Marketing & Management*, *19*(3), 203–216. doi:10.1080/19368621003591319

Munar, A. M. (2012). Social media strategies and destination management. *Scandinavian Journal of Hospitality and Tourism*, *12*(2), 101–120. doi:10.1080/15022250.2012.679047

Standing, C., Tang-Taye, J., & Boyer, M. (2014). The impact of internet in travel and tourism: A research review 2001–2010. *Journal of Travel & Tourism Marketing, 31*(1), 82–113. doi:10.1080/10548408.2014.861724

KEY TERMS AND DEFINITIONS

Adventure Marketing: Advertising that focuses on a type of niche tourism involving an outdoor activity, travel excursion, and exploration with a certain degree of risk.

Destination Image: The appearance of all objective knowledge in combination with subjective impressions, imagination, and emotional thoughts a person can have about a place (whether positive or negative).

Destination Management: A form of coordinated management of all elements that make up a destination—elements such as activities, attractions, amenities, access, marketing, and pricing of products and services.

Destination Marketing: A type of advertising in order to promote tourism to a specific place (such as a city, region, district, or site) with the aim of creating a tourism impact.

Information Technology: A process of developing and maintaining computer systems, software, and networks for the processing and distributing of a firmware products and services to its customers.

Social Media Marketing: A modern technological use of communicating a firm's products and services to potential customers such as Twitter, YouTube, and Instagram.

Tour Operator: A firm that arranges tourists' holidays in terms of travel, accommodation, activities, and sightseeing.

Tourism: A pleasure- or business-oriented activity that involves people traveling from one place to another for and staying there for over a short period of time.

Tourism Marketing: A continuous, sequential process by which firms manage the planning, research, implementation, control, and evaluation of tourism activities designed in order to satisfy the customers' needs and wants and the firm's plans and objectives.

Tourist: A person who travels to another place outside their normal place of residence, doing so for either business or leisure—and who spends at least 24 hours (but no more than 265 days) there.

APPENDIX 1

Table 1. A list of tour operators used in the case studies

Names of Tour Operators	
Fisherman's Rest Tours	Misuku Expeditions
Kiboko Safari	Robin Pope Safari
Ulendo Safari	Land and Lake Safari
Bon Voyage Tours Limited	Central African Wilderness Safari
Sunrise Ground Tours	Jambo Africa Ltd.
Lilongwe Wildlife Trust	Barefoot Safari and Adventure Tours
Responsible Safari Company	Kayak Africa
Malawian Style and Tours	Sunset Safari and Events
Ultimate Travel Malawi	The Travel Center
Baobab Travel	Budget Safari

APPENDIX 2

Table 2. Some of the technological marketing strategies of tour (resident) operators based in Malawi

No.	Name of Tour Operator	Opened	Website	Twitter	Facebook	Instagram	Brochures	Guides	Pinterest		Other Media	
1	Misuku Expeditions	2013	Y	Y	Y	N	Y	Y	Y	Blogs	Video	Networking
2	Robin Pope Safari	1985	Y	Y	Y	Y	Y	Y	Y	Blogs	Video	Networking
3	Land and Lake Safari	1986	Y	Y	Y	Y	Y	Y	Y	Blogs	Video	Networking
4	Central African Wilderness Safari	1987	Y	Y	Y	Y	Y	Y	N	blogs	Video	Networking
5	Jambo Africa Ltd	1991	Y	Y	Y	Y	Y	Y	Y	Blogs	Video	Networking
6	Barefoot Safari and Adventure	1992	Y	Y	Y	Y	Y	Y	Y	Blogs	Video	Networking
7	Kayak Africa	1996	Y	Y	Y	Y	Y	Y	Y	Blogs	Video	Networking
8	Fisherman's Rest Tours (Malawi)	1997	Y	Y	Y	Y	Y	Y	N	Blogs	Video	Networking
9	Kiboko Safari (Malawi)	1998	Y	Y	Y	Y	Y	Y	Y	video	Blogs	Networking
10	Ulendo Safari	1998	Y	Y	Y	Y	Y	Y	Y	Blogs	Video	Networking
11	Bon Voyage Tours Limited	2001	Y	Y	Y	N	Y	N	Y	Video	Blog	Networking
12	Sunrise Ground Tours	2007	Y	N	Y	N	Y	Y	N	N/A	N/A	N/A
13	Lilongwe Wildlife Trust	2008	Y	Y	Y	Y	Y	Y	Y	Flicker	Video	Networking
14	Responsible Safari Company	2008	Y	Y	Y	Y	Y	Y	Y	Blogs	You Tube	Networking
15	Malawian Style and Tours	2009	Y	Y	Y	Y	Y	Y	N	Skype	Blogs	Networking
16	Ultimate Travel Malawi	2010	Y	Y	Y	Y	Y	Y	Y	Skype	Blogs	Networking
17	Baobab Travel	N/A	Y	Y	Y	Y	Y	Y	Y	Skype	Video	Networking
18	Budget Safari (Malawi)	N/A	Y	Y	Y	Y	Y	Y	N	Blogs	Video	Networking
19	Sunset Safari and Events (Malawi)	N/A	Y	Y	Y	Y	Y	Y	Y	Skype	Video	Networking
20	The Travel Centre	N/A	Y	Y	Y	Y	Y	Y	N	Skype	Skype	Networking

Source: Researchers' data, 2017

Chapter 13
Sustaining Tourism and Branding:
The Core Responsibilities of Stakeholders in Destination Development

Caner Çalişkan
Adiyaman University, Turkey

Bekir Bora Dedeoglu
Nevsehir Haci Bektas Veli University, Turkey

ABSTRACT

Branding with local dynamics is crucial to sustain tourism for a destination's existence and future. In this case, many stakeholder groups are responsible for the participation, social cohesion, economy, and environment. Thus, the authors conducted face-to-face interviews with seven key persons related to regional tourism development in the research area, Adıyaman. Research results show that in Adıyaman, a strong partnership, cooperation, and cohesion for sustainable tourism and branding is needed. The use of local dynamics—such as values, natural resources, education, and manpower—is an important variable of sustainable tourism and branding process.

DOI: 10.4018/978-1-5225-5835-4.ch013

INTRODUCTION

Tourism-driven mobility of people throughout the world creates natural, social, cultural, and economic impacts on different geographical places. In this regard, the discourse of sustainable tourism focuses on sustaining the tourism through fundamental principles, such as environmental protection, social welfare, and economic development (Neto, 2003; Budeanu, 2003) and equilibration among them (Clarke, 1997). One of the approaches to successful sustainable tourism, especially in developing regions, is branding with the help of local dynamics, such as cultural values, natural resources, and local manpower.

Branding through local dynamics plays a key role in ensuring sustainable tourism and creating a final brand. Within this context, a collective action including each stakeholder group in every region is required to be able to have more significant results and acquisitions from the tourism development. If a common ground could be established among the different stakeholder groups, tourism could develop using the local resources and sustain the locality in the region (Woodland & Acott, 2007). To ensure the sustainability of the existing tourism activities and adapt them to the local features of the region, common tasks and responsibilities at each hierarchical level should be determined, defined, analyzed, and performed. From this point of view, the present study focused on Adıyaman, which is one of the important historical and cultural cities in Turkey, and how to promote sustainable tourism with the help of local dynamics and how to brand the city in this way were discussed within the framework of stakeholder participation. Located in the Southeastern Anatolia Region and famous for its National Park of Mountain Nemrut included in the World Cultural Heritage list, Adıyaman is one of the cities with an important tourism potential with its natural resources (Çalışkan, 2014). Despite its important tourism potential, Adıyaman needs a sustainable tourism perspective and significant efforts during the branding process, and the problems faced in stakeholder collaboration and participation are observed to hinder its development (Yılmaz & Çalışkan, 2015).

BACKGROUND

Sustainable Tourism as a Driving Force of Destination

The facts discovered because of tourism activities since the late 19th century have brought along particular changes on the paradigms related to tourism development. In the late periods of the past century, especially because of the increases in income levels and the technological advancement in the Western world, a mass tourism model, where the resources are generally utilized in an unplanned way, has emerged in a short period. Both environmental and social adverse impacts of mass tourism started to attract attention, and new environment-friendly paradigms came to the forefront in the borders of development in tourism(Camilleri, 2018). This situation shifted tourism—a global phenomenon supposed to be under control—toward sustainable development (Carrillo & Jorge, 2017). Thus, in the sustainable tourism approach, the practices with which tourism is directly or indirectly in interaction were adopted within the framework outlined by sustainable development (Garrod & Fyall, 1998).

As understood, tourism is a powerful sector, and ensuring the sustainability of this power is essential (Garrod & Fyall, 1998). In most of the current strategic tourism plans, sustainability issues occupy an additional reference point (Hardy, Beeton, & Perarson, 2002). Sustainable tourism is basically based on the principle of local resource management. However, the tourism industry has a complicated system and challenging implementation practices; therefore, the stakeholder participation is of vital importance (Hunter, 1997).

Tourism has different types, and it has a nature of creating common interest areas ranging from local issues to general ones (L'Etang, Falkheimer, & Lugo, 2006). Furthermore, the sustainable tourism approach gathers all kinds of local-regional values, activities, and events under a single identity and brings today's comfort to the future (Beyhan & Ünügür, 2005). Redesigning of tourism and the implementation models requires sustainability (Lozano-Oyola, Blancas, González & Caballero, 2012). More clearly, sustainable tourism requires analyzing technicalities, regulating sociopolitics, and defining the interaction networks among the sub-elements of the sector; however, obligatory policies are needed as well to actualize the mentioned points.

Tourism is not independent from the system where it is located, although it has a complicated structure as indicated before. Therefore, sustainability of tourism is related to its integrity with the systems with which it has organic ties (Gössling, Hall, & Weaver, 2009). In other words, tourism is closely linked to the social processes, and the motivations underlying its practices cannot be assessed, ignoring the justifications observed in global life (Çalışkan, 2017).

Stakeholder Participation and Sustainable Tourism Development

The key element underlying the success of sustainable tourism is stakeholder participation. The heterogeneous nature of tourism and different interest groups' participation in the planning process related to the sustainability, the definition of potential groups, and, particularly, the coordination and collaboration between the relevant variables are among the most needed conditions (Aas, Ladkin, & Fletcher, 2005). When the tourism sector does not adopt the sustainability principles, or the stakeholders show unwilling behaviors, the stakeholder participation would be interrupted (Butler, 1999). The stakeholders' sense of responsibility is the fundamental dynamic under the socio-political practices. Thus, a wide variety of examples can be given, ranging from political balances of power at the national and international levels to local responsibility (Camilleri, 2015; Dodds & Butler, 2008). Hence, analyzing the complicated political system and the power structure in a country is vital to understand the sustainable tourism policy, planning, and implementation (Yasarata, Altinay, Burns, & Okumus, 2010).

"Sustainable tourism development" and "stakeholder" are related to implementing what, when, and how. The primary aim is to institutionalize sustainable tourism (Camilleri, 2014; Weaver, 2006). Stakeholder participation can be categorized under two dimensions in terms of institutionalization: the full participation and the active participation of the local people who form the biggest stakeholder group into the decision-making processes (Choi & Sırakaya, 2005). From a similar perspective, the purpose is to ensure that tourism becomes a part of enhancing the power of society (Cole, 2007). Moreover, the main factor on which the tourism is based is society itself; however, factors such as demographical and cultural characteristics, organizational forms, attitudes, and educational levels are crucial variables in the success of tourism-related efforts (Avcıkurt, 2009). On the other hand, the tendencies and approaches of the local authorities are the determining parameters, although society is the main influential factor in tourism development. Thus, the variables influencing the decision-making processes of the local authorities and the extent of society's benefit from tourism are other points that can be examined.

Sustaining Local Dynamics and Responsibilities

The tendency to responsible management, sustainable development, and similar subjects shows a remarkable increase in literature. Despite the difference, the common point in each concept is to pacify the negative effects and obtain a maximum output from the tourism. What matters is that tourism becomes sustainable within the framework of responsible management and contributes to society in which it takes its current shape (Frey & George, 2010). Sustainability is important because societies need to support one another through the available resources (Richards & Hall, 2002). On the other hand, sustainable tourism is related to which dynamics are used. This case also indicates the responsibility of effectively using all direct and indirect tourism-related components in the region. At this point, the priority is to establish the local-global connection and to analyze how the economic, cultural, and environmental components in this context would affect the local development outputs. Certainly, the starting point of those efforts is to ensure that the implementation practices would benefit society. Thus, local dynamics should accumulate around a system so that tourism becomes sustainable and each component creates an output (Milne & Ateljevic, 2001; Booyens, 2010).

Examining the local dynamics within a system requires the public and private institutions to have an organized structure (Jackson, 2006). Maintaining the local dynamics over the system to be developed and the responsibilities of the stakeholders in this regard should be considered from a multidimensional perspective (Camilleri, 2016). As partially mentioned before, how the local economies would develop without destroying the sociocultural and environmental resources in a globalizing world is open to discussion (Milne & Ateljevic, 2001).

Building Local Economics

Economy is a set of institutions producing products and services put into market for public consumption. The tourism industry aims to create an economic value for consumers through providing touristic product or services, including food-and-drink activities, accommodation, and transportation. This value is also intended to provide income to the employees and investors. Labor, wages, and earnings are the main income elements in the tourism sector (Reece, 2010). In this regard, it can be indicated that the tourism development stimulates economic growth. Tourist incomes and its increases increase economic growth, enhance the investment in the sector, increase the income of the existing labor force, and create new job opportunities in the sector; thus, they accelerate the economic growth process.

It can also be argued that a decrease observed in touristic activities might result in economic stagnation. Tourism is an important power plant for the economy (Doğru & Bulut, 2017). Regarding the multidimensional interaction area of the economy, a movement taking its power from local sources can be considered as a reference point. Local economic development refers to the management of the available resources, creation of new job opportunities, and, finally, economic recovery and increase in the competitive power (Ecereal & Özmen, 2009). At this point, indicating that the present status of the local economy not only determines the way the benefits and costs are perceived but also affects the support given by society to the sectors with a major impact area such as tourism is necessary (Gursoy & Rutherford, 2004).

The increase observed in the volume of competition as an expected result of the globalized economy has enhanced the importance of local dynamics. Similarities among the societies, places, and even the lifestyles and the distinctive features becoming indistinctive take away the advantages the region has in the global competitive environment. Considering the current situation, the development sequence ranging from general to specific has diminished, and a new development perspective taking its strength from the local sources has become more forefront (Çetin, 2007). However, the same case is seen in tourism planning as well. Traditional top-down planning fell from favor, particularly for the social and environmental subjects (Scheyvens, 2002). Each component of the available regional power should take its strength from local resources, and the conditions where the local actors could have more autonomy should be established (Canzanelli, 2001).

Social Cohesion and Collaboration

Social cohesion is a harmony introduced by individuals, institutions, groups, and classes sharing common values in a social structure through showing the same behavioral patterns continuously. Each society that establishes the harmony ensures the social cohesion in an easier way (Avcıoğlu, 2013). Society is crucial among the social life, individuals (person/family), and nonindividual elements (institutions). Society-based tourism efforts actualized within the scope of social collaboration and cohesion are the focus points of the development plans, and local collaboration, trust, and network provide successful touristic development outputs (Milne & Ateljevic, 2001).

Considering the global picture, the inclusion of different stakeholder groups into the tourism planning and management has become more important. Similarly, tourism-based collaborations of the direct or indirect interest groups act as a driving force for the development and implementation of tourism plans and policies. When the collaborations in question are examined, the interaction among semiprivate, private, public institutions, and nongovernmental organizations, including the pressure and interest groups, are seen. The interaction occurred in the framework of local collaboration could enable the provision of mutually acceptable offers on how to develop tourism through social dialogue. Collaborations in tourism planning gather the different parties of the same objective located in different places and join the mutual benefits together under the common objective (Bramwell & Lane, 2000).

Respect to Environment

Protection of the environment is an issue, which has been the focus of global tourism for years and where local actors take joint actions (Erkuş-Öztürk & Eraydın, 2010). Despite its remarkable contributions to economy, it causes environmental destruction at a large extent and negative impacts on the sociocultural structure. Unplanned development of tourism has destroyed the natural and sociocultural environments in many tourism destinations. Those undesired impacts have raised concerns regarding the protection of natural resources and human and economic welfare of the societies in the long run (Choi & Sirakaya, 2006). Indicating that the fundamental objective of tourism to create economic value is necessary; however, the framework is the protection and development of the environment, and this is also the ethical principle underlying economic success (Cater, 1991; Ham & Weiler, 2012). On the other hand, within the scope of responsible tourism, each activity carried out in the field of tourism aims to minimize the social, economic, and environmental impacts and maximize the positive impacts of the developments in tourism (Frey & George, 2010).

This objective can be reached through sustainable development. A sustainable development strategy can be defined and implemented only if the environmental and social dynamics in a system are well-known. The implementation process of the strategy is required to be followed by each direct and indirect addressee (Ianos, Peptenatu, & Zamfir, 2009). It is likely that the society-environment relationship, which has been re-formed in a critical time where human beings have the opportunity to alter the patterns of the nature, would affect the scope of environment in tourism. Considering its enlarging borders and extending environmental impacts, the tourism phenomenon is an important link in the relationship between society and nature (Holden, 2009).

Environment is a sine qua non of tourism. One of the factors directing the touristic demands is the environmental resources that the destinations have. For what and how those resources are used is influential on the visitors' preferences as well. Through the interaction between tourism and environment, each environmental element creates a touristic product (Kahraman & Türkay, 2006). This case can also be considered as one of the steps to be taken in the branding process based on the local environmental dynamics. As mentioned above, local-based economy needs to be shaped by stakeholder engagement based on social cohesion and respect for the environment. This situation also refers to sustainable tourism and branding (Camilleri, 2014). Because in developing regions, the starting point of sustainable tourism must be local. Sustainable tourism development and the local design of sustainability are also important in regional branding and destination branding, respectively (Bowman, 2011).

BUILDING A DESTINATION BRAND AND SUSTAINABILITY

A brand is an impression of a product and service in the mind of a consumer. That impression is the total of all physical and nonphysical components making the preference unique (Moilanen & Rainisto, 2009). In branding studies, it is particularly focused on the differences of the product and services from the others, and the differences of physical and nonphysical components are tried to be emphasized (Kotler & Keller, 2012). On the other hand, in destination branding processes, the destination marketing organization should focus on unique cultural, natural, and local characteristics as local dynamics.

Destination branding can be defined as an identity and a personality development process that will distinguish the destination from its rivals (Morrison & Anderson, 2002). Hence, destination branding aims at rendering the identity more visible, thus providing tourists with the opportunities of having unique experiences (Blain, Levy, & Ritchie, 2005). At this point, unique social, cultural, and natural characteristics create the basic destination identity or personality.

Destination identity or personality is a very important concept to unearth the distinguishing features of the destination. However, rather than the importance of the term, the sustainability of the elements contributing to its formation is vital in destination branding. If the unique identity (or features) of the destination starts to disappear in time, the elements distinguishing the destination from others will start to disappear as well, and it will cause the destination not perceived successful and special.

Another point that needs to be taken into consideration is that destination branding has a more complicated branding process compared to the product and service brandings because of being more multidimensional than product brand, having heterogeneous stakeholders and facing problems in funding in both scale and consistency (Pike, 2005). To continuously ensure this dynamism, the sustainability term should particularly be noticed.

The sustainability approach can contribute to the branding efforts in a destination in two ways. First, physical protection should be ensured. As mentioned before, destination features can be maintained within the framework of sustainability. More clearly, physical protection refers to the protection of unique social and natural features in a destination. Natural beauties or sociocultural values in a destination belong to only that destination, and imitating those features is difficult or impossible. Even though they could be imitated, providing the same competitive advantage is impossible for those imitated features. Since the characteristics of the local people—who are one of the most crucial stakeholders in a destination—also improve within the framework of the cultural and developmental processes in the destination, they remarkably contribute to the formation of the destination identity.

Kavaratsiz (2004) emphasized that particular changes are observed after shifting from regional marketing toward regional branding, and regional branding not only provides competitive advantage but also contributes to community development, reinforcing local identity and identification of the citizens with their city and activating all social forces to avoid social exclusion and unrest. On the other hand, according to Anholt (2005), destination branding is not as simple as designing a logo, motto, etc. that bring attractiveness to the destination. Destination branding is about the public, which embodies the economic and political elements of the region as well as its cultural and social environment. A destination should maintain its brand value and competitive advantage by protecting its physical unique social and natural features. Accordingly, destinations should ensure the permanence of those features to be successful at their branding attempts. Therefore, they should pay special attention to the sustainability approach.

Secondly, looking after the interest of local people can help a more successful branding process go through. Compared to the branded product and services, destinations could face many problems in branding processes because of having many stakeholders and challenging management control (Morgan & Pritchard, 2005). However, those problems can be eliminated with the help of the inputs of the stakeholders in the destination (Morgan, Pricthard & Piggott, 2003). Thus, it can be benefitted from internal branding. Thanks to internal branding, not only sustainable improvement can be achieved, but it can also contribute to the destination branding process in bottom-up terms. In other words, it should be focused on sustainable improvement. Interests of the stakeholders should be taken into consideration, and the branding process should be followed accordingly. After that, a successful destination branding can be achieved.

Zouganeli et al. (2012) indicate that stakeholders in a destination not only provide an important infrastructure but are also an important determinative factor for the sustainability approach in tourism. More clearly, residents in a destination can establish the basis for the destination branding. Destination branding can become sustainable, only if the harmonization is ensured among the residents, the administrative purposes, and the tourist demands. On the other hand, Anholt (2007) mentioned that the branding strategy developed within the framework of the local people's cultures, aspirations, and capabilities can be reliable, sustainable, and effective. Nevertheless, the tourists' increasing expectations to reach a level that cannot be satisfied or the misleading comments on the characteristics of the region could result in undesired conditions/states/situations in both the projected induced image and the destination branding. The organic image to be developed, considering the feelings of the residents about the region and the social marketing approach, can look after the tourist's demands and the local people's interests (Jamrozy & Walsh, 2008). Hence, it can be indicated that the sustainable improvement approach embodying the benefits of the local people should be adopted to achieve a successful destination branding.

METHODOLOGY

Creating a brand using the local dynamics and, at the same time, promoting sustainable tourism fall under the responsibility of the stakeholders. The responsibility in question—which emerges from the local actors in consciousness, awareness, and practicing—indicates that the branding creates a value within the framework of tourism development as well. Thus, the stakeholder approach, on which the study is based, and the examination of this approach are at the heart of the subject. Because of research design, the qualitative method that facilitates the collection of data rich in content and enables the flexible examination of the results was utilized in the study (Yüksel & Yüksel, 2004).

Seven key persons in tourism were interviewed. The interviews were conducted face-to-face and lasted for 15–30 minutes, and semi-structured questions covering and elaborating the research topic were used. The face-to-face interviews were conducted from October to December, with seven key actors consisting of academicians, hotel managers, local government, and opinion leaders. The face-to-face interviews gathered more detailed information. The consistency between the information gathered and the observed body language of the respondents were also accepted as a parameter for data reliability (Güven, 2006; Sönmez & Alacapınar, 2014). Descriptive analysis was used for data processing, and the statements were reviewed and interpreted within the context of the meanings of the responses (Şimşek & Yıldırım, 2011).

RESULTS

In terms of the number of employees and its contributions to the socioeconomic development of a region or country, tourism is among the most important sectors. It is an industry that helps solving unemployment and poverty problems, particularly in the developing countries or regions, through using the available resources in the region or the country (Holjevac, 2003). With regard to the relationship between tourism and future, a respondent mentioned the following statements:

Such an internationally important sector like tourism can change the future in a city. It is of vital importance to turn the cities into "brand city," which is today's trend motto. International recognition will pave the way for the other necessary investments into other sectors in the city. At this point, decision-makers in the region should accelerate the incentives on tourism and support the investors.

So that the sustainable tourism agenda can come into existence for the different stakeholder groups, opportunities and obstacles should be better understood, and the tourism-related attempts should be adapted to this agenda. The foundation of this agenda is a branding approach, including the core sustainability standards (Woodland & Acott, 2007). For instance, one of respondents mentioned the following statement:

In order to improve the tourism in Adıyaman, all available efforts should be gathered under a single roof. In this way, it would be possible to quantitatively examine the values which the tourism would contribute to the socioeconomic structure of the region. On the other hand, the nonexistence of the systematic information about the region would bring along the never-ending discussions.

Another forefront issue is the use of local resources to create a unique value. The subject of economic and environmental sustainability has started to focus on the local alternative products lately (Sims, 2009). The following is the opinions of one of the respondents:

So that Adıyaman could have a touristic identity, it should be able to utilize its unique features. Thus, the local resources are used, become more valuable, and the awareness is established. In addition, it would also be possible to inherit those resources to the new generations.

Similarly, another respondent stressed out the efficient use of the local values in the city and drew attention to the cooperation among the stakeholders:

Touristic supply sources—such as local festivals, bird watching, photography, trekking, camping, canoe, sailing, rowing, and waterboarding—do exist in Adıyaman. Efficient use of those local sources could be the driving force for the city to have a touristic brand. At this point, it can be indicated that each local stakeholder bears different responsibilities for both sustainable tourism and branding (Camilleri, 2014).

Tourism sustainability, branding, and the role equation among the stakeholders can be considered as a whole (Camilleri, 2016). Planning and implementing of those plans create the framework. Nevertheless, the challenging point is planning and the coordinating afterwards. On the other hand, as claimed by Jamal and Getz (1995), the lack of coordination and harmonization render more difficult to move a step further in an already complicated structure of tourism, and it becomes a chronic dilemma for destination managers and planners. A similar opinion by one of respondents is as follows:

Instead of organizing events to save the day, it is necessary to prepare short-, medium-, and long-term tourism road maps and to lay down the priorities of the government, craftsman, nongovernmental organizations, and education institutions on the subject matter. Following the education plans and strategies, it would become possible for the city to have a brand in tourism. Otherwise, it does not seem possible to develop the tourism in Adıyaman through short-term and non-sustainable approaches.

Stakeholder participation means actualizing the tourism phenomenon at the local consciousness level and the necessary steps to be taken accordingly. As emphasized by Çalışkan (2015), the developmental goal of the regions wishing for the utilization of the tourism potential is to establish a strong society based on local partnership. Regardless of the field, the available sources would be materialized in the regions with the sufficient social infrastructure, and this would create a justification for the purpose of development only within this framework. One respondent's opinion supporting this idea is as follows:

Financing the costs of sustainability practices, the divided structure of the sector, and the political needs put a great responsibility on the shoulders of the local administrations. In order to adopt the sustainable tourism approach (Camilleri, 2014), all stakeholders should take joint action . . . In this regard, it is of vital importance that the trainings are organized for the target groups. The businesses do benefit from the local resources and the local people consider touristic values more than an economic output.

Establishing the term *tourism* in the developing regions such as Adıyaman and ensuring the local people's adaptation to the tourism are also matters to be considered. Establishing a common consciousness on tourism and, if possible, its better perception through practices are prerequisites of social participation (Moscardo, 2008). Within the context of local people and tourism, the opinion of one of the participants is as follows:

For the developing cities, it is no doubt that the local dynamics have an impact on the tourism sector. Tourism affects the whole structure of the city. What is important here is the direction of this impact. In cities where the sector is not welcomed and the local dynamics have negative impacts, tourism cannot develop in a sustainable way.

Utilizing manpower in the region could provide remarkable benefits and acquisitions in using local sources and could be an important prescription for the recovery of the social conditions in the region. This can also be considered as a fundamental variable for the sustainability of tourism (Klintman, 2012). Regarding the importance of local manpower, one of participants mentioned the following statement:

The most important point is to find the human resource in the city. The human resource in question not only would have a direct effect on the economy but also shape the future of the city in terms of the sector. As long as the enterprises get profit, they will stay in the region. However, it is an undeniable fact that the stories of the cultural assets and their historical meanings can be better told by the well-educated and experienced local people. Professional representatives in the sector have difficulties with finding human resource, especially in the developing cities. Therefore, most of the time, they tend to make investments into human resources that might create many opportunities in the region.

Although tourism creates direct or indirect economic resources for many fields, it brings along some problems as well. Hence, developing applicable resource management strategies is vital (Connell, Stephen & Bentley, 2009). Here is the approach of one of the participants on the resource management and sustainable tourism:

The efficient use of local dynamics is one of the leading factors having enabled the sustainable tourism activities turning into mass touristic activities in many regions. Therefore, in order to ensure that sustainable tourism efforts yield the expected results and the touristic regions maintain their natural characteristics, it is of importance that local dynamics—such as local authorities, local people, nongovernmental organizations, and professional associations—embodies the sustainable tourism activities in a collective way and manage the touristic resources in a wise way. In this way, sustainable tourism activities can reach a significance level.

Tourism has a structure that is continuously developing, transforming, and taking shape over the natural and local resources, and it affects the resources that it is based on. Therefore, various challenges are faced with the management, use, and sustainability of the local sources (Budowski, 1976), and the source efficacy, the use of local values, and all other factors mentioned above are important variables of sustainable tourism and branding process.

SOLUTIONS AND RECOMMENDATIONS

Tourism is a large-scaled industry that largely affects areas, shapes the socioeconomic life, and transforms the environment positively and negatively (Mathieson & Wall, 1988). Hence, sustainable tourism indicates an approach where all available resources and dynamics work coordinately (Clarke, 1997). As emphasized by Budeanu (2003), success of tourism in practice shows linearity with its position within the sustainable development policies. It is beside the point to mention about tourism without understanding how tourism is perceived by stakeholders and how the resources can be managed. Thus, sustainable tourism planning should be considered with a proactive and holistic approach in short and long terms (Hardy & Beetoon, 2001). As seen in Dwyer, Forsyth, and Spurr's (2009) approach, the main question of the local power to be formed with stakeholder participation is what should be in the future rather than what will it be.

In the present study, the local dynamics' role on tourism sustainability and the subject of branding based on those dynamics were discussed. Within the scope of the study, key persons were interviewed, and their opinions were reflected. Examining the approaches of Aas, Ladkin, and Fletcher (2005) on stakeholder collaboration, the present study supports the following implementation projections:

The first one is the utilization of the available resources and the establishment of the communication channels among the relevant tourism groups, the second one is about how to make income for the resources in question and the protection and management of the resources, the third one is how to integrate the local people into the process, and the last one is the evaluation of the success of stakeholder participation and collaboration (Aas, Ladkin, & Fletcher, 2005).

As seen in the interview results, the stakeholders should gather and take a joint action for sustainable tourism and branding. Although tourism is considered as an important opportunity, particularly for the developing small cities like Adıyaman, the opportunity in question should be actualized with the help of medium- and long-term plans, and the local dynamics should be used as a basis for those plans. The main motivation underlying the tourism identity and branding process of Adıyaman lies in processing the unique values in the city. At this point, Woodland and Acott (2007) mentioned about the following points in their local branding strategies:

Developing and implementing a local tourism brand strategy covering sustainability – facilitating the cohesion among the stakeholders and the harmony of brand plan and implementation processes with the sustainability. In this context, understanding the relations between the local factors forming the brand is necessary (Gelder, 2004).

Cooperation between public and sector – organizing consultation meetings and training to understand the criteria and requirements of a sustainable tourism approach. In parallel with sustainability, branding efforts based on local values should be able to oversee the importance of the balance among the traditional, the new, the environmental, and the developmental, or between the internal and the external environment (Go & Trunfio, 2011).

Local tourism network – establishing the local tourism network including the representatives from different sectors. The ability to share information and act collectively in the local tourism network is important (Iorio & Wall, 2011).

From the interview's result, the recommendations reflect the ongoing regional problems. Accordingly, the main problem in Adıyaman is not about the necessary potential for sustainability and branding but about the challenges faced with the utilization of the potential in practical life. Many communication problems in a large area range from using local manpower, educating, and using natural attractions to taking joint actions. As mentioned in the interviews, correctly understanding where the sustainability intersects with the branding, even though the economic interests have priority, is essential.

Gartner (2014) emphasized that it should not be focused only on the economic outputs of the destination branding. The author draws attention to the unique features and the required factors that each destination should have. On the other hand, the utilization of the local resources during the branding process is an important element; however, the successful utilization of the resources could be quite challenging within the framework of sustainability. In addition to the implementation practices, the external environment of the destination could be significant in the equation of branding and sustainability. Thus, particular indicators have been developed to understand whether sustainability is successfully achieved by the destinations (Dinnie, 2007), and these indicators can be an important guide for developing destinations in particular.

Although differences might bring competitive advantage (Jamrozy & Walsh, 2008), unique geographical and cultural features in the destination could subject to deformation in time. Therefore, ways to protect and maintain the unique features that would bring competitive advantage to the destination within the scope of the destination branding should be overemphasized. Tourism branding is vital, particularly for overcoming the problems faced in the protected areas in sustainable tourism (Woodland & Acott, 2007).

The disadvantageous part is where the phenomenon of tourism that has not been so widespread and had an identity stands in the minds of local people. This case indicates the absence of *a driving sectorial power that brings income at a large scale, therefore, needs to be maintained*. The ambiguity observed in the tourism-oriented development perceptions of the local people and the local authorities halt the acceptance, internalization, and start-up processes as well (Çalışkan, 2015).

When the subject is thoroughly examined, the possible problems about the harmonization of the planning and practices with the local patterns attract attention. Although a tourism destination, as an assumption, would be successful at a branding process, establishing the brand awareness and brand creation principles that are coherent with the existing tourism goal is crucial because ignoring sensitive points such as social, geographical or cultural structures in the region might negatively affect the region's identity and the individuals' senses of place (Konecnik & Go, 2008). It also requires the harmonization between economic and political structures in the region (Önen, 2000).

Therefore, a holistic approach on sustainable tourism development should be ecologically liable, socially compatible, culturally suitable, politically equal, technologically supportive, and economically applicable for the hosting community (Choi & Sirakaya, 2006).

FUTURE RESEARCH DIRECTIONS

The concepts of branding and sustainable tourism are widely discussed in the literature. Both concepts are still current and will quite likely stay up-to-date in destination management. The authors have tackled the issue of branding, sustainable tourism, and stakeholders in the common ground, also evaluated as intercorrelated in barriers and solutions. Research topics can be correlated with national/international policies and implementations and examined by considering different variables, such as local branding strategies, globalization, and decentralization.

CONCLUSION

Indicating important statements for the sustainable tourism and branding process in Adıyaman is essential. For instance, the tourism activities in the city are limited, and the available potential does not have the risk of harming the local resources yet. This case can be examined considering the advantages and disadvantages.

The tourism activities that have not been so widespread and risky are suitable for more reasonable and realistic plans. Hence, implementing initial precautions and practices would be possible. Moreover, the tourism outputs could become more widespread, thanks to the systemization of the resource utilization and the branding process. Local tourism branding is an initiative bringing the main activity network together. Thanks to this initiative, increasing the sales rate of the local touristic product and services through branding them under a specific region or area is tried. Moreover, it contributes to local branding, the quality standards are ensured, and the market recognition increases. This aim can be benefitted from the common marketing technique, which would ensure the local sustainable development (Woodland & Acott, 2007).

REFERENCES

Aas, C., Ladkin, A., & Fletcher, J. (2005). Stakeholder collaboration and heritage management. *Annals of Tourism Research*, *32*(1), 28–48. doi:10.1016/j.annals.2004.04.005

Avcıkurt, C. (2009). *Turizm Sosyolojisi, Genel ve Yapısal Yaklaşım*. Ankara: Detay.

Avcıoğlu, G. Ş. (2013). Kriz Dönemlerinde Sosyal Bütünleşme: Millî Mücadele Örneği. *Uluslararası Tarih ve Sosyal Araştırmalar Dergisi*, *5*(10), 155–170.

Beyhan, Ş. G. & Ünügür, S. M. (2010). Çağdaş gereksinmeler bağlamında sürdürülebilir turizm ve kimlik modeli. *İtü Dergisi*, *4*(2), 79-87.

Booyens, I. (2010). Rethinking township tourism: Towards responsible tourism development in South African townships. *Development Southern Africa*, *27*(2), 273–287. doi:10.1080/03768351003740795

Bowman, K. S. (2011). Sustainable tourism certification and state capacity: Keep it local, simple, and fuzzy. *International Journal of Culture, Tourism and Hospitality Research*, *5*(3), 269–281. doi:10.1108/17506181111156961

Bramwell, B., & Lane, B. (2000). Collaboration and partnerships in tourism planning. *Tourism collaboration and partnerships*. In B. Bramwell & B. Lane (Eds.), *Politics, practice and sustainability* (pp. 1–19). Channel View Publications.

Buckley, R. (1996). Sustainable Tourism: Technical Issues and Information Needs. *Annals of Tourism Research, Volume*, 23(4), 1996.

Budeanu, A. (2003). Impacts and responsibilities for sustainable tourism: A tour operator's perspective. *Journal of Cleaner Production, 13*(2), 89–97. doi:10.1016/j.jclepro.2003.12.024

Budowski, G. (1976). Tourism and environmental conservation: Conflict, coexistence, or symbiosis? *Environmental Conservation, 3*(1), 27–31. doi:10.1017/S0376892900017707

Butler, R. W. (1999). Sustainable tourism: A state-of-the-art review. *Tourism Geographies, 1*(1), 7–25. doi:10.1080/14616689908721291

Çalışkan, C. (2014). Evaluation of Protected Areas from the Perspective of Sustainable Tourism: Case Study of Mount Nemrut National Park/Adıyaman. *Global International Conference on Business Tourism and Sciences*, Tampa, FL.

Çalışkan, C. (2015). Turizm Potansiyeli Olan Bölgelerin Kalkınma Sürecinde Toplumsal Kapasiteyi Güçlendirme Stratejileri: Adıyaman Örneği. Nevşehir Hacı Bektaş Veli Üniversitesi Sosyal Bilimler Enstitüsü, yayınlanmamış Doktora Tezi, Nevşehir.

Çalışkan, C. (2017). Sürdürülebilir Turizmin Çevre İkilemi: Toplum ve Tüketim. *İnsan ve Toplum Bilimleri Araştırmaları Dergisi, 6*(2), 1123-1136.

Camilleri, M. A. (2014). Advancing the sustainable tourism agenda through strategic CSR perspectives. *Tourism Planning & Development, 11*(1), 42–56. doi:10.1080/21568316.2013.839470

Camilleri, M. A. (2015). Valuing stakeholder engagement and sustainability reporting. *Corporate Reputation Review, 18*(3), 210–222. doi:10.1057/crr.2015.9

Camilleri, M. A. (2016). Responsible tourism that creates shared value among stakeholders. *Tourism Planning & Development, 13*(2), 219–235. doi:10.1080/21568316.2015.1074100

Camilleri, M. A. (2018). The Marketing Environment. In *Travel Marketing, Tourism Economics and the Airline Product* (pp. 3–27). Cham, Switzerland: Springer. doi:10.1007/978-3-319-49849-2_1

Canzanelli, G. (2001). *Overview and learned lessons on local economic development, human development, and decent work.* Universitas Working Papers, ILO (Organización Internacional del Trabajo).

Carrillo, M., & Jorge, J. M. (2017). Multidimensional Analysis of Regional Tourism Sustainability in Spain. *Ecological Economics*, *140*, 89–98. doi:10.1016/j.ecolecon.2017.05.004

Cater, E. (1991). *Sustainable tourism in the Third World: Problems and prospects.* London: University of Reading.

Çetin, M. (2007). Yerel ekonomik kalkınma yaklaşımı ve uluslararası organizasyonlar. *Yönetim ve Ekonomi: Celal Bayar Üniversitesi İktisadi ve İdari Bilimler Fakültesi Dergisi*, *14*(1), 153–170.

Choi, H. C., & Sirakaya, E. (2005). Measuring residents' attitude toward sustainable tourism: Development of sustainable tourism attitude scale. *Journal of Travel Research*, *43*(4), 380–394. doi:10.1177/0047287505274651

Choi, H. C., & Sirakaya, E. (2006). Sustainability indicators for managing community tourism. *Tourism Management*, *27*(6), 1274–1289. doi:10.1016/j.tourman.2005.05.018

Clarke, J. (1997). A Framework of Approaches to Sustainable Tourism. *Journal of Sustainable Tourism*, *5*(3), 224–233. doi:10.1080/09669589708667287

Cole, S. (2006). Information and empowerment: The keys to achieving sustainable tourism. *Journal of Sustainable Tourism*, *14*(6), 629–644. doi:10.2167/jost607.0

Connell, J., Page, S. J., & Bentley, T. (2009). Towards sustainable tourism planning in New Zealand: Monitoring local government planning under the Resource Management Act. *Tourism Management*, *30*(6), 867–877. doi:10.1016/j.tourman.2008.12.001

Dodds, R., & Butler, R. W. (2008). 4 *Inaction More than Action. Barriers to the Implementation of Sustainable Tourism Policie.* In S. Gossling, C. M. Hall, & D. B. Weaver (Eds.), *Sustainable Tourism Futures Perspectives on Systems* (pp. 43–57). Routledge, UK: Restructuring and Innovations. doi:10.4324/9780203884256.pt2

Dogru, T., & Bulut, U. (2017). Is tourism an engine for economic recovery? Theory and empirical evidence. *Tourism Management*, 1-10. (in press)

Dwyer, L., Forsyth, P., & Spurr, R. (2004). Evaluating tourism's economic effects: New and old approaches. *Tourism Management*, *25*(3), 307–317. doi:10.1016/S0261-5177(03)00131-6

Eceral, T. Ö., & Özmen, C. A. (2009). *Beypazarı'nda turizm gelişimi ve yerel ekonomik kalkınma*. AİBÜ-İİBF Ekonomik ve Sosyal Araştırmalar Dergisi.

Erkuş-Öztürk, H., & Eraydın, A. (2010). Environmental governance for sustainable tourism development: Collaborative networks and organisation building in the Antalya tourism region. *Tourism Management, 31*(1), 113–124. doi:10.1016/j.tourman.2009.01.002

Frey, N., & George, R. (2010). Responsible tourism management: The missing link between business owners' attitudes and behaviour in the Cape Town tourism industry. *Tourism Management, 31*(5), 621–628. doi:10.1016/j.tourman.2009.06.017

Garrod, B., & Fyall, A. (1998). Beyond the rhetoric of sustainable tourism? *Tourism Management, 19*(3), 199–212. doi:10.1016/S0261-5177(98)00013-2

Gössling, S., Hall, C. M., & Weaver, D. B. (2008). Synthesis and Conclusions. In S. Gossling, C. M. Hall, & D. B. Weaver (Eds.), *Sustainable Tourism Futures Perspectives on Systems* (pp. 300–306). Routledge, UK: Restructuring and Innovations.

Gursoy, D., & Rutherford, D. G. (2004). Host attitudes toward tourism: An improved structural model. *Annals of Tourism Research, 31*(3), 495–516. doi:10.1016/j.annals.2003.08.008

Güven, S. (2006). *Toplumbiliminde Araştırma Yöntemleri*. Bursa: Ezgi Kitabevi Yayınları.

Ham, S. H., & Weiler, B. (2012). Interpretation as the centerpiece of sustainable wildlife tourism. In R. Harris, T. Griffin, & P. Williams (Eds.), *Sustainable Tourism* (pp. 35–44). Oxford, UK: Butterworth-Heinemann.

Hardy, A., Beeton, R. J., & Pearson, L. (2002). Sustainable tourism: An overview of the concept and its position in relation to conceptualisations of tourism. *Journal of Sustainable Tourism, 10*(6), 475–496. doi:10.1080/09669580208667183

Hardy, A. L., & Beeton, R. J. (2001). Sustainable tourism or maintainable tourism: Managing resources for more than average outcomes. *Journal of Sustainable Tourism, 9*(3), 168–192. doi:10.1080/09669580108667397

Holden, A. (2009). The environment-tourism nexus: Influence of market ethics. *Annals of Tourism Research, 36*(3), 373–389. doi:10.1016/j.annals.2008.10.009

Holjevac, I. A. (2003). A vision of tourism and the hotel industry in the 21st century. *International Journal of Hospitality Management, 22*(2), 129–134. doi:10.1016/S0278-4319(03)00021-5

Hunter, C. (1997). Sustainable tourism as an adaptive paradigm. *Annals of Tourism Research, 24*(4), 850–867. doi:10.1016/S0160-7383(97)00036-4

Ianos, I., Peptenatu, D., & Zamfir, D. (2009). Respect for environment and sustainable development. *Carpathian Journal of Earth and Environmental Sciences, 4*(1), 81–93.

Iorio, M., & Wall, G. (2011). Local museums as catalysts for development: Mamoiada, Sardinia, Italy. *Journal of Heritage Tourism, 6*(1), 1–15. doi:10.1080/1743873X.2010.515311

Jackson, J. (2006). Developing regional tourism in China: The potential for activating business clusters in a socialist market economy. *Tourism Management, 27*(4), 695–706. doi:10.1016/j.tourman.2005.02.007

Jamal, T. B., & Getz, D. (1995). Collaboration theory and community tourism planning. *Annals of Tourism Research, 22*(1), 186–204. doi:10.1016/0160-7383(94)00067-3

Joppe, M. (1996). Sustainable community tourism development revisited. *Tourism Management, 17*(7), 475–479. doi:10.1016/S0261-5177(96)00065-9

Kahraman, N., & Türkay, O. (2006). *Turizm ve Çevre*. Ankara: Detay Yayıncılık.

Klintman, M. (2012). Issues of scale in the global accreditation of sustainable tourism: schemes toward harmonized re-embeddedness? *Sustainability: Science, Practice, & Policy, 8*(1).

Konecnik, M., & Go, F. (2008). Tourism destination brand identity: The case of Slovenia. *Journal of Brand Management, 15*(3), 177–189. doi:10.1057/palgrave.bm.2550114

L'Etang, J., Falkheimer, J., & Lugo, J. (2007). Public relations and tourism: Critical reflections and a research agenda. *Public Relations Review, 33*(1), 68–76. doi:10.1016/j.pubrev.2006.11.008

Lozano-Oyola, M., Blancas, F. J., González, M., & Caballero, R. (2012). Sustainable tourism indicators as planning tools in cultural destinations. *Ecological Indicators, 18*, 659–675. doi:10.1016/j.ecolind.2012.01.014

Milne, S., & Ateljevic, I. (2001). Tourism, economic development and the global-local nexus: Theory embracing complexity. *Tourism Geographies, 3*(4), 369–393. doi:10.1080/14616680110070478

Moscardo, G. (Ed.). (2008). *Building community capacity for tourism development*. Cabi. doi:10.1079/9781845934477.0000

Neto, F. (2003). A new approach to sustainable tourism development: Moving beyond environmental protection. *Natural Resources Forum*, *27*(3), 212–222. doi:10.1111/1477-8947.00056

Önen, O. M. (2000). *Türkiye'nin Turizm Sektöründeki Gelişmeler, Dünya Turizmindeki Yeri ve Türkiye Kalkınma Bankası'nın Rolü*. Türkiye Kalkınma Bankası.

Reece, W. S. (2009). *The economics of tourism*. Pearson Education Inc.

Richards, G., & Hall, D. (2002). The community: a sustainable concept in tourism development? In G. Richards & D. Hall (Eds.), *Tourism and Sustainable Community Development* (pp. 1–15). Routledge.

Scheyvens, R. (2002). *Tourism for development: Empowering communities*. Pearson Education.

Sims, R. (2009). Food, place and authenticity: Local food and the sustainable tourism experience. *Journal of Sustainable Tourism*, *17*(3), 321–336. doi:10.1080/09669580802359293

Şimşek, H., & Yıldırım, A. (2011). Sosyal bilimlerde nitel araştırma yöntemleri. Ankara: Seçkin Yayıncılık.

Sönmez, V., & Alacapınar, F.G. (2014). Bilimsel Araştırma Yöntemleri. Ankara: Anı Yayıncılık.

Van Gelder, S. (2004). Global brand strategy. *Journal of Brand Management*, *12*(1), 39–48. doi:10.1057/palgrave.bm.2540200

Weaver, D. B. (2006). *Sustainable tourism: Theory and practice*. Routledge.

Woodland, M., & Acott, T. G. (2007). Sustainability and local tourism branding in England's South Downs. *Journal of Sustainable Tourism*, *15*(6), 715–734. doi:10.2167/jost652.0

Yasarata, M., Altinay, L., Burns, P., & Okumus, F. (2010). Politics and sustainable tourism development–Can they co-exist? Voices from North Cyprus. *Tourism Management*, *31*(3), 345–356. doi:10.1016/j.tourman.2009.03.016

Yılmaz, İ., & Çalışkan, C. (2015). Turizm Potansiyeli Olan Bölgelerde Toplumsal Kapasite Algısı: Adıyaman Örneği. *Journal of Yasar University*, *10*(39).

Yüksel, A., & Yüksel, F. (2004). Turizmde Bilimsel Araştırma Yöntemleri. Ankara: Turhan Kitabevi.

Compilation of References

Aaker, D. A. (1991). *Managing brand equity*. New York: Free Press.

Aaker, D. A. (2002). *Building strong brands*. New York, NY: Free Press.

Aaker, D. A., & Joachimsthaler, E. (2000). *Brand leadership*. New York: The Free Press.

Aas, C., Ladkin, A., & Fletcher, J. (2005). Stakeholder collaboration and heritage management. *Annals of Tourism Research*, *32*(1), 28–48. doi:10.1016/j.annals.2004.04.005

Abrate, G., Fraquelli, G., & Viglia, G. (2012). Dynamic pricing strategies: Evidence from European hotels. *International Journal of Hospitality Management*, *31*(1), 160–168. doi:10.1016/j.ijhm.2011.06.003

Abrate, G., & Viglia, G. (2016). Strategic and tactical price decisions in hotel revenue management. *Tourism Management*, *55*, 123–132. doi:10.1016/j.tourman.2016.02.006

ACS Distance Education (ACSEDU). (n.d.). *Marketing adventure tourism: Ecotourism and adventure tourism*. Retrieved August 19, 2017, from http://www.acsedu.com/courses/ecotourism-and-adventure-activities-courses.aspx

Adams, J. S. (1963). Towards an understanding of inequity. *Journal of Abnormal and Social Psychology*, *67*(5), 422–436. doi:10.1037/h0040968 PMID:14081885

Adeyinka-Ojo, S. F., & Khoo-Lattimore, C. (2013). Slow food events as a high yield strategy for rural tourism destinations: The case of Bario, Sarawak. *Worldwide Hospitality and Tourism Themes*, *5*(4), 353–364. doi:10.1108/WHATT-03-2013-0012

Agapito, D., do Vale, P., & Mendes, J. (2014). The sensory dimension of tourist experiences: Capturing meaningful sensory-informed themes in Southwest Portugal. *Tourism Management*, *42*, 224–237. doi:10.1016/j.tourman.2013.11.011

Agapito, D., Valle, P. O., & Mendes, J. C. (2013). The cognitive-affective-conative model of destination image: A confirmatory analysis. *Journal of Travel & Tourism Marketing*, *30*(5), 471–481. doi:10.1080/10548408.2013.803393

Ahmed, Z. U., Johnson, J. P., Ling, C. P., & Fang, T. W. A. K. (2002). Country-of-Origin and Brand Effects on Consumers' Evaluations of Cruise Lines. *International Marketing Review*, *19*(2/3), 279–323. doi:10.1108/02651330210430703

Ahmed, Z. U., Sohail, M. S., Myers, C., & Chan Pui, S. (2006). Marketing of Australia to Malaysian Consumers. *Services Marketing Quarterly*, *28*(2), 57–78. doi:10.1300/J396v28n02_04

Aicher, J., Asiimwe, F., Batchuluun, B., Hauschild, M., Zöhrer, M., & Egger, R. (2016). Online Hotel Reviews: Rating Symbols or Text… Text or Rating Symbols? That Is the Question! In Information and Communication Technologies in Tourism 2016 (pp. 369–382). Springer.

Aitken, R., & Campelo, A. (2011). The fours Rs of place branding. *Journal of Marketing Management*, *27*(9), 913–933. doi:10.1080/0267257X.2011.560718

Alaeddinoglu, F., & Can, A. S. (2010). Destination image from the perspective of travel intermediaries. *Anatolia: An International Journal of Tourism and Hospitality Research*, *21*(2), 339–350. doi:10.1080/13032917.2010.9687107

Alcañiz, E. B., García, I. S., & Blas, S. S. (2009). The functional-psychological continuum in the cognitive image of a destination: A confirmatory analysis. *Tourism Management*, *30*(5), 715–723. doi:10.1016/j.tourman.2008.10.020

Alegre, J., & Sard, M. (2015). When demand drops and prices rise. Tourist packages in the Balearic Islands during the economic crisis. *Tourism Management*, *46*, 375–385. doi:10.1016/j.tourman.2014.07.016

Alhemoud, A. M., & Armstrong, E. G. (1996). Image of Tourism Attractions in Kuwait. *Journal of Travel Research*, *34*(4), 76–80. doi:10.1177/004728759603400413

Allcock, J. B. (1989). Seasonality. In S. F. Witt & L. Moutinho (Eds.), *Tourism marketing and management handbook* (pp. 387–392). Englewood Cliffs, NJ: Prentice-Hall.

Almeida, F., Peláez, M. A., Balbuena, A., & Cortés, R. (2016). Residents' perceptions of tourism development in Benalmadena (Spain). *Tourism Management*, *54*, 259–274. doi:10.1016/j.tourman.2015.11.007

Alon, I., Jaffe, E., Prange, C., & Vianelli, D. (2016). *Global Marketing: Contemporary theory, practice and cases*. New York: Routledge-Taylor & Francis.

Alvarez, M. D., & Campo, S. (2014). The Influence of Political Conflicts on Country Image and Intention to Visit: A Study of Israel's Image. *Tourism Management*, *40*, 70–78. doi:10.1016/j.tourman.2013.05.009

Amuquandoh, F. E. (2010). Residents' perceptions of the environmental impacts of tourism in the Lake Bosomtwe Basin, Ghana. *Journal of Sustainable Tourism*, *18*(2), 223–238. doi:10.1080/09669580903298531

Compilation of References

Andereck, K. L., & Nyaupane, G. P. (2011). Exploring the nature of tourism and quality of life perceptions among residents. *Journal of Travel Research*, *50*(3), 248–260. doi:10.1177/0047287510362918

Andereck, K. L., Valentine, K. M., Knopf, R. C., & Vogt, C. A. (2005). Residents' perceptions of community tourism impacts. *Annals of Tourism Research*, *32*(4), 1056–1076. doi:10.1016/j.annals.2005.03.001

Anderson, C. (2012). The Impact of Social Media on Lodging Performance. *Cornell Hospitality Report*, *12*(15), 6–11.

Andersson, D. E. (2010). Hotel attributes and hedonic prices: An analysis of internet-based transactions in Singapore's market for hotel rooms. *The Annals of Regional Science*, *44*(2), 229–240. doi:10.100700168-008-0265-4

Andrews, C. G. (2015). Ten reasons why adventure travel is good for you. *Good Nature Travel—The Official Travel Blog of Natural Habitat Adventures & WWF*. Retrieved July 4, 2017, from http://goodnature.nathab.com/ten-reasons-why-adventure-travel-is-good-for-you

Andriotis, K., & Vaughan, R. D. (2003). Urban residents' attitudes toward tourism development: The case of Crete. *Journal of Travel Research*, *42*(2), 172–185. doi:10.1177/0047287503257488

Anholt, S. (2010). *Handbook on tourism destination branding*. Madrid: ETC/UNWTO.

Antigua and Barbuda Tourism Development. (2003). *Tourism's economic impacts increasing the contribution to prosperity. Antigua LP*. Antigua and Barbuda: KPMG Consulting.

Ap, J. (1992). Residents' perceptions on tourism impacts. *Annals of Tourism Research*, *19*(4), 665–690. doi:10.1016/0160-7383(92)90060-3

Ap, J., & Crompton, J. L. (1993). Residents' strategies for responding to tourism impacts. *Journal of Travel Research*, *32*(1), 47–50. doi:10.1177/004728759303200108

Archer, B., Cooper, C., & Ruhanen, L. (2005). *The Positive and Negative Impacts of Tourism*. Oxford, UK: Elsevier. doi:10.1016/B978-0-7506-7789-9.50011-X

Aref, F., & Gill, S. (2009). Rural tourism development through rural cooperatives. *Nature and Science*, *7*(1), 670–673.

Arnott, R., De Palma, A., & Lindsey, R. (1993). A structural model of peak-period congestion: A traffic bottleneck with elastic demand. *The American Economic Review*, 161–179.

Ashworth, G. (2002). The Image of Georgian Bath 1700–2000: Towns, Heritage and History. *Journal of Historical Geography*, *28*(2), 303–304. doi:10.1006/jhge.2002.0433

Ashworth, G., & Kavaratzis, M. (2009). Beyond the logo: Brand management for cities. *Journal of Brand Management*, *16*(8), 520–531. doi:10.1057/palgrave.bm.2550133

Atadil, H. A., Sarıkaya, E., & Altıntaş, V. (2017). An Analysis of Destination Image for Emerging Markets of Turkey. *Journal of Vacation Marketing*, *23*(1), 37–54. doi:10.1177/1356766715616858

Avcıkurt, C. (2009). *Turizm Sosyolojisi, Genel ve Yapısal Yaklaşım*. Ankara: Detay.

Avcıoğlu, G. Ş. (2013). Kriz Dönemlerinde Sosyal Bütünleşme: Millî Mücadele Örneği. *Uluslararası Tarih ve Sosyal Araştırmalar Dergisi, 5*(10), 155–170.

Ayeh, J. K., Au, N., & Law, R. (2013). "Do We Believe in TripAdvisor?" Examining Credibility Perceptions and Online Travelers' Attitude toward Using User-Generated Content. *Journal of Travel Research, 52*(4), 437–452. doi:10.1177/0047287512475217

Ayuntamiento de Barcelona. (2015). *Tourism Activity Report of Barcelona*. Barcelona, Spain: Ayuntamiento de Barcelona.

Babbie, E. R. (2010). *The practice of social research* (12th ed.). Belmont, CA: Wadsworth Cengage.

Baggio, R., & Sainaghi, R. (2016). Mapping time series into networks as a tool to assess the complex dynamics of tourism systems. *Tourism Management, 54*, 23–33. doi:10.1016/j.tourman.2015.10.008

Baker, M. J., & Cameron, E. (2008). Critical success factors in destination marketing. *Tourism and Hospitality Research, 8*(2), 79–97. doi:10.1057/thr.2008.9

Balakrishnan, M. S. (2009). Strategic branding of destinations: A framework. *European Journal of Marketing, 43*(5/6), 611–629. doi:10.1108/03090560910946954

Bala, P. (2002). *Changing borders and identities in the Kelabit highlands: anthropological reflections on growing up in a Kelabit village near the international border*. Kuching, Malaysia: Unit Penerbitan Universiti Malaysia, Sarawak.

Ball, R. M. (1989). Some aspects of tourism, seasonality and local labour markets. *Area, 21*(1), 35–45.

Baloglu, S. (1999). A path analytic model of visitation intention involving information sources, socio-psychological motivations, and destination image. *Journal of Travel & Tourism Marketing, 8*(3), 81–90. doi:10.1300/J073v08n03_05

Baloglu, S., & Brinberg, D. (1997). Affective Images of Tourism Destinations. *Journal Of Tourism Research, 35*(4), 11–15.

Baloglu, S., & Mangaloglu, M. (2001). Tourism destination images of Turkey, Egypt, Greece, and Italy as perceived by US-based tour operators and travel agents. *Tourism Management, 22*(1), 1–9. doi:10.1016/S0261-5177(00)00030-3

Baloglu, S., & McCleary, K. W. (1999a). A model of destination image formation. *Annals of Tourism Research, 26*(4), 868–897. doi:10.1016/S0160-7383(99)00030-4

Baloglu, S., & McCleary, K. W. (1999b). U.S. international pleasure travelers' images of four Mediterranean destinations: A comparison of visitors and non-visitors. *Journal of Travel Research, 38*(2), 144–152. doi:10.1177/004728759903800207

Banja, V. (2016). Tourism in Function of Development of the Republic of Serbia: Spa Tourism in Serbia and Experiences of other countries. *1st International Scientific Conferences.*

BarOn. R.V. (1975). Seasonality in tourism. London: The Economic Intelligence Unit.

Bar-On, R. R. (1999). The measurement of seasonality and its economic impacts. *Tourism Economics*, *5*(4), 437–458. doi:10.1177/135481669900500409

Barreto, A. M. (2014). The word of mouth phenomenon in the social media era. *International Journal of Market Research*, *56*(5), 631–654. doi:10.2501/IJMR-2014-043

Bath and North-East Somerset Council. (2016). *The Roman Baths Bath.* Available at: http://www.romanbaths.co.uk/visit

Bauer, A. (2010). *Marketing adventure tourism: What works and what doesn't.* Munich, Germany: Munich University of Applied Sciences. Accessible from the Shannon College of Hotel Management. Retrieved from http://www.shannoncollege.com/wp-content/uploads/2009/12/A.-Bauer-THRIC-2010-Full-Paper.pdf

Baum, T. (1999). Seasonality in tourism: Understanding the challenges. *Tourism Economics*, *5*(1), 5–8. doi:10.1177/135481669900500101

Baum, T., & Hagen, L. (1999). Responses to seasonality: The experiences of peripheral destinations. *International Journal of Tourism Research*, *1*(5), 232–299. doi:10.1002/(SICI)1522-1970(199909/10)1:5<299::AID-JTR198>3.0.CO;2-L

Beerli, A., & Martín, J. D. (2004). Tourists' characteristics and the perceived image of tourist destinations: A quantitative analysis—a case study of Lanzarote, Spain. *Tourism Management*, *25*(5), 623–636. doi:10.1016/j.tourman.2003.06.004

Beerli, A., & Martín, J. D. (2004a). Factors influencing destination image. *Annals of Tourism Research*, *31*(3), 657–681. doi:10.1016/j.annals.2004.01.010

Benckendorff, P. J., & Black, N. L. (2000). Destination marketing on the Internet: A case study of Australian Regional Tourism Authorities. *Journal of Tourism Studies*, *11*(1), 11–21.

Berger, P. D., Weinberg, B., & Hanna, R. C. (2003). Customer lifetime value determination and strategic implications for a cruise-ship company. *Journal of Database Marketing & Customer Strategy Management*, *11*(1), 40–52. doi:10.1057/palgrave.dbm.3240204

Besanko, D., Dubé, J.-P., & Gupta, S. (2003). Competitive price discrimination strategies in a vertical channel using aggregate retail data. *Management Science*, *49*(9), 1121–1138. doi:10.1287/mnsc.49.9.1121.16565

Besse, B. A. (2015). *The situation of the Hagymatikum of Makó on the Hungarian spa market, possible ways of attracting more visitors there* (Doctoral dissertation, bgf).

Beyhan, Ş. G. & Ünügür, S. M. (2010). Çağdaş gereksinmeler bağlamında sürdürülebilir turizm ve kimlik modeli. *İtü Dergisi, 4*(2), 79-87.

Bigley, J. D., Lee, C. K., Chon, J., & Yoon, Y. (2010). Motivations for War-related Tourism: A Case of DMZ Visitors in Korea. *Tourism Geographies*, *12*(3), 371–394. doi:10.1080/14616688.2010.494687

Bigné, J. E., Sánchez, M. I., & Sánchez, J. (2001). Tourism image, evaluation variables and after purchase behaviour: Inter-relationship. *Tourism Management*, *22*(6), 607–616. doi:10.1016/S0261-5177(01)00035-8

Bilgihan, A., Barreda, A., Okumus, F., & Nusair, K. (2016). Consumer perception of knowledge-sharing in travel-related online social networks. *Tourism Management*, *52*, 287–296. doi:10.1016/j.tourman.2015.07.002

Bill, J. (2010). Perceptions of Tourism Products. *Tourism Management*, *31*(5), 607–610. doi:10.1016/j.tourman.2009.06.011

Blackshaw, P., & Nazarro, M. (2006). *Consumer-generated media (CGM) 101: Word-of-mouth in the age of the web-fortified consumer*. New York: Nielsen.

Blum, V., & Fallon, J. (2001). Welsh visitor attraction web sites: Multipurpose tools or technological tokenism? *Information Technology & Tourism*, *4*(3-1), 191-201.

Bolton, L. E., Warlop, L., & Alba, J. W. (2003). Consumer Perceptions of Price (Un)Fairness. *The Journal of Consumer Research*, *29*(4), 474–491. doi:10.1086/346244

Boniface, B. G., & Cooper, C. (2005). *Worldwide destinations: The geography of travel and tourism*. Oxford, UK: Butterworth-Heinemann.

Bonn, M. A., Joseph, S. M., & Dai, M. (2005). International versus domestic visitors: An examination of destination image perceptions. *Journal of Travel Research*, *43*(3), 294–301. doi:10.1177/0047287504272033

Booyens, I. (2010). Rethinking township tourism: Towards responsible tourism development in South African townships. *Development Southern Africa*, *27*(2), 273–287. doi:10.1080/03768351003740795

Bowman, K. S. (2011). Sustainable tourism certification and state capacity: Keep it local, simple, and fuzzy. *International Journal of Culture, Tourism and Hospitality Research*, *5*(3), 269–281. doi:10.1108/17506181111156961

Boyd, S. (2002). Cultural and heritage tourism in Canada: Opportunities, principles and challenges. *Tourism and Hospitality Research*, *3*(3), 211–233. doi:10.1177/146735840200300303

Boyne, S., Hall, D., & Williams, F. (2003). Policy, Support and Promotion for Food-Related Tourism Initiatives. *Journal of Travel & Tourism Marketing*, *14*(3-4), 131–154. doi:10.1300/J073v14n03_08

Bradley, K. (2016). *2016 Annual Tourism Conference and Exhibition*. Derbyshire, UK: Marketing Peak District and Derbyshire.

Compilation of References

Bramwell, B., & Lane, B. (2000). Collaboration and partnerships in tourism planning. *Tourism collaboration and partnerships*. In B. Bramwell & B. Lane (Eds.), *Politics, practice and sustainability* (pp. 1–19). Channel View Publications.

Braun, B. M., Xander, J. A., & White, K. R. (2002). The impact of the cruise industry on a region's economy: A case study of Port Canaveral, Florida. *Tourism Economics*, *8*(3), 281–288. doi:10.5367/000000002101298124

Braun, E., Kavaratzis, M., & Zenker, S. (2010). My city – my brand: the role of residents in place branding. *50th European Regional Science Association Congress*.

Braun, V., & Clarke, V. (2006). Using thematic analysis in psychology. *Qualitative Research in Psychology*, *3*(2), 77–101. doi:10.1191/1478088706qp063oa

Bray, J., Schetzina, C., & Steinbrick, S. (2006). *Six travel trends for 2006*. PhoCusWright.

Breejen, L. (2007). The experiences of long distance walking: A case study of the West Highland Way in Scotland. *Tourism Management*, *28*(6), 1417–1427. doi:10.1016/j.tourman.2006.12.004

Briggs, P. B., & Turay, S. (2016). *Malawi: The Bradt travel guide* (7th ed.). Guilford, CT: Globe Pequot Press.

Brinzan, D. (2016). *How to Respond Properly to Online Hotel Reviews*. Retrieved 24 November 2017, from https://www.hermesthemes.com/respond-properly-online-hotel-reviews/

Brons, M., Pels, E., Nijkamp, P., & Rietveld, P. (2002). Price elasticities of demand for passenger air travel: A meta-analysis. *Journal of Air Transport Management*, *8*(3), 165–175. doi:10.1016/S0969-6997(01)00050-3

Brown, L. (2013). Tourism: A catalyst for existential authenticity. *Annals of Tourism Research*, *40*, 176–190. doi:10.1016/j.annals.2012.08.004

Bruwer, J. (2015). Service performance and satisfaction in a South African festivalscape. *Anatolia – An International Journal of Tourism and Hospitality Research, 26*(3), 434-446.

Buckley, R. (1996). Sustainable Tourism: Technical Issues and Information Needs. *Annals of Tourism Research, Volume*, *23*(4), 1996.

Buckley, R. C. (2010). *Adventure tourism management*. Oxford, UK: Butterworth-Heinemann.

Budeanu, A. (2003). Impacts and responsibilities for sustainable tourism: A tour operator's perspective. *Journal of Cleaner Production*, *13*(2), 89–97. doi:10.1016/j.jclepro.2003.12.024

Budowski, G. (1976). Tourism and environmental conservation: Conflict, coexistence, or symbiosis? *Environmental Conservation*, *3*(1), 27–31. doi:10.1017/S0376892900017707

Budruk, M., White, D. D., Wodrich, J. A., & Van Riper, C. (2008). Connecting Visitors to People and Place: Visitors' Perceptions of Authenticity at Canyon de Chelly National Monument, Arizona. *Journal of Heritage Tourism*, *3*(3), 185–202. doi:10.1080/17438730802139004

Buhalis, D. (1998). Strategic use of information technologies in the tourism industry. *Tourism Management, 19*(5), 409–421. doi:10.1016/S0261-5177(98)00038-7

Buhalis, D. (2000). Marketing the competitive destination of the future. *Tourism Management, 21*(1), 97–116. doi:10.1016/S0261-5177(99)00095-3

Buhalis, D., & Law, R. (2008). Progress in information technology and tourism management: 20 years on and 10 years after the Internet—The state of eTourism research. *Tourism Management, 29*(4), 609–623. doi:10.1016/j.tourman.2008.01.005

Buhalis, D., & Michopoulou, E. (2011). Information-enabled tourism destination marketing: Addressing the accessibility market. *Current Issues in Tourism, 14*(2), 145–168. doi:10.1080/13683501003653361

Bujosa, A., & Rossello, J. (2007). Modelling environmental attitudes toward tourism. *Tourism Management, 28*(3), 688–695. doi:10.1016/j.tourman.2006.04.004

Butler, R. W. (1994). Seasonality in tourism: issues and problems. In A.V., Seaton (Eds.), Tourism: the State of the Art. Chichester, UK: Wiley.

Butler, R. W. (1974). Social implications of tourism development. *Annals of Tourism Research, 2*(2), 100–111. doi:10.1016/0160-7383(74)90025-5

Butler, R. W. (1980). The concept of a tourist area cycle of evolution: Implications for management and resources. *Canadian Geographer, 25*(1), 5–12. doi:10.1111/j.1541-0064.1980.tb00970.x

Butler, R. W. (1994). Seasonality in tourism: Issues and problems. In A. V. Seaton (Ed.), *Tourism. The state of the art* (pp. 332–340). Chichester, UK: Wiley.

Butler, R. W. (1999). Sustainable tourism: A state-of-the-art review. *Tourism Geographies, 1*(1), 7–25. doi:10.1080/14616689908721291

Butler, R., & Mao, B. (1997). Seasonality in Tourism: Problems and Measurement. In P. Murphy (Ed.), *Quality Management in Urban Tourism* (pp. 9–23). Chichester, UK: Wiley.

Buxton CHS and Thermal Spa. (2016). *Buxton CHS and Thermal Spa*. Available at: http://buxtonCHS.com/

Cai, L. A. (2002). Cooperative branding for rural destinations. *Annals of Tourism Research, 29*(3), 720–742. doi:10.1016/S0160-7383(01)00080-9

Cai, L. A. (2009). Tourism branding in a social exchange system. In L. A. Cai, W. C. Gartner, & A. M. Munar (Eds.), *Tourism branding: Communities in action* (pp. 89–104). Emerald Group Publishing Limited. doi:10.1108/S2042-1443(2009)0000001009

Çalışkan, C. (2015). Turizm Potansiyeli Olan Bölgelerin Kalkınma Sürecinde Toplumsal Kapasiteyi Güçlendirme Stratejileri: Adıyaman Örneği. Nevşehir Hacı Bektaş Veli Üniversitesi Sosyal Bilimler Enstitüsü, yayınlanmamış Doktora Tezi, Nevşehir.

Compilation of References

Çalışkan, C. (2017). Sürdürülebilir Turizmin Çevre İkilemi: Toplum ve Tüketim. *İnsan ve Toplum Bilimleri Araştırmaları Dergisi, 6*(2), 1123-1136.

Çalışkan, C. (2014). Evaluation of Protected Areas from the Perspective of Sustainable Tourism: Case Study of Mount Nemrut National Park/Adıyaman. *Global International Conference on Business Tourism and Sciences*, Tampa, FL.

Camilleri, M. A. (2018a). The Tourism Industry: An Overview. In Travel Marketing, Tourism Economics and the Airline Product (pp. 3-27). Cham: Springer.

Camilleri, M. A. (2018b). Tourism Distribution Channels. In Travel Marketing, Tourism Economics and the Airline Product (pp. 105-115). Cham: Springer. doi:10.1007/978-3-319-49849-2_6

Camilleri, M. A. (2018c). Tourism Supply and Demand. In Travel Marketing, Tourism Economics and the Airline Product (pp. 139-154). Cham: Springer. doi:10.1007/978-3-319-49849-2_8

Camilleri. (2018a). The Tourism Industry: An Overview. In *Travel Marketing, Tourism Economics and the Airline Product* (pp. 3-27). Cham, Switzerland: Springer.

Camilleri. (2018b). Integrated Marketing Communications. In *Travel Marketing, Tourism Economics and the Airline Product* (pp. 3-27). Cham, Switzerland: Springer.

Camilleri, M. A. (2014). Advancing the sustainable tourism agenda through strategic CSR perspectives. *Tourism Planning & Development, 11*(1), 42–56. doi:10.1080/21568316.2013.839470

Camilleri, M. A. (2015). Valuing stakeholder engagement and sustainability reporting. *Corporate Reputation Review, 18*(3), 210–222. doi:10.1057/crr.2015.9

Camilleri, M. A. (2016). Responsible tourism that creates shared value among stakeholders. *Tourism Planning & Development, 13*(2), 219–235. doi:10.1080/21568316.2015.1074100

Camilleri, M. A. (2018a). The Tourism Industry: An Overview. In *Travel Marketing, Tourism Economics and the Airline Product* (pp. 3–27). Cham, Switzerland: Springer. doi:10.1007/978-3-319-49849-2_1

Camilleri, M. A. (2018b). Integrated Marketing Communications. In *Travel Marketing, Tourism Economics and the Airline Product*. Cham: Springer. doi:10.1007/978-3-319-49849-2_5

Camilleri, M. A. (2018b). Pricing and Revenue Management. In *Travel Marketing, Tourism Economics and the Airline Product* (pp. 155–163). Cham: Springer. doi:10.1007/978-3-319-49849-2_9

Campbell, M. C. (1999). Perceptions of Price Unfairness: Antecedents and Consequences. *JMR, Journal of Marketing Research, 36*(2), 187–199. doi:10.2307/3152092

Cano, V., & Prentice, R. (1998). Opportunities for endearment to place through electronic 'visiting': WWW homepages and the tourism promotion of Scotland. *Tourism Management, 19*(1), 67–73. doi:10.1016/S0261-5177(97)00092-7

Cantallops, A. S., & Salvi, F. (2014). New consumer behavior: A review of research on eWOM and hotels. *International Journal of Hospitality Management*, *36*, 41–51. doi:10.1016/j.ijhm.2013.08.007

Canzanelli, G. (2001). *Overview and learned lessons on local economic development, human development, and decent work*. Universitas Working Papers, ILO (Organización Internacional del Trabajo).

Capó, J., Riera, A., & Rosselló, J. (2007). Accommodation determinants of seasonal patterns. *Annals of Tourism Research*, *34*(2), 422–436. doi:10.1016/j.annals.2006.10.002

Carneiro, M. J. (2007). *Modelação da escolha de destinos turísticos: Uma análise de posicionamento* (PhD thesis). University of Aveiro, Aveiro, Portugal.

Carrillo, M., & Jorge, J. M. (2017). Multidimensional Analysis of Regional Tourism Sustainability in Spain. *Ecological Economics*, *140*, 89–98. doi:10.1016/j.ecolecon.2017.05.004

Carter, C. (2006). World adventure capital. In R. Buckley (Ed.), Adventure Tourism (pp. 429-442). Wallington, Australia: The Centre for Agriculture and Bioscience International (CABI) Publishing.

Cartwright, R., & Baird, C. (1999). *The development and growth of the cruise industry*. Oxford, UK: Butterworth-Heinemann.

Cassady, R. Jr. (1946a). Some Economic Aspects of Price Discrimination under non-perfect market conditions. *Journal of Marketing*, *11*(1), 7–20. doi:10.2307/1246801

Cassady, R. Jr. (1946b). Techniques and purposes of price discrimination. *Journal of Marketing*, *11*(2), 135–150. doi:10.2307/1246769

Castro, C. B., Armario, E. M., & Ruiz, D. M. (2007). The influence of market heterogeneity on the relationship between a destination's image and tourists' future behavior. *Tourism Management*, *28*(1), 175–187. doi:10.1016/j.tourman.2005.11.013

Cater, E. (1991). *Sustainable tourism in the Third World: Problems and prospects*. London: University of Reading.

Cavlek, N. (2002). Tour operators and destination safety. *Annals of Tourism Research*, *29*(2), 478–496. doi:10.1016/S0160-7383(01)00067-6

Çetin, M. (2007). Yerel ekonomik kalkınma yaklaşımı ve uluslararası organizasyonlar. *Yönetim ve Ekonomi: Celal Bayar Üniversitesi İktisadi ve İdari Bilimler Fakültesi Dergisi*, *14*(1), 153–170.

Chase, G. L. (2002). *The economic impact of cruise ships in the 1990s: Some evidence from the Caribbeans*. Published Doctoral Thesis, UMI 3041166.

Chen, C. C., & Schwartz, Z. (2008a). Room rate patterns and customers' propensity to book a hotel room. *Journal of Hospitality & Tourism Research (Washington, D.C.)*, *32*(3), 287–306. doi:10.1177/1096348008317389

Compilation of References

Chen, C. C., & Schwartz, Z. (2008b). Timing matters: Travelers' advanced-booking expectations and decisions. *Journal of Travel Research*, *47*(1), 35–42. doi:10.1177/0047287507312413

Chen, C. C., Schwartz, Z., & Vargas, P. (2011). The search for the best deal: How hotel cancellation policies affect the search and booking decisions of deal-seeking customers. *International Journal of Hospitality Management*, *30*(1), 129–135. doi:10.1016/j.ijhm.2010.03.010

Chen, C. F., & Rothschild, R. (2010). An application of hedonic pricing analysis to the case of hotel rooms in Taipei. *Tourism Economics*, *16*(3), 685–694. doi:10.5367/000000010792278310

Chen, C., & Chiou-Wei, S. Z. (2009). Tourism expansion, tourism uncertainty and economic growth: New evidence from Taiwan and Korea. *Tourism Management*, *30*(6), 812–818. doi:10.1016/j.tourman.2008.12.013

Chen, C.-F., & Tsai, D. (2007). How destination image and evaluative factors affect behavioral intentions? *Tourism Management*, *28*(4), 1115–1122. doi:10.1016/j.tourman.2006.07.007

Chen, J. S., & Hsu, C. (2000). Measurement of Korean tourists' perceived images of overseas destinations. *Journal of Travel Research*, *38*(4), 411–416. doi:10.1177/004728750003800410

Chiappa, G. D., & Dall'Aglio, S. (2012). Factors influencing Travellers' e-Ratings and e-Complaints about Hotel Services: Insights from an Italian Tourism Destination. In *Information and Communication Technologies in Tourism 2012* (pp. 448–459). Vienna: Springer; doi:10.1007/978-3-7091-1142-0_39

Chi, C. G., & Qu, H. (2008). Examining the structural relationships of destination image, tourist satisfaction and destination loyalty: An integrated approach. *Tourism Management*, *29*(4), 624–636. doi:10.1016/j.tourman.2007.06.007

Chi-Cheng, W., Yi-Fen, L., Ying-Ju, C., & Chih-Jen, W. (2012). Consumer responses to price discrimination: Discriminating bases, inequality status, and information disclosure timing influences. *Journal of Business Research*, *65*(1), 106–116. doi:10.1016/j.jbusres.2011.02.005

Chilembwe, J. M., & Mweiwa, V. (2014, September 14). Tour guides: Are they tourism promoters and developers? Case study of Malawi. *International Journal of Research in Business Management*, *2*(9), 29–45.

Chilembwe, J. M., & Sepula, M. B. (2017). Corporate social responsibility practices in the tourism and hospitality industry in Malawi. In C. Koutra (Ed.), *Social Responsibility: Application of Good Practices and Malpractices in Tourism and Hospitality Industry in the Developing World*. New York, NY: Nova Science Publishers.

Choi, Y. S. (2003). The Web marketing strategy for fine dining restaurants. *Advances in Hospitality and Tourism Research,* Volume 8*: Proceedings of the Annual Graduate Education and Graduate Student Research Conference in Hospitality and Tourism*, 98-99.

Choi, H. C., & Sirakaya, E. (2005). Measuring residents' attitude toward sustainable tourism: Development of sustainable tourism attitude scale. *Journal of Travel Research*, *43*(4), 380–394. doi:10.1177/0047287505274651

Choi, H. C., & Sirakaya, E. (2006). Sustainability indicators for managing community tourism. *Tourism Management, 27*(6), 1274–1289. doi:10.1016/j.tourman.2005.05.018

Choi, S., & Mattila, A. S. (2004). Hotel revenue management and its impact on customers' perceptions of fairness. *Journal of Revenue and Pricing Management, 2*(4), 303–314. doi:10.1057/palgrave.rpm.5170079

Chon, K. (1990). The role of destination image in tourism: A review and discussion. *Tourism Review, 45*(2), 2–9.

Chon, K. (1991). Tourism destination image modification process: Marketing implications. *Tourism Management, 12*(1), 68–72. doi:10.1016/0261-5177(91)90030-W

Chon, K. (1992). The role of destination image in tourism: An extension. *Tourism Review, 47*(1), 2–8.

Christou, E., Sigala, M., & Gretzel, U. (2012). *Social Media in Travel, Tourism and Hospitality: Theory, Practice and Cases*. Farnham, UT: Routledge.

Chung, J. Y. (2009). Seasonality in tourism: A review. *Ereview of Tourism Research, 7*(5), 82–96.

Chung, N. K., & Koo, C. (2015). The use of social media in travel information search. *Telematics and Informatics, 32*(2), 215–229. doi:10.1016/j.tele.2014.08.005

Chung, T., & Law, R. (2003). Developing a performance indicator for hotel Websites. *International Journal of Hospitality Management, 22*(1), 119–125. doi:10.1016/S0278-4319(02)00076-2

Cisneros, J. D., & Fernandez, A. (2015). Cultural tourism as tourist segment for reducing seasonality in a coastal area: The case study of Andalusia. *Current Issues in Tourism, 18*(8), 765–784. doi:10.1080/13683500.2013.861810

Clarke, J. (1997). A Framework of Approaches to Sustainable Tourism. *Journal of Sustainable Tourism, 5*(3), 224–233. doi:10.1080/09669589708667287

Clerides, S. K. (2004). Price discrimination with differentiated products: Definition and identification. *Economic Inquiry, 42*(3), 402–412. doi:10.1093/ei/cbh069

Clia. (2017). *2016 Annual Report, Statistics and Markets*. Retrieved from http://www.cruising.org/about-the-industry/research/2016-annual-report

Cloquet, I. (2013). Looking into the overlooked: Incoming tour operators and early tourism Development in Gabon. *Current Issues in Tourism, 16*(7-8), 647–663. doi:10.1080/13683500.2013.785480

CMA. (2016). *Online reviews: letting your customers see the true picture - GOV.UK*. Retrieved 24 November 2017, from https://www.gov.uk/government/publications/online-reviews-and-endorsements-advice-for-businesses/online-reviews-giving-consumers-the-full-picture

Coenders, G., Espinet, J., & Saez, M. (2003). Predicting random level and seasonality of hotel prices: A latent growth curve approach. *Tourism Analysis, 8*(1), 15–31. doi:10.3727/108354203108750148

Compilation of References

Cohen, E. (1984). The sociology of tourism: Approaches, issues, and findings. *Annual Review of Sociology*, *10*(1), 373–392. doi:10.1146/annurev.so.10.080184.002105

Colantonio, A., & Potter, R. B. (2006). *Urban tourism and development in the socialist state: Havana during the 'special period*. La Habana, Cuba: Ashgate Publishing.

Cole, S. (2006). Information and empowerment: The keys to achieving sustainable tourism. *Journal of Sustainable Tourism*, *14*(6), 629–644. doi:10.2167/jost607.0

Conde Nest Publication Ltd. (2017). *Best of Bath*. Available at: http://www.cntraveller.com/recommended/uk/best-of-bath-somerset-uk

Connell, J., Page, S. J., & Bentley, T. (2009). Towards sustainable tourism planning in New Zealand: Monitoring local government planning under the Resource Management Act. *Tourism Management*, *30*(6), 867–877. doi:10.1016/j.tourman.2008.12.001

Connell, J., Page, S. J., & Meyer, D. (2015). Visitor attractions and events: Responding to seasonality. *Tourism Management*, *46*, 283–298. doi:10.1016/j.tourman.2014.06.013

Cooper, C. (2008). *Tourism: Principles and practice*. London, UK: Pearson Education.

Cooper, C. (2012). *Essentials of Tourism*. Pearson Education Limited.

Cooper, D. R., & Schindler, P. S. (2003). *Business research methods*. New York: McGraw Hill.

Corigliano, M. A., & Baggio, R. (2006). On the significance of tourism website evaluations. *Information and Communication Technologies in Tourism*, *2006*, 320–331.

Countryman, C. C. (1999). Content analysis of state tourism Websites and the application of marketing concepts. *Advances in Hospitality and Tourism Research,* Volume 4*: Proceedings of the Annual Graduate Conference in Hospitality and Tourism*, 210-218.

Cox, J., & Dale, B. G. (2002). Key quality factors in Web site design and use: An examination. *International Journal of Quality & Reliability Management*, *19*(7), 862–888. doi:10.1108/02656710210434784

Cresswell, J. W. (2007). *Qualitative inquiry and research design: Choosing among five approaches* (2nd ed.). Thousand Oaks, CA: Sage.

Cresswell, J. W. (2014). *Research Design: Qualitative, quantitative, and mixed methods approaches* (4th ed.). Thousand Oaks, CA: Sage Publications Inc.

Crompton, J. L. (1979). An Assessment of the Image of Mexico as a Vacation Destination and the Influence of Geographical Location upon that Image. *Journal of Travel Research*, *17*(4), 18–24. doi:10.1177/004728757901700404

Crompton, J. L. (1992). Structure of vacation destination choice sets. *Annals of Tourism Research*, *19*(3), 420–434. doi:10.1016/0160-7383(92)90128-C

Crompton, J. L., & Ankomah, P. K. (1993). Choice set propositions in destination decisions. *Annals of Tourism Research*, *20*(3), 461–476. doi:10.1016/0160-7383(93)90003-L

Cuccia, T., & Rizzo, I. (2011). Tourism seasonality in cultural destinations: Empirical evidence from Sicily. *Tourism Management*, *32*(3), 589–595. doi:10.1016/j.tourman.2010.05.008

Custódio, M. J., & Gouveia, P. M. (2007). Evaluation of the cognitive image of a country/destination by the media during the coverage of mega-events: The case of UEFA EURO 2004 in Portugal. *International Journal of Tourism Research*, *9*(4), 285–296. doi:10.1002/jtr.615

D'Angella, F., De Carlo, M., & Sainaghi, R. (2010). Archetypes of destination governance: A comparison of international destinations. *Tourism Review*, *65*(4), 61–73. doi:10.1108/16605371011093872

Da Silveira, C., Lages, C., & Simões, C. (2013). Reconceptualizing brand identity in a dynamic environment. *Journal of Business Research*, *66*(1), 28–36. doi:10.1016/j.jbusres.2011.07.020

Daniel, R. H. (1961, September). Management data crisis. *Harvard Business Review*, 111–112.

Davidson, R., & Rogers, T. (2012). *Marketing Destinations and Venues for Conferences and Conventions* (2nd ed.). Routledge.

Daye, M. (2010). Challenges and prospects of differentiating destination brands: The case of the Dutch Caribbean islands. *Journal of Travel and Marketing*, *27*(1), 1–13. doi:10.1080/10548400903534725

De Chernatony, L. (1999). Brand management through narrowing the gap between brand identity and brand reputation. *Journal of Marketing Management*, *15*(1–3), 157–179. doi:10.1362/026725799784870432

De la Vina, L., & Ford, J. (2001). Logistic regression analysis of cruise vacation market potential: Demographic and trip attribute perception factors. *Journal of Travel Research*, *39*(4), 406–410. doi:10.1177/004728750103900407

Deccio, C., & Baloglu, S. (2002). Non-host community resident reactions to the 2001 Winter Olympics: The spillover impacts. *Journal of Travel Research*, *41*(1), 46–56. doi:10.1177/0047287502041001006

Decrop, A. (1999). Triangulation in qualitative tourism research. *Tourism Management*, *20*(1), 157–161. doi:10.1016/S0261-5177(98)00102-2

Delgado, C. (2014). El huésped 2.0 siempre tiene la razón. *El País*. Retrieved from https://elpais.com/economia/2014/08/09/actualidad/1407601275_385548.html

Dellarocas, C. (2003). The digitization of word of mouth: Promise and challenges of online feedback mechanisms. *Management Science*, *49*(10), 1407–1424. doi:10.1287/mnsc.49.10.1407.17308

Denizci Guillet, B., Law, R., & Xiao, Q. (2014). Rate fences in hotel revenue management and their applications to Chinese leisure travelers: A fractional factorial design approach. *Cornell Hospitality Quarterly*, *55*(2), 186–196. doi:10.1177/1938965513507497

Compilation of References

Denizci Guillet, B., Liu, W., & Law, R. (2014). Can setting hotel rate restrictions help balance the interest of hotels and customers? *International Journal of Contemporary Hospitality Management*, *26*(6), 948–973. doi:10.1108/IJCHM-01-2013-0020

Dickson, P., & Kalapurakal, R. (1994). The Use and Perceived Fairness of Price-Setting Rules in the Bulk Electricity Market. *Journal of Economic Psychology*, *15*(3), 427–448. doi:10.1016/0167-4870(94)90023-X

Diedrich, A., & García, E. (2009). Local perceptions of tourism as indicators of destination decline. *Tourism Management*, *30*(4), 512–521. doi:10.1016/j.tourman.2008.10.009

Dilley, J. (2015). *The Peak District and Derbyshire Growth Strategy for the Visitor Economy 2015-2020*. Available at: http://mediafiles.thedms.co.uk/Publication/DS/cms/pdf/Growth%20Plan%20draft%20v1.pdf

Dimitriviski, P., & Todorovic, A. (2015). Clustering Wellness Tourists in spa Environment. *Tourism Management Perspectives*, *16*, 259–265. doi:10.1016/j.tmp.2015.09.004

Djurica, M. 2010). Tourism destination marketing management. *Proceedings of the Tourism and Hospitality Management 2010 Conference*, 890-901.

Do Valle, P. O., Mendes, J., & Guerreiro, M. (2012). Residents' participation in events, events image, and destination image: A correspondence analysis. *Journal of Travel & Tourism Marketing*, *29*(7), 647–664. doi:10.1080/10548408.2012.720151

Dodds, R., & Butler, R. W. (2008). 4 *Inaction More than Action. Barriers to the Implementation of Sustainable Tourism Policie*. In S. Gossling, C. M. Hall, & D. B. Weaver (Eds.), *Sustainable Tourism Futures Perspectives on Systems* (pp. 43–57). Routledge, UK: Restructuring and Innovations. doi:10.4324/9780203884256.pt2

Dogru, T., & Bulut, U. (2017). Is tourism an engine for economic recovery? Theory and empirical evidence. *Tourism Management*, 1-10. (in press)

Dohse, K. (2013). *Fabricating Feedback: Blurring the Line Between Brand Management and Bogus Reviews (SSRN Scholarly Paper No. ID 2333170)*. Rochester, NY: Social Science Research Network. Retrieved from https://papers.ssrn.com/abstract=2333170

Dolnicar, S., & Grün, B. (2013). Validly Measuring Destination Image in Survey Studies. *Journal of Travel Research*, *52*(1), 3–14. doi:10.1177/0047287512457267

Doughty, D., & Zwimer, W. (2003). Urban Setting. The Urban Experience: A People-Environment Perspective, 135.

Doughty, D., & Zwirner, W. (1994). *A spa culture for the nineties and thereafter: Health and relaxation in an urban setting*. Academic Press.

Douglas, N., & Douglas, N. (2004). Cruise ship passenger spending patterns in Pacific Island ports. *International Journal of Tourism Research*, *6*(4), 251–261. doi:10.1002/jtr.486

Doxey, G. V. (1975). Leisure, tourism and Canada's aging population tourism in Canada: Selected issues and options. *Western Geographical Series*, *21*, 57–72.

Dryglas, D. (2016). Profile of tourists visiting European spa resorts a case study of Poland. *Journal of Policy Research in Tourism, Leisure and Events, 9*(3), 298-317.

Duman, T. (2002). *A model of perceived value for leisure travel products*. Published Doctoral Thesis in Leisure Studies, UMI 3065879.

Duman, T., & Mattila, A. S. (2003). A logistic regression analysis of discount receiving behavior in the cruise industry: Implications for cruise marketers. *International Journal of Hospitality & Tourism Administration*, *4*(4), 45–57. doi:10.1300/J149v04n04_03

Duman, T., & Mattila, A. S. (2005). The role of affective factors on perceived cruise vacation value. *Tourism Management*, *26*(3), 311–323. doi:10.1016/j.tourman.2003.11.014

Du, R., Gerrie, H. E., & Alberts, N. (2003). The Role of Local and Regional Food in Destination Marketing. *Journal of Travel & Tourism Marketing*, *14*(3-4), 97–112.

Dwyer, F. R., Schurr, P. H., & Oh, S. (1987). Developing buyer-seller relationship. *Journal of Marketing*, *51*(2), 11–27. doi:10.2307/1251126

Dwyer, L., Forsyth, P., Fredline, L., Jago, L., Deery, M., & Lundie, S. (2006). *Concepts of Tourism yield and their measurement – technical reports*. Cooperative Research Centre for Sustainable Tourism.

Dwyer, L., Forsyth, P., & Spurr, R. (2004). Evaluating tourism's economic effects: New and old approaches. *Tourism Management*, *25*(3), 307–317. doi:10.1016/S0261-5177(03)00131-6

Dyer, P., Gursoy, D., Sharma, B., & Carter, J. (2007). Structural modeling of resident perceptions of tourism and associated development on the Sunshine Coast, Australia. *Tourism Management*, *28*(2), 409–422. doi:10.1016/j.tourman.2006.04.002

Eceral, T. Ö., & Özmen, C. A. (2009). *Beypazarı'nda turizm gelişimi ve yerel ekonomik kalkınma*. AİBÜ-İİBF Ekonomik ve Sosyal Araştırmalar Dergisi.

Echtner, C. M., & Ritchie, J. B. (1993). The measurement of destination image: An empirical assessment. *Journal of Travel Research*, *31*(4), 3–13. doi:10.1177/004728759303100402

Echtner, C. M., & Ritchie, J. R. (1991). The meaning and measurement of destination image. *Journal of Tourism Studies*, *2*(2), 2–12.

Echtner, C. M., & Ritchie, J. R. B. (1991). The Meaning and Measurement of Destination Image. *Journal of Tourism Studies*, *2*(2), 37–48.

Elliot, S., Papadopoulos, N., & Kim, S. (2011). An integrative model of place image: Exploring relationships between destination, product, and country images. *Journal of Travel Research*, *50*(5), 520–534. doi:10.1177/0047287510379161

Compilation of References

Erdeli, G., Dinca, A. I., Gheorghilas, A., & Surugiu, C. (2011). Romanian spa tourism: A communist paradigm in a post communist era. *Human Geographies*, *5*(2), 41–56. doi:10.5719/hgeo.2011.52.41

Erkuş-Öztürk, H., & Eraydın, A. (2010). Environmental governance for sustainable tourism development: Collaborative networks and organisation building in the Antalya tourism region. *Tourism Management*, *31*(1), 113–124. doi:10.1016/j.tourman.2009.01.002

Espinet, J. M., Saez, M., Coenders, G., & Fluvià, M. (2003). Effect on prices of the attributes of holiday hotels: A hedonic prices approach. *Tourism Economics*, *9*(2), 165–177. doi:10.5367/000000003101298330

Esu, B. B., & Arrey, V. M. E. (2009). Branding cultural festival as a destination attraction: A case study of Calabar carnival festival. *International Business Research*, *2*(3), 182–192. doi:10.5539/ibr.v2n3p182

European Best Destinations. (2017). Retrieved October 1, 2017, from https://www.europeanbestdestinations.com/best-of-europe/european-best-destinations-2017/

Evans, J. R., & King, V. E. (1999). Business-to-business marketing and the world wide web: Planning, managing, and assessing web sites. *Industrial Marketing Management*, *28*(4), 343–358. doi:10.1016/S0019-8501(98)00013-3

Exceltur. (2016). *Valoración turística empresarial de 2015*. Madrid, Spain: Exceltur.

Ezeuduji, I. O., & Rid, W. (2011). Rural tourism offer and local community participation in The Gambia. *Tourismos: An International Multidisciplinary Journal of Tourism*, *6*(2), 187–211.

Faba-Pérez, C., Zapico-Alonso, F., Guerrero-Bote, V. P., & Moya-Anegón, F. D. (2005). Comparative analysis of webometric measurements in thematic environments. *Journal of the American Society for Information Science and Technology*, *56*(8), 779–785. doi:10.1002/asi.20161

Fakeye, P., & Crompton, J. (1991). Image differences between prospective, first-time, and repeat visitors to the lower Rio Grande valley. *Journal of Travel Research*, *30*(2), 10–16. doi:10.1177/004728759103000202

Fan, D. X., Qiu, H., Hsu, C. H., & Liu, Z. G. (2015). Comparing Motivations and Intentions of Potential Cruise Passengers from Different Demographic Groups: The Case of China. *Journal of China Tourism Research*, *11*(4), 461–480. doi:10.1080/19388160.2015.1108888

Feng, R., Morrison, A. M., & Ismail, J. A. (2003). East versus west: A comparison of online destination marketing in China and the U.S. *Journal of Vacation Marketing*, *10*(1), 43–56. doi:10.1177/135676670301000105

Fennell, D. A. (2007). *Ecotourism*. New York: Routledge.

Fereday, J., & Muir-Cochrane, E. (2006). Demonstrating rigor using thematic analysis: A hybrid approach of inductive and deductive coding and theme development. *International Journal of Qualitative Methods*, *5*(1), 1–11. doi:10.1177/160940690600500107

Fernández-Morales, A., & Mayorga-Toledano, M. C. (2008). Seasonal concentration of the hotel demand in Costa del Sol: A decomposition by nationalities. *Tourism Management, 29*(5), 940–949. doi:10.1016/j.tourman.2007.11.003

Fernback, J., & Thompson, B. (2014). *Virtual communities: abort, retry, failure?* Retrieved from http://www. well. com/user/hlr/texts/vccivil. html

Ferrara, E., Varol, O., Davis, C., Menczer, F., & Flammini, A. (2016). The Rise of Social Bots. *Communications of the ACM, 59*(7), 96–104. doi:10.1145/2818717

Fick, G. R., & Brent Ritchie, J. R. (1991). Measuring service quality in the travel and tourism industry. *Journal of Travel Research, 30*(2), 2–9. doi:10.1177/004728759103000201

Field, J. M., Heim, G. R., & Sinha, K. K. (2004). Managing Quality in the E-service System: Development and Application of a Process Model. *Production and Operations Management, 13*(4), 291–306. doi:10.1111/j.1937-5956.2004.tb00219.x

Filieri, R., Alguezaui, S., & McLeay, F. (2015). Why do travelers trust TripAdvisor? Antecedents of trust towards consumer-generated media and its influence on recommendation adoption and word of mouth. *Tourism Management, 51*, 174–185. doi:10.1016/j.tourman.2015.05.007

Fishbein, M., & Ajzen, I. (1975). *Belief, attitude, intention, and behavior*. Reading, MA: Addison-Wesley.

Flanagin, A. J., Metzger, M. J., Pure, R., Markov, V., & Hartsell, E. (2014, March). Mitigating risk in eCommerce transactions: Perception of information credibility and the role of user-generated ratings in product quality and purchase intention. *Electronic Commerce Research, 14*(1), 1–13. doi:10.100710660-014-9139-2

Flognfeldt, T. (2001). Long-term positive adjustments to seasonality: consequences of summer tourism in the Jotunheimen Area, Norway. In T. Baum & S. Lundtorp (Eds.), *Seasonality in Tourism* (pp. 109–117). Oxford, UK: Pergamon. doi:10.1016/B978-0-08-043674-6.50010-6

Foley, M., & Lennon, J. J. (1996). JFK and dark tourism: A fascination with assassination. *International Journal of Heritage Studies, 2*(4), 198–211. doi:10.1080/13527259608722175

Font, X., & Carey, B. (2005). *Marketing sustainable tourism products*. Leeds, UK: Leeds Metropolitan University.

Ford, R. C., Wang, Y., & Vestal, A. (2012). Power asymmetries in tourism distribution networks. *Annals of Tourism Research, 39*(2), 755–779. doi:10.1016/j.annals.2011.10.001

Forgas-Coll, S., Palau-Saumell, R., Sánchez-García, J., & Maria Caplliure-Giner, E. (2014). The role of trust in cruise passenger behavioral intentions: The moderating effects of the cruise line brand. *Management Decision, 52*(8), 1346–1367. doi:10.1108/MD-09-2012-0674

Frey, N., & George, R. (2010). Responsible tourism management: The missing link between business owners' attitudes and behaviour in the Cape Town tourism industry. *Tourism Management, 31*(5), 621–628. doi:10.1016/j.tourman.2009.06.017

Compilation of References

Frias, D. M., Rodriguez, M. A., Castaneda, J. A., Sabiote, C. M., & Buhalis, D. (2012). The formation of tourist destination's image via information sources; The moderating effect of culture. *International Journal of Tourism Research, 14*(5), 437–450. doi:10.1002/jtr.870

Frost, W. (2006). Brave hearted Ned Kelly: Historic films, heritage tourism and destination image. *Tourism Management, 27*(2), 247–254. doi:10.1016/j.tourman.2004.09.006

Frost, W., & Laing, J. (2016). *History of spa tourism*. The Routledge Handbook of Health Tourism.

Fyall, A., Garrod, B., & Wang, Y. (2012). Destination collaboration: A critical review of theoretical approaches to a multi-dimensional phenomenon. *Journal of Destination Marketing & Management, 1*(1), 10–26. doi:10.1016/j.jdmm.2012.10.002

Gabe, T. M., Lynch, C. P., & McConnon, J. C. Jr. (2006). Likelihood of cruise ship passenger return to a visited port: The case of Bar Harbor, Maine. *Journal of Travel Research, 44*(3), 281–287. doi:10.1177/0047287505279107

Gallarza, M. G., Saura, I. G., & García, H. C. (2002). Destination image: Towards a conceptual framework. *Annals of Tourism Research, 29*(1), 56–78. doi:10.1016/S0160-7383(01)00031-7

Gambetta, D. (1988). Can we trust? In D. Gambetta (Ed.), *Trust: Making and Breaking Cooperative Relations*. Oxford, UK: Basil Blackwell.

Garbarino, E., & Johnson, M. S. (1999). The different roles of satisfaction, trust, and commitment in customer relationships. *Journal of Marketing, 63*(2), 70–87. doi:10.2307/1251946

García, J. A., Gómez, M., & Molina, A. (2012). A destination-branding model: An empirical analysis based on stakeholders. *Tourism Management, 33*(3), 646–661. doi:10.1016/j.tourman.2011.07.006

Garrod, B., & Fyall, A. (1998). Beyond the rhetoric of sustainable tourism? *Tourism Management, 19*(3), 199–212. doi:10.1016/S0261-5177(98)00013-2

Gartner, & Hunt, J. D. (1987). An analysis of state image change over a twelve-year period (1971-1983). *Journal of Travel Research, 26*(2), 15–19.

Gartner. (1994). Image formation process. *Journal of Travel & Tourism Marketing, 2*(2-3), 191–216.

Gartner, C. W. (1989). Tourism Image: Attribute Measurement of State Tourism Products Using Multidimensional Scaling Techniques. *Journal of Travel Research, 28*(2), 16–20. doi:10.1177/004728758902800205

Gavalas, D., Konstantopoulos, C., Mastakas, K., & Pantziou, G. (2014). Mobile recommender systems in tourism. *Journal of Network and Computer Applications, 39*, 319–333. doi:10.1016/j.jnca.2013.04.006

Gee, C. Y., Choy, D. J., & Makens, J. C. (1984). *The travel industry*. Westport, CT: AVI Publishing.

George, D., & Mallery, P. (2003). *SPSS for Windows step by step: A simple guide and reference. 11.0 update* (4th ed.). Boston: Allyn & Bacon.

Getz, D., & Page, S. (2015). Progress and Prospects for Event Tourism Research. *Tourism Management*, *52*, 593–631. doi:10.1016/j.tourman.2015.03.007

Ghaderi, Z., & Henderson, J. C. (2012). Sustainable rural tourism in Iran: A perspective from Hawraman Village'. *Tourism Management Perspectives*, *2-3*, 47–54. doi:10.1016/j.tmp.2012.03.001

Gjerald, O. (2005). Sociocultural Impacts of Tourism: A Case Study from Norway. *Journal of Tourism and Cultural Change*, *3*(1), 36–58. doi:10.1080/14766820508669095

Goldsmith, R. E., & Horowitz, D. (2006). Measuring Motivations for Online Opinion Seeking. *Journal of Interactive Advertising*, *6*(2), 2–14. doi:10.1080/15252019.2006.10722114

Gordon, B. M. (2012). Reinventions of a spa town: The unique case of Vichy. *Journal of Tourism History*, *4*(1), 35–55. doi:10.1080/1755182X.2012.671377

Gössling, S., Hall, C. M., & Weaver, D. B. (2008). Synthesis and Conclusions. In S. Gossling, C. M. Hall, & D. B. Weaver (Eds.), *Sustainable Tourism Futures Perspectives on Systems* (pp. 300–306). Routledge, UK: Restructuring and Innovations.

Government of Malaysia. (2010). *Tenth Malaysia Plan. The Economic Planning Unit*. Putrajaya, Malaysia: Prime Minister's Department.

Govers, R., & Go, F. M. (2003). Deconstructing destination image in the information age. *Information Technology & Tourism*, *6*(1), 13–29. doi:10.3727/109830503108751199

Govers, R., & Go, F. M. (2004). Projected destination image online: Website content analysis of pictures and text. *Information Technology & Tourism*, *7*(2), 73–89. doi:10.3727/1098305054517327

Govers, R., Go, M., & Kumar, K. (2007). Promoting tourism destination image. *Journal of Travel Research*, *46*(1), 15–23. doi:10.1177/0047287507302374

Grant, M., Human, B., & Le Pelley, B. (1997). Seasonality. In *Insights. Tourism Intelligence Papers*. London, UK: British Tourist Authority.

Gravili, S., & Rosato, P. (2017). Italy's Image as a Tourism Destination in the Chinese Leisure Traveler Market. *International Journal of Marketing Studies*, *9*(5), 28–55. doi:10.5539/ijms.v9n5p28

Greaves, N., & Skinner, H. (2010). The importance of destination image analysis to UK rural tourism. *Marketing Intelligence & Planning*, *28*(4), 486–507. doi:10.1108/02634501011053586

Greenberg, J. (1987). A taxonomy of organizational justice theories. *Academy of Management Review*, *12*(1), 9–22.

Greenberg, J. (1990). Organizational justice: Yesterday, today, and tomorrow. *Journal of Management*, *16*(2), 399–432. doi:10.1177/014920639001600208

Gretzel, U., & Yoo, K. H. (2008). Use and impact of online travel reviews. *Information and Communication Technologies in Tourism*, *2008*, 35–46.

Compilation of References

Grosspietsch, M. (2006). Perceived and projected images of Rwanda: Visitor and international tour operator perspectives. *Tourism Management*, *27*(2), 225–234. doi:10.1016/j.tourman.2004.08.005

Guba, E. G., & Lincoln, Y. S. (1994). Competing paradigms in qualitative research. In N. K. Denzin & Y. S. Lincoln (Eds.), *Handbook of Qualitative Research*. Thousand Oaks, CA: Sage Publications Inc.

Gubrium, J. A., & Holsten, J. A. (2001). *Handbook of interview research: Context and method*. Thousand Oaks, CA: Sage. doi:10.4135/9781412973588

Guizzardi, A. Mariani, & Prayag, G. (2017). Environmental impacts and certification: evidence from the Milan World Expo 2015. *International Journal of Contemporary Hospitality Management*, *29*(3), 1052-1071.

Gunn, A. C. (1989). *Tourism Planning*. New York: Taylor and Francis.

Gunn, C. A. (1988). *Vacationscape: Designing tourist regions*. University of Minnesota: Van Nostrand Reinhold.

Guo, Y., Denizci Guillet, B., Kucukusta, D., & Law, R. (2016). Segmenting spa customers based on rate fences using conjoint and cluster analyses. *Asia Pacific Journal of Tourism Research*, *21*(2), 118–136. doi:10.1080/10941665.2015.1025085

Gursoy, D., Chen, J., & Chi, C. G.-Q. (2014). Theoretical examination of destination loyalty formation. *International Journal of Contemporary Hospitality Management*, *26*(5), 809–827. doi:10.1108/IJCHM-12-2013-0539

Gursoy, D., Chi, C. G., & Dyer, P. (2010). Locals' attitudes toward mass and alternative tourism: The case of Sunshine Coast, Australia. *Journal of Travel Research*, *49*(3), 381–394. doi:10.1177/0047287509346853

Gursoy, D., Jurowski, C., & Uysal, M. (2002). Resident attitudes. A structural modeling approach. *Annals of Tourism Research*, *29*(1), 79–105. doi:10.1016/S0160-7383(01)00028-7

Gursoy, D., & Rutherford, D. G. (2004). Host attitudes toward tourism: An improved structural model. *Annals of Tourism Research*, *31*(3), 495–516. doi:10.1016/j.annals.2003.08.008

Gustafson, P. (2012). Managing business travel: Developments and dilemmas in corporate travel management. *Tourism Management*, *33*(2), 276–284. doi:10.1016/j.tourman.2011.03.006

Güven, S. (2006). *Toplumbiliminde Araştırma Yöntemleri*. Bursa: Ezgi Kitabevi Yayınları.

Hair, J. F., Tatham, R. L., Anderson, R. E., & Black, W. (2010). *Multivariate data analysis* (7th ed.). Englewood Cliffs, NJ: Prentice Hall.

Halkier, H., Kozak, M., & Svensson, B. (2014). Innovation and Tourism Destination Development. *European Planning Studies*, *22*(8), 1547–1550. doi:10.1080/09654313.2013.784571

Hallab, Z., & Kim, K. (2006). US travelers' perceptions of Mississippi as a tourist destination. *Tourism Analysis*, *10*(4), 393–403. doi:10.3727/108354206776162822

Hall, C. M. (2008). *Tourism planning: policies, processes and relationships*. London, UK: Pearson Education.

Hamari, J., Koivisto, J., & Sarsa, H. (2014). Does gamification work? A literature review of empirical studies on gamification. In *Proceedings of the 47th Hawaii International Conference on System Sciences*, 3025-3034. Institute of Electrical and Electronics Engineers (IEEE). Retrieved from http://doi.ieeecomputersociety.org/10.1109/HICSS.2014.377

Hamilton, J. M. (2007). Coastal landscape and the hedonic price of accommodation. *Ecological Economics*, *62*(3), 594–602. doi:10.1016/j.ecolecon.2006.08.001

Ham, S. H., & Weiler, B. (2012). Interpretation as the centerpiece of sustainable wildlife tourism. In R. Harris, T. Griffin, & P. Williams (Eds.), *Sustainable Tourism* (pp. 35–44). Oxford, UK: Butterworth-Heinemann.

Hanks, R. D., Cross, R. G., & Noland, R. P. (1992). Discounting in the hotel industry: A new approach. *The Cornell Hotel and Restaurant Administration Quarterly*, *33*(1), 15–23.

Hardwick, J. C. R., & MacKenzie, F. M. (2003). Information contained in miscarriage-related websites and the predictive value of website scoring systems. *European Journal of Obstetrics, Gynecology, and Reproductive Biology*, *106*(1), 60–63. doi:10.1016/S0301-2115(02)00357-3 PMID:12475583

Hardy, A. L., & Beeton, R. J. (2001). Sustainable tourism or maintainable tourism: Managing resources for more than average outcomes. *Journal of Sustainable Tourism*, *9*(3), 168–192. doi:10.1080/09669580108667397

Hardy, A., Beeton, R. J., & Pearson, L. (2002). Sustainable tourism: An overview of the concept and its position in relation to conceptualisations of tourism. *Journal of Sustainable Tourism*, *10*(6), 475–496. doi:10.1080/09669580208667183

Harroate Borough Council Department of Economy and Culture. (2017). *Culture Five Year Forward Plan 2017-2021*. Available at: https://localdemocracy.harrogate.gov.uk/ViewSelectedDocument.asp?DocumentID=38883

Harrogate Borough Council Department of Economy and Culture. (2017). *Culture Five Year Forward Plan 2017-2021*. Available at: https://localdemocracy.harrogate.gov.uk/ViewSelectedDocument.asp?DocumentID=38883

Harrogate Turkish Baths and Spa. (2016). *Turkish Baths and Health Spa*. Available at: http://www.turkishbathsharrogate.co.uk/

Hartmann, R. (1986). Tourism, seasonality and social change. *Leisure Studies*, *5*(1), 25–33. doi:10.1080/02614368600390021

Hashim, N. H., Murphy, J., & Law, R. (2007). A review of hospitality website design frameworks. *Information and communication technologies in tourism 2007*, 219-230.

Compilation of References

Hassanien, A., Dale, C., & Clarke, A. (2010). *Hospitality Business Development*. Oxford, UK: Butterworth Heinemann.

Hassan, S. S. (2000). Determinants of Market Competitiveness in an Environmentally Sustainable Tourism Industry. *Journal of Travel Research*, *38*(3), 239–245. doi:10.1177/004728750003800305

Hatch, M. J., & Schultz, M. (2002). The Dynamics of Organisational Identity'. *Human Relations*, *55*(8), 989–1018. doi:10.1177/0018726702055008181

Haven-Tang, C., & Sedgley, D. (2014). Partnership working in enhancing the destination brand of rural areas: A case study of made in Monmouthshire, Wales, UK. *Journal of Destination Marketing & Management*, *3*(1), 59–67. doi:10.1016/j.jdmm.2013.12.001

Heldal, F., Sjøvold, E., & Heldal, A. F. (2004). Success on the Internet—optimizing relationships through the corporate site. *International Journal of Information Management*, *24*(2), 115–129. doi:10.1016/j.ijinfomgt.2003.12.010

Hennig-Thurau, T., Gwinner, K. P., Walsh, G., & Gremler, D. D. (2004). Electronic word-of-mouth via consumer-opinion platforms: What motivates consumers to articulate themselves on the internet? *Journal of Interactive Marketing*, *18*(1), 38–52. doi:10.1002/dir.10073

Hensens, W. (2015). The future of hotel rating. *Journal of Tourism Futures*, *1*(1), 69–73. doi:10.1108/JTF-12-2014-0023

Heo, C. Y., & Hyun, S. S. (2015). Do luxury room amenities affect guests' willingness to pay? *International Journal of Hospitality Management*, *46*, 161–168. doi:10.1016/j.ijhm.2014.10.002

Heo, C. Y., & Lee, S. (2009). Application of revenue management practices to the theme park industry. *International Journal of Hospitality Management*, *28*(3), 446–453. doi:10.1016/j.ijhm.2009.02.001

Heo, C. Y., & Lee, S. (2010). Customers' Perceptions of Demand-driven Pricing in Revenue Management Context: Comparisons of Six Tourism and Hospitality Industries. *International Journal of Revenue Management*, *4*(3/4), 382–402. doi:10.1504/IJRM.2010.036030

Heo, C. Y., & Lee, S. (2011). Influences of consumer characteristics on fairness perceptions of revenue management pricing in the hotel industry. *International Journal of Hospitality Management*, *30*(2), 243–251. doi:10.1016/j.ijhm.2010.07.002

Hepp, M., Siorpaes, K., & Bachlechner, D. (2006). Towards the semantic web in e-tourism: can annotation do the trick? *14th European Conference on Information System (ECIS 2006)*.

High Peak Borough Council. (2012). *Buxton*. Available at: http://www.highpeak.gov.uk/hp/council-services/profile-of-the-main-areas/buxton

Higham, J., & Hinch, T. D. (2002). Tourism, sport and seasons: The challenges and potential of overcoming seasonality in the sport and tourism sectors. *Tourism Management*, *23*(2), 175–185. doi:10.1016/S0261-5177(01)00046-2

Hinch, T. D., & Jackson, E. L. (2000). Leisure Constraints Research: Its Value as a Framework for Understanding Tourism Seasonability. *Current Issues in Tourism*, *3*(2), 87–106. doi:10.1080/13683500008667868

Hine, C. (2000). *Virtual ethnography*. Sage. doi:10.4135/9780857020277

Hofstede, G., Hofstede, G. J., & Minkov, M. (2010). *Cultures and organizations: software of the mind*. McGraw-Hill Professional.

Holden, A. (2006). *Tourism studies and the social sciences*. New York: Routledge.

Holden, A. (2009). The environment-tourism nexus: Influence of market ethics. *Annals of Tourism Research*, *36*(3), 373–389. doi:10.1016/j.annals.2008.10.009

Holjevac, I. A. (2003). A vision of tourism and the hotel industry in the 21st century. *International Journal of Hospitality Management*, *22*(2), 129–134. doi:10.1016/S0278-4319(03)00021-5

Holloway, J. C., & Taylor, N. (2006). *The business of tourism*. London, UK: Pearson Education.

Hong, J.-Y., & Lee, W.-N. (2008). Consumer Complaint Behavior in the Online Environment. In *Web Systems Design and Online Consumer Behaviour*. Idea Group Inc (IGI). Retrieved from https://www.igi-global.com/chapter/consumer-complaint-behavior-online-environment/18274

Hopkinson, M. (2014). *Yorkshire Market Towns: not just for shopping: A research survey by PLACE*. Academic Press.

Hosany, S., Ekinci, Y., & Uysal, M. (2006). Destination image and destination personality: An application of branding theories to tourism places. *Journal of Business Research*, *59*(5), 638–642. doi:10.1016/j.jbusres.2006.01.001

Hosteltur. (2016). *Informe de Coyuntura Turística 2015*. Madrid, Spain: Hosteltur.

Hsu, C. H. C., Wolfe, K., & Kang, S. K. (2004). Image assessment for a destination with limited comparative advantages. *Tourism Management*, *25*(1), 121–126. doi:10.1016/S0261-5177(03)00062-1

Huang, S. S., & Gross, M. J. (2010). Australia's destination image among mainland Chinese travelers: An exploratory study. *Journal of Travel & Tourism Marketing*, *27*(1), 63–81. doi:10.1080/10548400903534923

Huei-Wen, L., & Huei-Fu, L. (2016). Valuing Residents' Perceptions of Sport Tourism Development in Taiwan's North Coast and Guanyinshan National Scenic Area. *Asia Pacific Journal of Tourism Research*, *21*(4), 398–424. doi:10.1080/10941665.2015.1050424

Hu, N., Bose, I., Koh, N. S., & Liu, L. (2012). Manipulation of online reviews: An analysis of ratings, readability, and sentiments. *Decision Support Systems*, *52*(3), 674–684. doi:10.1016/j.dss.2011.11.002

Hung, W. T., Shang, J. K., & Wang, F. C. (2010). Pricing determinants in the hotel industry: Quantile regression analysis. *International Journal of Hospitality Management*, *29*(3), 378–384. doi:10.1016/j.ijhm.2009.09.001

Hunt, D. J. (1975). Image as a Factor In Tourism Development. *Journal of Tourism Research*, *13*(3), 1–7.

Hunter, C. (1997). Sustainable tourism as an adaptive paradigm. *Annals of Tourism Research*, *24*(4), 850–867. doi:10.1016/S0160-7383(97)00036-4

Hunter, W. C., Chung, N., Gretzel, U., & Koo, C. (2015). Constructivist research in smart tourism. *Asia Pacific Journal of Information Systems*, *25*(1), 105–120. doi:10.14329/apjis.2015.25.1.105

Hylleberg, S. (1992). General introduction. In S. Hylleberg (Ed.), *Modelling Seasonality* (pp. 3–14). Oxford, UK: Oxford University Press.

Ianos, I., Peptenatu, D., & Zamfir, D. (2009). Respect for environment and sustainable development. *Carpathian Journal of Earth and Environmental Sciences*, *4*(1), 81–93.

Ibrahim, E. E., & Gill, J. (2005). A positioning strategy for a tourist destination, based on analysis of customers' perceptions and satisfactions. *Marketing Intelligence & Planning*, *23*(2), 172–188. doi:10.1108/02634500510589921

İçöz, O. (2005). *Turizm Ekonomisi*. Ankara: Turhan Kitabevi.

Inan, H. (2002). *Measuring the success of your Website*. Frenchs Forest, NSW: Pearson Education Australia.

Intercampus. (2013). *Estudo satisfação de turistas – Análise de resultados*. Lisbon: Turismo de Portugal, IP.

Ioannides, D., & Petersen, T. (2003). Tourism 'non-entrepreneurship' in peripheral destinations: A case study of small and medium tourism enterprises on Bornholm, Denmark. *Tourism Geographies*, *5*(4), 408–435. doi:10.1080/1461668032000129146

Iorio, M., & Wall, G. (2011). Local museums as catalysts for development: Mamoiada, Sardinia, Italy. *Journal of Heritage Tourism*, *6*(1), 1–15. doi:10.1080/1743873X.2010.515311

Ismail, J. A., Labropoulos, T., Mills, J. E., & Morrison, A. M. (2002). A snapshot in time: The marketing of culture in European Union NTO Websites. *Tourism, Culture & Communication*, *3*(3), 165–179. doi:10.3727/109830401108750760

Ivanov, S., & Ivanova, M. (2011, September). *Triple bottom line analysis of potential sport tourism impacts on local communities – a review*. Paper presented at the Black Sea Tourism Forum. Sport tourism – Possibilities to extend the tourist season, Varna, Bulgaria.

Ivanov, S. (2014). *Hotel Revenue Management: From Theory to Practice*. Varna: Zangador.

Jackson, J. (2006). Developing regional tourism in China: The potential for activating business clusters in a socialist market economy. *Tourism Management*, *27*(4), 695–706. doi:10.1016/j.tourman.2005.02.007

Jafari, J. (Ed.). (2002). *Encyclopedia of tourism*. Oxford, UK: Routledge.

Jakkilinki, R., Sharda, N., & Ahmad, I. (2005). *Ontology-based Intelligent Tourism Information Systems: An overview of development methodology and applications*. Paper presented at the International Conference TES2005 (Tourism Enterprise Strategies: Thriving – and Surviving – in an Online Era), Victoria University, Melbourne, Australia.

Jamal, T., & Getz, D. (1995). Collaboration theory and community tourism planning. *Annals of Tourism Research*, *22*(1), 186–204. doi:10.1016/0160-7383(94)00067-3

Jang, S. (2005). The past, present, and future research of online information search. *Journal of Travel & Tourism Marketing*, *17*(2-3), 41–47. doi:10.1300/J073v17n02_04

Jedidi, K., & Zhang, Z. J. (2002). Augmenting conjoint analysis to estimate consumer reservation price. *Management Science*, *48*(10), 1350–1368. doi:10.1287/mnsc.48.10.1350.272

Jenkins, O. (1999). Understanding and measuring tourist destination. *International Journal of Tourism Research*, *1*(1), 1–15. doi:10.1002/(SICI)1522-1970(199901/02)1:1<1::AID-JTR143>3.0.CO;2-L

Jenkins, O. (2003). Photography and travel brochures: The circle of representation. *Tourism Geographies*, *5*(3), 305–328. doi:10.1080/14616680309715

Jennings, G. (2010). Tourism research (2nd ed.). Milton, Australia: Wiley & Sons Australia Limited.

Jeong, M., & Lambert, C. (2001). Adaptation of an information quality framework to measure customers' behavioral intentions to use lodging Web sites. *International Journal of Hospitality Management*, *20*(2), 129–146. doi:10.1016/S0278-4319(00)00041-4

Jiang, Y., Ramkissoon, H., Mavondo, F. T., & Feng, S. (2017). Authenticity: The Link Between Destination Image and Place Attachment. *Journal of Hospitality Marketing & Management*, *26*(2), 105–124. doi:10.1080/19368623.2016.1185988

Jónás-Berki, M., Csapó, J., Pálfi, A., & Aubert, A. (2015). A Market and Spatial Perspective of Health Tourism Destinations: The Hungarian Experience. *International Journal of Tourism Research*, *17*(6), 602–612. doi:10.1002/jtr.2027

Jones, R. A. (1996). *Research methods in the social and behavioral sciences*. New York: Sinauer Associates.

Jones, S. (2005). Community-based ecotourism: The significance of social capital. *Annals of Tourism Research*, *32*(2), 303–324. doi:10.1016/j.annals.2004.06.007

Joppe, M. (1996). Sustainable community tourism development revisited. *Tourism Management*, *17*(7), 475–479. doi:10.1016/S0261-5177(96)00065-9

Jorgensen, D. L. (1989). *Participant observation: A methodology for human studies.* Newbury Park, CA: Sage Publications. doi:10.4135/9781412985376

Joukes, V. (2016). Efficient Networking Makes Mineral Spa Towns More Attractive: A Handful of Examples. Cultural Management and Tourism in European Cultural Routes: from theory to practice, 136.

Juaneda, C., Raya, J. M., & Sastre, F. (2011). Pricing the time and location of a stay at a hotel or apartment. *Tourism Economics, 17*(2), 321–338. doi:10.5367/te.2011.0044

Jurowski, C., Uysal, M., & Williams, D. R. (1997). A theoretical analysis of host community resident reactions to tourism. *Journal of Travel Research, 36*(2), 3–11. doi:10.1177/004728759703600202

Kahneman, D., Knetsch, J. L., & Thaler, R. (1986). Fairness and the Assumptions of Economics. *The Journal of Business, 4*(59), 285–300. doi:10.1086/296367

Kahraman, N., & Türkay, O. (2006). *Turizm ve Çevre.* Ankara: Detay Yayıncılık.

Kaiser, H. F. (1974). An index of factorial simplicity. *Psychometrika, 39*(1), 31–36. doi:10.1007/BF02291575

Kalish, S., & Nelson, P. (1991). A comparison of ranking, rating and reservation price measurement in conjoint analysis. *Marketing Letters, 2*(4), 327–335. doi:10.1007/BF00664219

Kalkstein-Silkes, C. A. (2007). *Food and food related festivals in rural destination branding* (Doctoral Thesis). Purdue University.

Kalyanaram, G., & Winer, R. S. (1995). Empirical generalizations from reference price research. *Marketing Science, 14*(3), G161–G169. doi:10.1287/mksc.14.3.G161

Kalyoncuoğlu, S. & Faiz, E. (2017). Akıllı Telefon Pazarı İçin Müşteri Sadakatinin Oluşturulmasında Memnuniyetin, Algılanan Değerin ve Değiştirme Maliyetinin Etkisi. *Üçüncü Sektör Sosyal Ekonomi, 52*(1), 128-149.

Kamata, H., & Misui, Y. (2015). Why do they choose a spa destination? The case of Japanese Tourists. *Tourism Economics, 21*(2), 283–305. doi:10.5367/te.2014.0450

Kapferer, J.-N. (2012). *The new strategic brand management. Advanced insights and strategic thinking.* London: Kogan Page.

Kaplan, R. S., & Norton, D. P. (1996). *Using the balanced scorecard as a strategic management system.* Academic Press.

Kaplan, A. M., & Haenlein, M. (2010). Users of the world, unite! The challenges and opportunities of Social Media. *Business Horizons, 53*(1), 59–68. doi:10.1016/j.bushor.2009.09.003

Kaplan, R. S., & Norton, D. P. (1992, January). The balanced scorecard–measures that drive performance. *Harvard Business Review,* 71–79. PMID:10119714

Kasavana, M. L. (2002). eMarketing: Restaurant websites that click. *Journal of Hospitality & Leisure Marketing, 9*(3/4), 161–178.

Kasavana, M. L., & Cahill, J. J. (1997). *Managing computers in the hospitality industry*. Educational Inst of the Amer Hotel.

Kastenholz, E., & Lima, J. (2011). The Integral Rural Tourism Experience From the Tourist's Point of View– A Qualitative Analysis of Its Nature and Meaning. *Tourism & Management Studies, 7*(8), 62–74.

Kavaratzis, M., & Hatch, M. J. (2013). The dynamics of place brands: An identity-based approach to place branding theory. *Marketing Theory, 13*(1), 69–86. doi:10.1177/1470593112467268

Kayat, K. (2008). Stakeholders' perspectives toward a community-based rural tourism development. *European Journal of Tourism Research, 1*(2), 94–111.

Kayat, K. (2011). *Homestay Programme as a Malaysian Tourism Product*. Sintok, Kedah: UUM Press.

Keeley-Browne, E. (2011). Cyber-Ethnography: The Emerging Research Approach for. In Handbook of Research on Transformative Online Education and Liberation: Models for Social Equality. Hershey, PA: Information Science Reference.

Keller, J. (1987). Development and Use of the ARCS Model of Instruction Design. *Journal of Instructional Development, 10*(3), 2–10. doi:10.1007/BF02905780

Keller, K. L. (2003). *Strategic brand management: Building, measuring and managing brand equity*. Upper Saddle River, NJ: Prentice Hall International.

Kenteris, M., Gavalas, D., & Economou, D. (2009). An innovative mobile electronic tourist guide application. *Personal and Ubiquitous Computing, 13*(2), 103–118. doi:10.100700779-007-0191-y

Keogh, B. (1989). Social Impact. In G. Wall (Ed.), *Outdoor recreation in Canada* (pp. 233–275). Toronto, Canada: Wiley.

Kerrigan, F., Shivanandan, J., & Hede, A. (2012). Nation Branding: A Critical Appraisal of Incredible India. *Journal of Macromarketing, 32*(3), 319–327. doi:10.1177/0276146712445788

Kester, J. (2003). Cruise Tourism. *Tourism Economics, 9*(3), 337–350. doi:10.1177/135481660300900307

Khadka, S. (2012). *Marketing of adventure and nature tourism—A case study of Shambala Trekking Agency in Nepal* (Thesis). Central Ostrobothnia University of Applied Sciences, Ostrobothnia, Finland. Retrieved from https://www.theseus.fi/bitstream/handle/10024/41135/Khadka%20Sujata.pdf

Kim, E., Chaing, L., & Tang, L. (2016). Investigating Wellness Tourists: Motivation, Engagement and Loyalty: In search of the Missing Link. *Journal of Travel and Tourism Marketing, 34*(7), 867-879.

Compilation of References

Kim, D. Y., Morrison, A. M., & Mills, J. E. (2003). (in press). Tiers or tears? An evaluation of the Web-based marketing efforts of major city convention centers in the U.S. *Journal of Convention & Exhibition Management.*

Kimes, S. E., & Chase, R. B. (1998). The Strategic Levers of Yield Management. *Journal of Service Research, 1*(2), 156–166. doi:10.1177/109467059800100205

Kimes, S. E., & Wirtz, J. (2003). Has Revenue Management Become Acceptable? *Journal of Service Research, 6*(2), 125–135. doi:10.1177/1094670503257038

Kim, H. W., & Kankanhalli, A. (2009). Investigating user resistance to information systems implementation: A status quo bias perspective. *Management Information Systems Quarterly, 33*(3), 567–582. doi:10.2307/20650309

Kim, H., & Jamal, T. (2007). Touristic quest for existential authenticity. *Annals of Tourism Research, 34*(1), 181–201. doi:10.1016/j.annals.2006.07.009

Kim, H., & Richardson, S. L. (2003). Motion picture impacts on destination images. *Annals of Tourism Research, 30*(1), 216–237. doi:10.1016/S0160-7383(02)00062-2

Kim, J., Natter, M., & Spann, M. (2009). Pay What You Want: A New Participative Pricing Mechanism. *Journal of Marketing, 73*(1), 44–58. doi:10.1509/jmkg.73.1.44

Kim, K., Hallab, Z., & Kim, J. N. (2012). The moderating effect of travel experience in a destination on the relationship between the destination image and the intention to revisit. *Journal of Hospitality Marketing & Management, 21*(5), 486–505. doi:10.1080/19368623.2012.626745

Kim, S., & Stoel, L. (2004). Apparel retailers: Website quality dimensions and satisfaction. *Journal of Retailing and Consumer Services, 11*(2), 109–117. doi:10.1016/S0969-6989(03)00010-9

Kim, S., & Yoon, Y. (2003). The hierarchical effects of affective and cognitive components on tourism destination image. *Journal of Travel & Tourism Marketing, 14*(2), 1–22. doi:10.1300/J073v14n02_01

King, R. A., Racherla, P., & Bush, V. D. (2014). What we know and don't know about online word-of-mouth: A review and synthesis of the literature. *Journal of Interactive Marketing, 28*(3), 167–183. doi:10.1016/j.intmar.2014.02.001

Klintman, M. (2012). Issues of scale in the global accreditation of sustainable tourism: schemes toward harmonized re-embeddedness? *Sustainability: Science, Practice, & Policy, 8*(1).

Knudsen, D. C., Rickly, J. M., & Vidon, E. S. (2016). The fantasy of authenticity: Touring with Lacan. *Annals of Tourism Research, 58*, 33–45. doi:10.1016/j.annals.2016.02.003

Koc, E., & Altinay, G. (2007). An analysis of seasonality in monthly per person tourist spending in Turkish inbound tourism from a market segmentation perspective. *Tourism Management, 28*(1), 227–237. doi:10.1016/j.tourman.2006.01.003

Koenig-Lewis, N., & Bischoff, E. E. (2005). Seasonality Research: The State of the Art. *International Journal of Tourism Research*, *7*(4-5), 201–219. doi:10.1002/jtr.531

Kokkranikal, J., Cronje, P., & Butler, R. (2011). Tourism policy and destination marketing in developing countries: The chain of influence. *Tourism Planning & Development*, *8*(4), 359–380. Retrieved from https://www.tandfonline.com/doi/figure/10.1080/21568316.2011.603885

Kolar, T. & Zabkar, V. (2010). A consumer-based model of authenticity: An oxymoron or the foundation of cultural heritage marketing? *Tourism Management*, *31*(5), 652–664. doi:.tourman.2009.07.01010.1016/j

Konecnik, M., & Gartner, W. C. (2007). Customer-based brand equity for a destination. *Annals of Tourism Research*, *34*(2), 400–421. doi:10.1016/j.annals.2006.10.005

Konecnik, M., & Go, F. (2008). Tourism destination brand identity: The case of Slovenia. *Journal of Brand Management*, *15*(3), 177–189. doi:10.1057/palgrave.bm.2550114

Kornum, N., Gyrd-Jones, R., Al Zagir, N., & Brandis, K. A. (2017). Interplay between intended brand identity and identities in a Nike related brand community: Co-existing synergies and tensions in a nested system. *Journal of Business Research*, *70*(January), 432–440. doi:10.1016/j.jbusres.2016.06.019

Kotler, P., & Armstrong, G. (2012). *Principles of marketing* (14th ed.). Upper Saddle River, NJ: Prentice Hall.

Kotler, P., Armstrong, G., Harris, L., & Piercy, N. (2013). *Principles of Marketing* (6th ed.). Essex, UK: Pearson Education Limited.

Kotler, P., & Gertner, D. (2002). Country as brand, product and beyond: A place marketing and brand management perspective. *Journal of Brand Management*, *9*(4/5), 249–261. doi:10.1057/palgrave.bm.2540076

Kotoua, S., & Ilkan, M. (2017a). Online tourism destination marketing in Kumasi Ghana. *Asia Pacific Journal of Tourism Research*, *22*(6), 666–680. doi:10.1080/10941665.2017.1308394

Kotoua, S., & Ilkan, M. (2017b). Tourism destination marketing and information technology in Ghana. *Journal of Destination Marketing & Management*, *6*(2), 127–135. doi:10.1016/j.jdmm.2017.04.007

Kozak, N. (2006). *Turizm Pazarlaması*. Ankara: Detay Yayıncılık.

Kozinets, R. V. (2002). The field behind the screen: Using netnography for marketing research in online communities. *JMR, Journal of Marketing Research*, *39*(1), 61–72. doi:10.1509/jmkr.39.1.61.18935

Kozinets, R. V., De Valck, K., Wajnicki, A. C., & Wilner, S. J. (2010). Networked narratives: Understanding word-of-mouth marketing in online communities. *Journal of Marketing*, *74*(2), 71–89. doi:10.1509/jmkg.74.2.71

Compilation of References

Kracht, J., & Wang, Y. C. (2010). Examining the tourism distribution channels: Evolution and transformation. *International Journal of Contemporary Hospitality Management, 22*(5), 736–757. doi:10.1108/09596111011053837

Krieger, B., Moskowitz, H., & Rabino, S. (2005). What customers want from a cruise vacation: Using internet-enabled conjoint analysis to understand the customer's mind. *Journal of Hospitality & Leisure Marketing, 13*(1), 83–111. doi:10.1300/J150v13n01_06

Kucukusta, D., & Denizci Gulliet, B. (2014). Measuring Spa-goers Preferences: A Conjoint Analysis Approach. *International Journal of Hospitality Management, 41*, 115–124. doi:10.1016/j.ijhm.2014.05.008

Kuokkanen, H. (2016). Behavioural pricing opportunities in tourism destinations: A collaborative approach. *International Journal of Revenue Management, 9*(2-3), 186–200. doi:10.1504/IJRM.2016.077020

Kuvan, Y., & Akan, P. (2005). Resident's attitudes toward general and forest-related impacts of tourism: The case of Belek, Antalya. *Tourism Management, 26*(5), 691–706. doi:10.1016/j.tourman.2004.02.019

Kuznets, S. S. (1933). *Seasonal variations in industry and trade (No. 22)*. New York: National Bureau of Economic Research.

Kwok, L., Xie, K. L., & Richards, T. (2017). Thematic framework of online review research: A systematic analysis of contemporary literature on seven major hospitality and tourism journals. *International Journal of Contemporary Hospitality Management, 29*(1), 307–354. doi:10.1108/IJCHM-11-2015-0664

Kylanen, M., & Mariani, M. M. (2012). Unpacking the temporal dimension of coopetition in tourism destinations: Evidence from Finnish and Italian theme parks. *Anatolia, 23*(1), 61–74. doi:10.1080/13032917.2011.653632

L'Etang, J., Falkheimer, J., & Lugo, J. (2007). Public relations and tourism: Critical reflections and a research agenda. *Public Relations Review, 33*(1), 68–76. doi:10.1016/j.pubrev.2006.11.008

Lake, L. (2015). *Marketing 101: What is branding?* Retrieved June 13, 2017, from http://www.marketing.abou.com/cs/brandmktg/a/whatisbranding.htm

Langkawi Development Agency (LADA). (2011). *The Langkawi tourism blueprint (2011-2015)*. Langkawi, Kedah, Malaysia: LADA Publications.

LaPlaca, P. J. (1997). Contributions to marketing theory and practice from industrial marketing management. *Journal of Business Research, 38*(3), 179–198. doi:10.1016/S0148-2963(96)00128-2

Lappas, T. (2012). Fake Reviews: The Malicious Perspective. In *Natural Language Processing and Information Systems* (pp. 23–34). Berlin: Springer. doi:10.1007/978-3-642-31178-9_3

Law, R., & Bai, B. (2006). Website development and evaluations in tourism: a retrospective analysis. *Information and communication technologies in tourism 2006*, 1-12.

Law, R., & Hsu, C. H. (2006). Importance of hotel website dimensions and attributes: Perceptions of online browsers and online purchasers. *Journal of Hospitality & Tourism Research (Washington, D.C.)*, *30*(3), 295–312. doi:10.1177/1096348006287161

Law, R., & Leung, R. (2000). A study of airlines' online reservation services on the Internet. *Journal of Travel Research*, *39*(2), 202–211. doi:10.1177/004728750003900210

Law, R., Qi, S., & Buhalis, D. (2010). Progress in tourism management: A review of website evaluation in tourism research. *Tourism Management*, *31*(3), 297–313. doi:10.1016/j.tourman.2009.11.007

Lawson, F., & Baud-Bovy, M. (1977). *Tourism and recreational development*. London: Architectural Pres.

Le Figaro. (2014). Retrieved October 1, 2017, from http://madame.lefigaro.fr/art-de-vivre/porto-insolite-charmante-240414-851138

Lebe, S. S., & Milfelner, B. (2006). Innovative organization approach to sustainable tourism development in rural areas. *Kybernetes*, *35*(7-8), 1136–1146. doi:10.1108/03684920610675139

Lee, B., Lee, C., & Lee, J. L. (2014). Dynamic Nature of Destination Image and Influence of Tourist Overall Satisfaction on Image Modification. *Journal of Travel Research*, *53*(2), 239–251. doi:10.1177/0047287513496466

Lee, C. K., Lee, Y. K., & Wicks, B. E. (2004). Segmentation of festival motivation by nationality and satisfaction. *Tourism Management*, *25*(1), 61–70. doi:10.1016/S0261-5177(03)00060-8

Lee, G., & Lee, C.-K. (2009). Cross-cultural comparison of the image of Guam perceived by Korean and Japanese leisure travelers: Importance–performance analysis. *Tourism Management*, *30*(6), 922–931. doi:10.1016/j.tourman.2008.11.013

Lee, K., Tamilarasan, P., & Caverlee, J. (2013). Crowdturfers, Campaigns, and Social Media: Tracking and Revealing Crowdsourced Manipulation of Social Media. *Seventh International AAAI Conference on Weblogs and Social Media*.

Lee, S. K., & Jang, S. (2011). Room rates of US airport hotels: Examining the dual effects of proximities. *Journal of Travel Research*, *50*(2), 186–197. doi:10.1177/0047287510362778

Lee, T. H. (2013). Influence analysis of community resident support for sustainable tourism development. *Tourism Management*, *34*, 37–46. doi:10.1016/j.tourman.2012.03.007

Letho, Y. X., Jang, S., Achana, F. T., & O'Leary, J. T. (2004). Tourist shopping preferences and expenditure behaviours: The case of the Taiwanese outbound market. *Journal of Vacation Marketing*, *10*(4), 320–332. doi:10.1177/135676670401000404

Leung, D., Law, R., Hoof, H. V., & Buhalis, D. (2013). Social media in tourism and hospitality: A literature review. *Journal of Travel & Tourism Marketing*, *30*(1), 3–22. doi:10.1080/10548408.2013.750919

Compilation of References

Levine, M. E. (2002). Price discrimination without market power. *Yale Journal on Regulation, 19*, 1.

Li, X. P. (2009). An examination of [the] effects of self-concepts, destination personality and SC-DP congruence on tourist behavior. Blacksburg, VA: Virginia Polytechnic Institute and State University.

Liang, T. P., & Lai, H. J. (2002). Effect of store design on consumer purchases: An empirical study of on-line bookstores. *Information & Management, 39*(6), 431–444. doi:10.1016/S0378-7206(01)00129-X

Li, M., Cai, L. A., Lehto, X. Y., & Huang, Z. J. (2010). A missing link in understanding revisit intention - The role of motivation and image. *Journal of Travel & Tourism Marketing, 27*(4), 335–348. doi:10.1080/10548408.2010.481559

Lin, C. H., Morais, B., Kerstetter, D. L., & Hou, J. S. (2007). Examining the Role of Cognitive and Affective Image in Predicting Choice across Natural, Developed, and Theme-Park Destinations. *Journal of Travel Research, 46*(2), 183–194. doi:10.1177/0047287507304049

Line, N. D., & Wang, Y. (2017). A multi-stakeholder market oriented approach to destination marketing. *Journal of Destination Marketing & Management, 6*(1), 84–93. doi:10.1016/j.jdmm.2016.03.003

Lin, Z., Chen, Y., & Filieri, R. (2017). Resident-tourist value co-creation: The role of residents' perceived tourism impacts and life satisfaction. *Tourism Management, 61*, 436–442. doi:10.1016/j.tourman.2017.02.013

Litvin, S. W., Goldsmith, R. E., & Pan, B. (2008). Electronic word-of-mouth in hospitality and tourism management. *Tourism Management, 29*(3), 458–468. doi:10.1016/j.tourman.2007.05.011

Litvin, S. W., Goldsmith, R. E., & Pan, B. (2017). A retrospective view of electronic word of mouth in hospitality and tourism management. *International Journal of Contemporary Hospitality Management*. doi:10.1108/IJCHM-08-2016-0461

Liu, J., Sheldon, P. J., & Var, T. (1987). Resident perception of the environmental impacts of tourism. *Annals of Tourism Research, 14*(1), 17–37. doi:10.1016/0160-7383(87)90045-4

Liu, J., & Var, T. (1986). Resident attitudes toward tourism impacts in Hawaii. *Annals of Tourism Research, 13*(2), 193–214. doi:10.1016/0160-7383(86)90037-X

Liu, W., Guillet, B. D., Xiao, Q., & Law, R. (2014). Globalization or localization of consumer preferences: The case of hotel room booking. *Tourism Management, 41*, 148–157. doi:10.1016/j.tourman.2013.09.004

Liu, X., Schuckert, M., & Law, R. (2016). Online incentive hierarchies, review extremity, and review quality: Empirical evidence from the hotel sector. *Journal of Travel & Tourism Marketing, 33*(3), 279–292. doi:10.1080/10548408.2015.1008669

Livi, E. (2009). Information technology and new business models in the tourism industry. In *Emerging Issues and Challenges in Business & Economics: Selected Contributions from the 8th Global Conference* (Vol. 24, p. 315). Firenze University Press.

Li, X., & Stepchenkova, S. (2012). Chinese Outbound Tourists' Destination Image of America: Part I. *Journal of Travel Research*, *51*(3), 250–266. doi:10.1177/0047287511410349

Li, Y. M., & Yeh, Y. S. (2010). Increasing trust in mobile commerce through design aesthetics. *Journal of Computers in Human Behavior*, *26*(4), 673–684. doi:10.1016/j.chb.2010.01.004

Lofland, J., & Lofland, L. H. (1995). Analysing social settings: A guide to qualitative observation and analysis (3rd ed.). Belmont, CA: Wadsworth.

Lo, M.-C., Songan, P., & Mohamad, A. Z. (2011). Rural destinations and tourists' satisfaction. *Journal of Services Research*, *11*(2), 59–74.

Long, T. P., & Perdue, R. R. (1990). The Economic Impact of Rural Festivals And Special Events: Assessing The Spatial Distribution of Expenditures. *Journal of Travel Research*, *28*(4), 10–14. doi:10.1177/004728759002800403

Lovelock, C. H., & Wirtz, J. (2004). *Services Marketing*. Englewood Cliffs, NJ: Prentice Hall.

Lozano-Oyola, M., Blancas, F. J., González, M., & Caballero, R. (2012). Sustainable tourism indicators as planning tools in cultural destinations. *Ecological Indicators*, *18*, 659–675. doi:10.1016/j.ecolind.2012.01.014

Luca, M., & Zervas, G. (2016). Fake It Till You Make It: Reputation, Competition, and Yelp Review Fraud. *Management Science*, *62*(12), 3412–3427. doi:10.1287/mnsc.2015.2304

Lu, L., Chi, C. G., & Liu, Y. (2015). Authenticity, involvement, and image: Evaluating tourist experiences at historic districts. *Tourism Management*, *50*, 85–96. doi:10.1016/j.tourman.2015.01.026

Lundtorp, S. (2001). Measuring tourism seasonality. In T. Baum & S. Lundtorp (Eds.), *Seasonality in Tourism* (pp. 23–50). Oxford, UK: Pergamon. doi:10.1016/B978-0-08-043674-6.50006-4

Lundtorp, S., Rassing, C. R., & Wanhill, S. (1999). The off-season is 'no season': The case of the Danish island of Bornholm. *Tourism Economics*, *5*(1), 49–68. doi:10.1177/135481669900500104

Lusseau, D., & Higham, J. E. S. (2004). Managing the impacts of dolphin-based tourism through the definition of critical habitats: The case of bottlenose dolphins (Tursiops spp.) in doubtful sound, New Zeeland. *Tourism Management*, *25*(6), 657–667. doi:10.1016/j.tourman.2003.08.012

Lytras, M. D., & Global, I. G. I. (2011). Geospatio-temporal semantic web for cultural heritage. In *Digital culture and e-tourism: Technologies, applications and management approaches* (pp. 12–14). Hershey, PA: IGI Global.

MacCannell, D. (1973). Staged authenticity: Arrangements of social space in tourist settings. *American Journal of Sociology*, *79*(3), 589–603. doi:10.1086/225585

Compilation of References

MacKay, K. J., & Fesenmaier, D. R. (1997). Pictorial element of destination in image formation. *Annals of Tourism Research*, *24*(3), 537–565. doi:10.1016/S0160-7383(97)00011-X

Mackenzie, L. (2016). *2016 Annual Tourism Conference and Exhibition*. Derbyshire: Marketing Peak District and Derbyshire.

Major, B., & Testa, M. (1989). Social Comparison Processes and Judgments of Entitlement and Satisfaction. *Journal of Experimental Social Psychology*, *25*(2), 101–120. doi:10.1016/0022-1031(89)90007-3

Makkonen, T. (2016). Cross-border shopping and tourism destination marketing: The case of Southern Jutland, Denmark. *Scandinavian Journal of Hospitality and Tourism*, *16*(Sup1), 36-50. 10.1080/15022250.2016.1244506

Malaysian Government. (2011). *Population and housing census of Malaysia: preliminary count Report 2010*. Retrieved from: https://www.statistics.gov.my

Mancini, M. (2000). *Cruising: A guide to the cruise line industry*. New York: Delmar Publishing.

Mano, A., Costa, R., & Moutinho, V. (2014). O estado atual e perspetivas futuras de investigação da imagem de destino turísticos: O caso de Portugal. *Revista Turismo & Desenvolvimento*, *2*(21/22), 391–402.

Marak, J., Oparka, S., & Wyrzykowski, J. (2014). *Factors conditioning the creation of the combined product "Health Resort, Spa and Wellness Tourism" in a region*. Tourism Role in the Regional Economy.

Mariani, M. M. (2016). Coordination in inter-network co-operation: Evidence from the tourism sector. *Industrial Marketing Management*, *53*, 103–123. doi:10.1016/j.indmarman.2015.11.015

Marien, C., & Pizan, A. (2005). Implementing sustainable tourism development through citizen participation in the planning process. In S. Wahab & J. J. Pigram (Eds.), *Tourism, development and growth: The challenge of sustainability*. London, UK: Routledge.

Marine-Roig, E. (2015). Identity and authenticity in destination image construction. *Anatolia*, *26*(4), 574–587. doi:10.1080/13032917.2015.1040814

Mariutti, F., & Giraldi, J. (2014). Country brand identity: An exploratory study about the Brazil brand with American travel agencies. *Tourism Planning & Development*, *11*(1), 13–26. doi:10.1080/21568316.2013.839469

Marti, B. E. (2005). Cruise line logo recognition. *Journal of Travel & Tourism Marketing*, *18*(1), 25–31. doi:10.1300/J073v18n01_03

Martinez, S. C., & Alvarez, D. M. (2010). Country Versus Destination Image in a Developing Country. *Journal of Travel & Tourism Marketing*, *27*(7), 748–764. doi:10.1080/10548408.2010.519680

Martin, J. M., Jimenez, J. D., & Molina, V. (2014). Impacts of seasonality on environmental sustainability in the tourism sector based on destination type: An application to Spain's Andalusia region. *Tourism Economics*, *20*(1), 123–142. doi:10.5367/te.2013.0256

Martin, J. M., Rodríguez, J. A., Zermeño, K. A., & Salinas, J. A. (2018). Effects of Vacation Rental Websites on the Concentration of Tourists—Potential Environmental Impacts. An Application to the Balearic Islands in Spain. *International Journal of Environmental Research and Public Health*, *15*(2), 347–333. doi:10.3390/ijerph15020347 PMID:29462863

Martin, J. M., Salinas, J. A., Rodríguez, J. A., & Jiménez, J. D. (2017). Assessment of the Tourism's Potential as a Sustainable Development Instrument in Terms of Annual Stability: Application to Spanish Rural Destinations in Process of Consolidation. *Sustainability*, *9*(10), 1692–1712. doi:10.3390u9101692

Martins, M., & Monroe, K. B. (1994). Perceived Price Fairness: A new Look at an Old Construct. *Advances in Consumer Research. Association for Consumer Research (U. S.)*, *21*(1), 75–78.

Masiero, L., Heo, C. Y., & Pan, B. (2015). Determining guests' willingness to pay for hotel room attributes with a discrete choice model. *International Journal of Hospitality Management*, *49*, 117–124. doi:10.1016/j.ijhm.2015.06.001

Masiero, L., Nicolau, J. L., & Law, R. (2015). A demand-driven analysis of tourist accommodation price: A quantile regression of room bookings. *International Journal of Hospitality Management*, *50*, 1–8. doi:10.1016/j.ijhm.2015.06.009

Maslow, A., & Lewis, K. J. (1987). *Maslow's hierarchy of needs*. Salenger Incorporated.

Mason, P. (2008). *Tourism impacts, planning and management*. Oxford, UK: Butterworth-Heinemann.

Mason, P. (2016). *Tourism Impacts Planning and Management* (3rd ed.). Oxon, UK: Routledge.

Mathieson, A., & Wall, G. (1982). *Tourism, economic, physical and social impacts*. London, UK: Pearson Longman.

Mathieson, A., & Wall, G. (1982). *Tourism: Economic, physical and social impacts*. Harlow, UK: Addison Wesley Longman.

Mauri, A. G. (2007). Yield management and perceptions of fairness in the hotel business. *International Review of Economics*, *54*(2), 284–293. doi:10.100712232-007-0015-4

Mauri, A. G. (2012a). *Hotel revenue management: Principles and practices*. Pearson.

Mauri, A. G. (2012b). *Hotel Revenue Management and Guests' Perceived Fairness. Theoretical Issues and Empirical Findings from a Multiple-Year Survey*. Smashwords.

Mauri, A. G. (2014). Foreword: marketing and pricing in the digital environment. In G. Viglia (Ed.), *Behavioral Pricing, Online marketing behavior, and analytics*. New York: Palgrave Macmillan.

Compilation of References

Mauri, A. G., & Soone, I. (2009). Yield/Revenue Management and Perceptions of Fairness in Hotel Business: Empirical Evidences. *Proceedings 12th International QMOD and Toulon-Verona Conference on Quality and Service Sciences (ICQSS)*.

Mawer, F. (2017). 36 Hours in…Bath. *Telegraph*. Available at: http://www.telegraph.co.uk/travel/destinations/europe/united-kingdom/england/somerset/bath/articles/36-hours-in-bath/

May, C. (2001). *From direct response to image with qualitative and quantitative research.* Presentation at the 32nd Annual Conference of the Travel and Tourism Research Association, Fort Myers, FL.

Mayzlin, D., Dover, Y., & Chevalier, J. (2014). Promotional reviews: An empirical investigation of online review manipulation. *The American Economic Review*, *104*(8), 2421–2455. doi:10.1257/aer.104.8.2421

McCartney, G. (2008). Does one culture all think the same? An investigation of destination image perceptions from several origins. *Tourism Review*, *63*(4), 13–26. doi:10.1108/16605370810912182

McEvilly, B. (2015). *How Online Review Sites Are Affecting Your Hotel*. Retrieved from https://www.hospitalitynet.org/opinion/4070901.html

McGill, J. I., & Van Ryzin, G. J. (1999). Revenue management: Research overview and prospects. *Transportation Science*, *33*(2), 233–256. doi:10.1287/trsc.33.2.233

McMahon-Beattie, U. (2006). Trust and revenue management. *Journal of Revenue and Pricing Management*, *4*(4), 406–407. doi:10.1057/palgrave.rpm.5170162

Mehmetoglu, M. (2004). *Kvalitativ Metode for Merkantile Fag [Qualitative Methods for Business Studies]*. Bergen, Norway: Fagbokforlaget.

Melián-González, S., Bulchand-Gidumal, J., & González López-Valcárcel, B. (2013). Online customer reviews of hotels: As participation increases, better evaluation is obtained. *Cornell Hospitality Quarterly*, *54*(3), 274–283. doi:10.1177/1938965513481498

Mendes, J. C., Valle, P. O., & Guerreiro, M. (2011). Destination image and events - A structural model for the Algarve case. *Journal of Hospitality Marketing & Management*, *20*(3-4), 366–384. doi:10.1080/19368623.2011.562424

Merriam, S. (1988). *Case Study Research in Education. A Qualitative Approach*. San Francisco, CA: Jossey-Bass Publishers.

Messick, D. M., & Sentis, K. P. (1979). Fairness and preference. *Journal of Experimental Social Psychology*, *15*(4), 418–434. doi:10.1016/0022-1031(79)90047-7

Mihalic, T. (2013). Performance of Environmental Resources of a Tourist Destination: Concept and Application. *Journal of Travel Research*, *52*(5), 614–630. doi:10.1177/0047287513478505

Mill, R. C., & Morrison, A. M. (1998). *The Tourism System, an Introductory Text*. Dubuque, IA: Kendall/Hunt.

Milman, A., & Pizam, A. (1995). The Role of Awareness and Familiarity with a Destination: The Central Florida Case. *Journal of Travel Research, 33*(3), 21–27. doi:10.1177/004728759503300304

Milne, S., & Ateljevic, I. (2001). Tourism, economic development and the global-local nexus: Theory embracing complexity. *Tourism Geographies, 3*(4), 369–393. doi:10.1080/146166800110070478

Ministry of Tourism. (2009). *National tourism policy for Malawi*. Lilongwe, Malawi: Malawi Government. Retrieved from http://www.e-travelworld.cn/malawi/Publications/documents/NATIONAL%20TOURISM%20POLICY.pdf

Mintel Group Ltd. (2011). *Spa Tourism – International – October - 2011*. Available at: http://academic.mintel.com.ezproxy.derby.ac.uk/display/545413/

Mintel Group Ltd. (2014a). *Inbound Tourism – UK – November 2016*. Available at: http://academic.mintel.com.ezproxy.derby.ac.uk/display/723354/

Mintel Group Ltd. (2014b). *Legacy of mega events in tourism – International – November 2010*. Available at: http://academic.mintel.com.ezproxy.derby.ac.uk/display/482892/

Mintel Group Ltd. (2016a). *Leisure Review – UK – December 2016*. Available at: http://academic.mintel.com.ezproxy.derby.ac.uk/display/809667/

Mintel Group Ltd. (2016b). *The Evolution of Wellness Tourism –August 2016*. Available at: http://academic.mintel.com.ezproxy.derby.ac.uk/display/786404/

Mintel Group Ltd. (2016c). *Travel and Tourism – China – February 2016*. Available at: http://academic.mintel.com.ezproxy.derby.ac.uk/display/764551/

Mintel Group Ltd. (2016d). *Travel and Tourism – Japan – February 2016*. Available at: http://academic.mintel.com.ezproxy.derby.ac.uk/display/764590/

Mintel Group Ltd. (2017). *Spa, Salon and In-store Treatments – UK – September 2017*. Available at: http://academic.mintel.com.ezproxy.derby.ac.uk/display/793777/

Mittila, T., & Lepsisto, T. (2013). The role of artists in place branding: A case study. *Place Branding and Public Diplomacy, 9*(3), 143–153. doi:10.1057/pb.2013.15

Mohammed, B. (2002). Strategic positioning of Malaysia as a tourism destinations: A review. In *Sustainable Tourism Research Cluster*. Universiti Sains Malaysia.

Mohammed, B., & Muhibudin, M. (2012). From idyllic fishing village to beach resorts: the case of Pangkor Island. *Proceedings of the Regional Symposium on Rural Tourism: Scaling up Community-Based Ecotourism.*

Moilanen, T., & Rainisto, S. (2009). *How to Brand Nations, cities and Destinations – a planning book for place branding*. Palgrave Macmillan. doi:10.1057/9780230584594

Moital, M., Costa, C., & Peres, R. (2005). Lisbon as a city break destination: Competitive analysis as perceived by London travel agents. *Journal of Tourism and Development, 2*(1), 67–80.

Compilation of References

Molnár, J. K. E. (2014). Potential for Tourism Development in Industrial Towns Based on Cultural Heritage, The Cases of Svit and Martfu. Enhancing Competitiveness of V4 Historic Cities to Develop Tourism, 178.

Monroe, K. B., & Xia, L. (2005). The Many Routes to Price Unfairness Perceptions. *Advances in Consumer Research. Association for Consumer Research (U. S.)*, *32*(1), 387–391.

Monty, B., & Skidmore, M. (2003). Hedonic pricing and willingness to pay for bed and breakfast amenities in Southeast Wisconsin. *Journal of Travel Research*, *42*(2), 195–199. doi:10.1177/0047287503257500

Moore, S. A., Rodger, K., & Taplin, R. H. (2013). Moving beyond visitor satisfaction to loyalty in nature-based tourism: A review and research agenda. *Current Issues in Tourism*, 1–17. doi:10.1080/13683500.2013.790346

Moorthy, K. S. (1984). Market segmentation, self-selection, and product line design. *Marketing Science*, *2*(4), 288–307. doi:10.1287/mksc.3.4.288

Moreira, A. C., Macedo, P., Lopes, M., & Moutinho, V. (2011). *Exercícios de estatística com recurso ao SPSS*. Lisbon: Sílabo.

Moreira, R., Santos, N. N., & Aires, E. (2014). *Porto*. Porto: Câmara Municipal do Porto.

Morgan, N., & Pritchard, A. (2010). Meeting the destination branding challenge. In N. Morgan, A. Pritchard, & R. Pride (Eds.), Destination Branding: Creating the unique destination proposition (2nd ed.). Oxford, UK: Elsevier Butterworth-Heinemann.

Morgan, N., Pritchard, A., & Pride, R. (Eds.). (2010). Destination Branding: Creating the unique destination proposition (2nd ed.). Oxford, UK: Elsevier Butterworth-Heinemann.

Morgan, N., Pritchard, A., & Piggott, R. (2002). New Zealand, 100% pure.the creation of a powerful niche destination brand. *Journal of Brand Management*, *9*(4-5), 335–354. doi:10.1057/palgrave.bm.2540082

Morrison, A. M., Taylor, J. S., & Douglas, A. (2004). *Website evaluation in tourism and hospitality*. Academic Press.

Morrison, A., & Anderson, D. (2002). *Destination branding*. Retrieved from: http://www.macvb.org/intranet/presentation/DestinationBranding

Morrison, A. (2013). Destination management and estimation marketing: The platform for excellence in tourism destinations. *Luyou Xuekan*, *28*(1), 6–9. Retrieved from http://www.lyxk.com.cn/EN/Y2013/V28/I1/6

Morrison, A. M. (2013). *Marketing and managing tourism destinations*. London: Routledge. PP.

Morrison, A. M., Taylor, J. S., Morrison, A. J., & Morrison, A. D. (1999). Marketing small hotels on the World Wide Web. *Information Technology & Tourism*, *2*(2), 97–113.

Morrisson, O., & Huppertz, J. W. (2010). External equity, loyalty program membership, and service recovery. *Journal of Services Marketing*, *24*(3), 244–254. doi:10.1108/08876041011040640

Moscardo, G. (Ed.). (2008). *Building community capacity for tourism development*. Cabi. doi:10.1079/9781845934477.0000

Mostowfi, B. (2000). *Agro-tourism and sustainable development, case study: Landscape design for Karyak village* (Master's thesis). University of Tehran, Tehran, Iran.

Mourdoukoutas, P. (1988). Seasonal employment and unemployment compensation: The case of the tourist industry of the Greek island. *American Journal of Economics and Sociology*, *47*(3), 315–329. doi:10.1111/j.1536-7150.1988.tb02044.x

Moutinho, L. (1987). Consumer behaviour in tourism. *European Journal of Marketing*, *21*(10), 5–44. doi:10.1108/EUM0000000004718

Murphy, J., Forrest, E. J., Wotring, C. E., & Brymer, R. A. (1996). Hotel management and marketing on the Internet: An analysis of sites and features. *The Cornell Hotel and Restaurant Administration Quarterly*, *37*(3), 770–782.

Murphy, J., Forrest, E., & Wotring, C. E. (1996). Restaurant marketing on the worldwide web. *The Cornell Hotel and Restaurant Administration Quarterly*, *37*(1), 61–71. doi:10.1177/001088049603700117

Murphy, L., Benckendorff, P., & Moscardo, G. (2007). linking travel motivation, tourist self-image and destination brand personality. *Journal of Travel & Tourism Marketing*, *22*(2), 45–59. doi:10.1300/J073v22n02_04

Murphy, P. E. (1985). *Tourism: A community approach*. London, UK: Methuen.

Murphy, P., Pritchard, M. P., & Smith, B. (2000). The destination product and its impact on traveller perceptions. *Tourism Management*, *21*(1), 43–52. doi:10.1016/S0261-5177(99)00080-1

Murray, K. B. (1991). A test of services marketing theory: Consumer information acquisition activities. *Journal of Marketing*, *55*(1), 10–25. doi:10.2307/1252200

Murray, N., Lynch, P., & Foley, A. (2014). Destination visioneering: A case study of best Practice. *Proceedings of the Irish Academy of Management Conference*. Limerick, Ireland: University of Limerick.

Murray, N., Lynch, P., & Foley, A. (2016). Unlocking the magic in successful tourism destination marketing: The role of sensing capability. *Journal of Marketing Management*, *32*(9), 877–899. doi:10.1080/0267257X.2016.1192557

Mütelcimler, E. (2005). *Korkak Abdul'den Coni Türk'e Gelibolu*. İstanbul: Alfa Basım Yayım Dağıtım.

Nagle, T. (1984). Economic Foundations for Pricing. *The Journal of Business*, *57*(1), 3–26. doi:10.1086/296232

Compilation of References

Nair, V. (2015). Langkawi's tourism blueprint (2011-2015): Transformation from rural tourism to developed rural tourism destination. *Proceeds of 21st Asia Pacific Tourism Association Conference*, 154-156.

Nair, V., Uma Thevi, M., Sushila Devi, R., & King, N. (2012). Redefining rural tourism in Malaysia: A conceptual perspective. *Asia Pacific Journal of Tourism Research*, *20*(3), 314–337. doi:10.1080/10941665.2014.889026

Naoi, T. (2004). Visitors' evaluation of a historic district: The roles of authentic city and manipulation. *Tourism and Hospitality Research*, *5*(1), 45–63. doi:10.1057/palgrave.thr.6040004

Nerhagen, L. (2003). Travel mode choice: Effect of previous experience on choice behavior and valuation. *Tourism Economics*, *9*(1), 5–30. doi:10.5367/000000003101298240

NetGenesis/SPSS Inc. (2003a). *E-metrics. Business metrics for the new economy*. Retrieved June 28, 2003, from http://www.spss.com/netgenesis

Neto, F. (2003). A new approach to sustainable tourism development: Moving beyond environmental protection. *Natural Resources Forum*, *27*(3), 212–222. doi:10.1111/1477-8947.00056

New York Times. (2016). Retrieved October 1, 2017, from https://www.nytimes.com/2016/02/10/t-magazine/travel/porto-portugal-hotels-galleries-restaurants.html

Nghiêm-Phú, B. (2014). A review of destination image studies from 2008 to 2012. *European Journal of Tourism Research*, *8*, 35–65.

Ng, I. C. L. (2006). Differentiation, self-selection and revenue management. *Journal of Revenue and Pricing Management*, *5*(1), 2–9. doi:10.1057/palgrave.rpm.5160019

Nicholas, L. N., Thapa, B., & Ko, Y. J. (2009). Residents' perspectives of a World Heritage Site: The Pitons Management Area, St. Lucia. *Annals of Tourism Research*, *36*(3), 390–412. doi:10.1016/j.annals.2009.03.005

Nichols, C. M., & Snepenger, D. J. (1988). Family decision-making and tourism behavior and attitudes. *Journal of Travel Research*, *26*(4), 2–6. doi:10.1177/004728758802600401

Nicolau, J. L., & Masiero, L. (2013). Relationship between price sensitivity and expenditures in the choice of tourism activities at the destination. *Tourism Economics*, *19*(1), 101–114. doi:10.5367/te.2013.0192

Nielsen. (2015). *The Nielsen Global Trust in Advertising Survey*. Retrieved from https://www.nielsen.com/content/dam/nielsenglobal/apac/docs/reports/2015/nielsen-global-trust-in-advertising-report-september-2015.pdf

Nielsen, J., & Tahir, M. (2002). *Homepage usability: 50 Websites deconstructed*. Indianapolis, IN: New Riders Publishing.

Niven, P. R. (2002). *Balanced scorecard step-by-step: Maximizing performance and maintaining results*. John Wiley & Sons.

Noone, B. M., & Mattila, A. S. (2009). Hotel revenue management and the Internet: The effect of price presentation strategies on customers' willingness to book. *International Journal of Hospitality Management*, *28*(2), 272–279. doi:10.1016/j.ijhm.2008.09.004

Northcote, J., & Macbeth, J. (2006). Conceptualising yield: Sustainable tourism management. *Annals of Tourism Research*, *33*(1), 199–220. doi:10.1016/j.annals.2005.10.012

Nunkoo, R., & Gursoy, D. (2012). Residents' support for tourism: An identity perspective. *Annals of Tourism Research*, *39*(1), 243–268. doi:10.1016/j.annals.2011.05.006

Nunkoo, R., & Ramkissoon, H. (2010). Modeling community support for a proposed integrated resort project. *Journal of Sustainable Tourism*, *18*(2), 257–277. doi:10.1080/09669580903290991

Nunkoo, R., & Ramkissoon, H. (2012). Power, trust, social exchange and community support. *Annals of Tourism Research*, *39*(2), 997–1023. doi:10.1016/j.annals.2011.11.017

O'Leary, S., & Deegan, J. (2005). Ireland's Image as a tourism destination in France: Attribute, importance and performance. *Journal of Travel Research*, *43*(3), 247–256. doi:10.1177/0047287504272025

O'reilly, T. (2005). *What is Web 2.0: Design patterns and business models for the next generation of software*. Sebastopol, CA: O'Reilly Media.

Obonyo, G. O., & Fwaya, E. V. O. (2012). Integrating tourism with rural development strategies in Western Kenya. *American Journal of Tourism Research*, *1*(1), 1–8.

Öğüt, H., & Onur Taş, B. K. (2012). The influence of internet customer reviews on the online sales and prices in hotel industry. *Service Industries Journal*, *32*(2), 197–214. doi:10.1080/02642069.2010.529436

Oh, H., & Jeong, M. (2010). Evaluating stability of the performance-satisfaction relationship across selected lodging market segments. *International Journal of Contemporary Hospitality Management*, *22*(7), 953–974. doi:10.1108/09596111011066626

Okumuş, B., Okumuş, F., & McKercher, B. (2007). Incorporating local and international cuisines in the marketing of tourism destinations: The cases of Hong Kong and Turkey. *Tourism Management*, *28*(1), 253–261. doi:10.1016/j.tourman.2005.12.020

Oliver, R. L. (2009). *Satisfaction: A Behavioral Perspective on the Consumer* (2nd ed.). Armonk: M.E. Sharpe.

Onder, I., & Marchiori, E. (2017). A Comparison of Pre-visit Beliefs and Projected Visual Images of Destinations. *Tourism Management Perspectives*, *21*, 42–53. doi:10.1016/j.tmp.2016.11.003

Önen, O. M. (2000). *Türkiye'nin Turizm Sektöründeki Gelişmeler, Dünya Turizmindeki Yeri ve Türkiye Kalkınma Bankası'nın Rolü*. Türkiye Kalkınma Bankası.

Opolskiej, Z. N. P., Migala, M., & Szczyrba, Z. (2006). Article. *Spas and Spa Tourism in the Czech Republic*, *1*(312), 147–162.

Compilation of References

Orel, F. D., & Kara, A. (2014). Supermarket self-checkout service quality, customer satisfaction, and loyalty: Empirical evidence from an emerging market. *Journal of Retailing and Consumer Services*, *21*(2), 118–129. doi:10.1016/j.jretconser.2013.07.002

Organisation for Economic Co-operation and Development (OECD). (1994). *Tourism strategies and rural development*. OECD.

Öztürk, Y., Yeşiltaş, M., Kozak, M., Özel, Ç. H., & Aksöz, O. (2013). *Destinasyon Yönetimi*. Eskişehir: Anadolu Üniversitesi Yayınları.

Page Size Checker | online Tool to check web page size. (n.d.). Retrieved from https://smallseotools.com/website-page-size-checker/

Page, S. L. (2007). *Tourism management: Managing for change*. Oxford, UK: Elsevier.

Pakurar, M., & Olah, J. (2008). Definition of rural tourism and its characteristics in the northern great plain region. *System*, *7*, 777–782.

Papatheodorou, A., Lei, Z., & Apostolakis, A. (2012). Hedonic price analysis. Handbook of research methods in tourism: Quantitative and qualitative approaches, 170-182. doi:10.4337/9781781001295.00015

Parasuraman, A., Zeithaml, V. A., & Berry, L. (1988). SERVQUAL: A multiple-item scale for measuring consumer perceptions of service quality. *Journal of Retailing*, *64*(1), 12–40.

Park, D. B., Lee, K. W., Choi, H. S., & Yoon, Y. (2012). Factors influencing social capital in rural tourism communities in South Korea. *Tourism Management*, *33*(6), 1511–1520. doi:10.1016/j.tourman.2012.02.005

Park, S., & Nicolau, J. L. (2015). Asymmetric effects of online consumer reviews. *Annals of Tourism Research*, *50*(Supplement C), 67–83. doi:10.1016/j.annals.2014.10.007

Park, Y. A., & Gretzel, U. (2007). Success factors for destination marketing web sites: A qualitative meta-analysis. *Journal of Travel Research*, *46*(1), 46–63. doi:10.1177/0047287507302381

Partners of Chatsworth. (2016). *Chatsworth on Film*. Available at: http://www.chatsworth.org/press-and-filming/filming

Paxson, M. C. (1995). Increasing survey response rates: Practical instructions from the total design method. *The Cornell Hotel and Restaurant Administration Quarterly*, *36*(4), 66–73.

Pearce, D. G. (2008). A needs-function model of tourism distribution. *Annals of Tourism Research*, *35*(1), 148–168. doi:10.1016/j.annals.2007.06.011

Petric, L. (2003). Constraints and possibilities of the rural development with special stress on the case of Croatia. European Regional Science Association, 1-28.

Petrick, J. F. (2004a). Are Loyal visitors desired visitors? *Tourism Management*, *25*(4), 463–470. doi:10.1016/S0261-5177(03)00116-X

Petrick, J. F. (2004b). First timers' and repeaters' perceived value. *Journal of Travel Research*, *43*(1), 29–38. doi:10.1177/0047287504265509

Petrick, J. F. (2004c). The roles of quality, value and satisfaction in predicting cruise passengers' behavioral intentions. *Journal of Travel Research*, *42*(4), 397–407. doi:10.1177/0047287504263037

Petrick, J. F. (2005). Segmenting cruise passengers with price sensitivity. *Tourism Management*, *26*(5), 753–762. doi:10.1016/j.tourman.2004.03.015

Petrick, J. F., Li, K., & Park, S. (2007). Cruise Passengers' Decision-Making Processes. *Journal of Travel & Tourism Marketing*, *23*(1), 1–15. doi:10.1300/J073v23n01_01

Phelps, A. (1986). Holiday destination image—the problem of assessment: An example developed in Menorca. *Tourism Management*, *7*(3), 168–180. doi:10.1016/0261-5177(86)90003-8

Phillips, R. (2005). *Pricing and Revenue Optimization*. Palo Alto, CA: Stanford University Press.

Pike, S. (2015, December 17). *Destination marketing: Essentials* (2nd ed.). New York, NY: Routledge.

Pike, S. (2002). Destination image analysis: A review of 142 papers from 1973-2000. *Tourism Management*, *23*(5), 541–549. doi:10.1016/S0261-5177(02)00005-5

Pike, S. (2008). *Destination marketing: An integrated marketing communication approach*. Oxford, UK: Butterworth-Heinemann, Elsevier.

Pike, S. (2009). Destination brand positions of a competitive set of near-home destinations. *Tourism Management*, *30*(6), 857–866. doi:10.1016/j.tourman.2008.12.007

Pike, S. (2015). *Destination Marketing Essentials* (2nd ed.). London: Taylor and Francis.

Pike, S., & Ryan, C. (2004). Destination positioning analysis through a comparison of cognitive, affective, and conative perceptions. *Journal of Travel Research*, *42*(4), 333–342. doi:10.1177/0047287504263029

Pizam, A. (1999). A Comprehensive Approach to Classifying Acts of Crime and Violence at Tourism Destinations. *Journal of Travel Research*, *38*(1), 5–12. doi:10.1177/004728759903800103

Pizam, A., & Mansfeld, Y. (Eds.). (1999). *Consumer behavior in travel and tourism*. Binghamtom. Haworth Press.

Pourová, M. (2002). *Agroturistika [Agrotourism]*. Praha: CREDIT.

Prayag, G., Hosany, S., Nunkoo, R., & Alders, T. (2013). London residents' support for the 2012 Olympic Games: The mediating effect of overall attitude. *Tourism Management*, *36*, 629–640. doi:10.1016/j.tourman.2012.08.003

Prem, C., Arrowsmith, C., & Jackson, M. (2004). Determining Hiking Experiences in Nature-based Tourist Destinations. *Tourism Management*, *25*(1), 31–43. doi:10.1016/S0261-5177(03)00057-8

Compilation of References

Puczkó, L., & Rátz, T. (2006). 10 Product Development and Diversification in Hungary. Tourism in the new Europe: The challenges and opportunities of EU enlargement, 116.

Puczkó, L., & Rátz, T. (2000). Tourist and resident perceptions of the physical impacts of tourism at Lake Balaton, Hungary: Issues for sustainable tourism management. *Journal of Sustainable Tourism*, *8*(6), 458–478. doi:10.1080/09669580008667380

Puri, A. (2007). The web of insights-The art and practice of webnography. *International Journal of Market Research*, *49*(3), 387–408. doi:10.1177/147078530704900308

Quan, S., & Wang, N. (2004). Towards a Structural Model of the Tourist Experience: An Illustration. *Tourism Management*, *25*(3), 297–305. doi:10.1016/S0261-5177(03)00130-4

Qu, H., Kim, L. H., & Im, H. H. (2011). A model of destination branding: Integrating the concepts of the branding and destination image. *Tourism Management*, *32*(3), 465–476. doi:10.1016/j.tourman.2010.03.014

Qu, H., & Ping, W. Y. E. (1999). A service performance model of Hong Kong Cruise travelers' motivation factors and satisfaction. *Tourism Management*, *20*(2), 237–244. doi:10.1016/S0261-5177(98)00073-9

Quinlan, T. (2008). *A stakeholder approach to the branding of urban tourism destinations* (Master Thesis). Waterford Institute of Technology, Ireland.

Quinn, B. (2006). Problematising 'festival tourism' arts festivals and sustainable development in Ireland. *Journal of Sustainable Tourism*, *14*(3), 288–306. doi:10.1080/09669580608669060

Qui, Y., & Qui, H. (2015). Nonutilitarian tourism destination positioning: A case study in China. *International Journal of Tourism Research*, *17*(4), 388–398. doi:10.1002/jtr.2005

Raab, C., Mayer, K., Kim, Y. S., & Shoemaker, S. (2009). Price-sensitivity measurement: A tool for restaurant menu pricing. *Journal of Hospitality & Tourism Research (Washington, D.C.)*, *33*(1), 93–105. doi:10.1177/1096348008329659

Rabanser, U., & Ricci, F. (2005). Recommender systems: Do they have a viable business model in e-tourism? *Information and Communication Technologies in Tourism*, *2005*, 160–171.

Radojevic, T., Stanisic, N., & Stanic, N. (2015). Solo travellers assign higher ratings than families: Examining customer satisfaction by demographic group. *Tourism Management Perspectives*, *16*, 247–258. doi:10.1016/j.tmp.2015.08.004

Rahman, S. (2017). Tourism destination marketing using Facebook as a promotional tool. *IOSR Journal of Humanities and Social Science*, *22*(2), 87–90. doi:10.9790/0837-2202018790

Ram, Y., Björk, P., & Weidenfeld, A. (2016). Authenticity and place attachment of major visitor attractions. *Tourism Management*, *52*, 110–122. doi:10.1016/j.tourman.2015.06.010

Rao, V. R. (2009). *Handbook of pricing research in marketing*. Edward Elgar Publishing. doi:10.4337/9781848447448

Rasmussen, S. E., Ostergaard, P., & Beckmann, C. S. (2006). *Essentials of social Science Research Methodology. Southern Denmark* University Press.

Rasoolimanesh, S. M., Ringle, C. M., Jaafar, M., & Ramayah, T. (2017). Urban vs. rural destinations: Residents' perceptions, community participation and support for tourism development. *Tourism Management*, *60*, 147–158. doi:10.1016/j.tourman.2016.11.019

Rawlinson, S., & Wiltshier, P. (2016). *Developing a wellness destination.* The Routledge Handbook of Health Tourism.

Raza, S. A. (2015). An integrated approach to price differentiation and inventory decisions with demand leakage. *International Journal of Production Economics*, *164*, 105–117. doi:10.1016/j.ijpe.2014.12.020

Reece, W. S. (2009). *The economics of tourism.* Pearson Education Inc.

Reeve, K. (2015). *Cultural and Creative Strategy Review: Bath and North-East Somerset 2015-2020.* Academic Press.

Reid, L. J., & Reid, S. D. (1993). Communicating tourism suppliers: Services building repeat visitor relationships. *Journal of Travel & Tourism Marketing*, *2*(2/3), 3–20.

Resnick, P., & Zeckhauser, R. (2002). Trust among strangers in Internet transactions: Empirical analysis of eBay's reputation system. In *The Economics of the Internet and E-commerce* (pp. 127–157). Emerald Group Publishing Limited. doi:10.1016/S0278-0984(02)11030-3

ReviewPro. (2017). *Destination Analytics.* Retrieved 30 October 2017, from https://www.reviewpro.com/products/destination-analytics/

Rezende-Parker, A. M., Morisson, A. M., & Ismail, J. A. (2003). Dazed and confused? An exploratory study of the image of Brazil as a travel destination. *Journal of Vacation Marketing*, *9*(3), 243–259. doi:10.1177/135676670300900304

Richards, G., & Hall, D. (2002). The community: a sustainable concept in tourism development? In G. Richards & D. Hall (Eds.), *Tourism and Sustainable Community Development* (pp. 1–15). Routledge.

Rickly Boyd, J. (2012). Authenticity & Aura: A Benjaminian approach to tourism. *Annals of Tourism Research*, *30*(1), 269–289. doi:10.1016/j.annals.2011.05.003

Ritchie, J. R. B., & Crouch, G. I. (2003). *The Competitive Destination: A Sustainable Tourism Perspective.* Wallingford, UK: CABI Publishing. doi:10.1079/9780851996646.0000

Rittichainuwat, B. N., & Chakraborty, G. (2009). Perceived Travel Risks Regarding Terrorism and Disease: The case of Thailand. *Tourism Management*, *30*(3), 410–418. doi:10.1016/j.tourman.2008.08.001

Robertson, D. M. H. (2015). Heritage interpretation, place branding and experiential marketing in the destination management of geotourism sites. *Translation Spaces*, *4*(2), 289–309. doi:10.1075/ts.4.2.06rob

Robinson, P., Fallon, P., Cameron, H., & Crotts, J. C. (Eds.). (2016). *Operations management in the travel industry*. Oxford, UK: Cabi. doi:10.1079/9781780646107.0000

Rockart, J. F. (1979). Chief executives define their own data needs. *Harvard Business Review*, *57*(2), 238–241. PMID:10297607

Rodríguez del Bosque, I., & San Martín, H. (2008). Tourist satisfaction a cognitive-affective model. *Annals of Tourism Research*, *35*(2), 551–573. doi:10.1016/j.annals.2008.02.006

Rogers Everett, M. (1995). Diffusion of innovations. New York: Academic Press.

Rogers, T., & Davidson, R. (2015). *Marketing destinations and venues for conferences, conventions and business events: A convention and event perspective (Events management)*. New York, NY: Routledge.

Rohm, H. (2002). Performance measurement in action. *Perform*, *2*(2), 2–5.

Roselló, J. A., Riera, A., & Sausó, A. (2004). The economic determinants of seasonal patterns. *Annals of Tourism Research*, *31*(3), 697–711. doi:10.1016/j.annals.2004.02.001

Rosen, S. (1974). Hedonic prices and implicit markets: Product differentiation in pure competition. *Journal of Political Economy*, *82*(1), 34–55. doi:10.1086/260169

Rosselló, J., & Sansó, A. (2017). Yearly, monthly and weekly seasonality of tourism demand: A decomposition analysis. *Tourism Management*, *60*, 379–389. doi:10.1016/j.tourman.2016.12.019

Russel, J., Ward, L., & Pratt, G. (1981). Affective quality attributed to environments: A factor analytic study. *Environment and Behavior*, *13*(3), 259–288. doi:10.1177/0013916581133001

Russell, J. (1980). A circumplex model of affect. *Journal of Personality and Social Psychology*, *39*(6), 1161–1178. doi:10.1037/h0077714

Russell, J., & Pratt, G. (1980). A description of the affective quality attributed to environments. *Journal of Personality and Social Psychology*, *38*(2), 311–322. doi:10.1037/0022-3514.38.2.311

Russell, J., & Snodgrass, J. (1987). Emotion and the environment. In D. Stokols & I. Altman (Eds.), *Handbook of Environmental Psychology* (Vol. 1, pp. 245–281). New York: John Wiley & Sons.

Russo, A. P. (2002). The "vicious circle" of tourism development in heritage cities. *Annals of Tourism Research*, *29*(1), 165–182. doi:10.1016/S0160-7383(01)00029-9

Ruzzier, K., & de Chernatony, L. (2013). Developing and applying a place brand identity model: The case of Slovenia. *Journal of Business Research*, *66*(1), 45–52. doi:10.1016/j.jbusres.2012.05.023

Ryan, C., & Gu, H. (2007). Destination branding and marketing: the role of marketing organisations. In H. Oh (Ed.), *The handbook of destination marketing*. Oxford, UK: Elsevier.

Sachs, S., & Ruhli, E. (2011). *Stakeholders Matter*. Cambridge, UK: Cambridge University Press. doi:10.1017/CBO9781139026963

Sainaghi, R., & De Carlo, M. (2016). How to Create Destination Capabilities in the Field of New Product Development. In H. Pechlaner & E. Innerhofer (Eds.), Competence-Based Innovation in Hospitality and Tourism (pp. 185-196). Routledge.

Sainaghi, R. (2006). From Contents to Processes: Versus a Dynamic Destination Management Model (DDMM). *Tourism Management*, *27*(5), 1053–1063. doi:10.1016/j.tourman.2005.09.010

Sainaghi, R. (2017). *Destination management e strategie competitive nel settore funiviario: il caso SIT (Alta Valcamonica)*. Milano: Edizioni LUMI.

Sainaghi, R., & Baggio, R. (2017). Complexity traits and dynamics of tourism destinations. *Tourism Management*, *63*, 368–382. doi:10.1016/j.tourman.2017.07.004

Sainaghi, R., & Canali, S. (2009a). Posizionamento competitivo delle urban destination e performance delle imprese alberghiere: Il caso Milano. *Economia & Management*, *9*(3), 83–100.

Sainaghi, R., & Canali, S. (2009b). *Commercial mix, seasonality and daily hotel performance: the case of Milan. Strategic management engineering: Enterprise, environment and crisis*. Chengdu, Sichuan, China: Sichuan University Press.

Sainaghi, R., & Canali, S. (2011). Exploring the effects of destination's positioning on hotels' performance: The Milan case. *Tourismos: An International Multidisciplinary Journal of Tourism*, *6*(2), 121–138.

Sainaghi, R., & Mauri, A. (2018). The Milan World Expo 2015: Hospitality operating performance and seasonality effects. *International Journal of Hospitality Management*, *72*, 32–46. doi:10.1016/j.ijhm.2017.12.009

San Martín, H., & del Bosque, I. R. (2008). Exploring the cognitive–affective nature of destination image and the role of psychological factors in its formation. *Tourism Management*, *29*(2), 263–277. doi:10.1016/j.tourman.2007.03.012

Sanders, L. (2011). *Developing New Products and Services: Learning, Differentiation, and Innovation*. Business Expert Press. doi:10.4128/9781606492420

Saunders, M., Lewis, P., & Thornhill, A. (2012). *Research methods for business students* (6th ed.). Harlow, UK: Pearson Education.

Saveriades, S. (2000). Establishing the social tourism carrying capacity for the tourist resorts of the east coast of the Republic of Cyprus. *Tourism Management*, *21*(2), 147–156. doi:10.1016/S0261-5177(99)00044-8

Schaal, D. (2013). *Travelers Visit 38 Sites Before Booking a Vacation, Study Says*. Retrieved 30 October 2017, from https://skift.com/2013/08/26/travelers-visit-38-sites-before-booking-a-vacation-study-says/

Compilation of References

Schamel, G. (2012). Weekend vs. midweek stays: Modelling hotel room rates in a small market. *International Journal of Hospitality Management, 31*(4), 1113–1118. doi:10.1016/j.ijhm.2012.01.008

Scheyvens, R. (2002). *Tourism for development: Empowering communities.* Pearson Education.

Schrader, K. (2013). *Types of Hotel Ratings Other Than the Star Rating.* Retrieved 24 November 2017, from http://traveltips.usatoday.com/types-hotel-ratings-other-star-rating-108407.html

Schubert, S. F., Brida, J. G., & Risso, W. A. (2011). The impacts of international tourism demand on economic growth of small economics dependent on tourism. *Tourism Management, 32*(2), 377–385. doi:10.1016/j.tourman.2010.03.007

Schuckert, M., Liu, X., & Law, R. (2015). Hospitality and tourism online reviews: Recent trends and future directions. *Journal of Travel & Tourism Marketing, 32*(5), 608–621. doi:10.1080/10548408.2014.933154

Schwartz, Z. (2000). Changes in hotel guests' willingness to pay as the date of stay draws closer. *Journal of Hospitality & Tourism Research (Washington, D.C.), 24*(2), 180–198. doi:10.1177/109634800002400204

Schwartz, Z. (2008). Time, price, and advanced booking of hotel rooms. *International Journal of Hospitality & Tourism Administration, 9*(2), 128–146. doi:10.1080/15256480801907885

Scott, J. (1990). *A matter of record: Documentary sources in social research.* Cambridge, UK: Polity Press.

Seaton, A. V. (1996). Guided by the Dark: From Thanatopsis to Thanatourism. *International Journal of Heritage Studies, 2*(4), 234–244. doi:10.1080/13527259608722178

Seddighi, H., Nuttall, M., & Theocharous, A. (2001). Does cultural background of tourists influence the destination choice? an empirical study with special reference to political instability. *Tourism Management, 22*(2), 181–191. doi:10.1016/S0261-5177(00)00046-7

Segaran, T. (2007). *Programming Collective Intelligence: Building Smart Web 2.0 Applications.* O'Reilly Media, Inc.

Shahzad, S. J. H., Shahbaz, M., Ferrer, R., & Kumar, R. R. (2017). Tourism-led growth hypothesis in the top ten tourist destinations: New evidence using the quantile-on-quantile approach. *Tourism Management, 60*, 223–232. doi:10.1016/j.tourman.2016.12.006

Shankar, V., Venkatesh, A., Hofacker, C., & Naik, P. (2010). Mobile marketing in the retailing environment: Current insights and future research avenues. *Journal of Interactive Marketing, 24*(2), 1–12. doi:10.1016/j.intmar.2010.02.006

Sharpley, R. (1994). *Tourism and tourist motivation.* Huntingdon, UK: Elm Publications.

Sharpley, R. (1994). *Tourism, Tourists and Society.* Huntingdon, UK: ELM Publishers.

Sharpley, R. (2014). Host perceptions of tourism: A review of the research. *Tourism Management, 42*, 37–49. doi:10.1016/j.tourman.2013.10.007

Sheldon, P. J., & Abenoja, T. (2001). Resident attitudes in a mature destination: The case of Waikiki. *Tourism Management, 22*(5), 435–443. doi:10.1016/S0261-5177(01)00009-7

Silva, M., Costa, R., & Moreira, A. (2018). The influence of travel agents and tour operators' perspectives on a tourism destination. The case of Portuguese intermediaries on Brazil's image. *Journal of Hospitality and Tourism Management, 34*, 93–104. doi:10.1016/j.jhtm.2018.01.002

Simonson, I. (2016). Imperfect Progress: An Objective Quality Assessment of the Role of User Reviews in Consumer Decision Making, A Commentary on de Langhe, Fernbach, and Lichtenstein. *The Journal of Consumer Research, 42*(6), 840–845. doi:10.1093/jcr/ucv091

Şimşek, H., & Yıldırım, A. (2011). Sosyal bilimlerde nitel araştırma yöntemleri. Ankara: Seçkin Yayıncılık.

Sims, R. (2009). Food, place and authenticity: Local food and the sustainable tourism experience. *Journal of Sustainable Tourism, 17*(3), 321–336. doi:10.1080/09669580802359293

Sinclair-Maragh, G. (2017). Demographic analysis of residents' support for tourism development in Jamaica. *Journal of Destination Marketing & Management, 6*(1), 5–12. doi:10.1016/j.jdmm.2016.03.005

Sirakaya, E., & Woodside, A. G. (2005). Building and testing theories of decision making by travelers. *Tourism Management, 26*(6), 815–832. doi:10.1016/j.tourman.2004.05.004

Siricharoen, W. V. (2008). Learning Semantic Web from E-Tourism. *Agent and Multi-Agent Systems: Technologies and Applications*, 516-525. doi:10.1007/978-3-540-78582-8_52

Skitka, L. J. (2009). Exploring the "lost and found" of justice theory and research. *Social Justice Research, 22*(1), 98–116. doi:10.100711211-009-0089-0

Slabbert, E., & Saayman, M. (2011). The influence of culture on community perceptions: The case of two South African arts festivals. *Event Management, 15*(2), 197–211. doi:10.3727/152599511X13082349958352

Smith, M., & Puczko, L. (2014). *Routledge Advances in Tourism*. London: Routledge.

Smith, S. J., Parsa, H. G., Bujisic, M., & van der Rest, J. P. (2015). Hotel cancelation policies, distributive and procedural fairness, and consumer patronage: A study of the lodging industry. *Journal of Travel & Tourism Marketing, 32*(7), 886–906. doi:10.1080/10548408.2015.1063864

Smith, V. L. (1998). War and Tourism: An American Ethnography. *Annals of Tourism Research, 25*(1), 202–227. doi:10.1016/S0160-7383(97)00086-8

Son, A., & Pearce, P. (2005). Multi-faceted image assessment. *Journal of Travel & Tourism Marketing, 18*(4), 21–35. doi:10.1300/J073v18n04_02

Compilation of References

Song, M., Noone, B. M., & Mattila, A. S. (2017). A Tale of Two Cultures: Consumer Reactance and Willingness to Book Fenced Rates. *Journal of Travel Research.*

Song, W., Cao, J., & Zheng, M. (2016). Towards an integrative framework of innovation network for new product development project. *Production Planning and Control, 27*(12), 967–978. doi:10.1080/09537287.2016.1167980

Sönmez, V., & Alacapınar, F.G. (2014). Bilimsel Araştırma Yöntemleri. Ankara: Anı Yayıncılık.

Sonmez, S. F. (1998). Tourism, Terrorism and Political Instability. *Annals of Tourism Research, 25*(2), 416–456. doi:10.1016/S0160-7383(97)00093-5

Sonmez, S., Apostolopoulos, Y., & Tarlow, P. (1999). Tourism in Crisis: Managing the Effects of Terrorism. *Journal of Travel Research, 38*(1), 13–18. doi:10.1177/004728759903800104

Sönmez, S., & Sirakaya, E. (2002). A distorted destination image? The case of Turkey. *Journal of Travel Research, 41*(2), 185–196. doi:10.1177/004728702237418

So, S.-I., & Morrison, A. M. (2003). Internet marketing in tourism in Asia: An evaluation of the performance of East Asian National Tourism Organization Websites. *Journal of Hospitality & Leisure Marketing.*

Souiden, N., Ladhari, R., & Chiadmi, N. (2017). Destination personality and destination image. *Journal of Hospitality and Tourism Management, 32*, 54–70. doi:10.1016/j.jhtm.2017.04.003

Spacilova, K. (2014). *Destination Spa Darkov: A study reviewing options for a full spa experience* (Maters Dissertation Thesis).

Stanisic, N. (2016). *Recent Trends in Quantitative Research in the Field of Tourism and Hospitality (SSRN Scholarly Paper No. ID 2875849).* Rochester, NY: Social Science Research Network.

Stankova, M., & Vassenska, I. (2015). Raising cultural awareness of local traditions through festival tourism. *Tourism & Management Studies, 11*(1).

Stathi, A., & Avgerinos, A. (2001). Bathing in the healing waters. A case-study of the development of thermal spas in Greece. *World Leisure Journal, 43*(1), 41–51. doi:10.1080/04419057.2001.9674218

Steiner, C. J., & Reisinger, Y. (2006). Understanding Existential Authenticity. *Annals of Tourism Research, 33*(2), 299–318. doi:10.1016/j.annals.2005.08.002

Stepchenkova, S., & Mills, J. E. (2010). Destination image: A meta-analysis of 2000 - 2007 Research. *Journal of Hospitality Marketing & Management, 19*(6), 575–609. doi:10.1080/19368623.2010.493071

Stepchenkova, S., & Morrison, A. M. (2008). Russia's destination image among American pleasure travelers: Revisiting Echtner and Ritchie. *Tourism Management, 29*(3), 548–560. doi:10.1016/j.tourman.2007.06.003

Sterne, E. (2002). *Web metrics. Proven methods for measuring Web site success*. New York: Wiley Publishing, Inc.

Stigler, G. (1987). *A Theory of Price*. New York: Macmillan.

Strauss, A. L., & Corbin, J. M. (2008). *Basics of qualitative research: Techniques and procedures for developing grounded theory*. London: Sage publications Limited.

Stylidis, D., Biran, A., Sit, J., & Szivas, E. (2014). Residents' support for tourism development: The role of residents' place image and perceived tourism impacts. *Tourism Management*, *45*, 260–274. doi:10.1016/j.tourman.2014.05.006

Suh, E., Lim, S., Hwang, H., & Kim, S. (2004). A prediction model for the purchase probability of anonymous customers to support real time web marketing: A case study. *Expert Systems with Applications*, *27*(2), 245–255. doi:10.1016/j.eswa.2004.01.008

Sun, A., Chi, C. G.-Q., & Xu, H. (2013). Developing destination loyalty: The case of Hainan Island, China. *Annals of Tourism Research*, *43*, 547–577.

Sun, S., Fong, L. H. N., Law, R., & Luk, C. (2016). An investigation of Gen-Y's online hotel information search: The case of Hong Kong. *Asia Pacific Journal of Tourism Research*, *21*(4), 443–456. doi:10.1080/10941665.2015.1062405

Supphellen, M., & Helgeson, J. G. (2004). A conceptual and measurement comparison of self-congruity and brand personality. *International Journal of Market Research*, *46*(2), 205–233. doi:10.1177/147078530404600201

Surowiecki, J. (2004). *The Wisdom of Crowds: Why the Many are Smarter Than the Few and how Collective Wisdom Shapes Business, Economies, Societies, and Nations*. Doubleday.

Swarbrooke, J., & Horner, S. (2001). *Business travel and tourism*. Oxford, UK: Routledge.

Tabacchi, M. (2010). Current Research and Events in the Spa industry. *Cornell University*, *51*(1), 102–117.

Tang, Y. (2014). Travel Motivation, Destination Image and Visitor Satisfaction of International Tourists After the 2008 Wenchuan Earthquake: A Structural Modelling Approach. *Asia Pacific Journal of Tourism Research*, *19*(11), 1260–1277. doi:10.1080/10941665.2013.844181

Tapachai, N., & Waryszak, R. (2000). An examination of the role of beneficial image in tourist destination selection. *Journal of Travel Research*, *39*(1), 37–44. doi:10.1177/004728750003900105

Tascı, A. D. A. (2007). Assessment of factors influencing destination image using a multiple regression model. *Tourism Review*, *62*(2), 23–30. doi:10.1108/16605370780000311

Tasci, A. D. A. (2011). Destination branding and positioning. In Y. Wang & A. Pizam (Eds.), *Destination marketing and management theories and applications*. Oxfordshire, UK: CABI. doi:10.1079/9781845937621.0113

Tasci, A. D. A., & Gartner, W. C. (2007). Destination image and its functional relationships. *Journal of Travel & Tourism Marketing, 45*(4), 413–425.

Tasci, A. D. A., & Gartner, W. C. (2007). Destination image and its functional relationships. *Journal of Travel Research, 45*(4), 413–425. doi:10.1177/0047287507299569

Taşçı, A. D. A., Gartner, W. C., & Cavusgil, S. T. (2007). Conceptualization And Operationalization of Destination Image. *Journal of Hospitality & Tourism Research (Washington, D.C.), 31*(2), 194–223. doi:10.1177/1096348006297290

Tasci, A. D. A., & Kozak, M. (2006). Destination brands vs destination images: Do we know what we mean? *Journal of Vacation Marketing, 12*(4), 299–317. doi:10.1177/1356766706067603

Taylor, D. T. F., Robert, R., & Clabaugh, T. (1993). A Comparison of Characteristics, Regional Expenditures, and Economic Impact of Visitors to Historical Sites with Other Recreational Visitors. *Journal of Travel Research, 32*(1), 30–35. doi:10.1177/004728759303200105

Telfer, D. J., & Sharpley, R. (2008). *Tourism and development in the developing world*. Abingdon, UK: Routledge.

Teye, V. B., & Leclerc, D. (1998). Product and service delivery satisfaction among north American cruise passengers. *Tourism Management, 19*(2), 153–160. doi:10.1016/S0261-5177(97)00107-6

The Guardian. (2017). Retrieved October 1, 2017, from https://www.theguardian.com/travel/2017/jul/31/destination-unknown-the-new-way-to-book-a-mystery-holiday-srprs-me

Thompson, K., & Schofield, P. (2007). An investigation of the relationship between public transport performance and destination satisfaction. *Journal of Transport Geography, 15*(2), 136–144. doi:10.1016/j.jtrangeo.2006.11.004

Thrane, C. (2005). Hedonic price models and sun-and-beach package tours: The Norwegian case. *Journal of Travel Research, 43*(3), 302–308. doi:10.1177/0047287504272034

Tierney, P. (2000). Internet-based evaluation of tourism web site effectiveness: Methodological issues and survey results. *Journal of Travel Research, 39*(2), 212–219. doi:10.1177/004728750003900211

Tilstone, C. (Ed.). (1998). *The technique of observation. In Observing teaching and learning: principle and practice* (pp. 32–53). London: David Fulton Publishers.

Trimi, S., & Berbegal-Mirabent, J. (2012). Business Model Innovation in Entrepreneurship. *International Entrepreneurship and Management Journal, 8*(4), 449-465.

TripAdvisor. (2014a). *More reviews, higher rating*. Retrieved from https://www.tripadvisor.com/TripAdvisorInsights/n2086/more-reviews-higher-rating

TripAdvisor. (2014b). *PhoCusWright insights plus TripAdvisor tips, Part 1*. Retrieved 29 October 2017, from https://www.tripadvisor.com/TripAdvisorInsights/n2121/phocuswright-insights-plus-tripadvisor-tips-part-1

TripAdvisor. (2014c). *What is considered fraud?* Retrieved from http://www.tripadvisorsupport.com/hc/en-us/articles/200615037-What-is-considered-fraud-

Tripbarometer. (2013). *TripBarometer Reveals Travel, Green and Mobile Trends.* Retrieved 29 October 2017, from https://www.tripadvisor.com/TripAdvisorInsights/n627/tripbarometer-reveals-travel-green-and-mobile-trends-infographic

Tso, A., & Law, R. (2005). Analysing the online pricing practices of hotels in Hong Kong. *International Journal of Hospitality Management, 24*(2), 301–307. doi:10.1016/j.ijhm.2004.09.002

Turismo de Portugal (2013). *Anuário das estatísticas do turismo 2012.* Lisbon: Turismo de Portugal, IP.

Turner, L., & Reisinger, Y. (2001). Shopping satisfaction for domestic tourists. *Journal of Retailing and Consumer Services, 8*(1), 15–27. doi:10.1016/S0969-6989(00)00005-9

Turtureanu, I. A. (2005). *Economic impact of tourism, Acta Universitatis Danubius.* Romania: University of Galati.

Ulrich, R. S., Simons, R. F., Losito B. D. & Fiorito, E. (1991). Stress recovery during exposure to natural and urban environments. *Journal of Environmental Psychology, 11*, 201-230.

United Nations World Tourism Organisation. (2007). *A practical guide to tourism destination Management UNWTO.* Madrid: Author.

United Nations World Tourism Organization. (2017). *Tourism for sustainable development in least developed countries: Leveraging resources for sustainable tourism with the enhanced integrated framework.* Geneva, Switzerland: United Nations Conference on Trade and Development. Retrieved from https://www.e-unwto.org/doi/pdf/10.18111/9789284418848

UNWTO. (2014). *Online Guest Reviews and Hotel Classification Systems: An Integrated Approach.* Madrid: UNWTO.

UNWTO. (2016). *World Tourism Organization UNWTO: Tourism Highlights.* Retrieved from http://www.e-unwto.org/doi/pdf/10.18111/9789284418145

Upchurch, R. S., & Teivane, U. (2000). Resident perceptions of tourism development in Riga, Latvia. *Tourism Management, 21*(5), 499–507. doi:10.1016/S0261-5177(99)00104-1

Upshaw, L. (1995). *Building brand identity.* New York: John Wiley.

Usakli, A., & Baloglu, S. (2011). Brand personality of tourist destinations: An application of self-congruity theory. *Tourism Management, 32*(1), 114–127. doi:10.1016/j.tourman.2010.06.006

Vallbona, M. C., & Dimitrovski, D. (2016). Well-being as driving force for economic recuperation of traditional spas, Lleida, Spain. *Tourism in Function of Development of The Republic of Serbia, 1st International Scientific Conferences,* 173.

Van Gelder, S. (2004). Global brand strategy. *Journal of Brand Management, 12*(1), 39–48. doi:10.1057/palgrave.bm.2540200

Compilation of References

Van Rensburg, M. J. (2014). Relevance of travel agents in the digital age. *African Journal of Hospitality, Tourism and Leisure*, *3*(2), 1–9. Retrieved from https://core.ac.uk/download/pdf/43178196.pdf

Vargas, A., Oom, P., Da Costa, J., & Albino, S. (2015). Residents' attitude and level of destination development: An international comparison. *Tourism Management*, *48*(3), 199–210. doi:10.1016/j.tourman.2014.11.005

Vargas, A., Plaza, M. A., & Porras, N. (2009). Understanding residents' attitudes toward the development of industrial tourism in a former mining community. *Journal of Travel Research*, *47*(3), 373–387. doi:10.1177/0047287508322783

Varian, H. R. (1989). Price discrimination. Handbook of industrial organization, 1, 597–654.

Varian, H. R. (1996). Differential pricing and efficiency. *First Monday*, *1*(2). doi:10.5210/fm.v1i2.473

Vergori, A. S. (2017). Patterns of seasonality and tourism demand forecasting. *Tourism Economics*, *23*(5), 1011–1027. doi:10.1177/1354816616656418

Vianelli, D. (2011). Il comportamento di scelta del prodotto crocieristico nel mercato italiano. *Micro & Macro Marketing*, *20*(1), 19–38.

Viglia, G., & Abrate, G. (2017). When distinction does not pay off-Investigating the determinants of European agritourism prices. *Journal of Business Research*, *80*, 45–52. doi:10.1016/j.jbusres.2017.07.004

Viglia, G., Mauri, A., & Carricano, M. (2016). The exploration of hotel reference prices under dynamic pricing scenarios and different forms of competition. *International Journal of Hospitality Management*, *52*, 46–55. doi:10.1016/j.ijhm.2015.09.010

Viglia, G., Minazzi, R., & Buhalis, D. (2016). The influence of e-word-of-mouth on hotel occupancy rate. *International Journal of Contemporary Hospitality Management*, *28*(9), 2035–2051. doi:10.1108/IJCHM-05-2015-0238

Vinod, B. (2004). Unlocking the value of revenue management in the hotel industry. *Journal of Revenue and Pricing Management*, *3*(2), 178–190. doi:10.1057/palgrave.rpm.5170105

Visit Bath. (2017a). *Executive Summary: Destination Marketing Strategy 2017-2020*. Available at: https://visitbath.co.uk/dbimgs/Summary%20of%20Bath%20Destination%20Marketing%20Strategy%20October%202017.pdf

Visit Bath. (2017b). *Executive Summary: Destination Marketing Strategy 2017-2020*. Available at: https://visitbath.co.uk/dbimgs/Summary%20of%20Bath%20Destination%20Marketing%20Strategy%20October%202017.pdf

Visit Buxton. (2016). *Visit Buxton Leading Spa Town*. Available at: http://www.visitbuxton.co.uk/

Visit Harrogate. (2016). *Visit Harrogate*. Available at: http://www.visitharrogate.co.uk/

Wall, G., & Yan, M. (2003). Disaggregating visitor flows — the example of China. *Tourism Analysis*, *7*(3/4), 191–205.

Wall-Reinius, A., Loannides, D., & Zampoukos, K. (2017). Does geography matter in all-inclusive resort tourism? An investigation of the marketing approach of major Scandinavian tourist operators. *Tourism Geographies: An International Journal of Tourism Space, Place and Environment*, 1-19. 10.1080/14616688.2017.1375975

Walton, J. K. (2012). Health, sociability, politics and culture. Spas in history, spas and history: An overview. *Journal of Tourism History*, *4*(1), 1–14. doi:10.1080/1755182X.2012.671372

Walton, J. K. (2014). Family firm, health resort and industrial colony: The grand hotel and mineral springs at Mondariz Balneario, Spain, 1873–1932. *Business History*, *56*(7), 1037–1056. doi:10.1080/00076791.2013.839661

Wan, C. S., Su, A. Y., & Shih, C. C. (2000). A study of Website content analysis of international tourist hotels and tour wholesalers in Taiwan. *Advances in Hospitality and Tourism Research, Volume 5: Proceedings of the Annual Graduate Conference in Hospitality and Tourism Research*, 132-137.

Wang, Y. C., & Pizam, A. (2011). Destination marketing and management: Theories and application. Oxford, UK: The Centre for Agriculture and Bioscience International (CABI) Publishing. doi:10.1079/9781845937621.0000

Wang, C., & Hsu, M. K. (2010). The relationships of destination image, satisfaction, and behavioral intentions: An integrated model. *Journal of Travel & Tourism Marketing*, *27*(8), 829–843. doi:10.1080/10548408.2010.527249

Wang, N. (1999). Rethinking authenticity in tourism experience. *Annals of Tourism Research*, *26*(2), 349–370. doi:10.1016/S0160-7383(98)00103-0

Wang, Y., & Davidson, M. C. G. (2010). Pre- and post-trip perceptions: An insight into Chinese package holiday market to Australia. *Journal of Vacation Marketing*, *16*(2), 111–123. doi:10.1177/1356766709357488

Wang, Y., & Krakover, S. (2008). Destination marketing: Competition, cooperation or coopetition? *International Journal of Contemporary Hospitality Management*, *20*(2), 126–141. doi:10.1108/09596110810852122

Wang, Y., Yu, Q., & Fesenmaier, D. R. (2002). Defining the virtual tourist community: Implications for tourism marketing. *Tourism Management*, *23*(4), 407–417. doi:10.1016/S0261-5177(01)00093-0

Ward, C., & Berno, T. (2011). Beyond social exchange theory: Attitudes toward tourists. *Annals of Tourism Research*, *38*(4), 1556–1569. doi:10.1016/j.annals.2011.02.005

Weaver, D. B. (2006). *Sustainable tourism: Theory and practice*. Routledge.

Weinreich, N. (1999). *Hands-On Social Marketing: A Step-by-Step Guide*. Thousand Oaks, CA: SAGE Publications.

Weiss, H. M., Suckow, K., & Cropanzano, R. (1999). Effects of justice conditions on discrete emotions. *The Journal of Applied Psychology*, *84*(5), 786–794. doi:10.1037/0021-9010.84.5.786

Wells, J. D., Valacich, J. S., & Hess, T. J. (2011). What signal are you sending? What website quality influences perceptions of product quality and purchase intentions. *Management Information Systems Quarterly*, *35*(2), 373–396. doi:10.2307/23044048

Wetzer, I. M., Zeelenberg, M., & Pieters, R. (2007). "Never eat in that restaurant, I did!": Exploring why people engage in negative word-of-mouth communication. *Psychology and Marketing*, *24*(8), 661–680. doi:10.1002/mar.20178

White, P. J., & Mulligan, G. F. (2002). Hedonic estimates of lodging rates in the four corners region. *The Professional Geographer*, *54*(4), 533–543. doi:10.1111/0033-0124.00348

Whitty, M. T., & Joinson, A. (2008). *Truth, Lies and Trust on the Internet* (1st ed.). London: Routledge.

Wiggins, J. (2004). Motivation, ability and opportunity to participate a reconceptualization of the RAND model of audience development. *Marketing Management*, *7*(1), 22-33.

Wirtz, J., & Kimes, S. E. (2007). The Moderating Role of Familiarity in Fairness Perceptions of Revenue Management Pricing. *Journal of Service Research*, *9*(3), 229–240. doi:10.1177/1094670506295848

Wirtz, J., Kimes, S. E., Ho Pheng Theng, J., & Patterson, P. (2003). Revenue management: Resolving potential customer conflicts. *Journal of Revenue and Pricing Management*, *2*(3), 216–228. doi:10.1057/palgrave.rpm.5170068

Wolfinbarger, M., & Gilly, M. C. (2003). ETailQ: Dimensionalizing, Measuring and Predicting eTail Quality. *Journal of Retailing*, *79*(3), 183–198. doi:10.1016/S0022-4359(03)00034-4

Woodland, M., & Acott, T. G. (2007). Sustainability and local tourism branding in England's South Downs. *Journal of Sustainable Tourism*, *15*(6), 715–734. doi:10.2167/jost652.0

Woodside, A., Mir, V. R., & Duque, M. (2011). Tourism's destination dominance and marketing website usefulness. *International Journal of Contemporary Hospitality Management*, *23*(4), 552–564. doi:10.1108/09596111111130038

Woo, E., Uysal, M., & Sirgy, M. J. (2018). Tourism Impact and Stakeholders' Quality of Life. *Journal of Hospitality & Tourism Research (Washington, D.C.)*, *42*(2), 260–286. doi:10.1177/1096348016654971

World Atlas. (2017). *Map of Malawi*. Retrieved September 18, 2017 from http://www.worldatlas.com/webimage/countrys/africa/mw.htm

Xia, L., Monroe, K. B., & Cox, J. L. (2004). The Price Is Unfair! A Conceptual Framework of Price Fairness Perceptions. *Journal of Marketing*, *68*(4), 1–15. doi:10.1509/jmkg.68.4.1.42733

Xiang, Y. (2013). The characteristics of independent Chinese outbound tourists. *Tourism Planning & Development*, *10*(2), 134–148. doi:10.1080/21568316.2013.783740

Xie, K. L., Zhang, Z., Zhang, Z., Singh, A., & Lee, S. K. (2016). Effects of managerial response on consumer eWOM and hotel performance: Evidence from TripAdvisor. *International Journal of Contemporary Hospitality Management*, *28*(9), 2013–2034. doi:10.1108/IJCHM-06-2015-0290

Xie, S., Wang, G., Lin, S., & Yu, P. S. (2012). Review Spam Detection via Temporal Pattern Discovery. In *Proceedings of the 18th ACM SIGKDD International Conference on Knowledge Discovery and Data Mining* (pp. 823–831). New York, NY: ACM. 10.1145/2339530.2339662

Xiong, J., Hashim, N. H., & Murphy, J. (2015). Multisensory image as a component of destination image. *Tourism Management Perspectives*, *14*, 34–41. doi:10.1016/j.tmp.2015.03.001

Xu, L., He, P., & Hua, Z. (2014). A new form of hotel to collaborate with a third-party website: Setting online-exclusive rooms. *Asia Pacific Journal of Tourism Research*, *20*(6), 635–655. doi:10.1080/10941665.2014.924975

Yang, H. (2013). Market mavens in social media: Examining young Chinese consumers' viral marketing attitude, eWOW motive, and behaviour. *Journal of Asia-Pacific Business*, *14*(2), 154–178. doi:10.1080/10599231.2013.756337

Yarnal, C. M., & Kerstetter, D. (2005). Casting off: An exploration of cruise ship space, group tour behavior, and social interaction. *Journal of Travel Research*, *43*(4), 368–379. doi:10.1177/0047287505274650

Yasarata, M., Altinay, L., Burns, P., & Okumus, F. (2010). Politics and sustainable tourism development–Can they co-exist? Voices from North Cyprus. *Tourism Management*, *31*(3), 345–356. doi:10.1016/j.tourman.2009.03.016

Yelkur, R., & Nêveda DaCosta, M. M. (2001). Differential pricing and segmentation on the Internet: The case of hotels. *Management Decision*, *39*(4), 252–262. doi:10.1108/00251740110391411

Ye, Q., Law, R., & Gu, B. (2009). The impact of online user reviews on hotel room sales. *International Journal of Hospitality Management*, *28*(1), 180–182. doi:10.1016/j.ijhm.2008.06.011

Ye, Q., Zhang, Z., & Law, R. (2009). Sentiment classification of online reviews to travel destinations by supervised machine learning approaches. *Expert Systems with Applications*, *36*(3), 6527–6535. doi:10.1016/j.eswa.2008.07.035

Yeung, W. L., & Lu, M. (2004). Functional characteristics of commercial web sites: A longitudinal study in Hong Kong. *Information & Management*, *41*(4), 483–495. doi:10.1016/S0378-7206(03)00086-7

Yılmaz, İ., & Çalışkan, C. (2015). Turizm Potansiyeli Olan Bölgelerde Toplumsal Kapasite Algısı: Adıyaman Örneği. *Journal of Yasar University*, *10*(39).

Compilation of References

Yılmaz, Y., Yılmaz, Y., Icigen, E. T., Ekin, Y., & Utku, D. B. (2009). Destination Image: A Comparative Study on Pre and Post Trip Image Variations. *Journal of Hospitality Marketing & Management*, *18*(5), 461–479. doi:10.1080/19368620902950022

Yin, R. K. (2009). Case study research: Design and methods (4th ed.). Thousand Oaks, CA: Sage Publications, Inc.

Yoo, K. H., & Gretzel, U. (2008). The influence of involvement on use and impact of online travel reviews. In Hospitality Information Technology Association (HITA) conference (pp. 15–16). Academic Press.

Yoo, I. Y., Lee, T. J., & Lee, C. K. (2015). Effect of health and wellness values on festival visit motivation. *Asia Pacific Journal of Tourism Research*, *20*(2), 152–170. doi:10.1080/10941665.2013.866970

Yoo, K.-H., Lee, Y., Gretzel, U., & Fesenmaier, D. R. (2009). Trust in travel-related consumer generated media. *Information and Communication Technologies in Tourism*, *2009*, 49–59.

Yoon, Y., Gursoy, D., & Chen, J. S. (1999). An investigation of the relationship between tourism impacts and host communities' characteristics. Anatolia: An International. *Journal of Tourism and Hospitality Research*, *10*(1), 29–44.

Yorkshire Tour Company. (2017). *Insider Tips Seven amazing experiences in Harrogate to make a great day out.* Available at: http://www.theyorkshiretourcompany.com/single-post/2017/03/13/Insider-tips---Seven-amazing-experiences-in-Harrogate-to-make-a-great-day-out

Yousaf, A., Amin, I., & Gupta, A. (2017). Conceptualising Tourist Based Brand-Equity Pyramid: An Application of Keller Brand Pyramid Model to Destinations. *Tourism and Hospitality Management*, *23*(1), 119–137. doi:10.20867/thm.23.1.1

Yüksel, A., & Yüksel, F. (2004). Turizmde Bilimsel Araştırma Yöntemleri. Ankara: Turhan Kitabevi.

Yuksel, A. (2004). Shopping experience evaluation: A case of domestic and international visitors. *Tourism Management*, *25*(6), 751–759. doi:10.1016/j.tourman.2003.09.012

Yuksel, Y., & Bilim, Y. (2009). Interactions between visual appeals, holiday motivations, destination personality and self-image: The implication for destination advertising. *Journal of Travel and Tourism Research*, *9*, 75–104.

Zeithaml, V. A., Parasuraman, A., & Malhotra, A. (2000). *A Conceptual Framework for Understanding E-service Quality: Implications for Future Research and Managerial Practice.* Marketing Science Institute Working Paper Series, Report NO. 00-115.

Zeithaml, V. A. (1988). Consumer perceptions of price, quality and value: A means-end model and synthesis of evidence. *Journal of Marketing*, *5*(3), 2–22. doi:10.2307/1251446

Zhang, Z. J. (2009). Competitive targeted pricing: perspectives from theoretical research. Handbook of Pricing Research in Marketing, 302. doi:10.4337/9781848447448.00023

Zhang, A., Zhong, L. Y., Xu, Y., Wang, H., & Dang, L. (2015). Tourists' Perception of Haze Pollution and the Potential Impacts on Travel: Reshaping the Features of Tourism Seasonality in Beijing, China. *Sustainability*, *7*(3), 2397–2414. doi:10.3390u7032397

Zhang, H., Fu, X., Cai, L. A., & Lu, L. (2014). Destination image and tourist loyalty: A meta-analysis. *Tourism Management*, *40*, 213–223. doi:10.1016/j.tourman.2013.06.006

Zhang, M. (2011). Fencing in the practice of revenue management. In I. Yeoman & U. McMahon-Beattie (Eds.), *Revenue management. A practical pricing perspective*. Basingstoke, UK: Palgrave Macmillan. doi:10.1057/9780230294776_11

Zhang, M., & Bell, P. (2012). Price fencing in the practice of revenue management: An overview and taxonomy. *Journal of Revenue and Pricing Management*, *11*(2), 146–159. doi:10.1057/rpm.2009.25

Zhang, Z., Ye, Q., & Law, R. (2011). Determinants of hotel room price: An exploration of travelers' hierarchy of accommodation needs. *International Journal of Contemporary Hospitality Management*, *23*(7), 972–981. doi:10.1108/09596111111167551

Zhou, L., Ye, S., Pearce, P. L., & Wu, M.-Y. (2014). Refreshing hotel satisfaction studies by reconfiguring customer review data. *International Journal of Hospitality Management*, *38*(Supplement C), 1–10. doi:10.1016/j.ijhm.2013.12.004

Zhu, Y. (2012). Performing heritage: Rethinking authenticity in tourism. *Annals of Tourism Research*, *39*(3), 1495–1513. doi:10.1016/j.annals.2012.04.003

About the Contributors

Mark Anthony Camilleri is a resident academic (Senior Lecturer) in the Department of Corporate Communication at the University of Malta. He successfully finalised his PhD (Management) in three years time at the University of Edinburgh in Scotland - where he was also nominated for his "Excellence in Teaching". During the past years, Mark taught business subjects at under-graduate, vocational and post-graduate levels in Hong Kong, Malta and the UK. Dr Camilleri is a member in the Global Reporting Initiative (GRI)'s Stakeholder Council, where he is representing Europe and Asia's CIS region. He is a scientific expert in research for the Ministero dell' Istruzione, dell' Universita e della Ricerca (in Italy). He is an editorial board member in a number of Springer and Inderscience journals. Mark has published his research in high impact peer-reviewed journals, chapters and conferences. He is a frequent speaker and reviewer at the British Academy of Management, Academy of Management (USA) and in the American Marketing Association's (AMA) annual gatherings. Dr Camilleri has published two Springer textbooks; "Corporate Sustainability, Social Responsibility and Environmental Management: An Introduction to Theory and Practice with Case Studies" (2017), and 'Travel Marketing, Tourism Economics and the Airline Product' (2018). Moreover, in 2017, he edited "CSR 2.0 and the New Era of Corporate Citizenship" (Indexed in Scopus).

* * *

Samuel Adeyinka-Ojo holds a PhD in Hospitality and Tourism from Taylor's University, Malaysia. He is the Head, Department of Marketing, Faculty of Business at Curtin University Malaysia. He teaches hospitality, marketing and tourism courses at the undergraduate programmes and project quality management at the postgraduate level. His research interests include social media marketing in hospitality and tourism, destination branding, guest behaviour, food festivals, green marketing, visitor memorable experience, virtual augmented reality, digital rural tourism, responsible and sustainable practices in rural and ecotourism destinations.

About the Contributors

Caner Çalişkan is an assistant professor and head of tourism management department in the Tourism Faculty of Adıyaman University. Dr. Çalişkan holds a PhD from the Social Sciences Institute of Nevşehir Hacı Bektaş Veli University in Tourism Management and a Master's degree in the Department of Tourism and Hotel Management from the Social Sciences Institute of Mustafa Kemal University. His research interests include tourism sociology, behavioural sciences and sustainable tourism.

Neslihan Cavlak holds a doctoral degree in of tourism and hotel management from Namık Kemal University, Tekirdağ-Turkey. Dr. Cavlak has a BA in Tourism and Hotel Management at Bilkent University (1999). He received his PhD in Business Administration with a thesis entitled as "The Effects of Customer Experience on Destination Image: A Comparable Study on Turkish and Anzac Tourists". His main research areas include: tourism and hotel management, tourism marketing and tourist behaviour.

Ruziye Cop is a professor of marketing in the department of business administration at Izzet Baysal University, Bolu, Turkey. Prof. Dr. Cop has BA at Gazi University (1984). She received PhD in Business Administration with her thesis entitled as "Physical distribution in enterprises, cost planning and application in pasta sector". Marketing, product and brand management and sales management are her main research areas.

Rui Augusto da Costa was born in Oliveira de Azeméis, district of Aveiro. He graduated in Management and Tourism Planning at the University of Aveiro in 1988. Afterwards, he completed his Master's degree in Innovation and Policy Development at the University of Aveiro. He also holds a PhD in Tourism from the same University. Currently, he is an Assistant Professor in Tourism within the Department of Economics, Management, Industrial Engineering and Tourism at University of Aveiro. He is member of the executive board of DEGEIT and he's also an Integrated Member of the Research Unit on Governance, Competitiveness and Public Policy in the Research Group on Tourism and Development. His research interests include; tourism planning, governance and public policy, territorial dynamics of investment and the financing of small and micro enterprises in the tourism sector. He has participated in several research projects, and he has authored and co-authored several articles in academic journals. He is also a member of the Editorial Board of the Journal of Tourism & Development and member of the Organizing Committee of the International Conference INVTUR.

About the Contributors

Bekir Bora Dedeoglu earned his Ph.D. degree from in the tourism management department at Akdeniz University and at the present time, is working in the Tourism Faculty at the Nevşehir Hacı Bektaş Veli University in Turkey. His research areas include destination marketing, destination branding, tourist behavior, and hospitality marketing. He has published articles in professional journals including the International Journal of Contemporary Hospitality Management, the Journal of Destination Marketing and Management, International Journal of Hospitality Management, the Journal of Travel & Tourism Marketing, and Anatolia: An International Journal of Tourism and Hospitality Research. Dr. Dedeoğlu has also served as reviewer for top tourism and hospitality journals such as Tourism Management, Tourism Management Perspectives, International Journal of Hospitality Management, among others.

James Malitoni Chilembwe is a PhD student at Glasgow Caledonian University, Scotland, United Kingdom and holds a Master of Science in International Tourism Enterprise from the same institution obtained in 2012 and possesses a number of IATA/UFTAA Travel and Tourism professional qualifications, Tourism Management and Teacher Training qualifications. He is also a lecturer in Tourism and Travel Management at Mzuzu University in the Faculty of Tourism, Hospitality and Management since May, 2014. Previously, he worked with Malawi Institute of Tourism as a lecturer in Travel and Tourism Management from January, 2005 to April, 2014. He has authored and published a number of journal tourism articles and two book chapters. His research interest is about tourism transport and travel, more specifically related to tourism sustainability, corporate social responsibility, and tourism marketing.

Elson Mankhomwa is a lecturer in Hospitality Management at the Malawi Institute of Tourism. He possesses an MSc degree in International Tourism Enterprise from Glasgow Caledonian University and a BTech degree in Food and Beverage Management from Cape Peninsula University of Technology. He is an author of two books and several articles in tourism, food and beverages and sports especially boxing. His research interest is in tourism marketing management, food and beverage service management and sports.

Ana Mano graduated in Tourism in 2012 and completed the Master's degree in Management in 2014, at the University of Aveiro. She worked in tourism consultancy in 2015, while developing some researches on destination image and tourism marketing. At the moment, she participates in several research projects and works on the organization of academic conferences. She is member of the Organizing Committee of the International Conference TOURISM promoted by Green Lines Institute for Sustainable Development. She is co-author of several papers in national and international journals.

About the Contributors

Jose Maria Martin is a senior lecturer at the International University of La Rioja, Spain; in the Department of Business. He is also a lecturer of Economic Structure within the School of Economics and Business at the University of Granada, Spain. The interests of his research focus on rural tourism, economic sustainability, seasonality and sustainable development. He is a consultant in tourist planning for diverse Spanish public agencies as well as private companies. His last projects focus on the evaluation of the socioeconomic impact of the tourist events and the design of anti-seasonality policies.

Maria Matiatou is a PhD candidate in Communication, Information and Technology in the Web Society at the Doctoral School of the University of Alcalá de Henares in Spain. She received her M.A. in Strategic Communication and Public Relations with the Graduate School Award from Deree College, the American College of Greece, and her BSc in Political and Economic Sciences from the Law School of the National and Kapodistrian University of Athens. She has held several administrative and teaching positions in the tertiary and secondary education, and currently serves as academic counselor at Deree College, The American College of Greece. Her research interests include Information Technology in the Tourism and Health Industries, Intercultural Communication and Web Design, Destination Marketing, Knowledge Management Systems, Social Marketing, Higher Education Management and Corporate Communication.

Aurelio G. Mauri is Associate Professor of Tourism and Services Marketing at IULM University, Milan, Italy. He has extensive and varied teaching experiences in various European universities. His research interests are service quality, customer satisfaction, revenue management, word-of-mouth and web reviews. He is author of several articles and books. He is the editor of the Italian version of the book "Marketing for Hospitality and Tourism" by Kotler, Bowen and Makens.

Jessica Emily Maxfield is a recent graduate of the University of Derby having gained a distinction in MSc Tourism Management. Her main interests in tourism management are the impacts of niche tourism and the classification of tourism typologies.

Juan Pedro Mellinas is a marketing professor at the Universidad Internacional de La Rioja. He holds a PhD in Business Administration and a Master in Tourism Business Administration.

About the Contributors

António C. Moreira obtained a Bachelor's degree in electrical engineering and a Master's degree in Management from the University of Porto, Portugal. He received his PhD in Management from UMIST-University of Manchester's Institute of Science and Technology, England. He has a solid international background in industry as he worked for a multinational company in Germany as well as in Portugal. He has also been involved in consultancy projects and in research activities. He is an Assistant Professor at the Department of Economics, Management, Industrial Engineering, and Tourism at the University of Aveiro, Portugal, where he is the Coordinator of the Management research area. He is also a member of GOVCOPP research unit.

Victor Ronald Mweiwa is a lecturer in Travel and Tourism Management at the Malawi Institute of Tourism. He holds a Bachelor degree in Tourism Strategic Management, Diploma in Tourism Management and IATA professional qualifications. He has published some research articles in tourism journals. His research interest is tourism marketing, travel agency and tour operations and sustainable tourism management.

Sofia Reino is a Senior Lecturer in Tourism Management at the University of Hertfordshire, UK. Her teaching and research expertise focuses around the application of ICT for improving the competitiveness of accommodation and tourism organisations. Sofia gained her Ph.D. at Queen Margaret University, Edinburgh, with the development of an Assessment Framework for eTourism Capability in Scotland.

Clarinda Rodrigues is a senior lecturer of marketing and head of retail and service management programme at the School of Business and Economics, Linnaeus University, Sweden. She is engaged in courses in brand management, sensory marketing, retail management and service management. Her on-going research projects concern global sensory branding in the field of places, luxury and consumer goods. More especially, it has a focus in understanding the impact of multi-sensory brand experiences on both brand love and brand hate. Furthermore, her research aims at developing a framework for brand-building strategies from a sensory perspective. She is member of the Sensory Studies Research Directory. She is also an experienced international marketing consultant and branding strategist, having worked in several firms before joining the Academia. Regular speaker at academic and business conferences about sensory branding and marketing.

Ruggero Sainaghi is an Associate Professor at IULM University, Milan, Italy. His research issues are destination management (strategic positioning, archetypes, corporate governance, performance measurement systems); competitive strategies of tourism firms (relationships between firm and destination strategy); firms' performance (operative and financial performance; determinants of operative performance).

Manuela Valta is a research fellow in marketing at the University of Trieste, Italy. She received a PhD in Business Studies at the University of Udine. She has published in several books, and presented her work at international conferences in the field of marketing and management. Her research focuses on retail management, brand management, and consumer behavior.

Donata Vianelli is a full professor of marketing and management at the University of Trieste, Italy. She received a PhD in management at Ca' Foscari University in Venice. She has authored four books and has published in a range of international journals. She researches global distribution and cross-cultural consumer behavior with a focus on Europe, the United States of America and Asia.

Giampaulo Viglia is a Reader at University of Portsmouth, UK. His research interests lie in the areas of pricing, consumer decision-making, and online reputation. Methodologically, he enjoys both quantitative studies and conducting experiments. His works have been published in many different journals.

Peter Wiltshier is a senior lecturer and programme leader for the courses in travel and tourism management at the University of Derby Buxton.

Index

A

accommodation 1-3, 5, 10-16, 18-23, 25, 44, 46, 126, 128-130, 156, 160, 200, 221, 230, 241-242, 245, 251-252, 254, 256, 259, 269, 297, 319, 326
Adventure Marketing 319
Airbnb 14-15, 191
airlines 6-8, 10, 18-19, 21, 117, 180, 211, 274, 297
Anzacs 256
attitude 72, 82-88, 93, 97, 99-100, 104, 191

B

Big Data 152, 173, 176
branding 29, 33, 198-201, 204-208, 210, 213, 229, 268-276, 278-285, 287-288, 300, 322-323, 328-332, 334-337
branding strategies 199, 204, 210, 335-336
Buxton 220-223, 225-226, 229-233

C

consumer behavior 32, 58-59, 64, 147, 181, 187
cruise destination 59
cruise industry 62, 64
cultural attractiveness 240-241, 257-259
cultural environment 200, 249, 258, 267

D

Derbyshire tourism 226
destination authenticity 198-199, 201, 208, 210-211
destination branding 33, 200, 205, 268-270, 272-276, 278-279, 281-285, 287-288, 300, 328-330, 335-336
destination image 29-35, 47-48, 175, 199-203, 205, 210, 240-254, 257-260, 267, 271, 273-274, 279, 283, 296-297, 299-300, 310-311, 319
destination management 29, 129, 188, 223, 240, 260, 273, 295-296, 302, 319, 336
destination marketing 174-175, 180, 185, 188, 223, 241, 250, 269, 273, 295-297, 299-303, 307, 309, 319, 328

E

e-tourism 174-177, 179-180
eWOM 143, 146-147, 155, 165, 173

F

fake reviews 155-159, 162, 164, 173
France 34, 38, 59-60, 211, 246

G

Germany 34, 38, 59-60, 72, 246, 281

H

hedonic pricing 113-114, 124-125, 128
hospitality 1, 11, 15, 17-18, 23, 43-44, 47, 85, 113-114, 116, 121, 125-126, 128, 174, 180, 185-186, 189-190, 200
hotels 6-7, 11-13, 15, 18, 20-21, 93, 95, 113-114, 116-118, 121, 124-126, 129-130, 144, 150-153, 157-158, 161-162, 185-186, 189, 225, 269-270, 297

I

image 12-13, 23, 28-36, 38, 42, 44-49, 63, 72, 86, 91, 162, 175, 199-205, 210, 213, 229, 240-254, 256-260, 267, 269-271, 273-274, 279-281, 283, 287, 296-297, 299-300, 303, 310-311, 319, 330
information sources 28, 34-36, 38, 40-41, 44-48, 62, 177, 180
information technology 14, 174-175, 300-301, 303, 308, 319
international markets 213-214, 221, 223, 225-227, 231, 233, 247
Italy 32, 59-60, 72

K

Knowledge Management 175-176

L

local dynamics 322-323, 325-326, 328, 330, 333-334

M

Malawi 295-296, 302-304, 306, 309-311
motivations 1, 4, 25, 28, 33-36, 38-40, 44-47, 61, 148-149, 222, 228, 232, 249, 324

N

natural environment 87, 226, 240-241, 247, 252-254, 258-259, 267, 271

O

OTAs 157, 173

P

participation 84-86, 88, 97, 148, 161, 277, 280, 322-325, 332-334
perceived destination image 47, 205, 240-243, 246, 248, 254, 257-260, 267
perceived image 29-32, 47-49, 204, 254
place brand identity 198-199, 201, 204-208, 210
place branding 199, 204-208, 210
planning 21, 81-82, 85, 87, 102, 104, 144, 156, 177, 180, 188, 223, 251, 269, 273, 284, 307, 319, 324-327, 332, 334, 336
political environment 240-241, 247-248, 257-259, 267, 280
Porto brand 198, 207-208, 210, 212-214
Portugal 28-29, 32, 34-36, 38-40, 42-45, 47-48, 187
price differentiation 113-116, 118, 120
pricing 62, 113-116, 118, 121, 123-126, 128, 230, 319
publicity 229, 278

R

rating 150, 158, 160-161, 242
recommender systems 174, 177-178, 181
reviews 15, 59, 126, 143-144, 146-162, 164-165, 173, 191, 303, 305-306, 308
rural destinations 81, 83, 97, 99-100, 103, 269-270, 273, 277
rural tourism 1, 25, 268-273, 276-277, 279-280, 282, 284-285, 287-288

S

scores 38, 44, 94, 100, 158, 160, 162, 164, 173, 187, 190
seasonality 81-83, 89-93, 97, 99-100, 103-104, 113-114, 126-130, 225
social environment 240-241, 247, 250, 257-259, 267, 329
social media marketing 300-301, 303, 306, 308, 311, 319
Spain 32, 34, 38, 59-60, 83, 95-97, 246
stakeholders 21, 33, 48, 93, 175, 186-187, 198-200, 204-208, 210-211, 213-214, 220, 226, 233, 268, 271-278, 280-285, 287-288, 322, 325-326, 329-330, 332-336
strategic framework 268, 282, 287-288
support 10, 18, 21, 23, 81-89, 92-94, 96-97, 102-103, 148, 157, 174, 179-180, 191, 205, 225-226, 241-242, 272, 281, 285, 287-288, 301-302, 325-326, 331
sustainable tourism 86, 296, 322-325, 328, 330-337

T

thana tourism 250
the Peak District 220-221, 223, 232
tour operator 16, 18-19, 296, 299, 319
Tourism 2.0 146, 173
tourism demand 247, 252
tourism destinations 47, 68, 151, 153, 163, 225-226, 240, 243, 247, 251, 253, 259, 269-272, 274, 281, 284, 288, 295, 297, 300, 302, 308-311, 327
tourism experience 6, 175
tourism intermediaries 29, 34, 39, 41, 47
tourism marketing 21, 47, 143, 146, 205, 243, 295, 307-308, 311, 319
tourism product 2, 5, 15, 18-22, 25, 61, 175, 226, 229, 231, 243, 271, 307
tourist destination image 29, 34-35, 48
tourist intermediaries 28-29, 34-35, 38-40, 42, 44-48
travel agencies 30, 32-35, 42, 47, 60, 62, 173, 180, 243-244, 256, 297
Turkey 32, 34, 240-241, 254, 256, 258, 323
Turkish 211, 229, 250, 254, 256-258, 260

U

UGC 146-147, 152, 156, 163-164, 173, 275, 283, 287-288

W

water festival 220-223, 225-228, 231-233
Web 2.0 146, 148, 173
website evaluation 175, 181, 185, 187-188, 191
word of mouth 63, 147, 173, 230, 278-279

Purchase Print, E-Book, or Print + E-Book

IGI Global books can now be purchased from three unique pricing formats:
Print Only, E-Book Only, or Print + E-Book. Shipping fees apply.

www.igi-global.com

Recommended Reference Books

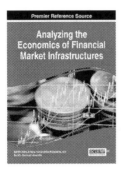

ISBN: 978-1-4666-8745-5
© 2016; 410 pp.
List Price: $220

ISBN: 978-1-4666-9604-4
© 2016; 378 pp.
List Price: $205

ISBN: 978-1-4666-9624-2
© 2016; 2,266 pp.
List Price: $2,200

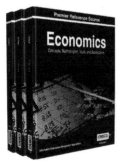

ISBN: 978-1-4666-8468-3
© 2015; 1,704 pp.
List Price: $2,395

ISBN: 978-1-4666-9484-2
© 2016; 514 pp.
List Price: $265

ISBN: 978-1-4666-8353-2
© 2015; 438 pp.
List Price: $310

Looking for free content, product updates, news, and special offers?
Join IGI Global's mailing list today and start enjoying exclusive perks sent only to IGI Global members.
Add your name to the list at **www.igi-global.com/newsletters**.

Publishing Information Science and Technology Research Since 1988

IGI Global
DISSEMINATOR OF KNOWLEDGE

www.igi-global.com   Sign up at www.igi-global.com/newsletters   facebook.com/igiglobal   twitter.com/igiglobal

Stay Current on the Latest Emerging Research Developments

Become an IGI Global Reviewer for Authored Book Projects

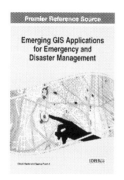

The overall success of an authored book project is dependent on quality and timely reviews.

In this competitive age of scholarly publishing, constructive and timely feedback significantly decreases the turnaround time of manuscripts from submission to acceptance, allowing the publication and discovery of progressive research at a much more expeditious rate. Several IGI Global authored book projects are currently seeking highly qualified experts in the field to fill vacancies on their respective editorial review boards:

Applications may be sent to:
development@igi-global.com

Applicants must have a doctorate (or an equivalent degree) as well as publishing and reviewing experience. Reviewers are asked to write reviews in a timely, collegial, and constructive manner. All reviewers will begin their role on an ad-hoc basis for a period of one year, and upon successful completion of this term can be considered for full editorial review board status, with the potential for a subsequent promotion to Associate Editor.

If you have a colleague that may be interested in this opportunity, we encourage you to share this information with them.

www.igi-global.com

InfoSci®-Books
A Database for Information Science and Technology Research

Maximize Your Library's Book Collection!

Invest in IGI Global's InfoSci®-Books database and gain access to hundreds of reference books at a fraction of their individual list price.

The InfoSci®-Books database offers unlimited simultaneous users the ability to precisely return search results through more than 80,000 full-text chapters from nearly 3,900 reference books in the following academic research areas:

Business & Management Information Science & Technology • Computer Science & Information Technology
Educational Science & Technology • Engineering Science & Technology • Environmental Science & Technology
Government Science & Technology • Library Information Science & Technology • Media & Communication Science & Technology
Medical, Healthcare & Life Science & Technology • Security & Forensic Science & Technology • Social Sciences & Online Behavior

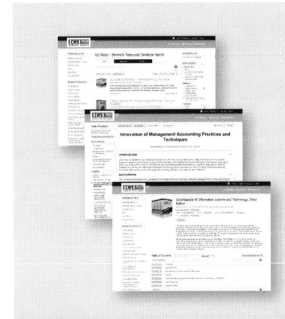

Peer-Reviewed Content:
- Cutting-edge research
- No embargoes
- Scholarly and professional
- Interdisciplinary

Award-Winning Platform:
- Unlimited simultaneous users
- Full-text in XML and PDF
- Advanced search engine
- No DRM

Librarian-Friendly:
- Free MARC records
- Discovery services
- COUNTER4/SUSHI compliant
- Training available

To find out more or request a free trial, visit:
www.igi-global.com/eresources

www.igi-global.com

IGI Global Proudly Partners with

Enhance Your Manuscript with eContent Pro International's Professional
Copy Editing Service

Expert Copy Editing

eContent Pro International copy editors, with over 70 years of combined experience, will provide complete and comprehensive care for your document by resolving all issues with spelling, punctuation, grammar, terminology, jargon, semantics, syntax, consistency, flow, and more. In addition, they will format your document to the style you specify (APA, Chicago, etc.). All edits will be performed using Microsoft Word's Track Changes feature, which allows for fast and simple review and management of edits.

Additional Services

eContent Pro International also offers fast and affordable proofreading to enhance the readability of your document, professional translation in over 100 languages, and market localization services to help businesses and organizations localize their content and grow into new markets around the globe.

IGI Global Authors Save 25% on eContent Pro International's Services!

Scan the QR Code to Receive Your 25% Discount

The 25% discount is applied directly to your eContent Pro International shopping cart when placing an order through IGI Global's referral link. Use the QR code to access this referral link. eContent Pro International has the right to end or modify any promotion at any time.

Email: customerservice@econtentpro.com

econtentpro.com

Information Resources Management Association

Advancing the Concepts & Practices of Information Resources Management in Modern Organizations

Become an IRMA Member

Members of the **Information Resources Management Association (IRMA)** understand the importance of community within their field of study. The Information Resources Management Association is an ideal venue through which professionals, students, and academicians can convene and share the latest industry innovations and scholarly research that is changing the field of information science and technology. Become a member today and enjoy the benefits of membership as well as the opportunity to collaborate and network with fellow experts in the field.

IRMA Membership Benefits:

- **One FREE Journal Subscription**
- **30% Off Additional Journal Subscriptions**
- **20% Off Book Purchases**
- Updates on the latest events and research on Information Resources Management through the IRMA-L listserv.
- Updates on new open access and downloadable content added to Research IRM.
- A copy of the Information Technology Management Newsletter twice a year.
- A certificate of membership.

IRMA Membership $195

Scan code or visit **irma-international.org** and begin by selecting your free journal subscription.

Membership is good for one full year.

www.irma-international.org

Available to Order Now
Order through www.igi-global.com with **Free Standard Shipping.**

The Premier Reference for Information Science & Information Technology

100% Original Content
Contains 705 new, peer-reviewed articles with color figures covering over 80 categories in 11 subject areas

Diverse Contributions
More than 1,100 experts from 74 unique countries contributed their specialized knowledge

Easy Navigation
Includes two tables of content and a comprehensive index in each volume for the user's convenience

Highly-Cited
Embraces a complete list of references and additional reading sections to allow for further research

Included in:
InfoSci®-Books

Encyclopedia of Information Science and Technology Fourth Edition
A Comprehensive 10-Volume Set

Mehdi Khosrow-Pour, D.B.A. (Information Resources Management Association, USA)
ISBN: 978-1-5225-2255-3; © 2018; Pg: 8,104; Release Date: July 31, 2017

The **Encyclopedia of Information Science and Technology, Fourth Edition** is a 10-volume set which includes 705 original and previously unpublished research articles covering a full range of perspectives, applications, and techniques contributed by thousands of experts and researchers from around the globe. This authoritative encyclopedia is an all-encompassing, well-established reference source that is ideally designed to disseminate the most forward-thinking and diverse research findings. With critical perspectives on the impact of information science management and new technologies in modern settings, including but not limited to computer science, education, healthcare, government, engineering, business, and natural and physical sciences, it is a pivotal and relevant source of knowledge that will benefit every professional within the field of information science and technology and is an invaluable addition to every academic and corporate library.

Scan for Online Bookstore

Pricing Information

Hardcover: **$5,695**   E-Book: **$5,695**   Hardcover + E-Book: **$6,895**

Recommend this Title to Your Institution's Library: www.igi-global.com/books